everything's an argument

with readings

Second Edition

EVERYTHING'S AN argument

with readings

Andrea A. Lunsford
Stanford University

John J. Ruszkiewicz
University of Texas at Austin

Keith Walters
University of Texas at Austin

BEDFORD/ST. MARTIN'S
BOSTON ■ NEW YORK

For Bedford/St. Martin's

Executive Editor: Marilyn Moller
Editorial Assistant: Priya Ratneshwar
Senior Production Editor: Michael Weber
Senior Production Supervisor: Joe Ford
Marketing Manager: Brian Wheel
Art Direction and Cover Design: Lucy Krikorian
Text Design: Anna George
Photo Research: Alice Lundoff
Cover Photos: Dilbert and Ruby slippers: Photofest; Breast Cancer Ribbon: Joel
    Gordon; Red Rose: Superstock; James Bond: Photofest.
Composition: Monotype Composition Company, Inc.
Printing and Binding: R.R. Donnelley & Sons Company

President: Charles H. Christensen
Editorial Director: Joan E. Feinberg
Editor in Chief: Nancy Perry
Director of Marketing: Karen R. Melton
Director of Editing, Design, and Production: Marcia Cohen
Managing Editor: Erica T. Appel

Library of Congress Control Number: 00-103338

Manufactured in the United States of America.
6 5 4 3 2
f e d

For information, write:
Bedford/St. Martin's
75 Arlington Street
Boston, MA 02116   (617-399-4000)

ISBN: 0-312-39739-9

ACKNOWLEDGMENTS

PREFACE

The first edition of *Everything's an Argument* was a labor of love, an introduction to rhetoric drawn directly from our experiences teaching persuasive writing. The book struck a chord with many students and instructors, and it immediately became the most widely taught brief guide to argument. At the same time, many instructors asked for an anthology of arguments to use with the rhetoric. So we are pleased now to offer an edition that includes a full anthology.

The title of this text sums up two key assumptions we share. First, language provides the most powerful means we have of understanding the world and of using that understanding to help shape our lives. Second, all language—including the language of visual images or of symbol systems other than writing—is persuasive, pointing in a direction and asking for response. From the cover of *Newsweek* to the pink ribbon commemorating those who have died of breast cancer, from the Nike swoosh to James Bond's BMW, we are surrounded by texts that beckon, that aim to persuade. In short, we walk, talk, and breathe persuasion very much as we breathe the air: **everything is an argument.**

For twenty-some years now, we have spent much time illustrating for our students the ways argument pervades our lives and thinking about how best to teach the arts and crafts of persuasion. We have also examined various argument textbooks carefully and have asked our students to work with many of them. As the influence of visual and electronic media has become everywhere more pervasive, we've looked for a text that would show students, directly and briefly, that "everything is an argument." We wanted a book that would focus less on complicated terminology and structures and more on concrete examples and that would engage students in understanding, criticizing, and—most important—

participating in arguments. These wishes crystallized for us during some intense discussions with students who told us, frankly, that they were unhappy with the textbooks we had been asking them to use—and in particular, that they disliked books that have more detail than they need and that focus on topics that are too broad or distant from their own lives.

With their words ringing in our ears, we began work on *Everything's an Argument*. We've aimed to present argument as something that's as everyday as an old pair of Levi's, as something we do almost from the moment we are born (in fact, an infant's first cry is as poignant a claim as we can imagine), and thus as something worthy of careful attention and practice. In pursuing this goal, **we've tried to use ordinary language whenever possible and to keep our use of specialized terminology to a minimum.** But we also see argument—and want students to see it—as a craft both delicate and powerful. So we have written *Everything's an Argument* to be itself an argument for argument, with a voice that aims to appeal to readers cordially but that doesn't hesitate to make demands on them when appropriate.

We've tried to pay attention to the critical *reading* of arguments (analysis) and the actual *writing* of arguments (production). And we have tried to demonstrate both with lively—and realistic—examples, on the principle that the best way to appreciate an argument may be to see it in action. To this end, we have added an anthology of arguments with questions for reflection and writing. We assume that the best training for writing effective arguments is analyzing many kinds of arguments, evaluating the elements of argumentation as they occur in real arguments, and responding to the issues arguments present and represent.

In selecting texts for the anthology, **we've tried to focus on topics of interest and concern to today's students.** Rather than focusing on abstract notions of gender rights, we include a cluster of arguments about Title IX and its consequences on campuses nationwide. Remembering our own students' complaints about chapters in other books on abortion and euthanasia, we instead ask students to consider how technology is redefining the meaning of life: What are the consequences of offering $50,000 for eggs from tall, athletic women with high SATs? What about the various choices we all may be forced to make at the end of our lives, from hospice care to officially requesting no care? Rather than asking students to consider "freedom of speech," we look at a specific incident at one campus when a conservative commentator was not allowed to speak. We think these are issues students will be familiar with, arguments they'll be interested in reading and writing.

And we have tried to broaden the context of argument to include visual media as well as the public spaces and electronic environments that students now inhabit so much of the time by adding a **chapter on visual argument** with advice about how to use images and design elements persuasively and a **chapter on spoken argument** with tips on presenting ideas to live audiences. And we, of course, have a **full chapter on arguing effectively in electronic environments.** Moreover, since electronic technology has made our world ever smaller and given writers more access to global audiences, we have added boxed discussions throughout offering **practical advice about argument across cultures.**

Our final goal has been to create a text that links the rhetorical treatment of argumentation to an **anthology of real world arguments.** What's "real world" about them? First, they're the kinds of arguments we encounter every day—ads, cartoons, email, news articles, radio programs, essays, and more—all demonstrating, we hope, that everything makes an argument. Second, we've tried as much as possible to reproduce these texts as they were when they were originally published. This "look," after all, is an important part of the argument they make, as Marshall McLuhan insisted when he said that "the medium's the message" or as Demosthenes argued when he said that the three most important parts of any message were "delivery, delivery, and delivery."

In pursuing all the above goals, we've tried hard to keep this book easy to use. To this end, we've designed it as **two books in one,** with the rhetoric chapters up front and the anthology in the back. You can teach with this book and focus on the elements of argumentation, supplemented with readings from the anthology, or you can focus on real arguments, referring back to the explanations in the front as necessary. To help you work with the two parts of the book, we have added links in the margins throughout, pointing out helpful examples of rhetorical elements found in the readings as well as useful explanations found in the rhetoric.

Even as we've added a full anthology of arguments, we've tried to retain the feature that many of our students have told us they like most about *Everything's an Argument*: the brevity of its explanations. Long-winded discussions and copious explanations can do more to confuse than clarify, more to *dissuade* than *persuade*. Students want basic information about argument, realistic examples of how it works, and then lots of space to maneuver in as they try producing arguments of their own. We hope that this book, like most effective arguments, will sustain interest and provoke dialogue.

Note: For instructors who do not want a full anthology, a shorter edition of this book, *Everything's an Argument*, is also available. This shorter version includes Chapters 1–22 of *Everything's an Argument, with Readings*.

Acknowledgments

We owe a debt of gratitude to many people for making possible *Everything's an Argument, with Readings*. Our first thanks must go to the students we have taught in our writing courses for more than two decades, particularly the first-year students at Ohio State University and the University of Texas at Austin. Almost every chapter in this book has been informed by a classroom encounter with a student whose shrewd observation or piercing question sent an ambitious lesson plan spiraling to the ground. (Anyone who has tried to teach claims and warrants on the fly to skeptical first-year students will surely appreciate why we have qualified our claims in the Toulmin chapter so carefully.) But students have also provided the motive for writing this book. More than ever, students need to know how to read and write arguments effectively if they are to secure a place in a world growing ever smaller and more rhetorically demanding.

After our students, our editor at Bedford/St. Martin's, Marilyn Moller, deserves the most sustained applause for bringing *Everything's an Argument, with Readings* to publication. We're still not entirely sure how she persuaded us to do the book in the first place, but we know it was Marilyn who nurtured and sustained the project and recognized, earlier and perhaps more clearly than we did, its full potential. Her creativity knows no bounds, and we are grateful for her intelligence, good will, and common sense. This book would not exist without her.

We are similarly grateful to others at Bedford/St. Martin's who contributed their talents to our book. Very special thanks to Priya Ratneshwar, for her great care in coordinating the many details of the arguments section—drafts, revisions, glosses, and endless questions from Keith. Her keen eye and memory helped head off many catastrophes before they had a chance to occur. Anna George's design breaks new ground in helping students consider the ways that layout is an important feature of argumentation. We likewise appreciate the patience of Michael Weber, who supervised the production of this textbook. His hard work with an often complex layout and design has resulted in a book that we hope will be interesting to read and valuable to use. Thanks also to Joe Ford, Lucy Krikorian, Alice Lundoff, Karen Melton, and Brian Wheel.

Finally, we thank Joan Feinberg and Chuck Christensen, for welcoming us into their lives and for their continuing support.

Thanks, too, to Ben Feigert who prepared most of the exercises for the first twenty-two chapters. Ben is the most enthusiastic teacher of Toulmin argument we know. He rocks. So do the students whose fine argumentative essays appear in our chapters.

Michal Brody is due very special thanks. Without her assistance—Web searches, question writing, textual links, proofreading, wit—the anthology and the *Instructor's Notes* simply wouldn't exist. A graduate student in linguistics at the University of Texas at Austin, Michal generously offered her help both in Austin and in Merida, Mexico, where she was conducting dissertation research on Yucatec Maya. "God pays you" is the Yucatec expression for conveying thanks (how's that for an argument?), and we trust God will continue to reward her richly.

And we thank those colleagues who reviewed *Everything's an Argument, with Readings* for their astute comments and suggestions: Jo-Anne Andre, University of Calgary; Diane Belcher, Ohio State University; Stuart C. Brown, New Mexico State University; Richard Bullock, Wright State University; Lauren Sewell Coulter, University of Tennessee at Chattanooga; Beth Daniell, Clemson University; Jane Mathison Fife, East Central University; Lynee Lewis Gaillet, Georgia State University; Paul Heilker, Virginia Polytechnic Institute and State University; Kathy M. Houff, University of Georgia; Elizabeth Anne Hull, William Rainey Harper College; Patty Kirk, John Brown University; Bonnie L. Kyburz, Utah Valley State College; Amy Muse, University of Minnesota; Julie Price, University of Illinois at Urbana-Champaign; Tammy Price, University of Minnesota; Lance Rubin, Arapahoe Community College; Andrea Sanders, Walters State Community College; Kathy Overhulse Smith, Indiana University; Lolly Smith, Everett Community College; Jo Koster Tarvers, Winthrop University; and Stephen Wilhoit, University of Dayton.

We hope that *Everything's an Argument, with Readings* responds to what students and instructors have told us they want and need. And we hope readers of this text will let us know how we've done: please share your opinions and suggestions with us at <www.bedfordstmartins.com /everythingsanargument>.

Andrea A. Lunsford
John J. Ruszkiewicz
Keith Walters

CONTENTS

PART 6 ARGUMENTS 369

Havin' a Good Time, or Just Chasin' the Benjamins?   509

What is the role of profit in movies, TV, and college athletics? Does it matter that companies pay to have their products appear in a movie? When college sports are "sold," who profits—and does anyone lose?

26. Who Owns What?   535

Who Owns the Body and Its Parts?   537

Have you ever thought of your body as property—or considered that your genes, embryos, organs, and remains can be bought, sold, patented, and traded? As this cluster of readings makes clear, the question of who owns the body is anything but simple.

Who Owns Words?   562

Can words and ideas be "owned"? If so, who owns "I Have a Dream"? And how do you feel knowing that someone else could own *your* next good idea?

29. **Technology Redefining the Meaning of Life**   694

Conception and Birth   696

$50,000 for eggs from a tall athletic coed with high SATs? This cluster of arguments examines some of the ways technology is changing the terms of public debates and private decisions about matters of conception and birth.

SPECIAL EGG DONOR NEEDED
$25,000

We are a loving, infertile couple hoping to find a compassionate woman to help us have a baby. We're looking for a healthy, intelligent college student, age 21-33, with blue eyes and blonde or light brown hair and SAT scores of at least 1400.

Compensation $25,000 plus expenses. You may contact us through our representative at 1-800-765-6789.

Death and Dying   712

What does it mean to die with dignity in light of technological advances in medicine and social movements encouraging hospice care or some form of physician-assisted suicide as alternatives to the biomedical model of dying?

everything's an argument
with readings

PART 1

INTRODUCING
argument

chapter one

Everything Is an Argument

"Best Ribs in Texas!" a sign in front of a restaurant promises.

A professor interrupts a lecture to urge her students to spend less time on the Internet and more in the company of thick, old books.

Claiming to have been a good boy for most of the year, a youngster asks Santa Claus for a bicycle with lots of gears.

A senator argues with a C-SPAN caller that members of Congress need a raise because most political perks have disappeared and it is expensive to maintain a home in Washington, D.C.

A nurse assures a patient eyeing an approaching needle, "This won't hurt one bit."

A sports columnist blasts a football coach for passing on fourth down and two in a close game—even though the play produces a touchdown.

A traffic sign orders drivers to **STOP**.

"Please let me make it through exams!" a student silently prays.

■ ■ ■

An argument can be any text—whether written, spoken, or visual—that expresses a point of view. When you write an argument, you try to influence the opinions of readers—or of yourself. Sometimes arguments can be aggressive, composed deliberately to change what readers believe, think, or do. At other times your goals may be more subtle, and your writing may be designed to convince yourself or others that specific facts are reliable or that certain views should be considered or at least tolerated.

In fact, some theorists claim that *every* text is an argument, designed to influence readers. For example, a poem that observes what little girls do in church may indirectly critique the role religion plays in women's lives, for good or ill:

> **I worry for the girls.**
> **I once had braids,**
> **and wore lace that made me suffer.**
> **I had not yet done the things**
> **that would need forgiving.**
>   **–Kathleen Norris, "Little Girls in Church"**

To take another example, observations about family life among the poor in India may suddenly illuminate the writer's life and the reader's experience, forcing comparisons that quietly argue for change:

> **I have learned from Jagat and his family a kind of commitment, a form of friendship that is not always available in the West, where we have become cynical and instrumental in so many of our relationships to others.**
>
>   **–Jeremy Seabrook, "Family Values"**

Even humor makes an argument when it causes readers to become aware—through bursts of laughter or just a faint smile—of the way things are and how they might be different:

> There is a serious question in my mind about whether guys actually *have* deep innermost feelings, unless you count, for example, loyalty to the Detroit Tigers, or fear of bridal showers.
>
> –Dave Barry, "Guys vs. Men"

More obvious as arguments are pieces that make a claim and present evidence to support it. Such writing often moves readers to recognize problems and to consider solutions. Suasion of this kind is usually easy to recognize:

> Discrimination against Hispanics, or any other group, should be fought and there are laws and a massive apparatus to do so. But the way to eliminate such discrimination is not to classify all Hispanics as victims.
>
> –Linda Chavez, "Towards a New Politics of Hispanic Assimilation"

> The real cultural fear is not that women are becoming too Victorian but that they are becoming too damn aggressive—in and out of bed.
>
> –Susan Faludi, "Whose Hype?"

> Resistance to science is born of fear. Fear, in turn, is bred by ignorance. And it is ignorance that is our deepest malady.
>
> –J. Michael Bishop, "Enemies of Promise"

ARGUMENT ISN'T JUST ABOUT WINNING

If in some ways all language has an "argumentative edge" that aims to make a point (after all, even saying "good morning" acknowledges that someone deserves a greeting and asks that you be acknowledged in return), not all language use aims to win out over others. In contrast to the traditional concept of "agonistic" or combative argument, communication theorists such as Sonja Foss and Josina Makau describe an invitational argument, which aims not to win over another person or group but to invite others to enter a space of mutual regard and exploration. In fact, as you'll see, writers and speakers have as many purposes for arguing as for using language, including—in addition to winning—to inform, to convince, to explore, to make decisions, even to meditate or pray.

Of course, many arguments *are* aimed at winning. Such is the traditional purpose of much writing and speaking in the political arena, in the business world, and in the law courts. Two candidates for office, for example, try to win out over each other in appealing for votes; the makers of

In a graduation speech at Wake Forest University, Cardinal Francis Arinze made an invitational argument, asking his listeners to explore the meaning and ramifications of what he terms "interreligious collaboration" and the extent to which it is possible for believers to "Join Hands Across the Divide of Faith."

LINK P. 635

one soft drink try to outsell their competitors by appealing to public tastes; and two lawyers try to defeat each other in pleading to a judge and jury. In your college writing, you may be also called on to make an argument that appeals to a "judge" and/or "jury" (your teacher and classmates). You might, for instance, argue that doctor-assisted suicide is a moral and legal right. In doing so, you may need to defeat your unseen opponents—those who oppose doctor-assisted suicide.

At this point, it may be helpful to acknowledge a common academic distinction between argument and persuasion. In this view, the point of argument is to discover some version of the truth, using evidence and reasons. Argument of this sort leads audiences toward conviction, an agreement that a claim is true or reasonable, or that a course of action is desirable. The aim of persuasion is to change a point of view, or to move others from conviction to action. In other words, writers or speakers argue to find some truth; they persuade when they think they already know it.

Argument (discover a truth) ⟶ **conviction**

Persuasion (know a truth) ⟶ **action**

In practice, this distinction between argument and persuasion can be hard to sustain. It is unnatural for writers or readers to imagine their minds divided between a part that pursues truth and a part that seeks to persuade. It is not surprising that people tend to admire those public figures whose lives embody the very principles they reasonably advocate; for example, Gandhi, Eleanor Roosevelt, Martin Luther King Jr., Margaret Thatcher. They move others to pursue the truths they have arrived at themselves.

And yet, you may want to reserve the term *persuasion* for writing that is aggressively designed to change opinions through the use of both reason and other appropriate techniques. For writing that sets out to persuade at all costs, abandoning reason, fairness, and truth altogether, the term *propaganda,* with all its negative connotations, seems to fit. Some would suggest that *advertising* often works just as well.

But, as we have already suggested, arguing isn't always about winning or even about changing others' views. In addition to invitational argument, another school of argument—called Rogerian argument, after the psychotherapist Carl Rogers—is based on finding common ground and establishing trust among those who disagree about issues, and on approaching audiences in nonthreatening ways. Writers who follow Rogerian approaches seek to understand the perspectives of those with whom they disagree, looking for "both/and" or "win/win" solutions (rather than "either/or" or "win/lose" ones) whenever possible. Much successful argument today follows such principles, consciously or not.

Some other purposes or goals of argument are worth considering in more detail.

Arguments to Inform

You may want or need to argue with friends or colleagues over the merits of different academic majors. But your purpose in doing so may well be to inform and to be informed, for only in such detailed arguments can you come to the best choice. Consider how Joan Didion uses argument to inform readers about the artist Georgia O'Keeffe:

> **This is a woman who in 1939 could advise her admirers that they were missing her point, that their appreciation of her famous flowers was merely sentimental. "When I paint a red hill," she observed cool-ly in the catalogue for an exhibition that year, "you say it is too bad that I don't always paint flowers. A flower touches almost everyone's heart. A red hill doesn't touch everyone's heart."**
> –Joan Didion, "Georgia O'Keeffe"

By giving specific information about O'Keeffe and her own ideas about her art, this passage argues that readers should pay close attention to the work of this artist.

Less subtle and more common as informative arguments are political posters featuring the smiling faces of candidates and the offices they are seeking: "Paretti 2000; Slattery for County Judge." Of course, these visual texts are usually also aimed at winning out over an unmentioned oppo-nent. But on the surface at least, they announce who is running for a specific office.

Arguments to Convince

If you are writing a report that attempts to identify the causes of changes in global temperatures, you would likely be trying not to conquer oppo-nents but to satisfy readers that you've thoroughly examined those causes and that they merit serious attention. As a form of writing, reports typical-ly aim to persuade readers rather than win out over opponents. Yet the presence of those who might disagree is always implied, and it shapes a writer's strategies. In the following passage, for example, Paul Osterman argues to convince readers of the urgency surrounding jobs for all citizens:

> Among employed 29- to 31-year-old high school graduates who did not go to college, more than 30 percent had not been in their position for even a year. Another 12 percent had only one year of tenure. The pattern was much the same for women who had remained in the labor force for the four years prior to the survey. These are adults who, for a variety of reasons — a lack of skills, training, or disposition — have not managed to secure "adult" jobs.
>
> —Paul Osterman, "Getting Started"

Osterman uses facts to report a seemingly objective conclusion about the stability of employment among certain groups, but he is also arguing against those who find that the current job situation is tolerable and not worthy of concern or action.

Arguments to Explore

Many important subjects call for arguments that take the form of exploration, either on your own or with others. If there's an "opponent" in such a situation at all (often there is *not*), it is likely the status quo or a current trend that — for one reason or another — is puzzling. Exploratory arguments may be deeply personal, such as E. B. White's often-reprinted essay "Once More to the Lake." Or the exploration may be aimed at solving serious problems in society. William F. Buckley Jr. opens just such an argument with a frank description of a situation he finds troubling:

> This is an exploratory column, its purpose to encourage thought on a question that badly needs thinking about.
>
> *The Problem:* The birth every year of one million babies to unwed mothers.
>
> *The Consequence:* One million children who, on reaching the age of 13, tend to run into difficulties. The statistics tell us that a child raised by a single parent is likelier by a factor of 600 per cent to commit crimes, consume drugs, quit school, and bear, or sire, children out of wedlock. Assume — if only to be hopeful — that the problems diminish after age 19; we are still left with six million teenagers who are a heavy social burden, as also, of course, a burden to themselves.
>
> —William F. Buckley Jr., "Should There Be a Law?"

Perhaps the essential argument in any such piece is the writer's assertion that a problem exists and that the writer or reader needs to solve it. Some exploratory pieces present and defend solutions. Others remain open-ended, as is the case with Buckley's column, which concludes with an unusually direct appeal to readers:

> **All these are designed as open questions, to flush out thought. Although commentary can't be acknowledged, I'd welcome having it, directed to me at *National Review.***

Arguments to Make Decisions

Closely allied to argument that explores is that which aims at making good, sound decisions. In fact, the result of your exploratory arguments may be to argue for a particular decision, whether that decision relates to the best computer for you to buy or to the "right" person for you to choose as your life partner. In the following paragraph from a novel, a minister's young daughter uses argument as a way to make her own personal decision not to undergo baptism:

Charles C. Mann challenges us to explore the definition of intellectual property and its consequences in our daily lives in his essay "Who Will Own Your Next Good Idea?"

LINK P. 564

> I bit my fingernails whenever I thought about baptism; the subject brought out a deep-rooted balkiness in me. Ever since I could remember, Matthew and I had made a game of dispelling the mysteries of worship with a gleeful secular eye: we knew how the bread and wine were prepared for Communion, and where Daddy bought his robes (Ekhardt Brothers, in North Philadelphia, makers also of robes for choirs, academicians, and judges). Yet there was an unassailable magic about an act as public and dramatic as baptism. I felt toward it the slightly exasperated awe a stagehand might feel on realizing that although he can identify with professional exactitude the minutest components of a show, there is still something indefinable in the power that makes it a cohesive whole. Though I could not have put it into words, I believed that the decision to make a frightening and embarrassing backward plunge into a pool of sanctified water meant that one had received a summons to Christianity as unmistakable as the blare of an automobile horn. I believed this with the same fervor with which, already, I believed in the power of romance, especially in the miraculous efficacy of a lover's first kiss. I had never been kissed by a lover, nor had I heard the call to baptism.
>
> –Andrea Lee, *Sarah Phillips*

Arguments to Meditate or Pray

Sometimes arguments can take the form of intense meditations on a theme, or of prayer. In such cases, the writer or speaker is most often hoping to transform something in him- or herself or to reach a state of equilibrium or peace of mind. If you know a familiar prayer or mantra, think for a moment of what it "argues" for and of how it uses quiet meditation to accomplish that goal. However, such meditations do not have to be formal prayers. Look, for example, at the ways in which Michael Lassell's poetry uses a kind of meditative language to reach understanding for himself and to evoke meditative thought in others:

> Feel how it feels to
> hold a man in your arms
> whose arms are used to holding men.
> Offer God anything to bring your brother back.
> Know you have nothing God could possibly want.
> Curse God, but do not
> abandon Him.
> —Michael Lassell, "How to Watch Your Brother Die"

Another sort of meditative argument can be found in the stained-glass windows of churches and other public buildings. Dazzled by a spectacle of light, people pause to consider a window's message longer than they might were the same idea conveyed on paper. The window engages viewers with a power not unlike that of poetry.

As all these examples suggest, the effectiveness of argument depends not only on the purposes of the writer but also on the context surrounding the plea and the people it seeks most directly to reach. Though we'll examine arguments of all types in this book, we'll focus chiefly on the kinds made in professional and academic situations.

Alicia Shepard's "The Long Goodbye," which chronicles her mother's death at home with hospice care, encourages readers to meditate on the consequences of hospice care for the meaning of life.

··· LINK TO P. 736

OCCASIONS FOR ARGUMENT

Another way of thinking about arguments is to consider the public occasions that call for them. In an ancient textbook of rhetoric, or the art of persuasion, the philosopher Aristotle provides an elegant scheme for classifying the purposes of arguments, one based on issues of time—past, future, and present. His formula is easy to remember and helpful in suggesting strategies for making convincing cases. But since all classifications overlap with others to a certain extent, don't be surprised to encounter many arguments that span more than one category—arguments about the past with implications for the future, arguments about the future with bearings on the present, and so on.

Arguments about the Past

Debates about what has happened in the past are called forensic arguments; such controversies are common in business, government, and academia. For example, in many criminal and civil cases, lawyers interrogate witnesses to establish exactly what happened at an earlier time: *Did the defendant sexually harass her employee? Did the company deliberately ignore evidence that its product was deficient? Was the contract properly enforced?*

The contentious nature of some forensic arguments is evident in this brief exchange between a defender of modern technology (Kevin Kelly) and an opponent (Kirkpatrick Sale):

> **KK: OK, then you tell me. What was the effect of printing technology? Did the invention of printing just allow us to make more books? Or did it allow new and different kinds of books to be written? What did it do? It did both.**
>
> **KS: That wasn't mass society back then, but what it eventually achieved was a vast increase in the number of books produced; and it vastly decreased forests in Europe so as to produce them.**
>
> **KK: I don't think so. The forests of Europe were not cut down to create books for Europe.**
>
> **–Kevin Kelly, "Interview with the Luddite"**

You can probably imagine how these claims and counterclaims will blossom, each speaker looking for evidence in the past to justify his conclusion. Obviously, then, forensic arguments rely on evidence and testimony to re-create what can be known about events that have already occurred.

Forensic arguments also rely heavily on precedents—actions or decisions in the past that influence policies or decisions in the present—and on analyses of cause and effect. Consider the ongoing controversy over Christopher Columbus: Are his expeditions to the Americas events worth celebrating, or are they unhappy chapters in human history? No simple exchange of evidence will suffice to still this debate; the effects of Columbus's actions beginning in 1492 may be studied and debated for the next five hundred years. As you might suspect from this case, arguments about history are typically forensic.

Martin Luther King Jr. uses a forensic argument when he invokes Abraham Lincoln and Lincoln's era in his famous "I Have a Dream" speech: "Five score years ago, a great American, in whose symbolic shadow we stand, signed the Emancipation Proclamation. This momentous decree came as a great beacon light of hope to millions of Negro slaves who had been seared in the flames of withering injustice."

LINK TO P. 666 ·············

Forensic cases may also be arguments about character, such as when someone's reputation is studied in a historical context to enrich current perspectives on the person. Allusions to the past can make present arguments more vivid, as in the following text about Ward Connerly, head of an organization that aims to dismantle affirmative action programs:

> **Despite the fact that Connerly's message seems clearly opposed to the Civil Rights Movement, some people are fond of pointing out that the man is black. But as far as politics goes, that is irrelevant. Before black suffrage, there were African Americans who publicly argued against their own right to vote.**
> **– Carl Villarreal, "Connerly Is an Enemy of Civil Rights"**

Such writing can be exploratory and open-ended, the point of argument being to enhance and sharpen knowledge, not just to generate heat or score points.

Arguments about the Future

Debates about the future are a form of deliberative argument. Legislatures, congresses, and parliaments are called deliberative bodies because they establish policies for the future: *Should Social Security be privatized? Should the United States build a defense against ballistic missiles?*

Because what has happened in the past influences the future, deliberative judgments often rely on prior forensic arguments. Thus, deliberative arguments often draw on evidence and testimony, as in this passage:

> **The labor market is sending a clear signal. While the American way of moving youngsters from high school to the labor market may be imperfect, the chief problem is that, for many, even getting a job no longer guarantees a decent standard of living. More than ever, getting ahead, or even keeping up, means staying in school longer.**
> **– Paul Osterman, "Getting Started"**

But since no one has a blueprint for what is to come, deliberative arguments also advance by means of projections, extrapolations, and reasoned guesses — *if X is true, Y may be true; if X happens, so may Y; if X continues, then Y may occur:*

> **If we liberate entrepreneurs and make it relatively easy for them to discover and invent our new world, we will be rearing a generation that increases our wealth and improves our lives to a degree that we can now barely imagine.**
> **– Newt Gingrich, "America and the Third Wave Information Age"**

Arguments about the Present

Arguments about the present are often arguments about contemporary values — the ethical premises and assumptions that are widely held (or contested) within a society. Sometimes called epideictic arguments or ceremonial arguments because they tend to be heard at public occasions, they include inaugural addresses, sermons, eulogies, graduation speeches, and civic remarks of all kinds. Ceremonial arguments can be passionate and eloquent, rich in anecdotes and examples. Martin Luther King Jr. was a master of ceremonial discourse, and he was particularly adept at finding affirmation in the depths of despair:

> Three nights later, our home was bombed. Strangely enough, I accepted the word of the bombing calmly. My experience with God had given me a new strength and trust. I know now that God is able to give us the interior resources to face the storms and problems of life.
> —Martin Luther King Jr., "Our God Is Able"

King argues here that the arbiter of good and evil in society is, ultimately, God. But not all ceremonial arguments reach quite so far.

More typical are values arguments that explore contemporary culture, praising what is admirable and blaming what is not. Sven Birkerts, for example, indirectly frames an argument against the current fascination with computers by posing some questions about contemporary values:

> [W]e may choose to become the technicians of our auxiliary brains, mastering not the information but the retrieval and referencing functions. At a certain point, then, we could become the evolutionary opposites of our forebears, who, lacking external technology, committed everything to memory. If this were to happen, what would be the status of knowing, of being educated? The leader of the electronic tribe would not be the person who knew the most, but the one who could exercise the widest range of technological functions. What, I hesitate to ask, would become of the already antiquated notion of wisdom?
> —Sven Birkerts, "Perseus Unbound"

By establishing and reinforcing common values in this way, ceremonial arguments can even be the means by which groups and coalitions form.

KINDS OF ARGUMENT

Yet another way of categorizing arguments is to consider their status or stasis — that is, the kinds of issues they address. This categorization system is called stasis theory. In ancient Greek and Roman civilizations, rhetoricians defined a series of questions by which to examine legal cases. The questions would be posed in sequence, since each depended on the question(s) preceding it. Together, the questions helped determine the point of contention in an argument, the place where disputants could focus their energy. A modern version of those questions might look like the following:

- Did something happen?
- What is its nature?
- What is its quality?
- What actions should be taken?

Here's how the questions might be used to explore a "crime."

Did Something Happen?

Yes. A young man kissed a young woman against her will. The act was witnessed by a teacher and friends and acquaintances of both parties. The facts suggest clearly that something happened.

What Is Its Nature?

Is Ebonics a separate language, a dialect of English, or something else? James Hill's "Say What? Watch Your Language" and John Rickford's "Suite for Ebony and Phonics" offer slightly different answers, basing their claims on different kinds of evidence.

·····················LINK TO PP. 608 AND 620

The act might be construed as "sexual harassment," defined as the imposition of unwanted or unsolicited sexual attention or activity on a person. The young man kissed the young woman on the lips. Kissing people who aren't relatives on the lips is generally considered a sexual activity. The young woman did not want to be kissed and complained to her teacher. The young man's act meets the definition of "sexual harassment."

What Is Its Quality?

Both the young man and young woman involved in the action are six years old. They were playing in a schoolyard. The boy didn't realize that kissing girls against their will was a violation of school policy; school sexual harassment policies had not in the past been enforced against first-graders. Most people don't regard six-year-olds as sexually culpable. Moreover, the girl wants to play with the boy again and apparently doesn't resent his action.

What Actions Should Be Taken?

The case has raised a ruckus among parents, the general public, and some feminists and anti-feminists. The consensus seems to be that the school overreached in seeking to brand the boy a sexual harasser. Yet it is important that the issue of sexual harassment not be dismissed as trivial. Consequently, the boy should probably be warned not to kiss little girls against their will. The teachers should be warned not to make federal cases out of schoolyard spats.

As you can see, each of the stasis questions explores different aspects of a problem and uses different evidence or techniques to reach conclusions. Stasis theory can be used to understand some common types of arguments.

Arguments of Fact — Did Something Happen?

An argument of fact usually involves a statement that can be proved or disproved with specific evidence or testimony. Although relatively simple to define, such arguments are often quite subtle, involving layers of complexity not apparent when the question is initially posed.

For example, the question of global warming — *Is it really occurring?* — would seem relatively easy to settle. Either scientific data prove that global temperatures are increasing as a result of human activity, or they don't. But to settle the matter, writers and readers would first have to agree on a number of points, each of which would have to be examined and debated: *What constitutes warming? How will global warming be measured? Over what period of time? Are any current temperature deviations unprecedented? How can one be certain that deviations are attributable to human action?*

Nevertheless, questions of this sort can be disputed primarily on the facts, complicated and contentious as they may be. (For more on arguments based on facts, see Chapter 7.)

Arguments of Definition — What Is the Nature of the Thing?

Just as contentious as arguments based on facts are questions of definition. An argument of definition often involves determining whether one known object or action belongs in a second — and more highly contested — category. One of the most hotly debated issues in American life today involves a question of definition: *Is a human fetus a human being?* If one argues that it is, then a second issue of definition arises: *Is abortion murder?*

As you can see, issues of definition can have mighty consequences—and decades of debate may leave the matter unresolved.

Consider Hector St. Jean de Crèvecoeur's famous response to the definitional question he posed to himself: *What is an American?* Today, his extended, idealized, and noticeably gendered reply would likely prompt disputes and objections among the many groups that bristle at the prospect of their assimilation into an American mainstream:

> He becomes an American by being received in the broad lap of our great *Alma Mater.* Here individuals of all nations are melted into a new race of men, whose labors and posterity will one day cause great changes in the world.
> —Hector St. Jean de Crèvecoeur, "What Is an American?"

Bob Costas, eulogizing Mickey Mantle, a great baseball player who had many human faults, advances his assessment by means of an important definitional distinction:

> In the last year, Mickey Mantle, always so hard upon himself, finally came to accept and appreciate the distinction between a role model and a hero. The first he often was not, the second he always will be.
> —Bob Costas, "Eulogy for Mickey Mantle"

But arguments of definition can be less weighty than these, though still hotly contested: *Is bowling a sport? Is Madonna an artist? Is ketchup a vegetable?* To argue such cases, one would first have to put forth definitions, and then those definitions would have to become the foci of debates themselves. (For more about arguments of definition, see Chapter 9.)

Arguments of Evaluation—What Is the Quality of the Thing?

Arguments of definition lead naturally into arguments of quality—that is, to questions about quality. Most auto enthusiasts, for example, would not be content merely to inquire whether the Corvette is a sports car. They'd prefer to argue whether it is a *good* sports car or a *better* sports car than, say, the Viper. Or they might wish to assert that it is the *best* sports car in the world, perhaps qualifying their claim with the caveat *for the price.* Arguments of evaluation are so common that writers sometimes take them for granted, ignoring their complexity and importance in establishing people's values and priorities.

Consider how Rosa Parks assesses Martin Luther King Jr. in the following passage. Though she seems to be defining the concept of "leader," she is measuring King against criteria she has set for "*true* leader," an important distinction:

> Dr. King was a true leader. I never sensed fear in him. I just felt he knew what had to be done and took the leading role without regard to consequences. I knew he was destined to do great things. He had an elegance about him and a speaking style that let you know where you stood and inspired you to do the best you could. He truly is a role model for us all. The sacrifice of his life should never be forgotten, and his dream must live on.
>
> –Rosa Parks, "Role Models"

Parks's comments represent a type of informal evaluation that is common in ceremonial arguments; because King is so well known, she doesn't have to burnish every claim with specific evidence. (See p. 13 for more on ceremonial arguments.) In contrast, Peggy Noonan in praising Ronald Reagan makes quite explicit the connections between her claim and the evidence:

> *He was right.* He said the Soviet Union was an evil empire, and it was; he said history would consign it to the ash heap, and it did. Thirty-one years ago . . . he said: high taxes are bad, heavy regulation is bad, bureaucracies cause more ills than they cure and government is not necessarily your friend. It could have been said by half the congressional candidates of 1994 — and was.

An argument of evaluation advances by presenting criteria and then measuring individual people, ideas, or things against those standards. Both the standards and the measurement can be explored argumentatively. And that's an important way to think of arguments — as ways to expand what is known, not just to settle differences. (For more about arguments of evaluation, see Chapter 10.)

Pondering the prospect of cosmetic surgery for her husband, Angela Neustatter writes an evaluative argument: "Yet I couldn't and wouldn't condemn it or him because no way do I want to join the band of puritans who deify their wrinkles and castigate, for their failure to age naturally, anyone who so much as has a collagen implant, because puritanism is a far nastier vice than narcissism."

LINK TO P. 422 ···

Proposal Arguments — What Actions Should Be Taken?

Arguments may lead to proposals for action when writers have succeeded in presenting problems in such a compelling way that readers ask: *What can we do?* A proposal argument often begins with the presentation of research to document existing conditions. Knowing and explaining the status quo enable writers to explore appropriate and viable alternatives and then to recommend one preferable course of action. David Thomas, for example, in arguing that reform is needed in the education of young boys, cites evidence that leads him to diagnose what he regards as a significant problem:

> **Do we, however, make the best of what nature has provided when the time comes to educate our young? Over the last few years, nationwide exam results have shown an increasing gap between the performances of girls and boys, in the girls' favor. Many more boys than girls leave school without any form of qualification.**
>
> –David Thomas, "The Mind of Man"

CULTURAL CONTEXTS FOR ARGUMENT

If you want to communicate effectively with people across cultures, then you need to try to learn something about the norms in those cultures — and to be aware of the norms guiding your own behavior.

- Be aware of the assumptions that guide your own customary ways of arguing a point. Remember that most of us tend to see our own way as the "normal" or "right" way to do things. Such assumptions guide your thinking and your judgments about what counts — and what "works" — in an argument.

- Keep in mind that if your own ways seem inherently right, then even without thinking about it you may assume that other ways are somehow less than right. Such thinking makes it hard to communicate effectively across cultures.

- Remember that ways of arguing are influenced by cultural contexts and that they differ widely across cultures. Pay attention to the ways people from cultures other than your own argue, and be flexible and open to the many ways of thinking you will no doubt encounter.

- Respect the differences among individuals within a given culture; don't expect that every member of a community behaves — or argues — in just the same way.

The best advice, then, might be *don't assume*. Just because you think a navy blazer and a knee-length skirt "argues" that you should be taken seriously as a job candidate at a multinational corporation, such dress may be perceived differently in other settings. And if in an interview a candidate does not look you in the eye, don't assume that this reflects any lack of confidence or respect; he or she may intend it as a sign of politeness.

Where a need for change is already obvious, writers may spend most of their energies describing and defending the solution. John Henry Newman, for example, in proposing a new form of liberal education in the nineteenth century, enumerates the benefits it will bring to society:

> [A] university education is the great ordinary means to a great but ordinary end; it aims at raising the intellectual tone of society, at cultivating the public mind, at purifying the national taste, at supplying true principles to popular enthusiasm and fixed aims to popular aspiration, at giving enlargement and sobriety to the ideas of the age, at facilitating the exercise of political power, and refining the intercourse of private life.
>
> –John Henry Newman, *The Idea of a University*

Americans in particular tend to see the world in terms of problems and solutions; indeed, Americans expect that any difficulty can be overcome by the proper infusion of technology and money. So proposal arguments seem especially appealing, even when quick-fix attitudes may themselves constitute a problem. (For more about proposal arguments, see Chapter 12.)

IS EVERYTHING AN ARGUMENT?

In a world where argument is as abundant as fast food, everyone has a role to play in shaping and responding to arguments. Debate and discussion are, after all, key components of the never-ending conversation about our lives and the world that is sometimes called academic inquiry. Its standards are rigorous: take no claim at face value, examine all evidence thoroughly, and study the implications of your own and others' beliefs. Developing an inquiring turn of mind like this can serve you well now and into the future. It might even lead you to wonder, with healthy suspicion, whether *everything* really is an argument.

RESPOND.

1. Can an argument really be any text that expresses a point of view? What kinds of arguments—if any—might be made about the following items?

    the embossed leather cover of a prayer book

    a newspaper masthead

a New York Yankees hat

the label on a best-selling rap CD

the health warning on a bag of no-fat potato chips

a belated birthday card

the nutrition label on a tub of margarine

the cover of a romance novel

a peace emblem worn on a chain

a Rolex watch

2. Decide whether each of the following items is an example of *argument, persuasion,* or *propaganda.* Be prepared to explain your categorization. Some of the items might be difficult to classify.

a proof in a geometry textbook

a flag burned at a protest rally

a U.S. president's State of the Union address

a sermon on the biblical Book of Job

a lawyer's opening statement at a jury trial

a movie by American film director Oliver Stone

the ABC television show *Politically Incorrect*

a lecture on race in an anthropology class

a marriage proposal

an environmental ad by a chemical company

3. Write short paragraphs describing times in the recent past when you've used language to inform, to convince, to explore, to make decisions, and to meditate or pray (write a paragraph for each of these purposes). Then decide whether each paragraph describes an act of argument, persuasion, or both, and offer some reasons in defense of your decisions.

In class, trade paragraphs with a partner, and decide whether his or her descriptions accurately fit the categories to which they've been assigned. If they do not, work with your partner to figure out why. Is the problem with the descriptions? The categories? Both? Neither?

4. In a recent newspaper or periodical, find three editorials—one that makes a ceremonial argument, one a deliberative argument, and one a forensic argument. Analyze the arguments by asking these questions: Who is arguing? What purposes are the writers trying to achieve? To whom are they directing their arguments?

Then consider whether the arguments' purposes have been achieved in each case. If they have, offer some reasons for the arguments' success.

5. If everything really *is* an argument, then one should be able to read poetry through the same lens, and with the same methods, as one reads more obviously argumentative writing. This means considering the occasions, purposes, and stasis of the poem—a process that may seem odd but that might reveal some interesting results.

   Find a poem that you like and that seems completely *nonargumen-tative* (you might even pick one that you have written). Then read it as a rhetorician, paying attention to the issues in this chapter, searching for claims, thinking about audience, and imagining occasions and purposes. Write a few paragraphs explaining why the poem is an argument.

   Next, for balance (and to make this a good argument), write a paragraph or two explaining why the poem is *not* an argument. Make sure you give good reasons for your position. Which of the two positions is more persuasive? Is there a middle ground—that is, a way of thinking about the poem that enables it both to be an argument and *not to be* an argument?

chapter two

Reading and Writing Arguments

"And ain't I a woman?" former slave Sojourner Truth is reported to have asked over and over again in a short speech arguing for women's rights. Her refrain punctuates descriptions of the difficult life she has endured, making it clear that women can do anything men can—and likely more:

Look at me! Look at my arm! I have ploughed and planted, and gathered into barns, and no man could head me. And ain't I a woman? . . . I have borne thirteen children, and seen most all sold off to slavery, and when I cried out with my mother's grief, none but Jesus heard me. And ain't I a woman?

–Sojourner Truth,
"Ain't I a Woman?"

To attribute the power of this passage to some particular method of argumentation would be extremely simplistic. Great arguments often arise from situations that no one can predict or control. Sojourner Truth's rhetoric soars because of her vivid images, her command of biblical cadences, and the authority she has earned sweating behind a plow.

Yet it still makes sense to try to examine arguments systematically, because one can, in fact, judge the scope of writers' claims, assess the reliability of their evidence, and react to the nuances of their language. Everyone evaluates arguments routinely, whenever they read editorials or listen to political speeches: *I don't see her point. Are those statistics up to date? Why did he have to resort to name-calling?* Most people know when a case is convincing or weak.

When people write arguments themselves, they are also aware of options and choices. Typically, they begin an argument knowing approximately where they stand. But they also realize they'll need evidence strong enough to convince both themselves and others more completely that their position makes sense. And often they surprise themselves by changing their views when they learn more about their subject.

Given the variety of arguments (see Chapter 1) and all the different readers and occasions they serve, we can't outline a simple process for writing a convincing argument. Moreover, no serious forms of writing can be reduced to formulas. But we can at least draw your attention to six key issues that readers and writers routinely face when dealing with arguments:

- connecting as reader or writer (Chapter 3)
- understanding lines of argument (Chapters 4–7)
- making a claim (Chapter 8)
- giving an argument shape (Chapters 9–13)
- giving an argument style (Chapters 14–17)
- managing the conventions of argument (Chapters 18–22)

As this list indicates, each of these matters is discussed in one or more chapters in this book.

CONNECTING AS READER OR WRITER

Just as "know thyself" is the philosopher's touchstone, "know thy *audience*" has long been the watchword among people who are interested in persuasion. You've probably heard of the demographic studies that advertisers and TV producers use to target their consumers—detailed surveys of consumers' likely ages, preferences, and habits. But understanding audiences isn't just a matter of figuring out the age, income level, reading preferences, and hair color of those for whom you expect to write. Connecting entails far more, whether you are a reader or a writer.

It should come as no surprise to you to learn that American society is riven by markers of race, gender, ethnicity, class, intelligence, religion, age, sexuality, ability, and so on. To some extent, *who* Americans are shapes what and how they write. And how readers imagine the writer affects how they receive what has been written. Neither writers nor readers are neutral parties handling information impassively. Life would be much less interesting if they were.

These complex relationships between readers and writers are always shifting. Sometimes as you read, you may be highly conscious of your gender and that of the writer; sometimes you may compose while thinking of yourself in terms of ethnicity or religion or economic class, alone or in combination with other factors. In the passage cited earlier, Sojourner Truth connects with many readers (particularly contemporary ones) in part because she is a former slave pleading for justice. But one can just as easily imagine other listeners turning deaf ears to her, precisely because of who she is.

In short, as you read or write arguments, you must be aware of points of contact between readers and writers—some friendly, others more troubled. And, of course, any writer or reader exploring a subject should come to it willing to learn that territory. Readers should ask what motivates writers to argue a case—what experiences they bring to the table. And writers, as they begin working with a subject, must consider how (and whether) they ought to convey to readers who they are. Consider how Shelby Steele, an African American who is worried about the voluntary resegregation of college campuses, positions himself within his argument to suggest what he knows about it:

> When I went to college in the mid-sixties, colleges were oases of calm and understanding in a racially tense society. . . . If I met whites who were not anxious to be friends with blacks, most were at least vaguely friendly to the cause of our freedom.
> –Shelby Steele, "The Recoloring of Campus Life"

Connecting means learning to identify with a writer or a reader, imagining yourself in someone else's shoes. Writers who fail to move beyond their own worlds or routines—who haven't considered alternative views—can be easily faulted. If you're reading an argument that strikes you as narrow, you might ask yourself: *What is the writer missing? Who is he or she excluding from the audience, deliberately or not?*

As a writer, you may want to connect with readers who share your own concerns. For example, Anthony Brandt, an author who wonders whether nonreligious parents owe their children religious training, aims his deliberative argument directly at parents in his situation, addressing them familiarly as *us* and *we*:

> **For those of us without faith it's not so easy. Do we send our kids to Sunday school when we ourselves never go to church? Do we have them baptized even though we have no intention of raising them as religious?**
>
> –Anthony Brandt, "Do Kids Need Religion?"

Brandt's technique illustrated here is just one of many ways to build an author-reader relationship. Yet some readers might find his appeal too overt, or aimed more at self-justification than at connecting with an audience. Argument is never easy.

Another bond between readers and writers involves building trust. In reading arguments, you should look for signals that writers are conveying accurate, honest information. You may find such reassurance in careful documentation of facts, in relevant statistics, or in a style that is moderate, balanced, and civil. Also look for indications of a writer's experience with the subject. You'd probably trust a student writing an essay about teaching who gave you the following reassurance:

> **I write this essay to offer a student perspective on the issues of power in the classroom. And although it is only one perspective, I've done a lot of thinking about teaching styles, about writing, and about conducting classes in my first year of college.**
>
> –Christian Zawodniak, "Teacher Power, Student Pedagogy"

After all, before you agree with an argument, you want to be sure it is presented by someone who knows what he or she is talking about. Needless to say, as a writer of arguments you have to pay attention to the very same issues—and do it right from the start of the writing process.

In short, connecting to an audience also means gaining authority over your subject matter—earning the right to write. (For more about connecting, see Chapter 3.)

In her article for the *National Review* about the effects of Title IX on male athletic programs, Kate O'Bierne signals her intention right up front to exclude readers with certain points of view. In the second sentence of the article, her use of quotation marks signals this intention: "In the name of 'gender equity,' colleges belonging to the NCAA have cut 20,900 male athletes from their rosters over the past five years."

LINK TO P. 497 ··

UNDERSTANDING LINES OF ARGUMENT

When you encounter an argument, your instinct as a reader should be to explore its premises, the statements or positions the writer assumes as true, and the evidence that supports it. Likewise, when you write an argument, you must decide on strategies to use to build your case. That case can usually be constructed by considering four types of appeals, or lines of argument:

- arguments from the heart
- arguments based on values
- arguments based on character
- arguments based on facts and reason

In considering these opportunities, you become involved in an important process of discovery and invention, finding what Aristotle described as "all the available means of persuasion."

Arguments from the Heart

Arguments from the heart are designed to appeal to readers' emotions and feelings. Readers are often told to be wary of such manipulation because emotions can lead them to make unwise judgments. And some emotional appeals are, in fact, just ploys to win readers' attention or consent.

But emotions can also direct readers in powerful ways to think more carefully about what they do. For example, persuading people not to drink and drive by making them fear death, injury, or arrest seems like a fair use of an emotional appeal. So writers need to consider what emotional appeals might be available when making an argument and whether these appeals are legitimate or appropriate. In arguing that wealthier Americans undervalue the academic abilities and achievements of those who are less well-off, Mike Rose evokes feelings of sympathy by describing an immigrant woman seeking to improve her life through education —an aspiration most native-born Americans will admire:

> There is another person in the sparse waiting room. She is thin, her gray hair pulled back in a tight bun, her black dress buttoned to her neck. She will tell you, if you ask her in Spanish, that she is waiting for her English class to begin. She might also tell you that the people here are helping her locate her son—lost in Salvadoran resettlement

camps—and she thinks if she learns a little English, it will help her
bring him to America.

–Mike Rose, *Lives on the Boundary*

In reading an argument that is heavy on emotional appeals, you'll
always want to question exactly how the emotions generated support the
claims a writer makes. Is there even a connection between the claim and
the emotional appeal? Sometimes there isn't. Most readers have seen
advertisements that promise an exciting life and attractive friends if only
they drink the right beer. Few are fooled when they think about such ads.
But sometimes emotional appeals move people away from thinking just
long enough to make a bad choice—and that's precisely the danger.

Finally, though people may not always realize it, humor, satire, and
parody are potent forms of emotional argument that can make ideas or
individuals seem foolish or laughable. (For more about emotional arguments, see Chapter 4.)

Alicia Shepard makes an argument very much from the heart in
"The Long Goodbye," her moving
description of the last months of
her mother's life.

LINK TO P. 736

Arguments Based on Values

Arguments that appeal to core values are closely related to emotional
appeals, but they work chiefly within specific groups of people—groups
as small as families or as large as nations. In such appeals, writers typically either (1) ask others to live up to higher principles, respected traditions, or even new values, or (2) complain that they have not done so.
Henry Scanlon, an entrepreneur who believes that President Clinton unfairly branded owners of small businesses as an "economic elite," makes
precisely such an appeal to core American principles:

> I expect that after I have spent decades creating jobs, never cheating
> anyone, constantly trying to make a positive contribution to the soci-
> ety in which I live, doing everything I can to treat employees, cus-
> tomers and suppliers fairly, honestly, and even generously, not only
> adhering to the founding principles of this country but actively trying
> to make an ongoing, positive contribution—that I would not be spo-
> ken of by the president of the country as if I were a reptile.
>
> –Henry Scanlon, "Suddenly, I'm the Bad Guy"

Scanlon's argument will succeed or fail depending on how readers react
to his catalog of values: hard work, honesty, fairness, generosity in business. Do they admire those virtues, or do they regard them as expressions
of an outdated and self-serving individualism?

Appeals based on values take many forms—from the Nike swoosh on a pair of basketball shoes to the peal of a trumpet playing taps at a military funeral. Such appeals can support many kinds of argument, especially ceremonial arguments, which, in fact, define or celebrate the ideals of a society. Any writer hoping to argue effectively needs a keen sense of the values operating within the community he or she is addressing. (For more on arguments based on values, see Chapter 5.)

Arguments Based on Character

Character matters when you read arguments, even when you don't know who the authors are. Readers tend to believe writers who seem honest, wise, and trustworthy. In examining an argument, you should look for evidence of these traits. *Does the writer have authority to write on this subject? Are all claims qualified reasonably? Is evidence presented in full, not tailored to the writer's agenda? Are important objections to the author's position acknowledged and addressed? Are sources documented?*

As a writer of arguments, you must anticipate the very same questions. And you must realize that everything you do in an argument sends signals to readers. Language that is hot and extreme can mark you as either passionate *or* intemperate. Organization that is tight can suggest that you are in control. Confusing or imprecise language can make you seem incompetent; technical terms and abstract phrases can characterize you as either knowledgeable *or* pompous.

Yet arguments based on character reach well beyond the shape and structure of a piece itself. Readers respond powerfully to the people behind arguments, to the experience and power they bring to their work. You can sense that authority in the sweep of the claims offered here by Pope John Paul II:

> **The Gospel contains a *fundamental paradox*: to find life, one must lose life; to be born, one must die; to save oneself, one must take up the cross. This is the essential truth of the Gospel, which always and everywhere is bound to meet with man's protest.**
> **–Pope John Paul II, *Crossing the Threshold of Hope***

A different but equally compelling appeal from character is evident in these sentences in which Terry Tempest Williams affirms a principle of resistance to officials who she believes concealed the dangers of nuclear testing in Utah:

> The officials thought it was a cruel joke to leave us stranded in the desert with no way to get home. What they didn't realize was that we were home, soul-centered and strong, women who recognized the sweet smell of sage as fuel for our spirits.
>
>   – Terry Tempest Williams, "The Clan of One-Breasted Women"

Of course, not everyone can write with Williams's power (or from the papal throne). But neither can writers ignore the power their own voices may have within an argument. (For more about arguments based on character, see Chapter 6.)

Where an argument appears also has a bearing on how seriously it is received. Not every such judgment will be fair, but it is hard to deny that a writer who is published in the *New Yorker* or *Commentary* or even *Newsweek* will be more respected than one who writes for a local paper or a supermarket tabloid. An argument that appears in a scholarly book thick with footnotes and appendices may seem more estimable than one that is offered in a photocopied newsletter handed out on the street corner. Likewise, facts and figures borrowed from the congressional Web site *Thomas* will carry more weight than statistics from *Jason's Gonzo Home Page.*

Arguments Based on Facts and Reason

In assessing most arguments, you'll have to judge first whether the linkages between claims and supporting reasons make sense.

Claim	Federal income taxes should be cut . . .
Reason	because the economy is growing too slowly.
Links	Tax cuts will stimulate the economy.
	A slow-growing economy is unhealthy.

Then you'll have to judge whether the writer provides enough evidence to support each part of the argument, in this case both the reason offered to support the claim (proof that the economy is growing too slowly for the good of the country) and the connections between the claim and the reason (evidence that tax cuts stimulate beneficial growth). In other words, when you assess an argument you should read skeptically, testing every assumption, claim, and linkage *between* assumption and claim as well as questioning the merit of every source and authority cited. (For more on arguments based on facts and reason, see Chapter 7.)

When you compose an argument you should write with this skeptical reader in mind. Offer logical arguments backed with the best evidence, testimony, and authority you can find. (For more about logical arguments, see Chapter 8.)

Logical appeals rely heavily on data and information from reliable sources. Knowing how to assess the quality of sources is more important now than ever because developments in information technology provide writers with access to more information than they have ever enjoyed before. The computer terminal is rapidly becoming the equivalent of a library reference room—except that the sources available on-screen vary much more widely in quality. As a consequence, both readers and writers of arguments these days must know the difference between reliable, first-hand, or fully documented sources and those that don't meet these standards. (For more on using and documenting sources, see Chapters 21 and 22.)

Mike McKee cites recent court decisions as reliable evidence in his article about the ownership and disposition of frozen embryos.

············· LINK TO P. 546

MAKING A CLAIM

Not every argument you read will package its claim in a neat sentence or thesis. A writer may tell a story from which you have to infer the claim or assemble it from various incidents. For instance, a much-admired passage in a novel by Maxine Hong Kingston describes how a girl's aunt who bears a child out of wedlock is compelled by a tradition-bound society to destroy herself and the infant because they have no means of support. The incident, starkly horrible, makes many indirect argumentative claims without the narrator having to state any one specifically, though she does comment on the fact that her family forbade anyone to speak of the aunt who had disgraced them:

> But there is more to this silence: they want me to participate in her punishment. And I have.
>
> In the twenty years since I heard this story I have not asked for details nor said my aunt's name; I do not know it.
>
> –Maxine Hong Kingston, *The Woman Warrior*

Cartoons are especially good at making claims implicitly. Check out, for example, "Sho 'Nuff" to see Garry Trudeau's Doonesbury commentary on Ebonics.

············· LINK TO P. 627

Readers cannot help being moved by the story of the aunt and the social conventions that made her a nonperson. An argument for justice is spoken even if the story itself is not designed as an argument.

In more traditional arguments, claims are liable to be more explicit. In such cases, writers stake out what they believe is true and what they expect to prove through reason and evidence. Here are three examples of explicit claims. The first comes near the beginning of an argument and previews the contents of an entire book; the second and third occur nearer the conclusion of articles and draw inferences from evidence already presented in great detail:

> **Multiculturalism, in short, has reached the point of *dérapage*. It is a universe of ambitious good intentions that has veered off the high road of respect for difference and plunged into a foggy chasm of dogmatic assertions, wishful thinking, and pseudoscientific pronouncements about race and sex.**
> –Richard Bernstein, *Dictatorship of Virtue*

> **[F]or the most part, the media coverage of the immune system operates largely in terms of the image of the body at war.**
> –Emily Martin, *Flexible Bodies*

> **What I do know, however, is that as a Mormon woman of the fifth generation of Latter-day Saints, I must question everything, even if it means losing my faith, even if it means becoming a member of a border tribe among my own people.**
> –Terry Tempest Williams, "The Clan of One-Breasted Women"

Wherever they are located, claims are, in some sense, focal points of energy in an argument—where writers decide to take their stands. Making a claim is an important early step in writing an argument, with the remainder of the process being involved in testing and refining that claim or thesis.

A lengthy essay may contain a series of related claims, each developed to support an even larger point. Indeed, every paragraph in an argument may develop a specific claim. Thus, in reading arguments you need to keep track of all these separate claims and the relationships among them. Likewise, in drafting an argument you must be sure that readers always understand the connections among individual claims you might make.

Yet a claim itself is not really an argument until it is attached to the reasons that support it and the premises that uphold it. Consider this claim from an article by Lynne Cheney, former head of the National Endowment for the Arts, who is writing about undergraduate education:

> **There are many reasons to be silent rather than to speak out on campuses today.**
> –Lynne Cheney, *Telling the Truth*

The sentence makes a point, but it doesn't offer an argument yet. The argument comes when the claim is backed by reasons that the author will then have to prove. To show the connection, we've inserted a "because" between the two sentences Cheney actually wrote:

> **There are many reasons to be silent rather than to speak out on campuses today. [because] Undergraduates have to worry not only about the power of professors to determine grades, but also about faculty members' ability to make the classroom a miserable place for the dissenting student.**

Now the author has a case she can set out to prove and a reader can test. When you read an argument, you'll always want to look for such claims and reasons, perhaps underlining them in the text you are reading or marking them in some other appropriate way. Then you can measure the argument against its claims—*Is the argument based on reasonable premises? Does the writer provide sufficient evidence to prove the claim?*

When you write an argument, you've got to be open to making changes in your claim, refining it from draft to draft. You'll want to be sure your core claim is clear, reasonable, disputable, and focused. (For more on making and developing claims, see Chapter 8.)

GIVING AN ARGUMENT SHAPE

Most arguments have a logical structure, even when they also rely on appeals to emotions, values, or character. Aristotle reduced the structure of argument to bare bones when he observed that an argument had only two parts:

- statement
- proof

You could do worse, in reading an argument, than just to make sure that every claim a writer makes is backed by sufficient evidence. When you can do so, underline every major statement in an article and then look for the evidence offered to support it. Weigh those individual claims, too, against the conclusion of the essay to determine whether the entire essay is coherent.

Most arguments you read and write will, however, be more than mere statements followed by proofs. Arguments typically require some background to clarify claims for readers who may not know every issue in contention. Arguments need qualifiers to limit claims to questions that writers can prove within the time and space available. They often need to acknowledge alternative views and to offer rebuttals to contrary claims and evidence.

Arguments may also contain various kinds of evidence. Some may open with anecdotes or incorporate whole narratives that, in fact, constitute the argument itself. Or the claim may be buttressed through charts, tables of statistics, diagrams, or photographs. Even sounds and short movies can now be incorporated into arguments when they appear on the World Wide Web, thanks to the capacity of computers to handle multiple types of media.

In any argument you write, all these elements must be connected in ways readers find logical and compelling. Just as a claim may be revised throughout the process of writing, so may the structure of an argument. (For more about structuring arguments, see Chapters 8–13.)

GIVING AN ARGUMENT STYLE

Even a well-shaped and coherent argument flush with evidence may not connect with readers if it is written in a dull, inappropriate, or offensive style. Indeed, as a reader, you probably judge the credibility of writers in part by how well they state their cases. Consider how these simple, blunt sentences from the opening of an argument shape your image of the author and probably determine whether you are willing to continue on and read the whole piece:

> **We are young, urban and professional. We are literate, respectable, intelligent and charming. But foremost and above all, we know what it's like to be unemployed.**
> —Julia Carlisle, "Young, Privileged and Unemployed"

Now consider how you would approach an argument that begins like the following:

> **This is a book about guys. It's *not* a book about men. There are already way too many books about men, and most of them are *way* too serious.**
> —Dave Barry, "Guys vs. Men"

Both styles probably work, but they signal that the writers are about to make very different kinds of cases. Style alone tells you what to expect.

Manipulating style also enables writers to shape readers' responses to their ideas. Devices as simple as repetition and parallelism can give sentences remarkable power. Consider this selection from Andrew Sullivan, who argues for greater tolerance of homosexuals in American culture:

> **Homosexuals in contemporary America tend to die young; they sometimes die estranged from their families; they die among friends who have become their new families; they die surrounded by young death and by the arch symbols of cultural otherness. Growing up homosexual was to grow up normally but displaced; to experience romantic love, but with the wrong person; to entertain grand ambitions, but of the unacceptable sort; to seek a gradual self-awakening, but in secret, not in public.**
>
> **–Andrew Sullivan, "What Are Homosexuals For?"**

The style of this passage asks readers to pay attention and perhaps to sympathize. But the entire argument can't be presented in this key without exhausting readers — and it isn't. Style has to be modulated almost like music to move readers appropriately.

Many writers prefer to edit for style after they've composed full drafts of their arguments. That makes sense, especially if you're a writer who likes to get lots of ideas on the page first. But the tone and spirit of an argument are also intimately related to subject matter, so style should not be a last-minute consideration. Often, how you express a thought can be as important as the thought itself. (For more about the style of arguments, see Chapters 14–17.)

MANAGING THE CONVENTIONS OF ARGUMENT

Because arguments rely on sources, many conventions of the genre involve proper presentation of borrowed material. You need to know how to present tables or graphs, how to document borrowed material, how to select and introduce quotations, how to tailor quotations to the grammar of surrounding sentences, how to shorten quoted passages, and so on. (For more about the conventions of argument, see Chapters 18–22.)

New conventions for argument are evolving in electronic environments. That's not surprising because computer forums such as email, Web pages, and MOOs certainly encourage the active sharing of ideas. Inevitably, you will discover that arguments themselves are changed by these environments, and you will have to learn new ways to connect ideas and to merge visual arguments with verbal ones. The prospects are quite exciting. (For more about visual and electronic arguments, see Chapters 15 and 16.)

RESPOND•

1. The opening paragraph of this chapter describes the argumentative power of Sojourner Truth's "Ain't I a Woman?" Describe a similarly persuasive moment you can recall from a speech, an article, an editorial, an advertisement, or your personal experience. Or research one of the following famous moments of persuasion and then describe the circumstances of the appeal: what the historical situation was, what issues were at stake, and what made the address memorable.

   Abraham Lincoln's "Gettysburg Address" (1863)

   Elizabeth Cady Stanton's draft of the "Declaration of Sentiments" for the Seneca Falls Convention (1848)

   Franklin Roosevelt's inaugural address (1933)

   Winston Churchill's addresses to the British people during the early stages of World War II (1940)

   Martin Luther King Jr.'s "Letter from Birmingham Jail" (1963)

   Ronald Reagan's tribute to the *Challenger* astronauts (1986)

   Toni Morrison's speech accepting the Nobel Prize (1993)

2. Before class, find an editorial argument in a recent newspaper or periodical. Analyze this argument with regard to the six components summarized in this chapter: write a few sentences describing and evaluating the author's success at

   connecting to his or her readers

   arguing from the heart, values, character, and facts

   making a claim

   giving the argument shape

   giving the argument style

   managing the conventions of argument

   In class, exchange editorials with a partner and analyze the one you've just been given along the same lines. Compare your analysis with your partner's: have you responded similarly to the editorials? If not, how do you account for the differences?

3. As suggested in Chapter 1, there are many ways of thinking about argument. Review the distinctions among purposes, occasions, and stases that were made in that chapter. Using these categories, how would you analyze the editorials you and your partner brought to class? Identify, if possible, the purposes, occasions, and stases of these arguments.

4. Find a paper you wrote for a previous class—it doesn't matter what kind of class or when you wrote the paper. Analyze this paper in the same way you did the editorials in exercises 1 and 2. You might find this assignment very easy, or it might be difficult—many academic papers make arguments that are hard to find. How do the editorials differ from the arguments you offered in your paper?

chapter three

Readers
and Contexts
Count

All argument calls for response, for the voices of others. Even in thinking through a choice you have to make—for example, one in which you create a kind of argument in your own mind—you will give response to yourself. And because argument is (at least) a two-way street, thinking hard about those people your argument will engage is crucial to effective communication. This kind of thinking is complicated, however, because those in a position to respond to your arguments or to join you in the argument —even if their number is very limited—are always individually complex and varied. In fact, if you can count on any one thing about people, it may be that they are infinitely varied, so varied that it is dangerous to make quick assumptions about what they do or do not think, or to generalize about what will or will not appeal to them.

MAPPING THE TERRITORY OF READERS

Readers or audiences for argument exist across a range of possibilities—from the flesh-and-blood person sitting right across the table from you, to the "virtual" participants in an online conversation, to the imagined ideal readers a written text invites. The sketch in Figure 3.1 may help you think about this wide range of possible readers or audiences.

As you consider your argument and begin to write, you will almost always be addressing an intended reader, one who exists in your own mind. As we write this textbook, we are certainly thinking of those who will read it: you are our intended reader, and ideally you know something about and are interested in the subject of this book. Though we don't know you personally, a version of you exists very much in us as writers, for we are *intending* to write for you. In the same way, the writer bell hooks indicates in an essay that she carries intended readers within her:

> **The most powerful resource any of us can have as we study and teach in university settings is full understanding and appreciation of the richness, beauty, and primacy of our familial and community backgrounds.**
> **–bell hooks, "Keeping Close to Home: Class and Education"**

This sentence reflects hooks's intention of talking to a certain "us"—those who "study and teach in university settings."

But if texts—including visual texts—have intended readers (those the writer consciously intends to address), they also have invoked readers (those who can be seen represented in the text). Later in this chapter, "you" are invoked as one who recognizes the importance of respecting readers. For another example, look at the first paragraph of Chapter 1; it invokes readers who are interested in the goals of argument, whether

FIGURE 3.1 READERS AND WRITERS IN CONTEXT

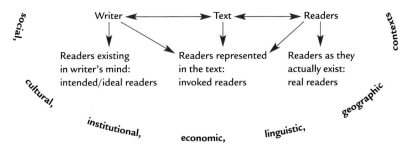

those goals are aggressive or subtle. And bell hooks's text also invokes or inscribes a particular reader within its lines: an open, honest person who regards education as what hooks calls the "practice of freedom" and is willing to build bridges to others without losing "critical consciousness." As she says, "It is important that we know who we are speaking to, who we most want to hear us, who we most long to move, motivate, and touch with our words." To invoke the readers hooks wants, her text uses the pronouns *us* and *we* throughout.

But this device can be dangerous: those who read hooks's text (or any text) and do not fit the mold of the reader invoked there can feel excluded from the text—left out and thus disaffected. Such is the risk that Susan Faludi takes when she opens an essay with this sentence:

> **Did you get the same irksome feeling of *déjà vu* as I did reading about Katie Roiphe's book, "The Morning After," that much ballyhooed attack on so-called victim feminism?**
> —Susan Faludi, "Whose Hype?"

The words *irksome* and *ballyhooed,* in particular, invoke readers who will agree with those terms. Those who do not agree are not invited into this piece of writing; there is little space made for them there.

In addition to intended readers and the readers invoked by the text of the argument, any argument will have "real" readers—and these real people may not be the ones intended or even the ones that the text calls forth. You may pick up a letter written to someone else, for instance, and read it even though it is not intended for you. Even more likely, you will read email not sent to you but rather forwarded (sometimes unwittingly) from someone else. Or you may read a legal brief prepared for a lawyer and struggle to understand it, since you are neither the intended reader nor the knowledgeable legal expert invoked in the text. As these examples suggest, writers can't always (or even usually) control who the real readers of any argument will be. Nevertheless, as a writer yourself, you would do well to think carefully about these real readers and to summon up what you do know about them.

When, in 1991, Julia Carlisle wrote an op-ed article for the *New York Times* about being "young, urban, professional, and unemployed," she intended to address readers who would sympathize with her plight; her piece invokes such readers through the use of the pronoun *we* and examples meant to suggest that she and those like her want very much to work at jobs that are not "absurd." But Carlisle ran into many readers who felt not only excluded from her text but highly offended by it. One reader,

Florence Hoff, made clear in a letter to the editor that she did not sympathize with Carlisle at all. In fact, she saw Carlisle as self-indulgent and as asking for entitlement to one kind of job while rejecting others—the jobs that Hoff and others like her are only too glad to hold. In this instance, Carlisle needed to think not only of her intended readers or of the readers her text invited in, but of all the various "real" readers who were likely to encounter her article in the *Times*.

No consideration of readers can be complete without setting those readers in context. In fact, reading always takes place in what one might think of as a series of contexts—concentric circles that move outward from the most immediate context (the specific place and time in which the reading occurs) to broader and broader contexts, including local and community contexts, institutional contexts (such as school, church, or business), and cultural and linguistic contexts. Julia Carlisle's article, for instance, was written at a specific time and place (in New York City in 1991), in certain economic conditions (during a recession), and from the point of view of white, college-educated, and fairly privileged people. As we have seen, such broader contexts always affect both you as a writer of arguments and those who will read and respond to your arguments. As such, they deserve your careful investigation.

ESTABLISHING CREDIBILITY

Because readers are so variable and varied, and because the contexts in which arguments are made are so complex, it's almost impossible to guarantee credibility. Nevertheless, careful writers can work toward establishing their credibility by listening closely to those they want to reach, by demonstrating to readers that they are knowledgeable, by highlighting shared values, by referring to common experiences related to the subject at hand, by using language to build common ground, by respecting readers—and by showing that they are trying hard to understand them. (See also Chapter 6, "Arguments Based on Character.")

Demonstrate Knowledge

One good way to connect with readers is by demonstrating that you know what you are talking about—that you have the necessary knowledge to make your case. Notice how Karen Lindsey uses examples and statistics to demonstrate her claims to knowledge and to bolster her argument:

CULTURAL CONTEXTS FOR ARGUMENT

Listening well is an essential element of effective argument. When you are arguing a point with people from cultures other than your own, make a special effort to listen for meaning: what is it that they're really saying? Misunderstandings sometimes occur when people hear only the words, and not the meaning.

- Ask people to explain or even repeat a point if you're not absolutely sure you understand what they're saying.
- Take care yourself to be explicit about what you mean.
- Invite response—ask if you're making yourself clear. This kind of back-and-forth is particularly easy (and necessary) in email.

A recent misunderstanding among a professor and two students helps to make these points. The issue was originality: the professor told the students to be more "original." One student (who was from the Philippines) thought this meant going back to the original and then relating her understanding of it in her own essay. The other student (who was from Massachusetts) thought it meant coming up with something on her own. The professor (who was French) had another definition altogether: he wanted students to read multiple sources and then come up with a point of their own about those sources. Once the students understood what he *meant,* they knew what they were supposed to do.

The traditional family isn't working. This should not come as a startling revelation to anyone who picks up this book: it may be the single fact on which every American, from the Moral Majority member through the radical feminist, agrees. Statistics abound: 50 percent of couples married since 1970 and 33 percent of those married since 1950 are divorced. One out of every six children under eighteen lives with only one parent. The number of children living in families headed by women more than doubled between 1954 and 1975.

–Karen Lindsey, *Friends as Family*

Highlight Shared Values

Even though all your readers will be somewhat different from you, they will not all be completely different. As a result, you can benefit from thinking about what values you hold and what values you may share with your readers. Jack Solomon is very clear about one value he hopes readers will share with him—the value of "straight talk":

> **There are some signs in the advertising world that Americans are getting fed up with fantasy advertisements and want to hear some straight talk. Weary of extravagant product claims and irrelevant associations, consumers trained by years of advertising to distrust what they hear seem to be developing an immunity to commercials.**
> –Jack Solomon, "Masters of Desire: The Culture of American Advertising"

Anthony Brandt faces a different kind of challenge in "Do Kids Need Religion?" for he assumes that his real readers will include those who would answer that question in very different ways. Since he wants to be attended to by readers on all sides of this issue, he highlights a widely shared value: the love for one's children and the wish for a good life for them. "I hope my children find a straighter road than I've found," he says near the end of the essay, concluding, "The longing for meaning is something we all share." To the extent that readers do share such a longing, they may be more receptive to Brandt's argument. (For more about arguments based on values, see Chapter 5.)

Refer to Common Experiences

Jennifer Ringley describes her reasons for broadcasting her life via webcam in an article from *Cosmopolitan*. She attributes the huge popularity of her Web site to the fact that people like to know they're not alone in their experiences, saying, "If you're having a bad hair day, just tune in —I probably am too."

LINK TO P. 464

In her article "The Signs of Shopping," Anne Norton draws on an experience common to many in her analysis of the ways symbolic messages are marketed to consumers: "A display window of Polo provides an embarrassment of semiotic riches. Everyone, from the architecture critic at the *New York Times* to kids in the hall of a Montana high school, knows what *Ralph Lauren* means." In a very different kind of essay, Susan Griffin draws on a common experience among men to build credibility with readers: "Most men can remember a time in their lives when they were not so different from girls, and they also remember when that time ended." Such references assume that readers have enough in common with the writer to read on and to accept—at least temporarily—the writer's credibility.

Build Common Ground

We've already mentioned the ways in which the use of pronouns can include or exclude readers and define the intended audience. Writers who want to build credibility need to be careful with pronouns and, in particular, to make sure that *we* and *our* are used accurately and deliberately. In her essay entitled "In Search of Our Mothers' Gardens," Alice Walker's use of pronouns reveals her intended audience. She uses first-person singular and plural pronouns in sharing recollections of her mother and demonstrating the way her heritage led her to imagine generations of black women and the "creative spark" they pass down. When she refers to "our mothers and grandmothers," she is primarily addressing other black women. This intended audience is even more directly invoked when she shifts to the second person: "Did you have a genius of a great-great-grandmother who died under some ignorant and depraved white overseer's lash?" Through this rhetorical direct address, Walker seeks solidarity and identification with her audience and builds her own credibility with them.

Respect Readers

Another very effective means of building credibility and of reaching readers comes through a little seven-letter word: *respect*. Especially when you wish to speak to those who may disagree with you, or who may not have thought carefully about the issues you wish to raise, such respect is crucial. In writing to a largely sighted audience, for example, Georgina Kleege, who is legally blind, wants to raise readers' consciousness about their dependence on and valuing of sight, but to do so without being accusatory or disrespectful of others' experiences. She accomplishes this goal through the extensive use of examples, through humor, and through a quiet and respectful challenge to her readers:

> **So go ahead. Close your eyes. It is not an unfamiliar condition for you. You experience it every time you blink. You are the same person with your eyes closed. You can still think, remember, feel. See? It's not so bad.**
> **–Georgina Kleege, "Call It Blindness"**

Of course, writers can also be deliberately *dis*respectful, particularly if they wish to be funny. P. J. O'Rourke uses this technique in his review of the book *Guidelines for Bias-Free Writing*, which was, he says, the product of "the pointy-headed wowsers at the Association of American University Presses, who in 1987 established a 'Task Force on Bias-Free Language' filled with cranks, pokenoses, blow-hards, four-flushers, and pettifogs." Thus, O'Rourke uses exaggerated and accusatory language to build up his credibility with an intended audience of readers he presumes are equally irritated by such guidelines.

Ed Madden expects some resistance from his readers in his "Open Letter to My Christian Friends," in which he describes the pain and difficulty he had in his home and church as a gay youth. He treats his audience with great respect, saying, "Regardless of what you think about homosexuality, please remember that you know homosexuals and lesbians, whether you are aware of them or not. . . . We are your invisible sons and daughters, your invisible brothers and sisters. Please at least think about that."

LINK TO P. 649

THINKING ABOUT READERS

The following questions may help you craft an argument that will be compelling to your readers:

- How could (or do) you describe your intended readers? What characterizes the group of people you most want to reach? What assumptions do you make about your readers—about their values, goals, and aspirations?

- How does your draft represent or invoke readers? Who are the readers that it invites into the text, and who are those that it may exclude? What words and phrases convey this information?

- What range of "real" readers might you expect to read your text? What can you know about them? In what ways might such readers differ from you? From one another? What might they have in common with you? With one another?

- Whether readers are intended, invoked, or "real," what is their stance or attitude toward your subject? What are they likely to know about it? Who will be most interested in your subject, and why?

- What is your own stance or attitude toward your subject? Are you a critic, an advocate, an activist, a detached observer, a concerned consumer or citizen? Something else? In what ways may your stance be similar to or different from that of your readers?

- What is your stance or attitude toward your readers? That of an expert giving advice? A subordinate offering recommendations? A colleague asking for support? Something else?

- What kinds of responses from readers do you want to evoke?

- Within what contexts are you operating as you write this text? College course? Workplace? Community group? Local or state or national citizenry? Religious or spiritual group? Something else?

- What might be the contexts of your readers? How might those contexts affect their reading of your text?

- How do you attempt to establish your credibility with readers? Give specifics.

Considering and connecting with readers inevitably draws you into understanding what appeals—and what does not appeal—to them, whether they are imagined, invoked, or "real." Even though appeals are as varied as readers themselves, it is possible to categorize those that have been traditionally and most effectively used in Western discourse. These appeals are the subject of Part 2, "Lines of Argument."

RESPOND.

1. Find an example of one of the following items. Explain the argument made by the piece and then describe, as fully as you can, the audience the text is designed to address or invoke.

   a request for a donation by a charitable or political group

   a film poster

   an editorial in a newspaper or magazine

   the cover of a political magazine or journal (such as the *New Republic, Weekly Standard, Nation,* or *National Review*)

   a bumper sticker

2. What common experiences—if any—do the following objects, brand names, and symbols evoke, and for what audiences in particular?

   the Nike swoosh

   golden arches

   a dollar bill

   a Tommy Hilfiger label

   a can of Coca-Cola

   Sleeping Beauty's castle on the Disney logo

   the Democrat donkey; the Republican elephant

   Martha Stewart

   the Lincoln Memorial

   the UN flag

3. Carry out an informal demographic study of the readership of a local newspaper. Who reads the paper? What is its circulation? What levels of education and income does the average reader have? Are readers politically conservative, moderate, or liberal? How old is the average reader? You'll likely have to do some research—phone calls, letters, follow-ups—to get this information, and some of it might be unavailable.

   Then select an article written by one of the paper's own reporters (not a wire-service story), and analyze it in terms of audience. Who seem to be its intended readers? How does it invoke or "hail" these readers? Does it seem addressed to the average reader you have identified?

PART 2

LINES OF argument

chapter four

Arguments from the Heart

Emotional appeals (sometimes called pathetic appeals) are powerful tools for influencing what people think and believe. Although it is sometimes taught that formal or academic arguments should rely chiefly on facts and logic, good ideas can be very powerful when they are supported by strong emotions. The civil rights struggle of the 1960s is a good example of a movement sustained equally by the reasonableness and the passionate justice of its claims.

But one doesn't have to look hard for less noble campaigns propelled by emotions such as hatred, envy, and greed. Untempered by reason, emotional arguments (and related fallacies such as personal attacks and name-calling) can wreak havoc in democratic societies divided by economic, racial, religious, and philosophical differences.

For that reason, writers who appeal to emotions must use care and restraint. (For more about emotional fallacies, see Chapter 19.)

UNDERSTANDING HOW EMOTIONAL ARGUMENTS WORK

No one doubts that words can generate emotions. Who hasn't been moved by a eulogy or stirred by a song? Such changes in disposition are critical to understanding how emotional arguments work. If writers can use words to rouse readers to specific feelings, they might also move them to sympathize with ideas associated with those feelings, and even to act on them. Make people hate an enemy, and they'll rally against him; help people to imagine suffering, and they'll strive to relieve it; make people feel secure or happy, and they'll buy products that promise such good feelings.

Emotional arguments probably count more when you are persuading than when you are arguing. Arguments make use of reasons and evidence to convince readers of some kind of truth. The aim of persuasion, however, is to move readers to action.

Argument (discover a truth) ⟶ conviction

Persuasion (know a truth) ⟶ action

The practical difference between being convinced and acting on a conviction can be enormous. Your readers may logically believe that contributing to charity is a noble act, but that conviction may not be enough to persuade them to part with their spare change. You need a spur sharper than logic, and that's when emotion might kick in. You can embarrass readers into contributing to a good cause ("Change a child's life for the price of a pizza") or make them feel the impact of their gift ("Imagine the smile on that little child's face"). Doubtless, you've seen such techniques work.

USING EMOTIONS TO BUILD BRIDGES

You may sometimes want to use emotions to establish a bond between yourself and readers. Such a bridge is especially important when your argument draws on personal experiences or when you are arguing about matters that readers might regard as sensitive. They'll want assurance that you understand the issues in depth. If you strike the right emotional note, raising feelings in readers they can share with you, you've established an important connection.

That's what bell hooks does in an essay that argues that working-class people shouldn't lose sight of their roots even as education changes their lives. To reinforce her point, hooks lets us peer into her strained relationship with her mother:

> She wants to know, "What hurts, what hurts are you talking about?" "Mom, I can't answer that. I can't speak for all of us, the hurts are different for everybody. But the point is you try to make the hurt better, to heal it, by understanding how it came to be. . . . You know that. And sometimes folk feel hurt about stuff and you just don't know or didn't realize it, and they need to talk about it. Surely you understand the need to talk about it."
> —bell hooks, "Keeping Close to Home: Class and Education"

In no obvious way is hooks's recollection an actual argument. But it prepares readers to accept the case she will make, knowing that hooks has experienced conflicts with her mother—as most readers have with their own.

A more obvious way to build an emotional tie is simply to help readers identify with your experiences. If, like Georgina Kleege, you were blind and wanted to argue for more sensible attitudes toward blind people, you might ask readers in the very first paragraph of your argument to confront their prejudices. Here is Kleege:

> I tell the class, "I am legally blind." There is a pause, a collective intake of breath. I feel them look away uncertainly and then look back. After all, I just said I couldn't see. Or did I? I had managed to get there on my own—no cane, no dog, none of the usual trappings of blindness. Eyeing me askance now, they might detect that my gaze is not quite focused. . . . They watch me glance down, or towards the door where someone's coming in late. I'm just like anyone else.
> —Georgina Kleege, "Call It Blindness"

Notice that although Kleege seems to be describing the reactions of a class she will be teaching, many readers are likely to feel the same uneasiness, imagining themselves sitting in that classroom and facing a sightless instructor.

Let's consider another rhetorical situation: How do you win over an audience when you regard a subject as more threatening than most readers realize, but you don't want to seem like Chicken Little either? Once again, a sensibly managed appeal to emotions on a personal level may work. That's the tack Richard Bernstein takes to confront what he regards as the dangers of multiculturalism, an intellectual perspective that many readers probably regard as harmless:

> I don't want to be melodramatic here. We are not reexperiencing the French Revolution, and we are not in danger of the guillotine or rule by a national-level Committee of Public Safety (though I think subsequent pages show the existence of rather smaller versions of the same committee). But we are threatened by a narrow orthodoxy—and the occasional outright atrocity—imposed, or committed, in the name of the very values that are supposed to define a pluralistic society.
>
> –Richard Bernstein, *Dictatorship of Virtue*

Look carefully at the passage and you'll find words designed to ratchet up your concerns *(guillotine, Committee of Public Safety, outright atrocity)* even while worst-case scenarios are dismissed. The bottom line according to Bernstein is that readers should feel threatened by multiculturalism. If they are, they'll want to know what they should do and will read on.

USING EMOTIONS TO SUSTAIN AN ARGUMENT

Emotional appeals can also work as a way of supporting actual claims made in an argument. Quite often the emotion is laid atop logical propositions to make them stronger or more memorable. The technique is tricky, however. Lay on too much anger or pity, and you offend the very readers you'd hoped to convince. But sometimes anger adds energy to a passage, as it does when feminist Susan Faludi accuses writer Katie Roiphe of minimizing the significance of date rape:

> Roiphe and others "prove" their case by recycling the same anecdotes of false accusations; they all quote the same "expert" who disparages reports of high rape rates. And they never interview any real rape victims. They advise us that a feeling of victimization is no longer a reasonable response to sexual violence; it's a hallucinatory state of mind induced by witchy feminists who cast a spell on impressionable co-eds. These date-rape revisionists claim to be liberating young women from the victim mind-set. But is women's sexual victimization just a mind trip—or a reality?
>
> –Susan Faludi, "Whose Hype?"

Here, the threat in Faludi's sarcasm becomes part of the argument: if you make the kind of suggestion Roiphe has, expect this sort of powerful response.

In the same way, emotions can be generated by presenting logical arguments in their starkest terms, stripped of qualifications or subtleties. Readers or listeners are confronted either with core issues (which may move them a great deal) or with a reduction of the matter to absurdity (which may anger them). Kevin Kelly (KK) takes this risk in the course of a debate he has with Kirkpatrick Sale (KS) over the benefits of technology:

> KK: Do you see civilization as a catastrophe?
>
> KS: Yes.
>
> KK: All civilizations?
>
> KS: Yes. There are some presumed benefits, but civilizations as such are all catastrophic, which is why they all end by destroying themselves and the natural environment around them.
>
> KK: You are quick to talk about the downsides of technological civilizations and the upsides of tribal life. But you pay zero attention to the downsides of tribal life or the upsides of civilizations. For instance, the downsides of tribal life are infanticide, tribal warfare, intertribal rape, slavery, sexism. Not to mention a very short lifespan, perpetual head lice, and diseases that are easily cured by five cents' worth of medicine now. This is what you get when you have tribal life with no civilization. This is what you want?
>
> —Kevin Kelly, "Interview with the Luddite"

You might imagine how you'd respond to Kelly at this point: would a more reasoned approach work, or would the reply have to be just as pointed as Kelly's barb?

It is possible, of course, for feelings to be an argument in themselves when they are powerfully portrayed. Here, for example, is Georgina Kleege again, describing the feelings of the blind in order to change the attitudes of the sighted:

> Face it. What you fear is not your inability to adapt to the loss of sight, it is the inability of people around you to see you the same way. It's not you, it's them. And it's not because you have an unduly malevolent view of human nature. Nor are you guiltily acknowledging this prejudice in yourself. You may not see it as prejudice. Pity and solicitude are not the same as prejudice, you assert. The disabled should be a little more gracious. But the words stick in your throat. You know that's not the only response people have to the disabled.
>
> —Georgina Kleege, "Call It Blindness"

As you can see, it is difficult to gauge how much emotion will work in a given argument. Some issues—such as date rape, abortion, gun control— provoke strong feelings and, as a result, are often argued on emotional terms. But even issues that seem deadly dull—such as funding for

In an article dominated by technical information, John Vidal and John Carvel add a very human dimension by relating the experiences of John Moore, a man whose spleen was removed by surgeons, who without his knowledge or permission, then patented his DNA. Says Moore, "They viewed me as a mine from which to extract biological material. I was harvested."

····· LINK TO P. 539

Medicare and Social Security—can be argued in emotional terms when proposed changes in these programs are set in human terms: cut benefits and Grandma will have to eat cat food; don't cut benefits and the whole system will collapse. Both alternatives evoke feelings strong enough to lead toward political action.

In exploring social and political matters, it is easy to get wrapped up in technical issues that are of interest chiefly to experts or insiders. If you want to make a case to a broad audience, you may sometimes want to "step outside the Beltway" and respond to the concerns of ordinary people. In other words, always consider how you can give presence to the human dimension of any problem in your arguments.

USING HUMOR

Just days after he lost the presidential election in 1996, Republican candidate Bob Dole appeared on the *Late Show with David Letterman,* grinning like a youngster and amusing the audience with self-deprecating humor. Some pundits commented that this was the real Bob Dole, who had been sadly absent from the campaign trail. Had more voters seen this easygoing, wry side of the candidate, the outcome of the election might have been different. That's highly speculative, of course. But, as the Dole case may suggest, you can't afford to ignore the persuasive power of humor.

You can certainly slip humor into an argument to put readers at ease, thereby making them well disposed toward a particular claim or proposal you offer. It is hard to say "no" when you're laughing. (Try it sometime.) Humor also has the effect of suspending sober judgment, perhaps because the surprise and naughtiness of wit are combustive: they provoke laughter or smiles, not reflection. Thus, it is possible to make a point through humor that might not work at all in more sober writing. Consider the gross stereotypes about men and women that Dave Barry presents with a decided chuckle:

> Other results of the guy need to have stuff are Star Wars, the recreational boat industry, monorails, nuclear weapons, and wristwatches that indicate the phase of the moon. I am not saying that women haven't been involved in the development or use of this stuff. I'm saying that, without guys, this stuff would probably not exist; just as, without women, virtually every piece of furniture in the world would still be in its original position.
>
> –Dave Barry, "Guys vs. Men"

Our laughter testifies to a kernel of truth in Barry's observations.

The power of laughter to cut to the bone can work in serious contexts as well, enabling the careful writer to deal with a sensitive issue that might otherwise have to be ignored. For example, sports commentator Bob Costas, given the honor of eulogizing the great baseball player Mickey Mantle, couldn't ignore well-known flaws in Mantle's character. So he argues for Mantle's greatness by confronting the man's weaknesses indirectly through humor:

> **It brings to mind a story Mickey liked to tell on himself and maybe some of you have heard it. He pictured himself at the pearly gates, met by St. Peter who shook his head and said "Mick, we checked the record. We know some of what went on. Sorry, we can't let you in. But before you go, God wants to know if you'd sign these six dozen baseballs."**
> –Bob Costas, "Eulogy for Mickey Mantle"

Not all humor is so well intentioned. In fact, among the most powerful forms of emotional argument is ridicule—humor aimed at a particular target. Lord Shaftesbury, an eighteenth-century philosopher, regarded humor as a serious test for ideas, believing that sound ideas would survive humorous broadsides. In our own time, comedians poke fun at politicians and their ideas almost nightly, providing an odd barometer of public opinion. Even bumper stickers can be vehicles for succinct arguments:

Vote Republican: It's easier than thinking.

Vote Democrat: It's easier than working.

But ridicule is a two-edged sword that requires a deft hand to wield it. Humor that reflects bad taste discredits a writer completely, as does ridicule that misses its mark. Unless your target deserves assault and you can be very funny, it's usually better to steer clear of humor. (For more on humorous arguments, see Chapter 13.)

In his essay "Bumper-Sticker Bravado," Michael Perry uses ridicule to make a point about a certain kind of driver: "Consider the case of the lump of gristle with a pulse who cut me off in traffic."

LINK TO P. 451 ·······················

RESPOND.

1. To what specific emotions do the following slogans, sales pitches, and maxims appeal?

    "Just do it." (ad for Nike)

    "Think different." (ad for Apple Computers)

    "Reach out and touch someone." (ad for a long-distance phone company)

"In your heart, you know he's right." (1964 campaign slogan for U.S. presidential candidate Barry Goldwater, a conservative)

"It's the economy, stupid!" (1992 campaign theme for U.S. presidential candidate Bill Clinton)

"By any means necessary." (a rallying cry from Malcolm X)

"When the going gets tough, the tough get going." (a maxim of many coaches)

"You can trust your car to the man who wears the star." (slogan for Texaco)

"We bring good things to life." (slogan for a large manufacturer)

"Know what comes between me and my Calvins? Nothing!" (tag line for Calvin Klein jeans)

"Don't mess with Texas!" (antilitter campaign slogan)

2. It's important to remember that argument—properly carried out—can be a form of *inquiry:* rather than a simple back-and-forth between established positions, good argument helps people *discover* their positions and modify them. Arguments from the heart can help in this process, as long as they are well tempered with reason.

   With this goal of inquiry in mind, as well as an awareness of the problems associated with emotional arguments, continue the argument between Kevin Kelly and Kirkpatrick Sale, writing their (imagined) responses and using reasonable arguments from the heart. Feel free to imagine Kelly or Sale discovering positions in the other man's statements that help him modify his own.

   You might also do this as a group exercise. Over several days, one group could work together to come up with lines of argument Kelly might use, while another group works to decide on Sale's lines. Then the groups could meet together to write the text of the argument itself. We hope you will find yourself modifying your preplanned statements as you hear what the other group has to say.

3. The Internet is a source of many arguments on the benefits of technology and its relationship to civilization. Using any search engine you feel comfortable with, find as many sites as you can that carry on the debate between Kelly and Sale. Divide the sites into three groups: those that make reasonable arguments from the heart, those that make emotional arguments with little or no rational support, and those that are hard to categorize.

   Make a list of the key words that each site uses to make its argument. Which words are logical? Which ones are emotional? What is the relative balance between logical and emotional words in each site?

chapter five

Arguments Based on Values

Arguments based on values usually occur among members of different groups. Whether they be clubs, sports teams, political parties, religious organizations, ethnic groups, or entire nations, groups come together because of values that individual members share. Lines of argument based on such values are related to both logical and emotional appeals, but they can be powerful enough in their own right to merit careful examination. To make a strong appeal to any group, you need to understand its core values as much as you possibly can since, in most cases, values themselves become the subject of debate. You also need to be critically aware of your own values — what they are as well as how they influence your understanding of the world.

UNDERSTANDING HOW VALUES ARGUMENTS WORK

Values are the principles shared by members of a group. Sometimes such principles are clearly spelled out in a creed or a document such as the Declaration of Independence. At other times, they evolve as part of the history and traditions of a club or movement or political party; for example, what it means to be a loyal Republican, a committed feminist, or an environmentalist may never be entirely clear, but it is always somehow understood. Moreover, the values to which groups and their members aspire are usually ideals all the more powerful for being neither fully attainable nor easily specified.

Such appeals to values are simple but powerful. They typically involve a comparison between what is and what ought to be:

- A person or group does not live up to current values.

- Past values were better or nobler than current ones.

- Future values can be better or worse than current ones.

USING VALUES TO DEFINE

You will likely find appeals to values whenever members of a society or group talk about that group. *What does it mean to be an American? An ecologist? A good Christian? A true Texan? A law-abiding citizen? A concerned liberal?* Everyone who belongs to such a group likely has an answer—as do people who stand outside—and their judgments are apt to be different enough to provoke interesting disagreement.

How would you define an American? Here is Hector St. Jean de Crèvecoeur, a Frenchman, trying in 1782 to do exactly that, speaking in the imagined voice of an American:

> **We are a people of cultivators, scattered over an immense territory, communicating with each other by means of good roads and navigable rivers, united by the silken bands of mild government, all respecting the laws without dreading their power, because they are equitable. We are all animated with the spirit of industry which is unfettered and unrestrained, because each person works for himself.**
>
> **–Hector St. Jean de Crèvecoeur, "What Is an American?"**

Crèvecoeur's themes are dated (few Americans are farmers now), but one still finds concepts that would resonate in arguments made to Americans today: limited government, fair laws, hard work, self-reliance. Appeals to such shared (and flattering) values are so common that even advertisers exploit them. In Texas, for example, one truck manufacturer advertises its products as "Texas tough," making a safe assumption that Texans like to think of themselves as rugged.

But let's consider an entirely different way of imagining American values, one far less idealistic. This time the commentator is Stanley Crouch, an African American social critic exploring the implications of the O. J. Simpson murder case:

> **So we end up in a big, fat, peculiarly American mess, the kind that allows us to understand why one writer said she would choose a good case of murder if her intent was to ascertain the broadest identity of a culture. In this case of blonde on black, omnipresent media magnification, wife-beating, sudden wealth, workout partners, golf courses, the disco life, Bentleys rolling into McDonald's, rumors of drug-spiced promiscuity, and the ugly punctuation marks of two bloody victims in a high rent district, we are forced to examine almost everything that crosses the T's of our American lives.**
> **–Stanley Crouch, "Another Long Drink of the Blues"**

Are hard work and personal responsibility compatible with "sudden wealth" and "the disco life"? Which of these "values" represent the real America? As a writer, you may find that the real America exists in the turbulence between such conflicting views—in the arguments about values that you, like Crèvecoeur and Crouch, will help to shape.

In writing an argument, you may find yourself defining the values you intend to champion and then presenting your claims in terms of those values. This process sounds complex, but it isn't. Consider the "Texas tough" truck mentioned earlier. In the ad, a cowboy slams the pickup down gullies and over cacti, trailing clouds of dust. If toughness is good, so is the truck. Case closed.

EMBRACING OR REJECTING VALUES

A straightforward form of arguments based on values involves identifying one's own beliefs or practices with well-accepted values. So when Terry Tempest Williams is arrested for protesting nuclear testing, she places her activity within an American custom as old and honorable as the Boston Tea Party:

> I crossed the line at the Nevada Test Site and was arrested with nine other Utahns for trespassing on military lands. They are still conducting nuclear tests in the desert. Ours was an act of *civil disobedience.* (emphasis added)
>> – Terry Tempest Williams, "The Clan of One-Breasted Women"

By linking her own arrest to the tradition of civil disobedience, she makes an argument in defense of her entire cause. Likewise, Meridel LeSueur justifies feminist political action by embracing the universality of women's struggles as almost a natural force:

> I feel we must be deeply rooted in the tribal family and in the social community. This is becoming a strong and universal force now in our society. Women speaking out boldly, going to jail for peace and sanctuary, defending the children against hunger. We still get half of what men get. But as I saw in Nairobi the struggle of women is now global. My Gramma and mother are not any more silenced and alone. Writing has become with women not a concealment, but an illumination. We are not alone.
>> – Meridel LeSueur, "Women and Work"

As you might guess, it is also possible to spin arguments based on values in the opposite direction, associating one's opponents with values that most readers reject. For instance, in a paragraph arguing for greater change in society, Newt Gingrich strategically associates government with the concept of monopoly, an idea unpalatable to most Americans:

> Why are governments so painfully slow at adjusting to change? Why are their agencies almost always obsolete? The basic reason is that governments aren't consumer driven. Governments almost always grant monopoly status to their own operations so they won't have to compete. Look at public education. Look at the post office. It's the same story everywhere. Consumers are too often stuck with inefficient service and poor products because they're not allowed to go anywhere else.
>> – Newt Gingrich, "America and the Third Wave Information Age"

COMPARING VALUES

Many arguments based on values involve comparisons. Something is faulted for not living up to an ideal, or the ideal is faulted for not reaching far enough, or one value is presented as preferable to another or in need of redefinition. It would be hard to find an argument based on values more clearly stated than the following example from a book by Stephen Carter that explores what Carter sees as a trend toward intolerance of religion among America's legal and political elites:

> **The First Amendment guarantees the "free exercise" of religion but also prohibits its "establishment" by the government. There may have been times in our history when we as a nation have tilted too far in one direction, allowing too much religious sway over politics. But in late-twentieth-century America, despite some loud fears about the weak and divided Christian right, we are upsetting the balance afresh by tilting too far in the other direction—and the courts are assisting in the effort.**
>
> –Stephen Carter, *The Culture of Disbelief*

In this case, a First Amendment balance between "free exercise" and "establishment" of religion is the value Carter uses to ground his argument. If readers share his interpretation of the First Amendment, they are also likely to agree with his inference that any deviation from this equilibrium is undesirable. Because of the high regard most Americans have for the First Amendment, Carter's argument is relatively easy to make. No extended defense of the basis for it is required. But consider how much more difficult it would be to get most readers to agree to the Second Amendment's protection of the right to bear arms. It provides a shakier premise for argument, one that requires more backing. (See Chapter 8 for more on using evidence.)

George Sim Johnston offers another example of such a values argument in action when, in describing the beliefs of Pope John Paul II, he suggests what the consequences might be of failing to embrace specific principles:

> **Above all, the pope objects to the notion of the individual conscience as a little god, a supreme tribunal making categorical decisions about right and wrong. Along with a new generation of Catholic intellectuals, he is suggesting that the modern world either rediscover the principles of natural law . . . or prepare itself for an increasingly fragmented and unhappy existence.**
>
> –George Sim Johnston, "Pope Culture"

Not every reader will accept the either/or choice that Johnston presents (natural law versus fragmentation), but the argument clearly champions a specific value over its alternatives: if people accept the reality of a natural law, they will enjoy more coherent and satisfying lives.

Adrienne Rich, a poet and writer, provides a clear example of a third type of value comparison, one in which a current value — in this case, power — is redefined for a different group so that it can be embraced in a new way. Watch especially how she unpacks the meaning of *power*:

> The word *power* is highly charged for women. It has been long associated for us with the use of force, with rape, with the stockpiling of weapons, with the ruthless accrual of wealth and the hoarding of resources, with the power that acts only in its own interest, despising and exploiting the powerless — including women and children. . . . But for a long time now, feminists have been talking about redefining power, about that meaning of power which returns to the root — *posse, potere, pouvoir:* to be able, to have the potential, to possess and use one's energy of creation — *transforming power.*
> – Adrienne Rich, "What Does a Woman Need to Know?"

As you can see, arguments based on values are challenging and sophisticated. That's because they often take you right into the heart of issues.

In an essay about issues of privacy and public accountability, David Brin makes a comparison in an argument of values, writing, "Despite uncountable flaws in our contemporary neo-Western world, there has never been a major urban society in which individuals of all social classes have had more freedom than we do today."

LINK TO P. 473

RESPOND •

1. Listed here are groups whose members likely share some specific interests and values. Choose a group you recognize (or find another special interest group on your own), research it on the Web or in the library, and, in a paragraph, explain its core values for someone less familiar with the group.

   parrotheads

   Harley Davidson owners

   Trekkies

   slackers

   Beanie Babies collectors

   log cabin Republicans

   PETA members

   hip-hop fans

   survivalists

   cacophonists

2. The first two extracted examples in this chapter focus on the values associated with the United States, both historically and in the present. Crèvecoeur has his list (industry, individualism, equity), and

Crouch presents a quite different one (spectacle, conspicuous consumption). Can you list 30 values—core values—associated with the people of the United States? 100? 200? List as many as you can, and then ask yourself when the list stops being representative of core values. Why does this problem arise?

Now make a list of core values for a small group—the members of your college's English department, for instance, or a church philanthropy committee, or an athletic team. Any small group will do. How many core values can you list? How does the list compare to the list you generated for the people of the United States?

3. Using the list of core values you've developed for the smaller group, write a paragraph arguing that a public figure—such as Jesse Jackson, Madonna, or Wayne Gretzky—meets the standards of that group.

4. Recently a group of animal rights activists raided a mink "ranch" and released several thousand minks from their cages. Many of the animals died during and after their release. Soon thereafter, other animal rights groups criticized this action, arguing that it did not represent the values of *true* animal rights activists.

What might these values be? And how would those responsible for the release characterize their own values? Write a statement from one of the other groups, using arguments based on values to express your disapproval of the release. Then write a statement from the releasing group, explaining why its actions were consonant with the values of true animal lovers. In each of these letters, you'll have to decide whether you're writing to a public audience or directly to the opposing group; the values you refer to might change, depending on the audience.

chapter six

Arguments Based on Character

In the preface to a book about men, Dave Barry tries to draw a line between men and guys. Naturally, in making such a distinction, he leads readers to expect that he'll explain each term. Here is what he has to say about the second:

And what, exactly, do I mean by "guys"? I don't know. I haven't thought much about it. One of the major characteristics about guyhood is that guys don't spend a lot of time pondering our deep innermost feelings.
–Dave Barry, "Guys vs. Men"

Such prattle probably makes you laugh if you understand that Barry is a renowned humorist (there was even a TV sitcom based on his life) and that he's not writing a piece intended for deep scrutiny, a fact he stresses in the very first line of his preface:

> **This is a book about guys. It's *not* a book about men. There are already way too many books about men and most of them are *way* too serious.**

But imagine for an unlikely moment that you have never heard of Dave Barry and missed all earlier signals of comic intention. What might you think of a writer who confessed, "I don't know. I haven't thought much about it," it being the subject matter of his book? Chances are you'd close the volume and select another one written by someone competent.

That's because in argument, as in politics, character matters. Readers want to be sure that an argument they are considering is the work of someone they can trust—which means that in composing an argument you have to convey authority and honesty through an appeal based on character, or ethos (sometimes called an ethical appeal). You can do so in various ways, both direct and subtle.

UNDERSTANDING HOW ARGUMENTS BASED ON CHARACTER WORK

Given life's complications, people often need shortcuts to help make choices; they can't weigh every claim to its last milligram or trace every fragment of evidence to its original source. Yet they often have to make judgments about weighty matters: *Which college or university should I attend? For whom should I vote in the next election? How do I invest my retirement funds?*

To answer these and hundreds of other similar questions, people typically rely on authorities and experts to give wise, well-informed, and honest advice. People also look to trustworthy individuals with experience and training to guide them in thousands of less momentous matters. Depending on the subject, an *expert* might be anyone with knowledge and experience, from a professor of nuclear physics at a local college to a short-order cook at the local diner.

When experts or authorities make claims, readers usually transfer their personal respect for the authorities to their arguments. If readers don't automatically accept what the experts and authorities say, they at least pause to listen, signaling a willingness to engage in dialogue. Readers give experts a hearing they might not automatically grant to a stranger or to someone who hasn't earned their respect. That's the power of arguments based on character.

CLAIMING AUTHORITY

When you read an argument, especially one that makes an aggressive claim, you have every right to wonder about the writer's authority: *What does he know about the subject? What experiences does she have that make her especially knowledgeable? Why should I pay attention to this writer?*

When you offer an argument yourself, you have to anticipate queries exactly like these and be able to answer them, directly or indirectly. Sometimes the claim of authority will be bold and uncompromising, as it is in the opening sentences of Terry Tempest Williams's essay indicting those who poisoned the Utah deserts with nuclear radiation:

> **I belong to the Clan of One-Breasted Women. My mother, my grand-mothers, and six aunts have all had mastectomies. Seven are dead. The two who survive have just completed rounds of chemotherapy and radiation.**
>
> **I've had my own problems: two biopsies for breast cancer and a small tumor between my ribs diagnosed as a "borderline malignancy."**
> **– Terry Tempest Williams, "The Clan of One-Breasted Women"**

What gives Williams the authority to speak on the hazards of living in areas affected by nuclear testing? Not scientific expertise, but gut-wrenching personal experience.

It's the same strategy Jill Frawley uses in reporting what she knows about appalling conditions in nursing homes. Hers is an attention-getting claim to authority, also delivered in the opening sentences of an essay:

> **I'm just one little nurse, in one little "care facility." Each shift I work, I carry in my soul a very big lie. I leave my job, and there aren't enough showers in the world to wash away my rage, my frustrations, my impotence.**
> **– Jill Frawley, "Inside the Home"**

Frawley knows what goes on inside nursing homes because she works there. But she tells us more. Her soul is troubled by what she sees, providing a rationale for her exposé. Readers are moved to trust her—especially if they identify with her sense of being just one person who is helpless to do much about the injustices she witnesses.

J. Michael Bishop, a scientist, also uses an argument based on character to defend the National Institutes of Health (NIH) against charges of mediocrity in its procedures:

> **I have assisted the NIH with peer review for more than twenty years. Its standards have always been the same: it seeks work of the highest originality and demands rigor as well. I, for one, have never knowingly punished initiative or originality, and I have never seen the agencies of the NIH do so.**
>
> **–J. Michael Bishop, "Enemies of Promise"**

Bishop might add, "Trust me," because as evidence of the NIH's integrity he offers his own character and experience as a respected scientist—not specific facts, objective evidence, or independent testimony. This argument in defense of an agency under attack depends on readers believing J. Michael Bishop personally.

When your readers are apt to be skeptical of both you and your claim—as is typically the problem when your subject is controversial—you may have to be even more specific about your credentials. That's exactly the strategy Richard Bernstein uses to establish his right to speak on the subject of multiculturalism. At one point in a lengthy argument, he challenges those who make simplistic pronouncements about non-Western cultures, specifically "Asian culture." But what gives a New York writer named Bernstein the authority to write about Asian peoples? Bernstein tells us in a sparkling example of an argument based on character:

> **The Asian culture, as it happens, is something I know a bit about, having spent five years at Harvard striving for a Ph.D. in a joint program called History and East Asian Languages and, after that, living either as a student (for one year) or a journalist (six years) in China and Southeast Asia. At least I know enough to know there is no such thing as the "Asian culture."**
>
> **–Richard Bernstein, *Dictatorship of Virtue***

Clearly, Bernstein understates the case when he says he knows "a bit" about Asian culture and then mentions a Ph.D. program at Harvard and years of living in Asia. But the false modesty may be part of his argumentative strategy, too.

When you write for readers who trust you and your work, you may not have to make such an explicit claim to authority. But you should know that making this type of appeal is always an option. A second lesson is that it certainly helps to know your subject when you are making a claim.

Even if an author does not step directly into the fray, authority can be conveyed through lots of tiny signals that readers may pick up almost subconsciously. Sometimes it comes just from a style of writing that presents ideas with robust confidence. For example, when Allan Bloom wrote a controversial book about problems in American education, he used tough, self-assured prose to argue for what needed to be done:

> **Of course, the only serious solution [to the problems of higher education] is the one that is almost universally rejected: the good old Great Books approach. . . . I am perfectly aware of, and actually agree with, the objections to the Great Books Cult. . . . But one thing is certain: wherever the Great Books make up a central part of the curriculum, the students are excited and satisfied.**
> **–Allan Bloom, *The Closing of the American Mind***

Bloom's "of course" seems arrogant; his concession—"I am perfectly aware"—is poised; his announcement of truth is unyielding—"one thing is certain." Writing like this can sweep readers along; the ideas feel carved in stone. Bloom was a professor at the University of Chicago, respected

In an essay reflecting on her life as a lesbian rabbi, La Escondida makes a powerful claim of authority: "I am a Jew. I am a woman. I am a rabbi. I am a lesbian."

······································ LINK TO P. 654

CULTURAL CONTEXTS FOR ARGUMENT

In the United States, students are often asked to establish authority in their arguments by drawing on certain kinds of personal experience, by reporting on research they or others have conducted, and by taking a position for which they can offer strong evidence and support. But this expectation about student authority is by no means universal. Indeed, some cultures regard student writers as novices who can most effectively make arguments by reflecting back on what they have learned from their teachers and elders—those who hold the most important knowledge, wisdom, and, hence, authority. Whenever you are arguing a point with people from cultures other than your own, therefore, you need to think about what kind of authority you are expected to have:

- Whom are you addressing, and what is your relationship with him or her?

- What knowledge are you expected to have? Is it appropriate or expected for you to demonstrate that knowledge—and if so, how?

- What tone is appropriate? If in doubt, always show respect: politeness is rarely if ever inappropriate.

and knowledgeable and often able to get away with such a style even when his ideas provoked strong opposition. Indeed, there is much to be said for framing arguments directly and confidently, as if you really mean them. (And it helps if you do.)

ESTABLISHING CREDIBILITY

Writers with authority seem smart; those with credibility seem trustworthy. As a writer you usually want to convey both impressions, but sometimes, to seem credible, you have to admit limitations: *this is what I know; I won't pretend to fathom more.* Readers pay attention to writers who are willing to be honest and modest (sometimes even falsely) about their claims.

Imagine, for instance, that you are the commencement speaker at a prestigious women's college. You want the graduates to question all the material advantages they have enjoyed. But you yourself have enjoyed many of the same privileges. How do you protect your argument from charges of hypocrisy? The poet Adrienne Rich defuses this very conflict simply by admitting her status:

> **And so I want to talk today about privilege and tokenism and about power. Everything I can say to you on this subject comes hard-won from the lips of a woman privileged by class and skin color, a father's favorite daughter, educated at Radcliffe.**
> **–Adrienne Rich, "What Does a Woman Need to Know?"**

Candor is a strategy that can earn writers immediate credibility.

It's a tactic used by people as respected in their fields as was the late biologist Lewis Thomas, who in this example ponders whether scientists have overstepped their bounds in exploring the limits of DNA research:

> **I suppose there is one central question to be dealt with, and I am not at all sure how to deal with it, although I am quite certain about my own answer to it. . . . Should we stop short of learning some things, for fear of what we, or someone, will do with the knowledge? My own answer is a flat no, but I must confess that this is an intuitive response and I am neither inclined nor trained to reason my way through it.**
> **–Lewis Thomas, "The Hazards of Science"**

When advancing an argument, many people might be reluctant to write "I suppose" or "I must confess," but those are the very concessions that might increase a reader's confidence in Lewis Thomas.

Thus, a reasonable way to approach an argument—especially an academic or personal one—is to be honest with your readers about who you are and what you do and do not know. If it is appropriate to create a kind of dialogue with readers, as Thomas does, then you want to give them a chance to identify with you, to see the world from your perspective, and to appreciate why you are making specific claims.

In fact, a very powerful technique for building credibility is to acknowledge outright any exceptions, qualifications, or even weaknesses in your argument. Making such concessions to objections that readers might raise, called conditions of rebuttal, sends a strong signal to the audience that you've scrutinized your own position with a sharp critical eye and can therefore be trusted when you turn to arguing its merits. W. Charisse Goodman, arguing that the media promote prejudice against people who aren't thin, points out that some exceptions do exist:

> **Television shows . . . occasionally make an effort. Ricki Lake, who has since lost weight, was featured in the defunct series *China Beach*; Delta Burke once co-starred in *Designing Women* and had her own series; and Roseanne's show has long resided among the Top 10 in the Nielsen ratings. Although these women are encouraging examples of talent overcoming prejudice, they are too few and far between. At best, TV shows typically treat large female characters as special cases whose weight is always a matter of comment, rather than integrating women of all sizes and shapes into their programs as a matter of course.**
>
> **–W. Charisse Goodman, "One Picture Is Worth a Thousand Diets"**

Notice how pointing out these exceptions helps build Goodman's credibility as a critic. Conceding some effort on the part of television shows allows her to make her final judgment more compellingly.

You can also use language in other ways to create a relationship of trust with readers. Speaking to readers directly, using *I* or *you*, for instance, enables you to come closer to them when that strategy is appropriate. Using contractions will have the same effect because they make prose sound more colloquial. Consider how linguist Robert D. King uses such techniques (as well as an admission that he might be wrong) to add a personal note to the conclusion of a serious essay arguing against the notion that language diversity is endangering the United States:

> **If I'm wrong, then the great American experiment will fail—not because of language but because it no longer means anything to be an American; because we have forfeited that "willingness of the heart"**

that F. Scott Fitzgerald wrote was America; because we are no longer joined by Lincoln's "mystic chords of memory."

We are not even close to the danger point. *I suggest* that we relax and luxuriate in our linguistic richness and our traditional tolerance of language differences. Language does not threaten American unity. Benign neglect is a good policy for any country when it comes to language, and it's a good policy for America. (emphasis added)
–Robert D. King, "Should English Be the Law?"

On the other hand, you may find that a more formal tone gives your claims greater authority. Choices like these are yours to make as you search for the ethos that best represents you in a given argument.

Another fairly simple way of conveying both authority and credibility is to back up your claims with evidence and documentation — or, in an electronic environment, to link your claims to sites with reliable information. Citing trustworthy sources and acknowledging them properly shows that you have done your homework.

Indeed, any signals you give readers to show that you have taken care to present ideas clearly and fairly will redound to your credit. A helpful graph, table, chart, or illustration may carry weight, just as does the physical presentation of your work (or your Web site, for that matter). Even proper spelling counts.

In his op-ed essay "If Only We All Spoke Two Languages," Ariel Dorfman establishes credibility for his argument about the methods of teaching English to immigrants in the United States by stating, "Both methods can work. I should know. I have endured them both. But my experience was unquestionably better with bilingual education."

LINK TO P. 581 ·································

RESPOND•

1. Consider the ethos of each of the following figures. Then describe one or two public arguments, campaigns, or products that might benefit from their endorsements as well as several that would not.

   Oprah Winfrey — TV talk-show host

   Jesse Ventura — governor of Minnesota and former professional wrestler

   Katie Holmes — actress featured on *Dawson's Creek*

   Ken Starr — special prosecutor during the Clinton era

   Jesse Jackson — civil rights leader

   Molly Ivins — political humorist and columnist

   Jeff Gordon — NASCAR champion

   Madeleine Albright — secretary of state in the Clinton administration

   Rush Limbaugh — radio talk-show host

   Marge Simpson — sensible wife and mother on *The Simpsons*

Jane Fonda—actress and political activist

Ricky Martin—pop singer from Puerto Rico

2. Voice is a choice. That is, writers modify the tone and style of their language depending on who they want to *seem to be*. Allan Bloom wants to appear poised and confident; his language aims to convince us of his expertise. Terry Tempest Williams wants to appear serious, knowledgeable, and personally invested in the problems of radiation poisoning; the descriptions of her family's illness try to convince us. In different situations, even when writing about the same topics, Bloom and Williams would adopt different voices. (Imagine Williams explaining "The Clan of One-Breasted Women" to a young girl in her family—she might use different words, a changed tone, and simpler examples.)

   Rewrite the Williams passage on p. 66, taking on the voice—the character—of someone speaking to a congressional committee studying nuclear experiments in Utah. Then rewrite the selection in the voice of someone speaking to a fourth-grade class in New Hampshire. You'll need to change the way you claim authority, establish credibility, and demonstrate competence as you try to convince different audiences of your character.

3. A well-known television advertisement from the 1980s featured a soap-opera actor promoting a pain relief medication. "I'm not a doctor," he said, "but I play one on TV." Michael Jordan trades on his good name to star in Nike advertisements. Actress Susan Sarandon uses the entertainment media to argue for political causes. Each of these cases relies on explicit or implicit arguments based on character.

   Develop a one-page print advertisement for a product or service you use often—anything from soap to auto repair to long-distance telephone service. There's one catch: your advertisement should rely on arguments based on character, and you should choose as a spokesperson someone who would seem the *least* likely to use or endorse your product or service (Elizabeth Taylor promoting a marriage-counseling program, for instance, or Al Gore promoting a gas-guzzling sport utility vehicle). The challenge is to turn an apparent disadvantage into an advantage by exploiting character.

chapter seven

Arguments Based on Facts and Reason

"Logic and practical information do not seem to apply here."

"You admit that?"

"To deny the facts would be illogical, Doctor."

–Spock and McCoy,
"A Piece of the Action"

When the choice is between logic and emotion, a great many of us are apt to side with *Star Trek*'s Dr. McCoy rather than the passionless Spock. Most people in Western society admire logical appeals—arguments based on facts, evidence, reason, and logic—but, like the good doctor, people are inclined to test the facts against their feelings. McCoy observes in another *Star Trek* episode, "You can't evaluate a man by logic alone."

The fortunate fact is that human beings aren't computers and most human issues don't present themselves like problems in geometry. When writers seek to persuade, they usually try their best to give readers or listeners good reasons to believe them or to enter into a dialogue with them. Sometimes their presentations get a sympathetic hearing; at other times, even their most reasonable efforts fail. Then they can try harder—by strengthening their good reasons with appeals to the heart and to authority. (For more on these types of appeals, see Chapters 4 and 6.)

Nevertheless, the resources of logical argument are formidable—far too numerous to catalog in a text this brief. Here we can only summarize some of the modes available to you. Aristotle provided one intriguing way of distinguishing among logical appeals when he divided them between inartistic and artistic. Inartistic appeals are those that people don't have to create themselves but find ready-made: facts, statistics, testimonies, witnesses. Artistic appeals are those shaped out of words, using informal logic and common understanding. We'll examine both types of appeals in this chapter.

INARTISTIC APPEALS

The term *inartistic appeal* sounds pejorative to modern ears, as if such an appeal comes up short in grace and subtlety. Nothing could be further from the truth. The arguments found in facts, statistics, and observations require just as much craft as artistic appeals invented by using informal logic. In fact, audiences today probably prefer evidence-based arguments to those grounded in reason. In a courtroom, for example, lawyers look for the "smoking gun"—the piece of *hard* evidence that ties a defendant unequivocally to a crime.

Often less compelling is the argument (perhaps about motive or opportunity) based on reason: *What is the likelihood that so wealthy a person would embezzle five thousand dollars? How could a defendant who had never shot a gun before kill the victim so readily with one clean shot through the heart?* After decades of exposure to science and the wonders of technology, people often have more faith in claims that can be counted, measured, photographed, or analyzed than in those that are merely defended with words.

Inartistic appeals come in many forms. Which ones you use will depend on the kind of argument you are writing.

Facts and Evidence

Facts can make compelling inartistic appeals, especially when readers believe they come from reputable sources. Assembling such evidence practically defines what contemporary writers mean by *scholarship*. Consider why a reviewer for the conservative journal *National Review* praises the work of William Julius Wilson, a liberal sociologist:

> In his eagerly awaited new book, Wilson argues that ghetto blacks are worse off than ever, victimized by a near-total loss of low-skill jobs in and around inner-city neighborhoods. In support of this thesis, he musters *mountains of data, plus excerpts from some of the thousands of surveys and face-to-face interviews* that he and his research team conducted among inner-city Chicagoans. It is a book that deserves a wide audience among thinking conservatives. (emphasis added)
> –John J. DiIulio Jr., "When Decency Disappears"

Wilson's book is recommended precisely because of its formidable mustering of evidence; the facts are trusted even above ideology.

When facts are compelling, they may stand on their own in an argument, supported by little more than a reliable source of the information. Consider the power of phrases such as "reported by the *New York Times*," "according to CNN," or "in a book published by Oxford University Press." Such sources gain credibility if they have, in readers' experience, reported facts accurately in most cases.

But arguing with facts often involves disputing existing claims. That's a tactic used by Christina Hoff Sommers, who challenges a story widely reported in reputable newspapers:

> A story in the *Boston Globe* written by Lynda Gorov reported that women's shelters and hotlines are "flooded with more calls from victims [on Super Bowl Sunday] than on any other day of the year." Miss Gorov cited "one study of women's shelters out West" that "showed a 40 per cent climb in calls, a pattern advocates said is repeated nationwide, including in Massachusetts."
>
> In this roiling sea of credulity was a lone island of professional integrity. Ken Ringle, a *Washington Post* staff writer, took the time to call around. When he asked Janet Katz—professor of sociology and criminal justice at Old Dominion . . .—about the connection between violence and football games, she said: "That's not what we found at all." Instead, she told him, they had found that an increase in emergency room admissions "was not associated with the occurrence of football games in general."
> –Christina Hoff Sommers, "Figuring Out Feminism"

In an ideal world, good evidence would always drive out bad. But as a writer, you'll soon learn that such is not always the case. That's why you have to present to readers not only the facts but also the contexts in which they make sense. You also must scrutinize any information you do collect before using it yourself, testing its reliability and reporting it with all appropriate qualifiers.

Providing evidence ought to become a habit whenever you write an argument. The evidence not only makes your case plausible; it also furnishes the details that make writing interesting. As noted earlier, Aristotle observed that arguments could be reduced to two basic parts:

Statement + Proof

These two basic parts of arguments are sometimes referred to as the claim and the supporting evidence. When you remember to furnish evidence for every disputable claim you make, you go a long way toward understanding argument. The process can be remarkably straightforward. For example, anthropologist Emily Martin believes that many scientific concepts—especially the operation of the human immune system—have been shaped by cultural metaphors that have racist, sexist, and classist implications. How does she prove such a thesis? She makes specific claims and then marshals supporting examples from professional literature, with each bit of evidence fully documented:

> *Although the metaphor of warfare against an external enemy dominates these accounts, another metaphor plays nearly as large a role: the body as police state.* **Every body cell is equipped with " 'proof of identity' . . . The human body's police corps is programmed to distinguish between bona fide residents and illegal aliens—an ability fundamental to the body's power of self-defense" (Nilsson 1985:21). What identifies a resident is likened to speaking a national language: "An immune cell bumps into a bacterial cell and says, 'Hey, this guy isn't speaking our language, he's an intruder.' That's defense" (Levy, quoted in Jaret 1986:733). (emphasis added)**
>
> –Emily Martin, "The Body at War"

Remember, too, that you want readers to understand and identify with your notions. That's why the examples that provide support for claims also make the claims engaging. For example, in writing about evidence of job insecurity among young people, Caryn James draws on interesting evidence from popular culture:

In music, alternative rock is the equivalent of the slacker film. In their song "Long View," the group Green Day proves there is no long view for its generation. The narrator watches television all day and sings: "My mother says to get a job/But she don't like the one she's got." A bleak future—a bad job or no job—is a legacy passed on from mom and dad.

–Caryn James, "Pop Culture: Extremes but Little Reality"

The specific details here both support James's thesis and help older readers understand a subject they may find alien. The song lyric in particular gives the argument both support and texture.

Statistics

Let's deal with a cliché right up front: *figures lie and liars figure.* Like all clichés, it contains a grain of truth. It is possible to lie with numbers, even those that are accurate. Anyone either using or reading statistics has good reason to ask how the numbers were gathered and how they have been interpreted. Both factors bear on the credibility of statistical arguments.

But the fact remains that contemporary culture puts great stock in tables, graphs, reports, and comparisons of numbers. People use such numbers to understand the past, evaluate the present, and speculate about the future. These numbers almost always need writers to interpret them. And writers almost always have agendas that influence their interpretations.

For example, you might want to herald the good news that unemployment in the United States stands just a tick over 5 percent. That means 95 percent of Americans have jobs, a figure much higher than that of most other industrial nations. But let's spin the figure another way. In a country as populous as the United States, unemployment at 5 percent means that millions of Americans are without a daily wage. Indeed, one out of every twenty adults who wants work can't find it. One out of twenty! As you can see, the same statistics can be cited as a cause for celebration or shame.

We don't mean to suggest that numbers are meaningless or untrustworthy or that you have license to use them in any way that serves your purposes. Quite the contrary. But you do have to understand the role *you* play in giving numbers a voice and presence.

Look at how W. Michael Cox and Richard Alm first present an economic experiment and then interpret its results to support their thesis that inequality in a nation's economy is not necessarily the result of inequity:

In the early 1970s, three groups of unemployed Canadians, all in their 20s, all with at least twelve years of schooling, volunteered to take up residence in a stylized economy where the only employment was making woolen belts on small hand looms. They could work as much or as little as they liked, earning $2.50 for each belt. After 98 days, the results were anything but equal: 37.2 percent of the economy's income went to the 20 percent with the highest earnings. The bottom 20 percent received only 6.6 percent.

This economic microcosm tells us one thing: even among people with identical work options, differences in talent, motivation and preferences will lead some workers to earn more than others. Income inequality isn't some quirk or some aberration. Quite the opposite, it's perfectly consistent with the economic laws that govern a free enterprise system.

–W. Michael Cox and Richard Alm, "By Our Own Bootstraps"

Notice that the interpretation depends on readers agreeing to a key claim: "This economic microcosm tells us one thing." If you wanted to dispute Cox and Alm's argument, you'd probably begin by challenging their reading of the data and offering a second (or third) way of explaining the same experiment. But in either case, the statistical results of the experiment don't become an argument until a writer uses them.

In his hilarious essay "Don't Make English Official — Ban It Instead," Dennis Baron uses a single statistic as powerful evidence for his argument, saying that "opponents of official English remind us that without legislation we have managed to get over 97 percent of the residents of this country to speak the national language."

·· LINK TO P. 213

Surveys, Polls, and Studies

Surveys and polls produce statistics. But they play so large a role in people's political and social lives that writers, whether using them or fashioning surveys themselves, need to give them special attention.

Surveys and polls provide persuasive appeals when they document the popularity of an idea or proposal since, in a democracy, majority opinion offers a compelling warrant: *a government should do what most people want.* Polls come as close to expressing the will of the people as anything short of an election — the most compelling and decisive poll of all. (For more on warrants, see Chapter 8, p. 95.)

However, surveys, polls, and studies can do much more than help politicians make decisions. They can also provide persuasive reasons for action or intervention. When studies show, for example, that most American sixth-graders don't know where France or Wyoming is on the map, that's an appeal for better instruction in geography. Here's Adrienne Rich arguing from a study for better education for women:

> [I]t is well for us to remember that, in an age of increasing illiteracy, 60 percent of the world's illiterates are women. Between 1960 and 1970, the number of illiterate men in the world rose by 8 million, while the number of illiterate women rose by 40 million.[1] And the number of illiterate women is increasing.
>
> –Adrienne Rich, "What Does a Woman Need to Know?"

By this point, however, you should appreciate the responsibility to question any cited study, even one offered to champion a cause as benign as improving education. What's Rich's source for these numbers? The superscript "1" provides the answer in a footnote: the United Nations' *Compendium of Social Statistics*. At this point, you might decide to trust the source or wonder whether the United Nations' numbers are influenced by a feminist social agenda. Perhaps you should also wonder why Rich doesn't use more recent figures. But you could check the date of her work: it turns out that the passage was written in 1979. And that fact might raise more questions about how relevant her numbers are today, decades later.

Are we picking on Rich? In fact, no. The scrutiny here is just the sort you should give to any claim in a study—and the sort you should anticipate from your readers whenever you use such material to frame an argument. Especially with polls and surveys, you should be confident that you or your source surveyed enough people to be accurate, that the people you chose for the study were representative of the selected population as a whole, and that you chose them randomly—not selecting those most likely to say what you hoped to hear.

Surveys and polls can be affected, too, by the way questions are asked. Professional pollsters generally understand that their reputations depend on asking questions in as neutral a way as possible. But some researchers aren't above skewing their results by asking leading questions. Consider how differently people might respond to the following queries on roughly the same subject:

Do you support cuts in Medicare to balance the budget?

Do you support adjustments in Medicare to keep the system solvent?

Do you support decisive action to prevent the bankruptcy of Medicare?

The simple lesson here is to use polls, surveys, and other studies responsibly.

Testimonies, Reports, and Interviews

We don't want to give the impression that numbers and statistics make the only good evidence. Writers support arguments with all kinds of human experiences, particularly those they or others have lived or reported. The testimony of reliable witnesses counts not only in courts but in almost any situation in which a writer seeks to make a case for action, change, or sympathetic understanding.

A writer's account of an event can support an argument when it helps readers identify with worlds otherwise unknown to them—as in the following passage, in which Maya Angelou explains what the black boxer Joe Louis meant to African Americans in the 1930s. The paragraph refers to a moment when Louis, facing a white opponent, seemed to be losing the fight that eventually earned him the heavyweight championship of the world:

> **My race groaned. It was our people falling. It was another lynching, yet another Black man hanging on a tree. One more woman ambushed and raped. A Black boy whipped and maimed. It was hounds on the trail of a man running through slimy swamps. It was a white woman slapping her maid for being forgetful.**
>
> **–Maya Angelou, "Champion of the World"**

Personal experience carefully reported can also support a claim convincingly, especially if a writer has earned the trust of readers. In the following excerpt, Christian Zawodniak describes his experiences as a student in a first-year college writing course. Not impressed by his instructor's performance, Zawodniak provides specific evidence of the instructor's failings:

> **My most vivid memory of Jeff's rigidness was the day he responded to our criticisms of the class. Students were given a chance anonymously to write our biggest criticisms one Monday, and the following Wednesday Jeff responded, staunchly answering all criticisms of his teaching: "Some of you complained that I didn't come to class prepared. It took me five years to learn all this." Then he pointed to the blackboard on which he had written all the concepts we had discussed that quarter. His responses didn't seem genuine or aimed at improving his teaching or helping students to understand him. He thought he was always right. Jeff's position gave him responsibilities**

that he officially met. But he didn't take responsibility in all the ways
he had led us to expect.
                    —Christian Zawodniak, "Teacher Power, Student Pedagogy"

Zawodniak's portrait of a defensive instructor gives readers details by
which to assess the argument. If readers believe Zawodniak, they learn
something about teaching. (For more on establishing credibility with readers, see Chapter 6.)

Shifting from personal experience to more distanced observations of
people and institutions, writers move into the arena of ethnographic
observation, learning what they can from the close study of human
behavior and culture. Ethnography is a discipline in itself with clearly
defined methods of studying phenomena and reporting data, but the
instinct to explore and argue from observation is widespread. Notice that
instinct in play as English professor Shelby Steele assembles evidence to
explain why race relationships on college campuses may be deteriorating:

> To look at this mystery, I left my own campus with its burden of famil-
> iarity and talked with black and white students at California schools
> where racial incidents had occurred: Stanford, UCLA, and Berkeley.
> I spoke with black and white students—not with Asians and
> Hispanics—because, as always, blacks and whites represent the
> deepest lines of division, and because I hesitate to wander into the
> complex territory of other minority groups. A phrase by William H.
> Gass—"the hidden internality of things"—describes, with maybe a
> little too much grandeur, what I hoped to find. But it is what I wanted
> to find, for this is the kind of problem that makes a black person nerv-
> ous, which is not to say that it doesn't unnerve whites as well. Once
> every six months or so someone yells "nigger" at me from a passing
> car. I don't like to think that these solo artists might soon make up a
> chorus, or worse, that this chorus might one day soon sing to me from
> the paths of my own campus.
>   —Shelby Steele, "The Recoloring of Campus Life"

Steele's method of observation also includes a rationale for his study,
giving it both credibility and immediacy. Chances are, readers will pay
attention to what he discovers. It may be worth noting that personal narratives and ethnographic reports can sometimes reach into the "hidden
internality of things" where more scientific approaches cannot inquire so
easily or reveal so much.

See Sherman Alexie's poem "The
Exaggeration of Despair" for a
good example of the use of testimony in the genre of poetry.

LINK TO P. 383

As you see, with appropriate caution and suitable qualifications you can offer personal experiences and careful observations as valid forms of argument.

ARTISTIC APPEALS

Artistic appeals are based on principles of reason rather than on specific pieces of evidence. In other words, writers base these cases on principles, assumptions, and habits of mind that they share with readers. Although these principles are formally known and studied as "logic," few people, except perhaps mathematicians and philosophers, present arguments using formal logic; the extent of what most people know about it is the most famous of all syllogisms (a vehicle of formal deductive logic):

All human beings are mortal.
Socrates is a human being.
Therefore, Socrates is mortal.

Fortunately, even as gifted a logician as Aristotle recognized that most people could argue very well using informal logic (some might say common sense). Consciously or not, people are constantly stating propositions, drawing inferences, assessing premises and assumptions, and deriving conclusions whenever they read or write.

In the next chapter, we describe a system of informal logic you'll find useful in shaping credible arguments—Toulmin argument. Here we want to examine the way informal logic works in people's daily lives.

Once again, we begin with Aristotle, who used the term *enthymeme* to describe a very ordinary kind of sentence, one that includes both a claim and a reason.

Enthymeme = Claim + Reason

Enthymemes are logical propositions that everyone makes almost effortlessly. The following sentences are all enthymemes:

We'd better cancel the picnic because it's going to rain.

Flat taxes are fair because they treat everyone in the same way.

I'll buy a Honda Civic because it's cheap and reliable.

Alex Rodriguez ought to be a baseball all-star because he's hitting over 300.

Enthymemes are persuasive statements when most readers agree with the assumptions hidden within them. Sometimes the statements seem so commonsensical that readers aren't even aware of the logical exercises they perform in accepting them. Consider the first example:

We'd better cancel the picnic because it's going to rain.

When a writer makes such a claim, it's usually derived from more specific information, so let's expand the enthymeme a bit to say what the writer really means:

We'd better cancel the picnic this afternoon because the weather bureau is predicting a 70 percent chance of rain for the remainder of the day.

Embedded in this little argument are all sorts of assumptions and bits of cultural information that help make it persuasive, among them:

Picnics are ordinarily held outdoors.

When the weather is bad, it's best to cancel picnics.

Rain is bad weather for picnics.

A 70 percent chance of rain means that rain is more likely than not.

When rain is more likely than not, it makes sense to cancel picnics.

The weather bureau's predictions are reliable enough to warrant action.

In most cases, it would be tedious and unnecessary to make all these points just to suggest that a picnic should be canceled because of rain. The enthymeme carries this baggage on its own; it is a *compressed* argument, acknowledging what audiences know and will accept.

Cultural Assumptions

Most logical arguments you are likely to make tote some of society's baggage in just this way—that is, the enthymemes likely rely on premises and assumptions that are acceptable to most readers. Where the premises or assumptions aren't acceptable, you'll have to make a conscious case for them. (After all, someone might object when you cancel the picnic that *you can't trust the weather bureau!*) Even when the premises are acceptable, you still have to prove that your particular claim is true—that the picnic will in fact be held outdoors and that the weather bureau has indeed predicted bad weather for the remainder of the day. So most informal arguments will involve presenting and proving enthymemes. And many enthymemes will be supported (consciously or not) by premises of argument widely endorsed by readers.

Some of those premises are grounded in culture and history. In the United States, for example, few arguments work better than those based on principles of fairness and equity. Most Americans believe that all people should be treated in the same way, no matter who they are or where they come from. That principle is announced even in the Declaration of Independence: *All men are created equal.*

Because fairness is culturally accepted, in American society enthymemes based on equity ordinarily need less support than those that challenge it. That's why, for example, both sides in debates over affirmative action programs seek the high ground of fairness: proponents claim that affirmative action is needed to correct enduring inequities from the past; opponents suggest that the preferential policies should be overturned because they cause inequity today. Here's Linda Chavez drawing deeply on this equity principle:

> **Ultimately, entitlements based on their status as "victims" rob Hispanics of real power. The history of American ethnic groups is one of overcoming disadvantage, of competing with those who were already here and proving themselves as competent as any who came before. Their fight was always to be treated the same as other Americans, never to be treated as special, certainly not to turn the temporary disadvantages they suffered into permanent entitlement. Anyone who thinks this fight was easier in the earlier part of this century when it was waged by other ethnic groups does not know history.**
> **–Linda Chavez, "Towards a New Politics of Hispanic Assimilation"**

Chavez expects Hispanics to accept her claims because she believes they do not wish to be treated differently than other ethnic groups in the society.

Other Artistic Appeals

Other lines of argument are less tightly bound to particular cultural assumptions. They seem to work on their own, making a plausible case that readers can readily comprehend—even when they don't necessarily agree with it. Arguments about *greater or lesser good* are of this type; they rarely need complex explanations. Consider the following argument from novelist Ayn Rand:

In an article about the allocation of transplant organs, Steven Walters and Marilynn Marchione appeal to our sense of fairness when they quote the head of a Wisconsin transplant program as saying, "We want to be good neighbors and play a fair game, but Chicago-area transplant programs won't agree to a payback system for organs sent to them from Wisconsin or other states."

LINK TO P. 550

If physical slavery is repulsive, how much more repulsive is the concept of servility of the spirit? The conquered slave has a vestige of
honor. He has the merit of having resisted and of considering his condition evil. But the man who enslaves himself voluntarily in the name
of love is the basest of creatures. He degrades the dignity of man and
he degrades the conception of love. But this is the essence of altruism.
— Ayn Rand, *The Fountainhead*

Although readers might disagree with this conclusion, the comparisons
posed help demonstrate why servility of spirit might be considered more
repulsive than physical slavery.

Gertrude Himmelfarb offers a less dramatic variation of this structure
when she presents a case for establishing orphanages to care for neglected children:

Orphanages are, to be sure, far more expensive than conventional
relief. But the cost is not so excessive when compared with that of
prisons, hospitals and asylums in which some of these children might
otherwise spend a great deal of their adult lives, to say nothing of the
cost of crime, delinquency, illiteracy and other social ills that these
children might inflict on society.
— Gertrude Himmelfarb, "The Victorians Get a Bad Rap"

Readers are much more likely to tolerate an expensive proposition if it
can be made to seem ultimately less costly than alternatives. This structure of support is one of the most common in deliberations about policy.

Analogies offer another appeal that people understand intuitively.
They usually involve illuminating something that is not well known by
comparing it to something much more familiar. We reject or accept such
analogies, depending on the quality of the comparison. For example, in
arguing that "full-body transplants" could present major ethical as well as
technical problems, Maia Szalavitz compares this operation to a horrifying fountain of youth:

Could full-body transplants become a macabre fountain of youth,
offering people a chance at near immortality as they continually
replace old bodies with new, younger ones? Will headless bodies be
cloned as replacements, or would people need other sources of
donors? Could this offer a bizarre new way to get a sex change? And
what does it say about identity, humanity and the soul?
— Maia Szalavitz, "Where's the Rest of Me?"

While the idea of a full-body transplant may offer attractions similar to
those connected with the fountain of youth, it may turn out not to be at

See how Charles Mann, in his
article "Who Will Own Your
Next Good Idea?" sets up a false
analogy about a friend's writing
being plagiarized in order to
frame his argument.

LINK TO P. 564

all like what we had traditionally imagined. Readers have to decide whether they are persuaded by the comparison.

As you can see, artistic appeals may require a bit of skill to construct and analyze. We give you a tool to do just that in the next chapter.

RESPOND•

1. Discuss whether the following statements are examples of inartistic or artistic appeals. Not all cases are clear-cut.

   "The bigger they are, the harder they fall."

   Drunk drivers are involved in more than 50 percent of traffic deaths.

   DNA tests of skin found under the victim's fingernails suggest that the defendant was responsible for the assault.

   Polls suggest that a large majority of Americans favor a constitutional amendment to ban flag burning.

   A psychologist testified that teenage violence could not be blamed on computer games.

   Honey attracts more flies than vinegar.

   Historical precedents demonstrate that cutting tax rates usually increases tax revenues because people work harder when they can keep more of what they earn.

   "We have nothing to fear but fear itself."

   Air bags ought to be removed from vehicles because they can kill young children and small adults.

2. We suggest in this chapter that statistical evidence—a kind of inartistic appeal—becomes useful only when responsible authors interpret the data fairly and reasonably. When Adrienne Rich argued in 1979 for better education for women, she used statistics to prove her point. Anyone making the same kind of argument today would need to do more statistical research before reaching a fair conclusion.

   Find several sources of information on men's and women's literacy rates worldwide (you might start with a recent edition of the United Nations' *Compendium of Social Statistics*). On the basis of your reading of the statistics, take a position on the need for more attention to women's literacy education, and write a paragraph for a general, educated audience arguing this position. Then write an opposing argument—many such arguments are available, not just simple pro versus con debates—using the same statistics.

We don't mean to suggest that you learn to use data disingenuously, but it is important that you see firsthand how the same statistics can serve a variety of arguments. After you've written the two opposing arguments, write a paragraph explaining which one you see as being fairer and more reasonable.

3. Testimony can be just as suspect as statistics. For example, movie reviews are often excerpted by advertising copywriters for inclusion in newspaper ads. A reviewer's stinging indictment of a shoot-'em-up film—"This summer blockbuster will be a great success at the box office; as a piece of filmmaking, though, it is a complete disaster"—could be reduced to "A great success."

   Bring to class a review of a recent film that you enjoyed. (If you haven't enjoyed any films lately, select a review of one you hated.) Using testimony from that review, write a brief argument to your classmates explaining why they should see that movie (or why they should avoid it at all costs). Be sure to use the evidence from the review fairly and reasonably, as support for a claim that you are making.

   Then exchange arguments with a classmate and decide whether the evidence in your peer's argument helps convince you about the movie. What is convincing about the evidence? If it does not convince you, why not?

4. For each excerpt in this chapter—from John J. Dilulio Jr.'s book review to Maia Szalavitz's passage on full-body transplants—determine the principal enthymeme (the claim and supporting reason) in the text. Remember that enthymemes are logical arguments that rely on assumptions the audience is likely to grant. For example, we could say that Linda Chavez's argument is built around the following enthymeme: Hispanics should not support policies that rely on their status as "victims" because such policies prevent them from proving themselves equal to other Americans. (This is just one version of the enthymeme; you might find other ways of stating the same general argument as a claim plus supporting reasons.)

   In the case of excerpts that are built on inartistic appeals, the enthymemes probably refer to the data. A few excerpts are logically very complex; you'll have to work hard to create simplified statements of claim and reasons without reducing the argument in an irresponsible way.

PART 3

WRITING arguments

chapter eight

Structuring Arguments

What do you do when you want to write an argument? The sheer variety of persuasive situations precludes simple guidelines: arguments serve too many audiences and purposes to wear one suit of clothes. All writing, moreover, is a process of discovery—thoroughly unpredictable and idiosyncratic. As a result, arguments can't be stamped out like sheet metal panels; they have to be treated like living things—cultivated, encouraged, and refined. Five-step plans for changing minds or scoring points don't work.

TOULMIN ARGUMENT

What we can offer, instead, is an informal method for constructing the kinds of arguments that can be expressed in thesis statements. This system—known as Toulmin argument after British philosopher Stephen Toulmin, who describes the method in *The Uses of Argument* (1958)—will help you think more clearly about basic elements of the writing process.

In the following pages, we'll introduce some key terms and processes of Toulmin argument as modified over the years by teachers of writing and rhetoric. Because it traces the ways many people really think rather than the paths of formal logic, Toulmin argument isn't airtight. But for exactly that reason, it has become a powerful and practical tool for shaping serious and persuasive prose. At the least, it opens up the dialogue at the heart of all inquiry.

Making Claims

In the Toulmin model, arguments begin with claims, which are statements of belief or truth. When you make an argument, you stake out a position others will likely find controversial and debatable. Notice that in this model the arguments depend on conditions set by others—your audience or readers. "It's raining" might be an innocent statement of fact in one situation; in another, it might provoke a debate: *No, it's not. That's sleet.* And in this way an inquiry begins, exploring a question of definition.

Claims worth arguing tend to be controversial; there's no point insisting on what most people freely acknowledge. For example, there are assertions in the statements *Twelve inches make a foot* or *Earth is the third planet from the sun.* But except in unusual circumstances, these claims aren't worth much debate. Life is too short to belabor the obvious.

Claims should also be debatable. That means that they can be demonstrated using logic or evidence, material offered to support an argument. Sometimes the line between what's debatable and what isn't can be thin. You push back your chair from the table in a restaurant and declare, "That was delicious!" A debatable point? Not really. If you thought the meal was appetizing, who can challenge your taste, particularly if your pronouncement touches no one but yourself?

But now imagine you're a restaurant critic working for the local newspaper, leaning back from the same table, making the same observation. Because of your job, your claim about the restaurant's cuisine has different status and wider implications. People's jobs may be at stake. "That was delicious!" suddenly becomes a matter for contention and demonstration, bite by bite.

CULTURAL CONTEXTS FOR ARGUMENT

In the United States, many people (especially those in the academic and business worlds) expect a writer to "get to the point" as directly as possible and to take on the major responsibility of articulating that point efficiently and unambiguously. Student writers are typically expected to make their claims explicit, leaving little unspoken. Such claims usually appear early on in an argument, often in the first paragraph. But not all cultures take such an approach. Some prefer that the claim or thesis be introduced subtly and indirectly, expecting that readers will be able to "read between the lines" to understand what is being said. Some even save the thesis until the very end of a written argument. Here are a couple of tips that might help you think about how explicitly you should (or should not) make your points:

- What general knowledge does your audience have about your topic? What information do they expect or need you to provide?

- Does your audience tend to be very direct, saying explicitly what they mean? Or are they more subtle, less likely to call a spade a spade? Look for cues to determine how much responsibility you have as the writer, and how you can most successfully argue your points.

Many writers stumble when it comes to making claims because facing issues squarely can take thought and guts. A claim answers the question: *What's your point?* If you haven't settled an issue in your own mind, it's hard to make a case to others. So writers and speakers sometimes avoid taking a stand, spewing out whole paragraphs to disguise the fact that they don't yet know enough about an issue to argue a case.

Is there a danger that a bold claim might oversimplify an issue? Of course. But making the claim is a logical first step toward complexity. Here are some fairly simple, undeveloped claims:

Grades in college should be abolished.

Flat taxes are fair.

NASA should launch a human expedition to Mars.

The federal government should support the arts.

Note that these claims are statements, not questions. There's nothing wrong with questions per se, but they're what you ask to reach a claim:

Questions	What should NASA's next goal be? Should the space agency establish a permanent moon base? Should NASA launch more robotic interstellar probes? Should NASA send people to Mars or Venus?
Statement	NASA should launch a human expedition to Mars.

Don't mistake one for the other.

Attaching Reasons

For every claim, there should be a reason—or two or three. A reason is a statement that offers evidence to support a claim. You can begin developing a claim, then, by drawing up a list of good reasons to support it. Doing so will provide a framework for your argument by generating a series of smaller claims that you can explore and, if necessary, shore up.

One student writer, for instance, wanted to gather good reasons in support of a claim that his college campus needed more space for motorcycle parking. He had been doing some research—gathering statistics about parking space allocation, numbers of people using particular parking lots, and numbers of motorcycles registered on campus. Before he went any further with this argument, however, he decided to list the good reasons he had identified for more motorcycle parking:

> *Personal experience:* At least three times a week for two terms, he had been unable to find a parking space for his bike.
>
> *Anecdotes:* Several of his best friends told similar stories; one had even sold her bike as a result.
>
> *Facts:* He had found out that the ratio of car to bike parking spaces was 200 to 1, whereas the ratio of cars to bikes registered on campus was 25 to 1.
>
> *Authorities:* The campus police chief had indicated in an interview with the college newspaper that she believed a problem existed for students trying to park motorcycles.

On the basis of his preliminary listing of possible reasons in support of the claim, this student decided that it would be worth his time to conduct extensive firsthand observation of campus parking conditions and to survey campus motorcycle owners. He was on the way to amassing a set of good reasons sufficient to support his claim.

In some arguments you read, claims might be widely separated from the reasons offered to support them. But in shaping your own arguments, try putting claims and reasons together early in the writing process to create what Aristotle called enthymemes, or arguments in brief. Think of these enthymemes as test cases:

> **Grades in college should be abolished** *because I don't like them!*

> **Flat taxes are fairer than progressive taxes** *because they treat all taxpayers in the same way.*

> NASA **should launch a human expedition to Mars** *because Americans need a unifying national goal.*

> *Since the federal government supports the military,* **the federal government should support the arts.**

As you can see, attaching a reason to a claim spells out the terms of an argument. In rare cases, the full enthymeme is all the argument you'll need:

> **Don't eat that mushroom—it's poisonous.**

> **We'd better stop for gas because the gauge has been reading empty for more than thirty miles.**

But more often, your work is just beginning when you've created an enthymeme. If your readers are capable—and you should always assume they are—they will then begin to question your enthymeme. At issue are the assumptions that connect your claim to the reason(s) you offer for supporting it. Also under scrutiny will be the evidence you introduce to make your case. You've got to address both issues: quality of assumptions, and quality of evidence. That connection between claim and reason(s) is a concern at the next level in Toulmin argument. (For more on enthymemes, see Chapter 7, p. 82.)

Determining Warrants

A crucial step in Toulmin argument is learning to state the warrants that support particular arguments. The warrant is the connection, often unstated and assumed, between your claim and your supporting reason(s), the glue that holds them together. Like the warrant in legal situations (a search warrant, for example), a sound warrant in an argument gives you authority to proceed with a case. If readers accept your warrant, you can then present specific evidence to prove your claim. If readers dispute your warrant, you'll have to defend it before you can move on to the claim itself.

James Hill makes the claim, in "Say What? Watch Your Language," that Ebonics is a dialect of English, not a separate language. He presents a definitional argument as his reason, providing evidence from the dictionary definition of *dialect* and from regional dialects in Minnesota and the U.S. South.

LINK TO P. 608

Stating warrants can be tricky because they can be phrased in various ways. What you are looking for is the general principle that enables you to move from the reason to the specific claim.

The warrant is the assumption that makes the claim seem plausible. Let's demonstrate this logical movement with an easy example.

Don't eat that mushroom—it's poisonous.

The warrant supporting this enthymeme can be stated in several ways, always moving from the reason ("it's poisonous") to the claim ("Don't eat that mushroom"):

That which is poisonous shouldn't be eaten.

If something is poisonous, it's dangerous to eat.

Here is the relationship, diagrammed:

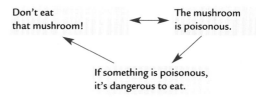

Perfectly obvious, you say? Exactly—and that's why the enthymeme is so convincing. If the mushroom in question is indeed a death angel or toadstool (and you might still need expert testimony to prove that's what it is), the warrant does the rest of the work, making the claim it supports seem logical and persuasive.

Let's look at a similar example, beginning with the argument in its enthymeme form:

We'd better stop for gas because the gauge has been reading empty for more than thirty miles.

There are at least two ways to express the warrant supporting this statement, beginning, as usual, with the reason ("because the gauge has been reading empty") and moving to the claim ("We'd better stop for gas"):

If the fuel gauge of a car has been reading empty for more than thirty miles, the tank is nearly empty.

When a fuel gauge has been reading empty for more than thirty miles, a car is about to run out of gas.

Since most readers would accept either of these warrants as reasonable, they would also likely accept the statement the warrants support.

Of course, cultural assumptions—beliefs considered obvious or commonsensical within a particular group—are operating in this statement. Such assumptions can function as warrants themselves: readers would understand without further explanation that running out of gas is no fun.

Naturally, factual information might undermine the whole argument—the fuel gauge might be broken, or the driver might know from previous experience that the car will go another ninety miles even though the fuel gauge reads empty. But in most cases, most readers would accept the warrant.

Let's look at a third easy case, one in which stating the warrant confirms the weakness of an enthymeme that doesn't seem convincing on its own merits:

Grades in college should be abolished *because I don't like them!*

Moving from stated reason to claim, we see that the warrant is a silly and selfish principle:

What I don't like should be abolished.

Most readers won't accept this assumption as a principle worth applying generally. It would produce a chaotic or arbitrary world, like that of the Queen of Hearts in *Alice in Wonderland*. (*Off with the heads of anyone I don't like!*)

So far so good. But how does understanding warrants make you better at writing arguments? Warrants suggest to you what arguments you have to make and at what level you have to make them. If your warrant isn't controversial, you can immediately begin to illustrate and defend your claim. If your warrant is controversial, you must explain the warrant—or modify it or shift your argument to different, more fertile grounds.

Let's consider how stating and exploring a warrant can help you determine the grounds on which you want to make a case. Here's a political enthymeme of a familiar sort:

Flat taxes are fairer than progressive taxes *because they treat all taxpayers in the same way.*

Warrants that follow from this enthymeme have power because they appeal to a core American value—equal treatment under the law:

> **That which treats all taxpayers in the same way is fair.**
>
> **Fair taxes are those that treat all taxpayers in the same way.**

You certainly could make an argument on these grounds. But stating the warrant should also put you on alert about this line of approach. If the principle is so obvious and universal, why are federal income taxes progressive, requiring people at higher levels of income to pay at higher tax rates than people at lower income levels? Could it be that the warrant isn't as universally endorsed as it might seem at first glance? To explore the argument further, try stating the contrary enthymeme and warrant:

> **Progressive taxes are fairer than flat taxes** *because they tax people according to their ability to pay.*
>
> **Fair taxes are those that tax people according to their ability to pay.**

Now you see how different the assumptions behind opposing positions really are. In making the flat tax argument, you'll almost certainly want to address the issue raised by the contrary warrant. Or you may want to shift grounds in your presentation of the claim. After all, you aren't obligated to argue any particular proposition. So you might explore an alternative rationale for flat taxes:

> **Flat taxes are preferable to progressive taxes** *because they simplify the tax code and reduce fraud.*

Now you have two stated reasons, supported by two new warrants:

> **Taxes that simplify the tax code are desirable.**
>
> **Taxes that reduce fraud are preferable.**

Consider Johnny Hart's *B.C.* cartoons, which address matters of faith from a Christian perspective. The warrant underlying these cartoons might be that the teachings of Jesus should be taken to heart.

LINK TO P. 641

You may find that warrants based on practicality provide surer grounds on which to erect your argument than warrants based on fairness. For example, middle-class taxpayers might question the equity of a flat tax system that expects them to pay at the same rate as wealthier people. But they might be willing to try out a simpler tax code if it actually relieved them of the burden of tax preparation and closed loopholes that made tax fraud possible. As always, you have to choose your warrant knowing your audience, the context of your argument, and your own feelings. But understanding how to state a warrant and how to assess its potential makes subsequent choices better informed.

Offering Evidence: Backing and Grounds

As you might guess, claims and warrants are only the skeleton of an argument; the bulk of a writer's work—the richest, most interesting part—still remains to be done after the argument has been assembled. Claims and warrants clearly stated do suggest the scope of the evidence you have yet to assemble.

An example will illustrate the point. Here's an enthymeme, suitably debatable and controversial, if somewhat abstract:

> NASA **should launch a human expedition to Mars** *because Americans need a unifying national goal.*

Here's the warrant that supports the enthymeme, at least one version of it:

> **What unifies the nation ought to be a national priority.**

To run with this claim and warrant, a writer needs, first, to place both in context because most points worth arguing have a rich history. Entering an argument can be like walking into a conversation already in progress. In the case of the politics of space exploration, the conversation has been a vigorous one, debated with varying intensity since the launch in 1957 of the Soviet Union's *Sputnik* satellite—the first human-engineered object to orbit the earth. A writer stumbling into this dialogue without a sense of history or context won't get far. Acquiring background knowledge (through reading, conversation, inquiry of all kinds) is the toll you have to pay to gain authority to speak on this subject. Without a minimum amount of information on this—or any comparable subject—all the subtleties of Toulmin argument won't do you much good. You've got to do the legwork before you're ready to make a case. (See Chapter 6 for more on gaining authority.)

Want examples of premature argument? Just listen to talk radio or C-SPAN phone-ins for a day or two. You'll soon learn that the better callers can hold a conversation with the host or guests, fleshing out their basic claims with facts, personal experience, and evidence. The weaker callers can usually offer a claim or even push as far as a full enthymeme. But then such callers begin to repeat themselves, as if saying over and over again that "Republicans are starving children" or "Democrats are scaring our senior citizens" will make the statement true.

If you are going to make a claim about the politics of space exploration, you need to defend both your warrant and your claim with authority, knowledge, and some passion (see Chapters 4–7), beginning with the warrant. Why? Because there is no point defending any claim until you've satisfied readers about the sturdiness of the foundation on which the claim is built. Evidence you offer in support of a warrant is called backing.

Warrant

What unifies the nation ought to be a national priority.

Backing

On a personal level, Americans want to be part of something bigger than themselves. (Emotional claim)

A country as regionally, racially, and culturally diverse as the United States of America needs common purposes and values to hold its democratic system together. (Ethical claim)

In the past, enterprises such as western expansion, World War II, and the Apollo moon program enabled many—though not all—Americans to work toward common goals. (Logical claim)

Once you are confident that most readers will grant your warrant, you can move on to demonstrate the truth of your enthymeme. Evidence you offer in support of your enthymeme is called the grounds.

Enthymeme

NASA should launch a human expedition to Mars *because Americans need a unifying national goal.*

Grounds

The American people are politically divided along racial, ethnic, religious, gender, and class lines. (Factual claim)

A common challenge or problem unites people to accomplish great things. (Emotional claim)

Successfully managing a Mars mission would require the cooperation of the entire nation—financially, logistically, and scientifically. (Logical claim)

A human expedition to Mars would be a worthwhile scientific project for the nation to pursue. (Logical claim)

Notice that backing and grounds may rely on information from outside sources—once again emphasizing the importance of context and background in any argument. Uninformed opinion doesn't have much status in argument.

Note, too, that backing and grounds can draw from a full range of argumentative claims. Appeals to values and emotions might be just as appropriate as appeals to logic and facts, and all such claims will be stronger if a writer presents a convincing ethos. Although one can study such appeals separately, they work together in arguments, reinforcing each other. (See Chapter 6 for more on ethos.)

Finally, evidence offered as either backing or grounds often involves additional enthymemes and, by implication, new warrants. For example, if you intend to back up the enthymeme

> NASA **should launch a human expedition to Mars** *because Americans need a unifying national goal.*

with the additional assertion that

> **A human expedition to Mars would be a worthwhile scientific project for the nation to pursue. (Logical claim)**

you've extended your argument. You may have to offer a supporting reason and possibly explore the resulting enthymeme:

Enthymeme

> **A human expedition to Mars would be a worthwhile scientific goal** *because human beings can explore the planet better than robots and other machines.*

Warrant

> **We should use the best possible means when pursuing scientific goals.**

If the warrant is convincing to most readers, the chain of argument can end here—if all factual claims are convincing. But, in fact, many planetary scientists would vigorously contest the claim that human beings can explore planets better than robots. So, as the writer, you would have to deal with this strong objection by either qualifying the supporting reason, defending it factually, or backing down from it entirely.

Jennifer Ringley, in "Why I Star in My Own *Truman Show*," defends her decision to broadcast her life to millions of people via webcam. What's her enthymeme? Her warrant? Her backing and grounds?

LINK TO P. 464

As you can see, arguments can readily shift downward from an original set of claims and warrants to deeper, more basic claims and reasons. In a philosophy course, you might dig many layers down to reach what seem to be first principles. In general, however, you need to pursue an argument only as far as critical readers require, always presenting them with adequate warrants and convincing evidence.

Using Qualifiers

If you begin to feel intimidated by the rigors of argument, remember that you control the terms of the argument. You can stipulate your responsibilities in an argument simply through the judicious use of qualifiers—terms and conditions that limit your claims and warrants. You can save yourself much time if you qualify a claim early in the writing process. But it often happens that the need to limit an argument becomes evident only as the argument develops.

One way to qualify an argument is by spelling out the terms of the claim as precisely as possible. Never assume that readers understand the limits you have in mind. Whenever you can, spell out what you mean precisely. You'll have less work to do as a result. In the following examples, the first claim in each pair would be much harder to argue convincingly and responsibly—and tougher to research—than the second claim.

Efforts to reduce drug use have failed. (Unqualified claim)

Most **efforts** *in Texas* **to reduce** *marijuana* **use** *among high school students* **have failed. (Qualified claim)**

Welfare programs should be cut. (Unqualified claim)

Ineffective federal **welfare programs should be** *identified, modified,* **and,** *if necessary, eliminated.* **(Qualified claim)**

Experienced writers cherish qualifying expressions because they make writing more precise and honest.

QUALIFIERS

few	it is possible
rarely	it seems
some	it may be
sometimes	more or less
in some cases	many
in the main	routinely

Check out the effects that Welch Suggs creates in his article about the fairness of cutting men's teams when he uses the phrases "almost everyone," "almost everybody," and "everyone."

·········· LINK TO P. 489

most	one might argue
often	perhaps
under these conditions	possibly
for the most part	if it were so

Understanding Conditions of Rebuttal

There's a fine old book on writing by Robert Graves and Alan Hodges entitled *The Reader over Your Shoulder* (1943). In it, Graves and Hodges advise writers always to imagine a crowd of "prospective readers" hovering over their shoulders, asking questions. At every stage in Toulmin argument—making a claim, offering a reason, or studying a warrant—you might converse with those nosy readers, imagining them as skeptical, demanding, even a bit testy. They may well get on your nerves. But they'll likely help you foresee the objections and reservations real readers will have regarding your arguments.

In the Toulmin system, potential objections to an argument are called conditions of rebuttal. Understanding and reacting to these conditions are essential not only to buttress your own claims where they are weak, but also to understand the reasonable objections of people who see the world differently.

For example, you may be a big fan of the Public Broadcasting Service (PBS) and the National Endowment for the Arts (NEA) and prefer that federal tax dollars be spent on these programs. So you offer the following claim:

> *Claim* The federal government should support the arts.

Of course, you need reasons to support this thesis, so you decide to present the issue as a matter of values:

> *Claim + Reason* The federal government should support the arts because it also supports the military.

Now you've got an enthymeme and can test the warrant, or the premises of your claim:

> *Warrant* If the federal government can support the military, it can also support other programs.

But the warrant seems frail—something is missing to make a convincing case. Over your shoulder you hear your skeptical friends wondering what wouldn't be fundable according to your very broad principle. They restate your warrant in their own mocking fashion: *Because we pay for a military, we should pay for everything!* You could deal with their objection in the body of your paper, but revising your claim might be a more intelligent way to parry the objections. You give it a try.

> **Revised Claim + Reason** If the federal government can spend huge amounts of money on the military, it can afford to spend much less on arts programs.

Now you've got a new warrant, too:

> **Revised Warrant** A country that can fund expensive programs can also afford less expensive programs.

This is a premise you feel more able to defend, believing strongly that the arts are just as essential to the well-being of the country as is a strong military. (In fact, you believe the arts are *more* important, but remembering those readers over your shoulder, you decide not to complicate your case by overstating it.) To provide backing for this new and more defensible warrant, you plan to illustrate the huge size of the federal budget and the proportion of that budget that goes to various programs.

But though the warrant seems solid, you still have to offer strong grounds to support your specific and controversial claim. Once again you cite statistics from reputable sources, this time specifically comparing the federal budgets for the military and the arts, breaking them down in ways readers can visualize, demonstrating that much less than a penny of every tax dollar goes to support the arts.

But once more you hear those voices over your shoulder, pointing out that the "common defense" is a federal mandate; the government is constitutionally obligated to support a military. Support for public television or local dance troupes is hardly in the same league. And we still have a huge federal debt.

Hmmm. You'd better spend a paragraph explaining all the benefits the arts provide for the very few dollars spent, and maybe you should also suggest that such funding falls under the constitutional mandate to "promote the general welfare." Though not all readers will accept these grounds, they will at least see that you haven't ignored their point of view. You gain credibility and authority by anticipating a reasonable objection.

As you can see, dealing with conditions of rebuttal is a natural part of argument. But it is important to understand rebuttal as more than mere opposition. Anticipating objections broadens your horizons and likely makes you more open to change. One of the best exercises for you or for any writer is to learn to state the views of others in your own *favorable* words. If you can do that, you're more apt to grasp the warrants at issue and the commonalities you may share with others, despite differences.

Fortunately, today's wired world is making it harder to argue in sublime (or silly) isolation. Newsgroups and listservs on the Internet provide quick and potent responses to positions offered by participants in discussions. Email, too, an almost instantaneous form of communication, makes cross-country connections feel almost like face-to-face conversations. Even the links on Web sites encourage people to think of communication as a network, infinitely variable, open to many voices and different perspectives. Within the Toulmin system, conditions of rebuttal—the voices over the shoulder—remind us that we're part of this bigger world. (For more on arguments in electronic environments, see Chapter 16.)

Brian Winter is sharply critical of an action taken by a political organization at the University of Texas—and he strengthens his argument criticizing that action by conceding the value of other activities undertaken by the same group.

LINK TO P. 680

BEYOND TOULMIN

Can most arguments be analyzed according to Toulmin's principles? The honest answer is no, if you expect most writers to express themselves in perfectly formulated enthymemes or warrants. The same neglect of Toulmin's conditions will likely be evident in arguments you compose yourself. Once you are into your subject, you'll be too eager to make a point to worry about whether you're buttressing the grounds or finessing a warrant.

But that's not a problem if you appreciate Toulmin argument for what it teaches:

- Claims should be stated clearly and qualified carefully.
- Claims should be supported with good reasons.
- Claims and reasons should be based on assumptions readers will likely accept.
- All parts of an argument need the support of solid evidence.
- Effective arguments anticipate objections readers might offer.

It takes considerable experience to write arguments that meet all these conditions. Using Toulmin's framework brings them into play automatically; if you learn it well enough, good arguments can become a habit.

James Hill presents a complete Toulmin argument that Ebonics is not a language. See paragraphs 8–11 in "Say What? Watch Your Language."

LINK TO P. 608

CULTURAL CONTEXTS FOR ARGUMENT

As you think about how to organize your writing, remember that cultural factors are at work: the patterns that you find satisfying and persuasive are likely ones that are deeply embedded in your culture. The organizational patterns favored by U.S. engineers, for example, hold many similarities to the system recommended by Cicero some two thousand years ago. It is a highly explicit pattern, leaving little or nothing unexplained: introduction and thesis, background, overview of the parts that follow, evidence, other viewpoints, and conclusion. If a piece of writing follows this pattern, Anglo-American readers ordinarily find it "well organized."

But writers who are accustomed to different organizational patterns may not. Those accustomed to writing that is more elaborate or that sometimes digresses from the main point may find the U.S. engineers' writing overly simple, even childish. Those from cultures that value subtlety and indirection tend to favor patterns of organization that display these values.

When arguing across cultures, think about how you can organize material to get your message across effectively, but here are a couple of points to consider:

- Determine when to state your thesis—at the beginning? at the end? somewhere else? not at all?

- Consider whether digressions are a good idea, a requirement, or best avoided.

RESPOND •

1. Claims aren't always easy to find—sometimes they are buried deep within an argument, and sometimes they are not present at all. An important skill in reading *and* writing arguments is the ability to identify claims, even when they are not obvious.

   Collect a sample of eight to ten letters to the editor of a daily newspaper. Read each letter and reduce it to a single sentence, beginning with "I believe that . . ."—this should represent the simplest version of the writer's claim.

   When you have compiled your list of claims, look carefully at the words the writers use when stating their positions. Is there a common vocabulary? Can you find words or phrases that signal an impending claim? Which of these seem most effective? Which seem least effective? Why?

2. At their simplest, warrants can be stated as "X is good" or "X is bad." Consider the example from p. 96, "Don't eat that mushroom—it's poisonous." In this case, the warrant could be reduced to "poison is bad." Of course, this is an oversimplification, but it may help you to see how warrants are based in shared judgments of value. If the audience members agree that poison is bad (as they are likely to do), they will accept the connection the writer makes between the claim and the reason.

   As you might expect, warrants are often hard to find, relying as they do on unstated assumptions about value. Return to the letters to the editor that you analyzed in exercise 1, this time looking for the warrant behind each claim. As a way to start, ask yourself these questions: *If I find myself agreeing with the letter writer, what assumptions about the subject matter do I share with the letter writer? If I disagree, what assumptions are at the heart of that disagreement?* The list of warrants you generate will likely come from these assumptions.

3. Toulmin logic is a useful tool for understanding existing arguments, but it can also help you through the process of inventing your own arguments. As you decide what claim you would like to make, you'll need to consider the warrants, different levels of evidence, conditions of rebuttal, and qualifiers. The argument about federal support for the arts provides a good illustration of the Toulmin system's inventional power. By coming to terms with the conditions of rebuttal, you revised your claim and reconsidered the evidence you'd use.

   Using a paper you are writing for this class—it doesn't matter how far along you are in the process—do a Toulmin analysis of the argument. At first, you may struggle to identify the key elements, and you might not find all the categories easy to fill. When you're done, see which elements of the Toulmin scheme are least represented. Are you short of evidence to support the warrant? Have you considered the conditions of rebuttal?

   Next, write a brief revision plan: How will you buttress the argument in the places where your writing is weakest? What additional evidence will you offer for the warrant? How can you qualify your claim to meet the conditions of rebuttal? Having a clearer sense of the logical structure of your argument will help you revise more efficiently.

   It might be instructive to show your paper to a classmate and have him or her do a Toulmin analysis, too. A new reader will probably see your argument in a very different way than you do and suggest revisions that may not have occurred to you.

4. Formulate a specific claim about one or more of the following subjects:

> a current controversial film or TV show
>
> an influential or controversial political figure
>
> affirmative action in college admissions
>
> state laws permitting the carrying of concealed firearms
>
> a controversial issue in sports (the designated hitter in baseball; high school graduates playing in the NBA; Title IX closures of men's sports teams)
>
> violence or sex in video games or song lyrics
>
> transportation issues (public transportation; the safety of small cars; fuel economy regulation)
>
> religion in public life
>
> the role of computers or the Internet in education
>
> the role of the family

5. Turn any claim you wrote for exercise 4 into a full enthymeme by attaching major supporting reasons.

6. State the warrant that connects your claim to its supporting reasons. If necessary, qualify your initial claim.

chapter nine

Arguments of Definition

A traffic committee must define what a small car is in order to enforce parking restrictions in a campus lot where certain spaces are marked "Small Car Only!" Owners of compact luxury vehicles, light trucks, and motorcycles have complained that their vehicles are being unfairly ticketed.

A panel of judges must decide whether computer-enhanced images will be eligible in a contest for landscape photography. At what point is an electronically manipulated image no longer a photograph?

A scholarship committee must decide whether the daughter of two European American diplomats, born while her parents were assigned to the U.S. embassy in Nigeria, will be eligible to apply for grants designated specifically for "African American students." The student claims that excluding her from consideration would constitute discrimination.

A priest chastises some members of his congregation for being "cafeteria Catholics" who pick and choose which parts of Catholic doctrine they will accept and follow. A member of that congregation responds to the priest in a letter explaining her view of what a "true Catholic" is.

A young man hears a classmate describe hunting as a "blood sport." He disagrees and argues that hunting for sport has little in common with "genuine blood sports" such as cockfighting.

A committee of the student union is accused of bias by a conservative student group, which claims that the committee has brought a disproportionate share of left-wing speakers to campus. The committee defends its program by challenging the definition of "left wing" used to classify its speakers.

■ ■ ■

UNDERSTANDING ARGUMENTS OF DEFINITION

When Adam names the animals in the biblical book of Genesis, he acquires authority over them because to name things is, partly, to control them. That's why arguments of definition are so important and so often contentious. They can be about the power to say *what* someone or something is. As such, they can also be arguments about inclusion and exclusion: a creature is a mammal or it isn't; an act is harassment or it isn't; an athlete ought or ought not to be a Hall of Famer.

Another way of approaching definitional arguments, however, is to explore the fertile middle ground between "is" and "is not." Indeed, the most productive definitional arguments probably occur in this realm. Consider the controversy over how to define human intelligence. Some might argue that human intelligence is a capacity measurable by tests of verbal and mathematical reasoning. Others might define it as the ability to perform specific practical tasks. Still others might interpret intelligence in emotional terms, as a competence in relating to other people. Any of these positions could be defended reasonably, but perhaps the wisest approach would be to construct a definition of intelligence that is rich enough to incorporate all three perspectives—and maybe more.

In fact, it's important to realize that many definitions in civil, political, and social (and some scientific) arenas are constantly "under construction," reargued and reshaped whenever they prove inaccurate or inadequate for the times. For example, Gretel Ehrlich's "About Men," one of the definitional essays included at the end of this chapter, reworks the meaning of a very familiar term, *cowboys*, and broadens readers' understanding of the storied ranch hands in light of the labor they actually do:

> Because these men work with animals, not machines or numbers, because they live outside in landscapes of torrential beauty, because they are confined to a place and a routine embellished with awesome variables, because calves die in the arms that pulled others into life, because they go to the mountains as if on a pilgrimage to find out what makes a herd of elk tick, their strength is also a softness, their toughness, a rare delicacy.
>
> – Gretel Ehrlich, "About Men"

And in case you are wondering, important arguments of definition usually *can't* be solved by consulting dictionaries. Indeed, dictionaries themselves are compilations that reflect the way words are used at a particular time and place by particular classes of people. Like any form of writing, dictionaries reflect the prejudices of their makers — as shown, perhaps most famously, in the entries of lexicographer Samuel Johnson (1709–1784), who gave the English language its first great dictionary. For example, Johnson defined *oats* as "a grain which in England is generally given to horses, but in Scotland supports the people." (To be fair, he also defined *lexicographer* as "a writer of dictionaries, a harmless drudge.") So it is quite possible to disagree with dictionary definitions or to regard them merely as starting points for new explorations of meaning.

CHARACTERIZING DEFINITION

The scope of a definitional argument is often determined by the kind of definition being explored. In most cases, you will probably not even recognize the specific type of definitional question at issue. Fortunately, identifying the type is less important than recognizing the fact that an issue of definition may be involved. Let's explore some common definitional issues.

Formal Definitions

The formal definition is what is typically encountered in dictionaries. It involves placing a term in its proper genus and species—that is, establishing the larger class to which it belongs and then specifying the features that distinguish it from other members of that class. For example, a violin might first be identified by placing it among its peers—musical instruments or stringed instruments. Then the definition would identify the features necessary to distinguish violins from other musical or stringed instruments—four strings, an unfretted fingerboard, a bow.

Given the genus-and-species structure of a formal definition, arguments might evolve from (1) the larger class to which a thing or idea is assigned, or (2) the specific features that distinguish it from other members of the class:

QUESTIONS RELATED TO GENUS

- What is a violin?
- Is tobacco a drug or a crop?
- Is female prostitution a freely chosen profession or an exploitation of women?
- Is *Nightline* a news program? A tabloid? Both?

QUESTIONS RELATED TO SPECIES

- Is a fiddle a type of violin?
- Is tobacco a harmless drug? A dangerously addictive one? Something in between?
- Is female prostitution a profession that empowers or that demeans the women involved?
- Do tabloids report or sensationalize the news?

John Rickford's essay "Suite for Ebony and Phonics" provides a good example of a definitional argument of species, considering the question of whether Ebonics is a dialect of English.

LINK TO P. 620

Operational Definitions

Operational definitions identify an object by what it does or by the conditions that create it: *A line is the shortest distance between two points; Sexual harassment is an unwanted and unsolicited imposition.* Arguments that evolve from operational definitions can be about the conditions that define the object or about whether those conditions have been met. (See also "Stasis Theory" in Chapter 1.)

QUESTIONS RELATED TO CONDITIONS

- Must sexual imposition be both unwanted and unsolicited to be considered harassment?
- Can institutional racism occur in the absence of individual acts of racism?
- Is a volunteer who is paid still a volunteer?
- Does someone who ties the record for home runs in one season deserve the title Hall of Famer?

QUESTIONS RELATED TO FULFILLMENT OF CONDITIONS

- Was the act sexual harassment if the accused believed the imposition was solicited?
- Has the institution kept in place traditions or policies that might lead to racial inequities?
- Was the compensation given to volunteers really "pay"?
- Has a person actually tied a home-run record if the player has hit the same number of homers in a long season that someone else has hit in a shorter season?

Definitions by Example

Resembling operational definitions are definitions by example, which define a class by listing its individual members. For example, one might define *planets* by listing all nine planets in orbit around the sun, or *true American sports cars* by naming the Corvette and the Viper.

Definitional arguments of this sort focus on what may or may not be included in a list of examples. Such arguments often involve comparisons and contrasts with the items most readers would agree from the start belong in this list. One might, for example, wonder why planet status is denied to asteroids, when both planets and asteroids are bodies in orbit around the sun. A comparison between planets and asteroids might suggest that size is one essential feature of the nine recognized planets that asteroids don't meet.

Similarly, one might define *great American presidents* simply by listing Washington, Lincoln, and Franklin Roosevelt. Does President Reagan belong in this company? You might argue that he does if he shares the qualities that place the other presidents in this select group.

QUESTIONS RELATED TO MEMBERSHIP IN A NAMED CLASS

- Is any rock artist today in a class with Chuck Berry, Elvis, Bob Dylan, the Beatles, or the Rolling Stones?
- Is the Mustang a Viper-class sports car?
- Who are the Freuds or Einsteins of the current generation?
- Does Washington, D.C., deserve the status of a state?

Other Issues of Definition

Many issues of definition cross the line between the types described here and some other forms of argument. For example, if you decided to explore whether banning pornography on the Internet violates First Amendment guarantees of free speech, you'd first have to establish a definition of *free speech*—either a legal one already settled on by, let's say, the Supreme Court, or another definition closer to your own beliefs. Then you'd have to argue that types of pornography on the Internet are (or are not) in the same class or share (or do not share) the same characteristics as free speech. In doing so, you'd certainly find yourself slipping into an evaluative mode since matters of definition are often also questions of value. (See Chapter 10.)

When exploring or developing an idea, you shouldn't worry about such slippage—it's a natural part of the process of writing. But do try to focus an argument on a central issue or question, and appreciate the fact that any definition you care to defend must be examined honestly and rigorously. Be prepared to explore every issue of definition with an open mind and with an acute sense of what will be persuasive to your readers.

See the cluster of readings in Chapter 28 about free speech on campus for various articles and letters about an incident at the University of Texas when a speaker with conservative views was heckled and interrupted to the point that he was unable to finish his speech.

⋯⋯⋯⋯⋯⋯⋯⋯⋯⋯ LINK TO P. 671

DEVELOPING A DEFINITIONAL ARGUMENT

Definitional arguments don't just appear out of the blue; they evolve out of the occasions and conversations of daily life, both public and private, such as the following:

- Watching *Washington Journal* on C-SPAN while breakfasting with the kids, you're drawn into a dialogue between two politicians during the "Newspaper Roundtable" segment. They're exploring whether a volunteer who is paid for services is, in fact, a volunteer. You send a fax to c-span expressing your opinion, and Brian Lamb reads it on the air!

- At work, you are asked your opinion about a job description your department is posting. Does it define the position adequately? Does the way the job is defined limit the pool of potential applicants too selectively or unfairly? You don't have many minority employees in your organization.

- Hot under the collar, Grandpa calls you long distance to complain that ten or twenty acres he intended to drain on his farm in Idaho are about to be declared "wetlands" by a busybody federal agent. He wants to know what the difference is between a no-good, mosquito-infested bog and a federally managed wetland.

- Your local newspaper claims, in an editorial, that a hefty new municipal fee on airport parking and hotel rooms shouldn't be considered a "tax." You vehemently disagree and decide to write a letter to the editor—after you cool down.

- Your favorite radio talk show host spends a whole segment explaining why Washington, D.C., ought not to be considered for statehood. "It's not a state," she says; "it's a city." You think about what makes a state a state.

- Just before you turn in one evening, you read an essay entitled "About Men" by Gretel Ehrlich. She says cowboys are the midwives of the plains. This shakes up your comfortable notions about cowboys.

In his essay "Divinity and Pornography," Dennis Prager develops a definitional argument around the invented term *heterophobia* in defense of a Harvard dean who was fired for having pornographic images on his office computer.

LINK TO P. 442 ···

Formulating Claims

In first addressing matters of definition, you'll likely formulate tentative claims—declarative statements that represent your first response to such situations. Note that these initial claims usually don't follow a single definitional formula.

CLAIMS OF DEFINITION

- A person paid to do public service is not a volunteer.
- Institutional racism can exist—maybe even thrive—in the absence of overt civil rights violations.
- A wetland is just a swamp with powerful friends.
- A municipal fee is the same darn thing as a tax.
- The District of Columbia has nothing in common with states.

- Gretel Ehrlich, who writes that "th[e] macho, cultural artifact the cowboy has become is simply a man who possesses resilience, patience, and an instinct for survival," may be on to something.

None of the claims listed here could stand on its own. The claims reflect first impressions and gut reactions because stating a claim is typically a starting point, a moment of bravura that doesn't last much beyond the first serious rebuttal or challenge. Statements of this sort aren't arguments until they're attached to reasons, warrants, and evidence. (See Chapter 8.)

Finding good reasons to support a claim of definition usually requires formulating a general definition by which to explore the subject. To be persuasive, the definition must be broad and *not* tailored to the specific controversy:

- A volunteer is . . .
- Institutional racism is . . .
- A wetland is . . .
- A tax is . . .
- A state is . . .
- A cowboy is . . .

Now consider how the following claims might be expanded in order to become full-fledged definitional arguments:

ARGUMENTS OF DEFINITION

- Someone paid to do public service is not a volunteer because volunteers are people who . . .
- Institutional racism can exist even in the absence of overt violations of civil rights because, by definition, institutional racism is . . .
- A swampy parcel of land becomes a federally protected wetland when . . .
- A municipal fee is the same darn thing as a tax. Both fees and taxes are . . .
- Washington, D.C., ought not to be considered eligible for statehood because states all . . .—and the District of Columbia doesn't!

Notice, too, that some of the issues here involve comparisons between things: swamp/wetland; fees/taxes.

Crafting Definitions

Imagine, now, that you decide to tackle the concept of "paid volunteer" in the following way:

> **Participants in the federal AmeriCorps program are not really volunteers because they are paid for their public service.** *Volunteers are people who work for a cause without compensation.*

In Toulmin terms, the argument looks like this:

Claim	Participants in AmeriCorps aren't volunteers . . .
Reason	. . . because they are paid for their service.
Warrant	Those who are paid for services are employees, not volunteers.

As you can see, the definition of *volunteers* will be crucial to the shape of the argument. In fact, you might think you've settled the matter with this tight little formulation. But now it's time to listen to the readers over your shoulder (see Chapter 8) pushing you further. Do the terms of your definition account for all pertinent cases of volunteerism, in particular any related to types of public service AmeriCorps volunteers might be involved in?

Consider, too, the word *cause* in your original statement of the definition:

> *Volunteers are people who work for a* **cause** *without compensation.*

Cause has political connotations that you may or may not intend. You'd better clarify what you mean by *cause* when you discuss your definition in your paper. Might a phrase such as "the public good" be a more comprehensive or appropriate substitute for "a cause"?

And then there's the matter of compensation in the second half of your definition:

> *Volunteers are people who work for a* **cause** *without* **compensation**.

Aren't people who volunteer to serve on boards, committees, and commissions sometimes paid, especially for their expenses? What about members of the so-called all-volunteer military? Certainly they are financially compensated for their years of service, and they enjoy substantial benefits after they complete their service.

As you can see, you can't just offer up a definition as part of your argument and assume that readers will understand or accept it. Every part of the definition has to be weighed, critiqued, and defended. That means you'll want to investigate your subject in the library, on the Internet, or in dialogue with others. You might then be able to present your definition in a single paragraph, or you may have to spend several pages coming to terms with the complexity of the core issue.

Were you to argue about the meaning of *wetlands*, for instance, you might have to examine a range of definitions from any number of sources before arriving at the definition you believe will be acceptable to your readers (or to Grandpa). Here are just three definitions of *wetlands* we found on the Internet, suggesting the complexity of the issue:

> **In general terms, wetlands are lands where saturation with water is the dominant factor determining the nature of soil development and the types of plant and animal communities living in the soil and on its surface.**
>
> – <http://www.nwi.fws.gov/contents.html#wetlands>
> **U.S. Fish and Wildlife Service**

> **WETLANDS are lands transitional between terrestrial and aquatic systems where the water table is usually at or near the surface or the land is covered by shallow water.**
>
> – <http://www.nwi.fws.gov/contents.html#wetlands>
> **U.S. Fish and Wildlife Service**

> **Part 303 of the Natural Resources and Environmental Protection Act, PA 451 of 1994, defines a wetland as "land characterized by the presence of water at a frequency and duration sufficient to support, and that under normal circumstances does support, wetland vegetation or aquatic life and is commonly referred to as a bog, swamp or marsh. . . ."**
>
> – <http://www.deq.state.mi.us/lwm/rrs/part303.html>

The definitions, taken together, do help distinguish the conditions that are essential and sufficient for determining wetlands. Essential conditions are those elements that must be part of a definition but that—in themselves—aren't enough to define the term. Clearly, the presence of water and land together in an environment is an essential component of a wetland, but not quite a sufficient condition since a riverbank or beach might meet that condition without being a wetland. In other words, land and water can be in proximity without being a wetland, but there can't be a wetland without there being land and water.

A sufficient condition is any element or conjunction of elements adequate to define a term. The sufficient condition for wetlands seems to be

What would be sufficient conditions for intellectual property to belong in the public domain? Four pieces in Chapter 26 argue about a court case that will decide whether Martin Luther King Jr.'s "I Have a Dream" speech should belong to the public.

···················· **LINK TO PP. 573–75**

a combination of land and water sufficient to form a regular (if sometimes temporary) ecological system.

One might add accidental conditions to a definition as well—elements that are often associated with a term but are not present in every case or sufficient to identify it. An important accidental feature of wetlands, for example, might be specific forms of plant life or species of birds.

After conducting research of this kind you might be in a position to write an extended definition sufficient to explain to your readers what you believe makes a wetland a wetland; a volunteer a volunteer; a tax a tax; and so on.

Matching Claims to Definitions

Once you've formulated a definition readers will accept—a demanding task in itself—you should place your particular subject in relationship to that general definition, providing evidence to show that

- it is a clear example of the class defined
- it falls outside the defined class
- it falls between two closely related classes

  or

- it defies existing classes and categories and requires an entirely new definition

Thus, your presentation of an issue of definition will depend on the presentation of evidence that may or may not support your initial claim. It is remarkable how often seemingly clear issues of definition become blurry—and open to compromise and accommodation—when the available evidence is examined. So as you assemble evidence, you should be willing to modify your original claim or at least be prepared to deal with objections to it. (See Chapter 8.)

Grandpa, for example, might insist that for half the year his soon-to-be-reclassified property doesn't have a bird on it and is as dry as a bone, so it can't possibly be a wetland. But the federal agent might point out that it meets the sufficient conditions for a wetland from January through June, when it's as mushy as a Slurpee and, moreover, serves as a breeding ground for several endangered species of birds. Needless to say, this kind of argument of definition is often resolved in court.

KEY FEATURES OF DEFINITIONAL ARGUMENTS

Arguments of definition take many shapes. A piece like Gretel Ehrlich's "About Men" (which appears at the end of this chapter) follows a logic of its own in defining *cowboy*, yet it evolves steadily from evidence offered to support a thesis in its first paragraph: "In our hellbent earnestness to romanticize the cowboy we've ironically disesteemed his true character." In writing an argument of definition of your own, consider that it is likely to include the following parts:

- a claim involving a question of definition
- an attempt to establish a general definition acceptable to readers
- an examination of the claim in terms of the accepted definition and all its conditions
- evidence for every part of the argument
- a consideration of alternative views and counterarguments
- a conclusion, drawing out the implications of the argument

It is impossible, however, to predict in advance what emphasis each of those parts ought to receive or what the ultimate shape of an argument of definition will be, especially if it appears in an electronic environment. In a listserv, for example, an argument might evolve over days or weeks, the property of no one person, each separate email message sharpening, qualifying, or complicating the argument. And certainly an argument of definition presented on the Web will offer possibilities that are simply not available on paper. (See Chapter 16.)

Whatever form an argument takes, the draft should be shared with others who can examine its claims, evidence, and connections. It is remarkably easy for a writer in isolation to conceive of ideas narrowly—and not to imagine that others might define *volunteer* or *institutional racism* in a completely different way. It is important to keep a mind open to criticism and suggestions. Look very carefully at the terms of any definitions you offer. Do they really help readers distinguish one concept from another? Are the conditions offered sufficient or essential? Have you mistaken accidental features of a concept or object for more important features?

Don't hesitate to look to other sources for comparisons with your definitions. If you can't depend on dictionaries to offer the last word about any serious or contested term, you can at least begin there to gain control over a concept. Check the meaning of terms in encyclopedias and other reference works. And search the Web intelligently to find how your key terms are presented there. (Searching for the definition of *wetland*, for example, you could type the following into a search engine like Excite and get a limited number of useful hits: *wetland + definition of*.)

Finally, be prepared for surprises in writing arguments of definition. That's part of the delight in expanding the way you see the world. "You're not a terrier; you're a police dog," exclaims fictional detective Nick Charles after his fox terrier, Asta, helps him solve a case. Such is the power of definition.

Finding a Topic

You are likely entering an argument of definition when you

- formulate a controversial definition: *Discrimination is the act of judging someone on the basis of unchangeable characteristics.*
- challenge a definition: *Judging someone on the basis of unchangeable characteristics is not discrimination.*
- try to determine whether something fits an existing definition: *Affirmative action is/is not discrimination.*

Look for issues of definition in your everyday affairs—for instance, in the way jobs are classified at work; in the way key terms are described in your academic major; in the way politicians characterize the social issues that concern you; in the way you define yourself or others try to define you. Be especially alert to definitional arguments that may arise whenever you or others deploy adjectives such as *true, real, actual,* or *genuine*: a *true* Texan, *real* environmental degradation, *actual* budget projections, *genuine* rap music.

Researching Your Topic

You can research issues of definition using the following sources:

- college dictionaries and encyclopedias
- unabridged dictionaries
- specialized reference works and handbooks, such as legal and medical dictionaries
- your textbooks (check their glossaries)
- newsgroups and listservs that focus on particular topics

Be sure to browse in your library reference room. Also, use the search tools of electronic indexes and databases to determine whether or how often controversial phrases or expressions are occurring in influential materials: major online newspapers, journals, and Web sites.

Formulating a Claim

After exploring your subject, begin to formulate a full and specific claim, a thesis that lets readers know where you stand and what issues are at stake. In moving toward this thesis, begin with the following types of questions of definition:

122

- questions related to genus: *Is assisting in suicide a crime?*
- questions related to species: *Is tobacco a relatively harmless drug or a dangerously addictive one?*
- questions related to conditions: *Must the imposition of sexual attention be both unwanted and unsolicited to be considered sexual harassment?*
- questions related to fulfillment of conditions: *Has our college kept in place traditions or policies that might constitute racial discrimination?*
- questions related to membership in a named class: *Is any rock artist today in a class with Elvis, Dylan, the Beatles, or the Rolling Stones?*

Your thesis should be an actual statement. In one sentence, you need to *make a claim of definition and state the reasons that support your claim.* In your paper or project itself, you may later decide to separate the claim from the reasons supporting it. But your working thesis should be a fully expressed thought. That means spelling out the details and the qualifications: *Who? What? Where? When? How many? How regularly? How completely?* Don't expect readers to fill in the blanks for you.

Preparing a Proposal

If your instructor asks you to prepare a proposal for your project, here's a format you might use:

State your thesis completely. If you are having trouble doing so, try outlining it in Toulmin terms:

> **Claim:**
>
> **Reason(s):**
>
> **Warrant(s):**

Explain why this argument of definition deserves attention. What is at stake? Why is it important for your readers to consider?

Explain whom you hope to reach through your argument and why this group of readers would be interested in it.

Briefly discuss the key challenges you anticipate in preparing your argument. Defining a key term? Establishing the essential and sufficient elements of your definition? Demonstrating that your subject will meet those conditions?

123

Determine what strategies you will use in researching your definitional argument. What sources do you expect to consult? Dictionaries? Encyclopedias? Periodicals? The Internet?

Consider what format you expect to use for your project. A conventional research essay? A letter to the editor? A Web page?

Thinking about Organization

Your argument of definition may take various forms, but it is likely to include elements such as the following:

- a claim involving a matter of definition: *Pluto ought not to be considered a genuine planet.*

- an attempt to establish a definition of a key term: *A genuine planet must be a body in orbit around the sun, spherical (not a rock fragment), large enough to sustain an atmosphere, and. . . .*

- an explanation or defense of the terms of the definition: *A planet has to be large enough to support an atmosphere in order to be distinguished from lesser objects within the solar system. . . .*

- an examination of the claim in terms of the definition and all its criteria: *Although Pluto does orbit the sun, it may not in fact be spherical or have sufficient gravity to merit planetary status. . . .*

- evidence for every part of the argument: *Evidence from radio telescopes and other detailed observations of Pluto's surface suggest . . . , and so. . . .*

- a consideration of alternative views and counterarguments: *It is true, perhaps, that Pluto is large enough to have a gravitational effect on. . . .*

Getting and Giving Response

All arguments benefit from the scrutiny of others. Your instructor may assign you to a peer group for the purpose of reading and responding to each other's drafts; if not, make the effort yourself to get some careful response. You can use the following questions to evaluate a draft. If you are evaluating someone else's draft, be sure to illustrate your points with specific examples. Specific comments are always more helpful than general observations.

The Claim

- Is the claim clearly a question of definition?

- Is the claim significant enough to interest readers?

- Are clear and specific criteria established for the concept being defined? Do the criteria define the term adequately? Using this definition, could most readers identify what is being defined and distinguish it from other related concepts?

Evidence for the Claim

- Is enough evidence furnished to explain or support the definition? If not, what kind of additional evidence is needed?
- Is the evidence in support of the claim simply announced, or are its significance and appropriateness analyzed? Is a more detailed discussion needed?
- Are all the conditions of the definition met in the concept being examined?
- Are any objections readers might have to the claim, criteria, or evidence, or to the way the definition is formulated, adequately addressed?
- What kinds of sources are cited? How credible and persuasive will they be to readers? What other kinds of sources might be more credible and persuasive?
- Are all quotations introduced with appropriate signal phrases (such as "As Himmelfarb argues,") and blended smoothly into the writer's sentences?

Organization and Style

- How are the parts of the argument organized? Is this organization effective, or would some other structure work better?
- Will readers understand the relationships among the claim, supporting reasons, warrants, and evidence? If not, what could be done to make those connections clearer? Are more transitional words and phrases needed? Would headings or graphic devices help?
- Are the transitions or links from point to point, paragraph to paragraph, and sentence to sentence clear and effective? If not, how could they be improved?
- Is the style suited to the subject? Is it too formal? Too casual? Too technical? Too bland?
- Which sentences seem particularly effective? Which ones seem weakest, and how could they be improved? Should some short sentences be combined, or should any long ones be separated into two or more sentences?
- How effective are the paragraphs? Do any seem too skimpy or too long?

- Which words or phrases seem particularly effective, vivid, and memorable? Do any seem dull, vague, unclear, or inappropriate for the audience or the writer's purpose? Are definitions provided for technical or other terms that readers might not know?

Spelling, Punctuation, Mechanics, Documentation, Format

- Are there any errors in spelling, punctuation, capitalization, and the like?

- Is an appropriate and consistent style of documentation used for parenthetical citations and the list of works cited or references? (See Chapter 22.)

- Does the paper or project follow an appropriate format? Is it appropriately designed and attractively presented? If it is a Web site, do all the links work?

RESPOND ●

1. Briefly discuss the criteria you might use to define the italicized terms in the following controversial claims of definition. Compare your definitions of the terms with those of classmates.

   Burning a nation's flag is a *hate crime.*

   The Kennedys are America's *royal family.*

   Matt Drudge and Larry Flynt are legitimate *journalists.*

   College sports programs have become *big businesses.*

   Plagiarism can be an act of *civil disobedience.*

   Satanism is a *religion* properly protected by the First Amendment.

   Wine (or beer) is a *health food.*

   Campaign contributions are acts of *free speech.*

   The District of Columbia should have all the privileges of an American *state.*

   Committed gay couples should have the legal privileges of *marriage.*

2. This chapter opens with sketches of six rhetorical situations that center on definitional issues. Select one of these situations, and write definitional criteria using the strategy of formal definition. For example, identify the features of a photograph that make it part of a larger class (art, communication method, journalistic technique). Next, identify the features of a photograph that make it distinct from other members of that larger class.

   Then use the strategy of operational definition to establish criteria for the same object: What does it *do?* Remember to ask questions related to conditions (*Is a computer-scanned photograph still a photograph?*) and questions related to fulfillment of conditions (*Does a good photocopy of a photograph achieve the same effect as the photograph itself?*).

3. In the essay at the end of this chapter, Gretel Ehrlich makes a variety of definitional claims — about men, about cowboys, about nature. Find the other terms that she defines, either explicitly or implicitly, and list all the criteria she uses to support her definitions.

   Keep in mind that since criteria are warrants, they are always audience-specific. What audiences are likely to accept Ehrlich's arguments about men? What audiences will likely not accept those arguments? Why not? Who is Ehrlich's *intended* audience? On what grounds do you make these judgments?

4. World chess champion Garry Kasparov lost a much-publicized match to a computer (IBM's "Deep Blue") in 1997. In the days following the

match, there was much speculation in the press and elsewhere over the computer's "intelligence" and its abilities relative to a human's.

Using Internet search engines, find several Web sites that discuss the results of the match between Kasparov and Deep Blue and that offer definitions of *intelligence*. What are the criteria that each site offers for the term? (You might have to analyze the sites carefully; not all arguments of definition provide obvious lists of criteria.)

Next, match the criteria to the sites' audiences. How have the authors of the various Web sites tailored their definitional arguments to the audiences they expect? What are the differences between chess-related sites that discuss the match and computer-related sites, or sites whose primary focus is artificial intelligence?

Before you begin, you might find it useful to make a short list of relevant terms to use during your searches. Start with the obvious terms *(intelligence, chess, Kasparov, Deep Blue)*, and then develop a more complete list as you search.

TWO SAMPLE ARGUMENTS OF DEFINITION

Creating a Criminal

....

MICHAEL KINGSTON

In reaction to the Vietnamese American practice of raising canines for food, Section 598b of the California Penal Code was recently amended to read as follows:

> (a) Every person is guilty of a misdemeanor who possesses, imports into this state, sells, buys, gives away, or accepts any carcass or part of any carcass of any animal traditionally or commonly kept as a pet or companion with the sole intent of using or having another person use any part of that carcass for food.

The California Penal Code defines what actions constitute a misdemeanor.

> (b) Every person is guilty of a misdemeanor who possesses, imports into this state, sells, buys, gives away, or accepts any animal traditionally or commonly kept as a pet or companion with the sole intent of killing or having another person kill that animal for the purpose of using or having another person use any part of the animal for food.

This is a fascinating new law, one that brings up a complex set of moral, political, and social questions. For example: What constitutes a "pet"? Do pets have special "rights" that other animals aren't entitled to? How should these "rights" be balanced with the real political rights of the human populace? How do we define the civil rights of an ethnic minority whose actions reflect cultural values that are at odds with those of the majority? Section 598b does not mention these issues. Rather, it seems to simply walk around them, leaving us to figure out for ourselves whose interests (if any) are being served by this strange new law.

All the questions Kingston raises here arise from an issue of definition: What is a pet?

Michael Kingston wrote "Creating a Criminal" while he was a student at the University of California, Riverside. Kingston argues that a law banning the consumption of animals regarded as pets targets specific immigrant groups. Key to the argument are definitions of *pet* and *racial discrimination*.

The first thing one might wonder is whether the purpose of Section 598b is to improve the lot of pets throughout California. What we do know is that it seeks to prevent people from eating animals traditionally regarded as pets (dogs and cats). But for the most part, the only people who eat dogs or cats are Vietnamese Americans. Furthermore, they don't consider these animals "pets" at all. So, pets aren't really being protected. Maybe Section 598b means to say (in a roundabout manner) that *all* dogs and cats are special and therefore deserve protection. Yet, it doesn't protect them from being "put to sleep" in government facilities by owners who are no longer willing to have them. Nor does it protect them from being subjected to painful, lethal experiments designed to make cosmetics safe for human use. Nor does it protect them from unscrupulous veterinarians who sometimes keep one or two on hand to supply blood for anemic pets of paying customers. No, the new law simply prevents Vietnamese Americans from using them as food.

Kingston compares the ostensible purpose of the new statutes with what he regards as their real purpose.

Is the consumption of dogs or cats so horrible that it merits its own law? One possible answer is that these practices pose a special threat to the trust that the pet-trading network relies upon. Or in other words: that strange man who buys one or more of *your* puppies might just be one of those dog-eaters. But this scenario just doesn't square with reality. A Vietnamese American, canine-eating family is no more a threat to the pet-trading industry than is a family of European heritage that chooses to raise rabbits (another popular pet) for its food. Predictably, there is a loophole in Section 598b that allows for the continued eating of pet rabbits. Its circular logic exempts from the new law any animal that is part of an *established* agricultural industry.

The case for prejudice can be built on a loophole in the law's definition of pet — *one that favors the culinary habits of the European American majority.*

It seems as though Vietnamese Americans are the only ones who can't eat what they want, and so it is hard not to think of the issue in terms of racial discrimination. And why shouldn't we? After all, the Vietnamese community in California has long been subjected to bigotry. Isn't it conceivable that latent xenophobia and racism have found their way into the issue of dog-eating? One needs only to look at the law itself for the answer. This law protects animals "traditionally . . . kept as a pet." *Whose* traditions? Certainly not the Vietnamese's.

The meaning of traditions now *becomes a key issue.*

Of course, the typical defense for racially discriminatory laws such as this one is that they actually protect minorities by forcing assimilation. The reasoning here is that everything will run much smoother if we can all just manage to fall in step with the dominant culture. This argument has big problems. First, it is morally bankrupt. How does robbing a culture of its uniqueness constitute a protection? Second, it doesn't defuse racial tensions at all. Racists will always find reasons for hating the Vietnamese. Finally, any policy that seeks to label minorities as the cause of the violence leveled against them is inherently racist itself.

A counterargument is considered and refuted.

Whatever the motives behind Section 598b, the consequences of the new law are all too clear. The government, not content with policing personal sexual behavior, has taken a large step toward dictating what a person can or cannot eat. This is no small infringement. I may never have the desire to eat a dog, but I'm rankled that the choice is no longer mine, and that the choice was made in a climate of racial intolerance. Whatever happened to the right to life, liberty, and the pursuit of happiness?

In this paragraph, Kingston draws on emotional and ethical appeals.

Unfortunately, we may suffer more than just a reduction in personal choice. Crimes such as dog-eating require a certain amount of vigilance to detect. More than likely, the police will rely upon such dubious measures as sifting through garbage left at curbside, or soliciting anonymous tips. Laws that regulate private behavior, after all, carry with them a reduction in privacy.

The threat the new law poses to privacy rights adds an emotional kick to the conclusion.

We sure are giving up a lot for this new law. It's sad that we receive only more criminals in return.

About Men

GRETEL EHRLICH

When I'm in New York but feeling lonely for Wyoming I look for the Marlboro ads in the subway. What I'm aching to see is horseflesh, the glint of a spur, a line of distant mountains, brimming creeks, and a reminder of the ranchers and cowboys I've ridden with for the last eight years. But the men I see in those posters with their stern, humorless looks remind me of no one I know here. In our hellbent earnestness to romanticize the cowboy we've ironically disesteemed his true character. If he's "strong and silent" it's because there's probably no one to talk to. If he "rides away into the sunset" it's because he's been on horseback since four in the morning moving cattle and he's trying, fifteen hours later, to get home to his family. If he's "a rugged individualist" he's also part of a team: ranch work is teamwork and even the glorified open-range cowboys of the 1880s rode up and down the Chisholm Trail in the company of twenty or thirty other riders. Instead of the macho, trigger-happy man our culture has perversely wanted him to be, the cowboy is more apt to be convivial, quirky, and softhearted. To be "tough" on a ranch has nothing to do with conquests and displays of power. More often than not, circumstances —like the colt he's riding or an unexpected blizzard—are overpowering him. It's not toughness but "toughing it out" that counts. In other words, this macho, cultural artifact the cowboy has become is simply a man who possesses resilience, patience, and an instinct for survival. "Cowboys are just like a pile of rocks—everything happens to them. They get climbed on, kicked, rained and snowed on, scuffed up by wind. Their job is 'just to take it,'" one old-timer told me.

A cowboy is someone who loves his work. Since the hours are long—ten to fifteen hours a day—and the pay is $30 he has to. What's required of him is an odd mixture of physical vigor and maternalism. His part of the beef-raising industry is to birth and nurture calves and take care of their mothers. For the most part his work is done on horseback and in a lifetime he sees and comes to know more animals than people. The iconic myth surrounding him is built on American notions of heroism: the index of a man's value as meas-

---

A filmmaker, poet, novelist, and essayist, Gretel Ehrlich lives on a ranch in Wyoming, ten miles from the nearest paved road. In this essay, from her collection *The Solace of Open Spaces* (1985), she sets out to define what she sees as the real qualities of a misunderstood American archetype—the cowboy.

ured in physical courage. Such ideas have perverted manliness into a self-absorbed race for cheap thrills. In a rancher's world, courage has less to do with facing danger than with acting spontaneously—usually on behalf of an animal or another rider. If a cow is stuck in a boghole he throws a loop around her neck, takes his dally (a half hitch around the saddle horn), and pulls her out with horsepower. If a calf is born sick, he may take her home, warm her in front of the kitchen fire, and massage her legs until dawn. One friend, whose favorite horse was trying to swim a lake with hobbles on, dove under water and cut her legs loose with a knife, then swam her to shore, his arm around her neck lifeguard-style, and saved her from drowning. Because these incidents are usually linked to someone or something outside himself, the westerner's courage is selfless, a form of compassion.

The physical punishment that goes with cowboying is greatly underplayed. Once fear is dispensed with, the threshold of pain rises to meet the demands of the job. When Jane Fonda asked Robert Redford (in the film *Electric Horseman*) if he was sick as he struggled to his feet one morning, he replied, "No, just bent." For once the movies had it right. The cowboys I was sitting with laughed in agreement. Cowboys are rarely complainers; they show their stoicism by laughing at themselves.

If a rancher or cowboy has been thought of as a "man's man"—laconic, hard-drinking, inscrutable—there's almost no place in which the balancing act between male and female, manliness and femininity, can be more natural. If he's gruff, handsome, and physically fit on the outside, he's androgynous at the core. Ranchers are midwives, hunters, nurturers, providers, and conservationists all at once. What we've interpreted as toughness—weathered skin, calloused hands, a squint in the eye and a growl in the voice—only masks the tenderness inside. "Now don't go telling me these lambs are cute," one rancher warned me the first day I walked into the football-field–sized lambing sheds. The next thing I knew he was holding a black lamb. "Ain't this little rat good-lookin'?"

So many of the men who came to the West were Southerners—men looking for work and a new life after the Civil War—that chivalrousness and strict codes of honor were soon thought of as western traits. There were very few women in Wyoming during territorial days, so when they did arrive (some as mail-order brides from places like Philadelphia) there was a stand-offishness between the sexes and a formality that persists now. Ranchers still tip their hats and say, "Howdy, ma'am" instead of shaking hands with me.

Even young cowboys are often evasive with women. It's not that they're Jekyll and Hyde creatures—gentle with animals and rough on women—but rather, that they don't know how to bring their tenderness into the house and lack the vocabulary to express the complexity of what they feel. Dancing wildly all night becomes a metaphor for the explosive emotions pent up inside, and when these are, on occasion, released, they're so battery-charged and potent that one caress of the face or one "I love you" will peal for a long while.

The geographical vastness and the social isolation here make emotional evolution seem impossible. Those contradictions of the heart between respectability, logic, and convention on the one hand, and impulse, passion, and intuition on the other, played out wordlessly against the paradisical beauty of the West, give cowboys a wide-eyed but drawn look. Their lips pucker up, not with kisses but with immutability. They may want to break out, staying up all night with a lover just to talk, but they don't know how and can't imagine what the consequences will be. Those rare occasions when they do bare themselves result in confusion. "I feel as if I'd sprained my heart," one friend told me a month after such a meeting.

My friend Ted Hoagland wrote, "No one is as fragile as a woman but no one is as fragile as a man." For all the women here who use "fragileness" to avoid work or as a sexual ploy, there are men who try to hide theirs, all the while clinging to an adolescent dependency on women to cook their meals, wash their clothes, and keep the ranch house warm in winter. But there is true vulnerability in evidence here. Because these men work with animals, not machines or numbers, because they live outside in landscapes of torrential beauty, because they are confined to a place and a routine embellished with awesome variables, because calves die in the arms that pulled others into life, because they go to the mountains as if on a pilgrimage to find out what makes a herd of elk tick, their strength is also a softness, their toughness, a rare delicacy.

chapter ten

Evaluations

A library patron who has never worked on the Internet asks a librarian to recommend several books that introduce a computer novice to the World Wide Web, email, and newsgroups. The patron says she wants the most authoritative books written in the most accessible language.

After a twenty-two-year stint, the president of a small liberal arts college finally decides to retire. After the announcement a committee is formed to choose a new leader, with representatives from the faculty, administration, alumni, and student body. The first task the group faces is to describe the character of an effective college president in the twenty-first century.

A senior is frustrated by the "C" he received on an essay written for a history class, so he makes an appointment to talk with the teaching assistant who graded the paper. "Be sure to review the assignment sheet first," she warns. The student notices that the sheet, on its back side, includes a checklist of requirements for the paper; he hadn't turned it over before.

"We have a lousy home page," a sales representative observes at a district meeting. "What's wrong with it?" the marketing manager asks. "Everything," she replies, then quickly changes the subject when she notices the manager's furrowed brow. But the manager decides to investigate the issue. Web sites are so new: Who knows what a good one looks like—or does?

The waiter uncorks the wine and pours a little into the diner's glass. The diner swirls the Merlot, sniffs its bouquet, and then sips gently, allowing the flavor to bloom on her tongue. "Very good," she nods, and the waiter fills her glass.

You've just seen *Citizen Kane* for the first time and want to share the experience with your roommate. Orson Welles's masterpiece is playing at the Student Union for only one more night, but *Die Hard X: The Battery* is featured across the street in THX sound. Guess which movie Bubba wants to see? You intend to set him straight.

■ ■ ■

UNDERSTANDING EVALUATIONS

By the time you leave home in the morning, you've likely made a dozen informal evaluations. You've selected dressy clothes because you have a job interview in the afternoon with a law firm; you've chosen low-fat yogurt and shredded wheat over artery-clogging eggs and bacon; you've spun the remote past cheery Matt Lauer for what you consider more adult programming on C-SPAN. In each case, you've applied criteria—standards used to measure the quality or value of something—to a particular problem and then made a decision.

Because all people have opinions and most people can—when pressed— even defend them, evaluations may in fact be the most familiar type of

argument. Some professional evaluations might require elaborate proto-
cols, but they don't differ much structurally from simpler choices that
people make routinely. And, of course, people do love to voice their opinions, and always have: a whole mode of classical rhetoric—called the ceremonial, or epideictic—was devoted entirely to speeches of praise and
blame. (See Chapter 1.)

Today, rituals of praise and blame are part of American life. Adults
who'd choke at the very notion of debating causal or definitional claims
will happily spend hours appraising the Dallas Cowboys or the Cleveland
Indians. Other evaluative spectacles in our culture include award shows,
beauty pageants, most-valuable-player presentations, lists of best-
dressed or worst-dressed celebrities, "sexiest people" magazine covers, literary prizes, political opinion polls, consumer product magazines, and—
the ultimate formal public gesture of evaluation—elections.

However, many arguments of evaluation do not produce simple rank-
ings, ratings, or winners. Instead, they lead people to make decisions,
explore alternative courses of action, or even change their lives. In such
cases, questions of evaluation can become arguments about core values
that affect the way people think and live. Identifying criteria of evaluation
can lead to individual insights into motives and preferences.

Why make such a big deal about criteria when many acts of evaluation
seem almost effortless? Because in social, cultural, and political realms,
evaluations need to be reexamined precisely when they become routine;
embedded in many acts of evaluation are important "why" questions that
typically go unasked:

- You may find yourself willing to dispute the grade you received in a
  course, but not the act of grading itself.

- You argue that Miss Alabama would have been a better Miss America
  than the contestant from New York, but perhaps you don't wonder
  loudly enough whether such competitions make sense at all.

- You argue passionately that a Republican Congress is better for
  America than a Democratic alternative, but you fail to ask why voters
  get only two choices.

- You may have good reasons for preferring a Ford pickup to a Chevy, but
  you never consider that a bike might be a better alternative than either
  truck.

- You prize books and reading over any other forms of cultural experience, but you never ask precisely why that should be the case.

How do we evaluate death? What would a "good" death be? In her book *The Good Death,* Marilyn Webb proposes that "those deaths that are good pull families together and leave a legacy of peace. Those that are bad leave a legacy of grief, anger, and pain that can continue across many generations."

··············· **LINK TO P. 712**

Push an argument of evaluation hard enough, and its relatively simple structure can raise deep questions about the values people hold in common and the consequences of those beliefs. Rosa Parks provides an effective example of the relationship between criteria and values when she points out, quite simply, what made Martin Luther King Jr. a hero to her:

> **Dr. King was a true leader. I never sensed fear in him. I just felt that he knew what had to be done and took the leading role without regard to consequences.**
>
> –Rosa Parks, "Role Models"

Her criterion for heroism could not be more evident or compelling: a fearless commitment to do what is right, regardless of the consequences. (For more on arguments based on values, see Chapter 5.)

CHARACTERIZING EVALUATION

For a society that regards itself as pluralistic, especially in matters of taste and values, U.S. citizens are remarkably feisty when it comes to making judgments. That's because even the strongest patrons of relativism—the belief that there are no absolute standards of value—find it hard to act on the principle. People prefer to think that their *own* beliefs are grounded in something more solid than mere rhetoric.

But "mere rhetoric," properly understood, is not to be sniffed at either. As an art of persuasion, rhetoric attunes writers to the power of audiences. Because audiences come to writers with values of their own, part of what writers must do is adjust their messages to the values of readers. But audiences can be moved as well by powerful words and good reasons, so writers also have the power to define values. This tension between existing values (tradition) and innovative perspectives (change) can spark healthy debates and move audiences toward new forms of consensus. That's what makes arguments of evaluation both powerful and exciting: they really do shape our worlds.

One way of classifying evaluative arguments is to consider the types of evidence they use. A distinction we explored in Chapter 7 between inartistic and artistic arguments is helpful here. You may recall that we defined inartistic arguments as those found ready-made as facts, statistics, testimony—what is sometimes now called "hard" evidence. Artistic arguments are those shaped chiefly in and through language, using informal logic. For evaluative arguments, the inartistic/artistic distinction can be expressed in terms of quantity versus quality. Quantitative arguments of evaluation rely on criteria that can be measured, counted, or demonstrated in a mechanical fashion. In contrast, qualitative arguments rely on nonnumerical criteria supported by reason, tradition, precedent, or logic. Needless to say, a claim of evaluation might be supported by arguments of both sorts. We separate them below merely to present them more clearly.

Quantitative Evaluations

At first glance, quantitative evaluations would seem to hold all the cards, especially in a society as enamored of science and technology as our own. Once you have defined a quantitative standard, making judgments should be as easy as measuring and counting—and in a few cases, that's the way things work out. *Who is the tallest or heaviest or loudest person in class?* If your colleagues allow themselves to be measured, you can find out easily enough, using the right equipment and internationally sanctioned standards of measurement: the meter, the kilo, or the decibel.

But what if you were to ask, *Who is the smartest person in class?* You could answer this more complex question quantitatively too, using IQ tests or college entrance examinations that report results numerically. In fact, almost every college-bound student in the United States submits to this kind of evaluation, taking either the SAT or ACT to demonstrate his or her verbal and mathematical prowess. Such measures are widely accepted by educators and institutions, but they are also vigorously challenged. Although scores generated by the SAT or ACT seem objective, they are based on responses to questions that measure particular kinds of skills, most of them related to academic success. Just how closely those numbers actually correlate with intelligence can be disputed, since many believe that academic achievement is far from the only measure of knowing, and that intelligence itself is not a single thing that can be measured quantitatively.

Like any standards of evaluation, quantitative criteria must be scrutinized carefully to make sure that what they measure relates to what is being evaluated. For example, in evaluating a car, you might use 0–60 mph times as a measure of acceleration, 60–0 mph distances as a measure of braking capability, skidpad numbers (0.85) as a measure of handling ability, and coefficient of drag (0.29) as a test of aerodynamic efficiency. But all these numbers are subject to error. A driver has to be on board to shift a manual transmission car through the gears, slam on the brakes, or

Check out the way Janice Turner uses both personal testimony and statistics on current trends in cosmetic surgery to support her argument that it should be acceptable for men to get face lifts, liposuction, and other cosmetic procedures.

LINK P. 416

steer a skidpad; the human variable tempers the absolute reliability of the measurements. Even when the numbers are gathered accurately and then compared, one vehicle with another, they may not tell the whole story, since some cars generate great test numbers and yet still feel less competent than vehicles with lower scores. The same disparity between numbers and feel occurs with other items—compact disc recordings, for example. CDs can produce awesome sonic accuracy numbers, but some listeners feel the music they produce may lack aural qualities important to listening pleasure. Educators, too, acknowledge that some students test better than others.

This is not to disparage quantitative measures of quality, only to offer a caveat: even the most objective measures have limits. They have been devised by fallible people looking at the world from their own inevitably limited perspectives. Just a few decades ago, teachers hoped that they might figure out how to measure quality of writing by applying quantitative measures relating to "syntactical maturity." The endeavor now seems almost comical because the more complex the human activity, the more it resists quantification. And writing is very complicated.

Yet experts in measurement assert with confidence that quantitative measures are almost always more reliable than qualitative criteria— no matter what is being evaluated. It is a sobering claim, and one not easily dismissed.

Qualitative Evaluations

Many issues of evaluation closest to people's hearts simply aren't subject to quantification. *What makes a movie great?* If someone suggested length, people would probably chuckle. Get serious! But what about box office receipts, especially if they could be adjusted to reflect changes in the value of the dollar over time? Would films that earned the most revenue—a definitely quantifiable measure—have a claim on the title "best picture"? In that select group would be movies such as *Star Wars, The Sound of Music, Gone with the Wind,* and *Titanic.* An interesting group of films, but the best? To argue for box office revenue as a criterion of film greatness, you'd have to defend the claim vigorously because many people in the audience would express doubts about it—substantial ones, based on prevailing prejudices that generally distinguish between artistic quality and popularity.

More likely, then, in defining the criteria for "great movie," you would look for standards to account for the merit of films such as *Citizen Kane,*

Casablanca, 8½, and *Jules et Jim*—works widely respected among serious critics. You might talk about directorial vision, societal impact, cinematic technique, dramatic rhythm—qualities that could be defined with some precision, but measured only with great difficulty. Lacking hard numbers, you would have to convince the audience to accept your standards and make your case rhetorically, providing evidence that connected artistic achievement to particular techniques or components. As you might guess, a writer using qualitative measures could spend as much time defending criteria of evaluation as providing evidence that these standards are present in the film under scrutiny.

But establishing subtle criteria is what can make arguments of evaluation so interesting if you take them seriously. They require you, time and again, to challenge conventional wisdom. Or they force you to give backbone to opinions you *think* you hold. In the following passage from one of the sample evaluative essays at the end of this chapter, the author provides a lively example of attacking a standard of evaluation she believes has survived too long:

> **Valorization of reading over television . . . is often based on the vague and groundless notion that reading is somehow "active" and television "passive." Why it is that the imaginative work done by a reader is more strenuous or worthwhile than that done by a viewer—or why watching television is more passive than, say, watching a play—is never explained.**
> **–Larissa MacFarquhar, "Who Cares If Johnny Can't Read?"**

Predictably, MacFarquhar's challenge to conventional wisdom provoked a strong response from readers when it appeared in the online magazine *Slate,* a response that generated perhaps more heat than light. Harvey Scodel writes in a letter to the editor: " 'Who Cares If Johnny Can't Read?' by Larissa MacFarquhar is a truly stupid article . . . a good example of supposedly skeptical and revisionist garbage." Ann W. Schmidt claims the article "is so off base that it is difficult to fathom that she [MacFarquhar] really believes what she is saying." Oh well, at least you know exactly where Scodel and Schmidt stand.

DEVELOPING AN EVALUATIVE ARGUMENT

Developing an argument of evaluation can seem like a simple process, especially if you already know what your claim is likely to be:

- *Citizen Kane* is the finest film ever made by an American director.
- Most serious drivers would prefer a 5-Series BMW to an E-Class Mercedes.
- A value-added tax would be a dreadful replacement for the federal income tax.
- John Paul II will likely be regarded as one of the three or four most important leaders of the twentieth century.

Having established a claim, you would then explore the implications of your belief, drawing out the reasons, warrants, and evidence that might support it.

Claim	**Citizen Kane is the finest film ever made by an American director . . .**
Reason	**. . . because it revolutionizes the way we see the world.**
Warrant	**Great films change viewers in fundamental ways.**
Evidence	**Shot after shot, Citizen Kane presents the life of its protagonist through cinematic images that viewers can never forget.**

The warrant here is, in effect, a statement of criteria—in this case, the quality that defines "great film" for the writer.

In developing an evaluative argument, you'll want to pay special attention to criteria, claims, and evidence.

Formulating Criteria

Personal ads present evaluation criteria distilled and condensed. W. Charisse Goodman quotes the following ad in her essay about weight prejudice in the United States: "Be any race, be yourself, but be beautiful."

·· LINK TO P. 408

Most often neglected in evaluations is the discussion of criteria. Although even casual evaluations ("Da Bears bite!") could be traced to reasonable criteria, most people don't bother defending their positions unless they are pressed ("Oh yeah?"). This reluctance to state criteria can be especially unfortunate whenever unexamined judgments are either inaccurate or indefensible to the point of stereotype or prejudice, as in the following examples:

It's an ugly sport coat, probably from off the rack at Kmart.

I doubt that the movie is any good. It stars Madonna.

Henley may not be the lawyer you want—she was admitted to law school only because of affirmative action.

Yet when writers address audiences whom they understand well or with whom they share core values, full statements of evaluative criteria are usually unnecessary. One wouldn't expect a film critic like Roger Ebert to restate all his principles every time he writes a movie review. Ebert assumes his readers will—over time—come to appreciate his standards.

Criteria are often embedded in statements rather than stated explicitly, because writers assume that readers will follow their meaning. For example, a newspaper columnist assessing President Clinton's policy toward North Korea might observe that "it lacks the imagination and risk of Nixon's China gambit." Packed in that clause is a wealth of implied meaning. First, there's implicit approval of a foreign policy widely agreed to have succeeded: in going to China in 1972, President Nixon reduced tensions between the United States and the huge Asian power. Since the China "gambit" worked, one can assume that the writer also approves of the "imagination" and "risk" that accompanied it. In other words, the writer is suggesting that foreign policy should be clever and daring: that's the implied criterion, a standard likely clear (even obvious) to readers familiar with the writer's historical allusion. But you can see the dangers of implied criteria. A reader who is ignorant of Nixon's policy won't appreciate the writer's point about President Clinton. So you see why you have to consider who your readers might be when you write arguments of evaluation. Readers must either share your criteria or be convinced to accept them.

Don't take criteria of evaluation for granted, especially when tackling a new subject. If you offer vague and unsupported principles, expect to be challenged. And you are most likely to be vague about your beliefs when you haven't thought enough about your subject. So push yourself at least as far as you imagine readers will. Imagine those readers over your shoulder, asking difficult questions.

Say, for example, that you intend to argue that serious drivers will obviously prefer a 5-Series BMW to an E-Class Mercedes. What standards would serious drivers apply to these sedans? Razor-sharp handling? But what does that mean? Perhaps it's the ability to hold the road in tight curves with minimal steering correction. That's a criterion you could defend. Serious drivers would likely expect precise braking, too. Might that mean that the brake pedal should be firm, responding linearly to driver input? Are such standards getting too technical? Or do you need to assert such sophisticated criteria to establish your authority to write about the subject? These are appropriate questions to ask.

Don't hesitate to be bold or idealistic in stating standards. Part of the appeal of Allan Bloom's now-classic discussion of American higher education, *The Closing of the American Mind,* was his ability to offer clear criteria to support the reforms he proposed:

A good program of liberal education feeds the student's love of truth and passion to live the good life. It is the easiest thing in the world to devise courses of study, adapted to the particular conditions of each university, which thrill those who take them. The difficulty is getting them accepted by the faculty. (emphasis added)

–Allan Bloom, "The Student and the University"

Making Claims

Claims can be stated directly or, in rare instances, strongly implied. For most writers the direct evaluative claim probably works better, with the statement carefully qualified. Consider the differences between the following claims and how much less the burden of proof would be for the second and third ones:

> **John Paul II is the most important leader of the twentieth century.**
>
> **John Paul II may be one of the three or four most influential leaders of the twentieth century.**
>
> **John Paul II may come to be regarded as one of the three or four most influential spiritual leaders of the twentieth century.**

The point of qualifying a statement is not to make evaluative claims bland, but to make them responsible and manageable. Of course, claims themselves might be more responsible if they were always written after a sober study of facts and evidence. But most people don't operate that way, particularly if they are working in isolation or within a closed community. Most people start with an opinion and then seek reasons and evidence to support it. If people are honest, though, they'll at least modify their claims in the face of contrary evidence.

But bringing strongly held claims to the table can work well in situations where different opinions meet. That's what makes discussions on listservs so potentially exciting: people with different values make contradictory claims and then negotiate their differences, sometimes over days and weeks. Committees and study groups can work in this way, too. For example, imagine Congress contemplating alternatives to the current federal income tax system. A committee assigned to explore better systems of taxation would likely work best if it included people willing to champion the merits of different plans, everything from a flat tax to the current progressive income tax. Each of these positions, well argued, would broaden the scope of what the committee knew and might help the group move toward consensus. Or it might not.

Presenting Evidence

The more evidence the better in an evaluation, provided that the evidence is relevant. In evaluating the performance of two computers, the speed of their processors would certainly be important, but the quality of their keyboards or the availability of service might be less crucial, perhaps irrelevant.

Just as important as relevance in selecting evidence is presentation. Not all pieces of evidence are equally convincing, nor should they be treated as such. Select evidence most likely to impress your readers, and arrange the paper to build toward your best material. In most cases, that *best material* will be evidence that is specific, detailed, and derived from credible sources. To support her point that reading is not inherently "better" than watching television, Larissa MacFarquhar points to examples that most readers will recognize and remember:

> **The best books might be better than the best television, but further down the pile the difference gets murkier. Most of the time the choice between books and television is not between Virgil and *Geraldo* but between *The Celestine Prophecy* and *Roseanne*. Who wouldn't pick *Roseanne?***
> —Larissa MacFarquhar, "Who Cares If Johnny Can't Read?"

Don't be afraid, either, to concede a point when evidence goes contrary to the overall claim you wish to make. If you are really skillful, you can even turn a problem into an argumentative asset, as Bob Costas does in acknowledging the flaws of baseball great Mickey Mantle in the process of praising him:

> **None of us, Mickey included, would want to be held to account for every moment of our lives. But how many of us could say that our best moments were as magnificent as his?**
> —Bob Costas, "Eulogy for Mickey Mantle"

When you are developing evidence for an evaluative paper, the Internet can be a remarkably helpful source, particularly when your subject falls within the realms of popular culture. By checking out particular newsgroups (even some that might not be considered authoritative sources for a traditional academic paper), you'll likely gain insight into popular feelings and attitudes. If, for example, you find the popularity of a show like *The X-Files* or *Roswell* puzzling, checking its Web site or related newsgroups may lead you to appreciate what has captured the imagination of fans. Evidence drawn from such material represents legitimate research.

For a discussion of who's a better sitcom dad — Homer Simpson or Ray Romano — see John Levesque's article "Sitcom Dads Rarely Know Best, Study of TV Laments."

LINK TO P. 385 ·····················

KEY FEATURES OF EVALUATIONS

In drafting an evaluation, you should consider three basic elements:

- an evaluative claim about a particular object, concept, or class related to the stated criteria

- a statement and (if necessary) an examination of criteria applicable to a given object, concept, or class: "This is what makes a *great film,* an *effective leader,* a *feasible solution:* . . ."

- evidence that the particular subject meets or falls short of the stated criteria

All these elements will be present in one way or another in arguments of evaluation, but they won't follow a specific order. In addition, you'll often need an opening paragraph to set the context for your evaluation, explaining to readers why they should care about the opinion you are about to present.

Nothing adds more depth to an opinion than offering it for discussion. When you can, use the resources of the Internet or more local online networks to get response to your opinions. It can be eye-opening to realize how strongly people react to ideas or points of view that you regard as perfectly conventional. When you are ready, share your draft with colleagues, asking them to identify places where you need additional support for your ideas, either in the discussion of criteria or in the presentation of evidence.

Finding a Topic

You are entering an argument of evaluation when you

- make a judgment about quality: *Citizen Kane is probably the finest film ever made by an American director.*
- challenge such a judgment: *Citizen Kane is vastly overrated by most film critics.*
- construct a ranking or comparison: *Citizen Kane is a more intellectually challenging movie than* Casablanca.

Issues of evaluation arise daily—in the judgments you make about public figures or policies; in the choices you make about instructors and courses; in the recommendations you make about books, films, or television programs; in the preferences you exercise in choosing products, activities, or charities. Be alert to evaluative arguments whenever you read or use terms that indicate value or rank: *good/bad, effective/ineffective, best/worst, competent/incompetent, successful/unsuccessful.* Finally, be aware of your own areas of expertise. Write about subjects or topics about which others regularly ask your opinion or advice.

Researching Your Topic

You can research issues of evaluation using the following sources:

- journals, reviews, and magazines (for current political and social issues)
- books (for assessing judgments about history, policy, etc.)
- biographies (for assessing people)
- research reports and scientific studies
- books, magazines, and Web sites for consumers
- periodicals and Web sites that cover entertainment and sports

Surveys and polls can be useful in uncovering public attitudes: *What books are people reading? Who are the most admired people in the country? What activities or businesses are thriving or waning?* You'll discover that Web sites, newsgroups, and listservs thrive on evaluation. Browse these public forums for ideas and, when possible, explore your own topic ideas there.

Formulating a Claim

After exploring your subject, begin to shape a full and specific claim, a thesis that lets readers know where you stand and on what criteria you will base your judgments. Look for a thesis that is challenging enough to attract readers' attention, not one that merely repeats views already widely held. In moving toward this thesis, you might begin with questions of this kind:

- What exactly is my opinion? Where do I stand?
- Can I make my judgment more specific?
- Do I need to qualify my claim?
- According to what standards am I making my judgment?
- Will readers accept my criteria, or will I have to defend them, too?
- What major reasons can I offer in support of my evaluation?

Your thesis should be a complete statement. In one sentence, you need to *make a claim of evaluation and state the reasons that support your claim.* Be sure your claim is specific enough. Anticipate the questions readers might have: *Who? What? Where? Under what conditions? With what exceptions? In all cases?* Don't expect readers to guess where you stand.

Preparing a Proposal

If your instructor asks you to prepare a proposal for your project, here's a format you might use.

State your thesis completely. If you are having trouble doing so, try outlining it in Toulmin terms:

Claim:

Reason(s):

Warrant(s):

Explain why this issue deserves attention. What is at stake?

Specify whom you hope to reach through your argument and why this group of readers would be interested in it.

Briefly discuss the key challenges you anticipate. Defining criteria? Defending them? Finding quantitative evidence to support your claim? Developing qualitative arguments to bolster your judgment?

Determine what research strategies you will use. What sources do you expect to consult?

Consider what format you expect to use for your project. A conventional research essay? A letter to the editor? A Web page?

Thinking about Organization

Your evaluation may take various forms, but it is likely to include elements such as the following:

- a specific claim: *Most sport utility vehicles (SUVs) are unsuitable for the kind of driving most Americans do.*
- an explanation or defense of the criteria (if necessary): *The overcrowding and pollution of American cities and suburbs might be relieved if more Americans drove small, fuel-efficient cars. Cars do less damage in accidents than heavy SUVs and are also less likely to roll over.*
- an examination of the claim in terms of the stated criteria: *Most SUVs are unsuitable for the kind of driving Americans do because they are not designed for contemporary urban driving conditions.*
- evidence for every part of the argument: *SUVs get very poor gas mileage; they are statistically more likely than cars to roll over in accidents. . . .*
- consideration of alternative views and counterarguments: *It is true, perhaps, that SUVs make drivers feel safer on the roads and give them a better view of traffic conditions because of their height. . . .*

Getting and Giving Response

All arguments benefit from the scrutiny of others. Your instructor may assign you to a peer group for the purpose of reading and responding to each other's drafts; if not, make the effort yourself to get some careful response. You can use the following questions to evaluate a draft. If you are evaluating someone else's draft, be sure to illustrate your points with specific examples. Specific comments are always more helpful than general observations.

The Claim

- Is the claim clearly an argument of evaluation? Does it make a judgment about something?
- Does the claim establish clearly what is being evaluated?
- Is the claim too sweeping? Does it need to be qualified?
- Will the criteria used in the evaluation be clear to readers? Do the criteria need to be defined more explicitly or precisely?
- Are the criteria appropriate ones to use for this evaluation? Are they controversial? Does evidence of their validity need to be added?

Evidence for the Claim

- Is enough evidence provided to ensure that what is being evaluated meets the criteria established for the evaluation? If not, what kind of additional evidence is needed?

- Is the evidence in support of the claim simply announced, or are its significance and appropriateness analyzed? Is a more detailed discussion needed?

- Are any objections readers might have to the claim, criteria, or evidence adequately addressed?

- What kinds of sources are cited? How credible and persuasive will they be to readers? What other kinds of sources might be more credible and persuasive?

- Are all quotations introduced with appropriate signal phrases (for instance, "As Will argues,") and blended smoothly into the writer's sentences?

Organization and Style

- How are the parts of the argument organized? Is this organization effective, or would some other structure work better?

- Will readers understand the relationships among the claims, supporting reasons, warrants, and evidence? If not, what could be done to make those connections clearer? Are more transitional words and phrases needed? Would headings or graphic devices help?

- Are the transitions or links from point to point, paragraph to paragraph, and sentence to sentence clear and effective? If not, how could they be improved?

- Is the style suited to the subject? Is it too formal? Too casual? Too technical? Too bland?

- Which sentences seem particularly effective? Which ones seem weakest, and how could they be improved? Should some short sentences be combined, or should any long ones be separated into two or more sentences?

- How effective are the paragraphs? Do any seem too skimpy or too long?

- Which words or phrases seem particularly effective, vivid, and memorable? Do any seem dull, vague, unclear, or inappropriate for the audience or the writer's purpose? Are definitions provided for technical or other terms that readers might not know?

Spelling, Punctuation, Mechanics, Documentation, Format

- Are there any errors in spelling, punctuation, capitalization, and the like?
- Is an appropriate and consistent style of documentation used for parenthetical citations and the list of works cited or references? (See Chapter 22.)
- Does the paper or project follow an appropriate format? Is it appropriately designed and attractively presented? If it is a Web site, do all the links work?

RESPOND.

1. Choose one item from the following list that you understand well enough to evaluate. Develop several criteria of evaluation you could defend to distinguish excellence from mediocrity in the area. Then choose another item from the list, this time one you do not know much about at all, and explain the research you might do to discover reasonable criteria of evaluation for it.

> fashion designers
>
> sport utility vehicles
>
> action films
>
> hip-hop music
>
> American presidents
>
> NFL quarterbacks
>
> landscape design
>
> contemporary painting
>
> professional journalists
>
> TV sitcoms
>
> fast food
>
> rock musicians

2. Local news-and-entertainment magazines often publish "best of" issues or articles that list readers' and editors' favorites in such categories as "best place to go on a first date," "best softball field," and "best dentist." Sometimes the categories are very specific: "best places to say, 'I was retro before retro was cool,'" or "best movie theater seats." Imagine that you are the editor of your own local magazine and that you want to put out a "best of" issue tailored to your hometown. Develop ten categories for evaluation. For each category, list the evaluative criteria you use to make your judgment. (You might want to review Chapter 9 to decide which of the criteria are essential, sufficient, or accidental to your evaluation.)

    Next, consider that since your criteria are warrants, they are especially tied to audience. (The criteria for "best dentist," for example, might be tailored to people whose major concern is avoiding pain, to those whose children will be regular visitors, or to those who want the cheapest possible dental care.) For several of your evaluative categories, imagine that you have to justify your judgments to a completely different audience. Write a new set of criteria for that audience.

3. Read Larissa MacFarquhar's article "Who Cares If Johnny Can't Read?" and the two readers' letters of response, both of which appear at the end of this chapter. MacFarquhar makes several evaluative claims, some of them more explicit than others. What are the categories that she evaluates? What are the criteria that she uses to evaluate them? Pick one category and list her evaluative criteria. Then turn to the readers' letters, and determine the criteria *they* use to evaluate the same category. Which criteria do the readers accept? Which do they not accept? How can you account for the strength of the readers' reactions?

The Simplsons: *A Mirror of Society*

BEN McCORKLE

The first paragraph offers a criterion for quality entertainment.

In recent years, a certain animated sitcom has caught the public's attention, evoking reactions that are both favorable and unfavorable, but hardly ever apathetic. As a brilliant, socially aware satire, Matt Groening's *The Simpsons* has effectively stirred different emotions from different factions of the culturally deadened American populace, and for this alone it should be recognized as "quality programming."

Effective parody exposes the flaws of society—another important standard for judging the show.

Often, *The Simpsons* is truly brutal parody, hurling barbs of hostile commentary at our materialistic and gluttonous American lifestyle. Many in the audience might be offended by this bullying, except that it seems like harmless fun. For example, when father Homer Simpson decides he would rather sleep in on a Sunday than attend church, Groening is obviously pointing out a corruption of traditional values within the family structure. But recognizing that people don't like to be preached to, the show takes a comic approach, having God come to talk to Homer, telling him to start his own religious sect. The hedonism that Homer extols in the name of the Lord is both ludicrous and hilariously funny, and viewers who might be offended are disarmed, so that even the most conservative Republican grandmother is receptive to the comic message.

McCorkle anticipates a potential objection to his argument.

Because it is a cartoon, some might scoff at *The Simpsons* and call it a children's show. But this cartoon is clearly meant for a mass audience, including adults: it is shown during prime time rather than on Saturday morn-

---

Ben McCorkle wrote "*The Simpsons*: A Mirror of Society" while he was a student at Augusta College in Augusta, Georgia. McCorkle argues that the television cartoon series *The Simpsons* merits serious attention because it exposes the deepest flaws in our society while making us laugh.

ings, and, moreover, it appears on the Fox network, that paragon of broadcast debauchery. The cartoon format allows for visual freedom artistically and, because many people believe cartoons to be childish and incapable of making any real commentary on social values, may aid as well in the subtle presentation of the show's message.

The Simpson family has occasionally been described as a "nuclear" family, which obviously has a double meaning: first, the family consists of two parents and three children, and, second, Homer works at a nuclear power plant with very relaxed safety codes. The overused label *dysfunctional,* when applied to the Simpsons, suddenly takes on new meaning. Every episode seems to include a scene in which son Bart is being choked by his father, the baby is being neglected, or Homer is sitting in a drunken stupor transfixed by the television screen. The comedy in these scenes comes from the exaggeration of commonplace household events (although some talk shows and news programs would have us believe that these exaggerations are not confined to the madcap world of cartoons).

The next several paragraphs provide detailed evidence to support the claim of evaluation.

While Bart represents the mischievous demon-spawn and Homer the dim-witted plow ox, the female characters serve as foils to counterbalance these male characters' unredeeming characteristics. Marge, the mother, is rational, considerate, and forgiving, always aware of her husband's shortcomings; younger sister Lisa is intelligent, well behaved, and an outstanding student; and baby Maggie is an innocent child. (Could the fact that the "good" members of the family all happen to be female reflect some feminist statements on Groening's part?)

It is said that "to err is human," in which case the Simpsons may appear to be a little more human than the rest of us. They are constantly surrounded by their failures, yet seemingly unaware that their lives are often less than ideal. Their ability to accept the hand dealt them and endure without complaint is their most charming quality. Although not very bright as a whole, the Simpsons are survivors. Moreover, they exhibit a patriotic dedication to life, liberty, and the pursuit of happiness that should make every true American proud.

The Simpsons'
targets are listed to
suggest the breadth
of the program's
satire.

Ultimately, viewers find this family to be unwitting heroes, enduring the incompetence and corruption of contemporary education, industry, government, religion, and, ironically, even television. Yet in spite of all the disheartening social problems it portrays, *The Simpsons* nevertheless remains funny. Whenever a scene threatens to turn melodramatic or raise an inescapably deep issue, the moment is saved by some piece of nonsense, often an absurdly gratuitous act of violence.

The conclusion
reinforces the
overall claim and
offers one final
rationale for the
show's success.

At a time when it seems that society is being destroyed by its own designs, it is good to be able to hold up a mirror that shows us the extent of our problems. Neither escapist nor preachy, *The Simpsons* provides such a satiric mirror, a metaphoric reflection of our dissolving social foundation. More than that, *The Simpsons* is therapeutic: to be able to laugh in the face of such problems is the ultimate catharsis.

Who Cares If Johnny Can't Read?

LARISSA MACFARQUHAR

Among the truisms that make up the eschatology of American cultural decline, one of the most banal is the assumption that Americans don't read. Once, the story goes—in the 1950s, say—we read much more than we do now, and read the good stuff, the classics. Now, we don't care about reading anymore, we're barely literate, and television and computers are rendering books obsolete.

None of this is true. We read much more now than we did in the '50s. In 1957, 17 percent of people surveyed in a Gallup poll said they were currently reading a book; in 1990, over twice as many did. In 1953, 40 percent of people

---

Larissa MacFarquhar is a contributing editor of *Lingua Franca,* a magazine about higher education, and an advisory editor at the *Paris Review,* a literary journal. In this article, which originally appeared in the online magazine *Slate* in 1997, she brashly challenges the traditional evaluation that the reading of books is the pinnacle of cultural achievement. As you might expect, the article provoked a torrent of outraged email to *Slate's* editors; two examples follow her piece here.

polled by Gallup could name the author of *Huckleberry Finn;* in 1990, 51 percent could. In 1950, 8,600 new titles were published; in 1981, almost five times as many.

In fact, Americans are buying more books now than ever before—over 2 billion in 1992. Between the early '70s and the early '80s, the number of bookstores in this country nearly doubled—and that was before the Barnes & Noble superstores and Amazon.com. People aren't just buying books as status objects, either. A 1992 survey found that the average adult American reads 11.2 books per year, which means that the country as a whole reads about 2 billion—the number bought. There are more than 250,000 reading groups in the country at the moment, which means that something like 2 million people regularly read books and meet to discuss them.

In his book about Jewish immigrants in America at the turn of the century, *World of Our Fathers,* Irving Howe describes a time that sounds impossibly antiquated, when minimally educated laborers extended their workdays to attend lectures and language classes. Howe quotes an immigrant worker remembering his adolescence in Russia: "How can I describe to you . . . the excitement we shared when we would discuss Dostoyevsky? . . . Here in America young people can choose from movies and music and art and dancing and God alone knows what. But we—all we had was books, and not so many of them, either."

Hearing so much about the philistinism of Americans, we think such sentiments fossils of a bygone age. But they're not. People still write like that about books. Of course, most aren't reading Dostoyevsky. The authors who attract thousands and thousands of readers who read everything they write and send letters to them begging for more seem to be the authors of genre fiction—romances, science fiction, and mysteries.

Romance readers are especially devoted. The average romance reader spends $1,200 a year on books, and often comes to think of her favorite authors as close friends. Romance writer Debbie Macomber, for instance, gets thousands of letters a year, and when her daughter had a baby, readers sent her a baby blanket and a homemade Christmas stocking with the baby's name embroidered on it. It's writers like Macomber who account for the book boom. In 1994, a full 50 percent of books purchased fell into the category of "popular fiction." (Business and self-help books were the next biggest group at 12 percent, followed by "cooking/crafts" at 11 percent, "religion" at 7 percent, and "art/literature/poetry" at 5 percent.)

These reading habits are not new. Genre fiction and self-help books have made up the bulk of the American book market for at least 200 years. A survey conducted in 1930 found that the No. 1 topic people wanted to read about was personal hygiene. And you just have to glance through a list of best sellers through the ages to realize how little we've changed: *Daily Strength for Daily Needs* (1895); *Think and Grow Rich* (1937); *Games People Play: The Psychology of Human Relationships* (1964); *Harlow: An Intimate Biography* (1964).

Romance writers tend to be cleareyed about what it is they're doing. They don't think they're creating subversive feminine versions of Proust. They're producing mass-market entertainment that appeals to its consumers for much the same reason as McDonald's and Burger King appeal to theirs: It's easy, it makes you feel good, and it's the same every time. The point of a romance novel is not to dazzle its reader with originality, but to stimulate predictable emotions by means of familiar cultural symbols. As romance writer Kathleen Gilles Seidel puts it: "My reader comes to my book when she is tired. . . . Reading may be the only way she knows how to relax. If I am able to give her a few delicious, relaxing hours, that is a noble enough purpose for me."

But then, if romance novels are just another way to relax, what, if anything, makes them different from movies or beer? Why should the activity "reading romances" be grouped together with "reading philosophy" rather than with "going for a massage"? The Center for the Book in the Library of Congress spends lots of time and money coming up with slogans like "Books Make a Difference." But is the mere fact of reading something—*anything*—a cultural achievement worth celebrating?

We haven't always thought so. When the novel first became popular in America in the latter half of the 18th century, it was denounced as a sapper of brain cells and a threat to high culture in much the same way that television is denounced today. In the 1940s, Edmund Wilson declared that "detective stories [are] simply a kind of vice that, for silliness and minor harmfulness, ranks somewhere between smoking and crossword puzzles." You almost never hear this kind of talk anymore in discussions of American reading habits: *Not all reading is worth doing. Some books are just a waste of time.*

As fears of cultural apocalypse have been transferred away from novels onto a series of high-tech successors (radio, movies, television, and now computers), books have acquired a reputation for educational and even moral worthiness. Books are special: You can send them through the mail for lower rates, and there are no customs duties imposed on books imported into this country. There have, of course, been endless culture wars fought over what kind of books should be read in school, but in discussions of adult reading habits these distinctions tend to evaporate.

The sentimentalization of books gets especially ripe when reading is compared with its supposed rivals: television and cyberspace. Valorization of reading over television, for instance, is often based on the vague and groundless notion that reading is somehow "active" and television "passive." Why it is that the imaginative work done by a reader is more strenuous or worthwhile than that done by a viewer—or why watching television is more passive than, say, watching a play—is never explained. Sven Birkerts' maudlin 1994 paean to books, *The Gutenberg Elegies: The Fate of Reading in an Electronic Age,* is a classic example of this genre. *Time* art critic Robert Hughes made a similarly sentimental and mysterious argument recently in the *New York Review of Books:*

> Reading is a collaborative act, in which your imagination goes halfway to meet the author's; you visualize the book as you read it, you participate in making up the characters and rounding them out. . . . The effort of bringing something vivid out of the neutral array of black print is quite different, and in my experience far better for the imagination, than passive submission to the bright icons of television, which come complete and overwhelming, and tend to burn out the tender wiring of a child's imagination because they allow no re-working.

I cannot remember ever visualizing a book's characters, but everyone who writes about reading seems to do this, so perhaps I'm in a minority. Still, you could equally well say that you participate in making up TV characters because you have to imagine what they're thinking, where in a novel, you're often provided with this information.

Another reason why books are supposed to be better than television is that books are quirky and individualistic and real, whereas television is mass-produced corporate schlock. But of course popular books can be, and usually are, every bit as formulaic and "corporatized" as television. The best books might be better than the best television, but further down the pile the difference gets murkier. Most of the time the choice between books and television is not between Virgil and *Geraldo* but between *The Celestine Prophecy* and *Roseanne.* Who wouldn't pick *Roseanne?*

If the fertility of our culture is what we're concerned about, then McLuhanesque musing on the intrinsic nature of reading (as if it had any such thing) is beside the point. Reading per se is not the issue. The point is to figure out why certain kinds of reading and certain kinds of television might matter in the first place.

LINKS

BookWeb, the site of the American Booksellers Association, includes a "Reference Desk," which tracks some trends in book selling, book buying, books as gifts, etc. You can get a quick summary of the Center for the Book and its campaigns to promote readership. Book groups have made their way onto the Web, and publishers are, quite understandably, promoting them. The Bantam Doubleday Dell site serves up a minihistory of book groups and tells you how to join or form one of your own. Not surprisingly, aficionados of romance fiction have a plethora of sites to choose from: For starters, try the Romance Reader, with its many reviews, and the online version of the magazine *Romance Times*. Mystery-fiction sites are equally abundant—see Mystery/Net.com and the Mysterious Home Page. You can read excerpts from Sven Birkerts' *The Gutenberg Elegies,* as well as a response to the book in the *Atlantic Monthly*. Finally, for some academic resources on reading, turn to the Society for the History of Authorship, Reading & Publishing.

Two Responses to This Article

"Who Cares If Johnny Can't Read?" by Larissa MacFarquhar is a truly stupid article, whose only point is that there is a big difference between basic reading and highbrow reading. But this is not a crucial distinction for people concerned about literacy in this country. There has been a palpable decline in literacy in America over the last 30 years. Even the average university student both knows less and, by common-sense measures, is less intelligent than his or her predecessors. And even if IQ has not declined on a mass scale (and I suspect that it has), there is a point at which lack of curiosity and sheer ignorance are indistinguishable from a deficiency of intelligence. This article was a good example of supposedly skeptical and revisionist garbage.

–Harvey Scodel, "Illiteracy Test"

"Who Cares If Johnny Can't Read?" by Larissa MacFarquhar is so off base that it is difficult to fathom that she really believes what she is saying. I am the president of the Literacy Council of Garland County, Ark., and I know that the functional illiteracy rate in our state is 52 percent.

Her data is obviously faulty. It is nonsense to ask an illiterate person if he's reading a book. Of course he's going to say "yes." The last thing an illiterate person wants to advertise is the fact that he can't read. Our culture is filled with ways to help people hide their illiteracy. Restaurants like Shoney's and Denny's feature pictures of their entrees on the menu so those who can't read can still order their meal. And people know who wrote *Huckleberry Finn* and other books because they have learned from television and the movies.

–Ann W. Schmidt, "Lying Illiterates"

chapter eleven

Causal Arguments

A local school board member notes that students at one high school consistently outscore all others in the district on standardized math tests. She decides to try to identify the cause(s) of these students' success.

Researchers at a national research laboratory note that a number of their colleagues have contracted skin cancer during the last five years. They decide to work together to investigate possible causes.

A large clothing manufacturer wants to increase its market share among teenage buyers of blue jeans. Its executives know that another company has been the overwhelming market leader for years—and they set out to learn exactly why.

Convinced that there is a strong and compelling causal link between smoking and lung cancer, you argue that your cousin should stop smoking immediately and at any cost.

A state legislator notes that gasoline prices are consistently between twenty-five and fifty cents higher in one large city in the state than elsewhere. After some preliminary investigation, the legislator decides to bring a class action lawsuit on behalf of the people of this city, arguing that price fixing and insider deals are responsible for the price difference.

■ ■ ■

UNDERSTANDING CAUSAL ARGUMENTS

Arguments about causes and effects inform many everyday decisions and choices: you decide to swear off desserts since they inevitably lead to weight gain; because you failed last week's midterm, you decide to work through all the problems with a group of other students in your class, convinced that the new study technique will bring about an improvement in your test scores. To take another example, suppose you are explaining, in a petition for a change of grade, why you were unable to submit the final assignment on time. You would probably try to trace the causes of your failure to submit the assignment—the death of your grandmother followed by an attack of the flu followed by the theft of your car—in hopes that the committee reading the petition would see these causes as valid and change your grade. In identifying the causes of the situation, you are implicitly arguing that the effect—your failure to turn in the assignment on time—should be considered anew.

Causal arguments exist in many forms and frequently appear as parts of other arguments (such as evaluations or proposals). But it may help focus your work on causal arguments to separate them into three major categories:

- arguments that state a cause and then examine its effect(s)
- arguments that state an effect and then trace the effect back to its cause(s)
- arguments that move through a series of links: A causes B, which leads to C and perhaps to D

Arguments that begin with a stated cause and then move to an examination of one or more of its effects

This type of argument might begin, for example, with a cause like putting women into combat and then demonstrate the effects that such a cause would have. In this type of argument, success depends on being able to show compellingly that the cause would indeed lead to the described effects. Producer Anita Gordon and zoologist David Suzuki mount such a causal argument in an essay about how current attempts to "engineer" nature will lead to environmental disaster. Here is the opening of their essay:

> **There's a strange phenomenon that biologists refer to as "the boiled frog syndrome." Put a frog in a pot of water and increase the temperature of the water gradually from 20°C to 30°C to 40°C . . . to 90°C and the frog just sits there. But suddenly, at 100°C (212°F), something happens: the water boils and the frog dies.**
>
> **Scientists studying environmental problems, particularly the greenhouse effect, see "the boiled frog syndrome" as a metaphor for the human situation: we have figuratively, and in some ways literally, been heating up the world around us without realizing the danger.**
> **–Anita Gordon and David Suzuki, "How Did We Come to This?"**

Arguments that begin with an effect and then trace the effect back to one or more causes

This type of argument might begin with a certain effect—for example, the facts of urban ghetto poverty—and then trace the effect or set of effects to the most likely causes—in this case, widespread racism and persistent job discrimination, or, from another point of view, an implicit but powerful class and economic system that demands a "bottom." Again, the special challenge of such arguments is to make the causal connection compelling to the audience. In 1962, scientist Rachel Carson seized the attention of millions with a causal argument about the effects of the overuse of chemical poisons in agricultural control programs. Here is an excerpt from the beginning of her book-length study of this subject:

> **. . . a strange blight crept over the area and everything began to change. Some evil spell had settled on the community: mysterious maladies swept the flocks of chickens; the cattle and sheep sickened and died. Everywhere was a shadow of death. The farmers spoke of much illness among their families. . . . There had been several sudden and unexplained deaths, not only among adults but even among children, who would be stricken suddenly while at play and die within a few hours. . . .**

A childless couple in California placed advertisements in selected college newspapers offering $50,000—ten times the going rate—for eggs donated by a tall, athletic, intelligent student. See Gina Kolata's article discussing the possible social consequences of such advertisements.

LINK TO P. 702 ···

Erica Goode's article explores the reasons behind a distressing new trend among young women in Fiji: "Just a few years after the introduction of television to [Fiji], eating disorders—once virtually unheard of there—are on the rise among girls."

LINK TO P. 398 ···

The roadsides, once so attractive, were now lined with browned and withered vegetation as though swept by fire. These, too, were silent, deserted by all living things. Even the streams were now lifeless. Anglers no longer visited them, for all the fish had died.

In the gutters under the eaves and between the shingles of the roofs, a white granular powder still showed a few patches; some weeks before it had fallen like snow upon the roofs and the lawns, the fields and streams.

No witchcraft, no enemy action had silenced the rebirth of new life in this stricken world. The people had done it themselves. . . .

What has already silenced the voices of spring in countless towns in America? This book is an attempt to explain.

–Rachel Carson, *Silent Spring*

Arguments that move through a series of links: Cause A leads to B, which leads to C and possibly to D

In an environmental science class, for example, you might decide to argue that a national law regulating smokestack emissions from utility plants is needed because (A) emissions from utility plants in the Midwest cause acid rain, (B) acid rain causes the death of trees and other vegetation in eastern forests, (C) powerful lobbyists have prevented midwestern states from passing strict laws to control emissions from these plants, and (D) as a result, acid rain will destroy most eastern forests by 2020. In this case, the first link is that emissions cause acid rain; the second, that acid rain causes destruction in eastern forests; and the third, that states have not acted to break the cause-effect relationship established by the first two points. These links set the scene for the fourth link, which ties the previous points together to argue from effect: unless X, then Y.

At their most schematic, then, causal arguments may be diagrammed in relatively straightforward ways, as shown in Figure 11.1.

FIGURE 11.1 CAUSAL ARGUMENTS

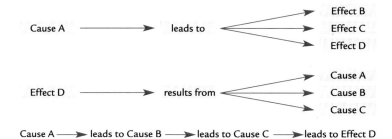

CHARACTERIZING CAUSAL ARGUMENTS

Causal arguments tend to share several characteristics.

They are often part of other arguments.

Causal arguments often work to further other arguments, especially proposals, so you should remember that they can be useful in establishing the good reasons for arguments in general. For example, a proposal to limit the amount of time children spend watching television would very likely draw on causal "good reasons" for support, ones that would attempt to establish that watching television causes negative results—such as increased violent behavior, decreased attention spans, and so on.

They are almost always complex.

The complexity of most causal arguments makes establishing causes and effects extremely difficult. For example, scientists and politicians continue to disagree over the extent to which acid rain is actually responsible for the so-called dieback of many eastern forests. If you can show that X *definitely* causes Y, though, you will have a powerful argument at your disposal. That is why, for example, so much effort has gone into establishing a definite link between smoking and cancer and between certain dietary habits and heart disease: providing the causal link amid the complex of factors that might be associated with cancer or heart disease would argue most forcefully for changing behavior in very significant ways.

They are often definition-based.

Part of the complexity of causal arguments arises from the need for very carefully worded definitions. Recent figures from the U.S. Department of Education, for example, indicate that the number of high school dropouts is rising and that this rise has caused an increase in youth unemployment. But exactly how does the study define *dropout*? A closer look may suggest that some students (perhaps a lot) who drop out actually "drop back in" later and go on to complete high school. Further, how does the study define *employment*? Until you can provide explicit definitions that answer such questions, you should proceed cautiously with a causal argument like this one.

They usually yield probable rather than absolute conclusions.

Because causal relationships are almost always extremely complex, they seldom yield more than a high degree of probability. Scientists in

In his article urging changes in the rules and organization of college basketball, Thad Williamson argues about the consequences of commercialism in the game.

LINK TO P. 519

particular are wary of making causal claims—that eating certain foods causes cancer, for example, since it is highly unlikely that a disease as resistant and persistent as cancer could be linked to any one cause. Even after an event, causation can be difficult to prove. No one would disagree that the Japanese bombing of Pearl Harbor took place on December 7, 1941, or that the United States entered World War II shortly thereafter. But what is the causal connection? Did the bombing "cause" the U.S. entry into the war? Even if one is convinced that the bombing was the most immediate cause, what of other related causes: the unstable and often hostile relationship between the U.S. and Japanese governments in the years leading up to the bombing; U.S. policies toward Japanese immigration; common U.S. stereotypes of "Oriental" peoples; U.S. reactions to the Japanese invasion of China; and so on? As another example, during the campus riots of the late 1960s, a special commission was charged with determining the "causes" of riots on a particular campus. After two years of work—and almost a thousand pages of evidence and reports—the commission was unable to pinpoint anything but a broad network of contributing causes and related conditions. Thus, causal claims must be approached with care and supported with the strongest evidence available in order to demonstrate the highest probability possible that A caused B.

DEVELOPING CAUSAL ARGUMENTS

Formulating a Claim

Although you might decide to write a wildly exaggerated or parodic causal argument for humorous purposes (such as *Dave Barry's Complete Guide to Guys: A Fairly Short Book,* in which Barry traces the "causes" of "guy-dom"), most of the causal reasoning you do will be related to serious subjects of significance to you, to your family and friends, or to your society. To begin creating a strong causal claim, try listing some of the effects—events or phenomena—you would like to know the causes of. *Why do you tend to panic immediately before exams? What's responsible for the latest tuition hike? What has led to the postings of "contamination" along your favorite creek?* Or try moving in the opposite direction, listing some events or causes you are interested in and then hypothesizing what kinds of effects they may produce. *What will happen if your academic major begins requiring a six-year program for a B.S.? What may be the effects of a balanced federal budget?*

When you find several possible causal relationships that interest you, try them out on friends and colleagues. Can they suggest ways to refocus or clarify what you want to do? Can they offer leads to finding information about your subject? If you have hypothesized various causes or effects, can they offer counterexamples or refutations?

Finally, map out a rough statement about the causal relationship you want to explore:

A causes (or is caused by) B for the following reasons:

1. _____

2. _____

3. _____

Read Michelle Cottle's article "Turning Boys into Girls" to see how she develops a claim about "how men's magazines are making guys as neurotic, insecure, and obsessive about their appearance as women."

LINK TO P. 428 ·····································

Developing the Argument

Once you have drafted a claim, you can explore the cause-effect relationship(s), drawing out the reasons, warrants, and evidence that can support the claim most effectively.

Claim	Losing seasons caused the football coach to lose his job.
Reason	The team lost more than half its games for three seasons in a row.
Warrant	Winning is the key to success for Big Ten college coaches.
Evidence	For the last ten years, coaches with more than two losing seasons in a row have lost their jobs.

Claim	Certain career patterns cause women to be paid less than men.
Reason	Women's career patterns differ from men's, and in spite of changes in the relative pay of other groups, women's pay still lags behind that of men.
Warrant	Successful careers are made during the period between ages 25 and 35.
Evidence	Women often drop out of or reduce work during the decade between ages 25 and 35 in order to raise families.

In further developing a causal argument, you can draw on many of the strategies we have already touched on in this book. In the article from which the following passage is excerpted, for instance, Stephen King uses dozens of examples—from *The Texas Chainsaw Massacre, The Gory Ones*, and *Invasion of the Body Snatchers* to *Night of the Living Dead, Psycho, The Amityville Horror*, and *The Thing*—in explaining why people love horror movies:

> **The mythic horror movie, like the sick joke, has a dirty job to do. It deliberately appeals to all that is worst in us. It is morbidity unchained, our most base instincts let free, our nastiest fantasies realized . . . and it all happens, fittingly enough, in the dark. For those reasons, good liberals often shy away from horror films. For myself, I like to see the most aggressive of them—*Dawn of the Dead*, for instance—as lifting a trap door in the civilized forebrain and throwing a basket of raw meat to the hungry alligators swimming around in that subterranean river beneath.**
>
> **Why bother? Because it keeps them from getting out, man. It keeps them down there and me up here. It was Lennon and McCartney who said that all you need is love, and I would agree with that.**
>
> **As long as you keep the gators fed.**
>
> **—Stephen King, "Why We Crave Horror Movies"**

Another way to support a causal argument is through the use of analogies. In such an argument, the strength will lie in how closely you can relate the two phenomena being compared. In exploring why Americans are now involved in what he calls "The Worship of Art," journalist Tom Wolfe draws an analogy between religion and art, and he argues that the causes that have long linked humans with religious belief now link them with the arts:

> **There was a time when well-to-do, educated people in America adorned their parlors with crosses, crucifixes, or Stars of David. These were marks not only of faith but of cultivation. Think of the great homes, built before 1940, with chapels. This was a fashionable as well as devout use of space. . . . Practically no one who cares about appearing cultivated today would display a cross or Star of David in the living room. It would be . . . *in bad taste*. Today the conventional symbol of devoutness is—but of course—the Holy Rectangle: the painting. The painting is the religious object we see today in the parlors of the educated classes.**
>
> **—Tom Wolfe, "The Worship of Art: Notes on the New God"**

Establishing causes for physical effects—like diseases—often calls for another means of support: testing hypotheses, or theories about possible causes. This kind of reasoning helped to determine the causes of school poisonings in California recently, and some years ago it helped to solve a

In his article arguing the merits of hospice care, Joe Loconte closes with this analogy: "hospice personnel could be to medical care what American GIs were to the Allied effort in Europe—the source of both its tactical and moral strength and, eventually, the foot soldiers for victory and reconciliation."

⋯⋯⋯⋯⋯⋯⋯⋯⋯⋯⋯⋯⋯⋯ LINK TO P. 729

mystery disease that had struck some fifty people in Quebec City. Puzzled by cases all involving the same effects (nausea, shortness of breath, cough, stomach pain, weight loss, and a marked blue-gray coloration), doctors at first investigated the hypothesis that the cause was severe vitamin deficiency. But too many cases in too short a time made this hypothesis unlikely, because vitamin deficiency does not ordinarily appear as a sudden epidemic. In addition, postmortem examinations of the twenty people who died revealed severe damage to the heart muscle and the liver, features that were inconsistent with the vitamin-deficiency hypothesis. The doctors therefore sought a clue to the mysterious disease in something the fifty victims were found to have shared: all fifty had been lovers of beer and had, in fact, drunk a particular brand of beer.

It seemed possible that the illness was somehow connected to the beer, brewed in Quebec City and Montreal. But Montreal had no incidence of the disease. The hypothesis, then, was further refined: perhaps the significant difference existed in the process of brewing. Eventually, this hypothesis was borne out. The Quebec brewery had added a cobalt compound to its product in order to enhance the beer's foaminess; the Montreal brewery had not. Furthermore, the compound had been added only a month before the first victims became ill.

In spite of the strength of this causal hypothesis, doctors in this case were still cautious, since the cobalt had not been present in sufficient quantities to kill a normal person. Yet twenty had died. After persistent study, the doctors decided that this fact must be related to the victims' drinking habits, which in some way reduced their resistance to the chemical. For those twenty people, a normally nonlethal dose of cobalt had been fatal.

The difficulties of such causal analysis were in the news a lot after the 1996 explosion of TWA flight 800. Those who followed this case in the news and on the Internet saw investigators test—and reject—a number of hypotheses about the cause of the crash: a bomb, a missile, "friendly fire," pilot error. Only in the summer of 1997 did the head investigator put forward a hypothesis that the team felt was sufficiently supported by all the data at hand. In their analysis, air conditioning packs that had been running for over two hours prior to the plane's departure heated up a small amount of fuel in an almost-empty center tank. This heating in turn may have caused vapor to form and eventually explode, blowing out the bottom center of the plane. According to the team, the first explosion led to subsequent explosions that destroyed the entire aircraft.

Deborah Tannen uses her own observation of gender differences in communication patterns to support her argument urging teachers to adopt new classroom strategies. She writes, "The classroom is a different environment for those who feel comfortable putting themselves forward in a group than it is for those who find the prospect of doing so chastening, or even terrifying."

LINK TO P. 595

Causal arguments can also be supported by experimental evidence that is based less on strictly scientific investigation than on ethnographic observation—the study of the daily routines of ordinary people in a particular community. In an argument that attempts to explain why, when people meet head-on, some step aside and some do not, investigators Frank Willis, Joseph Gier, and David Smith observed "1,038 displacements involving 3,141 persons" at a Kansas City shopping mall. In results that surprised the investigators, "gallantry" seemed to play a significant role in causing people to step aside for one another—more so than other causes the investigators had anticipated (such as deferring to someone who is physically stronger or higher in status).

Yet another method of supporting a causal argument is through the use of one or more correlations. In such an argument you try to show that if A occurs, B is also likely to occur. You may be most familiar with correlations from statistical procedures that allow you to predict, within a degree of certainty, how likely it is that two elements or events will occur together. Recent advances in the human genome project, for example, have identified "clusters" of genes that, when found in correlation with one another, strongly suggest the occurrence of certain cancers. But correlation works in more informal ways as well. Robert Coles, internationally known for his studies of childhood development, uses such a strategy in his study of affluent children in which he traces the effects that a correlation between wealth and power has on young people:

> **Wealth does not corrupt nor does it ennoble. But wealth does govern the minds of privileged children, gives them a peculiar kind of identity which they never lose, whether they grow up to be stockbrokers or communards, and whether they lead healthy or unstable lives. There is, I think, a message that virtually all quite well-off American families transmit to their children—an emotional expression of those familiar, classbound prerogatives, money and power. I use the word "entitlement" to describe that message.**
> —Robert Coles, *Privileged Ones*

Finally, you may want to consider using personal experience in support of a causal argument. Indeed, people's experiences generally lead them to seek out or to avoid various causes and effects. If you are consistently praised for your writing ability, chances are that you will look for opportunities to produce that pleasant effect. If three times in a row you get sick after eating shrimp, you will almost certainly identify the shellfish as the cause of your difficulties and stop eating it. Personal experience can also help build your credibility as a writer, gain the empathy of your listeners, and thus support your cause. Although one person's experiences cannot ordinarily be universalized, they can still argue eloquently for causal relationships. Terry Tempest Williams explores one causal relationship, asking "If we poison Mother Earth, our home, will our own mothers (and we as well) not also be poisoned?" In pursuing this question, Williams draws on her own personal experience:

> **I belong to a Clan of One-Breasted Women. My mother, my grand-mothers, and six aunts have all had mastectomies. Seven are dead. The two who survive have just completed rounds of chemotherapy and radiation. . . .**
>
> **I've had my own problems: two biopsies for breast cancer and a small tumor between my ribs diagnosed as "borderline malignancy."**
>
> **This is my family history.**
>
> **Most statistics tell us breast cancer is genetic, hereditary, with rising percentages attached to fatty diets, childlessness, or becoming pregnant after thirty. What they don't say is living in Utah may be the greatest hazard of all. . . .**
>
> **I cannot prove that my mother, Diane Dixon Tempest, or my grand-mothers, Lettie Romney Dixon and Kathryn Blackett Tempest, along with my aunts developed cancer from nuclear fallout in Utah. But I can't prove they didn't.**
>
> **– Terry Tempest Williams, "The Clan of One-Breasted Women"**

All these strategies—the use of examples, analogies, testing hypotheses, experimental evidence, correlations, and personal experience—can help you build good reasons in support of a causal argument. However, the success of the argument may ultimately depend on your ability to convince your readers that the reasons you offer are indeed good ones. In terms of causal arguments, that will mean distinguishing among immediate, necessary, and sufficient reasons. In the case of the mysterious illness in Quebec City, the immediate reasons for illness were the symptoms themselves: nausea, shortness of breath, and so on. But they were not the base or root causes of the disease. Drinking the particular beer in question served as a necessary reason: without the tainted beer, the illness would not have occurred. However, the researchers had to search much harder for the sufficient reason—the reason that will cause the effect (the illness) if it is present. In the case of the Quebec City beer, that reason turned out to be the addition of cobalt.

This example deals with the scientific investigation of a disease, but everyday causal analysis can draw on this distinction among reasons as

In a Latino USA radio program segment about the Taco Bell chihuahua, María Martin interviews people who hold various ideas about the "necessary and sufficient" reasons for offensive stereotyping.

LINK TO P. 391 ···

well. What caused you, for instance, to pursue a college education? Immediate reasons might be that you needed to prepare for a career of some kind or that you had planned to do so for years. But what are the necessary reasons, the ones without which your pursuit of higher education could not occur? Adequate funds? Good test scores and academic record? The expectations of your family? You might even explore possible sufficient reasons, those that—if present—will guarantee the effect of your pursuing higher education. In such a case, you may be the only person with enough information to determine what sufficient reasons might be.

KEY FEATURES OF CAUSAL ARGUMENTS

In drafting a causal argument, consider the following five elements:

- examination of each possible cause and effect
- description and explanation of the relationship among any links, especially in an argument based on a series of links in a causal chain
- evidence that your description and explanation are accurate and thorough
- evidence to show that the causes and effects you have identified are highly probable and that they are backed by good reasons, usually presented in order of their strength and importance
- consideration of alternative causes and effects, and evidence that you have considered them carefully before rejecting them

Fully developing a causal argument will probably call for addressing each of these elements, though you may order them in several ways. You may want to open your essay with a dramatic description of the effect, for example, and then "flash back" to multiple causes. Or you might decide to open with a well-known phenomenon, identify it as a cause, and then trace its effects. In the same way, you might decide to lead off the body of the argument with your strongest, most compelling piece of evidence, or to hold that evidence for the culmination of your argument. In any case, you should make a careful organizational plan and get a response to that plan from your instructor, friends, and colleagues before proceeding to a full draft. When the draft is complete, you should again seek a response, testing out the strength of your causal argument on at least several readers.

Finding a Topic

Chances are that a little time spent brainstorming—either with friends or other students, or on paper—will turn up some good possibilities for causal arguments of several kinds, including those that grow out of your personal experience. *Just exactly what did lead to your much higher GPA last term?* Beyond your own personal concerns, you may find a good number of public issues that lend themselves to causal analysis and argument: *What factors have led to the recent decline in reported cases of HIV infection? What will happen if the United States signs the Comprehensive Nuclear Test Ban Treaty? What effects have been caused by the move to pay professional basketball players astronomical sums of money?* Finally, as you are brainstorming possibilities for a causal argument of your own, don't ignore important current campus issues: *What have been the effects of recent increases in tuition (or what factors caused the increases)? What are the likely outcomes of shifting the academic calendar from a quarter to a semester system? If, as some argue, there has been a significant increase of racism and homophobia on campus, what has caused that increase? What are its consequences?*

Researching Your Topic

Causal arguments will lead you to a number of different resources:

- current news media—especially magazines and newspapers (online or in print)
- scholarly journals
- books written on your subject (here you can do a keyword search, either in your library or online)
- Web sites, listservs, or newsgroups devoted to your subject

In addition, you may decide to carry out some field research of your own—to conduct interviews with appropriate authorities on your subject, for instance, or to create a questionnaire aimed at getting a range of opinion on a particular aspect of your subject.

Formulating a Claim

You may begin to formulate your claim by identifying the particular kind of causal argument you want to make—one moving from cause(s) to effect(s); one moving from effect(s) to cause(s); or one involving a series of links, with cause A leading to B, which then leads to C. (See pp. 162–64 for a review of these kinds of arguments.)

Your next move may be to explore your own relationship to your subject. What do you know about the subject and its causes and effects? On what basis do you agree with the claim? What significant reasons can you offer in support of it?

In short, you should end this process of exploration by formulating a brief claim or thesis about a particular causal relationship. It should include *a statement that says, in effect, A causes (or is caused by) B, and a summary of the reasons supporting this causal relationship.* Remember to make sure that your thesis is as specific as possible and that it is sufficiently controversial or interesting to hold your readers' interest.

Preparing a Proposal

If your instructor asks you to prepare a proposal for your project, here's a simple format that may help.

State the thesis of your argument fully, perhaps using the Toulmin schema:

> Claim:
>
> Reason(s):
>
> Warrant(s):

Explain why this argument deserves attention. Why is it important for your readers to consider?

Specify those whom you hope to reach with this argument, and explain why this group of readers is an appropriate audience. What interest or investment do they have in the issue? Why will they (or should they) be concerned?

Briefly identify and explore the major challenges you expect to face in supporting your argument. Will demonstrating a clear causal link between A and B be particularly difficult? Will the data you need to support the claim be hard to obtain?

What strategies do you expect to use in researching your argument— Interviewing? Surveying opinion? Library or online searches? Other? What are the major sources you will need to consult—and are they readily available to you?

Briefly identify and explore the major counterarguments you might expect in response to your argument.

What format or genre do you expect to use for your argument? A press release? An editorial for the local newspaper? A Web site?

Thinking about Organization

Whatever genre or format you decide to use, your causal argument should address the following elements:

- a specific causal claim: *Devastating flash floods associated with El Niño were responsible for the dramatic loss of homes in central California in early 1998.*

- an explanation of the claim's significance or importance: *Claims for damage from flooding put some big insurance companies out of business; as a result, homeowners couldn't get coverage and many who lost their homes had to declare bankruptcy.*

- supporting evidence sufficient to support each cause or effect—or, in an argument based on a series of causal links, evidence to support the relationships among the links: *The amount of rain that fell in central California in early 1998 was 200 percent above normal, leading inexorably to rapidly rising rivers and creeks.*

- consideration of alternative causes and effects, and evidence that you understand these alternatives and have thought carefully about them before rejecting them: *Although some say that excessive and sloppy logging and poor building codes were responsible for the loss of homes, the evidence supporting these alternative causes is not convincing.*

Getting and Giving Response

All arguments can benefit from the scrutiny of others. Your instructor may assign you to a peer group for the purpose of reading and responding to each other's drafts; if not, make the effort yourself to get some careful response. You can use the following questions to evaluate a draft. If you are evaluating someone else's draft, be sure to supply specific examples to illustrate your points. Specific comments are always more helpful than general observations.

The Claim

- What is most effective about the claim? What are its strengths?

- Is the claim sufficiently qualified?

- Is the claim specific enough to be clear? Could it be narrowed and focused more clearly?

- How strong is the relationship between the claim and the reasons given to support it? Could that relationship be made more explicit?

- Is it immediately evident why the claim is important? Could it be rephrased in a way that more forcefully and clearly suggests its significance?

- Does the claim reveal a causal connection? Could it be revised to make the causal links clearer?

Evidence for the Claim

- What is the strongest evidence offered for the claim? Does any of the evidence need to be strengthened?

- Is enough evidence offered that these particular causes are responsible for the effect that has been identified, that these particular effects result from the identified cause, or that a series of causes and effects are linked? If not, what kind of additional evidence is needed? What kinds of sources might provide this evidence?

- How credible and persuasive will the sources likely be to potential readers? What other kinds of sources might be more credible and persuasive?

- Is the evidence in support of the claim simply announced, or is it analyzed in terms of its appropriateness and significance? Is a more detailed discussion necessary?

- Have all the major alternative causes and effects as well as objections to the claim been considered? What support is offered for rejecting these alternatives? Where is additional support needed?

Organization and Style

- How are the parts of the argument organized? Is this organization effective, or would some other structure work better?

- Will readers understand the relationships among the claims, supporting reasons, warrants, and evidence? If not, what could be done to make those connections clearer? Are more transitional words and phrases needed? Would headings or graphic devices help?

- Are the transitions or links from point to point, paragraph to paragraph, and sentence to sentence clear and effective? If not, how could they be improved?

- Is the style suited to the subject? Is it too formal? Too casual? Too technical? Too bland?

- Which sentences seem particularly effective? Which ones seem weakest, and how could they be improved? Should some short sentences be combined, or should any long ones be separated into two or more sentences?

- How effective are the paragraphs? Do any seem too skimpy or too long?

- Which words or phrases seem particularly effective, vivid, and memorable? Do any seem dull, vague, unclear, or inappropriate for the audience or the writer's purpose? Are definitions provided for technical or other terms that readers might not know?

Spelling, Punctuation, Mechanics, Documentation, Format

- Are there any errors in spelling, punctuation, capitalization, and the like?
- Is an appropriate and consistent style of documentation used for parenthetical citations and the list of works cited or references? (See Chapter 22.)
- Does the paper or project follow an appropriate format? Is it appropriately designed and attractively presented? If it is a Web site, do all the links work?

RESPOND.

1. The causes of the following events and phenomena are quite well known and frequently discussed. But do you understand them well enough yourself to spell out the causes to someone else? Working in a group, see how well (and in how much detail) you can explain each of the following events or phenomena. Which explanations are relatively clear-cut and which seem more open to debate?

   rain

   the collapse of communism in 1989

   earthquakes

   the common cold

   the popularity of the film *The Blair Witch Project*

   the itching caused by a mosquito bite

   the economic boom of the 1990s

   a skid in your car on a slippery road

   the explosion of the space shuttle *Challenger*

   the election of Minnesota Governor Jesse Ventura in 1998

2. One of the fallacies of argument discussed in Chapter 19 is the *post hoc, ergo propter hoc* fallacy: "after this, therefore because of this." Causal arguments are particularly prone to this kind of fallacious reasoning, in which a writer asserts a causal relationship between two entirely unconnected events. After Elvis Presley's death, for instance, oil prices in the United States rose precipitously—but it would be a real stretch to argue that the King's passing *caused* gas prices to skyrocket.

   Because causal arguments can easily fall prey to this fallacy, you might find it useful to take absurd causal positions and see where they go—if only to learn how to avoid such mistakes. As a class, create an argument that goes from cause to effect—or from effect to cause—in a series of completely ridiculous steps (A leads to B leads to C leads to D). Start with one person stating a cause (such as someone sleeping late or missing a test) and move on one by one through the class, building effects on effects. (For example: "Because I slept in, I missed my flight home for Thanksgiving break." Next person: "Because I missed my flight home, I had to call my parents and explain." Next person: "Because I was talking to my parents on the phone, . . .")

3. In the article at the end of this chapter, Lester C. Thurow tests a variety of hypotheses about the causes of gender-based wage inequality.

He rejects all but one of the hypotheses, claiming that they don't hold up as causal explanations. Using Toulmin logic, analyze the competing causal claims Thurow offers, the role that evidence plays in them, and the reasons he decides against them. (Incidentally, the latest government statistics reveal that women now earn 76 percent as much as men. What causes might have accounted for this change? Do you think they are related to the changes Thurow predicts would have to take place for the wage differential to diminish?)

TWO SAMPLE CAUSAL ARGUMENTS

What Makes a Serial Killer?

....

LA DONNA BEATY

Jeffrey Dahmer, John Wayne Gacy, Mark Allen Smith, Richard Chase, Ted Bundy—the list goes on and on. These five men alone have been responsible for at least ninety deaths, and many suspect that their victims may total twice that number. They are serial killers, the most feared and hated of criminals. What deep, hidden secret makes them lust for blood? What can possibly motivate a person to kill over and over again with no guilt, no remorse, no hint of human compassion? What makes a serial killer?

Serial killings are not a new phenomenon. In 1798, for example, Micajah and Wiley Harpe traveled the backwoods of Kentucky and Tennessee in a violent, year-long killing spree that left at least twenty—and possibly as many as thirty-eight—men, women, and children dead. Their crimes were especially chilling as they seemed particularly to enjoy grabbing small children by the ankles and smashing their heads against trees (Holmes and DeBurger 28). In modern society, however, serial killings have grown to near epidemic proportions. Ann Rule, a respected author and expert on serial murders, stated in a seminar at the University of Louisville on serial murder that between 3,500 and 5,000 people become victims of serial murder each year in the United States alone (qtd. in Holmes and DeBurger 21). Many others estimate that there are close to 350 serial killers currently at large in our society (Holmes and DeBurger 22).

The cause-effect relationship is raised in a question: What (the causes) makes a serial killer (the effect)?

An important term (serial killer) is defined through examples.

Authority is cited to emphasize the importance of the causal question.

La Donna Beaty wrote this essay while she was a student at Sinclair Community College in Dayton, Ohio. In the essay, she explores the complex web of possible causes—cultural, psychological, genetic, and others—that may help to produce a serial killer. The essay follows MLA style.

180

Fascination with murder and murderers is not new, but researchers in recent years have made great strides in determining the characteristics of criminals. Looking back, we can see how naive early experts were in their evaluations: in 1911, for example, Italian criminologist Cesare Lombrosco concluded that "murderers as a group [are] biologically degenerate [with] bloodshot eyes, aquiline noses, curly black hair, strong jaws, big ears, thin lips, and menacing grins" (qtd. in Lunde 84). Today, however, we don't expect killers to have fangs that drip human blood, and many realize that the boy-next-door may be doing more than woodworking in his basement. While there are no specific physical characteristics shared by all serial killers, they are almost always male and 92 percent are white. Most are between the ages of twenty-five and thirty-five and often physically attractive. While they may hold a job, many switch employment frequently as they become easily frustrated when advancement does not come as quickly as expected. They tend to believe that they are entitled to whatever they desire but feel that they should have to exert no effort to attain their goals (Samenow 88, 96). What could possibly turn attractive, ambitious human beings into cold-blooded monsters?

Evidence about general characteristics of serial killers is presented.

One popular theory suggests that many murderers are the product of our violent society. Our culture tends to approve of violence and find it acceptable, even preferable, in many circumstances (Holmes and DeBurger 27). According to research done in 1970, one out of every four men and one out of every six women believed that it was appropriate for a husband to hit his wife under certain conditions (Holmes and DeBurger 33). This emphasis on violence is especially prevalent in television programs. Violence occurs in 80 percent of all prime-time shows, while cartoons, presumably made for children, average eighteen violent acts per hour. It is estimated that by the age of eighteen, the average child will have viewed more than 16,000 television murders (Holmes and DeBurger 34). Some experts feel that children demonstrate increasingly aggressive behavior with each violent act they view (Lunde 15) and become so accustomed to violence that these acts

One possible cause is explored: violence in society.

Evidence, including statistics and authority, is offered to support the first cause.

seem normal (35). In fact, most serial killers do begin to show patterns of aggressive behavior at a young age. It is, therefore, possible that after viewing increasing amounts of violence, such children determine that this is acceptable behavior; when they are then punished for similar actions, they may become confused and angry and eventually lash out by committing horrible, violent acts.

A second possible cause is introduced: family context.

Another theory concentrates on the family atmosphere into which the serial killer is born. Most killers state that they experienced psychological abuse as children and never established good relationships with the male figures in their lives (Ressler, Burgess, and Douglas 19). As children, they were often rejected by their parents and received little nurturing (Lunde 94; Holmes and DeBurger 64–70). It has also been established that the families of serial killers often move repeatedly, never allowing the child to feel a sense of stability; in many cases, they are also forced to live outside the family home before reaching the age of eighteen (Ressler, Burgess, and Douglas 19–20). Our culture's tolerance for violence may overlap with such family dynamics: with 79 percent of the population believing that slapping a twelve-year-old is either necessary, normal, or good, it is no wonder that serial killers relate tales of physical abuse (Holmes and DeBurger 30; Ressler, Burgess, and Douglas 19–20) and view themselves as the "black sheep" of the family. They may even, perhaps unconsciously, assume this same role in society.

Evidence is offered in support of the second cause.

An alternative analysis of the evidence in support of the second cause is explored.

While the foregoing analysis portrays the serial killer as a lost, lonely, abused, little child, another theory, based on the same information, gives an entirely different view. In this analysis, the killer is indeed rejected by his family but only after being repeatedly defiant, sneaky, and threatening. As verbal lies and destructiveness increase, the parents give the child the distance he seems to want in order to maintain a small amount of domestic peace (Samenow 13). This interpretation suggests that the killer shapes his parents much more than his parents shape him. It also denies that the media can influence a child's mind and turn him into something that he doesn't already long to be. Since most children view similar amounts of violence, the argument goes, a responsible child filters what he sees and will not resort to criminal activity no matter how acceptable it seems to be (Samenow 15–18). In 1930, the noted psychologist Alfred Adler seemed to find this true of any criminal. As he put it, "With criminals it is different: they have a private logic, a private intelligence. They are suffering from a wrong outlook upon the world, a wrong estimate of their own importance and the importance of other people" (qtd. in Samenow 20).

Most people agree that Jeffrey Dahmer or Ted Bundy had to be "crazy" to commit horrendous multiple murders, and scientists have long maintained that serial killers are indeed mentally disturbed (Lunde 48). While the percentage of murders committed by mental hospital patients is much lower than that among the general population (35), it cannot be ignored that the rise in serial killings happened at almost the same time as the deinstitutionalization movement in the mental health care system during the 1960s (Markman and Bosco 266). While reform was greatly needed in the mental health care system, it has now become nearly impossible to hospitalize those with severe problems. In the United States, people have a constitutional right to remain mentally ill. Involuntary commitment can only be accomplished if the person is deemed dangerous to self, dangerous to others, or gravely disabled. However, in the words of Ronald Markman, "According to the way that the law is interpreted, if you can go to the mailbox to pick up your Social Security check, you're not gravely disabled even if you think you're living on Mars"; even if a patient is thought to be dangerous, he or she cannot be held longer than ninety days unless it can be proved that the patient actually committed dangerous acts while in the hospital (Markman and Bosco 267). Many of the most heinous criminals have had long histories of mental illness but could not be hospitalized due to these stringent requirements. Richard Chase, the notorious Vampire of Sacramento, believed that he needed blood in order to survive, and while in the care of a psychiatric hospital, he often killed birds and other small animals in order to quench this desire. When he was

A third possible cause is introduced: mental instability.

Evidence in support of the third cause, including a series of examples, is offered.

released, he went on to kill eight people, one of them an eighteen-month-old baby (Biondi and Hecox 206). Edmund Kemper was equally insane. At the age of fifteen, he killed both of his grandparents and spent five years in a psychiatric facility. Doctors determined that he was "cured" and released him into an unsuspecting society. He killed eight women, including his own mother (Lunde 53–56). The world was soon to be disturbed by a cataclysmic earthquake, and Herbert Mullin knew that he had been appointed by God to prevent the catastrophe. The fervor of his religious delusion resulted in a death toll of thirteen (Lunde 63–81). All of these men had been treated for their mental disorders, and all were released by doctors who did not have enough proof to hold them against their will.

A fourth possible cause is introduced: genetic makeup.

Recently, studies have given increasing consideration to the genetic makeup of serial killers. The connection between biology and behavior is strengthened by research in which scientists have been able to develop a violently aggressive strain of mice simply through selective inbreeding (Taylor 23). These studies have caused scientists to become increasingly interested in the limbic system of the brain, which houses the amygdala, an almond-shaped structure located in the front of the temporal lobe. It has long been known that surgically altering that portion of the brain, in an operation known as a lobotomy, is one way of controlling behavior. This surgery was used frequently in the 1960s but has since been discontinued as it also erases most of a person's personality. More recent developments, however, have shown that temporal lobe epilepsy causes electrical impulses to be discharged directly into the amygdala. When this electronic stimulation is re-created in the laboratory, it causes violent behavior in lab animals. Additionally, other forms of epilepsy do not cause abnormalities in behavior, except during seizure activity. Temporal lobe epilepsy is linked with a wide range of antisocial behavior, including anger, paranoia, and aggression. It is also interesting to note that this form of epilepsy produces extremely unusual brain waves. These waves have been found in only 10 to 15 percent of the general population, but over 79 percent of known serial killers test positive for these waves (Taylor 28–33).

Statistical evidence in support of the fourth cause is offered.

The look at biological factors that control human behavior is by no means limited to brain waves or other brain abnormalities. Much work is also being done with neurotransmitters, levels of testosterone, and patterns of trace minerals. While none of these studies are conclusive, they all show a high correlation between antisocial behavior and chemical interactions within the body (Taylor 63–69).

One of the most common traits that all researchers have noted among serial killers is heavy use of alcohol. Whether this correlation is brought about by external factors or whether alcohol is an actual stimulus that causes certain behavior is still unclear, but the idea deserves consideration. Lunde found that the majority of those who commit murder had been drinking beforehand and commonly had a urine alcohol level of between .20 and .29, nearly twice the legal level of intoxication (31–32). Additionally, 70 percent of the families that reared serial killers had verifiable records of alcohol abuse (Ressler, Burgess, and Douglas 17). Jeffrey Dahmer had been arrested in 1981 on charges of drunkenness and, before his release from prison on sexual assault charges, his father had written a heartbreaking letter which pleaded that Jeffrey be forced to undergo treatment for alcoholism, a plea that, if heeded, might have changed the course of future events (Davis 70, 103). Whether alcoholism is a learned behavior or an inherited predisposition is still hotly debated, but a 1979 report issued by Harvard Medical School stated that "[a]lcoholism in the biological parent appears to be a more reliable predictor of alcoholism in the children than any other environmental factor examined" (qtd. in Taylor 117). While alcohol was once thought to alleviate anxiety and depression, we now know that it can aggravate and intensify such moods (Taylor 110), which may lead to irrational feelings of powerlessness that are brought under control only when the killer proves he has the ultimate power to control life and death.

A fifth possible cause—heavy use of alcohol—is introduced and immediately qualified.

"Man's inhumanity to man" began when Cain killed Abel, but this legacy has grown to frightening proportions, as evidenced by the vast number of books that line the shelves of modern bookstores—row after row of titles

The complexity of causal relationships is emphasized: one cannot say for certain what produces a particular serial killer.

dealing with death, anger, and blood. We may never know what causes a serial killer to exact his revenge on an unsuspecting society. But we need to continue to probe the interior of the human brain to discover the delicate balance of chemicals that controls behavior. We need to be able to fix what goes wrong. We must also work harder to protect our children. Their cries must not go unheard. Their pain must not become so intense that it demands bloody revenge. As today becomes tomorrow, we must remember the words of Ted Bundy, one of the most ruthless serial killers of our time: "Most serial killers are people who kill for the pure pleasure of killing and cannot be rehabilitated. Some of the killers themselves would even say so" (qtd. in Holmes and DeBurger 150).

The conclusion looks toward the future: the web of causes examined here suggests that much more work needs to be done to understand, predict, and ultimately control the behavior of potential serial killers.

WORKS CITED

Biondi, Ray, and Walt Hecox. *The Dracula Killer.* New York: Simon, 1992.

Davis, Ron. *The Milwaukee Murders.* New York: St. Martin's, 1991.

Holmes, Ronald M., and James DeBurger. *Serial Murder.* Newbury Park, CA: Sage, 1988.

Lunde, Donald T. *Murder and Madness.* San Francisco: San Francisco Book, 1976.

Markman, Ronald, and Dominick Bosco. *Alone with the Devil.* New York: Doubleday, 1989.

Ressler, Robert K., Ann W. Burgess, and John E. Douglas. *Sexual Homicide—Patterns and Motives.* Lexington, MA: Heath, 1988.

Samenow, Stanton E. *Inside the Criminal Mind.* New York: Times, 1984.

Taylor, Lawrence. *Born to Crime.* Westport, CT: Greenwood, 1984.

Why Women Are Paid Less Than Men

LESTER C. THUROW

In the 40 years from 1939 to 1979 white women who work full time have with monotonous regularity made slightly less than 60 percent as much as white men. Why?

Over the same time period, minorities have made substantial progress in catching up with whites, with minority women making even more progress than minority men. Black men now earn 72 percent as much as white men (up 16 percentage points since the mid-1950s) but black women earn 92 percent as much as white women. Hispanic men make 71 percent of what their white counterparts do, but Hispanic women make 82 percent as much as white women. As a result of their faster progress, fully employed black women make 75 percent as much as fully employed black men while Hispanic women earn 68 percent as much as Hispanic men.

This faster progress may, however, end when minority women finally catch up with white women. In the bible of the New Right, George Gilder's *Wealth and Poverty*, the 60 percent is just one of Mother Nature's constants like the speed of light or the force of gravity. Men are programmed to provide for their families economically while women are programmed to take care of their families emotionally and physically. As a result men put more effort into their jobs than women. The net result is a difference in work intensity that leads to that 40 percent gap in earnings. But there is no discrimination against women—only the biological facts of life.

The problem with this assertion is just that. It is an assertion with no evidence for it other than the fact that white women have made 60 percent as much as men for a long period of time.

"Discrimination against women" is an easy answer but it also has its problems as an adequate explanation. Why is discrimination against women not

Professor of economics at the Massachusetts Institute of Technology and former dean of the Sloan School of Management, Lester C. Thurow is noted for his many writings on U.S. and global economic issues. He is author or coauthor of more than sixteen books, including *The Future of Capitalism: How Today's Economic Forces Shape Tomorrow's World* (1997) and *Economics Explained: Everything You Need to Know about How the Economy Works and Where It's Going* (1998). In this brief essay, originally published in the *New York Times* in March 1981, Thurow examines possible reasons that women earn less money than men and predicts the conditions that must exist if the gap between earnings is to be reduced.

declining under the same social forces that are leading to a lessening of discrimination against minorities? In recent years women have made more use of the enforcement provisions of the Equal Employment Opportunities Commission and the courts than minorities. Why do the laws that prohibit discrimination against women and minorities work for minorities but not for women?

When men discriminate against women, they run into a problem. To discriminate against women is to discriminate against your own wife and to lower your own family income. To prevent women from working is to force men to work more.

When whites discriminate against blacks, they can at least think that they are raising their own incomes. When men discriminate against women they have to know that they are lowering their own family income and increasing their own work effort.

While discrimination undoubtedly explains part of the male-female earnings differential, one has to believe that men are monumentally stupid or irrational to explain all of the earnings gap in terms of discrimination. There must be something else going on.

Back in 1939 it was possible to attribute the earnings gap to large differences in educational attainments. But the educational gap between men and women has been eliminated since World War II. It is no longer possible to use education as an explanation for the lower earnings of women. Some observers have argued that women earn less money since they are less reliable workers who are more apt to leave the labor force. But it is difficult to maintain this position since women are less apt to quit one job to take another and as a result they tend to work as long, or longer, for any one employer. From any employer's perspective they are more reliable, not less reliable, than men.

Part of the answer is visible if you look at the lifetime earnings profile of men. Suppose that you were asked to predict which men in a group of 25-year-olds would become economically successful. At age 25 it is difficult to tell who will be economically successful and your predictions are apt to be highly inaccurate. But suppose that you were asked to predict which men in a group of 35-year-olds would become economically successful. If you are successful at age 35, you are very likely to remain successful for the rest of your life. If you have not become economically successful by age 35, you are very unlikely to do so later.

The decade between 25 and 35 is when men either succeed or fail. It is the decade when lawyers become partners in the good firms, when business managers make it onto the "fast track," when academics get tenure at good universities, and when blue collar workers find the job opportunities that will lead to training opportunities and the skills that will generate high earnings. If there is any one decade when it pays to work hard and to be consistently in the labor force, it is the decade between 25 and 35. For those who succeed, earnings will rise rapidly. For those who fail, earnings will remain flat for the rest of their lives.

But the decade between 25 and 35 is precisely the decade when women are most apt to leave the labor force or become part-time workers to have children. When they do, the current system of promotion and skill acquisition will extract an enormous lifetime price.

This leaves essentially two avenues for equalizing male and female earnings. Families where women who wish to have successful careers, compete with men, and achieve the same earnings should alter their family plans and have their children either before 25 or after 35. Or society can attempt to alter the existing promotion and skill acquisition system so that there is a longer time period in which both men and women can attempt to successfully enter the labor force. Without some combination of these two factors, a substantial fraction of the male-female earnings differentials are apt to persist for the next 40 years, even if discrimination against women is eliminated.

chapter twelve

Proposals

A couple looking forward to a much-needed vacation writes to four friends proposing that they all charter a sailboat for two weeks of exploring the Greek islands.

A blue-ribbon commission works for two years to develop a plan for instituting a national health care policy.

The members of a club for business majors begin to talk about their common need to create informative and appealing résumés. After lengthy discussion, three members suggest that the club develop a Web site that will guide members in building résumés and provide links to other resources.

A project team at a large consulting engineering firm works for three months developing a proposal in response to an RFP (request for proposal) to convert a military facility to a community camp.

Members of a church take up a question brought to them by their youth organization: Why are women disallowed from taking on certain roles in the church? After a series of discussions, the youth group decides to propose a change in church policy.

The undergraduate student organization at a large state university asks the administration for information about how long it takes to complete a degree in each academic major. Following an analysis of this information, the group recommends a reduction in the number of hours needed to graduate.

■ ■ ■

UNDERSTANDING AND CATEGORIZING PROPOSALS

Much everyday activity is related to proposals you make or consider, many of them very informal: your roommate suggests skipping breakfast in order to get in an extra hour of exercise; you and a colleague decide to go out to dinner rather than work late once again; you call your best friend to propose checking out a new movie; you decide to approach your boss about implementing an idea you've just had. In each case, the proposal implies that some action *should* take place and implicitly suggests that there are good reasons *why* it should.

In their simplest form, then, proposal arguments look something like this:

A should do B because of C.

```
┌A┐┌─────────────B─────────────┐
```
We should see Branagh's *Hamlet* tonight
```
┌──────────────────C──────────────────┐
```
because the NPR reviewer said it is the best film version yet.

Because proposals are so pervasive in people's lives, it's no surprise that they cover a dizzyingly wide range of possibilities, from very local and concrete practices (*A company should switch from one supplier of paper to another*) to very broad matters of policy (*The United States should adopt a more inclusive immigration policy*). Thus, it may be helpful to think of proposal arguments as divided roughly into two kinds—those that focus on practices and those that focus on policies. Here are several examples:

PROPOSALS ABOUT PRACTICES

- The city should use brighter lightbulbs in employee parking garages.
- The college should adopt a new procedure allowing students to pay tuition on a month-by-month basis.
- The community center staff should authorize funds for a new interior paint job.

PROPOSALS ABOUT POLICIES

- Congress should institute a national youth service plan.
- The college should adopt a "forgiveness" policy allowing students to have one course each semester not count in their grade point average.
- The state should end affirmative action policies in every state agency.

CHARACTERIZING PROPOSALS

Proposals have three main characteristics:

- They are action-oriented.
- They are focused on the future.
- They are audience-centered.

Proposals always call for some kind of action; they aim at *getting something done.* Thus, although proposals may rely on analysis and on careful reflection about ideas and information, these strategies are in the service of urging a decision about what to do. This feature of proposals almost always presents a challenge to the writer or speaker. Most simply, this challenge is the one expressed in the old saying, "You can lead a horse to water, but you can't make it drink." You can present a proposal as cogently and compellingly as possible—but most of the time you can't *make* the audience take the action you propose. Thus, proposal arguments must stress the ethos of the writer: if your word and experience and judgment are all credible, the audience is more likely to carry out the action you propose.

In addition, proposal arguments focus on the future, which the actions proposed will affect. Aristotle referred to such arguments as "deliberative" and associated them with the work of government, which is most often concerned with what a society should do over the upcoming few years or decades. This future orientation also presents special challenges, since writers have no crystal balls that enable them to predict the future with absolute confidence. Proposal arguments must therefore concentrate on marshaling all available evidence to demonstrate that the proposed action is very likely to produce the effects it sets out to achieve.

Finally, proposal arguments are highly focused on audience and audience response, since the success of the argument often (if not always) depends on the degree to which the audience agrees to carry out the proposed action.

Let's say that as president of your church youth organization, you decide to propose that the group take on a community tutoring project. Your proposal aims at action: you want members to do volunteer tutoring in an after-school program at the local community center. Your proposal is also future-oriented: you believe that such a project would help teach your group's members about conditions in the inner city as well as help inner-city children in ways that could make them more successful in future schooling. And certainly your proposal is heavily audience-dependent, because only if you can convince members that such service is needed, that it is feasible and likely to achieve the desired effects, and that it will be beneficial to members and to the organization, is your proposal likely to be acted on positively.

Julia Fein Azoulay's article "Getting Product Placed in Film and TV" is a good example of a nuts-and-bolts proposal for business purposes.

LINK TO P. 513 ⋯⋯⋯⋯⋯⋯⋯⋯⋯⋯⋯⋯⋯⋯⋯⋯⋯

In a proposal argument called "Let's Put Pornography Back in the Closet," Susan Brownmiller likewise focuses on action, on what she wants to happen—which is for legislatures and courts to draw a "distinction between permission to publish and permission to display publicly." Brownmiller argues that government restrictions on the public display of pornography would not endanger the free-speech guarantees of the First Amendment and would contribute to social harmony by removing from public view what she sees as a major vehicle for expression of hatred in our society. Her argument is thus action- and future-oriented. But it is also strongly audience-centered, for in it she mentions objections that readers might have and tries to answer them in a fair and evenhanded way.

DEVELOPING PROPOSALS

Developing effective proposals requires you to make a strong and clear claim, to show that the proposal meets a specific need or solves a significant problem, to present good reasons why adopting the proposal will effectively address the need or problem, and finally to show that the proposal is feasible and should therefore be adopted.

Making a Strong and Clear Claim

Formulating a strong claim means crafting a statement that features a claim (what X or Y should do) followed by the reason(s) why X or Y should act and the effects of adopting the proposal:

Claim	Communities should encourage the development of charter schools
Reason	because they are not burdened by the bureaucracy associated with most public schooling, and
Effects	because instituting such schools will bring more effective educational progress to the community and offer a positive incentive to the public schools to improve their programs as well.

Having established a claim, you can explore its implications by drawing out the reasons, warrants, and evidence that can support it most effectively:

Claim	Parents should shed old taboos and deal with new realities by providing extensive sex education at home and encouraging additional education in community centers and schools.
Reason	More than a million teenagers become pregnant each year, almost all of them unintentionally.
Warrant	Sex education helps prevent unwanted pregnancies.
Evidence	Evidence from Sweden, the Netherlands, France, and Canada demonstrates that extensive sex education results in reduced numbers of teenage pregnancies.

In this proposal argument the reason sets up the need for the proposal, whereas the warrant and evidence demonstrate that the proposal could indeed meet its objective.

Relating the Claim to a Need or Problem

To be effective, claims must be clearly related to a significant need or problem. Thus, establishing that the need or problem exists is one of the most important tasks the writer of a proposal argument faces. For this reason, you should explore this part of any proposal you wish to make very early on; if you can't establish a clear need for the proposal or show that it solves an important problem, you should probably work toward a revision or a new claim.

In practice, establishing the need or problem may occur at the beginning of your introduction as a way of leading up to your claim. Alternatively, it might appear right after your introduction as the major reason for adopting the proposal. In the preceding examples about charter schools and sex education, the writer might choose either strategy. Regardless of the practical choices about organization, the task of establishing a need or problem calls on you to

- evoke the need or problem in concrete and memorable ways
- show how the need or problem affects the larger society or group in general and the audience in particular
- indicate why the need or problem is significant

In an argument proposing that a state board of higher education institute courses that involve students in community service in all state colleges, a writer might begin by painting a fairly negative picture of a "me first and only" society that is self-absorbed and concentrated only on self-gratification. After evoking such a scene, the writer might explore how this particular problem affects society in general and the state's colleges in particular: it results in hypercompetition that creates a highly stressful "pressure-cooker" atmosphere on campuses; it leaves many of society's most vulnerable members without resources or helping hands; it puts the responsibility of helping these people solely in the hands of government, thereby adding to the size and cost of government and raising taxes for all; it deprives many of the satisfaction that helping others can bring, a satisfaction that should be a part of every student's education. Finally, the writer might demonstrate this problem's importance by relating it to the needs of the many people who would be benefited by various kinds of volunteer service: child care, elder care, health care, community learning, arts and cultural projects—the list of those affected could go on and on.

Note the way Craig R. Dean, a lawyer and executive director of the Equal Marriage Rights Fund, relates his claim—that the United States should legalize same-sex marriage—to a significant problem (and how he evokes, or renders, the problem):

> **In November 1990, my lover, Patrick Gill, and I were denied a marriage license because we are gay. In a memorandum explaining the District's decision, the clerk of the court wrote that "the sections of the**

In "The Cost of Hoop Dreams," William Hytche proposes a new basketball league as a solution to problems existing in college basketball. He opens his article by laying out a major problem: "Let's admit that the bottom line is money—even in college. There's a new and alarming trend in college basketball: young men forgoing college eligibility to enter the pros."

LINK TO P. 526

District of Columbia code governing marriage do not authorize marriage between persons of the same sex." By refusing to give us the same legal recognition that is given to heterosexual couples, the District has degraded our relationship as well as that of every other gay and lesbian couple.

At one time, interracial couples were not allowed to marry. Gays and lesbians are still denied this basic civil right in the U.S.—and around the world. Can you imagine the outcry if any other minority group was denied the right to legally marry today?

Marriage is more than a piece of paper. It gives societal recognition and legal protection to a relationship. It confers numerous benefits to spouses; in the District alone, there are more than 100 automatic marriage-based rights. In every state in the nation, married couples have the right to be on each other's health, disability, life insurance and pension plans. Married couples receive special tax exemptions, deductions and refunds. Spouses may automatically inherit property and have rights of survivorship that avoid inheritance tax. Though unmarried couples—both gay and heterosexual—are entitled to some of these rights, they are by no means guaranteed.

For married couples, the spouse is legally the next of kin in case of death, medical emergency or mental incapacity. In stark contrast, the family is generally the next of kin for same-sex couples. In the shadow of AIDS, the denial of marriage rights can be even more ominous. . . .

Some argue that gay marriage is too radical for society. We disagree. According to a 1989 study by the American Bar Association, eight to 10 million children are currently being reared in three million gay households. Therefore, approximately 6 percent of the U.S. population is made up of gay and lesbian families with children. Why should these families be denied the protection granted to other families?

Allowing gay marriage would strengthen society by increasing tolerance. It is paradoxical that mainstream America perceives gays and lesbians as unable to maintain long-term relationships while at the same time denying them the very institutions that stabilize such relationships.

—Craig R. Dean, "Legalize Gay Marriage"

Showing That the Proposal Addresses the Need or Problem

A very important but potentially tricky part of making a successful proposal lies in relating the claim to the need or problem it seeks to address. Everyone you know may agree that rising tuition costs at your college constitute a major problem. But will your spur-of-the-moment letter to the college newspaper proposing to reduce the size of the faculty and eliminate all campus bus services really address the problem effectively? Chances are, you would have a very hard time making this connection. On the other hand, proposing that the college establish a joint commission of students, administrators and faculty, and legislative leaders charged with studying the problem and proposing a series of alternatives for solving it would be much more likely to establish a clear connection between the problem and the claim.

In the earlier example about charter schools, the writer would need to show that establishing such schools could significantly address at least one of the problems identified with currently available public education. And in the passage from "Legalize Gay Marriage," the writer must show explicitly how carrying out the recommended action would directly affect the problems he has identified.

Showing That the Proposal Is Feasible

To be effective, proposals must be feasible—the action proposed must be able to be carried out in a reasonable way. Demonstrating feasibility calls on you to present more evidence—from analogous cases, from personal experience, from observational data, from interview or survey data, from Internet research, or from any other sources that help show that what you propose can indeed be done. In addition, it will help your case if you can show that the proposal can be carried out with the resources available. If instead the proposal calls for personnel or funds far beyond reach or reason, the audience is unlikely to accept it. As you think about revising your proposal argument, you can test its feasibility against these criteria. In addition, you can try to think of proposals that others might say are better, more effective, or more feasible than yours—and you can ask colleagues and friends to help you think of such counterproposals. If your own proposal argument can stand the test of counterproposals, it is a strong one indeed.

Using Personal Experience

If you have personally had an experience that demonstrates the need or problem your proposal aims to address, or that can serve as backing for your claim, consider using it to develop your proposal (as Craig R. Dean does in the opening of his proposal to legalize gay marriage). Consider the

Proposing changes in the U.S. customs policies vis-à-vis strip searches, Daria MonDesire uses her own experience as powerful evidence of problems in the current system, saying "There have, in my life, been two occasions when underwear was removed against my will. The first occurred at the hands of a rapist. The second time was at the hands of my government."

LINK TO P. 448

following questions in deciding when to include your own experiences in making a proposal:

- Is your experience directly related to the need or problem you seek to address, or to your proposal?
- Will your experience be appropriate and speak powerfully to the audience? Will the audience immediately understand its significance, or will it require explanation?
- Does your personal experience fit logically with the other reasons you are using to support your claim?

KEY FEATURES OF PROPOSALS

In drafting a proposal, remember to include each of the following elements:

- a claim that proposes a practice or policy to address a problem or need and that is oriented toward action, directed at the future, and appropriate to your audience
- statements that clearly relate the claim to the problem or need
- evidence that the proposal will effectively address the need or solve the problem, and that it is feasible

Fully developing your proposal will call for addressing all these elements, though you may choose to order them in several different ways. As you organize your proposal, you may want to open with an introductory paragraph that evokes as dramatically as possible the problem you are addressing, and you may decide to conclude by recalling this opening dramatic scene in your final paragraphs. Or you may choose to start right off with your claim and offer strong support for it before showing the ways in which your proposal addresses a need or solves a problem. In any case you should organize your proposal carefully, seeking response to your organizational plan from your instructor and colleagues.

Considering Design

Since proposals often address very specific audiences, they can take any number of forms: a letter or memo, a feasibility report, a brochure, a prospectus. Each form has different design requirements; indeed, the design may add powerfully to—or detract significantly from—the effectiveness of the proposal. Even in a college essay that is produced on a computer, the use of white space and margins, headings and subheadings, and variations in type (such as boldface or italics) can guide readers through the proposal and enhance its persuasiveness. So before you produce a final copy of any proposal, make a careful plan for its design. Then get response to the proposal in terms of its content *and* its design, asking friends, colleagues, or instructors to read the proposal and give you their responses. Finally, revise to address all the concerns they raise.

Finding a Topic

Your everyday experience probably calls on you to make proposals all the time; for example, to spend the weekend doing a special activity, to change your academic major for some very important reasons, or to add to the family income by starting a small, home-based business. In addition, your community group work or your job may require you to make proposals—to a boss, a board of directors, the local school board, and so on. And in this age of electronic communication, you may have an opportunity or a need to make proposals to online groups or to Web sites you visit. In all these cases some sort of action is called for, which is the hallmark of proposal arguments. Why not make an informal list of proposals you'd like to explore in a number of different areas? Or do some freewriting on a subject of great interest to you and see if it leads to a proposal? Either method of exploration is likely to turn up several possibilities for a good proposal argument.

Researching Your Topic

Proposals often call for some research. Even a simple one like "Let's all paint the house this weekend" would raise questions that require some investigation: *Who has the time for the job? What sort of paint will be the best? How much will the job cost?* A proposal that your school board adopt block scheduling would call for careful research into evidence supporting the use of such a system. *Where has it been effective, and why?* And for proposals about social issues (for example, that information on the Internet be freely accessible to everyone, even youngsters), extensive research would be necessary to provide sufficient support. For many proposals, you can begin your research by consulting the following types of sources:

- newspapers, magazines, reviews, and journals (online and print)
- online databases
- government documents and reports
- Web sites and listservs or newsgroups
- books
- experts in the field, some of whom may be right on your campus

In addition, you may decide to carry out some field research: a survey of student opinion on Internet accessibility, for example, or online interviews with people who are well informed about your subject.

Formulating a Claim

As you are thinking about and exploring your topic, you can also begin formulating a claim about it. To do so, try to draft a clear and complete thesis that *makes a proposal and states the reasons why this proposal should be followed.* To get started on formulating a claim, explore and respond to the following questions:

- What do I know about the proposal I am making?
- What reasons can I offer to support my proposal?
- What evidence do I have that implementing my proposal will lead to the results I want?

Preparing a Proposal

If your instructor asks you to prepare a proposal for your project, here's a format that may help:

State the thesis of your proposal completely. If you are having trouble doing so, try outlining it in terms of the Toulmin system:

Claim:

Reason(s):

Warrant(s):

Explain why your proposal is important. What is at stake in taking, or not taking, the action you propose?

Identify and describe those whom you most hope to reach with your proposal. Why is this group of readers most appropriate for your proposal? What are their interests in the subject?

Briefly discuss the major difficulties you foresee in preparing your argument. Demonstrating that the action you propose is necessary? Demonstrating that it is feasible? Moving the audience beyond agreement to action? Something else?

List the research you intend to do. What kinds of sources do you expect to consult? What formats or genre do you expect to use? An academic essay? A formal report? A Web site?

Thinking about Organization

Proposals can take many different forms, generally including the following elements:

- a clear and strong proposal, including the reasons for taking the action proposed and the effects that taking this action will have: *Our neighborhood should establish a "Block Watch" program that will help reduce break-ins and vandalism, and involve our children in building neighborhood pride.*

- a clear connection between the proposal and a significant need or problem: *Break-ins and vandalism have been on the rise in our neighborhood for the last three years.*

- a demonstration of ways in which the proposal addresses the need: *A Block Watch program establishes a rotating monitor system for the streets in a neighborhood and a voluntary plan to watch out for others' homes.*

- evidence that the proposal will achieve the desired outcome: *Block Watch programs in three other areas have significantly reduced break-ins and vandalism.*

- consideration of alternative ways to achieve the desired outcome, and a discussion of why these are not preferable: *We could ask for additional police presence, but funding would be hard to get.*

- a demonstration that the proposal is feasible and practical: *Because Block Watch is voluntary, our own determination and commitment are all we need to make it work.*

Getting and Giving Response

All arguments can benefit from the scrutiny of others. Your instructor may assign you to a peer group for the purpose of reading and responding to each other's drafts; if not, make the effort yourself to get some careful response. You can use the following questions to evaluate a draft. If you are evaluating someone else's draft, be sure to illustrate your points with specific examples. Specific comments are always more helpful than general observations.

The Claim

- Does the claim clearly call for action? Is the proposal as clear and specific as possible?

- Is the proposal too sweeping? Does it need to be qualified? If so, how?

- Does the proposal clearly address the problem it intends to solve? If not, how could the connection be strengthened?
- Is the claim likely to get the audience to act rather than just to agree? If not, how could it be revised to do so?

Evidence for the Claim

- Is enough evidence provided to get the audience to support the proposal? If not, what kind of additional evidence is needed? Does any of the evidence provided seem inappropriate or otherwise ineffective? Why?
- Is the evidence in support of the claim simply announced, or are its significance and appropriateness analyzed? Is a more detailed discussion needed?
- Are any objections readers might have to the claim or evidence adequately addressed?
- What kinds of sources are cited? How credible and persuasive will they be to readers? What other kinds of sources might be more credible and persuasive?
- Are all quotations introduced with appropriate signal phrases ("As Ehrenreich argues") and blended smoothly into the writer's sentences?

Organization and Style

- How are the parts of the argument organized? Is this organization effective, or would some other structure work better?
- Will readers understand the relationships among the claims, supporting reasons, warrants, and evidence? If not, what could be done to make those connections clearer? Are more transitional words and phrases needed? Would headings or graphic devices help?
- Are the transitions or links from point to point, paragraph to paragraph, and sentence to sentence clear and effective? If not, how could they be improved?
- Is the style suited to the subject? Is it too formal? Too casual? Too technical? Too bland?
- Which sentences seem particularly effective? Which ones seem weakest, and how could they be improved? Should some short sentences be combined, or should any long ones be separated into two or more sentences?
- How effective are the paragraphs? Do any seem too skimpy or too long?

- Which words or phrases seem particularly effective, vivid, and memorable? Do any seem dull, vague, unclear, or inappropriate for the audience or the writer's purpose? Are definitions provided for technical or other terms that readers might not know?

Spelling, Punctuation, Mechanics, Documentation, Format

- Are there any errors in spelling, punctuation, capitalization, and the like?
- Is an appropriate and consistent style of documentation used for parenthetical citations and the list of works cited or references? (See Chapter 22.)
- Does the paper or project follow an appropriate format? Is it appropriately designed and attractively presented? If it is a Web site, do all the links work?

RESPOND•

1. For each problem and solution, explain readers' likely objections to the outrageous solution offered. Then propose a more defensible solution of your own and explain why you think it is more feasible.

   Problem   Future bankruptcy of the Social Security system in the United States.

   Solution   Raise the age of retirement to eighty.

   Problem   Traffic gridlock in major cities.

   Solution   Allow only men to drive on Mondays, Wednesdays, and Fridays and only women on Tuesdays, Thursdays, and Saturdays. Everyone can drive on Sunday.

   Problem   Increasing rates of obesity in the general population.

   Solution   Ban the sale of all high-fat items in fast-food restaurants, including hamburgers, fries, and shakes.

   Problem   Threats of violence in schools.

   Solution   Authorize teachers and students to carry handguns.

   Problem   Unmanageable credit card debt among college students.

   Solution   Limit credit card use to people over age twenty-five.

2. People write proposal arguments to solve problems; when writers face some kind of practical or policy issue, they develop arguments that will (they hope) change the way things are. But problems are not always obvious; what troubles some people might be no problem at all to others.

   To get an idea of the range of problems people face on your campus—some of which you may not even have thought of as problems —divide into groups and brainstorm about things that annoy you on and around campus, including everything from short crosswalk-light timers to long lines at the registrar's office. Each group should aim for a list of twenty gripes. Then choose one problem and, as a group, discuss how you would go about writing a proposal to deal with it. Remember that you will need to (a) make a strong and clear claim, (b) show that the proposal meets a clear need or solves a significant problem, (c) present good reasons why adopting the proposal will effectively address the need or problem, and (d) show that the proposal is feasible and should be adopted.

3. In the essay "Don't Make English Official—Ban It Instead" at the end of this chapter, Dennis Baron makes a tongue-in-cheek proposal to

outlaw the English language. Using the Toulmin model discussed in Chapter 8, analyze the proposal's structure. What claim does Baron make, and what reasons does he give to support the claim? What are the warrants that connect the reasons to the claim? What evidence does he provide?

TWO SAMPLE PROPOSALS

Auto Liberation

....

BRENT KNUTSON

The driver of a late-model Japanese sports car grins as he downshifts into third gear, blips the throttle with his heel, and releases the clutch. The car's rear end abruptly steps out in the wide, sweeping corner. He cranks the wheel, gathering the tail while eagerly stabbing the accelerator. The engine emits a metallic wail and barks angrily as the driver pulls the gearshift into fourth. Controlled pandemonium ensues as the secondary turbocharger engages and slams the driver's cranium against the headrest. With adrenaline thumping in his temples, he watches the needle on the speedometer sweep urgently toward the end of the scale. The driver then flicks the turn signal and blasts onto the interstate like a guided missile launching from a fighter jet. Today, he will not be late for work.

An opening vignette captures readers' attention and piques interest in the title.

This scenario may seem a bit far-fetched, enough so that one might conclude that the driver is unnecessarily risking his life and the lives of other people on the road. But, on Germany's autobahns, people normally drive in excess of 80 miles per hour. Yet, these German superhighways are the safest in the world, filled with German drivers who are skilled, competent, and courteous. Using the autobahn system as a model, it is possible to examine whether national speed limits in the United States are necessary.

Background information on driving in Germany is presented.

In fact, there is solid reasoning to support the claim that the speed limits on U.S. interstate highways should be repealed. Not only are American speed limits unnecessarily restrictive, they also infringe upon the personal

The claim—that U.S. interstate speed limits should be repealed—is introduced and followed by a summary of reasons in support of the claim.

Brent Knutson wrote this essay while he was a student at Boise State University in Boise, Idaho. He calls for an end to speed limits on U.S. interstate highways—a proposal that requires him to spend much of the essay in refuting opposing views.

207

freedoms of American citizens. Although there are locations where speed limits are appropriate, in most cases these limits are arbitrarily imposed and sporadically enforced. Modern automobiles are capable of traveling safely at high speeds, and, despite what the auto-insurance consortium would have us believe, speed does not kill. With proper training, American drivers could be capable of driving "at speed" responsibly. Perhaps the most compelling reason to lift the national speed limit is the simplest: driving fast is enjoyable.

Those opposed to lifting the national speed limit argue that removing such restrictions would result in mayhem on the freeway; they're convinced that the countryside would be littered with the carcasses of people who achieved terminal velocity only to careen off the road and explode into flames. Speed limit advocates also argue that American drivers do not possess the skill or capacity to drive at autobahn speeds. They contend that our driver-education programs do not sufficiently prepare drivers to operate vehicles, and obtaining a driver's license in most states is comically easy; therefore, lifting the speed limit would be irresponsible.

The major objection to the proposal—that repeal will lead to an increase in deaths—is considered, and a statistical counter-argument is offered.

The belief that a "no speed limit" highway system would result in widespread carnage appears to be based more on fear than fact. In 1987, Idaho senator Steve Symms introduced legislation allowing states to raise speed limits on rural interstates to 65 miles per hour (Csere, "Free" 9). Auto-insurance industry advocates responded that the accident rates would skyrocket and the number of fatalities caused by auto accidents would increase accordingly. Ironically, the Insurance Institute for Highway Safety (IIHS) reported in July 1994 that "[o]nly 39,235 deaths resulting from auto-related accidents were reported during 1992, the lowest number since 1961. The institute found that 1992 was the fourth year in which automotive deaths consistently declined" (qtd. in "Highways" 51). Coincidentally, that decline in fatalities began two years after many states raised interstate speed limits. Unfortunately, the insurance industry has made it a habit to manipulate statistics to suit its purposes. Later in the essay, I'll discuss evidence of this propensity to deceive.

The contention that American drivers are not capable of driving safely at higher speeds has some merit. During a drive around any city in this country, one is bound to witness numerous displays of behind-the-wheel careless-ness. Because of poor driver-education programs, as well as general apathy, Americans have earned their standing among the worst drivers in the world. Regarding our poor driving habits, automotive journalist Csaba Csere wrote in the April 1994 issue of *Car and Driver:* "American drivers choose their lanes randomly, much in the way cows inex-plicably pick a patch of grass on which to graze" ("Drivers" 9). Fortunately, Americans' poor driving habits can be remedied. Through intensive driver-education programs, stringent licensing criteria, and public-service announce-ment campaigns, we can learn to drive more proficiently.

Knutson concedes that Americans are poor drivers, but he offers a remedy.

I recently returned from a four-year stay in Kaiser-slautern, Germany. While there, I learned the pleasure of high-speed motoring. I was particularly impressed by the skill and discipline demonstrated by virtually all drivers traveling on the network of superhighways that make up the autobahn system. Germany's automobile regulatory laws are efficient, practical, and serve as an example for all countries to follow. It is striking that automobiles and driving fast are such integral components of German culture. Germans possess a passion for cars that is so con-tagious I didn't want to leave the country. German chan-cellor Helmut Kohl summed up the German attitude regarding speed limits quite concisely: "For millions of people, a car is part of their personal freedom" (qtd. in Cote 12).

A comparison is offered as logical evidence: Germany has both high-speed motoring and efficient and responsible drivers.

It is apparent in the United States that there are not many old, junky cars left on the road. The majority of vehi-cles operating in the United States are newer cars that have benefited from automotive engineering technology designed to increase the performance of the average vehi-cle. With the advent of independent suspension, electronic engine-management systems, passive restraints, and

Factual evidence (improvements in automotive technology and stringent safety requirements) supports the proposal to repeal speed limits.

other technological improvements, modern automobiles are more capable than ever of traveling at high speeds, safely. Indeed, the stringent safety requirements imposed by the Department of Transportation for vehicles sold in the United States ensure that our cars and trucks are the safest in the world.

A mini-argument of definition is offered in support of the proposal argument: driving fast does not itself constitute a "hazard."

One of the biggest fallacies perpetrated by the auto-insurance industry and car-fearing legislators is that "speed kills." Driving fast in itself, however, is not a hazard; speed combined with incompetence, alcohol, or hazardous conditions is dangerous. A skilled motor-vehicle operator traveling at 90 miles per hour, in light traffic, on a divided highway does not present a significant risk. Psychologist and compensation theorist G. J. Wilde "developed the RHT (Risk Homeostasis Theory) to account

An authority is cited in support of the proposal: drivers try to keep their level of risk constant, regardless of speed limits.

for the apparent propensity of drivers to maintain a constant level of experienced accident risk" (qtd. in Jackson and Blackman 950). During a driving simulation experiment in which he changed "non-motivational factors," Wilde determined that "[n]either speed limit nor speeding fine had a significant impact on accident loss" (qtd. in Jackson and Blackman 956). Wilde's theory is convincing because he emphasizes the human tendency towards self-preservation. The impact of RHT could be far-reaching. As Wilde says, "The notion that drivers compensate fully for non-motivational safety countermeasures is significant because it is tantamount to the claim that most legislated safety measures will not permanently reduce the total population traffic accident loss" (qtd. in Jackson and Blackman 951). What this means is that drivers would not increase their personal risk by driving faster than their capabilities dictate, regardless of the speed limit.

Opposing statistical evidence is refuted.

Unfortunately, the IIHS doesn't see things this way. It has been busy manipulating statistics in an attempt to convince people that raising the interstate speed limits to 65 miles per hour has resulted in a veritable bloodbath. A headline in a recent edition of the IIHS status report states, "For Sixth Year in a Row, Deaths on U.S. Rural Interstates Are Much Higher Than before Speed Limits Were Raised to 65 mph" (qtd. in Bedard 20). That statistic is more than a little misleading because it does not compensate for the increased number of drivers on the road. Patrick Bedard explains: "What's the real conclusion? Rural interstate fatalities over the whole United States increased 19 percent between 1982 and 1992. But driving increased 44 percent. So the fatality rate is on a definite downward trend from 1.5 to 1.2 [percent]" (21).

One might ask what the insurance industry stands to gain by misrepresenting auto fatality statistics. The real issue is what it stands to lose if speed limits are deregulated. The lifting of speed limits translates into fewer traffic citations issued by police. Fewer tickets means fewer points assessed on Americans' driving records, which would remove the insurance industry's primary tool for raising premiums. Needless to say, the industry isn't thrilled about the prospect of less money in its coffers.

The credibility of opponents is challenged: insurance companies make a lot of money from enforcement of speed limits.

There is one lucid and persuasive argument to abolish interstate speed limits: Driving fast is pure, unadulterated, rip-snortin' fun. I experienced the thrill of a lifetime behind the wheel of a 1992 Ford Mustang while chasing a BMW 525i on the Frankfurt-Mainz Autobahn. I remember my heart racing as I glanced at my speedometer, which read 120 mph. When I looked up, I saw the high-beam flash of headlights in my rearview mirror. Moments after I pulled into the right lane, a bloodred Ferrari F-40 passed in a surreal symphony of sound, color, and power, dominated by the enraged howl of a finely tuned Italian motor at full tilt. At that moment, I was acutely aware of every nerve ending in my body, as I experienced the automotive equivalent of Zen consciousness. It was a sort of convergence of psyche and body that left me light-headed and giddy for ten minutes afterwards. I was glad to discover that my reaction to driving fast was not unique:

An appeal to emotion—that driving fast is fun— is supported by evidence from personal experience.

> Few people can describe in words the mixture of sensations they experience, but for some the effect is so psychologically intense that no other experience can match it [. . .]. For some people the psychological effects are experienced as pure fear. For others, however, this basic emotional state is modified to give a sharply tingling experience which is perceived as intensely

pleasurable. The fear, and the state of alertness are still there—but they have been mastered. (Marsh and Collett 179)

Conclusion reiterates proposal and emotional appeal to personal freedom.

Repealing interstate speed limits is an objective that every driver should carefully consider. At a time when our elected officials are striving to control virtually every aspect of our lives, it is imperative that we fight to regain our freedom behind the wheel. Like Germans, Americans have a rich automotive culture and heritage. The automobile represents our ingenuity, determination, and independence. It is time to return control of the automobile to the driver, and "free us from our speed slavery once and for all" (Csere, "Free" 9).

WORKS CITED

Bedard, Patrick. "Auto Insurance Figures Don't Lie, but Liars Figure." Editorial. *Car and Driver* Mar. 1994: 20–21.

Cote, Kevin. "Heartbrake on Autobahn." *Advertising Age* 26 Sept. 1994: 1+.

Csere, Csaba. "Drivers We Love to Hate." Editorial. *Car and Driver* Apr. 1994: 9.

———. "Free the Speed Slaves." Editorial. *Car and Driver* Nov. 1993: 9.

"Highways Become Safer." *Futurist* Jan.–Feb. 1994: 51–52.

Jackson, Jeremy S. H., and Roger Blackman. "A Driving Simulator Test of Wilde's Risk Homeostasis Theory." *Journal of Applied Psychology* 79.6 (1994): 950–58.

Marsh, Peter, and Peter Collett. *Driving Passion.* Winchester: Faber, 1987.

Don't Make English Official—Ban It Instead

DENNIS BARON

Congress is considering, and may soon pass, legislation making English the official language of the United States. Supporters of the measure say that English forms the glue that keeps America together. They deplore the dollars wasted translating English into other languages. And they fear a horde of illegal aliens adamantly refusing to acquire the most powerful language on earth.

On the other hand, opponents of official English remind us that without legislation we have managed to get over ninety-seven percent of the residents of this country to speak the national language. No country with an official language law even comes close. Opponents also point out that today's non-English-speaking immigrants are picking up English faster than earlier generations of immigrants did, so instead of official English, they favor "English Plus," encouraging everyone to speak both English and another language.

I would like to offer a modest proposal to resolve the language impasse in Congress. Don't make English official, ban it instead.

That may sound too radical, but proposals to ban English first surfaced in the heady days after the American Revolution. Anti-British sentiment was so strong in the new United States that a few superpatriots wanted to get rid of English altogether. They suggested replacing English with Hebrew, thought by many in the eighteenth century to be the world's first language, the one spoken in the garden of Eden. French was also considered, because it was thought at the time, and especially by the French, to be the language of pure reason. And of course there was Greek, the language of Athens, the world's first democracy. It's not clear how serious any of these proposals were, though Roger Sherman of Connecticut supposedly remarked that it would be better to keep English for ourselves and make the British speak Greek.

Denis Baron is professor of English and linguistics at the University of Illinois at Urbana-Champaign and head of the department of English. His books include *Grammar and Good Taste: Reforming the American Language* (1982) and the *Guide to Home Language Repair* (1994). He writes often on questions of language and efforts to reform it or legislate its use. This essay, originally published in the *Washington Post*, parodies the genre of proposals—and is a great model of an academic proposal.

Even if the British are now our allies, there may be some benefit to banning English today. A common language can often be the cause of strife and misunderstanding. Look at Ireland and Northern Ireland, the two Koreas, or the Union and the Confederacy. Banning English would prevent that kind of divisiveness in America today.

Also, if we banned English, we wouldn't have to worry about whose English to make official: the English of England or America? of Chicago or New York? of Ross Perot or William F. Buckley?

We might as well ban English, too, because no one seems to read it much lately, few can spell it, and fewer still can parse it. Even English teachers have come to rely on computer spell checkers.

Another reason to ban English: it's hardly even English anymore. English started its decline in 1066, with the unfortunate incident at Hastings. Since then it has become a polyglot conglomeration of French, Latin, Italian, Scandinavian, Arabic, Sanskrit, Celtic, Yiddish and Chinese, with an occasional smiley face thrown in.

More important, we should ban English because it has become a world language. Remember what happened to all the other world languages: Latin, Greek, Indo-European? One day they're on everybody's tongue; the next day they're dead. Banning English now would save us that inevitable disappointment.

Although we shouldn't ban English without designating a replacement for it, there is no obvious candidate. The French blew their chance when they sold Louisiana. It doesn't look like the Russians are going to take over this country any time soon—they're having enough trouble taking over Russia. German, the largest minority language in the U. S. until recently, lost much of its prestige after two world wars. Chinese is too hard to write, especially if you're not Chinese. There's always Esperanto, a language made up a hundred years ago that is supposed to bring about world unity. We're still waiting for that. And if you took Spanish in high school you can see that it's not easy to get large numbers of people to speak another language fluently.

In the end, though, it doesn't matter what replacement language we pick, just so long as we ban English instead of making it official. Prohibiting English will do for the language what Prohibition did for liquor. Those who already use it will continue to do so, and those who don't will want to try out what has been forbidden. This negative psychology works with children. It works with speed limits. It even worked in the Garden of Eden.

chapter thirteen

Humorous Arguments

When the local city council passes an ordinance requiring bicyclists to wear helmets to protect against head injuries, a cyclist responds by writing a letter to the editor of the local newspaper suggesting other requirements the council might impose to protect citizens—including wearing earplugs in dance clubs, water wings in city pools, and blinders in City Hall.

After staging a successful academic conference, participants in a listserv begin exchanging messages of congratulations, praising the cooperation and fine work done by members of the group. After the seventh or eighth syrupy communication, a member of the group posts a tongue-in-cheek message suggesting that his conference paper was the only one he found bearable and that he spent the other sessions sleeping—along with most other members of the audience.

An undergraduate who thinks his school's new sexual harassment policy amounts to puritanism parodies it for the school literary magazine by describing in a short fictional drama what would happen if Romeo and Juliet strayed onto campus.

Under fire for inviting political contributors to stay at the White House overnight, the president of the United States jokes that while he's sad his only child is going away to college, it does free up another bedroom!

Tired of looking at the advertisements that cover every square inch of the campus sports arena walls, a student sends the college newspaper a satirical "news" article entitled "Sports Arena for Sale—to Advertisers!"

■ ■ ■

UNDERSTANDING HUMOR AS ARGUMENT

Though tough to define and even harder to teach, humor can be a powerful form of argument. You can use humor as a strategy to make readers well disposed toward your own projects or to ridicule people and concepts you don't like. In recent years, late-night talk show hosts have become the barometers of political opinion, the day's events fodder for their comic monologues. A somber two minutes from Dan Rather probably does a politico less harm than a couple of zingers from Jay Leno.

By its very nature, humor is risky. Playing fast and loose with good taste and sound reason, writers turn what is comfortable and familiar inside out and then hope readers get the joke. Play it too safe with humor, and audiences groan; step over an unseen line, and they hiss or hurl tomatoes. Because of such pitfalls, humor may be the most rhetorically intense form of argument, requiring a shrewd assessment of audience, language, and purpose. At its best, humor amazes readers with its evanescent clarity. But one cannot revise bad humor or save it with better evidence or more careful documentation.

Neither can humor afford to be less than razor sharp. (John Dryden described great satire as severing the head from a body so cleanly as to leave it standing in place.) Comic timing is, in fact, a rhetorical skill, the ability to find suitable words for unanticipated situations. Because humor

Ted Rall's article on office jargon, written during the height of public debate on Ebonics, takes risks with a volatile topic, considering whether the language spoken in suburban office parks is a dialect—and whether the upper-middle-class workers who speak it need help learning to speak "proper" English.

LINK TO P. 611

is so attached to the moment of its delivery and to the cultural context, retelling a funny story often ends with the comment, "You just had to be there." It's also why topical humor wears so poorly—and why even Shakespeare's comedies require so many footnotes. To manage humor, you must appreciate the rhetorical situation as well as the foibles of human nature. You've got to be fresh and witty, not crude and obscene (which reflects the most juvenile form of humor).

Obviously, then, humor cannot be learned quickly or easily. But it is too powerful a tool to leave to comedians. For writers and speakers, humor can quicken the major rhetorical strategies—appeals of the heart, character, and reason.

Humor is not itself an emotion, but it can be used to rouse powerful feelings in readers. In some circumstances, humor can simply make people feel good and, thus, move them to do what others ask. That's the rationale behind many "soft sell" commercials, from classic VW pitches of a generation ago ("Think small") to more recent, thoroughly silly spots for Mentos mint candies. Advertisers hope to associate the pleasure of a smile with particular products.

But humor has a darker side, too; it can make people feel superior to targets of ridicule. Naturally, one doesn't want to associate with people or ideas one finds ridiculous. So if a health care reform proposal can be lampooned as a ludicrously tangled web of government agencies, perhaps it won't be taken seriously by citizens who might fear a medical delivery system with the efficiency of the post office and the charm of the IRS.

Humor plays a large role, too, in arguments of character. One of the easiest ways to win the goodwill of readers is to make them laugh. It is no accident that all but the most serious speeches ritually begin with a few jokes or anecdotes. The humor puts listeners at ease and helps them identify with the speaker—*She's just a regular guy, who can crack a smile.* A little self-deprecating wit can endear writers or speakers to the toughest audience. You'll likely listen to people confident enough to make fun of themselves because their wit suggests both intelligence and an appealing awareness of their own limitations. After all, no one likes a stuffed shirt.

Humor also is related to reason and good sense. A funny remark usually has, at its core, an element of truth:

Political correctness is . . . another form of American insanity that forbids people from speaking their minds for fear they'll say exactly what everyone else is thinking.

–John Ruszkiewicz, "Politics, Political Correctness, and Sex"

Or humor may work off a particular logical structure. Dave Barry, for example, opens the sample argument at the end of this chapter with a carefully constructed, rather artful analogy between—odd as it may seem—Amtrak and sports:

> I mean, suppose you have a friend who, for no apparent reason, suddenly becomes obsessed with Amtrak. He babbles about Amtrak constantly, citing obscure railroad statistics from 1978; he puts Amtrak bumper stickers on his car; and when something bad happens to Amtrak, such as a train crashes and investigators find that the engineer was drinking and wearing a bunny suit, your friend becomes depressed for weeks. You'd think he was crazy, right? "Bob," you'd say to him as a loving and caring friend, "you're a moron. Amtrak has NOTHING TO DO WITH YOU."
>
> But if Bob is behaving exactly the same deranged way about, say, the Pittsburgh Penguins, it's considered normal guy behavior. He could name his child "Pittsburgh Penguin Johnson" and be considered only mildly eccentric.
>
> —Dave Barry, "A Look at Sports Nuts—And We Do Mean Nuts"

Many forms of humor, especially satire and parody, get their power from twists of logic. When Jonathan Swift in the eighteenth century suggested that Ireland's English rulers consider a diet of Irish children, he depended on readers perceiving the parallel between his outrageous proposal and actual policies of an oppressive English government. The satire works precisely because it is perfectly logical, given the political realities of Swift's time—though some of his contemporaries missed the joke.

> I profess, in the sincerity of my heart, that I have not the least personal interest in endeavoring to promote this necessary work, having no other motive but the public good of my country, by advancing our trade, providing for infants, relieving the poor, and giving some pleasure to the rich.
>
> —Jonathan Swift, "A Modest Proposal"

In our own era, columnist Molly Ivins, taking on opponents of gun control on a television talk show, seems to submit to their position—but then extends it with a twist that makes her own point and ridicules her opponents at the same time:

> I think that's what we need: more people carrying weapons. I support the legislation but I'd like to propose one small amendment. Everyone

should be able to carry a concealed weapon. But everyone who carries a weapon should be required to wear one of those little beanies on their heads with a little propeller on it so the rest of us can see them coming.

–Molly Ivins

CHARACTERIZING KINDS OF HUMOR

It's possible to write entire books about comic form, exploring variations such as satire, parody, burlesque, travesty, pastiche, lampoon, caricature, farce, and more. Almost every type of humor entails a kind of argument, laughter usually aiming at some purpose grander than a chuckle. Not all such purposes are laudable; schoolyard taunts and vicious editorial cartoons may share an intent to hurt or humiliate. But humor can also break down pretensions or barriers of prejudice and help people see the world in new ways. When it is robust and honest, humor is a powerful rhetorical form.

Humor

Though serious academic writing generally avoids sustained moments of comedy, humor can contribute to almost any argument. Appreciating when it is appropriate isn't always easy, however. One has to sense what humor can do before deploying it.

For instance, humor inserted in an otherwise serious piece readily catches a reader's attention and changes the tone. Here, for example, is the African American writer Zora Neale Hurston addressing the very real issue of discrimination, with a nod and a wink:

> Sometimes I feel discriminated against, but it does not make me angry. It merely astonishes me. How *can* any deny themselves the pleasure of my company? It's beyond me.
>
> –Zora Neale Hurston, "How It Feels to Be Colored Me"

Or a fairly serious point can be illustrated with comic examples that keep a reader engaged in the message, aware that what the author is describing comports with reality. Consider the following lengthy passage in which Prudence Makintosh, mother of three sons, illustrates, in part, why she believes that nurture and socialization alone don't account for certain differences between girls and boys:

Ellen Goodman deals with the serious topics of eating disorders and school killings, yet she uses humor to hold readers' attention and goodwill. She opens her deadly serious argument by asking readers to "imagine a place [where] women greet one another at the market with open arms, loving smiles, and a cheerful exchange of ritual compliments: 'You look wonderful! You've put on weight.'"

LINK TO P. 401

> How can I explain why a little girl baby sits on a quilt in the park thoughtfully examining a blade of grass, while my baby William uproots grass by handfuls and eats it? Why does a mother of very bright and active daughters confide that until she went camping with another family of boys, she feared that my sons had a hyperactivity problem? I am sure there are plenty of noisy, rowdy little girls, but I'm not just talking about rowdiness and noise. I'm talking about some sort of primal physicalness that causes the walls of my house to pulsate on rainy days. I'm talking about something inexplicable that makes my sons fall into a mad, scrambling, pull-your-ears-off-kick-your-teeth-in heap just before bedtime, when they're not even mad at each other. I mean something that causes them to climb the doorjamb with honey and peanut butter on their hands while giving me a synopsis of *Star Wars* that contains only five unintelligible words. . . . When Jack and Drew are not kicking a soccer ball or each other, they are kicking the chair legs, the cat, the baby's silver rattle, and inadvertently, Baby William himself, whom they have affectionately dubbed "Tough Eddy."
>
> –Prudence Makintosh, "Masculine/Feminine"

The rich detail of the description is part of the argumentative strategy, capturing perfectly the exasperation of a mother who apparently thought she could raise her boys to be different. Readers chuckle at little William eating grass, the house pulsating, doorjambs sticky with peanut butter— and see Makintosh's point, whether they agree with it or not. Her intention, however, is not so much to be funny but to give her opinion presence.

That seems to be George Felton's strategy, too, in the following passage from his meditation on the American obsession with healthy living and natural foods. In this case, the humor may be gaining the upper hand, yet readers understand the writer's point (at least those readers of a certain age):

> The cereal aisle at the grocery store now presents us with one trail mix after another designed for the long march through our large intestines, each another grainy way to combat cancer, cholesterol, our own weak desire for pleasure. I now walk down the aisle trying, not to satisfy my hunger, but to represent my colon. What would *it* like? What does *it* need? I wonder. "Bran!" the shelves shout back.
>
> –George Felton, "The Selling of Pain"

Exaggeration of the kind evident in Felton's piece is an essential technique of humor. Sometimes readers see the world more clearly when a writer blows up the picture. Here's Dave Barry, again, arguing that computer enthusiasts might be just a tad odd:

> **I am not the only person who uses his computer mainly for the purpose of diddling with his computer. There are millions of others. I know because I encounter them on the Internet, which is a giant international network of intelligent informed computer enthusiasts, by which I mean, "people without lives."**
>
> —Dave Barry, "You Have to Be a Real Stud
> Hombre Cybermuffin to Handle 'Windows'"

Satire

Satire is a more focused form of humor, a genre in its own right. In satire, a writer uses humor and wit to expose—and possibly correct—human problems or failings. The most famous piece of satire in English literature is probably Jonathan Swift's *Gulliver's Travels,* which pokes fun at all human pretensions, targeting especially politics, religion, science, and sexuality. This satire is a sustained argument for change in human character and institutions.

Not all satires reach as far as Swift's masterpiece, but the impulse to expose human foibles to ridicule is quite strong. Political and social satire thrive on television programs such as *Saturday Night Live* and *Politically Incorrect.* Most editorial cartoons, like the one shown in Figure 13.1, also fall into the realm of satire when they highlight a defect in society that the cartoonist feels needs to be remedied.

Satire often involves a shift in perspective that compels readers to examine a situation in a new way. In *Gulliver's Travels,* for example, we see human society reduced in scale (in Lilliput), exaggerated in size (in Brobdingnang), even through the eyes of a superior race of horses (the Houyhnhnms). In the land of the giants, Gulliver comments on the defects of the ladies when he sees them up close in their boudoirs:

> **Their skins appeared so coarse and uneven, so variously coloured, when I saw them near, with a mole here and there as broad as a trencher, and hairs hanging from it thicker than pack-threads, to say nothing further concerning the rest of their persons.**
>
> —Jonathan Swift, *Gulliver's Travels*

So much for human beauty. You'll note that there's nothing especially funny in Gulliver's remarks. That's because satire is more likely to employ

Responding to the movement to make English the official language of the United States, Dennis Baron makes a satirical proposal to ban English altogether. As he argues, "Prohibiting English will do for the language what Prohibition did for liquor. . . . This negative psychology works with children. It works with speed limits. It even worked in the Garden of Eden."

LINK TO P. 213 ·····································

Figure 13.1

"Do you solemnly swear to be truth-oriented?"

wit than humor, the point of a piece being to open readers' eyes rather than to make them laugh out loud. People are amused that the author of a satire is not altogether serious, but they also understand that there is a larger point to be made—if the satire works.

You can see this balancing act between satiric form and message in the following proposal to eliminate grades in college. Roberta Borkat, a college English instructor fed up with her students' whining about grades, is sure there's a better way to handle evaluation and offers a scheme:

> **The plan is simplicity itself: at the end of the second week of the semester, all students enrolled in each course will receive a final grade of A. Then their minds will be relieved of anxiety, and they will be free to do whatever they want for the rest of the term.**
>
> **The benefits are immediately obvious. Students will be assured of high grade point averages and an absence of obstacles in their march toward graduation. Professors will be relieved of useless burdens and will have time to pursue their real interests. Universities will have achieved the long-desired goal of molding individual professors into interchangeable parts of a smoothly operating machine. Even the environment will be improved because education will no longer consume vast quantities of paper for books, compositions and examinations.**
>
> **–Roberta Borkat, "A Liberating Curriculum"**

Readers know Borkat doesn't mean what she says, but they don't exactly laugh at her proposal either. For many teachers and some students, no doubt, the satire strikes too close to home. Borkat has made her case.

Parody

Like satire, parody typically offers an argument. What distinguishes the two forms is that parody makes its case by transforming the familiar—be it songs, passages of prose, TV shows, poems, films, even people—into something new. The argument sparkles in the tension between the original work and its imitation. That's where the humor lies, too.

Needless to say, parodies work best when audiences make that connection. Imagine how pointless a parody of the sitcom *Friends* might seem fifty years from now. Even today, allusions to President Gerald Ford's clumsiness seem about as funny (and topical) as digs at William Howard Taft's prodigious weight. Indeed, context is everything.

But if the half-life of parody is brief, the form is potent in its prime. Just a few years ago, when a men's movement danced briefly in the national consciousness, Joe Bob Briggs brought the nascent trend to its knees with a ruthless parody of Wild Man weekends, when boorish males finally got in touch with their inner selves:

> **I'll never forget it. I sweated a lot. I cried. I sweated *while* I was crying. Of course, I was crying because they made me sweat so much. We had this one part of the weekend where we went into a giant sauna and turned it up to about, oh, 280, until everybody's skin turned the color of strawberry Jell-O and the veins of our heads started exploding, and it turned into this communal out-of-body *male* thing, where everybody was screaming, "I want *out* of my body!"**
> **–Joe Bob Briggs, "Get in Touch with Your Ancient Spear"**

When a subject or work becomes the object of a successful parody, it's never seen in quite the same way again.

Signifying

One distinctive kind of humor found extensively in African American English is signifying, in which a speaker cleverly and often humorously needles the listener. In the following passage, two African American men (Grave Digger and Coffin Ed) signify on their white supervisor (Anderson), who ordered them to discover the originators of a riot:

"I take it you've discovered who started the riot," Anderson said.

"We knew who he was all along," Grave Digger said.

"It's just nothing we can do to him," Coffin Ed echoed.

"Why not, for God's sake?"

"He's dead," Coffin Ed said.

"Who?"

"Lincoln," Grave Digger said.

"He hadn't ought to have freed us if he didn't want to make provisions to feed us," Coffin Ed said. "Anyone could have told him that."

—Chester Himes, *Hot Day, Hot Night*

Coffin Ed and Grave Digger demonstrate the major characteristics of effective signifying: indirection, ironic humor, fluid rhythm—and a surprising twist at the end. Rather than insulting Anderson directly by pointing out that he's asked a dumb question, they criticize the question indirectly by ultimately blaming a white man (and not just *any* white man, but one they're all supposed to revere). This twist leaves the supervisor speechless, teaching him something *and* giving Grave Digger and Coffin Ed the last word.

You will find examples of signifying in the work of many African American writers. You may also hear signifying in NBA basketball, for it is an important element of trash talking; what Grave Digger and Coffin Ed do to Anderson, Reggie Miller regularly does to his opponents on the court.

DEVELOPING HUMOROUS ARGUMENTS

It's doubtful anyone can offer a formula for being funny; some would suggest that humor is a gift. But at least the comic perspective is a trait widely distributed among the population. Most people can be funny, given the right circumstances.

But the stars may not always be aligned when you need them in composing an argument. And just working hard may not help: laughter arises from spirited, not labored, insights. Yet once you strike the spark, a blaze usually follows.

Look for humor in obvious situations. Bill Cosby began a stellar career as a humorist with a comedy album that posed the rather simple question: *Why Is There Air?* The late columnist and author Erma Bombeck, too, endeared herself to millions of people by pointing out the humor in daily routines.

Look for humor in incongruity or in *what if* situations, and then imagine the consequences. *What if men had monthlies? What if reading caused flatulence? What if students hired special prosecutors to handle their grade complaints? What if broccoli tasted like chocolate? What if politicians always told the truth? What if the Pope wasn't Catholic?*

Don't look for humor in complicated ideas. You're more apt to find it in simple premises, like Barry's potent question: "How come guys care so much about sports?" There are, of course, serious answers to the question. But the humor practically bubbles up on its own once you ponder men and their games. You can write a piece of your own just by listing details: *Monday Night Football, sports bars, beer commercials, sagging couches, fantasy camps, Little League, angry wives.* Push a little further, relate such items to personal insights and experiences, and you are likely to discover some of the incongruities and implausibilities at the heart of humor.

Let us stress detail. Abstract humor probably doesn't work for anyone except German philosophers and inebriated graduate students. Look for humor in concrete and proper nouns, in people and places readers will recognize but not expect to encounter. Consider Barry's technique in defending himself against those who might question his attack on sports:

> **And before you accuse me of being some kind of sherry-sipping ascot-wearing ballet-attending MacNeil-Lehrer-NewsHour-watching wussy, please note that I am a sports guy myself, having had a legendary athletic career consisting of nearly a third of the 1965 season on the track team at Pleasantville High School ("Where the Leaders of Tomorrow Are Leaving Wads of Gum on the Auditorium Seats of Today").**
> —Dave Barry, "A Look at Sports Nuts—And We Do Mean Nuts"

Remove the lively details from the passage and this is what's left:

> **And before you accuse me of being some kind of wussy, please note that I am a sports guy myself, having had an athletic career on the track team at Pleasantville High School.**

Enough said?

KEY FEATURES OF HUMOROUS ARGUMENTS

Drafting humor and revising humor are yin-yang propositions—opposites that complement each other. Think Democrats and Republicans.

Creating humor is, by nature, a robust, excessive, and egotistical activity. It requires assertiveness, courage, and often a (temporary) suspension

Complaining about the proliferation of T-shirts bearing humorous insults, Steve Rushin takes the climate of "clever contempt" even further in order to argue against it. He suggests that "on our one-dollar bill George Washington ought to smirk like Mona Lisa. On the five, Lincoln's fingers could form a *W*, the international symbol for *whatever*."

LINK TO P. 602

of good judgment and taste. Whereas drafting more material than necessary usually makes good sense for writers, you can afford to be downright
prodigal with humor. Pile on the examples and illustrations. Take all the
risks you can with language. Indulge in puns. Leap into innuendo. Be
clever, but not childishly obscene. Push your vocabulary. Play with words
and have fun.

Then, when you revise, do the opposite. Recall that Polonius in
Shakespeare's *Hamlet* is right about one thing: "Brevity is the soul of wit."
Once you have written a humorous passage, whether a tooting horn or a
full symphonic parody, you must pare your language to the bone. Every
noun must be a thing, every verb an action. Think: less is more. Cut, then
cut again.

That's all there is to it.

Finding a Topic

You may use humor in an argument to

- point out flaws in a policy, proposal, or argument
- suggest a policy of your own
- set people in a favorable frame of mind
- admit weaknesses or deflect criticism
- satirize or parody a position, point of view, or style

Opportunities to use humor in daily life are too numerous to catalog, but they are much rarer in academic and professional writing. You can find amusing topics everywhere if you think about the absurdities of your job, home life, or surrounding culture. Try to see things you take for granted from radically different perspectives. Or flip-flop the normal order of affairs: make a small issue cosmic; chop a huge matter to fritters.

Researching Your Topic

You can't exactly research a whimsical argument, but humor does call for some attention to detail. Satires and parodies thrive on actual events, specific facts, telling allusions, or memorable images that can be located in sources or recorded in discussions and conversations. Timeliness is a factor, too; you need to know whom or what your readers will recognize and how they might respond. Seek inspiration for humor in these sources:

- popular magazines, especially weekly journals (for current events)
- TV, including commercials (especially for material about people)
- classic books, music, films, artwork (as inspiration for parodies)
- comedians (to observe how they make a subject funny)

Formulating a Claim

With humorous arguments, satires, and parodies, you won't so much develop a thesis as play upon a theme. But humor of the sort that can grow for several pages does need a focal point, a central claim that requires support and evidence—even if that support strains credulity. (In fact, it probably should.) Here are lines to kick-start a humorous argument:

- What if . . . ?
- What would happen if . . . ?
- Why is it that . . . ?
- How come . . . never happens to . . . ?
- When was the last time you tried to . . . ?
- Why is it that men/women . . . ?
- Can you believe that . . . ?

Preparing a Proposal

If your instructor asks you to prepare a proposal for a satire, parody, or other humorous argument, here's a format you might use (or parody!).

Explain the focus of your project.

Articulate the point of your humor. What is at stake? What do you hope to accomplish?

Specify any models you have for your project. Who or what are you trying to emulate? If you are writing a parody, what is your target or inspiration?

Explain whom you hope to reach by your humor and why this group of readers will be amused.

Briefly discuss the key challenges you anticipate. Defining a point? Finding comic ideas?

Identify the sources you expect to consult. What facts might you have to establish?

Determine the format you expect to use for your project. A conventional paper? A letter to the editor? A Web page?

Thinking about Organization

Humorous arguments can be structured exactly like more serious ones — with claims, supporting reasons, warrants, evidence, qualifiers, and rebuttals. In fact, humor has its own relentless logic. Once you set an argument going, you should press it home with the same vigor you see in serious pieces.

If you write a parody, you need to be thoroughly familiar with the work on which it is based, particularly its organization and distinctive features. In parodying a song, for example, you've got to be sure listeners recognize familiar lines or choruses. In parodying a longer piece, boil it down to essential elements — the most familiar actions in the plot, the most distinctive characters, the best-known passages of dialogue — and then arrange those elements within a compact and rapidly moving design.

Getting and Giving Response

All arguments can benefit from the scrutiny of others. Your instructor may assign you to a peer group for the purpose of reading and responding to each other's drafts; if not, go out of your way to get some careful response. You can use the following questions to evaluate your own draft, to secure response to it from others, or to prepare a response to a colleague's work. If you are evaluating someone else's draft, be sure to supply specific examples to illustrate your points. Most writers respond better to specific comments than to general observations.

Focus

- Is the argument funny? Would another approach to the topic — even a nonhumorous one — be more effective?
- Does the humor make a clear argumentative point? Is its target clear?
- If the piece is a satire, does it suggest a better alternative to the present situation? If not, does it need to?

Logic, Organization, and Format

- Is there logic to the humor? If so, will readers appreciate it?
- Are the points in the argument clearly connected? Are additional or clearer transitions needed?
- Does the humor build toward a climax? If not, would saving the best laughs for last be more effective?
- Is the piece too long, making the humor seem belabored? If so, how might it be cut?

- Does the format of the piece contribute to the humor? Would it be funnier if it were formatted to look like a particular genre—an advertisement, an email message, a sports column, a greeting card? If you've used illustrations, do they enhance the humor? If there are no illustrations, would adding some help?

Style and Detail

- Is the humor too abstract? Does it need more details about specific people, events, and so on?
- If the piece is a parody, does it successfully imitate the language and idioms of whatever is being parodied?
- Are the sentences wordy or too complex for the type of humor being attempted?
- Are there any problems with spelling, grammar, punctuation, or mechanics?

RESPOND ●

1. For each of the following items, list particular details that might contribute to a humorous look at the subject. (For an example, see Dave Barry's essay about sports fanatics at the end of this chapter.)

   zealous environmentalists

   clueless builders and developers

   aggressive drivers

   violent Hollywood films

   hemp activists

   drivers of big sport utility vehicles

   Martha Stewart

   high school coaches

   college instructors

   malls and the people who visit them

2. Spend some time listening to a friend who you think is funny. What kind of humor does he or she use? What sorts of details crop up in it? Once you've put in a few days of careful listening, try to write down some of the jokes and stories just as your friend told them. Writing humor may be excruciating at first, but you might find it easier with practice.

   After you've written a few humorous selections, think about how well they translate from the spoken word to the written. What's different? Do they work better in one medium than in another? Show your written efforts to your funny friend and ask for comments. How would he or she revise your written efforts?

3. Using Internet search tools, find a transcript of a funny television or radio show. Read the transcript a few times, paying attention to the places where you laugh the most. Then analyze the humor, trying to understand what makes it funny. This chapter suggests several possible avenues for analysis, including normality, incongruity, simplicity, and details. How does the transcript reflect these principles? Or does it operate by a completely different set of principles? (Some of the best humor is funny because it breaks all the rules.)

TWO SAMPLE HUMOROUS ARGUMENTS

The Road to Acme Looniversity

KIRSTEN DOCKENDORFF

With a "click," the television set goes on. You hear that familiar music and see the Warner Brothers logo indicating it's time for *Looney Toons*. We've all watched them, including the many episodes of Wyle E. Coyote and his never-ending quest to catch the Road Runner. Secretly, we've all wanted Wyle E. to succeed, although long before the end of every episode we know that his hard work will only be rewarded by his being dropped from a cliff, smashed by a falling rock, *and* run over by a truck. As if that's not bad enough, Wyle E.'s defeat is also made more miserable by the Road Runner driving over him with his tongue stuck out and a shrill "Beep! Beep!" One thing is clear: Wyle E. has a problem, and it is time for him to solve it.

Like a typical proposal argument, the parody opens with a problem.

One of the easiest ways to get rid of the bird would be for Wyle E. to hire an assassin. This way, he could rest easily knowing a professional was at work. Wyle E. could use the money usually spent on Acme products to cover the assassin's fee. This would also save additional money because Wyle E. would no longer have to buy Acme equipment or pay all of those expensive hospital bills that result when the Acme equipment fails. A professional would be a quick, easy, and cost-effective solution. The major drawback is that Wyle E. would miss the satisfaction of doing the job himself. After so many years of working so hard to catch the Road Runner, he might want to be part of the event.

The parody suggests, assesses, then rejects various solutions to Wyle E. Coyote's problem — just like a real essay.

Kirsten Dockendorff wrote this essay while she was a student at Bowling Green State University in Bowling Green, Ohio. In the essay, Dockendorff parodies the structure of conventional proposal arguments (see Chapter 12) by applying it to the dilemma of cartoon character Wyle E. Coyote.

A better way for Wyle E. to kill the Road Runner and still participate might be to get some help from his friends. Wyle E. could call on Elmer Fudd, Yosemite Sam, Sylvester the Cat, and Taz, the Tasmanian Devil. By constructing a plan in which he and his friends combine their natural talents, Wyle E. would have the satisfaction of being part of the bird's demise. Taz, with speed equal to the Road Runner's, could chase the bird into a trap designed by Yosemite Sam: a small mound of birdseed in the Road Runner's path. When the bird stops to eat, a cage would drop. Then Sylvester's natural bird-catching instincts could be of use in disabling the bird to prevent escape, perhaps by breaking its legs. After that, Elmer could use his extraordinary hunting skills to finish him off. The only flaw in this plan might be that his friends don't have much of a record of success: Elmer, Sam, and Taz have never caught Bugs Bunny; Sylvester has never caught Tweety; and you know the results of all Wyle E.'s plans. The chance would thus seem infinitesimal at best that even together they might catch the Road Runner.

To appreciate the humor, a reader has to recognize a host of cartoon characters.

Wyle E.'s major problem in his pursuit of the Road Runner never seems to be the plan itself, but the products he uses to carry out the plan. None of the equipment he buys from Acme ever works correctly. It may work fine in a test run, but when the Road Runner actually falls into the trap, everything goes crazy or fails completely. In one recurring episode, Wyle E. buys a rocket and a pair of roller skates. His plan is to strap the rocket to his back and the skates to his feet, and thus overtake his speedy prey. The test run is fine. Then the bird runs by, and Wyle E. starts the rocket, which immediately runs out of fuel, blows up, or does not go off. If Wyle E. used a company other than Acme, he might avoid the injuries he suffers from faulty Acme equipment. Of course, one obstacle to this plan is the cost of doing business with a new company. Since Wyle E. probably receives a sizable discount from Acme because of his preferred customer status, he perhaps would not get the same treatment from a new company, at least for a while. On his cartoon-character salary, Wyle E. may not be able to afford higher prices.

The humor also depends on readers going along with the joke, regarding Wyle E. Coyote as a person and Acme as a company.

Now the parody mocks actors, too.

Given the range of possibilities for catching the Road Runner, the best solution to the problem might be for Wyle E. to use his superior intellect. Wyle E. could undoubtedly convince the Road Runner that a dramatic death scene on the show might win him an Emmy. Since roadrunners are known for their vanity, this Road Runner would seem likely to leap at the prospect of winning fame and fortune for his fine acting skills. With such a prestigious award, the Road Runner could do what every actor dreams of doing: direct. He would win not only fame and fortune, but the respect of his hero, Big Bird.

Real proposal arguments ponder the feasibility of their solutions — and so does this one.

If and when Wyle E. catches the Road Runner, the cartoon, of course, would end. Although this might at first seem tragic, the consequences are really not tragic at all. Wyle E. would have more time to pursue his movie career and perhaps even teach at Acme Looniversity. He would have more time to devote to his family, friends, and fans. And he could finally stop paying a therapist since his psychological issues would be resolved. Wyle E. would gain self-confidence and no longer doubt his ability as he did when the birdbrain outsmarted him. He would finally recognize his own genius and realize his lifelong dream of opening a theme restaurant.

Even the conclusion follows a formula.

After years and years of torment and humiliation, it is time for Wyle E. Coyote to catch the Road Runner. Although it is feasible for Wyle E. to pay an assassin to kill the bird, to enlist his friends for help, or to stop using Acme products, the best solution is for Wyle E. to use the immeasurable power of his brain to trick the imbecilic bird. Regardless of the method Wyle E. chooses, one thing is clear: the bird must *die!*

A Look at Sports Nuts—And We Do Mean Nuts

DAVE BARRY

Today in our continuing series on How Guys Think, we explore the question: How come guys care so much about sports?

This is a tough one, because caring about sports is, let's face it, silly. I mean, suppose you have a friend who, for no apparent reason, suddenly becomes obsessed with Amtrak. He babbles about Amtrak constantly, citing obscure railroad statistics from 1978; he puts Amtrak bumper stickers on his car; and when something bad happens to Amtrak, such as a train crashes and investigators find that the engineer was drinking and wearing a bunny suit, your friend becomes depressed for weeks. You'd think he was crazy, right? "Bob," you'd say to him as a loving and caring friend, "you're a moron. Amtrak has NOTHING TO DO WITH YOU."

But if Bob is behaving exactly the same deranged way about, say, the Pittsburgh Penguins, it's considered normal guy behavior. He could name his child "Pittsburgh Penguin Johnson" and be considered only mildly eccentric.

There is something wrong with this. And before you accuse me of being some kind of sherry-sipping ascot-wearing ballet-attending MacNeil-Lehrer-NewsHour-watching wussy, please note that I am a sports guy myself, having had a legendary athletic career consisting of nearly a third of the 1965 season on the track team at Pleasantville High School ("Where the Leaders of Tomorrow Are Leaving Wads of Gum on the Auditorium Seats of Today"). I competed in the long jump, because it seemed to be the only event where afterward you didn't fall down and throw up. I probably would have become an Olympic-caliber long-jumper except that, through one of those "bad breaks" so common in sports, I turned out to have the raw leaping ability of a convenience store.

So, okay, I was not Jim Thorpe, but I care as much about sports as the next guy. If you were to put me in the middle of a room, and in one corner was Albert Einstein, in another corner was Abraham Lincoln, in another corner was Plato, in another corner was William Shakespeare, and in another corner (this room is a pentagon) was a TV set showing a football game between

Dave Barry is a syndicated columnist and the author of numerous books, including *Dave Barry's Complete Guide to Guys: A Fairly Short Book* (1995), *Dave Barry Is from Mars and Venus* (1997), and *Dave Barry Talks Back* (1991), from which this piece is taken. In it, Barry offers a not entirely serious answer to an age-old question: "How come guys care so much about sports?"

teams that have no connection whatsoever with my life, such as the Green Bay Packers and the Indianapolis Colts, I would ignore the greatest minds in Western thought, gravitate toward the TV, and become far more concerned about the game than I am about my child's education. And SO WOULD THE OTHER GUYS. I guarantee it. Within minutes, Plato would be pounding Lincoln on the shoulder and shouting in ancient Greek that the receiver did NOT have both feet in bounds.

Obviously, sports connect with something deeply rooted in the male psyche, dating back to prehistoric times, when guys survived by hunting and fighting, and they needed many of the skills exhibited by modern athletes—running, throwing, spitting, renegotiating their contracts, adjusting their private parts on nationwide television, etc. So that would explain how come guys like to PARTICIPATE in sports. But how come they care so much about games played by OTHER guys? Does this also date back to prehistoric times? When the hunters were out hurling spears into mastodons, were there also prehistoric guys watching from the hills, drinking prehistoric beer, eating really bad prehistoric hot dogs and shouting "We're No. 1!" but not understanding what it meant because this was before the development of mathematics?

There must have been, because there is no other explanation for such bizarre phenomena as:

- Sports-talk radio, where guys who have never sent get-well cards to their own mothers will express heartfelt, near-suicidal anguish over the hamstring problems of strangers.
- A guy in my office who appears to be a normal middle-age husband and father until you realize that he spends most of his waking hours managing a PRETEND BASEBALL TEAM. This is true. He and some other guys have formed a league where they pay actual money to "draft" major league players, and then they have their pretend teams play a whole pretend season, complete with trades, legalistic memorandums, and heated disputes over the rules. This is crazy, right? If these guys said they were managing herds of pretend caribou, the authorities would be squirting lithium down their throats with turkey basters, right? And yet we all act like it's PERFECTLY NORMAL. In fact, eavesdropping from my office, I find myself getting involved in the discussions. That's how pathetic I am: I'm capable of caring about a pretend sports team that's not even my OWN pretend sports team.

So I don't know about the rest of you guys, but I'm thinking it's time I got some perspective in my life. First thing after the Super Bowl, I'm going to start paying more attention to the things that should matter to me, like my work, my friends, and, above all, my family, especially my little boy, Philadelphia Phillies Barry.

PART 4

STYLISH argument

chapter fourteen

Figurative Language and Argument

Open any magazine or newspaper and you will see figurative language working on behalf of arguments. When the writer of a letter to the editor complains that "Donna Haraway's supposition that because we rely on cell phones and laptops we are cyborgs is [like] saying the Plains Indians were centaurs because they relied on horses," he is using an analogy to rebut (and perhaps ridicule) Haraway's claim. When another writer says that "the digital revolution is whipping through our lives like a Bengali typhoon," she is making an implicit argument about the speed and strength of the digital revolution. When still another writer calls Disney World a "smile factory," she begins a stinging critique of the way pleasure is "manufactured" there.

Just what is figurative language? Traditionally, the terms *figurative language* and *figures of speech* refer to language that differs from the ordinary—that calls up, or "figures," something else. But in fact, all language could be said to call up or figure something else. The word *table,* for example, is not itself a table; rather, it calls up a table in our imaginations. Thus, just as all language is by nature argumentative, so too is it all figurative. Far from being mere decorations or embellishments (something like icing on the cake of thought), figures of speech are indispensable to language use.

More specifically, figurative language brings two major strengths to arguments. First, it often aids understanding by likening something unknown to something known. For example, in arguing for the existence of DNA as they had identified and described it, scientists Watson and Crick used two familiar examples—a helix (spiral) and a zipper—to make their point. Today, arguments about new computer technologies are filled with similar uses of figurative language. Indeed, Microsoft's entire word-processing system depends on likening items to those in an office (as in Microsoft Office) to make them more understandable and familiar to users. Second, figurative language can be helpful in arguments because it is often extremely memorable. Someone arguing that slang should be used in formal writing turns to this memorable definition for support: "Slang is language that takes off its coat, spits on its hands, and gets to work." In a brief poem that carries a powerful argument, Langston Hughes uses figurative language to explore the consequences of unfulfilled dreams:

What happens to a dream deferred?

Does it dry up
Like a raisin in the sun?
Or fester like a sore—
And then run?
Does it stink like rotten meat?
Or crust and sugar over—
Like a syrupy sweet?

Maybe it just sags
Like a heavy load.

Or does it explode?
            –Langston Hughes, "Harlem—A Dream Deferred"

In a famous speech in 1963, Martin Luther King Jr. used figurative language to make his argument unmistakably clear as well as memorable:

> **In a sense we have come to our nation's capital to cash a check. When the architects of our republic wrote the magnificent words of the Constitution and the Declaration of Independence, they were signing a promissory note to which every American was to fall heir. This note was a promise that all men would be guaranteed the unalienable rights of life, liberty, and the pursuit of happiness.**
>
> **It is obvious today that America has defaulted on this promissory note insofar as her citizens of color are concerned. Instead of honoring this sacred obligation, America has given the Negro people a bad check; a check which has come back marked "insufficient funds." But we refuse to believe that the bank of justice is bankrupt. We refuse to believe that there are insufficient funds in the great vaults of opportunity in this nation. So we have come to cash this check—a check that will give us upon demand the riches of freedom and the security of justice.**
>
> **–Martin Luther King Jr., "I Have a Dream"**

The figures of the promissory note and the bad check are especially effective in this passage because they suggest financial exploitation, which fits in well with the overall theme of King's speech.

You may be surprised to learn that during the European Renaissance, schoolchildren sometimes learned and practiced using as many as 180 figures of speech. Such practice seems more than a little excessive today, especially since figures of speech come so naturally to native speakers of the English language; you hear of "nipping a plot in the bud," "getting our act together," "blowing your cover," "marching to a different drummer," "seeing red," "smelling a rat," "being on cloud nine," "throwing in the towel," "tightening our belts," "rolling in the aisles," "turning the screws," "turning over a new leaf"—you get the picture. We don't aim for a complete catalog of figures of speech here, much less for a thorough analysis of the power of figurative language. What we can offer, however, is a brief listing—with examples—of some of the most familiar kinds of figures, along with a reminder that they can be used to extremely good effect in the arguments you write.

Figures have traditionally been classified into two main types: tropes, which involve a change in the ordinary signification, or meaning, of a word or phrase; and schemes, which involve a special arrangement of words. Here we will exemplify the most frequently used figures in each category, beginning with the familiar tropes of metaphor, simile, and analogy.

TROPES

Metaphor

One of the most pervasive uses of figurative language, metaphor offers an implied comparison between two things and thereby clarifies and enlivens many arguments. In the following passage, bell hooks uses the metaphor of the hope chest to enhance her argument that autobiography involves a special kind of treasure hunt:

> **Conceptually, the autobiography was framed in the manner of a hope chest. I remembered my mother's hope chest, with its wonderful odor of cedar, and thought about her taking the most precious items and placing them there for safekeeping. Certain memories were for me a similar treasure. I wanted to place them somewhere for safekeeping. An autobiographical narrative seemed an appropriate place.**
>
> **–bell hooks, *Bone Black***

In another argument, lawyer Gerry Spence opens "Easy in the Harness: The Tyranny of Freedom" with a question—"What is freedom?"—to which he shortly replies with a metaphor: "Freedom is . . . a blank, white canvas where no commitments, no relationships, no plans, no values, no moral restraints have been painted on the free soul." (As Spence makes clear in his discussion, his title calls on another metaphor—one used by poet Robert Frost, who likened freedom to "being easy in the harness.")

English language use is so filled with metaphors that these powerful, persuasive tools often zip by native speakers unnoticed, so be on the lookout for effective metaphors in everything you read. For example, when a reviewer of new software that promises complete filtering of advertisements on the World Wide Web refers to the product as "a weedwhacker for the Web," he is using a metaphor to advance an argument about the nature and function of that product.

Simile

A direct comparison between two things, simile is pervasive in written and spoken language. You may even have your own favorites: someone's hair is "plastered to him like white on rice," for instance, or, as one of our

Metaphors can work powerfully in an argument. Consider the metaphoric use of the verb *pump* in John Levesque's article about the poor image of fatherhood conveyed by many TV sitcoms: ". . . because we have a crisis in fatherhood today, we have to take seriously the kinds of images we pump into kids' homes." What underlying statement does this metaphor make?

LINK TO P. 385

grandmothers used to say, "prices are high as a cat's back," or, as a special compliment, "you look as pretty as red shoes." Similes are also at work in many arguments, as you can see in this excerpt from a brief *Wired* magazine review of a new magazine for women:

> Women's magazines occupy a special niche in the cluttered infoscape of modern media. Ask any *Vogue* junkie: no girl-themed Web site or CNN segment on women's health can replace the guilty pleasure of slipping a glossy fashion rag into your shopping cart. Smooth as a pint of chocolate Häagen-Dazs, feckless as a thousand-dollar slip dress, women's magazines wrap culture, trends, health, and trash in a single, decadent package.
>
> But like the diet dessert recipes they print, these slick publications can leave a bad taste in your mouth.
>
> —Tiffany Lee Brown, "En Vogue"

Here three similes are in prominent display: "smooth as a pint of chocolate Häagen-Dazs" and "feckless as a thousand-dollar slip dress" in the third sentence, and "like the diet dessert recipes" in the fourth. Together, the similes add to the image the writer is trying to create of mass-market women's magazines as a mishmash of "trash" and "trends."

Analogy

Analogies compare two different or dissimilar things for special effect, arguing that if two things are alike in one way they are probably alike in other ways as well. Often extended to several sentences, paragraphs, or even whole essays, analogies can help clarify and emphasize points of comparison. Here Maya Angelou uses an analogy to begin an exploration of one area of Harlem:

> One Hundred and Twenty-fifth Street was to Harlem what the Mississippi was to the South, a long traveling river always going somewhere, carrying something.
>
> —Maya Angelou, "The Heart of a Woman"

And in an argument about the failures of the aircraft industry, another writer uses an analogy for potent contrast:

> If the aircraft industry had evolved as spectacularly as the computer industry over the past twenty-five years, a Boeing 767 would cost five hundred dollars today, and it would circle the globe in twenty minutes on five gallons of fuel.

Other Tropes

Several other tropes deserve special mention.

Hyperbole is the use of overstatement for special effect, a kind of pyrotechnics in prose. The tabloid papers whose headlines scream at shoppers in the grocery checkout line probably qualify as the all-time champions of hyperbole (journalist Tom Wolfe once wrote a satirical review of a *National Enquirer* writers' convention that he titled "Keeps His Mom-in-Law in Chains *meets* Kills Son and Feeds Corpse to Pigs"). Everyone has seen these overstated arguments and, perhaps, marveled at the way they seem to sell.

Hyperbole is also the trademark of more serious writers. In a column arguing that men's magazines fuel the same kind of neurotic anxieties about appearance that have plagued women for so long, Michelle Cottle uses hyperbole and humor to make her point:

> **What self-respecting '90s woman could embrace a publication that runs such enlightened articles as "Turn Your Good Girl Bad" and "How to Wake Up Next to a One-Night Stand"? Or maybe you'll smile and wink knowingly: What red-blooded hetero chick *wouldn't* love all those glossy photo spreads of buff young beefcake in various states of undress, ripped abs and glutes flexed so tightly you could bounce a check on them? Either way you've got the wrong idea. My affection for *Men's Health* is driven by pure gender politics. . . . With page after page of bulging biceps and Gillette jaws, robust hairlines and silken skin, *Men's Health* is peddling a standard of male beauty as unforgiving and unrealistic as the female version sold by those dewy-eyed pre-teen waifs draped across covers of *Glamour* and *Elle*.**
>
> **—Michelle Cottle, "Turning Boys into Girls"**

As you can well imagine, hyperbole of this sort can easily backfire, so it pays to use it sparingly and for an audience whose reactions you believe you can effectively predict.

Understatement, on the other hand, requires a quiet, muted message to make its point effectively. In her memoir, Rosa Parks—an African American civil rights activist who made history in 1955 by refusing to give up her bus seat to a white passenger—uses understatement so often that it might be said to be characteristic of her writing, a mark of her ethos. She refers to Martin Luther King Jr. simply as "a true leader," to Malcolm X as a person of "strong conviction," and to her own lifelong efforts as simply a small way of "carrying on."

Quiet understatement can be particularly effective in arguments. When Watson and Crick published their first article on the structure of DNA, they felt that they had done nothing less than discover the secret of life. (Imagine what the *National Enquirer* headlines might have been for this story!) Yet in an atmosphere of extreme scientific competitiveness they chose to close their article with a vast understatement, using it purposely to gain emphasis: "It has not escaped our notice," they wrote, "that the specific pairing we have postulated immediately suggests a possible copying mechanism for the genetic material." Forty-some years later, considering the profound developments that have taken place in genetics, the power of this understatement resonates even more strongly.

Rhetorical questions don't really require answers. Rather, they are used to help assert or deny something about an argument. In a review of a book-length argument about the use and misuse of power in the Disney dynasty, the reviewer uses a series of rhetorical questions to sketch in part of the book's argument:

> **If you have ever visited one of the Disney theme parks, though, you have likely wondered at the labor—both seen and unseen—necessary to maintain these fanciful environments. How and when are the grounds tended so painstakingly? How are the signs of high traffic erased from public facilities? What keeps employees so poised, meticulously groomed, and endlessly cheerful?**
> —Linda S. Watts, Review of *Inside the Mouse*

Antonomasia is probably most familiar to you from the sports pages: "His Airness" means Michael Jordan; "The Great One," Wayne Gretzky; "The Sultan of Swat," Babe Ruth; and "Fraulein Forehand," Steffi Graf. Such shorthand substitutions of a descriptive word or phrase for a proper name can pack arguments into just one phrase. What does calling Jordan "His Airness" argue about him?

Irony, the use of words to convey a meaning in tension with or opposite to their literal meanings, also works powerfully in arguments. One of the most famous sustained uses of irony in literature occurs in Shakespeare's *Julius Caesar*, as Mark Antony punctuates his condemnation of Brutus with the repeated ironic phrase "But Brutus is an honourable man." In an argument about the inadequacies and dangers of nursing homes, Jill Frawley uses irony in describing herself as "just one little nurse, in one little care facility"; the statement is ironic since as "one little nurse" she has actually made very big differences in nursing home care.

Margaret Curtis opposes the suit brought by the family of Martin Luther King Jr. to copyright his "I Have a Dream" speech, noting that many elements of his speech were drawn from the Bible. She asks the following rhetorical question: "How can the speech be divided into which part was his invention and which was not?"

LINK TO P. 573 ·······································

John Anderson's article in Chapter 23 laments the problems independent filmmakers face in trying to find distributors for films that do not appeal neatly to established audiences that can be marketed to, noting ironically that "black people . . . have the chutzpah to go to the movies in numbers far beyond their population percentile (thus showing insufficient fealty to marketing analysts or other Masters of the Universe)."

LINK TO P. 388 ·······································

SCHEMES

Schemes, figures that depend on word order, can add quite a bit of syntactic "zing" to arguments. Here we present the ones you are likely to see most often at work.

Parallelism uses grammatically similar words, phrases, or clauses for special effect:

> **The Wild Man process involves five basic phases: Sweating, Yelling, Crying, Drum-Beating, and Ripping Your Shirt off Even If It's Expensive.**
>
> > –Joe Bob Briggs, "Get in Touch with Your Ancient Spear"
>
> **We die. That may be the meaning of life. But we *do* language. That may be the measure of our lives.**
>
> > –Toni Morrison, Nobel Prize acceptance speech
>
> **The laws of our land are said to be "by the people, of the people, and for the people."**

Antithesis is the use of parallel structures to mark contrast or opposition:

> **That's one small step for a man, one giant leap for mankind.**
>
> > –Neil Armstrong
>
> **Those who kill people are called murderers; those who kill animals, sportsmen.**
>
> **Love is an ideal thing; marriage a real thing.**

Inverted word order, in which the parts of a sentence or clause are not in the usual subject-verb-object order, can help make arguments particularly memorable:

> **Into this grey lake plopped the thought, I know this man, don't I?**
>
> > –Doris Lessing
>
> **One game does not a championship make.**
>
> **Good looking he was not; wealthy he was not; but brilliant—he was.**

As with anything else, however, too much of such a figure can quickly become, well, too much.

Anaphora, or effective repetition, can act like a drumbeat in an argument, bringing the point home. In an argument about the true meaning of freedom, June Jordan uses repetition to focus on students and the ideals in which they want to believe:

Martin Luther King Jr.'s "I Have a Dream" speech in Chapter 28 uses many anaphoric threads to strong effect. Find five.

········· LINK TO P. 666

CULTURAL CONTEXTS FOR ARGUMENT

Style is always affected by language, culture, and rhetorical tradition. What constitutes effective style, therefore, varies broadly across cultures and depends on the rhetorical situation—purpose, audience, and so on. There is at least one important style question to consider when arguing across cultures: what *level of formality* is most appropriate? In the United States a fairly informal style is often acceptable, even appreciated. Many cultures, however, tend to value more formality. If in doubt, therefore, it is probably wise to err on the side of formality, especially in communicating with elders or with those in authority.

- Take care to use proper titles as appropriate—Ms., Mr., Dr., and so on.

- Do not use first names unless invited to do so.

- Steer clear of slang. Especially when you're communicating with members of other cultures, slang may be seen as disrespectful— and it may not even be understood.

Beyond formality, stylistic preferences vary widely, and when arguing across cultures, the most important stylistic issue might be clarity, especially when you're communicating with people whose native languages are different from your own. In such situations, analogies and similes almost always aid in understanding and can be especially helpful when you're communicating across cultures. Likening something unknown to something familiar can help make your argument forceful—and understandable.

They believe that there is a mainstream majority America that will try to be fair, and that will respect their courage, and admire the intelligence of their defense. They believe that there is a mainstream majority America that will overwhelm the enemies of public and democratic education. They believe that most of us, out here, will despise and resist every assault on freedom in the United States.

–June Jordan, "Freedom Time"

Reversed structures for special effect have been used widely in political argumentation since President John F. Kennedy's Inaugural Address in 1961 charged citizens, "Ask not what your country can do for you; ask what you can do for your country." Like the other figures we have listed here, this one can help make arguments memorable:

The Democrats won't get elected unless things get worse, and things won't get worse until the Democrats get elected.

–Jeanne Kirkpatrick

The Negro needs the white man to free him from his fears. The white man needs the Negro to free him from his guilt.

–Martin Luther King Jr.

When the going gets tough, the tough get going.

DANGERS OF UNDULY SLANTED LANGUAGE

Although all arguments depend on figurative language to some degree, if the words used call attention to themselves as "stacking the deck" in unfair ways, they will not be particularly helpful in achieving the goals of the argument. In preparing your own arguments, you will want to pay special attention to the connotations of the words you choose—those associations that words and phrases always carry with them. The choices you make will always depend on the purpose you have in mind and those to whom you wish to speak. Should you choose *skinny* or *slender* in describing someone? Should you label a group *left-wing agitators, student demonstrators,* or *supporters of human rights?*

A good example of the power of such choices came in an exchange between Jesse Jackson and Michael Dukakis at the 1988 Democratic National Convention. Jackson was offended that Dukakis, who had defeated Jackson for the Democratic presidential nomination, had asserted his leadership of the party by describing himself as "the quarterback on this team," a phrase that reminded many African Americans of an old stereotype that African Americans were not intelligent enough to play quarterback on football teams. For his part, Dukakis was upset when Jackson told the new voters he had brought into the party that they were being used to "carry bales of cotton" up to "the big house," because the connotations of that language were intended to suggest that Dukakis was like a white plantation owner profiting from the labor of African American slaves. Both speakers later voiced second thoughts about their choice of figurative language in such an important public setting.

The lesson for writers of arguments is a simple one that can be devilishly hard to follow: know your audience and be respectful of them, even as you argue strenuously to make your case.

RESPOND•

1. Identify the types of figurative language used in the following advertising slogans—metaphor, simile, analogy, hyperbole, understatement, rhetorical question, antonomasia, irony, parallelism, antithesis, inverted word order, anaphora, or reversed structure.

   "Good to the last drop." (Maxwell House coffee)

   "It's the real thing." (Coca-Cola)

   "Melts in your mouth, not in your hands." (M&M's)

   "Be all that you can be." (U.S. Army)

   "Does she . . . or doesn't she?" (Clairol)

   "Breakfast of champions." (Wheaties)

   "Double your pleasure; double your fun." (Doublemint gum)

   "Let your fingers do the walking." (the Yellow Pages)

   "Think small." (Volkswagen)

   "We try harder." (Avis)

2. We mentioned in this chapter that during the Renaissance, students would memorize and practice more than a hundred figures of speech. As part of their lessons, these students would be asked to write whole paragraphs using each of the figures *in order,* in what might be called "connected discourse": the paragraph makes sense, and each sentence builds on the one that precedes it. Use the following list of figures to write a paragraph of connected discourse on a topic of your choice. Each sentence should use a different figure, starting with metaphor and ending with reversed structure.

metaphor	irony
simile	parallelism
analogy	antithesis
hyperbole	inverted word order
understatement	anaphora
rhetorical question	reversed structure
antonomasia	

   Now rewrite the paragraph, still on the same topic but using the list of figures in *reverse order.* The first sentence should use reversed structure and the last should use metaphor.

3. Some public speakers are well known for their use of tropes and schemes. (Jesse Jackson comes to mind, as does Ross Perot, who

employs folksy sayings to achieve a certain effect.) Using the Internet, find the text of a recent speech by a speaker who uses figures liberally. Pick a paragraph that seems particularly rich in figures, and rewrite it, eliminating every trace of figurative language. Read the two paragraphs—the original and your revised version—aloud to your class. With the class's help, try to imagine rhetorical situations in which the figure-free version would be most appropriate.

Now find some prose that seems dry and completely unfigurative. (A technical manual, instructions for operating appliances, or a legal document might serve.) Rewrite a part of the piece in the most figurative language you can muster. Then try to list rhetorical situations in which this newly figured language might be most appropriate.

chapter fifteen

Visual Arguments

You know you shouldn't buy camping gear just because you see it advertised in a magazine. But what's the harm in imagining yourself on that Arizona mesa, the sun setting, the camp stove open, the tent up and ready? That could be you reminiscing about the rugged trek that got you there, just like the tanned campers in the ad. Now what's that brand name again, and what's its URL?

A student government committee is meeting to talk about campus safety. One member has prepared a series of graphs showing the steady increase in the number of on-campus attacks over the last five years, along with several photographs that really bring these crimes to life.

It turns out that the governor and now presidential candidate who claims to be against taxes actually raised taxes in his home state—according to his opponent, who is running thirty-second TV spots to make that point. The ads feature a plainly dressed woman who sure looks credible; she's got to be a real person, not an actor, and she says he raised taxes. She wouldn't lie—would she?

You've never heard of the trading firm. But the letter, printed on thick bond with smart color graphics, is impressive and, hey, the company CEO is offering you $75 just to open an online account. The $75 check is right at the top of the letter, and it sure looks real. The company's Web site seems quite professional—quick-loading and easy to navigate. Somebody's on the ball. Perhaps you should sign up?

A glittering silver coupe passes you effortlessly on a steep slope along a curving mountain interstate. It's moving too fast for you to read the nameplate, but on the trunk lid you see a three-pointed star. Hmmmm . . . Maybe after you graduate from law school and your student loans are paid off . . .

You've always thought that the jams on the supermarket shelves taste pretty much alike. But those preserves stocked at eye level—the ones from France—look especially appetizing in their squat little jars with the fancy labels and golden lids. They're probably worth the extra dollar.

■ ■ ■

THE POWER OF VISUAL ARGUMENTS

We need not be reminded that visual images have clout. We see the evidence everywhere, from T-shirts to billboards to computer screens. Everyone is trying to get our attention and they are doing it with images as well as words. Technology is also making it easier for people to create and transmit images. And those images are more compelling than ever, brought to us via DVD and HDTV on our computers, on our walls, in our pockets, even in our cars.

But let's put this in perspective. Visual arguments weren't invented by Bill Gates, and they've always had power. The Pharaohs of Egypt lined the Nile with statues of themselves to assert their authority, and Roman emperors stamped their portraits on coins for the same reason.

In our own era, two events marked turning points in the importance of media images. The first occurred in 1960, when presidential candidates John F. Kennedy and Richard M. Nixon met in a nationally televised debate. (See Figure 15.1.) Kennedy, robust and confident in a dark suit, faced a pale and haggard Nixon barely recovered from an illness. Kennedy looked cool and "presidential"; Nixon did not. Many believe that the contrasting images Kennedy and Nixon presented on that evening radically changed the direction of the 1960 election campaign, leading to Kennedy's narrow victory. For better or worse, the debate also established television as the chief medium for political communication in the United States.

FIGURE 15.1   RICHARD NIXON AND JOHN KENNEDY BEFORE A TELEVISED DEBATE, 1960

The second event is more recent—the introduction in the early 1980s of personal computers with graphic interfaces. These machines, which initially seemed strange and toylike, operated with icons and pictures rather than through arcane commands. Subtly at first, and then with the smack of a tsunami, graphic computers (the only kind we use now) moved people away from an age of print into an era of electronic, image-saturated communications.

So that's where we are at the start of a new millennium. People today are adjusting rapidly to a world of seamless, multichannel communications. Our prophet is Marshall McLuhan, the guru of *Wired* magazine who proclaimed some forty years ago that "the medium is the message." Is the medium also the massage—an artful manipulator of how we think and feel? Anyone reading and writing today has to be prepared to deal with arguments that shuffle more than words.

SHAPING THE MESSAGE

Images make arguments of their own. A photograph, for example, isn't a faithful representation of reality; it's reality shaped by the photographer's point of view. Photographic and video arguments can be seen at work everywhere, but perhaps particularly so during political campaigns. Staff photographers and handlers work to place candidates in settings that will show them in the best possible light—shirtsleeves rolled up, surrounded by smiling children and red-white-and-blue bunting—while their opponents look for opportunities to present them in a bad light. Closer to home, perhaps, you may well have chosen photographs that showed you at your best to include in your college applications. Employers often judge potential employees by the image their clothing helps to create, and universities hire special consultants to help them create attractive "brand" images.

If those producing images shape the messages these images convey—and they certainly do—those "reading" them are by no means passive. Human vision is selective: to some extent, we actively shape what we see. Much of what we see is laden with cultural meanings, too, and we must have "learned" to see them in certain ways. Consider the Statue of Liberty welcoming immigrants to America's shores—and then imagine her instead as Bellona, the goddess of war, guarding New York Harbor with a blazing torch. For a moment at least, she's a different statue.

Of course, we don't always see things the same way, which is one reason eyewitnesses to the same event often report it differently. Or why even instant replays don't always solve disputed calls on football fields.

The visual images that surround us today—and that argue forcefully for our attention and often for our time and money—are constructed to invite, perhaps even coerce, us into seeing them just one way. But each of us has our own powers of vision, our own frames of reference. So visual arguments might best be described as a give-and-take, a dialogue, or even a tussle.

Consider the photo of Calista Flockhart that illustrates Ellen Goodman's article about changing notions of body image in Fiji. What does this photo contribute to Goodman's argument and to its persuasiveness?

LINK TO P. 402 ···

ACHIEVING VISUAL LITERACY

Why take images so seriously? Because they matter. Images change lives and shape behavior. When advertisements for sneakers are powerful enough to lead some kids to kill for the coveted footwear, when five- and ten-second images and sound bites are deciding factors in presidential elections, when the image of Joe Camel is credibly accused of enticing youngsters to smoke, or when a cultural icon like Oprah Winfrey can sell more books in one TV show than a hundred writers might do—it's high time to start paying careful attention to visual elements of argument.

How text is presented affects how it is read—whether it is set in fancy type, plain type, or handwritten; whether it has illustrations or not; whether it looks serious, fanciful, scholarly, or commercial. Figure 15.2 shows one short passage from Martin Luther King Jr.'s "I Have a Dream" speech presented four different ways—as poetry, as an excerpt in newspaper coverage of the speech, as part of a poster, and as it appears in plain text off the Web. Look at the four different versions of this text and consider in each case how the presentation affects the way you perceive and read King's argument. Do the photographs, for example, make King's words seem more—or less—powerful? Does the version set as poetry have more—or less— impact on you? The point, of course, is that as you read any text, you need to consider its presentation—a crucial element in any written argument.

FIGURE 15.2 FOUR DIFFERENT PRESENTATIONS OF THE SAME TEXT FROM "I HAVE A DREAM" (A) AS POETRY; (B) AS NEWSPAPER TEXT; (C) AS A POSTER; (D) AS WEB TEXT

from "I Have a Dream"

I say to you today, my friends,
That in spite of the difficulties
And frustrations of the moment,

I still have a dream. It is a dream
Deeply rooted in the American dream.

I have a dream that one day
This nation will rise up and live
out the true meaning of its creed:

"We hold these truths to be self-evident:
that all men are created equal."

a

I say to you today, my friends, that in spite of the difficulties and frustrations of the moment, I still have a dream. It is a dream deeply rooted in the American dream. I have a dream that one day this nation will rise up and live out the true meaning of its creed: "We hold these truths to be self-evident: that all men are created equal."

b

I say to you today, my friends, that in spite of the difficulties and frustrations of the moment, I still have a dream. It is a dream deeply rooted in the American dream.

I have a dream that one day this nation will rise up and live out the true meaning of its creed: "We hold these truths to be self-evident: that all men are created equal."

c

I say to you today, my friends, that in spite of the difficulties and frustrations of the moment, I still have a dream. It is a dream deeply rooted in the American dream.

I have a dream that one day this nation will rise up and live out the true meaning of its creed: "We hold these truths to be self-evident: that all men are created equal."

d

257

ANALYZING VISUAL ELEMENTS OF ARGUMENTS

We've probably said enough to suggest that analyzing the visual elements of argument is a challenge, one that's even greater as we begin to encounter multimedia appeals as well, especially on the Web. Here are some questions that can help you recognize—and analyze—visual and multimedia arguments:

ABOUT CONTENT

- What argumentative purpose does the visual convey? What do its creators intend for its effects to be? What is it designed to convey?

- What media does the visual use—print, screen, photographs, drawings, video clips, graphs, charts? Is there sound as well? What are the strengths (or limits) of the media chosen?

- What cultural values or ideals does the visual evoke or suggest? The good life? Love and harmony? Sex appeal? Youth? Adventure? Economic power or dominance? Freedom? Does the visual reinforce these values or question them? What do the visuals do to strengthen the argument?

- What emotions does the visual evoke? Which ones do you think it intends to evoke? Desire? Envy? Empathy? Shame or guilt? Pride? Nostalgia? Something else?

ABOUT DESIGN

- What is your eye drawn to first? Why? How do other media come into play?

- What is in the foreground? In the background? What is in or out of focus? What is moving? What is placed high, and what is placed low? What is to the left, in the center, and to the right? What effect do these placements have on the message?

- Is any particular information highlighted (such as a name, face, or scene) to attract your attention?

- How are light and color used? What effect(s) are they intended to have on you? What about video? Sound?

- What details are included or emphasized? What details are omitted or deemphasized? To what effect? Is anything downplayed, ambiguous, confusing, distracting, or obviously omitted? To what ends?

- Does the visual evoke positive—or negative—feelings about individuals, scenes, or ideas?

- Is anything in the visual repeated, intensified, or exaggerated? Is anything presented as "supernormal" or idealistic? What effects are intended by these strategies, and what effects do they have on you as a viewer?

- What is the role of any words that accompany the visual? How do they clarify or reinforce (or blur or contradict) the message?

- How are you directed to move within the argument? Are you encouraged to read further? Click on a link? Scroll down? Fill out a form? Provide your email address? Place an order?

Take a look at the Web page in Figure 15.3, the 1999–2000 home page of United Colors of Benetton, a company that sells sportswear, handbags,

FIGURE 15.3 BENETTON HOME PAGE, JANUARY 2000 <**http://benetton.com**>

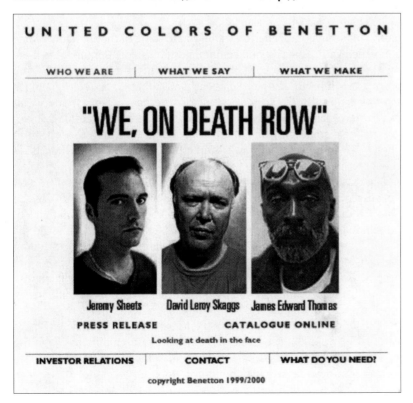

shoes, and more. You might expect a company that sells eighty million items of clothing and accessories annually to feature garments on its home page or to make a pitch to sell you something. And you would find many of those items if you probed the Benetton site more deeply. But here on the company's main page, you see three death-row inmates staring out from under the bold headline, "WE, ON DEATH ROW." The phrase suggests a kind of community, an odd recasting of "We, the people . . ." The convicts are all men—two white, one black—and they seem calm, resigned. The photographs present the men, carefully lighted, framed by soft but potent colors. Clearly, these aren't prison snapshots, but the art of a skilled professional working to make a point with these images.

The portraits so dominate the Web page that it might take you a few moments to notice the actual heading of the page—the name of the company poised above three helpful links: "Who We Are," "What We Say," and "What We Make." Clicking "What We Say" takes you to a page headed by this claim: "ALL HUMAN BEINGS ARE BORN FREE AND EQUAL IN DIGNITY AND RIGHTS." It seems that Benetton wants you to think of the company as one concerned with issues beyond commerce and fashion. Commerce is there on the Benetton home page as well. Beneath the photographs of the convicts are links to "Investor Relations" and "What Do You Need?" But it's hard to ignore those faces or to escape the nagging question—what exactly have the convicts to do with Benetton's core mission? Maybe then you notice a small gray line of type: "Looking at death in the face." You click it for more information. Nothing happens: it is not a link. It's a thought: these men are going to die.

That's what Benetton wants you to ponder as it creates for itself an aura of involvement and concern for social issues. Or, to use the company's own words, available under its "Press Release" link (hard to miss in red): "Benetton has once again chosen to look reality in the face by tackling a social issue, as it did in previous campaigns that focused on war, AIDS, discrimination and racism." So the manufacturer of clothing and accessories promotes its wares through an involvement in social activism. And so its images challenge you to judge the character of the company by looking reality in the face. Do you admire its concerns and its willingness to take controversial stands? Do you consider what's not on the Web page —images of the convicts' victims—which could boldly challenge the statement Benetton is making? Or do you do some of both as you begin to weigh the various perspectives on this argument?

Check out the three men's underwear ads from the last fifty years in Chapter 23. What do they tell you about the changing attitudes about the male body in America?

LINK TO P. 432

USING VISUALS IN YOUR OWN ARGUMENTS

You too can, and perhaps must, use visuals in your writing. Many college classes now call for projects to be posted on the Web, which almost always involves the use of images. Many courses also require students to make multimedia presentations using software such as PowerPoint, or even good, old-fashioned overhead projectors with transparencies.

Here we sketch out some basic principles of visual rhetoric. To help you appreciate the argumentative character of visual texts, we examine them under some of the same categories we use for written and oral arguments earlier in this book (Chapters 4, 6, and 7), though in a different order. You may be surprised by some of the similarities you will see in visual and verbal arguments.

Visual Arguments Based on Character

What does character have to do with visual argument? Consider two argumentative essays submitted to an instructor. One is scrawled in thick pencil on pages ripped from a spiral notebook, little curls of paper still dangling from the left margin. The other is neatly typed on bond and in a form the professor likely regards as "professional." Is there much doubt about which argument will (at least initially) get the more sympathetic reading? You might object that appearances *shouldn't* count for so much, and you would have a point. The argument scratched in pencil could be the stronger piece, but it faces an uphill battle because its author has sent the wrong signals. Visually, the writer seems to be saying "I don't much care about this message or the people to whom I am sending it."

There may be times when you want to send exactly such a signal to an audience. Some TV advertisements aimed at young people are deliberately designed to antagonize older audiences with their noisy soundtracks, MTV-style quick cuts, and in-your-face style. The point is that the visual rhetoric of any piece you create ought to be a deliberate choice, not an accident. Also keep control of your own visual image. In most cases, when you present an argument, you want to appear authoritative and credible.

Look for images that reinforce your authority and credibility.

For a brochure about your new small business, for instance, you would need to consider images that prove your company has the resources to do its job. Consumers might feel better seeing that you have an actual office, up-to-date equipment, and a competent staff. Similarly, for a Web site about a company or organization you represent, you would consider including its logo or emblem. Such emblems have authority and weight. That's why university Web sites so often include the seal of the institution somewhere on the home page, or why the president of the United States always travels with a presidential seal to hang upon the speaker's podium. The emblem or logo, like the hood ornament on a car, can convey a wealth of cultural and historical implications. (See Figure 15.4.)

Consider how design reflects your character.

Almost every design element sends signals about character and ethos, so be sure you control them. For example, the type fonts you select for a document can mark you as warm and inviting or efficient and contemporary. The warm and readable fonts often belong to a family called *serif.* The serifs are those little flourishes at the ends of their strokes that make the fonts seem handcrafted and artful:

> warm and readable (New York)
>
> warm and readable (Times New Roman)
>
> **warm and readable (Bookman)**

Cleaner and modern are fonts without the flourishes, rather predictably called *sans serif.* These fonts are colder and simpler—and, some argue, more readable on a computer screen (depending on screen resolution):

> efficient and contemporary (Helvetica)
>
> **efficient and contemporary (Arial Black)**
>
> efficient and contemporary (Geneva)

FIGURE 15.4 THREE IMAGES: THE U.S. PRESIDENTIAL SEAL, THE MCDONALD'S LOGO, AND THE BMW ORNAMENT

You may also be able to use decorative fonts. These are appropriate for special uses, but not for extended texts:

decorative and special uses (Zapf Chancery)

decoratiue and special uses (Chicago)

Other typographic elements shape your ethos as well. The size of type, for one, can make a difference. You'll seem to be shouting if your headings or text is boldfaced and too large. Tiny type might make you seem evasive.

Lose weight! Pay nothing!*

*Excludes the costs of enrollment and required meal purchases. Minimum contract: 12 months.

Similarly, your choice of color—especially for backgrounds—can make a statement about your taste, personality, and common sense. For instance, you'll make a bad impression with a Web page whose background colors or patterns make reading difficult. If you want to be noticed, you might use bright colors—the same sort that would make an impression in clothing or cars. But more discrete shades might be a better choice in many situations.

Don't ignore the impact of illustrations and photographs. What you picture can send powerful signals about your preferences, sensitivities, and inclusiveness—and it's not always easy. A few years ago, the organizers of a national meeting of writing teachers created a convention program alive with images of women and minorities. But it had more pictures of elephants than of white men—a laughable gaffe in this case, but one that illustrates the problem of reaching all audiences.

Even your choice of medium says something about you. If you decide to make an appeal on a Web site, you send signals about your technical skills and contemporary orientation. A presentation that relies on an overhead projector gives a different impression than one presented on an LCD projector with software. Even the way you dress can affect a spoken argument, enhancing your appeal—or distracting viewers from your message.

Follow required design conventions.

Many kinds of writing have required design conventions. When that's the case, follow them to the letter. It's no accident that lab reports for science courses are sober and unembellished. Visually, they reinforce the serious character of scientific work. The same is true of a college research paper. You might resent the tediousness of placing page numbers in the right place or aligning long quotations just so, but these visual details help convey your competence. So whether you are composing a term paper, résumé, screen-play, or Web site, look for authoritative models and follow them.

Visual Arguments Based on Facts and Reason

We tend to associate facts and reason with verbal arguments, but here too visual elements play an essential role. Indeed, it is hard to imagine a compelling presentation these days that does not rely, to some degree, on visual elements to enhance or even make the argument.

Many readers and listeners now expect ideas to be represented graphi-cally. Not long ago, media critics ridiculed the colorful charts and graphs in newspapers like *USA Today*. Today, comparable features appear in even the most traditional publications *because they work*. They convey informa-tion efficiently.

Organize information visually.

A design works well when readers can look at an item and understand what it does. A brilliant, much-copied example of such an intuitive design is a seat adjuster invented many years ago by Mercedes-Benz. It is shaped like a tiny seat. Push any element of the control and the real seat moves the same way—back and forth, up and down. No instructions are necessary.

Good visual design can work the same way in an argument, conveying information without elaborate instructions. Titles, headings, subheadings, pull quotes, running heads, boxes, and so on are some common visual signals. When you present parallel headings in a similar type font, size, and color, you make it clear that the information under these headings is in some way related. So in a conventional term paper, you should use headings and subheadings to group information that is connected or par-allel. Similarly, on a Web site, you might create two or three types of head-ings for groups of related information.

You should also make comparable inferences about the way text should be arranged on a page: look for relationships among items that should look alike. In this book, for example, bulleted lists are used to offer specific guidelines. You might use a list or a box to set off information that should be treated differently from the rest of the presentation, or you might visually mark it in other ways—by shading, color, or typography.

An item presented in large type or under a larger headline should be more important than one that gets less visual attention. Place illustra-tions carefully: what you position front and center will appear more important than items in less conspicuous places. On a Web site, key head-ings should usually lead to subsequent pages on the site.

Needless to say, you take a risk if you violate the expectations of your audience or if you present a visual text without coherent signals. Particularly for Web-based materials that may be accessible to people around the world, you can't make many assumptions about what will count as "coherent" across cultures. So you need to think about the roadmap you are giving viewers whenever you present them with a visual text. But design principles do evolve and change from medium to medium. A printed text or an overhead slide, for example, ordinarily works best when its elements are easy to read, simply organized, and surrounded by restful white space. But some types of Web pages seem to thrive on visual clutter, attracting and holding audiences by the variety of information they can pack onto a relatively limited screen. Check out the way the opening screens of most search engines assault a viewer with enticements (Google is a notable exception). Yet, look closely, and you will also see logic in these designs.

Use visuals to convey information efficiently.

Words are immensely powerful and capable of enormous precision and subtlety. But the simple fact is that some information is conveyed more efficiently by charts, graphs, drawings, maps, or photos than by words. When making an argument, especially to a large group, consider what information should be delivered in nonverbal form.

A pie chart is an effective way of comparing a part to the whole. You might use a pie chart to illustrate the ethnic composition of your school, the percentage of taxes paid by people at different income levels, or the consumption of energy by different nations. Pie charts depict such information memorably. (See Figure 15.5.)

FIGURE 15.5 PIE CHART SHOWING RACIAL AND ETHNIC ORIGIN IN THE UNITED STATES, **1990.** *SOURCE:* U.S. BUREAU OF THE CENSUS, 1991.

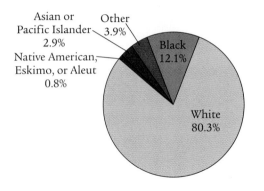

A graph is an efficient device for comparing items over time or other variables. You could use a graph to trace the rise and fall of test scores over several decades, or to show the growth of churches, as in Figure 15.6.

Diagrams or drawings are useful for drawing attention to details. You can use drawings to illustrate complex physical processes or designs of all sort. Indeed, it might have been the artful renderings of President Reagan's proposed Star Wars missile shield in the 1980s that helped to sell the country on the project. Defense Department films showed incoming missiles being destroyed by lasers and smart projectiles—even though no hardware had been built.

You can use maps to illustrate location and spatial relationships—something as simple as the distribution of office space in your student union or as complex as the topography of Utah. Such information might be far more difficult to explain using words alone.

Follow professional guidelines for presenting visuals.

Charts, graphs, tables, and illustrations play such an important role in many fields that professional groups have come up with specific guidelines for labeling and formatting these items. You need to become famil-

FIGURE 15.6 CHURCH GROWTH BY DENOMINATION, 1700–1780. *SOURCE:* JAMES HENRETTA ET AL., *AMERICA'S HISTORY.* NY: WORTH, 1997.

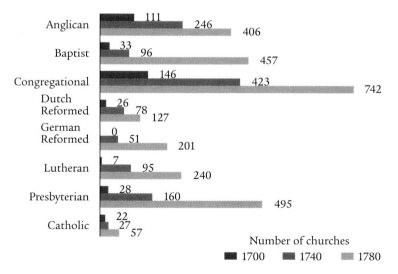

iar with those conventions as you advance in a field. A guide such as the *Publication Manual of the American Psychological Association* (4th edition) or the *MLA Style Manual and Guide to Scholarly Publishing* (2nd edition) describes these rules in detail.

You also must be careful to respect copyright rules when you use visual items created by someone else. It is relatively easy now to download visual texts of all kinds from the Web. Some of these items—like clip art—may be in the public domain, meaning that you are free to use them without paying a royalty. But other visual texts may require permission, especially if you intend to publish your work or use the item commercially. And remember: anything you place on a Web site is considered "published."

Visual Arguments That Appeal to Emotion

To some extent, we tend to be suspicious of arguments supported by visual and multimedia elements because they can seem to manipulate our senses. And many advertisements, political documentaries, rallies, marches, and even church services do in fact use visuals to trigger our emotions. Who has not teared up at a funeral when members of a veteran's family are presented with the flag, a bugler blowing Taps in the distance? Who doesn't recall the public service announcement that featured a fried egg ("This is your brain on drugs")? You might also have seen or heard about *Triumph of the Will,* a Nazi propaganda film from the 1930s that powerfully depicts Hitler as the benign savior of the German people, a hero of Wagnerian dimensions. It is a chilling reminder of how images can be manipulated and abused.

Yet you cannot flip through a magazine without being cajoled or seduced by images of all kinds—most of them designed in some way to attract your eye and mind. Not all such seductions are illicit, nor should you avoid them when emotions can support the legitimate claims you hope to advance.

Appreciate the emotional power of images.

Images can bring a text or presentation to life. Sometimes the images have power in and of themselves to persuade. This was the case with images in the 1960s that showed civil rights demonstrators being assaulted by police dogs and water hoses. Images of starving children in Somalia in the early 1990s had similar power, leading to relief efforts. (See Figure 15.7.)

FIGURE 15.7 SOMALI CHILD, 1992

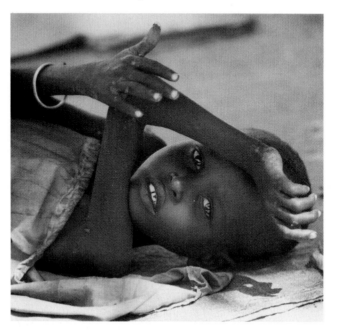

Images you select for a presentation may be equally effective if the visual text works well with other components of the argument. Indeed, a given image might support many different kinds of arguments. Take, for example, the famous *Apollo 8* photograph of our planet as a big blue marble hanging above the horizon of the moon (Figure 15.8). You might use this image to introduce an argument about the need for additional investment in the space program. Or it might become part of an argument about the need to preserve our frail natural environment, or part of an argument against nationalism: *from space, we are one world.* You could, of course, make any of these claims without the image. But the photograph—like most images—may touch members of your audience more powerfully than words alone could.

Appreciate the emotional power of color.

Consider the color red. It attracts hummingbirds—and cops. It excites the human eye in ways that other colors don't. You can make a powerful

FIGURE 15.8 EARTH SHINING OVER THE MOON

statement with a red dress or a red car—or red shoes. In short, red evokes emotions. But so do black, green, pink, and even brown. That we respond to color is part of our biological and cultural makeup. So it makes sense to consider carefully what colors are compatible with the kind of argument you are making. You might find that the best choice is black on a white background.

In most situations, you can be guided in your selection of colors by your own good taste (guys—check your ties), by designs you admire, or by the advice of friends or helpful professionals. Some design and presentation software will even help you choose colors by offering you dependable "default" shades or by offering an array of preexisting designs and compatible colors—for example, of presentation slides.

The colors you choose for a design should follow certain commonsense principles. If you are using background colors on a poster, Web site, or slide, the contrast between words and background should be vivid enough to make reading easy. For example, white letters on a yellow background will likely prove illegible. Any bright background color should be avoided for a long document. Indeed, reading seems easiest with dark letters against a light or white background. Avoid complex patterns, even though they might look interesting and be easy to create. Quite often, they interfere with other, more important elements of your presentation.

As you use visuals in your college projects, test them on prospective readers. That's what professionals do because they appreciate how delicate the choices about visual and multimedia texts can be. These responses will help you analyze your own arguments as well as improve your success with them.

RESPOND.

1. Find an advertisement with both verbal and visual elements. Analyze the ad's visual argument by answering some of the questions on pp. 258–59, taking care to "reread" its visual elements just as carefully as you would its words. After you've answered each question as thoroughly as possible, switch ads with a classmate and analyze the new argument in the same way. Then compare your own and your classmate's responses to the two advertisements. If they are different—and there is every reason to expect they will be—how do you account for the differences? What is the effect of audience on the argument's reception? What are the differences between your own active reading and your classmate's?

2. Criticism of Camel cigarettes "spokesman" Joe Camel has led Camel's manufacturer to agree to severe restrictions on its ad campaign. Obviously, the image of an ultra-cool, pool-playing camel has great power over children, enticing them to begin smoking at ever-younger ages. Or does it? Debates about Joe's persuasive power are far from settled, with reasonable people weighing in on both sides.

   Write a letter to the editor of a general-circulation newspaper arguing that visual images like Joe Camel do not influence viewers to the degree that antismoking advocates claim. As an alternative, write a one-paragraph topic proposal—a plan for a longer paper—for an English class, in which you argue that such visual arguments do carry great weight and should be regulated. To write either of these documents, you'll need to do some research on the current conversation about advertising images and regulation. You'll also need to provide compelling reasons to support your claim. Remember that you should use this process as a form of inquiry, and not just to find information; develop your own arguments as a result of listening to others'.

3. If you have used the World Wide Web, you have no doubt noticed the relationships between visual design and textual material. In the best Web pages, the elements work together rather than simply competing for space. In fact, even if you have not used the Web, you still know a great deal about graphic design: newspapers, magazines, and your own college papers make use of design principles to create effective texts.

   Find three or four Web or magazine pages that you think exemplify good visual design—and then find just as many that do not. When you've picked the good and bad designs, draw a rough sketch of their physical layout. Where are the graphics? Where is the text? What are the relative size and relationship of text blocks to graphics? How is color used? Can you discern common principles among the pages, or does each good page work well in its own way? Write a brief explanation of what you find, focusing on the way the visual arguments influence audiences.

4. If you have access to the Internet, go to the Pulitzer Prize Archives at <http://www.pulitzer.org/archive/>. Pick a year to review and then study the images of the winners in three categories: editorial cartooning, spot news photography, and feature photography. (Click on "Works" to see the images.) From among the images you review, choose one you believe makes a strong argument. Then, in a paragraph, describe that image and the argument it makes.

chapter sixteen

Arguments in Electronic Environments

A student who's just loaded a new Web browser goes looking for online sources to develop a research assignment about a contemporary political issue. Looking for newsgroups, she notices that the default service on the browser offers many discussion groups sponsored by a big software company. But many of the groups she ordinarily consults don't seem to be available. She contemplates writing her research paper on the way commercial interests can shape and limit political discussion on the Web.

You send email to a friend questioning the integrity of your state's high school competency examinations. You mention irregularities you yourself have witnessed in testing procedures. A week later, you find passages from your original email circulating in a listserv. The remarks aren't attributed to you, but they are sure stirring up a ruckus.

One of the news-talk channels is exploring the issue of genetically engineered foods. Unfortunately, the experts being interviewed have to squeeze in their opinions among interruptions from two aggressive hosts, questions from generally hostile callers, and commercials for Viagra. Meanwhile, the hosts are urging viewers to participate in an online poll on the subject posted on the network's Web site. The results, they admit, are unscientific.

Browsing the <humanities.lit.authors.Shakespeare> newsgroup, you are annoyed to read a flurry of postings arguing that someone other than William Shakespeare of Stratford-upon-Avon wrote the plays. You join the fray by suggesting that these anti-Stratfordians "get a life." Your insult provokes an angry discussion that settles down only when a writer from California offers a much more detailed defense of Shakespeare's authorship than you did. You are relieved to be off the hook.

You've been discussing gender roles on a MOO with a woman who calls herself Sue. She sure seems to have your number, almost anticipating the arguments you make. Even though you find her positions untenable, you admire her intuition and perception. Then you discover that Sue is really your roommate Mike! He says he has enjoyed playing with your mind.

■ ■ ■

If ancient Greece provided classical Western models for oral arguments, and the European Renaissance gave birth to the printed book, the current era will surely be remembered for the electronic expression of ideas. Within the last decade or so, computers have fostered new environments where ideas can be examined, discussed, and debated in configurations many might never have imagined—some beautifully suited to the give-and-take of argument. Is there a special rhetoric of argument for such environments, a way of making effective and honest claims in this brave new world? Clearly there is, but it's a work in progress, evolving gradually as people learn to cross boundaries among written, aural, and visual texts.

It's an exciting time for extending the reach of the human mind. What follows are some observations and speculations about the play of argument online, including email and discussion groups, synchronous communications, and the World Wide Web.

EMAIL AND DISCUSSION GROUPS

Email, Usenet groups, and listservs all transmit electronic messages via the Internet from person to person. Sometimes the messages go from one individual to another; in other cases, they are distributed to groups or to anyone with Internet access. (But this rapid communication has changed more than the speed by which individuals can share ideas.)

Email

Ed Madden's piece was written originally as an email message to many of his friends and colleagues in response to the many questions and comments he heard after Ellen DeGeneres came out on her TV show.

LINK TO P. 649

Like the telephone, microwave, and VCR, email has earned its place as an essential technology, supporting instant and reliable communication around the globe. An email message can be a private communication to one person or a message distributed among groups, large and small, creating communities linked by information. Unlike regular ("snail") mail, email makes back-and-forth discussions easy and quick: people can speak their minds, survey opinion, or set agendas for face-to-face meetings. And they can meet at all hours, since electronic messages arrive whenever a server routes them. Increasingly, email communication will be wireless, available via cell phone or other mobile devices.

An email message has a character of its own, halfway between the formality of a letter and the intimacy of a telephone conversation. It can feel less intrusive than a phone call, yet at the same time be more insistent— the person too shy to say something in person or on the phone may speak up boldly in email. Like a letter, email preserves a textual record of all thoughts and comments, an advantage in many situations. Yet because it is less formal than a business letter, readers tend to ignore or forgive slips in email (misspellings, irregular punctuation and capitalization) that might disturb them in another type of message.

Arguments in email operate by some new conventions. First, they tend to be "dialogic," with a rapid back-and-forth of voices in conversation. When you send an email, you can usually anticipate a quick reply. In fact, "reply" is an automatic function in email; select it, and your response to a message is attached to the original communication. Second, the very ease and speed of response in email invite rebuttals that may be less carefully considered than those sent by snail mail. Third, because email can be easily forwarded, your arguments may travel well beyond your intended audience, a factor to consider before clicking on "send."

Much advice about email is obvious once you've used it for a while. For one thing, although email messages can be quite lengthy, most people won't tolerate an argument that requires them to scroll through page after page of unrelieved print. You'll likely make a stronger impression with a concise claim, one that fits on a single screen if possible. If you are replying to an email message, send back just enough of the original posting so that your reader knows what you are responding to; this will set your claim within a context.

Remember, too, that your email messages need to be verbally powerful, since the medium may not support some of the formatting options you might otherwise use to enhance your authority. Not all email software supports boldface, italics, multiple fonts, or graphics. But you can highlight your ideas by skipping lines between paragraphs to open some white space, bulleting key ideas or short lists, drawing lines, and following the email convention of using asterisks before and after text you want to emphasize: "Do *not* delete this message before printing it out." In general, don't use all capital letters, LIKE THIS, for emphasis. The online equivalent of shouting, it will alienate many readers — as will using all lowercase letters, which makes text harder to read.

Your email signature, known as a .sig file, can influence readers, too. Automatically attached to the bottom of every email you send (unless you switch this function off), your .sig file might include your address, phone numbers, fax numbers, and professional credentials. You can use the signature as a way to reinforce your credibility by explaining who you are and what you do. Here is an example:

Celia Garcia
Executive Secretary
Students for Responsive Government
University of Texas at San Antonio

Usenet Newsgroups and Listservs

Usenet is an electronic network that provides access to thousands of newsgroups, interactive discussion forums classified by subject and open to anyone with email access to the network. Listservs also use the

Internet to bring together people with common interests, but they are more specialized: you have to subscribe to a particular listserv to receive its messages. In both newsgroups and listservs, messages consist of email-like postings that can be linked topically to form threads exploring particular subjects.

Newsgroups and listservs would seem to be a natural environment for productive argument—where knowledgeable people worldwide can bring and exchange their perspectives and work toward consensus. Unfortunately, not all group discussions live up to this potential. The relative anonymity of online communication removes an important rhetorical component from some debates—the respectable ethos. The result has often been a dumbing down of discussions, especially in newsgroups with the less-regulated "alt." designation. And because postings are so easy in either type of forum, even more responsible groups can be inundated or spammed with pointless messages, unwanted advertisements, and irrational diatribes.

Nevertheless, newsgroups and listservs can be stimulating places for interchanges, particularly where the subject matter is specialized enough to attract informed and interested participants. Before posting, you owe it to the group to learn something about it, either by reading some messages already posted in a newsgroup or by subscribing to a listserv and lurking for enough time to gain a feel for the way issues are introduced, discussed, and debated. If a group offers a file of frequently asked questions (known as FAQs), read what it has to say about the group's rules of discourse and print it out for later reference.

When you decide to join in a conversation, be sure your posting contains enough information to make a smooth transition between the message to which you are responding and your own contribution to the group. If you have little to contribute, don't bother posting. A comment such as "I agree" wastes the time of everyone in the group who bothers to download your item—as some of the members may tell you in none-too-polite terms. In fact, if you are new to the Internet, you may be surprised at the temper of some online conversation participants. You can get *flamed*—bombarded with email—for asking a question that has already been asked and answered repeatedly by other members, for veering too far from the topic of discussion, or just for sending a message someone doesn't like. Flaming is unfortunate, but it is also a reality of newsgroups and listservs.

As sources for academic work, listservs are probably more reliable than newsgroups, though both forums can help you grasp the range of opinion

WEB SITES

Web sites make arguments of a different sort. These sites consist of electronic pages of information (which may include any combination of words, images, sounds, and film clips) that are linked hypertextually, meaning that you can move from one page to another by clicking your computer's mouse button on parts of a page that are identified as links. Generally, there's no prescribed sequence to those links; you browse through the pages of a site or the entire World Wide Web according to your interests. Therefore, someone coming to a site that you create may not follow the links you provide in the order you had imagined. Readers become participants in your site, with critical agendas of their own.

What are the implications for argument? The Web would seem to suit many traditional components of argument and then to complicate them. Web pages might include conventional claims supported in traditional ways with evidence and good reasons. But instead of merely summarizing or paraphrasing evidence and providing a source citation, a Web author might furnish links to the primary evidence itself—to statistics borrowed directly from a government Web site or to online documents at a university library. Indeed, links within a Web page can be a version of documentation, leading to the very material the original author examined, full and complete.

A site might also provide links to other sites dealing with the same issue, usher readers to discussion groups about it, or (if it's a sophisticated site like those operated by the national political parties) even support chatrooms of its own where anyone can offer an opinion in real time. Perhaps most revolutionary of all, a Web site can incorporate visual and aural elements of diverse kinds into its argument, not as embellishments but as actual persuasive devices. Indeed, writers today need to learn these new techniques of document design if they expect to communicate in this complex medium.

How do arguments actually get made on the Web? The fact is that people are still learning. Already, almost every political group, interest group, academic institution, corporation, and government entity has a Web presence. The home page or full Web site is the "face" an institution uses to present its ethos to readers, a version of what we have called "arguments based on character." Here we can find intriguing differences in the ways arguments may be offered. In 1997, an "off year" in election cycles, the home pages for both the Republican and Democratic National Committees featured many soft-sell elements, crafted to make people feel good about the political parties. The Republicans displayed an image of a Republican Main Street that included, for instance, a red brick schoolhouse topped by a huge American flag. The Democratic Party site unfolded in bold red, white, and blue hues and featured an eye-catching photograph of President Clinton and the first lady sharing a picture book with a group of children. By 2000, however, a presidential election year, the character of both sites had evolved and the arguments presented had harder edges. Most of the inviting graphics were gone, replaced by links that made direct attacks on opposition candidates: "Bush Lite"; Al Gore as Flipper. Whereas the earlier sites seemed to welcome everyone, the election-year pages looked as if they were aimed at true believers.

Beyond home pages of this kind, Web sites typically contain more substantive information. Many sites include extended prose arguments supported by the same kinds of charts, statistics, and graphs you might find in books or newsmagazines. For instance, in 1998 a site sponsored by Common Cause, a progressive citizens' group <http://www.common cause.org/laundromat/index.htm>, provided a series of studies of what it called "the money trail in politics," which were designed to direct readers to information about financial influence in national politics. As shown in Figure 16.1, the page used a simple layout and clever graphics to make its points.

When crafting a Web site designed to present an argument of your own, you will want not only to take full advantage of the electronic medium but also to meet its distinctive challenges. Your pages need to be graphically interesting to persuade readers to enter your site and to encourage them to read your lengthier arguments. If you just post a traditional argument, thick with prose paragraphs that have to be scrolled endlessly, readers might ignore it. Check out the way the online periodical *Slate* <http://www.slate.com> arranges its articles to make them Web readable, or examine the design of other sites you find especially effective in presenting an argument.

Since the Web encourages browsing and surfing, you also need to consider how to cluster ideas so that they retain their appeal. In a traditional print argument, though you can't prevent readers from skipping around and looking ahead, you can largely control the direction they take through your material, from claim to warrant to evidence. On a Web page, however, readers usually want to choose their own paths. Inevitably that means they will play a larger role in constructing *your* argument. You lose an element of control, but your argument gains a new dimension, particularly if you provide links that help readers understand how you came to

"If Plan A Fails, Go to Plan B," a Web site shown in Chapter 29, is an advertisement for a morning-after contraception program. Contraception is a very private topic; notice how the site has been designed to accommodate readers who may not be viewing it in a very private place.

······························· LINK TO P. 698

FIGURE **16.1** COMMON CAUSE WEB PAGE

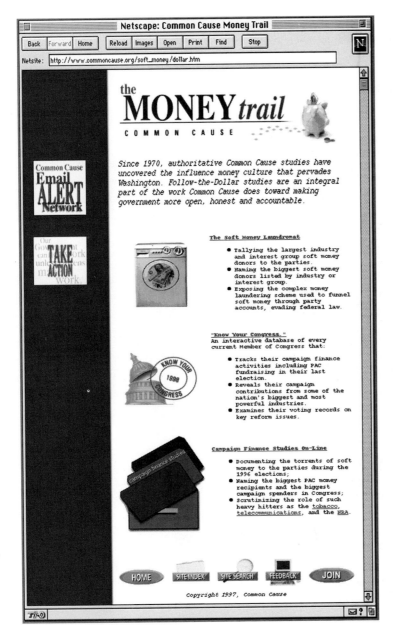

your own conclusions. Sometimes that may mean including links to sites that don't necessarily support your views. But you enhance your credibility by recognizing a full range of ideas, hoping that on their own, readers will reach the same conclusions you have reached.

KEY POINTS TO REMEMBER IN ARGUING ELECTRONICALLY

EMAIL

- Keep your remarks short and pertinent.
- Think twice before replying immediately to an argumentative message. Don't lose your cool.
- Remember that email is easily forwarded. Your actual audience may prove to be much larger than you initially intended.

NEWSGROUPS, LISTSERVS, IRCS, AND MOOS

- Get a feel for groups before posting to them.
- Post concise messages directly related to the interests of the group.
- Consider whether your posting should go to everyone on the list. Would an individual email message be more appropriate?
- Resist the temptation to flame or be impolite, especially when an argument heats up.

WEB SITES

- Plan your site carefully. Use your home page to direct readers to more detailed information within the site.
- Think of design in terms of pages. When you can, chunk a claim to fit within a single page. If your argument is highly readable, readers won't mind some scrolling, but don't expect them to advance through more than four or five screens' worth of material.
- Shape pages according to their purpose. A page of useful links will differ in arrangement from a page of prose argument.
- When your argument requires a lot of text, break it up with helpful headings and white space.
- At the bottom of the home page, include your name, your email address, and the date you created or last updated the site. This information will help other readers cite your work or reach you one-on-one to continue a discussion.

GRAPHICS

- Use graphics purposefully to support an argument. Images should make points you can't convey as effectively in prose.

- Keep graphics to a minimum. It takes time to download pages heavy in graphics—time readers might not have.

- Avoid images that pulse, rotate, or blink. Such glitz will likely distract readers from your argument.

- Graphics taken from the Web may be copyrighted items. Be sure to request permission from and to credit the source for any materials you import into your own pages.

LINKS

- Use links to guide readers to evidence that explains your ideas.

- Be sure your links are diverse. You'll gain credibility by acknowledging alternative views.

- Be sure readers can understand from the context what the links you create will do or where they will lead.

RESPOND •

1. Newcomers to a newsgroup or listserv normally lurk for a while, reading postings and getting to know the people who participate in the group, before entering the conversation themselves. Over the next several days, pick a group that interests you—there are thousands to choose from—and read as many of its postings as you can. For some groups, this might entail a tremendous amount of work, so limit your reading to those threads (topics within a group) that interest you.

   When you have a sense of the direction of the group, pick a single thread and follow the postings on that topic. Read all the postings that you can, making special note of quoting techniques—how writers refer to previous postings—and other interplay between writers. On the basis of the small evidence that you have (the group may have existed for several years), try to reconstruct the "conversation" on this thread that went on before you arrived. Who were the most common writers? What did they claim? How did others respond to those claims? What is the current state of the conversation? Are people in general agreement or disagreement?

2. FAQs can tell a careful reader a lot about a particular newsgroup or listserv and its contributors. Find the FAQs of three different groups

and read them carefully. What suppositions about audience are inherent in these texts? Write an audience analysis of each FAQ, based on the kinds of questions and answers you see there, their tone, and their length. Who are the FAQ's intended readers? What kinds of rules about argument does each FAQ offer?

3. Find several Web sites that make explicit argumentative claims, and evaluate them on the basis of a set of criteria you develop. What constitutes a good Web-based argument? What are the characteristics of effective Web rhetoric? Do these sites exhibit those characteristics? How does the nonlinear nature of the site affect your reading, or its persuasiveness? If your instructor requests, make a presentation to the class, showing printouts of the site (or directing the class to look at it if you are in a networked classroom) and explaining why the Web-based arguments are effective or ineffective.

4. Take an argumentative paper you've written for any class—it should be longer than two pages—and literally cut it up into separate paragraphs. Shuffle the stack of paragraphs so that they are completely reordered. Then read the paragraphs in their new order, from top to bottom. How is the argument affected? Is your claim still clear? Is your evidence powerful?

   Now imagine that those paragraphs were separate pages on a Web site that readers could browse through in any order. Would the site's argument be effective? If not, how could you rearrange the argument so that readers could move among its sections without being confused? Try to make an arrangement that could translate well to the Web's hypertextual environment. You might need to create headings that point readers in appropriate directions, or you might write transitions that help readers make decisions about what to read next.

chapter seventeen

Spoken Arguments

In the wake of a devastating hurricane, local ministers search for just the right words to offer comfort and inspire hope in their congregations.

At a campus rally, student leaders call for the administration to provide increased access for students with handicaps.

A customer looking for a good buy on a new car settles in for some tough negotiations with the salesperson and manager.

At the half, the team is down by ten. In the locker room, the captain calls on all her persuasive powers to rebuild morale and help seize the momentum.

For a course in psychology, a student gives a multimedia presentation on the work of neuroscientist Constance Pert.

During their wedding, a couple exchanges the special vows they have worked together to create.

■ ■ ■

As these examples suggest, people are called on every day to present spoken arguments of one kind or another. Successful speakers point to several crucial elements in that success: whenever possible, they have thorough knowledge of their subjects; they pay very careful attention to the values, ideas, and needs of their listeners; and they use structures and styles that make their spoken arguments easy to follow. Equally important, they keep in mind the interactive nature of spoken arguments (live audiences can argue back!) and, whenever possible, they practice, practice—and then practice some more.

CONTEXTS FOR SPOKEN ARGUMENTS

Perhaps the most common context for spoken argument takes place in ordinary discussions, whether you're trying to persuade your parents that you need a new computer for your college work, to explore the meaning of a poem in class, or to make a decision about a new company health plan. In such everyday contexts, many people automatically choose the tone of voice, kind of evidence, and length of speaking time to suit the situation. You can improve your own performance in such contexts by observing closely other speakers you find effective and by joining in on conversations whenever you possibly can: the more you participate in lively discussions, the more comfortable you will be doing so.

Formal Presentations

You may well be asked to make more formal spoken arguments. In such cases, you need to consider the full context carefully. Note how much time you have to prepare and how long the presentation should be. You want to use the allotted time effectively, while not infringing on the time of others. Consider also what visual aids, handouts, or other materials might help make the presentation successful. Will you have an overhead projector? Can you use PowerPoint or other computer presentation tools? A statistical pie chart may carry a lot of weight in one argument while photographs will make your point better in another. (See Chapter 15.)

Think about whether you are to make the presentation alone or as part of a group—and plan and practice accordingly. Especially with a group, turn-taking will need to be worked out carefully. Check out where your presentation will take place—in a classroom with fixed chairs? A lecture or assembly hall? An informal sitting area? Will you have a lectern? An overhead projector? Will you sit or stand? Remain in one place or move around? What will the lighting be, and can you adjust it? Finally, note any criteria for evaluation: how will your spoken argument be assessed?

Whenever you make a formal presentation, you need to consider several key elements:

- Determine your major argumentative *purpose*. Is it to inform? Convince or persuade? Explore? Make a decision? Something else?

- Who is your *audience*? Your instructor may be one important member, in addition to other class members. Think carefully about what they will know about your topic and what opinions they are likely to hold.

- Consider your own *stance* toward your topic and audience. Are you an expert? Novice? Fairly well informed? Interested observer? Peer?

- *Structure* your presentation to make it easy to follow, and remember to take special care to plan an introduction that gets the audience's attention and a conclusion that makes your argument memorable.

Cardinal Francis Arinze's article in Chapter 28 was part of a commencement address at Wake Forest University. How does he make his tone appropriate to the occasion?

LINK TO P. 635 ·················

ARGUMENTS TO BE HEARD

Even if you rely on a printed text, that text must be written to be *heard* rather than *read*. Such a text—whether in the form of an overhead list, note cards, or a full written-out text—should feature a strong introduction and conclusion, a clear structure with helpful signposts, straightforward syntax, and concrete diction.

Introductions and Conclusions

Like readers, listeners tend to remember beginnings and endings most readily. Work hard, therefore, to make these elements of your spoken argument especially memorable. Consider including a provocative or puzzling statement, opinion, or question; a vivid anecdote; a powerful quotation; or a vivid visual image. If you can refer to the interests or experiences of your listeners in the introduction or conclusion, do so.

Amy Tan used some of these techniques in the opening of a talk she gave in 1989 to the Language Symposium in San Francisco. In addressing this group of language experts, Tan began with a puzzling statement—given that she was speaking to a group of language scholars—and then related that statement to the interests of her audience:

See the rest of Amy Tan's speech in Chapter 27.

················· LINK TO P. 589

> **I am not a scholar of English or literature. I cannot give you much more than personal opinions on the English language and its variations in this country or others.**
>
> —Amy Tan, "Mother Tongue"

Structures and Signposts

For a spoken argument, you want your organizational structure to be crystal clear. Offer an overview of your main points toward the beginning of your presentation and make sure that you have a clearly delineated beginning, middle, and end to the presentation. Throughout, remember to pause between major points and to use helpful signposts to mark your movement from one topic to the next. Such signposts act as explicit transitions in your spoken argument and thus should be clear and concrete: *The second crisis point in the breakup of the Soviet Union occurred hard on the heels of the first* rather than *The breakup of the Soviet Union came to another crisis. . . .* In addition to such explicit transitions as *next, on the contrary,* or *finally,* you can offer signposts to your listeners by carefully repeating key words and ideas as well as by carefully introducing each new idea with concrete topic sentences.

Diction and Syntax

Avoid long, complicated sentences, and use straightforward syntax (subject-verb-object, for instance, rather than an inversion) as much as possible. Remember, too, that listeners can hold onto concrete verbs and nouns more easily than they can grasp a steady stream of abstractions. So when you need to deal with abstract ideas, try to illustrate them with concrete examples.

Take a look at the following paragraph from Ben McCorkle's essay on the Simpsons in Chapter 10, first as he wrote it for his essay and then for an oral presentation:

Written Version

The Simpson family has occasionally been described as a "nuclear" family, which obviously has a double meaning: first, the family consists of two parents and three children, and, second, Homer works at a nuclear power plant with very relaxed safety codes. The overused label *dysfunctional,* when applied to the Simpsons, suddenly takes on new meaning. Every episode seems to include a scene in which son Bart is being choked by his father, the baby is being neglected, or Homer is sitting in a drunken stupor transfixed by the television screen. The comedy in these scenes comes from the exaggeration of commonplace household events (although some talk shows and news programs would have us believe that these exaggerations are not confined to the madcap world of cartoons).

–Ben McCorkle, "The Simpsons: A Mirror of Society"

Spoken Version

What does it mean to describe the Simpsons as a *nuclear* family? Clearly, a double meaning is at work. First, the Simpsons fit the dictionary meaning—a family unit consisting of two parents and some children. The second meaning, however, packs more of a punch. You see, Homer works at a nuclear power plant [pause here] with *very* relaxed safety codes!

Still another overused family label describes the Simpsons. Did everyone guess I was going to say *dysfunctional?* And like "nuclear," when it comes to the Simpsons, "dysfunctional" takes on a whole new meaning.

Remember the scene when Bart is being choked by his father?

How about the many times the baby is being neglected?

Or the classic view—Homer sitting in a stupor transfixed by the TV screen!

My point here is that the comedy in these scenes often comes from double meanings—and from a lot of exaggeration of everyday household events.

Note that the revised paragraph presents the same information, but this time it is written to be heard. See how the revision uses helpful signposts, some repetition, a list, italicized words to prompt the speaker to give special emphasis, and simple syntax to help make it easy to listen to.

Radio reports are edited very tightly; even very technical information needs to be presented in a crisp and straightforward manner, as Bob Edwards and Christopher Joyce do in a radio news feature on a new gender-selection process for prospective parents: "The technique was invented in 1989 to breed livestock. A device called a flow cytometer distinguishes between sperm carrying X chromosomes— those are the ones that make girls—and Y-bearing sperm. Those make the boys. The machine can distinguish the two because the X chromosome is 2.8 percent heavier than the Y."

LINK TO P. 707

ARGUMENTS TO BE REMEMBERED

You can probably think of spoken arguments that still stick in your memory—a song like Bruce Springsteen's "Born in the USA," for instance, or a political call to arms like Martin Luther King Jr.'s "I Have a Dream." These arguments are memorable in part because they call on the power of figures of speech and other devices of language. In addition, careful repetition can make spoken arguments memorable, especially when linked with parallelism and climactic order. (See Chapter 14 for more on using figurative language to make arguments more vivid and memorable.)

Repetition, Parallelism, and Climactic Order

Whether they are used alone or in combination, repetition, parallelism, and climactic order are especially appropriate for spoken arguments that sound a call to arms or that seek passionate engagement from the audience. Perhaps no person in this century has used them more effectively than Martin Luther King Jr., whose sermons and speeches helped to spearhead the civil rights movement. Standing on the steps of the Lincoln Memorial in Washington, D.C., on August 28, 1963, with hundreds of thousands of marchers before him, King called on the nation to make good on the promissory note represented by the Emancipation Proclamation. Look at the way he uses repetition, parallelism, and climactic order in the following paragraph to invoke a nation to action:

The full text of "I Have a Dream" appears in Chapter 28.

······································ LINK TO P. 666

> It is obvious today that America has defaulted on this promissory note insofar as her citizens of color are concerned. Instead of honoring this sacred obligation, America has given the Negro people a bad check which has come back marked "insufficient funds." But *we refuse* to believe that the bank of justice is bankrupt. *We refuse* to believe that there are insufficient funds in the great vaults of opportunity of this nation. So *we have come* to cash this check—a check that will give us upon demand the riches of freedom and the security of justice. *We have also come* to this hallowed spot to remind America of the fierce urgency of now. This *is no time* to engage in the luxury of cooling off or to take the tranquilizing drug of gradualism. Now *is the time* to rise from the dark and desolate valley of segregation to the sunlit path of racial justice. *Now is the time* to open the doors of opportunity to all of God's children. *Now is the time* to lift our nation from the quicksands of racial injustice to the solid rock of brotherhood. (emphasis added)
> —Martin Luther King Jr., "I Have a Dream"

The italicized words highlight the way King uses repetition to drum home his theme. But along with that repetition, King sets up a powerful set of parallel verb phrases, calling on all "to rise" from the "dark and desolate valley of segregation" to the "sunlit path of racial justice" and "to open the doors of opportunity" for all. The final verb phrase ("to lift") leads to a strong climax, as King moves from what each individual should do to what the entire nation should do: "to lift our nation from the quicksands of racial injustice to the solid rock of brotherhood." These stylistic choices, together with the vivid image of the "bad check" help to make King's speech powerful, persuasive—and memorable.

Thank goodness you don't have to be as highly skilled as Dr. King, however, to take advantage of the power of repetition and parallelism: simply repeating a key word in your argument can help impress it on your audience, as can arranging parts of sentences or items in a list in parallel order.

Amalia Mesa-Bains uses repetition effectively to drive home her point about the Taco Bell chihuahua in a radio interview on *Latino USA:* ". . . you have to look at the context in which that dog appears. That dog appears near a brothel, that's a love hotel. That dog appears with low-riders. That dog appears with black people sitting in armchairs, snacking away while they watch television all day. What is that about?"

LINK TO P. 393

THE ROLE OF VISUALS

Visuals often play an important part in spoken arguments and they should be prepared with great care. Don't think of them as add-ons but rather as a major means of getting across your message and supporting the claims you are making. In this regard, a visual—like a picture—can be worth a thousand words, helping your audience *see* examples or illustrations or other data that make your argument compelling. Test the effectiveness of your visuals on classmates, friends, or family members, asking them specifically to judge whether the visuals help advance your argument.

Whatever visuals you use—charts, graphs, photographs, summary statements, sample quotations, lists—must be large enough to be readily seen by your audience. If you use PowerPoint or other overhead projections, be sure that the information on each frame is simple, clear, and easy to read and process. The same rule holds true for posters, flip charts, or a chalkboard. And remember not to turn your back on your audience while you refer to any of these visuals. Finally, if you prepare supplementary materials for your audience—bibliographies or other texts—distribute these at the end of the presentation so that they will not distract the audience from your spoken argument.

For a talk about how best to make an effective oral presentation, one writer used the PowerPoint slide shown in Figure 17.1. Note how easy this visual is to read: uncluttered, plenty of white space pulling readers from

FIGURE 17.1 SAMPLE POWERPOINT SLIDE

the top—where the main topic is announced—through a series of supporting points and then to an eye-catching photograph that demonstrates these points.

THE IMPORTANCE OF DELIVERY

When an orator in ancient times was asked to rank the most important parts of effective rhetoric, he said, "Delivery, delivery, delivery." Indeed, most effective spoken arguments are *performances* that call on you to pay very careful attention to the persuasive effects your clothing, body language, voice, and so on will have on the audience. Many practiced speakers say that they learned to improve the performance of spoken arguments through extensive practice. To make this advice work for you, get a draft of your spoken argument, including all visuals, together enough in advance to allow for several run-throughs. Some speakers audiotape or videotape these rehearsals and then revise the argument and the performance based on a study of the tapes. Others practice in front of a mirror, watching every movement with a critical eye. Still others practice in front of friends. Any of these techniques can work; the main thing is to practice.

One point of all that practice is to make sure you can be heard clearly. Especially if you are at all soft-spoken, you will need to concentrate on projecting your voice. Or you may need to practice lowering the pitch or speaking more slowly or enunciating each word more clearly. Tone of voice can dispose audiences for—or against—speakers. Those who sound sarcastic, for instance, usually win few friends. For most spoken arguments, you want to develop a tone that conveys interest and commitment to your position as well as respect for your audience.

The way you dress, the way you move, as well as the sound of your voice make arguments of their own that can either add to or detract from the main one you are trying to make. How to dress for an effective presentation, of course, depends on what is appropriate for your topic, audience, and setting, but most experienced speakers like to wear clothes that are simple and comfortable and that allow for easy movement—but that are not overly casual: "dressing up" a little indicates that you take pride in your appearance, that you have confidence in your argument, and that you respect your audience.

Most speakers make a stronger impression standing than sitting. Stand with your hands resting lightly on the lectern or at your side (don't fidget with anything!) and with both feet solidly on the floor—and move about a little, even if you are using a lectern. Moving a bit may also help you make good eye contact with members of your audience. And according to several studies, making eye contact is especially important for spoken arguments, since audiences perceive those who look at them directly to be more honest, friendly, and informed than others who do not.

Last but not at all least: time your presentation carefully to make sure you will stay within the allotted time. If you are working from a written text, a good rule of thumb is to allow roughly two and a half minutes for every double-spaced 8-1/2 x 11-inch page of text (or one and a half minutes for every 5 x 7-inch card). The only way to make sure of your time, however, is to set a clock and time the presentation precisely. Knowing that you will not intrude on the time allotted to other speakers not only signals your respect for their presentations but will also help you relax

Choose a few paragraphs from Amy Tan's speech in Chapter 27 or Cardinal Arinze's in Chapter 28, and try delivering them the way you think it might have been done originally. What do you notice about the ways you modify your voice and manner of speaking?

LINKS PP. 589 AND 635 ··

and gain self-confidence; and when your audience senses your self-confidence, they will become increasingly receptive to your message.

Some Helpful Presentation Strategies

In spite of your best preparation, you may feel some anxiety before your presentation. (According to the Gallup Poll, Americans often identify public speaking as a major fear, scarier than attacks from outer space!) Experienced speakers say they have strategies for dealing with anxiety—and even that a little anxiety (and accompanying adrenalin) can act to a speaker's advantage.

The most effective strategy seems to be knowing your topic and material through and through. Confidence in your own knowledge goes a long way toward making you a confident speaker. In addition to being well prepared, you may wish to try some of the following strategies:

- Visualize your presentation. Go over the scene of the presentation in your mind, and think it through completely.

- Get some rest before the presentation, and avoid consuming excessive amounts of caffeine.

- Concentrate on relaxing. Consider doing some deep-breathing exercises right before you begin.

- Pause before you begin, concentrating on your opening lines.

- Remember to interact with the audience whenever possible; doing so will often help you relax and even have some fun.

Finally, remember to allow time for audience members to respond and ask questions. Try to keep your answers brief so that others may get in on the conversation. And at the very end of your presentation, thank your audience for attending so generously to your arguments.

RESPOND●

1. Take a brief passage—one or two paragraphs—from an essay you've written. Then, following the guidelines in this chapter, rewrite the passage to be heard. Finally, make a list of every change you made.

2. Look in the TV listings for a speech or oral presentation you'd like to hear. Check out C-SPAN or Sunday morning news shows such as *Meet the Press*. Watch and listen to the presentation, making notes of the strategies the speaker uses to good effect—signpost language, repetition, figurative language, and so on.

PART 5

CONVENTIONS OF argument

chapter eighteen

What Counts
as Evidence

A downtown office worker who can never find a space in the company lot to park her motorcycle decides to argue for a designated motorcycle parking area. In building her argument, she decides to conduct a survey to find out exactly how many employees drive cars to work and how many ride motorcycles.

A business consultant wants to identify characteristics of effective teamwork so that he can convince his partners to adopt these characteristics as part of their training program. To begin gathering evidence for this argument, the consultant decides to conduct on-site observations of three effective teams, followed by in-depth interviews with each member.

For an argument aimed at showing that occupations are often unconsciously thought of as masculine or feminine, a student decides to carry out an experiment: she will ask fifty people chosen at random to draw pictures of a doctor, a police officer, a nurse, a CEO, a lawyer, and a secretary—and see which are depicted as men, which as women. The results of this experiment will become evidence for (or against) the argument.

Trying to convince her own family not to put their elderly grandmother into a "home," a former nursing home administrator offers her twelve years of personal experience in three different nursing homes as part of the evidence in support of her contention.

In arguing that virtual reality technology may lead people to ignore or disregard the most serious of "real" world problems, a student writer cites sixteen library sources that review and critique cyberspace and virtual reality as one way of providing evidence for his claim.

■ ■ ■

EVIDENCE AND THE RHETORICAL SITUATION

As the examples above demonstrate, people use all kinds of evidence in making and supporting claims. But the evidence they use does not exist in a vacuum; instead, it becomes part of the larger context of the argument and the argument's situation: when, where, and to whom it is made. Remembering the rhetorical situation into which evidence enters suggests an important point regarding argumentative evidence: it may be persuasive in one time and place but not in another; it may convince one kind of audience but not another; it may work with one genre of discourse but not another.

To be most persuasive, then, evidence should match the time in which the argument takes place. For example, arguing that a military leader should employ a certain tactic because that very tactic worked effectively for George Washington is likely to fail if Washington's use of the tactic is the only evidence provided. After all, a military tactic that was effective in 1776 is more than likely an *ineffective* one today. In the same way, a writer may achieve excellent results by using her own experience as well as an extensive survey of local leaders and teenagers as evidence to support a proposal for a new teen center in her small-town community—but she may have far less success in arguing for the same thing in a distant, large inner-city area.

Careful writers also need to consider the disciplinary context in which they plan to use evidence, since some disciplines privilege certain kinds of evidence and others do not. Observable, quantifiable data may constitute the best evidence in, say, experimental psychology, but the same kind of data may be less appropriate—or impossible to come by—in a historical study. As you become more familiar with a particular discipline or area of study, you will gain a sense of just what it takes to prove a point or support a claim in that field. The following questions will help you begin understanding the rhetorical situation of a particular discipline:

- How do other writers in the field use precedence and authority as evidence? What or who counts as an authority in this field? How are the credentials of authorities established?

- What kinds of data seem to be preferred as evidence? How are such data gathered and presented?

- How are statistics or other numerical information used and presented as evidence? Are tables, charts, or graphs commonly used? How much weight do they carry?

- How are definitions, causal analyses, evaluations, analogies, and examples used as evidence?

- How does the field use firsthand and secondhand sources as evidence?

- How is personal experience used as evidence?

- How are quotations used as part of evidence?

As these questions suggest, evidence may not always travel well from one field to another. As you consider the kinds of evidence surveyed in the rest of this chapter, consider in which contexts—in which rhetorical situations—each kind of evidence would be most (or least) effective.

FIRSTHAND EVIDENCE

Firsthand evidence comes from research you have carried out or been closely involved with, and much of this kind of research requires you to collect and examine data. Here we will discuss the kinds of firsthand research most commonly conducted by student writers.

Observations

"What," you may wonder, "could be any easier than observing something?" You just choose a subject, look at it closely, and record what you see and hear. If observing were so easy, eyewitnesses would all provide reliable accounts. Yet experience shows that several people who have observed the same phenomenon generally offer contradictory evidence on the basis of those observations. Trained observers say that getting down a faithful record of an observation requires intense concentration and mental agility.

Before you begin an observation, then, decide exactly what you want to find out and anticipate what you are likely to see. Do you want to observe an action repeated by many people (such as pedestrians crossing a street, in relation to an argument for putting in a new stoplight), a sequence of actions (such as the stages involved in student registration, which you want to argue is far too complicated), or the interactions of a group (such as meetings of the campus Young Republicans, which you want to see adhere to strict parliamentary procedures)? Once you have a clear sense of what you will observe and what questions you wish to answer through the observation, use the following guidelines to achieve the best results:

- Make sure the observation relates directly to your claim.
- Brainstorm about what you are looking for, but don't be rigidly bound to your expectations.
- Develop an appropriate system for collecting data. Consider using a split notebook or page: on one side, record the minute details of your observations directly; on the other, record your thoughts or impressions.
- Be aware that the way you record data will affect the outcome, if only in respect to what you decide to include in your observational notes and what you leave out.
- Record the precise date, time, and place of the observation.

In the following brief excerpt, editor Nell Bernstein uses information drawn from careful observation to introduce an argument about why some teenagers are drawn to taking on a new identity:

> **Her lipstick is dark, the lip liner even darker, nearly black. In baggy pants, a blue plaid Pendleton, her bangs pulled back tight off her forehead, 15-year-old April is a perfect cholita, a Mexican gangsta girl.**
>
> **But April Miller is Anglo. "And I don't like it!" she complains. "I'd rather be Mexican."**
>
> **–Nell Bernstein, "Goin' Gangsta, Choosin' Cholita"**

W. Charisse Goodman monitored a number of magazines to gather evidence for her claim that the media render large women invisible: "A survey of merely eleven mainstream magazines, including *Vogue, Redbook, Time, McCall's,* even *Audubon* and *Modern Maturity,* turned up an astounding 645 pictures of thin women as opposed to 11 of heavy women."

······· LINK TO P. 408

Interviews

Some evidence is best obtained through direct interviews. If you can talk with an expert—in person, on the phone, or online—you might get information you could not have obtained through any other type of research. In addition to getting expert opinion, you might ask for first-hand accounts, biographical information, or suggestions of other places to look or other people to consult. The following guidelines will help you conduct effective interviews:

- Determine the exact purpose of the interview, and be sure it is directly related to your claim.

- Set up the interview well in advance. Specify how long it will take, and if you wish to tape-record the session, ask permission to do so.

- Prepare a written list of both factual and open-ended questions. (Brainstorming with friends can help you come up with good questions.) Leave plenty of space for notes after each question. If the interview proceeds in a direction that you had not expected but that seems promising, don't feel you have to cover every one of your questions.

- Record the subject's full name and title, as well as the date, time, and place of the interview.

- Be sure to thank those you interview, either in person or with a follow-up letter or email message.

In arguing that alternative athletic venues such as the Gay Games do not pose a major challenge to the dominant structure of sports, Michael Messner uses data drawn from extensive interviews with participants in the Gay Games, including the following remarks from one of his subjects, Mike T:

> "You don't win by beating someone else. We defined winning as doing your very best. That way, everyone is a winner. And we have age-group competition, so all ages are involved. We have parity: if there's a men's sport, there's a women's sport to complement it. And we go out and recruit in Third World and minority areas. All these people are gonna get together for a week, they're gonna march in protest together, they're gonna hold hands."
>
> –Michael Messner, "In Living Color"

Messner uses this quotation from an interview subject to illustrate his contention that the Gay Games focus on bridging differences and overcoming prejudices of all kinds.

Surveys and Questionnaires

Surveys usually require the use of questionnaires. On any questionnaire, the questions should be clear, easy to understand, and designed so that respondents' answers can be analyzed easily. Questions that ask respondents to say "yes" or "no" or to rank items on a scale (1 to 5, for example, or "most helpful" to "least helpful") are particularly easy to tabulate. Here are some guidelines to help you prepare for and carry out a survey:

- Write out your purpose in conducting the survey, and make sure its results will be directly related to your claim.

- Brainstorm potential questions to include in the survey, and ask how each relates to your purpose and claim.

- Figure out how many people you want to contact, what the demographics of your sample should be (men in their twenties, or an equal number of men and women?), and how you plan to reach these people.

- Draft questions, making sure that each calls for a short, specific answer.

- Test the questions on several people, and revise those that are ambiguous, hard to answer, or too time-consuming to answer.

- If your questionnaire is to be sent by mail or email, draft a cover letter explaining your purpose and giving a clear deadline. For mail, provide an addressed, stamped return envelope.

- On the final draft of the questionnaire, leave plenty of space for answers.

- Proofread the final draft carefully; typos will make a bad impression on those whose help you are seeking.

In an argument about the way computers are misused in schools, LynNell Hancock uses information drawn from several surveys, including the one she mentions in the following paragraph:

> Having enough terminals to go around is one problem. But another important question is what the equipment is used for. Not much beyond rote drills and word processing, according to Linda Roberts, a technology consultant for the U.S. Department of Education. A 1992 National Assessment of Educational Progress survey found that most fourth-grade math students were using computers to play games "like Donkey Kong." By the eighth grade, most math students weren't using them at all.
>
> –LynNell Hancock, "The Haves and the Have-Nots"

Experiments

Some arguments may be supported by evidence gathered through experiments. In the sciences, experimental data are highly valued—if the experiment is conducted in a rigorously controlled situation. For other kinds of writing, "looser" and more informal experiments can be acceptable, especially if they are intended to provide only part of the support for an argument. If you want to argue that the recipes in *Gourmand* magazine are impossibly tedious to follow and take far more time than the average person wishes to spend, you might ask five or six people to conduct a little experiment with you: following two recipes apiece from a recent issue and recording and timing every step. The evidence you gather from this informal experiment could provide some concrete support—by way of specific examples—for your contention. But such experiments should be taken with a grain of salt; they may not be effective with certain audiences, and if they can easily be attacked as skewed or sloppily done ("The people you asked to make these recipes couldn't cook their way out of paper bags!"), then they may do more harm than good.

In an essay about computer hackers and the threats they pose to various individuals and systems, Winn Schwartau reports on an experiment performed by an ex-hacker he knows:

> One afternoon in Newport Beach, Jesse [the ex-hacker] put on a demonstration to show how easy it was to rob a bank.
>
> Jesse took his audience to a trash bin behind Pacific Bell, the Southern California Baby Bell service provider. Dumpster diving proved to be an effective means of social engineering because within minutes, an internal telephone company employee list was dredged out of the garbage. On it, predictably, were handwritten notes with computer passwords.
>
> In the neighborhood was a bank, which shall go nameless. After some more dumpster diving, financial and personal profiles of wealthy bank customers surfaced. That was all Jesse said he needed to commit the crime.
>
> At a nearby phone booth, Jesse used a portable computer with an acoustic modem to dial into the telephone company's computer. Jesse knew a lot about the telephone company's computers, so he made a few changes. He gave the pay phone a new number, that of one of the wealthy clients about whom he now knew almost everything. He also turned off the victim's phone with that same number. Jesse then called the bank and identified himself as Mr. Rich, an alias.
>
> "How can we help you, Mr. Rich?"

"I would like to transfer $100,000 to this bank account number."

"I will need certain information."

"Of course."

"What is your balance?"

"About _____," he supplied the number accurately.

"What is your address?"

Jesse gave the address.

"Are you at home, Mr. Rich?"

"Yes."

"We'll need to call you back for positive identification."

"I understand. Thank you for providing such good security."

In less than a minute the phone rang.

"Hello, Rich here."

The money was transferred, then transferred back to Mr. Rich's account again, to the surprise and embarrassment of the bank. The money was returned and the point was made.

–Winn Schwartau, "Hackers: The First Information Warriors"

Personal Experience

Personal experience can serve as powerful evidence when it is appropriate to the subject, to your purpose, and to the audience. Remember that if it is your *only* evidence, however, personal experience probably will not be sufficient to carry the argument. Nevertheless, it can be especially effective for drawing listeners or readers into an argument, as Sam Fulwood III demonstrates in the opening of an essay about the black middle class:

Race awareness displaced my blissful childhood in 1969.

I was then in the sixth grade at Oaklawn Elementary, a three-year-old school built on the edge of my neighborhood in Charlotte, N.C. Everybody knew that one day little white boys and girls would attend classes there, but at the time, the sparkling new rooms contained only black students and teachers. . . .

Mrs. Cunningham, a proper and proud black woman, knew that my father was a Presbyterian minister and my mother was an elementary school teacher, the perfect pair of parents for unchallenged credentials into black society's elite. She was convinced, on the advice of my teachers, that I should be among the first students from her elementary school to attend the nearest white junior high school the following year. This was an honor, she declared. Mrs. Cunningham countered any arguments I attempted about staying at the neighborhood school. As I needed additional persuading, she stated: "I am

CULTURAL CONTEXTS FOR ARGUMENT

Personal experience counts in making academic arguments in some but not all cultures. Showing that you have personal experience with a topic can carry strong persuasive appeal with many English-speaking audiences, however, so it will probably be a useful way to argue a point in the United States. As with all evidence used to make a point, evidence based on your own experience must be pertinent to the topic, understandable to the audience, and clearly related to your purpose and claim.

absolutely certain that you can hold your own with the best [white students] at Ransom Junior High." . . .

I evolved that day into a race-child, one who believed that he would illuminate the magnificent social changes wrought by racial progress. Overt racial barriers were falling, and I, among the favored in Charlotte's black middle class, thought my future would be free of racism, free of oppression. I believed I was standing on the portico of the Promised Land.

–Sam Fulwood III, "The Rage of the Black Middle Class"

SECONDHAND EVIDENCE

Secondhand evidence comes from sources beyond yourself—books, articles, films, online sources, and so on.

Library Sources

Your college library has not only a great number of print materials (books, periodicals, reference works) but also computer terminals that provide access to electronic catalogs and indexes as well as to other libraries' catalogs via the Internet. Although this book isn't designed to give a complete overview of library resources, we can offer a few key questions that can help you use the library most efficiently:

- What kinds of sources do you need to consult? Check your assignment to see whether you are required to consult different kinds of sources. If you must use print sources, find out whether they are readily available in your library or whether you must make special arrangements (such as an interlibrary loan) to use them. If you need to locate nonprint sources, find out where those are kept and whether you need special permission to examine them.

- How current do your sources need to be? If you must investigate the very latest findings about a new treatment for Alzheimer's, you will probably want to check periodicals, medical journals, or the Web. If you want broader, more detailed coverage and background information, you may need to depend more on books. If your argument deals with a specific time period, you may need to examine newspapers, magazines, or books written during that period.

- How many sources should you consult? Expect to look over many more sources than you will end up using. The best guideline is to make sure you have enough sources to support your claim.

- Do you know your way around the library? If not, ask a librarian for help in locating the following resources in the library: general and specialized encyclopedias; biographical resources; almanacs, yearbooks, and atlases; book and periodical indexes; specialized indexes and abstracts; the circulation computer or library catalog; special collections; audio, video, and art collections; the interlibrary loan office.

- Do you know how to conduct subject heading searches about your topic? Consult the *Library of Congress Subject Headings* (LCSH) for a list of standard subject headings related to your topic. This reference work is a helpful starting point because it lists the subject headings used in most library catalogs and indexes.

Online Sources

Today, most students have fairly easy access to online sources from the college library or from a campus computer center. In addition, some dormitory rooms are now wired for immediate Internet connections to your own computer. But in many instances in dorms, and almost certainly at home, you will need a modem and a software package (usually available at the campus bookstore at low cost) to get access to the Internet. With a modem connection, you can link to the college computer system and thus get access. Or you may need to subscribe to an Internet service provider (ISP), such as America Online, CompuServe, or Prodigy. These companies often offer bonus features in addition to access to the Internet, such as encyclopedias and various kinds of software. However, commercial services can be expensive, so you may want to check local sources, such as a Freenet.

Many important resources for argument are now available in databases, either online or on CD-ROM. To search such databases, you must provide a list of authors, titles, or keywords (sometimes called "descriptors"). Especially if you have to pay a fee for such searches, limit the search as much as you can. To be most efficient, choose keywords very carefully. Sometimes you can search just by author or title; then the keywords are obvious. More often, however, you will search with subject headings. For an argument about the fate of the hero in contemporary films, for example, you might find that *film* and *hero* produce far too many possible matches or "hits." You might further narrow the search by adding a third keyword, say, *American* or *current*.

In doing such searches, you will need to observe the search logic for a particular database. Using *and* between keywords (*movies and heroes*) usually indicates that both terms must appear in a file for it to be called up. Using *or* between keywords usually instructs the computer to locate every file in which either one word or the other shows up, whereas using *not* tells the computer to exclude files containing a particular word from the search results (*movies not heroes*).

Software programs called browsers allow you to navigate the contents of the Web and to move from one Web site to another. Today, most browsers—such as Netscape Navigator, Mosaic, and Microsoft Internet Explorer—are graphics browsers that display both text and visual images.

Web-based search engines can be used to carry out keyword searches or view a list of contents available in a series of directories. Here are a few of the most popular search engines:

AltaVista	<http://www.altavista.digital.com>
Ask Jeeves	<http://www.askjeeves.com>
Dogpile	<http://www.dogpile.com>
Google	<http://www.google.com>
Infoseek	<http://www.infoseek.com>
Lycos	<http://www.lycos.com>
WebCrawler	<http://webcrawler.com>
Yahoo!	<http://www.yahoo.com>

USING EVIDENCE EFFECTIVELY

You may gather an impressive amount of evidence on your topic—from firsthand interviews, from careful observations, and from intensive library and online research. But until that evidence is woven into the fabric of your own argument, it is just a pile of data. Using your evidence effectively calls for turning data into information that will be persuasive to your intended audience.

Considering Audiences

The ethos you bring to an argument is crucial to your success in connecting with your audience. You want to present yourself as reliable and credible, naturally, but you also need to think carefully about the way your evidence relates to your audience. Is it appropriate to this particular group of readers or listeners? Does it speak to them in ways they will understand and respond to? Does it acknowledge and appeal to where they are "coming from"? It's hard to give any definite advice for making sure that your evidence is appropriate to the audience. But in general, timeliness is important to audiences: the more up-to-date your evidence, the better. In addition, evidence that is representative is usually more persuasive than evidence that is extreme or unusual. For example, in arguing for a campus-wide escort service after 10 P.M., a writer who cites numbers of students frightened, threatened, or attacked on their way across campus after dark and numbers of calls for help from campus phone boxes will probably be in a stronger position than one who cites only an attack that occurred four years ago.

Although the ownership of frozen embryos is of interest to physicians, scientists, prospective parents, and many other groups, Mike McKee writes for an audience of attorneys in "Weighing the Right to Own an Embryo" and virtually all of his evidence comes from court cases.

LINK TO P. 546

Building a Critical Mass

Throughout this chapter we have stressed the need to discover as much evidence as possible in support of your claim. If you can find only one or two pieces of evidence, only one or two reasons to back up your contention, then you may be on weak ground. Although there is no magic number, no definite way of saying how much is "enough" evidence, you should build toward a critical mass, a number of pieces of evidence all pulling in the direction of your claim. Especially if your evidence relies heavily on personal experience or on one major example, you should stretch your search for additional sources and good reasons to back up your claim.

Arranging Evidence

You can begin to devise a plan for arranging your evidence effectively by producing a rough outline or diagram of your argument, a series of hand-written or computer note cards that can be grouped into categories, or

CULTURAL CONTEXTS FOR ARGUMENT

How do you decide what evidence will best support your claims? The answer depends, in large part, on how you define evidence. Differing notions of what counts as evidence can lead to arguments that go nowhere fast.

One example of such a failed argument occurred in 1979, when Oriana Fallaci, an Italian journalist, was interviewing the Ayatollah Khomeini. Fallaci argued in a way common in North American and Western European cultures: she presented what she considered strong assertions backed up with facts ("Iran denies freedom to people. . . . Many people have been put in prison and even executed, just for speaking out in opposition."). In response, Khomeini relied on very different kinds of evidence: analogies ("Just as a finger with gangrene should be cut off so that it will not destroy the whole body, so should people who corrupt others be pulled out like weeds so they will not infect the whole field.") and, above all, the authority of the Q'uran. Partly because of these differing beliefs about what counts as evidence, the interview ended in a shouting match.

People in the United States tend to give great weight to factual evidence, but as this example shows, the same is not true in some other parts of the world. In arguing across cultures, you need to think carefully about how you are accustomed to using evidence—and to pay attention to what counts as evidence to members of other cultures.

- Do you rely on facts? Examples? Firsthand experience?

- Do you include testimony from experts—and which experts are valued most (and why)?

- Do you cite religious or philosophical texts? Proverbs or everyday wisdom?

- Do you use analogies as evidence? How much do they count?

Once you determine what counts as evidence in your own arguments, ask these same questions about the use of evidence by members of other cultures.

anything else that makes the major points of the argument very clear. Then review your evidence, deciding which pieces support which points in the argument. In general, try to position your strongest pieces of evidence in key places—near the beginning of paragraphs, at the end of the introduction, or where you build toward a powerful conclusion. In addition, try to achieve a balance between your own argument and your own words, and the sources you use or quote in support of the argument. The sources of evidence are important props in the structure, but they should not overpower the structure (your argument) itself.

RESPOND.

1. What counts as evidence depends in large part on the rhetorical situation. One audience might find personal testimony compelling in a given case, whereas another might require data that only experimental studies can provide. The Christine Hoff Sommers excerpt in Chapter 7 (see p. 75) offers a good example of audience-specific responses to evidence. Lynda Gorov, the author of the *Boston Globe* piece Sommers quotes, believed the evidence she found in "one study of women's shelters out West" that pointed toward a rise in spousal abuse on the day of the Super Bowl. Another writer Sommers mentions, Ken Ringle, did not accept that evidence and went looking for expert testimony.

   Imagine that you want to argue for a national anti-abuse educational campaign composed of television ads to air before and during the Super Bowl—and you want the National Football League to pay for those ads. Make a list of reasons and evidence to support your claim, aimed at NFL executives. What kind of evidence would be most compelling to that group? How would you rethink your use of evidence if you were writing for the newsletter of a local women's shelter? This is not an exercise in pulling the wool over anyone's eyes; your goal is simply to anticipate the kind of evidence that different audiences would find persuasive given the same case.

2. Finding, evaluating, and arranging evidence in an argument is often a *discovery* process: sometimes you're concerned not only with digging up support for an already established claim but also with creating and revising tentative claims. Surveys and interviews can help you figure out what to argue, as well as provide evidence for a claim.

   Interview a classmate with the goal of writing a brief proposal argument about his or her career goals. The claim should be "My classmate should be doing X five years from now." Limit yourself to ten questions; write them ahead of time and do not deviate from them. Record the results of the interview (written notes are fine—you don't need a tape recorder).

Then interview another classmate, with the same goal in mind. Ask the same first question, but this time let the answer dictate the rest of the questions. You still get only ten questions.

Which interview gave you more information? Which one helped you learn more about your classmate's goals? Which one better helped you develop claims about his or her future?

3. Imagine that you're trying to decide whether to take a class with a particular professor, but you don't know if he or she is a good teacher. You might already have an opinion, based on some vaguely defined criteria and dormitory gossip, but you're not sure if that evidence is reliable. You decide to observe a class to inform your decision.

Visit a class in which you are not a student, and make notes on your observations following the guidelines in this chapter (p. 300). You probably only need a single day's visit to get a sense of the note-taking process, though you would, of course, need much more time to write an honest evaluation of the professor.

Write a short evaluation of the professor's teaching abilities on the basis of your observations. Then write an analysis of your evaluation. Is it honest? Fair? What other kinds of evidence might you need if you wanted to make an informed decision about the class and the teacher?

chapter nineteen

Fallacies of Argument

"Either you eat your broccoli or you don't get dessert!"

"But if you don't give me an "A," I won't get into medical school."

"You would if you loved me."

"Make love, not war."

"All my friends have AOL. I'm the only one who can't get instant messages!"

■ ■ ■

Fallacies are arguments supposedly flawed by their very nature or structure; as such, you should avoid them in your own writing and question them in arguments you read. That said, it's important to appreciate that one person's fallacy may well be another person's stroke of genius.

How can that be, if fallacies are faulty arguments? Remember that arguments ordinarily work in complex social, political, and cultural environments where people are far more likely to detect the mote in someone else's eye than the beam in their own.

Consider, for example, the fallacy termed *ad hominem* argument—"to the man." It describes a strategy of attacking the character of those with whom one disagrees rather than the substance of their arguments: *So you think government entitlement programs are growing out of control? Well, you're an idiot.* It's an argument of a kind everyone has blurted out at some time in their lives.

But there are also situations when an issue of character *is* germane to an argument. If that weren't so, appeals based on character would be pointless. The problem arises in deciding when such arguments are legitimate and when they are fallacious. You are much more likely to regard attacks on people you admire as *ad hominem,* and attacks on those you disagree with as warranted. Moreover, debates about character can become quite ugly and polarizing; consider Anita Hill and Clarence Thomas, Paula Jones and Bill Clinton, Pete Rose and major league baseball. (For more on arguments based on character, see Chapter 6.)

It might be wise to think of fallacies not in terms of errors you can detect and expose in someone else's work, but as strategies hurtful to everyone (including the person advancing them) because they make civil argument more difficult. Fallacies are impediments to the kind of rich conversations experienced writers ought to cultivate—regardless of their differences.

To help you understand fallacies of argument, we've classified them according to three rhetorical appeals discussed in earlier chapters: emotional arguments, arguments based on character, and logical arguments. (See Chapters 4, 6, and 7.)

FALLACIES OF EMOTIONAL ARGUMENT

In Western tradition, emotional arguments have long been dismissed as "womanish" and, therefore, weak and suspect. But such views are not only close-minded and sexist; they're flat-out wrong. Emotional arguments can be both powerful and appropriate in many circumstances, and most writers use them as a matter of course. However, writers who attempt to evoke either excessive or inappropriate feelings on the part of their audiences violate the good faith on which legitimate argument depends. The essential connection between writers and readers won't last if it is built on deception or manipulation.

Scare Tactics

Corrupters of children, the New Testament warns, would be better off dropped into the sea with millstones around their necks. Would that the same fate awaited politicians, advertisers, and public figures who peddle ideas by scaring people. It is the essence of demagoguery to reduce complicated issues to threats or to exaggerate a possible danger well beyond its statistical likelihood. Yet scare tactics, which do just that, are remarkably common in everything ranging from ads for life insurance to threats of audits by the Internal Revenue Service. Such tactics work because it is usually easier to imagine a dire consequence than to appreciate its remote probability. That may be why so many people fear flying, despite the fine safety record of commercial aviation.

Scare tactics can also be used to magnify existing, sometimes legitimate fears into panic or prejudice. People who genuinely fear losing their jobs can be persuaded, easily enough, to mistrust all immigrants as people who might work for less money; people living on fixed incomes can be convinced that even minor modifications of entitlement programs represent dire threats to their standard of living. Such tactics have the effect of closing off thinking because people who are scared seldom act rationally.

Even well-intended fear campaigns—like those directed against drugs or HIV infection—can misfire if their warnings prove too shrill. When AIDS failed to occur within the heterosexual population at the rate health professionals originally predicted, many people became suspicious of the establishment's warnings and grew unduly careless about their own sexual behavior, thereby greatly increasing their risk of exposure to infection.

Either-Or Choices

Presenting arguments that require people to choose one of only two alternatives can be a kind of scare tactic. The preferred option is drawn in the warmest light, whereas the alternative is cast as an ominous shadow. Sometimes *either-or* choices are benign strategies to get something accomplished: *Either you eat your broccoli or you don't get dessert*. Such arguments become fallacious when they reduce a complicated issue to excessively simple terms or when they deliberately obscure other alternatives.

To suggest that Social Security must be privatized or the system will go broke may have rhetorical power, but the choice is too simple. The fiscal problems of Social Security can be addressed in any number of ways, including privatization. To defend privatization, fallaciously, as the only possible course of action is to lose the support of people who know better.

But then *either-or* arguments—like most scare tactics—are often purposefully designed to seduce those who aren't well informed about a subject. And that cynical rationale is yet another reason the tactic violates principles of civil discourse. Argument should enlighten people, making them more knowledgeable and more capable of acting intelligently and independently.

Slippery Slope

The slippery slope fallacy is well named, describing an argument that casts a tiny misstep today as tomorrow's avalanche. Of course, not all arguments aimed at preventing dire consequences are slippery slope fallacies: the parent who corrects a child for misbehavior now is acting sensibly to prevent more serious problems as the child grows older. And like the homeowner who repairs a loose shingle to prevent an entire roof from rotting, businesses and institutions that worry about little problems often prevent bigger ones. The city of New York learned an important lesson in the 1990s about controlling crime by applying what had become known as "the broken window theory": after the mayor directed police to crack down on petty crimes that make urban life especially unpleasant, major crimes declined as well.

The slippery slope fallacy arises when a writer exaggerates the future consequences of an action, usually with the intention of frightening readers. As such, slippery slope arguments are also scare tactics. But people encounter them so often that they come to seem almost reasonable. For instance, defenders of free speech typically regard even mild attempts to govern behavior as constitutional matters: for example, a school board's request that a school pupil cut his ponytail becomes a direct assault on the child's First Amendment rights, litigated through the courts. Similarly, opponents of gun control warn that any legislation regulating firearms is just a first step toward the government knocking down citizens' doors and seizing all their weapons. Ideas and actions do have consequences, but they aren't always as dire as writers fond of slippery slope tactics would have you believe.

Sentimental Appeals

Sentimental appeals are arguments that use emotions excessively to distract readers from facts. Quite often, such appeals are highly personal and individual—focusing attention on heart-warming or heart-wrenching situations that make readers feel guilty about raising legitimate objections to related proposals or policies. Emotions become an impediment to civil discourse when they keep people from thinking clearly.

Yet, sentimental appeals are a major vehicle of television news, where it is customary to convey ideas through personal tales that tug at viewers' heartstrings. For example, a camera might document the day-to-day life of a single mother on welfare whose on-screen generosity, kindness, and tears come to represent the spirit of an entire welfare clientele under attack by callous legislators; or the welfare recipient might be shown driving a Cadillac and trading food stamps for money while a lower-middle-class family struggles to meet its grocery budget. In either case, the conclusion the reporter wants you to reach is supported by powerful images that evoke emotions in support of that conclusion. But though the individual stories presented may be genuinely moving, they seldom give a complete picture of a complex social or economic issue.

Bandwagon Appeals

Bandwagon appeals are arguments that urge people to follow the same path everyone else is taking. Curiously, many American parents seem endowed with the ability to refute bandwagon appeals. When their kids whine that *Everyone else is going camping overnight without chaperones,* the parents reply instinctively, *And if everyone else jumps off a cliff (or a railroad bridge, or the Empire State Building), you will too?* The children stomp and groan—and then try a different line of argument.

Unfortunately, not all bandwagon approaches are so transparent. Though Americans like to imagine themselves as rugged individualists, they're easily seduced by ideas endorsed by the mass media and popular culture. Such trends are often little more than harmless fashion statements. At other times, however, Americans become obsessed by issues selected for their attention by politicians or by media or cultural elites. In recent years, issues of this kind have included the "war on drugs," health care reform, AIDS prevention, gun control, tax reform, welfare reform, teen smoking, and campaign finance reform. Everyone must be concerned by this issue-of-the-day, and something—*anything*—must be done! More often than not, enough people jump on the bandwagon to achieve a measure of reform. And when changes occur because people have become sufficiently informed to exercise good judgment, then one can speak of "achieving consensus," a rational goal for civil argument.

But sometimes bandwagons run downhill and out of control, as they did in the 1950s when many careers were destroyed by "witch hunts" for suspected communists during the McCarthy era and in the late 1980s when concerns over child abuse mushroomed into indiscriminate prosecutions of parents and child care workers. In a democratic society, the bandwagon appeal is among the most potentially serious and permanently damaging fallacies of argument.

FALLACIES OF ETHICAL ARGUMENT

The presence of an author in an argument is called ethos. To build connections with readers, writers typically seek an ethos that casts themselves as honest, well informed, and sympathetic. Not surprisingly, readers pay closer attention to authors whom they respect. But *trust me* is a scary warrant. People usually need more than promises to move them to action—and they don't like to be intimidated by writers who exploit issues of character to limit how readers can respond to complex problems. When choice is constricted, civil discourse usually ends. (For more on ethos, see Chapter 6.)

Appeals to False Authority

One of the best strategies a writer can employ to support an idea is to draw on the authority of widely respected people, texts, or institutions. Relying on respected voices, past and present, is a mainstay of civil discourse; in fact, some academic research papers are essentially exercises in finding and reflecting on the work of reputable authorities. Writers may introduce these authorities into their arguments through allusions, citations, or direct quotations. (See Chapter 21 for more on assessing the reliability of sources.)

False authority occurs chiefly when writers offer themselves, or other authorities they cite, as *sufficient* warrant for believing a claim:

Claim	X is true because I say so.
Warrant	What I say must be true.
Claim	X is true because Y says so.
Warrant	What Y says must be true.

Rarely will you see authority asserted quite so baldly as in these examples, because few readers would accept a claim stated in either of these ways. Nonetheless, claims of authority drive many persuasive campaigns. American pundits and politicians are fond of citing the U.S. Constitution or Bill of Rights, a reasonable practice when the documents are interpreted respectfully. However, as often as not, the constitutional rights claimed aren't in the texts themselves or don't mean what the speakers think they do. And most constitutional issues are self-evidently debatable.

Likewise, the claims of religion are often based on texts or teachings of great authority within a community of believers. However, the power of these texts is usually more limited outside that group and, hence, less capable of persuading solely on the grounds of their authority—though arguments of faith often have power on other grounds.

Institutions can be cited as authorities within their proper spheres. Certainly, serious attention should be paid to claims supported by authorities one respects or recognizes—the White House, the FBI, the FDA, the National Science Foundation, the *New York Times,* the *Wall Street Journal,* and so on. But one ought not to accept facts or information *simply* because they have the imprimatur of such agencies. To quote a Russian proverb made famous by Ronald Reagan, "Trust, but verify."

Dogmatism

A writer who attempts to persuade by asserting or assuming that a particular position is the only one conceivably acceptable within a community is trying to enforce dogmatism. Dogmatism is a fallacy of ethos because the tactic undermines the trust that must exist between those who would make and those who would receive arguments. In effect, arbiters of dogmatic opinion imply that there are no arguments to be made: the truth is self-evident to those who know better.

Doubtless, there are arguments beyond the pale of civil discourse—positions and claims so outrageous or absurd that they are unworthy of serious attention. Attacks on the historical reality of the Holocaust fall into this category. But relatively few subjects in a free society ought to be off the table—certainly none that can be defended with facts, testimony, and good reasons. In general, therefore, the suggestion that merely raising an issue for debate is somehow "politically incorrect"—whether racist or sexist, unpatriotic or sacrilegious, or insensitive or offensive in some other way—may well represent a fallacy of argument deployed to constrict the range of acceptable opinion.

Moral Equivalence

A fallacy of argument perhaps more common today than a decade ago is moral equivalence—that is, suggesting that serious wrongdoings don't differ in kind from more minor offenses. A warning sign that this fallacy is likely to come into play is the retort of the politician or bureaucrat accused of wrongdoing: *But everyone else does it too!* Richard Nixon insisted that the crimes that led to his resignation did not differ in kind from the activities of previous presidents; Bill Clinton made similar claims about the fund-raising and other scandals of his administration. Regardless of the validity of these particular defenses, there is a point at which the scale of a morally questionable act overwhelms even its shady precedents.

Moral equivalence can work both ways. It is not uncommon to read arguments in which relatively innocuous activities are raised to the level of major crimes. Some would say that the national campaign against smoking falls into this category—a common and legally sanctioned behavior now given the social stigma of serious drug abuse. And if smoking is almost criminal, should one not be equally concerned with people who use and abuse chocolate—a sweet and fatty food responsible for a host of health problems? You see how easy it is to make an equivalence argument. Yet suggesting that all behaviors of a particular kind—in this case, abuses of substances—are equally wrong (whether they involve cigarettes, alcohol, drugs, or fatty foods) blurs the subtle distinctions people need to make in weighing claims.

Ad Hominem Arguments

One obviously gendered term that feminists have not been eager to neuter—probably with good reason—is the argument *ad hominem,* "to the man." *Ad hominem* arguments are attacks directed at the character of a person rather than at the claims he or she makes. The theory is simple: destroy the credibility of your opponents, and you either destroy their ability to present reasonable appeals or you distract from the successful arguments they may be offering. Critics of Rush Limbaugh's conservative stances rarely fail to note his heft; opponents of Bill Clinton's military policies just as reliably mention "draft dodging."

In such cases, *ad hominem* tactics turn arguments into ham-fisted, two-sided affairs with good guys and bad guys. Civil argument resists this destructive nastiness, though the temptation to use such tactics persists even (some would say, especially) in colleges and universities.

Of course, character does matter in argument. People expect the proponent of peace to be civil, the advocate of ecology to respect the environment, the champion of justice to be fair even in private dealings. But it is fallacious to attack an idea by exposing the frailties of its advocates or attacking their motives, backgrounds, or unchangeable traits.

FALLACIES OF LOGICAL ARGUMENT

Logical fallacies are arguments in which the claims, warrants, and/or evidence are invalid, insufficient, or disconnected. In the abstract, such problems seem easy enough to spot; in practice, they can be camouflaged by artful presentations. Indeed, logical fallacies pose a challenge to civil argument because they often seem quite reasonable and natural, especially when they appeal to people's self-interests. Whole industries (such as phone-in psychic networks) depend on one or more of the logical fallacies for their existence; political campaigns, too, rely on them to prop up that current staple of democratic interchange—the fifteen-second TV spot.

Hasty Generalization

Among logical fallacies, only faulty causality might be able to challenge hasty generalization for the crown of most prevalent. A hasty generalization is an inference drawn from insufficient evidence: *Because my Honda broke down, all Hondas must be junk.* It also forms the basis for most stereotypes about people or institutions: because a few people in a large group are observed to act in a certain way, one infers that all members of that group will behave similarly. The resulting conclusions are usually sweeping claims of little merit: *Women are bad drivers; men are boors; Scots are stingy; Italians are romantic; English teachers are tweedy; scientists are nerds.* You could, no doubt, expand this roster of stereotypes by the hundreds.

To draw valid inferences, you must always have sufficient evidence: a random sample of a population, a selection large enough to represent fully the subjects of your study, an objective methodology for sampling the population or evidence, and so on (see Chapter 18). And you must qualify your claims appropriately. After all, people do need generalizations to help make reasonable decisions in life; and such claims can be offered legitimately if placed in context and tagged with appropriate qualifiers: *some, a few, many, most, occasionally, rarely, possibly, in some cases, under certain circumstances, in my experience.*

You should be especially alert to the fallacy of hasty generalization when you read reports and studies of any kind, especially case studies based on carefully selected populations. Be alert for the fallacy, too, in the interpretation of poll numbers. Everything from the number of people selected to the time the poll was taken to the exact wording of the questions may affect its outcome.

Faulty Causality

In Latin, the fallacy of faulty causality is described by the expression *post hoc, ergo propter hoc,* which translates word-for-word as "after this, therefore because of this." Odd as the translation may sound, it accurately describes what faulty causality is—the fallacious assumption that because one event or action follows another, the first necessarily causes the second.

Some actions, of course, do produce reactions. Step on the brake pedal in your car, and you move hydraulic fluid that pushes calipers against disks to create friction that stops the vehicle. Or, if you happen to be chair of the Federal Reserve Board, you raise interest rates to increase the cost of borrowing to slow the growth of the economy in order to curb inflation—you hope. Causal relationships of this kind are reasonably convincing because one can provide evidence of relationships between the events sufficient to convince most people that an initial action did, indeed, cause others.

But as even the Federal Reserve example suggests, causality can be difficult to control when economic, political, or social relationships are involved. That's why suspiciously simple or politically convenient causal claims should always be subject to scrutiny.

Begging the Question

There's probably not a teacher in the country who hasn't heard the following argument from a student: *You can't give me a "C" in this course; I'm an "A" student.* The accused felon's version of the same argument goes this way: *I can't be guilty of embezzlement; I'm an honest person*. In both cases, the problem with the claim is that it is made on grounds that cannot be accepted as true because those grounds are in doubt. How can the student claim to be an "A" student when she just earned a "C"? How can the accused felon defend himself on the grounds of honesty when that honesty is now suspect? Setting such arguments in Toulmin terms helps to expose the fallacy:

Claim + Reason	**You can't give me a "C" in this course because I'm an "A" student.**
Warrant	**An "A" student is someone who can't receive "C"s.**
Claim + Reason	**I can't be guilty of embezzlement because I'm an honest person.**
Warrant	**An honest person cannot be guilty of embezzlement.**

With the warrants stated, you can see why begging the question—that is, assuming as true the very claim that is disputed—is a form of circular argument, divorced from reality. If you assume that an "A" student can't receive "C"s, then the first argument stands. But no one is an "A" student *by definition*; that standing has to be earned by performance in individual courses. Otherwise, there would be no point for a student who once earned an "A" to be taking additional courses; "A" students can only get "A"s, right?

Likewise, even though someone with an honest record is unlikely to embezzle, a claim of honesty is not an adequate defense against specific charges. An honest person won't embezzle, but merely claiming to be honest does not make it so. (For more on Toulmin argument, see Chapter 8.)

Equivocation

Both the finest definition and the most famous literary examples of equivocation come from Shakespeare's tragedy *Macbeth*. In the drama, three witches, representing the fates, make prophecies that seem advantageous to the ambitious Macbeth, but that prove disastrous when understood more fully. He is told, for example, that he has nothing to fear from his enemies "till Birnam wood/Do come to Dunsinane" (*Mac.* V.v.44–45); but these woods do move when enemy soldiers cut Birnam's boughs for camouflage and march on Macbeth's fortress. Catching on to the game, Macbeth begins "[t]o doubt the equivocation of the fiend/That *lies like truth*" (V.v.43–44, emphasis added). An equivocation, then, is an argument that gives a lie an honest appearance; it is a half-truth.

Equivocations are usually juvenile tricks of language, the kind children relish when claiming "I don't even have a nickel," knowing that they have dimes. Consider the plagiarist who copies a paper word-for-word from a source and then declares—honestly, she thinks—that "I wrote the entire paper myself," meaning that she physically copied the piece on her own. But the plagiarist is using "wrote" equivocally—that is, in a limited sense, knowing that most people would understand "writing" as something more than the mere copying of words.

As you might suspect, equivocations are artful dodges that work only as long as readers or listeners don't catch on. But once they do, the device undermines both the logic of the appeal and the good character of the writer. A writer who equivocates becomes, to use yet another Shakespearean phrase, a "corrupter of words."

Non Sequitur

A *non sequitur* is an argument in which claims, reasons, or warrants fail to connect logically; one point does not follow from another. As with other fallacies, children are notably adept at framing *non sequiturs*. Consider this familiar form: *You don't love me or you'd buy me that bicycle!* It might be more evident to harassed parents that no connection exists between love and Huffys if they were to consider the implied warrant:

Claim	**You must not love me**
Reason	**. . . because you haven't bought me that bicycle.**
Warrant	**Buying bicycles for children is essential to loving them.**

A five-year-old might endorse that warrant, but no responsible adult would because love does not depend on buying things, at least not a particular bicycle. Activities more logically related to love might include feeding and clothing children, taking care of them when they are sick, providing shelter and education, and so on.

In effect, *non sequiturs* occur when writers omit a step in an otherwise logical chain of reasoning, assuming that readers agree with what may be a highly contestable claim. For example, it is a *non sequitur* simply to argue that the comparatively poor performance of American students on international mathematics examinations means the country should spend more money on math education. Such a conclusion *might* be justified if a correlation were known or found to exist between mathematical ability and money spent on education. But the students' performance might be poor for reasons other than education funding, so a writer should first establish the nature of the problem before offering a solution.

Faulty Analogy

Comparisons give ideas greater presence or help clarify concepts. Consider all the comparisons packed into this reference to Jack Kennedy from a tribute to Jacqueline Kennedy by Stanley Crouch:

> **The Kennedys had spark and Jack had grown into a handsome man, a male swan rising out of the Billy the Kid version of an Irish duckling he had been when he was a young senator.**
>
> > –**Stanley Crouch, "Blues for Jackie"**

When comparisons are extended, they become analogies — ways of understanding unfamiliar ideas by comparing them with something that is already known. Some argue that it is through comparisons, metaphors, and analogies that people come to understand the universe. Neil Postman draws readers' attention to the importance of analogies when he asks them to consider how the brain works:

> **Is the human mind, for example, like a dark cavern (needing illumination)? A muscle (needing exercise)? A vessel (needing filling)? A lump of clay (needing shaping)? A garden (needing cultivation)? Or, as some may say today, is it like a computer that processes data?**
>
> > –**Neil Postman, "The Word Weavers/The World Makers"**

Useful as such comparisons are, they may prove quite false either on their own or when pushed too far or taken too seriously. At this point they become faulty analogies, inaccurate or inconsequential comparisons between objects or concepts. To think of a human mind as a garden has charm: gardens thrive only if carefully planted, weeded, watered, pruned, and harvested; so too the mind must be cultivated, if it is to bear fruit. But gardens also thrive when spread with manure. Need we follow the analogy down that path? Probably not.

RESPOND●

1. Following is a list of political slogans or phrases that may be examples of logical fallacies. Discuss each item to determine what you may know about the slogan and then decide which, if any, fallacy might be used to describe it.

   "It's the economy, stupid." (sign on the wall at Bill Clinton's campaign headquarters)

   "Nixon's the one." (campaign slogan)

   "Fifty-four forty or fight."

   "Make love, not war." (antiwar slogan during the Vietnam War)

"A chicken in every pot."

"No taxation without representation."

"No Payne, your gain." (aimed at an opponent named Payne)

"Loose lips sink ships."

"Guns don't kill, people do." (NRA slogan)

"If you can't stand the heat, get out of the kitchen."

2. We don't want you to argue fallaciously, but it's fun and good practice to frame argumentative fallacies in your own language. Pick an argumentative topic—maybe even one that you've used for a paper in this class—and write a few paragraphs making nothing but fallacious arguments in each sentence. Try to include all the fallacies of emotional, ethical, and logical argument that are discussed in this chapter. It will be a challenge, since some of the fallacies are difficult to recognize, much less produce. Then rewrite the paragraphs, removing all traces of fallacious reasoning, rewriting for clarity, and improving the quality of the argument. This may be an even greater challenge— sometimes fallacies are hard to fix.

3. Choose a paper you've written for this or another class, and analyze it carefully for signs of fallacious reasoning. Once you've tried analyzing your own prose, find an editorial, a syndicated column, and a political speech and look for the fallacies in them. Which fallacies are most common in the four arguments? How do you account for their prevalence? Which are the least common? How do you account for their absence? What seems to be the role of audience in determining what is a fallacy and what is not? Did you find what seem to be fallacies other than the kinds discussed in this chapter?

4. Arguments on the Web are no more likely to contain fallacies than are arguments in any other text, but the fallacies *can* take on different forms. The hypertextual nature of Web arguments and the ease of including visuals along with text make certain fallacies more likely to occur there. Find a Web site sponsored by an organization, business, government entity, or other group (such as the sites of the Democratic and Republican National Committees that were discussed in Chapter 16), and analyze the site for fallacious reasoning. Among other considerations, look at the relationship between text and graphics, and between individual pages and the pages that surround or are linked to them. How does the technique of separating information into discrete pages affect the argument? Then send an email message to the site's creators, explaining what you found and proposing ways the arguments in the site could be improved.

chapter twenty

Intellectual Property

A student writing an essay about Title IX's effect on college athletic programs finds some powerful supporting evidence for her argument on a Web site. Can she use this information without gaining permission?

Day care centers around the country receive letters arguing that they will be liable to lawsuit if they use representations of Disney characters without explicit permission or show Disney films "outside the home."

In California, one large vintner sues another, claiming that the second "stole" the idea of a wine label from the first, although a judge later found that even though the labels were similar, the second was not "copied" from the first.

Musicians argue against other musicians, saying that the increasingly popular use of "sampling" in songs amounts to a form of musical "plagiarism."

On the electronic frontier, the development of digital "watermarks" makes it possible to trace not only documents printed out but those read online as well; as a result, some lawyers argue that millions of Internet users are probably guilty of copyright infringement.

■ ■ ■

In an age of agriculture and industrialization, products that can provide a livelihood are likely to be concrete things: crops, automobiles, houses. But in an age of information such as the current one, *ideas* (intellectual property) are arguably society's most important products. Hence the growing importance of—and growing controversies surrounding—what counts as "property" in an information age.

Perhaps the framers of the Constitution foresaw such a shift in the bases of the nation's economy. At any rate, they articulated in the Constitution a delicate balance between the public's need for information and the incentives necessary to encourage people to produce work—both material and intellectual. Thus, the Constitution empowers Congress "[t]o promote the progress of Science and useful Arts, by securing for limited Times to Authors and Inventors the exclusive Right to their respective Writings and Discoveries" (Article 1, Section 8, Clause 8). This passage allows for *limited* protection (copyright) of the expression of ideas ("Writings and Discoveries"), and through the years that time limit has been extended to up to lifetime plus seventy-five years (and it may be extended yet again to lifetime plus one hundred years).

Why is this historical information important to student writers? First, because writers need to know that ideas themselves cannot be copyrighted—only the *expression* of those ideas. Second, this information explains why some works fall out of copyright and are available for students to use without paying a fee (as you have to do for copyright-protected material in a coursepack, for instance). Third, this information is crucial to the current debates over who owns online materials—materials that may never take any form of concrete *expression*. The debate will certainly be raging during and after the publication of this book—and the

A cluster of arguments in Chapter 26 considers the matter of who owns words, presenting several different arguments about intellectual property. Charles Mann writes about the future of intellectual property in general, and four other pieces consider who should have the rights to use Martin Luther King Jr.'s "I Have a Dream" speech.

LINK TO P. 564 ··

way in which it is resolved will have many direct effects on students and teachers. For up-to-date information about copyright law, see the Digital Future Coalition site at <http://www.dfc.org> or the U.S. Copyright site at <http://lcweb.loc.gov/copyright/>.

RECOGNIZING PLAGIARISM

In a way, it is completely true that there is "nothing new under the sun." Indeed, whatever you think or write or say draws on everything you have ever heard or read or experienced. Trying to recall every influence or source of information you have drawn on, even in one day, would take so long that you would have little time left in which to say anything at all. Luckily, people are seldom if ever called on to list every single influence or source of their ideas and writings.

Certainly, recognizing and avoiding plagiarism is a good deal easier and more practical than that. And avoiding plagiarism is very important, for in Western culture *the use of someone else's words or ideas without acknowledgment and as your own is an act of dishonesty that can bring devastating results.* In some cases, students who plagiarize fail courses or are expelled. Eminent political, business, and scientific leaders have lost positions, appointments, or awards following charges of plagiarism. You might want to check out some sites on the Web that offer further information:

- <http://www.indiana.edu/~wts/wts/plagiarism.html>
- <http://www.guilford.edu/ASC/honor.html>
- <http://www.willamette.edu/wu/policy/cheat.html>

CULTURAL CONTEXTS FOR ARGUMENT

Not all cultures accept Western notions of plagiarism, which rest on a belief that language can be owned by writers. Indeed, in many countries, and in some communities within the United States, using the words of others is considered a sign of deep respect and an indication of knowledge—and attribution is not expected or required. In writing arguments in the United States, however, you should credit all materials but those that are common knowledge, that are available in a wide variety of sources, or that are your own findings from field research.

ACKNOWLEDGING YOUR USE OF SOURCES

The safest way to avoid charges of plagiarism is to acknowledge as many of your sources as possible, with the following three exceptions:

- *common knowledge,* a specific source of information most readers will know (that Bill Clinton won the 1996 presidential election, for instance)
- *facts available from a wide variety of sources* (that the Japanese bombing of Pearl Harbor occurred on December 7, 1941, for example)
- *your own findings from field research* (observations, interviews, experiments, or surveys you have conducted), which should simply be announced as your own

For all other source material you should give credit as fully as possible, placing quotation marks around any quoted material, citing your sources according to the documentation style you are using, and including them in a list of references or works cited. Include in material to be credited all of the following:

- *direct quotations*
- *facts not widely known or arguable statements*
- *judgments, opinions, and claims made by others*
- *statistics, charts, tables, graphs, or other illustrations* from any source
- *collaborations,* the help provided by friends, colleagues, instructors, supervisors, or others

(See Chapters 21 and 22 for more on using and documenting sources.)

Giving full credit to your sources needn't be awkward or interfere with the flow of your writing. Check out the way Joshua Gamson smoothly weaves fully credited quotes into his article about privacy—sometimes two or three in a single paragraph.

LINK TO P. 456 ···

ACKNOWLEDGING COLLABORATION

We have already noted the importance of acknowledging the inspirations and ideas you derive from talking with others. Such help counts as one form of collaboration, and you may also be involved in more formal kinds of collaborative work—preparing for a group presentation to a class, for example, or writing a group report. Writers generally acknowledge all participants in collaborative projects at the beginning of the presentation, report, or essay—in print texts, often in a footnote or brief prefatory note. The fifth edition of the *MLA Handbook for Writers of Research Papers* (1999) calls attention to the growing importance of collaborative work and gives the following advice on how to deal with issues of assigning fair credit all around:

> **Joint participation in research and writing is common and, in fact, encouraged in many courses and in many professions, and it does not constitute plagiarism provided that credit is given for all contributions. One way to give credit, if roles were clearly demarcated or were unequal, is to state exactly who did what. Another way, especially if roles and contributions were merged and truly shared, is to acknowledge all concerned equally. Ask your instructor for advice if you are not certain how to acknowledge collaboration.**

USING COPYRIGHTED INTERNET SOURCES

If you've done any surfing on the Net, you already know that it opens the doors to worldwide collaborations, as you can contact individuals and groups around the globe and have access to whole libraries of information. As a result, writing (most especially, online writing) seems increasingly to be made up of a huge patchwork of materials that you alone or you and many others weave together. (For a fascinating discussion of just how complicated charges and countercharges of plagiarism can be on the Internet, see <http://www.ombuds.org/narrative1.html>, where you can read a description of a mediation involving a Web site that included summaries of other people's work.) But when you use information gathered from Internet sources in your own work, it is subject to the same rules that govern information gathered from other types of sources.

Thus, whether or not the material includes a copyright notice or symbol ("© 2000 by John J. Ruszkiewicz and Andrea A. Lunsford," for example), it is more than likely copyrighted—and you may need to request permission to use part or all of it. Although they are currently in danger, "fair use" laws still allow writers to use brief passages from published works (generally up to 300 words from a book, 150 from a periodical article, or 4 lines from a poem) without permission from the copyright holder *if* the use is for educational or personal, noncommercial reasons *and* full credit is given to the source. For personal communication such as email or for listserv postings, however, you should ask permission of the writer before you include any of his or her material in your own argument. For graphics, photos, or other images you wish to reproduce in your text, you should also request permission from the creator or owner (except when you are using them in work only turned into an instructor, which is "fair use"). And if you are going to disseminate your work beyond your classroom—especially online—you must ask permission for any material you borrow from an Internet source.

Here are some examples of student requests for permission:

To: litman@mindspring.com
CC: lunsford.2@osu.edu
Subject: Request for permission

Dear Professor Litman:

I am writing to request permission to quote from your essay "Copyright, Owners' Rights and Users' Privileges on the Internet: Implied Licences, Caching, Linking, Fair Use, and Sign-on Licences." I want to quote some of your work as part of an essay I am writing for my composition class at Ohio State University to explain the complex debates over ownership on the Internet and to argue that students in my class should be participating in these debates. I will give full credit to you and will cite the URL where I first found your work: <http://www.msen.com/~litman/dayton/htm>.

    Thank you very much for considering my request.

Raul Sanchez <sanchez.32@osu.edu>

To: fridanet@aol.com
CC: lunsford.2@osu.edu
Subject: Request for permission

Dear Kimberley Masters:

I am a student at Ohio State University writing to request your permission to download and use a photograph of Frida Kahlo in a three-piece suit <fridanet/suit.htm#top> as an illustration in a project about Kahlo that I and two other students are working on in our composition class. In the report on our project, we will cite <http://members.aol.com/fridanet/kahlo.htm> as the URL, unless you wish for us to use a different source.

    Thank you very much for considering our request.

Jennifer Fox <fox.360@osu.edu>

CREDITING SOURCES IN ARGUMENTS

Acknowledging your sources and giving full credit is especially important in argumentative writing because doing so helps establish your ethos as a writer. In the first place, saying "thank you" to those who have been of help to you reflects gratitude and openness, qualities that audiences generally respond to very well. Second, acknowledging your sources demonstrates that you have "done your homework," that you know the conversation surrounding your topic and are familiar with what others have thought and said about it, and that you want to help readers find other contributions to the conversation and perhaps join it themselves. Finally, acknowledging sources reminds you to think very critically about your own stance in your argument and about how well you have used your sources. Are they timely and reliable? Have you used them in a biased or overly selective way? Have you used them accurately, double-checking all quotations and paraphrases? Thinking through these questions will improve your overall argument.

RESPOND ●

1. Not everyone agrees with the concept of intellectual material as property, as something to be protected. Lately the slogan "information wants to be free" has been showing up in popular magazines and on the Internet, often along with a call to readers to take action against forms of protection such as data encryption and further extension of copyright.

   Using a Web search engine, look for pages where the phrase "free information" appears. Find several sites that make arguments in favor of free information, and analyze them in terms of their rhetorical appeals. What claims do the authors make? How do they appeal to their audience? What is the site's ethos, and how is it created? Once you have read some arguments in favor of free information, return to this chapter's arguments about intellectual property. Which do you find more persuasive? Why?

2. Although this text is principally concerned with ideas and their written expression, there are other forms of protection available for intellectual property. Scientific and technological developments are protectable under patent law, which differs in some significant ways from copyright law.

Find the standards for protection under U.S. copyright law and U.S. patent law. You might begin by visiting the U.S. copyright Web site at <http://lcweb.loc.gov/copyright/>. Then, imagine that you are the president of a small, high-tech corporation and are trying to inform your employees of the legal protections available to them and their work. Write a paragraph or two explaining the differences between copyright and patent and suggesting a policy that balances employees' rights to intellectual property with the business's needs to develop new products.

3. Using the definitions of *patent* and *copyright* that you found for the previous exercise, write a few paragraphs speculating on the reasons behind the differences in protection granted by each. Be sure to consider the application process, too. How does a person go about getting copyright or patent protection? Why are the processes different?

chapter twenty-one

Assessing and Using Sources

ASSESSING SOURCES

As many examples in this text have shown, the quality of an argument often depends to a large degree on the quality of the sources used to support or prove it. As a result, careful evaluation and assessment of *all* your sources is important, including those you gather in libraries or from other print sources, in online searches, or in field research you conduct yourself.

Print Sources

Since you want the information you glean from sources to be reliable and persuasive, it pays to evaluate thoroughly each potential source. The following principles can help you in conducting such an evaluation for print sources:

- *Relevance.* Is the source closely related to your argumentative claim? For a book, the table of contents and the index may help you decide. For an article, check to see if there is an abstract that summarizes the contents.

- *Credentials and stance of author/publisher.* Is the author an expert on the topic? What is the author's stance on the issue(s) involved, and how does this stance influence the information in the source? Does the author's stance support or challenge your own views? If the source was published by a corporation, government agency, or interest group, what is the publisher's position on the topic? If you are evaluating an article, what kind of periodical published it? Popular? Academic? Alternative? Right- or left-leaning in terms of political perspective? If only *one* perspective is presented, do you need to balance or expand it?

- *Date of publication.* Recent sources are often more useful than older ones, particularly in the sciences. However, in some fields such as history or literature, the most authoritative works can be the older ones.

- *Level of specialization.* General sources can be helpful as you begin your research, but later in the project you may need the authority or currentness of more specialized sources. On the other hand, keep in mind that extremely specialized works on your topic may be too difficult for your audience to understand easily.

- *Audience.* Was the source written for a general readership? For specialists? For advocates or opponents?

- *Cross-referencing.* Is the source cited in other works? If it is, do the citations refer to it as an "authority"?

- *Length.* Is the source long enough to provide adequate detail in support of your claim?

- *Availability.* Do you have access to the source? If it is not readily accessible, your time might be better spent looking elsewhere.

- *Omissions.* What is missing or omitted from the source? Might such exclusions affect whether or how you can use the source as evidence?

Electronic Sources

You will probably find working on the Internet and the World Wide Web both exciting and frustrating, for even though these tools have great potential, they are still in a fairly primitive state. Unlike most library-based sources, much material on the Internet in general and on the Web in particular is still the work of enthusiastic amateurs; sloppy research, commercial advertisements, one-sided statements, even false information all rub elbows with good, reliable evidence in cyberspace. As a result, some scholars refuse to trust anything on the Net and look for corroboration before accepting evidence they find there. In such an environment, you must be the judge of how accurate and trustworthy particular electronic sources are. In making these judgments you should rely on the same kind of careful thinking you would use to assess any source. In addition, you may find some of the following questions helpful in evaluating online sources:

- Who has posted the document or message or created the site? An individual? An interest group? A company? A government agency? Does the URL offer any clues? Note especially the final suffix in a domain name —.com (commercial); .org (nonprofit organization); .edu (educational institution); .gov (government agency) — or the geographical domains that indicate country of origin, as in .ca (Canada) or .ar (Argentina).

- What can you determine about the credibility of the author? Can the information in the document or site be verified in other sources? How accurate and complete is it?

- Who can be held accountable for the information in the document or site? How well and thoroughly does it credit its own sources?

- How current is the document or site? Be especially cautious of undated materials.

- How effectively is the document or site designed? How "friendly" is it? Are its links, if any, helpful? What effects do design, visuals, and/or sound have on the message? (See Chapters 15 and 16.)

- What perspectives are represented? If only one perspective is represented, how can you balance or expand this point of view?

Field Research

If you have conducted experiments, surveys, interviews, observations, or any other field research in developing and supporting an argument, make sure to review your own results with a critical eye. The following questions can help you evaluate your own field research:

- Have you rechecked all data and all conclusions to make sure they are accurate and warranted?

- Have you identified the exact time, place, and participants in all field research?
- Have you made clear what part you played in the research and how, if at all, your role could have influenced the results or findings?
- If your research involved other people, have you gotten their permission to use their words or other material in your argument? Have you asked whether you could use their names or whether the names should be kept confidential?

USING SOURCES

As you locate, examine, and evaluate sources in support of an argument, remember to keep a careful record of where you have found them. For print sources, you may want to keep a working bibliography on your computer—or a list in a notebook you can carry with you. In any case, make sure you take down the *name of the author;* the *title* of the book or periodical and article, if any; the *publisher* and *city of publication;* the *date of publication;* relevant *volume, issue,* and *page numbers;* and any other information you may later need in preparing a works-cited or references list. In addition, for a book, note where you found it—the section of the library, for example, along with the call number for the book.

For electronic sources, you should also keep a careful record of the information you will need in your works-cited or references list—particularly the *name of the database or online source,* the full *electronic address or URL,* and several potentially important dates: (1) the *date the document was first produced;* (2) the *date the document was published on the Web*—this may be a version number or a revision date; and (3) the *date you accessed the document.* In general, the simplest way to ensure that you have this information is to get a printout of the source.

Signal Words and Introductions

Because your sources will probably be extremely important to the success of your arguments, you need to introduce them carefully to your readers. Doing so usually calls for beginning a sentence in which you are going to use a source with a signal phrase of some kind: *According to noted child psychiatrist Robert Coles, children develop complex ethical systems at extremely young ages.* In this sentence, the signal phrase tells readers that you are about to draw on the work of a person named Robert Coles and that this person is a "noted child psychiatrist." Here is an example that uses a quotation from a source in more than one sentence (note that in the MLA style, ellipsis marks are enclosed in brackets):

> In *Job Shift,* consultant William Bridges worries about "dejobbing and about what a future shaped by it is going to be like." Even more worrisome, Bridges argues, is the possibility that "the sense of craft and of professional vocation [. . .] will break down under the need to earn a fee" (228).

"Worries" and "argues" add a sense of urgency to the message Bridges offers and suggest that the writer either agrees with—or is neutral about—these points. Other signal verbs have a more negative slant, indicating that the point being introduced in the quotation is open to debate and that others (including the writer) might disagree with it. If the writer of the passage above had said, for instance, that Bridges "unreasonably contends" or that he "fantasizes," these signal verbs would carry quite different connotations from those associated with "argues." In some cases, a signal verb may require more complex phrasing to get the writer's full meaning across:

> Bridges recognizes the dangers of changes in work yet refuses to be overcome by them: "The real issue is not how to stop the change but how to provide the necessary knowledge and skills to equip people to operate successfully in this New World" (229).

As these examples illustrate, the signal verb is important because it allows you to characterize the author's or source's viewpoint or perspective as well as your own—so choose these verbs with care. Other frequently used signal verbs include *acknowledges, advises, agrees, allows, asserts, believes, charges, claims, concludes, concurs, confirms, criticizes, declares, disagrees, discusses, disputes, emphasizes, expresses, interprets, lists, objects, observes, offers, opposes, remarks, replies, reports, responds, reveals, states, suggests, thinks,* and *writes.*

Quotations

For supporting argumentative claims, you will want to quote—that is, to reproduce an author's precise words—in at least three kinds of situations: when the wording is so memorable or expresses a point so well that you cannot improve it or shorten it without weakening it; when the author is a respected authority whose opinion supports your own ideas particularly well; and when an author challenges or disagrees profoundly with others in the field. The following guidelines can help you make sure that you quote accurately:

- Copy quotations carefully, being sure that punctuation, capitalization, and spelling are exactly as they are in the original.

- Enclose the quotation in quotation marks; don't rely on your memory to distinguish your own words from those of your source. If in doubt, recheck all quotations for accuracy.

- Use square brackets if you introduce words of your own into the quotation or make changes to it. *("And [more] brain research isn't going to define further the matter of 'mind.'")*

- Use ellipsis marks if you omit material and enclose them in brackets. *("And brain research isn't going to define [. . .] the matter of 'mind.'")*

- Make sure you have all the information necessary to create an in-text citation as well as an item in your works-cited or references list.

- If you're quoting a short passage (four lines or less, MLA style; forty words or less, APA style), it should be worked into your text, enclosed by quotation marks. Longer quotations should be set off from the regular text. Begin such a quotation on a new line, indenting every line one inch or ten spaces (MLA) or five to seven spaces (APA). Set-off quotations do not need to be enclosed in quotation marks.

- If the quotation extends over more than one page, indicate page breaks in case you decide to use only part of the quotation in your argument.

- Label the quotation with a note that tells you where and/or how you think you will use it.

Paraphrases

Paraphrases involve putting an author's material (including major and minor points, usually in the order they are presented in the original) into *your own words and sentence structures*. Here are some guidelines that can help you paraphrase accurately:

- Include all main points and any important details from the original source, in the same order in which the author presents them.

- State the meaning in your own words and sentence structures. If you want to include especially memorable or powerful language from the original source, enclose it in quotation marks.

- Make sure you have all the information necessary to create an in-text citation as well as an item in your works-cited or references list.

- If you are paraphrasing material that extends over more than one page, indicate page breaks if possible in case you decide to use only part of the paraphrase in your argument.

- Label the paraphrase with a note suggesting where and/or how you intend to use it in your argument.

Summaries

A summary is a significantly shortened version of a passage—or even a whole chapter of a work—that captures the main ideas *in your own words.* Unlike a paraphrase, a summary uses just enough information to record the points you want to emphasize. Summaries can be extremely valuable in supporting arguments. Here are some guidelines to help you prepare accurate and helpful summaries:

- Include just enough information to recount the main points you want to cite. A summary is usually much shorter than the original.

- Use your own words. If you include any language from the original, enclose it in quotation marks.

- Make sure you have all the information necessary to create an in-text citation as well as an item in your works-cited or references list.

- If you are summarizing material that extends over more than one page, indicate page breaks in case you decide to use only part of the summary in your argument.

- Label the summary with a note that suggests where and/or how you intend to use it in your argument.

RESPOND•

1. Select one of the essays at the end of Chapters 9–13, such as Gretel Ehrlich's "About Men" (Chapter 9) or Larissa MacFarquhar's "Who Cares If Johnny Can't Read?" (Chapter 10). Then write a brief summary

of the essay that includes both direct quotations and paraphrases. Be careful to attribute the ideas properly, even when you paraphrase.

Trade summaries with a partner, and compare the passages you selected to quote and paraphrase, and the signal phrases you used to introduce them. How do your choices create an ethos for the original author that differs from the one your partner has created? How do the signal phrases shape a reader's sense of the author's position? Which summary best represents the author's argument? Why?

2. Imagine that you are in the beginning stages of research for a paper on the history of race relations in the United States. You have an initial bibliography, but you need to shorten the list so that you can begin reading—you need to make some tough decisions about which works to cut.

   Turn to the examples for a list of works cited (MLA style) and a list of references (APA style) in Chapter 22. Use the criteria in this chapter to help you select five of these sources for inclusion in your short list. For each source that you pick, write a few sentences explaining your decision. How relevant is the source? How recent? How specialized?

3. Return to the Internet sites you found in exercise 1 of Chapter 20 that discuss free information. Using the criteria in this chapter for evaluating electronic sources, judge each of those sites. Select three that you believe are most trustworthy, and write a paragraph summarizing their arguments and recommending them to an audience unfamiliar with the debate.

chapter twenty-two

Documenting Sources

What does documenting sources have to do with argument? First, the sources themselves form part of the argument, showing that a writer has done some homework, knows what others have said about the topic, and understands how to use these sources as support for a claim. The list of works cited or references makes an argument, saying, perhaps, "Look at how thoroughly this essay has been researched" or "Note how up-to-date I am!" Even the style of documentation makes an argument, though in a very subtle way. You will note in the instructions that follow, for example, that for a print source the Modern Language Association (MLA) style for a list of works cited requires putting the date of publication at or near the end of an entry, whereas the American Psychological Association (APA) style for a list of references involves putting the date near the beginning. (The exercise at the end of this chapter asks you to consider what argument this difference represents.) And when a documentation style calls for listing only the first author and et al. in citing works by multiple authors, it is subtly arguing that only the first author really matters—or at least that acknowledging the others is less important than keeping citations brief. Pay attention to the fine points of documentation and documentation style, always asking what these elements add (or do not add) to your arguments.

MLA STYLE

Documentation styles vary from discipline to discipline, with different formats favored in the social sciences and the natural sciences, for example. Widely used in fields in the humanities, the MLA style is fully described in the *MLA Handbook for Writers of Research Papers* (5th edition, 1999) and the *MLA Style Manual and Guide to Scholarly Publishing* (2nd edition, 1998). In this discussion, we provide guidelines drawn from the *MLA Handbook* for in-text citations, notes, and entries in the list of works cited.

The essays by La Donna Beaty and Brent Knutson both use MLA style.

LINK TO PP. 180 AND 207

In-Text Citations

The MLA style calls for in-text citations in the body of an argument to document sources of quotations, paraphrases, summaries, and so on. Keep an in-text citation short, but include enough information for readers to locate the source in the list of works cited. Place the citation as near to the relevant material as possible without disrupting the flow of the sentence, as in the following examples.

1. Author Named in a Signal Phrase

Ordinarily, use the author's name in a signal phrase—to introduce the material—and cite the page number(s) in parentheses.

> Loomba argues that Caliban's "political colour" (emphasis hers) is black, given his stage representations, which have varied from animalistic to a kind of missing link (143).

2. Author Named in Parentheses

When you don't mention the author in a signal phrase, include the author's last name before the page number(s) in the parentheses.

> Renaissance visions of "other" worlds, particularly in plays and travel narratives, often accentuated the differences of the Other even when striking similarities to the English existed (Bartels 434).

3. Two or Three Authors

Use all authors' last names.

> Kiniry and Rose maintain that a curriculum focused on critical thinking and writing strategies will help students improve their academic writing abilities (v).

4. Four or More Authors

The MLA allows you to use all authors' last names, or to use only the first author's name with *et al.* (in regular type, not underlined or italicized). Although either format is acceptable when applied consistently throughout a paper, in an argument it may be better to name all authors who contributed to the work.

> Similarly, as Goldberger, Tarule, Clinchy, and Belenky note, their new book builds on their collaborative experiences (xii).

5. Organization as Author

Give the full name of a corporate author if it is brief or a shortened form if it is long.

> Clements sold Nancy to Henry Waring, another Catholic slaveholder (Montgomery County 77).

6. Unknown Author

Use the full title of the work if it is brief or a shortened form if it is long.

> Hollywood executives insisted that the second kiss between the men be cut from the film ("The New Wave" 53).

7. Author of Two or More Works

When you use two or more works by the same author, include the title of the work or a shortened version of it in the citation.

> Green challenges the conception of blacks that the whites in Wellington want to force on him when he declares "I ain't no w'ite folks' nigger, I ain'. I don' call no man 'marster'" (qtd. in Chesnutt, Marrow of Tradition 304).

8. Authors with the Same Last Name

When you use works by two or more authors with the same last name, include each author's first initial in the citation.

> Father Divine's teachings focused on eternal life, salvation, and socio-economic progress (R. Washington 17).

9. Multivolume Work

Note the volume number first and then the page number(s), with a colon and one space between them.

> Aristotle's "On Plants" is now available in a new translation, edited by Barnes (2: 1252).

10. Literary Work

Because literary works are often available in many different editions, you need to include enough information for readers to locate the passage in any edition. For a prose work such as a novel or play, first cite the page number from the edition you used, followed by a semicolon; then indicate the part or chapter number (114; *ch.* 3) or act or scene in a play (42; *sc.* 2). For verse plays, omit the page number and give instead the act, scene, and line numbers, separated by periods.

> Before he takes his own life, Othello says he is "one that loved not wisely but too well" (5.2.348).

For a poem, cite the stanza and line numbers. If the poem has only line numbers, use the word *line(s)* in the first reference (*lines 33–34*).

> Looking back, Lenore Keeshig-Tobias recalls growing up on the reserve, "thinking it was the most/beautiful place in the world" (I.2-3).

11. Works in an Anthology

For an essay, short story, or other short work within an anthology, use the name of the author of the work, not the editor of the anthology; but use the page number(s) from the anthology.

> In the end, if the black artist accepts any duties at all, that duty is to express the beauty of blackness (Hughes 1271).

12. Bible

Identify quotations by chapter and verse (*John* 3.16). Spell out the names of books mentioned in your text. In a parenthetical citation, use standard scholarly abbreviations for books of the Bible with five or more letters (*Gen.* for *Genesis*).

13. Indirect Source

Use the abbreviation *qtd. in* to indicate that what you are quoting or paraphrasing is quoted (as part of a conversation, interview, letter, or excerpt) in the source you are using.

> As Catherine Belsey states, "to speak is to have access to the language which defines, delimits and locates power" (qtd. in Bartels 453).

14. Two or More Sources in the Same Citation

Separate the information for each source with a semicolon.

> Adefunmi was able to patch up the subsequent holes left in worship by substituting various Yoruba, Dahomean, or Fon customs made available to him through research (Brandon 115-17; Hunt 27).

15. Entire Work or One-Page Article

Include the citation in the text without any page numbers or parentheses.

> The relationship between revolutionary innocence and the preservation of an oppressive post-revolutionary regime is one theme Milan Kundera explores in The Book of Laughter and Forgetting.

16. Work without Page Numbers

If the work is not paginated, include instead the section (*sec.*), part (*pt.*), or paragraph (*par.*) numbers, if available.

Zora Neale Hurston is one of the great anthropologists of the twentieth century, according to Kip Hinton (par. 2).

17. Other Nonprint Source

Give enough information in a signal phrase or parenthetical citation for readers to locate the source in the list of works cited. Usually give the author or title under which you list the source.

In his film version of Hamlet, Zefferelli highlights the sexual tension between the prince and his mother.

Explanatory and Bibliographic Notes

The MLA recommends using explanatory notes for information or commentary that does not readily fit into your text but is needed for clarification, further explanation, or justification. In addition, the MLA allows bibliographic notes for information about a source. Use superscript numbers in your text at the end of a sentence to refer readers to the notes, which usually appear as endnotes (with the heading *Notes*) on a separate page before the list of works cited. Indent the first line of each note five spaces, and double-space all entries.

Text with Superscript Indicating a Note

Heilbrun describes her decision to choose life over death and notes her affinity to artist Käthe Kollwitz's love of work.[2]

Note

[2] Kollwitz, like Heilbrun, identified work as the essence of life: "The readiness forms in waves inside myself," and "I need only be on the alert [. . .]" (10).

List of Works Cited

A list of works cited is an alphabetical listing of the sources you cite in your essay. The list appears on a separate page at the end of your argument, after any notes, with the heading *Works Cited*. (If you are asked to list everything you have read as background, call the list *Works Consulted*.)

The first line of each entry should align on the left; subsequent lines indent one-half inch or five spaces. Double-space.

Books

The basic information for a book includes three elements, each followed by a period: the author's name, last name first; the title and subtitle, underlined or (if your instructor permits) italicized; and the publication information, including the city, a shortened form of the publisher's name, and the date. For a book with multiple authors, only the first author's name is inverted.

1. One Author

Jacobs, Jane. The Death and Life of Great American Cities. New York: Vintage, 1992.

2. Two or More Authors

Arbib, Michael, and Mary Hesse. The Construction of Reality. Cambridge: Cambridge UP, 1986.

3. Organization as Author

American Cancer Society. The Dangers of Smoking, the Benefits of Quitting. New York: Amer. Cancer Soc., 1972.

4. Unknown Author

The Spanish Republic. London: Eyre, 1933.

5. Two or More Books by the Same Author

List the works alphabetically by title.

Gaines, Ernest. A Gathering of Old Men. New York: Viking, 1984.
---. A Lesson before Dying. New York: Vintage, 1994.

6. Editor

Rorty, Amelie Oksenberg, ed. Essays on Aristotle's Poetics. Princeton: Princeton UP, 1992.

7. Author and Editor

Shakespeare, William. The Tempest. Ed. Frank Kermode. London:
Routledge, 1994.

8. Selection in an Anthology or Chapter in an Edited Book

Brown, Paul. "'This thing of darkness I acknowledge mine': The Tempest
and the Discourse of Colonialism." Political Shakespeare: Essays
in Cultural Materialism. Ed. Jonathan Dillimore and Alan Sinfield.
Ithaca: Cornell UP, 1985. 48-71.

9. Two or More Works from the Same Anthology

Gates, Henry Louis, Jr., and Nellie McKay, eds. The Norton Anthology of
African American Literature. New York: Norton, 1997.
Neal, Larry. "The Black Arts Movement." Gates and McKay 1960-1972.
Karenga, Maulana. "Black Art: Mute Matter Given Force and Function."
Gates and McKay 1973-1977.

10. Translation

Kundera, Milan. The Book of Laughter and Forgetting. Trans. Michael
Henry Haim. New York: Penguin, 1984.

11. Edition Other than the First

Stoessinger, John G. Why Nations Go to War. 6th ed. New York: St.
Martin's, 1993.

12. One Volume of a Multivolume Work

Byron, Lord George. Byron's Letters and Journals. Ed. Leslie A.
Marchand. Vol. 2. London: J. Murray, 1973-1982.

13. Two or More Volumes of a Multivolume Work

Byron, Lord George. Byron's Letters and Journals. Ed. Leslie A.
Marchand. 12 vols. London: J. Murray, 1973-1982.

14. Preface, Foreword, Introduction, or Afterword

Walker, Alexander. Introduction. Film Censorship. By Guy Phelps.
London: Gollancz, 1975. vii-xi.

15. Article in a Reference Work

"Carolina Campaign." The Columbia Encyclopedia. 5th ed. 1993.

16. Book That Is Part of a Series

Shakespeare, William. Othello. Ed. M. R. Ridley. The Arden Shakespeare Ser. 3. London: Routledge, 1993.

17. Government Document

United States. Cong. House Committee on the Judiciary. Impeachment of the President. 40th Cong., 1st sess. H. Rept. 7, 1867. Washington: GPO, 1867.

18. Pamphlet

An Answer to the President's Message to the Fiftieth Congress. Philadelphia: Manufacturer's Club of Philadelphia, 1887.

19. Published Proceedings of a Conference

Edwards, Ron, ed. Proceedings of the Third National Folklore Conference. Canberra, Austral.: Australian Folk Trust, 1988.

20. Title within a Title

Tauernier-Courbin, Jacqueline. Ernest Hemingway's A Moveable Feast: The Making of a Myth. Boston: Northeastern UP, 1991.

Periodicals

The basic entry for a periodical includes the following three elements, separated by periods: the author's name, last name first; the article title, in quotation marks; and the publication information, including the periodical title (underlined or italicized), the volume and issue numbers (if any), the date of publication, and the page number(s). For works with multiple authors, only the first author's name is inverted. Note, too, that the period following the article title goes *inside* the closing quotation mark.

21. Article in a Journal Paginated by Volume

Wood, Winifred J. "Double Desire: Overlapping Discourses in a Film Writing Course." College English 60 (1998): 278-300.

22. Article in a Journal Paginated by Issue

Radavich, David. "Man among Men: David Mamet's Homosocial Order."
American Drama 1.1 (1991): 46-66.

23. Article in a Monthly Magazine

Heartney, Eleanor. "Portrait of a Decade." Art in America Oct. 1997:
102-05.

24. Article in a Newspaper

Mitchell, Alison. "Campaign Finance Bill Approaches Deadlock." New
York Times 26 Feb. 1998, late ed.: A16.

25. Editorial or Letter to Editor

Danto, Arthur. "'Elitism' and the N.E.A." Editorial. The Nation 17 Nov.
1997: 6-7.

26. Unsigned Article

"Court Rejects the Sale of Medical Marijuana." New York Times 26 Feb.
1998, late ed.: A21.

27. Review

Partner, Peter. "The Dangers of Divinity." Rev. of The Shape of the Holy:
Early Islamic Jerusalem, by Oleg Grabar. New York Review of
Books 5 Feb. 1998: 27-28.

Electronic Sources

Most of the following models are based on the MLA's guidelines for
citing electronic sources in the *MLA Handbook* (5th edition, 1999) as well as
on up-to-date information available at <http://www.mla.org/style/
sources.htm>. Formats not covered by the MLA are based on Andrew
Harnack and Eugene Kleppinger, *Online! A Reference Guide to Using Internet
Sources* (2000 edition).

The MLA requires that URLs be enclosed in angle brackets. Also, if a
URL will not all fit on one line, it should be broken only after the second
slash in the opening protocol *http://* or after a slash later in the URL, with
no hyphen at the line break.

The basic MLA entry for most electronic sources should include the following elements:

- name of the author, editor, or compiler
- title of the work, document, or posting
- date of electronic publication or last update, if available
- date of access
- URL in angle brackets

28. *CD-ROM, Diskette, or Magnetic Tape, Single Issue*

> McPherson, James M., ed. The American Heritage New History of the Civil War. CD-ROM. New York: Viking, 1996.

29. *Periodically Revised CD-ROM*

Include the author's name; publication information for the print version of the text (including its title and date of publication); the title of the database; the medium (CD-ROM); the name of the company producing it; and the electronic publication date (month and year, if possible).

> Heyman, Steven. "The Dangerously Exciting Client." Psychotherapy Patient 9.1 (1994): 37-46. PsycLIT. CD-ROM. SilverPlatter. Nov. 1996.

30. *Scholarly Project or Reference Database*

Include the title of the project or database, underlined or italicized; the name of the editor, if any, preceded by *Ed.*; the version number, if relevant and not part of the title; the date of electronic publication or of the latest update; the name of any sponsoring institution or organization; the date of access; and the URL.

> The Orlando Project: An Integrated History of Women's Writing in the British Isles. 1997. U of Alberta. 1 Mar. 2000 <http://www.ualberta.ca/ORLANDO/>.

31. *Professional or Personal Web Site*

Include the name of the person who created the site, if relevant; the title of the site (underlined) or (if there is no title) a description such as *Home page*; the name of any institution or organization associated with the site; the date of access; and the URL.

<u>Classical Myth: The Ancient Sources</u>. 24 June 1999. Dept. of Greek and
 Roman Studies, U of Victoria. 1 Mar. 2000 <http://web.uvic.ca/
 grs/bowman/myth/index.html>.
Bays, Carter L. Home page. 3 Jan. 1998. 1 Mar. 2000 <http://
 www.con.wesleyan.edu/~cbays/homepage.html>.

32. Online Book

Begin with the name of the author—or, if only an editor, a compiler, or a
translator is identified, the name of that person followed by *ed., comp.,* or
trans. Then give the title and the name of any editor, compiler, or translator not listed earlier, preceded by *Ed., Comp.,* or *Trans.* If the online version
of the text has not been published before, give the date of electronic
publication and the name of any sponsoring institution or organization.
Then give any publication information (city, publisher, and/or year) for
the original print version that is given in the source; the date of access;
and the URL.

Maugham, W. Somerset. <u>Of Human Bondage</u>. London: Macmillan, 1972.
 1 Mar. 2000 <http://www.bibliomania.com/Fiction/Maugham/
 Human/index.html>.

For a poem, an essay, or other short work within an online book, include
its title after the author's name. Give the URL of the short work, not of the
book, if they differ.

Dickinson, Emily, "The Grass." <u>Poems: Emily Dickinson</u>. Boston: Roberts
 Brothers, 1891. <u>Humanities Text Initiative American Verse
 Collection</u>. Ed. Nancy Kushigian. 1995. U of Michigan.
 1 Mar. 2000 <http://www.hti.umich.edu/bin/
 amv-idx.pl?type=HTML&rgn=DIV1&byte=9559331>.

33. Article in an Online Periodical

Follow the formats for citing articles in print periodicals, but adapt them
as necessary to the online medium. Include the page numbers of the article or the total number of pages, paragraphs, parts, or other numbered
sections, if any; the date of access; and the URL.

White, Richard B. "The Mahar Movement's Military Component." <u>South
 Asia Graduate Research Journal</u> 1.1 (May 1994). 1 Mar. 2000
 <http://asnic.utexas.edu/asnic/sagar/spring.1994/
 richard.white.art.html>.

Gwande, Atul. "Drowsy Docs." Slate 9 Oct. 1997. 1 Mar. 2000
<http://www.slate.com/MedicalExaminer/97-10-09/
MedicalExaminer.asp>.

34. Listserv Posting

Begin with the author's name, the title of the posting, and the description
Online posting. Then give the date of the posting, the name of the listserv,
the date of access, and either the URL of the listserv or (preferably) the
URL of an archival version of the posting. If a URL is unavailable, give the
email address of the list moderator.

Chagall, Nancy. "Web Publishing and Censorship." Online posting. 2 Feb.
1997. ACW: Alliance for Computers and Writing Discussion List.
10 Oct. 1997 <http://english.ttu.edu/acw-1/archive.htm>.

35. Newsgroup Posting

Give the author's name and the title of the posting followed by *Online posting,* the date of the posting, and the date of access. Then give the name of
the newsgroup with the prefix *news:.*

Martin, Jerry. "The IRA & Sinn Fein." Online posting. 31 Mar. 1998.
31 Mar. 1998 <news:soc.culture.irish>.

36. Email Message

Include the writer's name, the subject line, the description *Email to the
author* or *Email to [the recipient's name],* and the date of the message.

DeLaRosa, Alexis. "Do This." Email to the author. 25 May 1997.

37. Synchronous Communication (MOO, MUD, or IRC)

Include the name of any specific speaker(s) you are citing; a description
of the event; its date; the name of the forum; the date of access; and the
URL of the posting (with the prefix *telnet:*) or (preferably) of an archival
version.

Patuto, Jeremy, Simon Fennel, and James Goss. The Mytilene debate.
9 May 1996. MiamiMOO. 28 Mar. 1998 <http://
moo.cas.muohio.edu/cgi-bin/moo?look+4085>.

38. Online Interview, Work of Art, or Film

Follow the general guidelines for the print version of the source, but also include information on the electronic medium, such as publication information for a CD-ROM or the date of electronic publication, the date of access, and the URL for a Web site.

> Dyson, Esther. Interview. Hotseat. 23 May 1997. 1 Mar. 2000
>   <http://www.hotwired.com/packet/hotseat/97/20/index4a.html>.
> Aleni, Guilio. K'un-yu t'u-shu. ca. 1620. Vatican, Rome. 28 Mar. 1998
>   <http://www.ncsa.uiuc.edu/SDG/Experimental/vatican.exhibit/
>   exhibit/full-images/i-rome-to-china/china02.gif>.
> John Woo, dir. Face Off. 1997. Hollywood.com. 8 Mar. 2000
>   <http://www.hollywood.com/multimedia/movies/faceoff/trailer/
>   mmindex.html>.

39. FTP (File Transfer Protocol), Telnet, or Gopher Site

Substitute *FTP, Telnet,* or *Gopher* for *http* at the beginning of the URL.

> Korn, Peter. "How Much Does Breast Cancer Really Cost?" Self Oct.
>   1994. 5 May 1997 <gopher://nysernet.org:70/00/BCTC/
>   Sources/SELF/94/how-much>.

Other Sources

40. Unpublished Dissertation

> West, Susan. "From Owning to Owning Up: 'Authorial' Rights and
>   Rhetorical Responsibilities." Diss. Ohio State U, 1996.

41. Published Dissertation

> Baum, Bernard. Decentralization of Authority in a Bureaucracy. Diss. U of
>   Chicago. Englewood Cliffs: Prentice-Hall, 1961.

42. Article from a Microform

> Sharpe, Lora. "A Quilter's Tribute." Boston Globe 25 Mar. 1989:
>   13. Newsbank: Social Relations 12 (1989): fiche 6, grids B4-6.

43. Personal Interview

> Harding, Sandra. Telephone interview. 14 May 2000.

44. Letter

Jacobs, Harriet. "Letter to Amy Post." 4 Apr. 1853. Incidents in the Life of a Slave Girl. Ed. Jean Fagan Yellin. Cambridge: Harvard UP, 1987. 234-35.

45. Film

He Got Game. Dir. Spike Lee. Perf. Denzel Washington and Ray Allen. Touchstone, 1998.

46. Television or Radio Program

King of the Hill. Writ. Jim Dauterive. Perf. Mike Judge and Pamela Seagall. FOX, New York. 29 Mar. 1998.

47. Sound Recording

Fugees. "Ready or Not." The Score. Sony, 1996.

48. Lecture or Speech

Higginbotham, Leon. "Baccalaureate Address." Wesleyan U, Middletown. 26 May 1996.

49. Performance

Freak. By John Leguizamo. Dir. David Bar Katz. Cort Theater, New York. 7 Mar. 1998.

50. Map or Chart

The Political and Physical World. Map. Washington: Natl. Geographic, 1975.

51. Cartoon

Cheney, Tom. Cartoon. New Yorker 16 Mar. 1998: 49.

52. Advertisement

Toyota. Advertisement. Discover Mar. 1998: 7.

APA STYLE

The *Publication Manual of the American Psychological Association* (4th edition, 1994) provides comprehensive advice to student and professional writers in the social sciences. Here we draw on the *Publication Manual's* guidelines to provide an overview of APA style for in-text citations, content notes, and entries in the list of references.

In-Text Citations

The APA style calls for in-text citations in the body of an argument to document sources of quotations, paraphrases, summaries, and so on. These in-text citations correspond to full bibliographic entries in the list of references at the end of the text.

1. Author Named in a Signal Phrase

Generally, use the author's name in a signal phrase to introduce the cited material, and place the date, in parentheses, immediately after the author's name. For a quotation, the page number, preceded by *p.*, appears in parentheses after the quotation. For electronic texts or other works without page numbers, paragraph numbers may be used instead, preceded by the ¶ symbol or the abbreviation "para." For a long, set-off quotation, position the page reference in parentheses two spaces after the punctuation at the end of the quotation.

> According to Brandon (1993), Adefunmi opposed all forms of racism and believed that black nationalism should not be a destructive force.

2. Author Named in Parentheses

When you do not mention the author in a signal phrase, give the name and the date, separated by a comma, in parentheses at the end of the cited material.

> Adefunmi opposed all forms of racism and believed that black nationalism should not be a destructive force (Brandon, 1993).

3. Two Authors

Use both names in all citations. Use *and* in a signal phrase, but use an ampersand (&) in parentheses.

Associated with purity and wisdom, Obatala is the creator of human beings, whom he is said to have formed out of clay (Edwards & Mason, 1985).

4. Three to Five Authors

List all the authors' names for the first reference. In subsequent references, use just the first author's name followed by *et al.* (in regular type, not underlined or italicized).

Lenhoff, Wang, Greenberg, and Bellugi (1997) cite tests that indicate that segments of the left brain hemisphere are not affected by Williams syndrome whereas the right hemisphere is significantly affected.

Shackelford drew on the study by Lenhoff et al. (1997).

5. Six or More Authors

Use only the first author's name and *et al.* (in regular type, not underlined or italicized) in *every* citation, including the first.

As Flower et al. (1990) demonstrate, reading and writing involve both cognitive and social processes.

6. Organization as Author

If the name of an organization or a corporation is long, spell it out the first time, followed by an abbreviation in brackets. In later citations, use the abbreviation only.

First Citation.   (Federal Bureau of Investigation [FBI], 1952)
Subsequent Citations.   (FBI, 1952)

7. Unknown Author

Use the title or its first few words in a signal phrase or in parentheses.

These ideas paralleled the tenets of New Thought and provided a bridge for ideological compatibility between the Bishop and the Fairmount Avenue Ministry (New Amsterdam News, 1932).

8. Authors with the Same Last Name

If your list of references includes works by different authors with the same last name, include the authors' initials in each citation.

C. McKay (1935) claimed that no men lived in the household, though at least one man lived in the Brooklyn collective.

9. Two or More Sources in the Same Citation

List sources by the same author chronologically by publication year. List sources by different authors in alphabetical order by the authors' last names, separated by semicolons.

While traditional forms of argument are warlike and agonistic, alternative models do exist (Foss & Foss, 1997; Makau, 1999).

10. Specific Parts of a Source

Use abbreviations (*chap., p.,* and so on) in a parenthetical citation to name the part of a work you are citing.

Bellah (1992, chap. 6) described the birth of New American myths.

11. World Wide Web Site

To cite an entire Web site, include its address in parentheses in your text (<http://www.gallup.com>); do not include it in your list of references. To cite part of a text found on the Web, indicate the chapter or figure, as appropriate. To document a quotation, include page or paragraph numbers, if available, or you may omit them if they are not available.

Shade argued the importance of "ensuring equitable gender access to the Internet" (1993, p. 6).

12. Personal Communication

Cite any personal letters, email messages, electronic bulletin-board correspondence, telephone conversations, or personal interviews by giving the person's initial(s) and last name, the identification *personal communication,* and the date.

V. Sweete (personal communication, March 7, 1983) supported these claims.

Content Notes

The APA recommends using content notes for material that will expand or supplement your argument but otherwise would interrupt the text.

Indicate such notes in your text by inserting superscript numerals. Type the notes themselves on a separate page headed *Footnotes,* centered at the top of the page. Double-space all entries. Indent the first line of each note five to seven spaces, and begin subsequent lines at the left margin:

Text with Superscript Indicating a Note

Data related to children's preferences in books were instrumental in designing the questionnaire.[1]

Note

[1] Rudine Sims Bishop and members of the Reading Readiness Research Group provided helpful data.

List of References

The alphabetical list of sources cited in your text is called *References.* (If your instructor asks you to list everything you have read as background — not just the sources you cite — call the list *Bibliography.*) The list of references appears on a separate page at the end of your paper.

For print sources, the APA style specifies the treatment and placement of four basic elements — author, publication date, title, and publication information.

- List all authors with last name first, and use only initials for first and middle names. Separate the names of multiple authors with commas, and use an ampersand (&) before the last author's name.
- Enclose the publication date in parentheses. Use only the year for books and journals; use the year, a comma, and the month or month and day for magazines. Do not abbreviate.
- Underline or italicize titles and subtitles of books and periodicals. Do not enclose titles of articles in quotation marks. For books and articles, capitalize only the first word of the title and subtitle and any proper nouns or proper adjectives. Capitalize all major words in a periodical title.
- For a book, list the city of publication (and the country or postal abbreviation for the state if the city is unfamiliar) and the publisher's name, dropping *Inc., Co.,* or *Publishers.* For a periodical, follow the periodical title with a comma, the volume number (underlined or italicized), the

issue number (if provided) in parentheses and followed by a comma, and the inclusive page numbers of the article. For newspaper articles and for articles or chapters in books, include the abbreviation *p.* ("page") or *pp.* ("pages").

The following APA-style examples appear double-spaced and in a "hanging indent" format, in which the first line aligns on the left and the subsequent lines indent one-half inch or five spaces.

Books

1. One Author

Jung, C. (1968). Analytical psychology: Its theory and practice. London: Routledge and K. Paul.

2. Two or More Authors

Steininger, M., Newell, J. D., & Garcia, L. (1984). Ethical issues in psychology. Homewood, IL: Dow Jones-Irwin.

3. Organization as Author

Use the word *Author* as the publisher when the organization is both the author and the publisher.

Pennsylvania Mental Health, Inc. (1960). Mental health education: A critique. Philadelphia: Author.

4. Unknown Author

National Geographic atlas of the world. (1996). Washington, DC: National Geographic Society.

5. Two or More Works by the Same Author

List the works in chronological order of publication. Repeat the author's name in each entry.

Rose, M. (1984). Writer's block: The cognitive dimension. Carbondale, IL: Southern Illinois University Press.

Rose, M. (1995). Possible lives: The promise of public education in America. Boston: Houghton Mifflin.

6. Editor

Greenbaum, S. (Ed.). (1977). <u>Acceptability in language.</u> The Hague, Netherlands: Mouton.

7. Selection in a Book with an Editor

Ong, W. J. (1988). Literacy and orality in our times. In G. Tate & E. P. J. Corbett (Eds.), <u>The writing teacher's sourcebook</u> (pp. 37-46). New York: Oxford University Press.

8. Translation

Konig, R. (1973). <u>A la mode: On the social psychology of fashion.</u> (F. Bradley, Trans.). New York: Seabury Press.

9. Edition Other than the First

Wrightsman, L. (1992). <u>Assumptions about human nature: Implications for researchers and practitioners</u> (2nd ed.). Newbury Park, CA: Sage.

10. One Volume of a Multivolume Work

Will, J. S. (1921). <u>Protestantism in France</u> (Vol. 2). Toronto: University of Toronto Press.

11. Article in a Reference Work

Chernow, B., & Vattasi, G. (Eds.). (1993). Psychomimetic drug. In <u>The Columbia encyclopedia</u> (5th ed., p. 2238). New York: Columbia University Press.

If no author is listed, begin with the title.

12. Republication

Sharp, C. (1978). <u>History of Hartlepool.</u> Hartlepool, UK: Hartlepool Borough Council. (Original work published 1816)

13. Government Document

U.S. Bureau of the Census. (1976). <u>Census of population and housing 1970.</u> Washington, DC: U.S. Government Printing Office.

Periodicals

14. Article in a Journal Paginated by Volume

Shuy, R. (1981). A holistic view of language. Research in the Teaching of
English, 15, 110-111.

15. Article in a Journal Paginated by Issue

Rudavich, D. (1991). Man among men: David Mamet's homosocial order.
American Drama, 1(1), 46-66.

16. Article in a Monthly Magazine

Cartmill, M. (1998, March). Oppressed by evolution. Discover, 78-83.

17. Article in a Newspaper

Glasser, R. J. (1998, March 4). As life ebbs, so does time to elect com-
forts of hospice. The New York Times, pp. A1, A8.

18. Editorial or Letter to the Editor

Seidel, M. C. (1998, January). Frankreich uber alles [Letter to the editor].
Harper's, 4.

19. Unsigned Article

Guidelines issued on assisted suicide. (1998, March 4). The New York
Times, p. A15.

20. Review

Richardson, S. (1998, February). [Review of the book The Secret
Family]. Discover, 88.

21. Published Interview

Shor, I. (1997). [Interview with A. Greenbaum]. Writing on the Edge,
8(2), 7-20.

Electronic Sources

Most of the following models are based on the APA's updated guidelines
for citing electronic sources posted at <http://www.apa.org/journals/

webref.html> as well as the *APA Publication Manual* (4th edition). Formats not covered by the APA guidelines are based on *Online! A Reference Guide to Using Internet Sources* (2000 edition), by Andrew Harnack and Eugene Kleppinger.

The basic APA entry for most electronic sources should include the following elements:

- name of the author, editor, or compiler
- date of electronic publication or most recent update
- title of the work, document, or posting
- publication information, including the title, volume or issue number, and page numbers
- a retrieval statement that includes date of access, followed by a comma, and retrieval method, followed by a colon
- URL, with no angle brackets and no closing punctuation

22. CD-ROM *Abstract*

Natchez, G. (1987). Frida Kahlo and Diego Rivera: The transformation of catastrophe to creativity. Psychotherapy Patient, 8, 153-174. Retrieved from PsycLIT database (SilverPlatter File, CD-ROM, 1999 release, Item 76-11344)

23. *Material from an Information Service or Online Database*

Belenky, M. F. (1984). The role of deafness in the moral development of hearing impaired children. In A. Areson & J. De Caro (Eds.), Teaching, learning and development. Rochester, NY: National Institute for the Deaf. Retrieved January 20, 2000, from ERIC online database (No. ED 248 646)

24. *Material from a Database Accessed via the Web*

Pryor, T., & Wiederman, M. W. (1998). Personality features and expressed concerns of adolescents with eating disorders. Adolescence, 33, 291-301. Retrieved February 7, 2000, from Electric Library database, on the World Wide Web: http://www.elibrary.com

25. Software or Computer Program

> Lotus Organizer (Version 2.1) [Computer software]. (1996). Cambridge,
>   MA: Lotus Development Corp.

26. World Wide Web Site

To cite a document from a Web site, include the document title and also the title of the complete work or site, if applicable, underlined or italicized.

> The Feminist Majority. (1995). Athletics in the lives of women and
>   girls. Empowering women in sports. Retrieved March 2, 2000,
>   from the World Wide Web: http://www.feminist.org/research
>   /sports2.html

27. FTP Site

Instead of the URL, you can use the abbreviation *ftp://* followed by the address of the FTP site and the full path to follow to find the document, with no closing punctuation.

> Altar, T. W. (1993). Vitamin B_{12} and vegans. Retrieved May 28, 1996,
>   from the World Wide Web: ftp://wiretap.spies.com/library
>   /article/food/b12.txt

28. Telnet Site

After the title of the document, include the title of the full work, if applicable, underlined or italicized and followed by a period. Then include the date of access, the complete telnet address, and directions to access the document.

> Aquatic Conservation Network. (n.d.). About the aquatic conservation
>   network. National capital freenet. Retrieved May 28, 1996, from
>   Freenet: telnet freenet.carleton.ca login as guest, go acn, press 1

29. Gopher Site

Include any print publication information, underlined or italicized where appropriate. Then give the date of retrieval and the gopher address.

> Korn, P. (1994, October). How much does breast cancer really cost? Self.
>   Retrieved May 5, 1997: gopher://nysernet.org:70/00/BCIC/Sources
>   /SELF/94/how-much

30. Listserv Posting

Include the author's name, the date and subject line of the posting, the date of access, and the listserv address.

> Gill, D. (1996, January 9). Environmental archaeology in the Aegean. Retrieved March 28, 1998, from the listserv: aegeanet@rome .classics.lsa.umich.edu

31. Newsgroup Posting

Include the author's name, the date and subject line of the posting, the access date, and the name of the newsgroup.

> Sand, P. (1996, April 20). Java disabled by default in Linux Netscape. Retrieved May 10, 1996, from the newsgroup: Keokuk.unh.edu

32. Email Message

The APA discourages including email messages in a list of references and suggests citing them as personal communications in your text.

33. Synchronous Communication (MOO, MUD, and IRC)

Provide the name(s) of the speaker(s), if known, or the name of the site; the date of the event, in parentheses; its title, if appropriate; the date of retrieval; and the URL.

> Patuto, J., Fennel, S., & Goss, J. (1996, May 9). The Mytilene debate. Retrieved March 29, 1998, from the World Wide Web: http://moo.cas.muohio.edu/cgi-vin/moo?look+4085

Other Sources

34. Technical or Research Reports and Working Papers

> Synott, T. J. (1979). Impact of human activities: IPAL technical reports (Tech. Rep. No. D2a, D2b, and D2c). Nairobi, Kenya: Integrated Project in Arid Lands, University of Nairobi EP.

35. Unpublished Paper Presented at a Meeting or Symposium

Welch, K. (1998, April). Electric rhetoric and screen literacy. Paper
presented at the Conference on College Composition and
Communication, Chicago.

36. Unpublished Dissertation

Barnett, T. (1997). Communities in conflict: Composition, racial discourse,
and the 60s revolution. Unpublished doctoral dissertation, Ohio
State University, Columbus.

37. Poster Presentation

Mensching, G. (1992, May). A simple, effective one-shot for disinterested
students. Poster session presented at the National LOEX Library
Instruction Conference, Ann Arbor, MI.

38. Film or Videotape

Stone, Oliver. (Director). (1995). Natural born killers [Film]. Los Angeles:
Warner Brothers.

39. Television Series, Single Episode

Begin with the names of the script writer(s), and give the name of the
director, in parentheses, after the episode title.

Nikulina, T. (1998, April 16). Top gun over Moscow (N. Schulz, Director).
In P. Apsell (Executive Producer), Nova. New York: WNET.

40. Sound Recording

For recordings by an artist other than the writer, begin with the writer's
name, followed by the date of copyright. Give the recording date if it is different from the copyright date.

Ivey, A., Jr., & Sall, R. (1995). Rollin' with my homies [Recorded by
Coolio]. On Clueless soundtrack [CD]. Hollywood, CA: Capitol
Records.

RESPOND•

1. The MLA and APA styles differ in several important ways, both for in-text citations and for lists of sources. You've probably noticed a few: the APA lowercases most words in titles and lists the publication date right after the author's name, whereas the MLA capitalizes most words and puts the publication date at the end of the works-cited entry. More interesting than the details, though, is the reasoning behind the differences. Placing the publication date near the front of a citation, for instance, reveals a special concern for that information in the APA style. Similarly, the MLA's decision to capitalize titles is not arbitrary: that style is preferred in the humanities for a reason.

   Find as many consistent differences between the MLA and APA styles as you can. Then, for each difference, try to discover the reasons these groups organize or present information in that way. The MLA and APA style manuals themselves may be of help. You might also begin by determining which academic disciplines subscribe to the APA style and which to the MLA.

arguments

chapter twenty-three

Mirror, Mirror . . .
Images and the Media

If you look in the mirror of media in America, what images do you see? Your own? Those of people who look or act like you in some way? Are the people you see like those you encounter in your daily life? Do the media serve as a mirror? Should they? How do some get to be the "fairest of them all" while others remain invisible— or are typecast in roles they contend are far from reality? Should these matters concern us? Do they affect us? How? These are the questions the readings in this chapter challenge you to consider.

The first cluster of arguments considers stereotypes in media and popular culture. Many argue that the media representations of various groups—ethnic groups, social classes, people of certain faiths, Americans from certain regions, even dads—are not accurate and, hence, not fair. These texts remind us that although such representations — stereotypes, really — may often go unnoticed, they are not without consequence. The readings in the second cluster examine a favorite American obsession — our bodies — and how the body is represented in popular culture. As the arguments demonstrate, media representations of the "perfect body" no longer concern only American women. The availability of U.S. TV programs around the world seems to be changing how women in distant lands see themselves. And from a very different perspective, men in this and other countries increasingly feel pressured to strive for a perfect body — or at least one that is more nearly perfect than the one they're currently occupying. In other words, questions of images and the media ultimately matter to each of us. If you see your image in the mirror of the media when you gaze at it, you probably have to work hard to stay there. Should you not see your image reflected in the media at all or should the image you see there bear little resemblance to who you are, what might the consequences be? After studying the arguments presented here, you'll likely agree that far more is at stake than an old ditty from a children's fairy tale.

If you check a dictionary, you'll find that the term *stereotype* originally referred to a plate for printing cast in metal from a mold of a page of set type. English borrowed the term from French, but its parts are ultimately of Greek origin, *stereo,* meaning "solid" or "three-dimensional," and *type,* meaning "model." By extension, a stereotype has come to mean a widely held conception of a group that is fixed and allows for little individuality among the group's members. Ironic, isn't it, that a term that originally referred to a three-dimensional printing plate has come to refer to one-dimensional representations of groups?

This cluster of readings focuses on issues of stereotypes, specifically **stereotypes in media and pop culture** in North America. These readings consider what many would argue are unsavory stereotypes of many groups. In "Fu Manchu on Naboo," John Leo examines stereotyping of African Americans, Asians, Middle Easterners, Republicans, and Catholics in a single film from the late 1990s—*The Phantom Menace.* James Sterngold writes about the movie *Smoke Signals,* the first feature-length film written, directed, and acted by Native Americans, in his *New York Times* article, "Able to Laugh at Their People, Not Just Cry for Them," and the efforts of Native Americans to question stereotypes about who they are. In "The Exaggeration of Despair," Sherman Alexie, author of the book that became the basis of *Smoke Signals,* writes a poem to argue with a member of his tribe about whether Alexie's representations of Indian life in one of his novels were exaggerated and, hence, stereotypical. John Levesque examines a 1999 study of fifteen television series that include fathers as characters; the results, he suggests, are not encouraging. An article that originally appeared in *Newsday* about the independent film *Side Streets* explains how a Merchant-Ivory production with a talented, ethnically diverse cast from around the world didn't get picked up for large-scale distribution because it dealt with "real people, people of color, people with accents, people with car payments" rather than with the problems of a single ethnic group to which the movie could be marketed. Finally, in the transcript of a *Latino USA* radio feature, "Taco Bell and Latino Stereotypes," María Martin asked a range of people, most of Hispanic background, to evaluate the extremely successful Taco Bell ad campaign featuring Dinky, a bilingual Chihuahua.

These arguments ask us to think hard about how various groups are represented in media and pop culture. They remind us that media and pop culture representations of various groups quickly become the topic of debate, whether or not you belong to the group in question. They also challenge us to consider how such representations become stereotypes and how those stereotypes ultimately influence us all. Originally, stereotypes were part of the printer's trade, enabling a printer to disseminate information quickly and relatively cheaply. No less a part of popular culture today, stereotypes of a different sort still disseminate information. You'll have to decide how much they matter and why.

▼ In this July 1999 essay from the "On Society" column in U.S. News & World Report, a weekly newsmagazine that generally takes a conservative stance, John Leo criticizes the most recent Star Wars movie, Episode I: The Phantom Menace. As you read, pay special attention to the structure of Leo's argument: specifically, how does he support his claim that the film perpetuates stereotypes of certain groups?

See "Giving an Argument Style" in Chapter 2 for examples of other opening paragraphs that grab readers' attention by breaking their expectations.

Fu Manchu on Naboo

LINK TO P. 33

BY JOHN LEO

Everyone's a victim these days, so America's touchiness industry is dedicated to seeing group slights everywhere. But sometimes even touchy people are right. Complaints about the new *Star Wars* movie, for instance, are valid. *Episode I: The Phantom Menace* is packed with awful stereotypes.

Consider the evil Neimoidians. They are stock Asian villains out of black-and-white B movies of the 1930s and 1940s, complete with Hollywood oriental accents, sinister speech patterns, and a space-age version of stock Fu Manchu clothing. Watto, the fat, greedy junk dealer with

"A stereotype on this level is more than an insult. It is a teaching instrument."

wings, is a conventional, crooked Middle Eastern merchant. This is a generic antisemitic image, Jewish if you want him to be, or Arab if you don't.

Law Prof. Patricia Williams says Watto looks strikingly like an anti-Jewish caricature published in Vienna at the turn of the century—round bellied, big nosed, with spindly arms, wings sprouting from his shoulders, and a scroll that says, "Anything for money." Perhaps Watto isn't supposed to be Jewish. Some people thought he sounded Italian. But by presenting the character as an unprincipled, hook-nosed merchant (and a slave owner, to boot), the movie is at least playing around with traditional antisemitic imagery. It shouldn't.

375

The loudest criticism has been directed at Jar Jar Binks, the annoying, computer-generated amphibian who looks like a cross between a frog and a camel and acts, as one critic put it, like a cross between Butterfly McQueen's Prissy° and Stepin Fetchit.° His voice, the work of a black actor, is a sort of slurred, pidgin Caribbean English, much of it impossible to understand. "Me berry, berry scayyud," says Jar Jar, in one of his modestly successful attempts at English. For some reason, he keeps saying "yousa" and "meesa," instead of "you" and "me." He is the first character in the four *Star Wars* movies to mess up Galactic Basic (the English language) on a regular basis.

RACIST CARICATURE

Fractured English is one of the key traits of a racist   5
caricature in America, from all the 19th-century characters named Snowball down to Amos 'n' Andy.° Whether endearing or pathetic, this trouble with language is supposed to demonstrate the intellectual inferiority of blacks. Childlike confusion is another familiar way of stereotyping blacks, and Jar Jar shows that trait too. He steps in alien-creature doo-doo, gets his tongue caught in a racing engine, and panics during the big battle scene. He is, in fact, a standard-issue, caricatured black who becomes hopelessly flustered when called upon to function in a white man's world.

A stereotype on this level is more than an insult. It is a teaching instrument and a powerful, nonverbal argument saying that racial equality is a hopeless cause. If blacks talk and act like this movie says they do, how can they possibly expect equal treatment?

What is going on in this movie? George Lucas, director of the *Star Wars* movies, says media talk about stereotypes is creating "a controversy out of nothing." But many visual cues support the charge that stereotypes are indeed built into the film. Jar Jar

Jar Jar Binks

Butterfly McQueen: the actress (1911–1995) who played Prissy, Scarlett O'Hara's young slave in *Gone with the Wind*. She is best remembered for the scene in which she tells O'Hara "Lawsy, Miss Scarlett — Lawsy, we's got ter have a doctah! Ah doan know nothin' 'bout birthin' babies!" Like many African American actors of the period, she refused to be filmed eating chicken or watermelon. Why might these actors have refused such a thing?

has head flaps drawn to look like dreadlocks. The ruler of his tribe, Boss Nass, wears what looks to be an African robe and African headdress. A Neimoidian senator named Lott (Trent Lott?), representing the evil viceroy Nute Gunray (Newt Gingrich?) wears a version of a Catholic bishop's mitre and a Catholic priest's stole over a dark robe. This can't be an accident. It duplicates, almost exactly, the appearance of a real bishop. It's a small reference but an unmistakable one. So Catholics, along with Asians and Republicans, are at least vaguely associated with Neimoidian treachery.

Lucas is a visually sophisticated and careful moviemaker. In a TV interview, he said that he researched imagery of Satan in every known culture before deciding on how the evil warrior Darth Maul should look in the film (tattooed, with horns). A *Star Wars* book, *The Visual Dictionary,* that came out with the movie describes in detail almost every image used in the film. So it's hard to believe that all the stereotyped imagery just happened.

One of the keys to Lucas's success is that his movies are made up of brilliantly re-imagined scenes from earlier films (World War II aerial dogfights, cowboys and Indians, swashbuckling sword fights, a *Ben-Hur* chariot race, etc.). After three very inventive *Star Wars* movies, the not-so-inventive fourth seems to have fallen back on some tired Hollywood ethnic themes he mostly avoided in the first three.

So *The Phantom Menace* offers us revived versions 10 of some famous stereotypes. Jar Jar Binks as the dithery Prissy; Watto, a devious, child-owning wheeler-dealer, as the new Fagin; the two reptilian Neimoidian leaders as the inscrutably evil Fu Manchu and Dr. No. What's next—an interplanetary version of the Frito Bandito? The *Star Wars* films deserve better than this. Let's put all these characters to sleep and start over in the next movie. ∎

Stepin Fetchit: the professional name of Theodore Monroe Andrew Perry (1902–1985), who was the first African American movie star. He first worked in stage revues and vaudeville shows for African American audiences and later became an international star in Hollywood films that cast him in roles where he played a lackey or provided comic relief. Much criticized for these roles, he in many ways paved the way for later generations of African Americans in Hollywood. The name, a play on the phrase "step and fetch it," has come to represent "slow-witted, shuffling servility," as Eric Lott puts it.

Fu Manchu *as played by Boris Karloff in the 1932 movie* The Mask of Fu Manchu.

Amos 'n' Andy: originally a radio show in which White actors took the roles of two African American men from the South who had moved to Chicago. The program began in 1926 and went on to become the most popular U.S. radio show. By 1951, when it became a television series, the actors were Black, but many Americans believe the program contributed to creating derogatory stereotypes of African Americans in the national consciousness for years to come.

RESPOND●

1. What kinds of evidence does Leo use in structuring his argument? How, specifically, does he use facts about earlier portrayals of various groups? (Why, for example, does he allude to Butterfly McQueen's Prissy, Stepin Fetchit, Snowball, and Amos 'n' Andy? How many of these characters do you recognize? Even if you recognize none of them, what can you imagine them to be like?) How does Leo use testimony? (What might his motivation be in citing law professor Patricia Williams when talking about an anti-Jewish caricature? How does he use testimony from Lucas, the filmmaker?)

2. Leo begins his argument by agreeing with the general criticism of those Americans who sometimes cast themselves as victims. He then immediately admits that some groups are justified in their complaints if *The Phantom Menace* is taken as evidence. Why is Leo's opening statement an appropriate way to begin his essay, particularly given the stance that *U.S. News & World Report* generally takes on issues?

3. Leo lets Lucas speak for himself. How does Leo use Lucas's own words and the existence of the *Star Wars Visual Dictionary* as evidence against Lucas's claim that "media talk about stereotypes is creating 'a controversy out of nothing'"?

4. Leo argues that the way movie characters speak is an important part of racist caricature; one imagines that Leo would be willing to extend his claim to cases of sexism and likely classism. **Write an essay** disagreeing with Leo's contention, presenting evidence why such portrayals do not reinforce racist (or sexist or classist or other) stereotypes — or supporting his claim, using evidence from familiar movies or television programs to back up your arguments.

▼ *James Sterngold's article originally appeared in the "Arts and Leisure" section of the* New York Times *in 1998 at about the time that* Smoke Signals *was released around the United States. In addition to providing background about the movie, which, as he notes, is the first film written, directed, and acted by Native Americans, the article raises many issues about the representation of American Indians in the media in general.*

Able to Laugh at Their People, Not Just Cry for Them

JAMES STERNGOLD

SLIAMMON INDIAN RESERVE, British Columbia—One morning recently, Evan Adams, a 31-year-old American Indian actor, was telling stories in the small living room of his parents' home on this beautiful, heavily wooded stretch of the Canadian coast. Surrounded by his mother, three sisters and a brother, he explained in his singsong voice how he had terrified some of the participants in a first-aid course he had taken by reacting with passionate alarm toward a doll that was supposedly choking and its inflatable mother.

He was telling the story as a testament to his acting ability, but his normally soft-spoken sister Maureen slyly deflated the boast by asking, "Was it acting or were you excited about that blow-up doll?"

This gentle gibe brought gales of laughter from Mr. Adams's family, and it was just one episode in a day of wordplay among a group of people clearly comfortable communicating through sometimes bawdy humor and irony. That, of course, would be unremarkable in such a close-knit family except for the fact that Indians have

LOOKING AT THEMSELVES *Adam Beach, right, and Evan Adams in "Smoke Signals," the first feature-length movie written, directed and acted by American Indians*

379

generally been depicted in popular culture, and especially in movies, as earnest and stoic, sometimes pathetic and at times bloodthirsty, but rarely wry.

Indians have also been pictured as living in poor, if not squalid conditions. And in fact Mr. Adams, a Coast Salish Indian, said that he had eaten so much salmon as a child growing up in a subsistence economy based on fishing that he took to calling it "Indian bologna." But the economic poverty has often been interpreted as cultural impoverishment — as an implication that Indian culture lacks a playful or a cerebral dimension.

That is one reason the new movie in which Mr. Adams is a co-star, "Smoke Signals," which opens Friday, is so distinctive. It's funny and complex, as well as poignant, casting a new light on the Indian sensibility.

"Smoke Signals," based on a book of short stories by Sherman Alexie titled "The Lone Ranger and Tonto Fistfight in Heaven," is the first feature-length movie written, directed and acted by American Indians. But the film, which won two awards at the Sundance festival in January and has been acclaimed by critics, is something more too: it is a step by a new generation of Indian artists toward finding an idiom for exploring their individual and cultural identities without resorting to self-pity, political correctness or Hollywood clichés.

The tone of "Smoke Signals," which documents the unexpected ways two young men living on the Coeur d'Alene reservation in Idaho come to terms with absent fathers,

is brash and self-confident in its self-examination. In one scene, for instance, Thomas Builds-the-Fire (Mr. Adams) notes as he watches a western, "The only thing more pathetic than Indians on TV is Indians watching Indians on TV."

This movie, which was directed by the 28-year-old Chris Eyre, is the

"Indian Killer," and he is completing a script for a movie in which he will also act later this year, with Loretta Todd, a Cree from Northern Alberta, directing.

But beyond all that, Mr. Adams — whose grandparents and several aunts died of tuberculosis — will begin medical school at the University of

"In 'Smoke Signals,' young American Indians make brash use of stereotypes, both to mock them and embrace them."

work not just of a group of creative people with full hearts but of aggressive achievers determined to stake their claim to high ground on the American cultural map. The best known of them is Mr. Alexie. A 31-year-old novelist and poet who grew up on the Spokane reservation in Washington, he was a producer of "Smoke Signals" and wrote its screenplay and is also producing a movie adapted from his recent novel "Indian Killer." He said in an interview that one of his primary goals was to take away from so-called white experts the responsibility for describing contemporary Indian culture. His aim, he said, is not to avoid criticism of Indian society but to make sure that it is Indians doing the criticizing and interpreting.

Mr. Adams, an athletic-looking man with a broad smile, a long ponytail and wire-framed glasses, is also a good example of restless ambition — but with a twist. He has acted in four full-length features; he will appear in

Calgary this fall, to fulfill a goal of bringing something back to his reservation, a hamlet of 650 people about 100 miles north of Vancouver amid mountains, towering cedars and rich blue waters.

The people involved in "Smoke Signals" are not, in short, willing to passively accept conventional images of Indian life.

"Smoke Signals" is a slow-moving, often wistful drama that turns into a road movie as Thomas, a confident nerd who maintains his people's storytelling tradition in an offbeat manner, accompanies the angry, self-conscious Victor Joseph (Adam Beach) on a journey to Arizona. But the story is enlivened by a self-deprecating sense of humor, one of the most enduring Indian cultural characteristics, particularly on the reservations, the filmmakers say.

"Smoke Signals" is clearly a product of a post-Wounded Knee generation. The filmmakers paid tribute to the American Indian Movement, saying that those angry demonstrators of the 1970's had helped establish a contemporary tradition of Indian pride that made a movie like "Smoke Signals" possible. But the film has a far different sensibility. The characters are angry, but they're also silly, loving, careless, vulnerable, witty and persistent. They play basketball. They laugh at their squalor. At one point the only way they can go forward is by driving a car backward. They mock Indian stereotypes, and they embrace them. In fact, they are much like the group of people who made the film.

Mr. Eyre, a graduate of the film school at New York University, is a Cheyenne-Arapaho who was adopted as a baby and brought up by a white family in Oregon. He has spent the last few years tracking down his biological parents and embracing his Indian heritage. "Smoke Signals," the first feature he has directed, was integral to that process. "In this movie, we're all searching for home to different degrees," he said.

was 8; she was eight months pregnant at the time. His father drowned two months later. "Living with that loss and not understanding it, you kind of feel you're not in the right place," said Mr. Beach, an avid hockey player and rock musician. "I'm kind of looking for the right place in this movie."

Mr. Beach also described the making of "Smoke Signals" as a means by which he could confront his own anger about the loss of his parents. "It was the first time in my life I was able to get that out of myself," said Mr. Beach in describing the filming of the tearful closing sequence of the movie. "I remember I was crying on Chris's shoulder and saying, 'It still hurts.' And he'd say, 'Well, you have to go do it again.'"

And then there is Mr. Adams, who has been almost frenetic in his efforts both to investigate his culture through writing and acting and to serve his people as a doctor. His parallel career paths reflect a tension that runs through the lives of many Indians, he

an actor's career when he can do movies that are life changing or magical," he said. "That's not enough for me. I need to do something that really helps my people all the time."

Mr. Adams's father, Les, the captain of a tugboat, said he had long contemplated these issues. As he sat bobbing on his boat, he explained that he knew many years ago that Evan was capable of extraordinary accomplishments. And he said that he had sternly instructed his son to focus his ambition on the world beyond the reservation. But, he admitted, Evan made it clear early on that he had his own ideas about heritage and creativity. As a teen-ager, for example, Evan learned and performed traditional dances that had been little seen for years. Les Adams recalled bringing a friend, the chief of a nearby tribe, to one of Evan's performances and being struck to see his friend cry at one point.

"He said he had not seen those 20 dances since he was a boy and that he never expected to see them again in his life," said Mr. Adams. "He was impressed that these young people wanted to bring them back."

Evan Adams did go away to a private high school when he was 14 and then to McGill University in Montreal. His father said he was crushed when Evan announced that he was leaving McGill after a year, to pursue acting.

The younger Mr. Adams said that part of his struggle over the years had come from his mixed feelings about living in a dominantly white society. "My family had a very high status on the reservation," he said, whose father

---

" 'We're all searching for home to different degrees,' the director says."

Mr. Beach, a 25-year-old Ojibway 15 from north of Winnipeg, bluntly described how much of his own personal history was reflected in that of his character, Victor, who is haunted by the absence of a parent. He said the defining element of his early life was the death of his mother, who was killed by a drunken driver when he

said: whether to concentrate on articulating a distinct cultural vision to the world outside the reservations or to focus on their own people. Mr. Adams is still undecided on which path will win out in his case, but he seems to be leaning in one direction.

"I do love acting and I'm working at it, but there are only a few times in

was the elected chief of his tribe for a number of years. "I was low status in the town. It was a constant source of irritation and humiliation."

Ultimately, Mr. Adams enrolled at the University of British Columbia in Vancouver and completed his premed studies, while continuing to write and act, doing everything from Shake- speare to a play he wrote, "Snapshots," about how two Indian families deal with illness and death.

He described his swings from one world to the other while showing a reporter an extraordinary collection of totem poles, masks and other ceremonial objects preserved in the glass and concrete Museum of Anthropology on the University of British Columbia campus. He insisted that he was trying to find a way of revering the past while shaping a new kind of future that was true to both the Indian spirit and the modern spirit.

"The Indian way," he concluded, 25 "is being adaptable and flexible."

Sterngold's interviews with Evan Adams, Chris Eyre, and Adam Beach provide nearly all of the information and evidence in this article. See the guidelines in Chapter 18 to help you plan and conduct your own interviews.

.... LINK TO P. 301

RESPOND •

1. One resource any writer has in constructing arguments is to appeal to readers' emotions, feelings, or values (including cultural values). How does Sterngold appeal to his readers' emotions? Which emotions in particular does he appeal to? Where do you see evidence of these appeals?

2. How does Sterngold's discussion of media representatives of Native Americans compare with John Leo's discussion of media representations of African Americans and other groups in his essay "Fu Manchu on Naboo" (p. 375)? How do the different purposes — writing a news article versus writing a column that takes a strong stance on an issue — influence the ways in which each author makes his main point?

3. Watch the movie *Smoke Signals*. Pay particular attention to the ways in which the movie and those in it "mock Indian stereotypes . . . and . . . embrace them" (paragraph 13). List any events or situations in the movie that call into question stereotypes about Native Americans you have seen in other media. In what ways is the Sterngold article useful background for seeing the film? If you had been in Sterngold's place, writing an article about the film *before* it appeared, what would you have told potential viewers? How would your comments differ from his? Why?

4. The Native Americans cited in this article raise several complex issues about representations of groups. One is the issue of authority: who has the right and the responsibility to represent a group? **Write an essay** discussing the advantages of representations crafted by insid- ers and by outsiders. One way to complete this assignment is to focus on a specific group of which you are — or are not — a member, using it as an example.

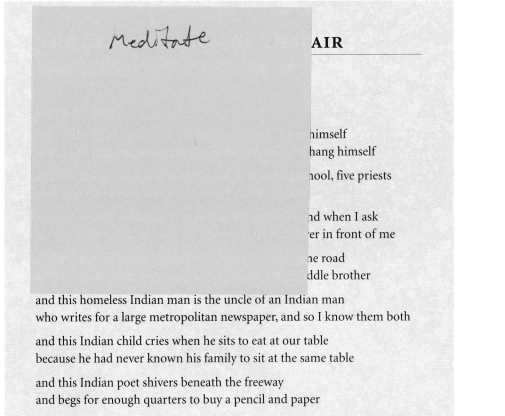

Sherman Alexie is the writer whose book of short stories, The Lone Ranger and Tonto Fistfight in Heaven (1993), became the basis for the film Smoke Signals. He wrote "The Exaggeration of Despair" as a response to a review of Reservation Blues, a novel he published in 1995. The reviewer, who belonged to the same tribe, argued that Alexie had been too negative in his portrayal of the reservation and of Indians generally. To voice disagreement with the review, Alexie chose to compose a poem "using negative language and imagery to create a chant-like quality," noting "Obviously, my poem cannot completely reproduce the despair and loss in the Indian world. For that matter, I could never write a poem that completely replicated the level of joy and magic in our lives. My poems are an attempt to capture moments, not whole lives or complete worlds." The poem was first published in Urbanus, a poetry magazine from San Francisco.

Meditate

AIR

himself
hang himself

nool, five priests

nd when I ask
er in front of me

ne road
ddle brother

and this homeless Indian man is the uncle of an Indian man
who writes for a large metropolitan newspaper, and so I know them both

and this Indian child cries when he sits to eat at our table
because he had never known his family to sit at the same table

and this Indian poet shivers beneath the freeway
and begs for enough quarters to buy a pencil and paper

and this fancydancer passes out at the powwow
and wakes up naked, with no memory of the evening, all of his regalia gone

and this is my sister, who waits years for an eagle, receives it
and stores it with our cousins, who then tell her it has disappeared

and this is my father, whose own father died on Okinawa, shot
by a Japanese soldier who must have looked so much like him

and this is my father, whose mother died of tuberculosis
not long after he was born, and so my father must hear coughing ghosts

and this is my grandmother who saw, before the white men came,
three ravens with white necks, and knew our God was going to change)

and invite the wind inside.

The style of repetition that Alexie uses in his poem is known as *anaphora*. Read more about anaphora and other structural schemes in Chapter 14.

·····································LINK TO P. 246

RESPOND.

1. This poem uses a common literary technique, providing a list or catalog of situations, events, individuals, and so on. What is the power of a catalog as argument? What particular themes recur in this particular catalog? How do they support the poet's argument?

2. What happens in this poem? (Hint: Read the first and last lines.) What is the relationship between these two events and the catalog, which is enclosed in parentheses? How is the title part of the poem's argument? What does it mean?

3. In what ways can poetry be an argument? In what ways is this particular poem an argument? What claim(s) do you think the poet is making? What evidence does the poet give for his claim(s)? Who are the poet's audiences? How do you know?

4. In James Sterngold's article, "Able to Laugh at Their People, Not Just Cry for Them," Alexie is noted as having said he seeks not to avoid criticism of Native American society but to ensure that Native Americans are speaking for themselves. In what ways is this poem an illustration of Alexie achieving his aim? How is criticism by an insider similar to—and different from—criticism by an outsider? You may wish to compare and contrast Alexie's poem with John Leo's critique of *The Phantom Menace* in "Fu Manchu on Naboo" (p. 375).

5. **Write an essay** describing and evaluating Alexie's argument. How does the poem's structure contribute to its success or failure as an argument?

▼ *In this article originally published in the entertainment section of the Seattle Post-Intelligencer in early June 1999, John Levesque reports on a 1999 study of the ways in which fathers are represented in television situation comedies. As you read, consider how the photograph from 7th Heaven and the chart on the next page contribute to Levesque's argument.*

Sitcom Dads Rarely Know Best, Study of TV Laments

JOHN LEVESQUE

Only nine shopping days [until Father's] Day, so let's decide once [and for all:] Who's the better sitcom [dad, Ray] Romano or Homer Simps[on?]

No contest, right? I [mean, Ray] Romano has never been [arrested for] trying to murder his boss[, never been] charged with sexual har[assment for] pulling a Gummi Venus d[e Milo off a] baby sitter's tush, and ne[ver been an] unwitting accomplice in [a corporate] takeover of the East Coast[...]

Homer Simpson has [been there,] done that. Many times ove[r...]

But with every precinc[t reporting,] the tabulations indicate [there's not] much to choose between R[omano and] Simpson on the fatherh[ood scale.] So says the National F[atherhood] Initiative in Gaithersburg, Md., which looked at 15 television series on five networks last fall and decided that— surprise!—father rarely knows best.

While comedian Ray Romano, 5 who plays himself on "Everybody Loves Raymond," does better than the bumbling patriarch of "The Simpsons" in areas of parental competence and guidance, Homer Simpson cleans Romano's clock when it comes to family involvement

[handwritten note: Inform? / convince]

Stephen Collins plays... Heaven... will not if two dads... portrayer scores in the apple of father to...

...and engagement. Stephen even has an edge in placing the role of father at the top of his priority list.

On a scale of 0 to 25, Romano and Simpson both tallied scores of 16 in NFI's "Fatherhood & TV" report, barely staying out of the "negative portrayal" range (see chart on page 386).

The fact that we're even comparing a live-action character with a cartoon figure seems a little goofy, but it was NFI that lumped them together, not I.

Founded in 1994, NFI is a nonprofit, non-partisan organization (www.fatherhood.org) that "encourages and supports family and father-friendly policies (and) develops national public education campaigns to highlight the importance of fathers in the lives of their children."

Wade Horn, a psychologist/ columnist who is NFI's president, intends to revisit the dads-on-TV report each year to see if there's any improvement at the networks, particularly in the area of comedies. Of the 15 shows studied by NFI, 12 are sitcoms and only three—"Smart Guy," "Two of a Kind" and "Mad About You"—were seen as portraying fatherhood positively. Ironically, none of the three will be back next season.

Two dramas, "Promised Land" 10 and "7th Heaven," got perfect scores, but the overall conclusion is that the typical portrayal of fathers on network television "is one of incompetence."

The report focused only on shows where a father was a recurring character, where the relationship between the father and his children was a defining feature, and where the father's children were 18 or younger.

Thus, dramas like "Profiler," "ER," "NYPD Blue" and "Law & Order," where parenthood is a

secondary or occasional story element, weren't evaluated. Nor was the
comedy "Frasier," in which a richly
drawn father-son relationship involves adults.

Horn says these shows will be
examined in future reports, as will
UPN, which was left out of this year's
study because NFI didn't consider
it to be on a par with the other networks.

It is not Horn's aim to have every
father on TV be the never-flustered
type played by Robert Young on
"Father Knows Best" in the '50s and
'60s. But he *would* like to see more
than four shows — out of the 100-plus
airing on the networks during a season — give dads a fair shake.

"I wouldn't make this argument in 15
1962," Horn said. "But because we

have a crisis in fatherhood today, we
have to take seriously the kinds of
images we pump into kids' homes."

Horn asks that the networks look
at their schedules and ask themselves:
"When one out of three kids is not
likely to have a father in the home, are
we doing enough, are we fulfilling
our public responsibility to ensure
that there are at least some positive
images of fatherhood coming into our
households?"

By the way, Horn is a fan of "The
Simpsons." He thinks it's clever and
funny, but he also knows his two
daughters have no illusions that
Homer Simpson is your typical dad.

"They can watch the Homer
Simpsons and laugh it off, and they
know that's not what real fatherhood
is about because they have a contrast-

ing model. But what about the one-
third who go to sleep without a
father? How easy is it for them to separate the entertainment image from
reality?"

And as for those who would dismiss the NFI study as just another
attempt by a special-interest group to
angle for some attention, Horn seeks
to distance himself from other
studies, such as a recent one suggesting that federal employees are also
treated shabbily in TV shows.

"I'm not suggesting every father 20
should be portrayed as a superhero,"
he said. "But . . . it's not the same as
negative stereotypes of government
workers. We as a society can survive
without government workers, but we
cannot survive without fathers."

Fatherhood Portrayals on Network TV

Network/Show	Involvement	Engagement	Guidance	Competence	Priority	Total
WB/7th Heaven	5	5	5	5	5	25
CBS/Promised Land	5	5	5	5	5	25
WB/Smart Guy	5	4	5	5	5	24
ABC/Two of a Kind	4.5	4.5	5	4	5	23
ABC/The Hughleys	4.75	3.75	3.75	2.75	4	19
NBC/Mad About You	4	4.3	3.7	2.3	4	18.3
Fox/Holding the Baby	3	3.5	3	3.5	4.5	17.5
Fox/King of the Hill	4.3	4	3	2	3.67	17
ABC/Home Improvement	4.25	4.5	2.5	2	3.5	16.75
CBS/Everybody Loves Raymond	3.67	2.67	3	3.67	3	16
Fox/The Simpsons	4.5	4	2	2	3.5	16
WB/Dawson's Creek	3	3	2.5	4	2.5	15
Fox/That '70s Show	2.5	1.5	1.5	4	2.5	12
ABC/Brother's Keeper	2.3	2.67	1.67	2.3	2	11
CBS/The Nanny	1	1	1.67	2.3	1.67	7.67

Scoring — *20 or more points:* positive fatherhood portrayal; *16 to 19 points:* mixed fatherhood portrayal;
15 or fewer points: negative fatherhood portrayal.

Source: National Fatherhood Initiative

RESPOND ●

1. Even though the primary function of Levesque's article is to report information about the National Fatherhood Initiative's (NFI) study of how fathers are portrayed on network TV, you might argue that by reporting the study and framing it as he does, Levesque is making an argument himself. How would you characterize his argument? (Hint: What is Levesque's stance toward the study he reports on? How do you know?)

2. Consider the chart that is part of the article. Does the chart make an argument? Why or why not? In what ways might you interpret the information given in the chart? Draw some generalizations about how fathers are represented on network television based on the information given in the chart.

3. Evaluate the categories—involvement, engagement, guidance, competence, priority, and total—used in the chart and the study. Do these seem to you to be the most relevant or appropriate categories to use in evaluating portrayals of fatherhood? Why or why not? Would you suggest others? Which ones? Why?

4. How does Levesque's argument about the portrayals of fatherhood reported in this article compare with the arguments made by John Leo (p. 375), James Sterngold (p. 379), and Sherman Alexie (p. 383) about the representation of various other groups? Which of these arguments do you find most convincing? Least convincing? Why?

5. If a writer argues that we should be concerned about the portrayals of fathers on network television, would it be inconsistent for that writer to contend that representations of ethnic minorities in movies or television are unimportant? Could another writer convincingly argue that we should be concerned about the representation of ethnic minorities while not paying attention to TV's portrayal of fathers? Why or why not? **Write an essay** in which you take a stance on media portrayal of various groups and their significance (or insignificance) for us all.

shibboleth: most often, a password or test word. The word's origin traces back to Judges 12:4-6, where the men of Gilead asked those they encountered a question whose answer required the word shibboleth, which meant "stream" in Hebrew. Because the enemy Ephraimites pronounced the sound sh as s, they immediately gave themselves away by their (mis)pronunciation of the word and paid with their lives.

Shot on Ethnic Grounds and Side Streets

JOHN ANDERSON

Ah, Diversity, the shibboleth° of the '90s.

You see its happy effects everywhere, but especially in the movies. And particularly last week: Kevin Kline, Will Smith, Salma Hayek and Bai Ling, the unelectable Rainbow Coalition of Wild Wild West (in which Kenneth Branagh plays pure evil as physically challenged).

Spike Lee, giving the once-over to insular Italian-Americans in Summer of Sam. Austin Powers, the Rosa Parks of the dentally handicapped. And, of course, Jar Jar Binks, the Star Wars creature currently giving voice to a truly disenfranchised minority, the intergalactic racial stereotype. What can you say? There's a lot of love out there.

But despite all these stirring examples of how far film has come in reflecting the triumph and bounty of the cultural mosaic, we all know it's a segregated cinema world.

Black people, who have the chutzpah to go to the movies in numbers far beyond   5
their population percentile (thus showing insufficient fealty to marketing analysts or other Masters of the Universe) are catered to, largely, with demeaning inanity.

Teenagers? For all the debate over violence in the cinema, it seems far more likely that any anger, resentment or lack of self-worth they feel would be rooted in the fact they're constantly portrayed as idiots.

Women? Don't get me started.

Other groups don't even get that much attention, not from movie companies. Hollywood, which is really interested only in "event" movies anyway, can put Will Smith in a blockbuster and feel good about itself (and the money he makes). Spike Lee, who still represents some kind of alternative vision, seems very happy being the only black filmmaker with his kind of publicity budget— even if he has to make a film about serial killers and Italians to get it. But what happens when directors make movies about real people, people of color, people with accents, people with car payments? Well, let's see. . . .

Director Tony Gerber and his wife, playwright/screenwriter Lynn Nottage, made their movie *Side Streets* last year, inspired by a discovery that sounds almost apocryphal: His father—of Romanian Jewish ancestry—and her mother—who was black—grew up in the same Brooklyn neighborhood, sharing many of the same memories of place. But each existed—as so many North Americans do—in what might be called a parallel galaxy.

So that's how Gerber and Nottage structured their film: five stories, each with characters of different ethnicities and economic standings whose lives and difficulties unfold within tantalizing proximity of the other—but who lead the kind of adjacent lives that seem all too true.

There's the Indian cab driver whose imperious, movie-star brother has taken over his home and alienated his wife; the Italian would-be fashion designer, suffering under her couturiere mother's reputation; the Caribbean wife who's taken the key to her husband's gold Cadillac, because he sold her heirloom china to buy it; the Romanian butcher with a gambling problem; and the Latino who needs to buy a pageant dress for the girlfriend who thinks he's married.

Nottage's dialogue and dramatic structure are totally believable, natural and at times painfully funny. Gerber has woven the varying plot lines together as seamlessly as this kind of thing has ever been done. A Merchant-Ivory production, *Side Streets* has a topflight international cast, including Art Malik *(A Passage to India)*, Valeria Golina *(Rain Man)*, Leon *(Waiting To Exhale)*, Shashi Kapoor *(Sammy and Rosie Get Laid)*, Shabana Azmi *(Fire)* and Mirjana Jokovic *(Underground)*. It's easy to see why these actors would be attracted to this film: So many of them have been shoehorned into so many clichéd characterizations it must be refreshing to play real people.

But the whole thing is, in a way, a setup: *Side Streets* isn't about ethnic diversity. It's about relationships between men and women (the men come off a bit less well than the women, but I can't imagine anyone's arguing with the portrayals). It's about emotional unity, not cultural difference. In this, Gerber and Nottage have triumphed, paying tribute to their own partnership and maybe even paying a little retroactive tribute to their parents.

And guess what? No one has picked the film up for distribution. Why? Too diverse.

10

What kind of humor is used in this article? Parody? Satire? Chapter 13 describes different types of humor and how to use them effectively in your writing.

LINK TO P. 219 ·······················

"In my discussions with distributors," Gerber said recently, "they've all said they   15
like it, but they also say, 'I don't know how to market it.' They feel they can't
market the film to the black community, because it's not an entirely black film;
same for the Latino and Indian communities. They feel the potential is divided
by five."

Which seems a silly assumption, and one that could easily be overcome with a
little creative marketing. But as this year has indicated, the paucity of creative
marketing, or creative risk-taking, has led to a number of very good films—*Go,
Rushmore, Election*—being hung out to dry at the local octoplex. And at least
one remarkable film has been relegated to the ghetto of orphaned indies.°

indies: independent films made by filmakers not affiliated with the larger Hollywood film studios.

RESPOND ●

1. What argument does this piece make about diversity in the films of
   the 1990s? How does the author support the claims made? Do you
   agree with the position taken? Why or why not? If you have not seen
   Side Streets, how does your answer support or call into question the
   author's claims?

2. The author casts marketing as the villain in this story about the fate
   of *Side Streets.* Is such a stance fair? What direct support is offered for
   this position? In what ways does the author indirectly support this
   position through the description of the film itself?

3. The style of writing here is quite effective in creating the author's
   ethos. How would you characterize that ethos? How does the writing
   style contribute to it?

4. What specific stylistic features in this text are inappropriate for most
   academic writing? Using the information in the first seven paragraphs, **rewrite the opening** of the article to produce the introductory
   paragraph of an academic essay on the extent to which the film world
   is segregated and the possible consequences of such segregation. (You
   might use some version of paragraph 4 as a thesis statement:
   "Although we can cite many examples of progress in cinematic representations of the diversity of our cultural mosaic, the world of film
   ultimately remains segregated" or "Despite the great progress films
   have made in representing cultural diversity, the world of cinema
   remains ultimately segregated, a situation that has negative consequences for us all." Then, in a paragraph or two, describe the changes
   you have made and why you made them.

Taco Bell and Latino Stereotypes

MARÍA MARTIN

The dog's name is Dinky, and he's just a few inches off the ground. But this Chihuahua, who Taco Bell says was rescued from a pound, has ignited something of a controversy about advertising images, subliminal messages, and what they say about Mexican culture. *Latino USA*'s María Martin has this report.

MARÍA MARTIN: Two young men ride in an older-model BMW while happily munching fast food from you-know-where. Above the back seat sits a bobbing plastic dog. Suddenly, the young men look in the rear-view mirror and the plastic canine's been replaced by a little pointy-eared Chihuahua with bulging eyes. This dog's very much alive, and he'll do just about anything to get his little canine teeth around some of that food.

DINKY: Yo quiero Taco Bell!

VADA HILL: It was a line that we thought was a cute line. I mean, it comes right out of our quasi-Mexican image. It comes right out of what's unique and distinctive about this brand.

MARÍA MARTIN: That's Vada Hill, in charge of the marketing campaign featuring 5 the Chihuahua called Dinky. The campaign's been very successful for Taco Bell. But in recent weeks, it's also stirred up some controversy, which appears to have begun with the comments of former Clearwater, Florida, Mayor Gabriel Cazares. He's the former president of the Tampa, Florida, chapter of LULAC, the League for United Latin American Citizens.

GABRIEL CAZARES: I think it was an unfortunate commercial. I think that the use of a dog to depict Mexicans was very demeaning. If Taco Bell wanted to depict someone that would reflect Mexican culture we have many live, two-legged artists, singers, dancers, musicians — some great people in America that could have been selected to give a testimonial for Taco Bell (and) say, "Yo quiero un taco." And that wouldn't have been offensive.

MARÍA MARTIN: But many other Latinos didn't respond so negatively to the ads, as did Mr. Cazares.

LISA NAVARRETE: People, when there's sort of a real thing that crosses the line, we hear from folks, and then we follow up on that. We hadn't heard at all.

This text is the transcript of a 1999 radio feature, a segment from Latino USA, a weekly half-hour program dedicated to information about Hispanic Americans. In this feature, María Martin, the host, discusses responses in the Hispanic community to the very successful Taco Bell marketing campaign that uses a bilingual Chihuahua to push its products. Martin reports mainly about two opposing stances on the topic being discussed and does not herself take an explicit stance on the issue. In our society, by refusing to take a stance on the issues they cover, journalists come to be characterized as "objective"; in so doing, they create an ethos of being fair and unbiased. In this feature, several arguments are going on simultaneously — the argument made by the journalist/ host and those made by the various people who give testimonies. Radio, TV, film, and the Internet are especially interesting in this regard because consumers can hear (and see with TV, film, and the Internet) those who are giving testimonies. You can listen to this feature at <www .bedfordstmartins.com /everythingsanargument>.

Martin could have asked almost anybody for their opinion about the Taco Bell Chihuahua, but each of the interviewees here contributes a specific kind of credibility to the piece. Adapt the criteria given in Chapter 21 for evaluating print sources to the task of evaluating Martin's choices of interview subjects with respect to their credentials and relevance.

·· LINK TO P. 334

MARÍA MARTIN: Lisa Navarrete is the deputy vice president for public information for the National Council of La Raza in Washington.

LISA NAVARRETE: I don't really see a problem with the commercial, but I think the   10 issue is a larger one, which is, this really points to how our community is so sensitive to its image. . . . Because our portrayals on television are so few and far between, and when they are on they're usually negative, that it's very understandable that people in our community would be very sensitive to any kind of portrayal on television. And I think this is one of those cases.

MARÍA MARTIN: As for the League of United Latin American Citizens, they quickly disavowed Mr. Cazares' statements and made clear he was speaking only as an individual. Cuauhtemoc Figueroa is the organization's director of policy and communications.

CUAUHTEMOC FIGUEROA: Mr. Cazares has every right to believe and think the way he does about those commercials, and there are probably others in our organization that believe the same way as Mr. Cazares, but they haven't brought that to the attention of our organization.

MARÍA MARTIN: Would you say that this is a non-issue?

CUAUHTEMOC FIGUEROA: I would say initially, that was the reaction of our president, that it was a non-issue, because it frustrated Belen Robles, our president. Because for her, I mean, she goes around the country and travels extensively to meet with our state directors and addressing the issues affecting various Hispanic communities, Dominicans, Puertorriqueños, Mexican Americans, Cubanos. And she extensively travels. And this wasn't on the radar screen. It hadn't come up.

MARÍA MARTIN: In other commercials, Dinky is seen walking up a fire escape,   15 passing by the open windows of many apartments.

DINKY: What is a logarithm?

MARÍA MARTIN: In one commercial, a couple is watching *Jeopardy* on television as he resolutely makes his way to get some of that food.

DINKY: Yo quiero Taco Bell!

AMALIA MESA-BAINS: Advertising has to have some elements of sexuality and aggression to be really successful, and people have known that on Madison Avenue since the 1950s. So advertising is never accidental.

MARÍA MARTIN: Amalia Mesa-Bains is the director for visual and public art at 20 California State University at Monterey Bay. She's a well-known artist and a scholar who studies advertising as a function of identity formation. For Mesa-Bains, negative images about Mexican culture are at the core of Taco Bell's message.

AMALIA MESA-BAINS: So I think to take a Chihuahua, which is of course a dog, it's an animal, and use it to articulate in Spanish is really to personify Mexicans as animals. So it has two sides, because it's so cute and seductive. But I always ask my students to look at it: What is a Chihuahua? It's a dog. What is a dog? It's an animal. What is a female dog? We all know what those things are.

MARÍA MARTIN: Some people would say this is not a negative image, because you have a little dog that is so clever that he can get from the balcony to the car because he's so interested in getting to eat the Taco Bell food. In another commercial, he answers the *Jeopardy* question correctly on his way to get the Taco Bell food. So it's a clever little dog, and maybe it represents Latinos as clever people.

AMALIA MESA-BAINS: But it also represents Latinos as animals that have to scamper for their food. And I maintain that you have to look at the context in which that dog appears. That a dog appears near a brothel, that's a love hotel. That dog appears with low-riders. That dog appears with black people sitting in armchairs, snacking away while they watch television all day. What is that about? And to look at the dog is to look at the campaign of Taco Bell over these years—transgressive, seductive images.

MARÍA MARTIN: In the 1970s, Latinos rallied to protest the use of the image of a sleepy bandit in a large sombrero as an advertising symbol in a commercial for Frito's corn chips. The so-called Frito Bandito was eventually taken off the air. Twenty years later, the images, says Mesa-Bains, are not so blatant. But even seemingly innocuous images, she says, are still capable of doing damage.

AMALIA MESA-BAINS: I mean, we live in segregated communities. Half the time, 25 people never meet us, but they certainly watch television. And this inundates endlessly. I'll give you a couple of scenarios about what the impact of it is. I have a friend who has a young boy, who's a teenager. And she overheard him talking to his friends, and in the voice of the Chihuahua he was speaking of a girl he liked. "Yo quiero," and then he named the girl. My husband had a student come into his class whose daughter came home from school in tears because she had been teased relentlessly by her peers as Miss Chihuahua,

because she was Mexican. So these images and this concept is probably one of the most profound influences that we need to deal with, and we have accepted it over and over again. And I really think it's time for the institutions that represent us to speak up.

MARÍA MARTIN: An informal on-line poll conducted recently by Latino Net found people equally split among those who were offended by the Chihuahua commercial, those who were not, and those who thought it was a non-issue.

For its part, Taco Bell says in a statement by their vice president that the company takes pride in the Mexican heritage of its food, and that their consumer research, including that done among Hispanics, indicates that people are being entertained and not offended.

For *Latino USA,* I'm María Martin.

RESPOND •

1. Characterize the stances of the parties who speak or are represented in this interview: Gabriel Cazares, Lisa Navarrete, Amalia Mesa-Bains, Vada Hill, Cuauhtemoc Figueroa, and the vice president of Taco Bell. What, for each of them, seems to be the "real issue"? Why? To what extent do the stances represent simple pro/con positions?

2. Discuss the role of humor in the Taco Bell controversy. How might the controversy be different if Dinky had been used as part of a marketing campaign that was serious rather than humorous? What particular dangers raised by the use of humor does this controversy highlight?

3. Evaluate the spoken arguments from the interviewees that Martin used in assembling this radio segment. (Most likely, the excerpts used here come from much longer taped interviews.) Using the criteria discussed in Chapter 17, analyze the specific elements of spoken argument used by the two interviewees you find most successful.

4. As this radio segment indicates, representing American ethnic groups in advertising is never simple. Compare the commercials for three to five fast-food chains, looking at how—and how well—they represent the diversity of American society. **Write an essay** in which you present your observations and evaluate the commercials' effectiveness. Part of your evidence will surely need to be descriptions of the commercials you analyze.

If the media become the mirror that reflects the fairest of us all, what sorts of bodies appear there, what sorts don't, and what might the consequences of this situation be? This cluster of readings asks you to consider the question **who's the fairest of them all** for and about yourself. It opens with a baby studying its reflection in a mirror and then moves on to two arguments that focus on research conducted in Fiji, an island in the Pacific, where, within a short while after the arrival of American television, adolescent girls began rejecting local notions about beauty, taking up instead an image of an "ideal body" based on the body type of contemporary Hollywood stars—thin, thin, thin. Erica Goode's *New York Times* news article, "Study Finds TV Alters Fiji Girls' View of Body," reports on the research study itself while Ellen Goodman's syndicated column "The Culture of Thin Bites Fiji" uses the study as the basis for claiming that little girls in this country learn to hate and harm themselves as a result of the unrealistic notions of beauty promoted by the media, television in particular. From a very different perspective, Carey Goldberg's *New York Times* news story "'People of Size' Gather to Promote Fat Acceptance" and W. Charisse Goodman's essay "One Picture Is Worth a Thousand Diets" document the struggle of Americans who are overweight, especially women, to combat what they term prejudice against fat people.

And it's not only women who find themselves under pressure because of the fair bodies represented in the media. Men of all ages are hitting the gym in record numbers, and as several texts make clear, they're also visiting the plastic surgeon. Janice Turner's "Cutting Edge: Men Are Having Cosmetic Surgery in Growing Numbers to Compete with Younger Guys" describes the new social pressures that encourage men to have cosmetic procedures. From a more critical perspective, Sandy Naiman's article, "Suck Out Your Gut," provides information about liposuction and its limitations. Reflecting on the men in their lives, Angela Neustatter and Louisa Young take opposing sides in answering the question, "Should they, or shouldn't they?" In her essay, "Turning Little Boys into Little Girls," Michelle Cottle, a self-acknowledged feminist, declares that magazines like *Men's Health,* which feed men's newly found obsessions with their bodies, are the greatest thing since spandex. Finally, "Selling Men's Underwear across the Decades" challenges you to examine three advertisements from the last fifty years—two from magazines and one from a billboard—and then to draw conclusions about how these ads reflect changing attitudes toward the male body and its representation in the media even as they've helped create new attitudes toward body image.

Look in the mirror. Are you pleased with what you see? Look in the media. Do you see bodies like yours? Should you be more worried if you do, or if you don't?

This cartoon, by artist P. Byrnes, appeared in a March 2000 issue of the New Yorker. As you study it, consider the argument we're making by using this cartoon to open the cluster about body image and the media.

RESPOND●

1. Is the baby in this cartoon male or female? Why do you think so?

2. What is the "it" of "It begins"?

3. Why is this cartoon humorous? What knowledge about American culture does it assume?

Study Finds TV Alters Fiji Girls' View of Body

BY ERICA GOODE

"You've gained weight" is a traditional compliment in Fiji, anthropologists say.

In accordance with traditional culture in the South Pacific nation, dinner guests are expected to eat as much as possible. A robust, nicely rounded body is the norm for men and women. "Skinny legs" is a major insult. And "going thin," the Fijian term for losing a noticeable amount of weight, is considered a worrisome condition.

But all that may be changing, now that Heather Locklear has arrived.

Just a few years after the introduction of television to a province of Fiji's main island, Viti Levu, eating disorders—once virtually unheard of there—are on the rise among girls, according to a study presented yesterday at the American Psychiatric Association meetings in Washington. Young girls dream of looking not like

their mothers and aunts, but like the slender stars of "Melrose Place" and "Beverly Hills 90210."

"I'm very heavy," one Fijian adolescent lamented during an interview with researchers led by Dr. Anne E. Becker, director of research at the

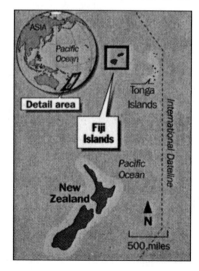

Harvard Eating Disorders Center of Harvard Medical School, who investigated shifts in body image and eating practices in Fiji over a three-year period.

The Fijian girl said her friends also tell her that she is too fat, "and sometimes I'm depressed because I always want to lose weight."

Epidemiological studies have shown that eating disorders are more prevalent in industrialized countries, suggesting that cultural factors play a role. But few studies have examined the effects of long-term cultural shifts on disordered eating in traditional societies.

Dr. Becker and her colleagues surveyed 63 Fijian secondary school girls, whose average age was 17. The work began in 1995, one month after satellites began beaming television signals to the region. In 1998, the researchers surveyed another group of 65 girls from the same schools, who were matched in age, weight and other characteristics with the subjects in the earlier group.

Fifteen percent in the 1998 survey reported that they had induced vomiting to control their weight, the researchers said, compared with 3 percent in the 1995 survey. And 29 percent scored highly on a test of eating-disorder risk, co[...] 13 percent three years be[...]

Girls who said they [...] vision three or more nig[...] the 1998 survey were 50 [...] likely to describe thems[...] big or fat" and 30 percen[...] to diet than girls who wa[...] sion less frequently.

Before 1995, Dr. F[...] there was little talk of di[...] "The idea of calories was [...] to them." But in the 199[...] percent said that at som[...] had been on a diet. In [...] liminary data suggest m[...] girls in Fiji diet than the[...] counterparts.

The results of the stu[...] been published, but were [...]reviewed by the psychiatric association's scientific program committee before being accepted for presentation at the meetings.

Several of the students told Dr. Becker and her colleagues that they wanted to look like the Western women they saw on television shows like "Beverly Hills 90210." One girl said that her friends "change their mood, their hairstyles, so that they can be like those characters." "So in order to be like them, I have to work on myself, exercising and my eating habits should change," she said.

Fiji schoolgirls in uniform

But Dr. Marshall Sahlins, Charles F. Grey professor emeritus of Anthropology at the University of Chicago, said that he doubts that television was the only factor in the changes. "I think that television is a kind of metaphor of something more profound," he said.

In contrast to the solitary couch-15 potato viewing style displayed by

Becker uses a combination of experimental evidence and ethnographic observation to support her causal argument. See Chapter 11 for examples of other ways to make an effective causal argument.

LINK TO P. 161

many Americans, watching television is a communal activity in Fiji, Dr. Becker said. Fijians often gather in households with television sets, and sit together, drinking kava and talking about their day's activities, the TV on in the background.

"What we noticed in 1995 is that people had a sort of curiosity, but it was a dismissive curiosity," Dr. Becker said. "But over the years they have come to accept it as a form of entertainment."

Fiji residents have access to only one television channel, she said, which broadcasts a selection of programs from the United States, Britain and Australia. Among the most popular are "Seinfeld," "Melrose Place," which features Ms. Locklear, "E.R.," "Xena, Warrior Princess," and "Beverly Hills 90210."

Dr. Becker said that the increase in eating disorders like bulimia may be a signal that the culture is changing so quickly that Fijians are having difficulty keeping up. Island teen-agers, she said, "are acutely aware that the traditional culture doesn't equip them well to negotiate the kinds of conflicts" presented by a 1990's global economy.

In other Pacific societies, Dr. Becker said, similar cultural shifts have been accompanied by an increase in psychological problems among adolescents. Researchers speculated, for example, that rapid social change played a role in a rash of adolescent suicides in Micronesia in the 1980's.

RESPOND ●

1. The arguments in news articles like this one are complex for several reasons. First, there are at least two arguments going on simultaneously, the one constructed by the author and the one put forth by the researcher whose work is being discussed. What arguments does each one make in this article? How does the Sahlins quotation in paragraph 14 contribute to the article? To the argument put forth by Becker in support of the study's findings?

2. How does Goode establish Becker as an authority? What reasons does Goode offer her audience for trusting Becker? Why does it matter that Sahlins is referred to as "Dr. Marshall Sahlins, Charles F. Grey professor emeritus of Anthropology at the University of Chicago" (paragraph 14)? What sorts of argument is Goode using in these instances, and why?

3. If your knowledge of America were based solely on *Seinfeld, Melrose Place, E.R., Xena, Warrior Princess,* and *Beverly Hills 90210,* what would your image of American women (or men) be? (After all, such images of America are the only ones many people around the globe have.) **Write an essay** in response to this question. If you are not familiar with these particular television programs, choose two or three other programs that you watch regularly as the basis for your argument.

▼ *Ellen Goodman, an award-winning columnist, writes regularly for the Boston Globe, where this article appeared in May 1999, a few days after Anne E. Becker discussed the findings of her research on the effects of American TV on adolescent Fijian girls' self-image. Becker's study is also discussed in the previous news article by Erica Goode (p. 398). Goodman's column generally appears on the op-ed (opinion-editorial) pages of newspapers across the country. As you read, consider how her discussion of Becker's research compares and contrasts with Goode's news report about the same study. Keep in mind as well that Goodman is writing shortly after the shootings at Columbine High School in Colorado, where two male students killed and wounded a number of students and teachers.*

The Culture of Thin Bites Fiji

ELLEN GOODMAN

First of all, imagine a place women greet one another at the market with open arms, loving smiles, and a cheerful exchange of ritual compliments:

"You look wonderful! You've put on weight!"

Does that sound like dialogue from Fat Fantasyland? Or a skit from fat-is-a-feminist-issue satire? Well, this Western fantasy was a South Pacific fact of life. In Fiji, before 1995, big was beautiful and bigger was more beautiful—and people really did flatter one another with exclamations about weight gain.

In this island paradise, food was not only love, it was a cultural imperative. Eating and overeating were rites of mutual hospitality. Everyone worried about losing weight—but not the way we do. "Going thin" was considered to be a sign of some social problem, a worrisome indication the person wasn't getting enough to eat.

The Fijians were, to be sure, a bit 5 obsessed with food; they prescribed herbs to stimulate the appetite. They were a reverse image of our culture. And that turns out to be the point.

Something happened in 1995. A Western mirror was shoved into the face of the Fijians. Television came to the island. Suddenly, the girls of rural coastal villages were watching the girls of "Melrose Place" and "Beverly Hills 90210," not to mention "Seinfeld" and "E.R."

Within 38 months, the number of teenagers at risk for eating disorders more than doubled to 29 percent. The number of high school girls who vomited for weight control went up five times to 15 percent. Worse yet, 74 percent of the Fiji teens in the study said they felt "too big or fat" at least some of the time and 62 percent said they had dieted in the past month.

This before-and-after television portrait of a body image takeover was drawn by Anne Becker, an 5 anthropologist and psychiatrist who directs research at the Harvard Eating Disorders Center. She presented her research at the American Psychiatric Association last week with all the usual caveats. No, you cannot prove a direct causal link between television and eating disorders. Heather Locklear doesn't cause anorexia. Nor does Tori Spelling cause bulimia.

Fiji is not just a Fat Paradise Lost. It's an economy in transition from subsistence agriculture to tourism and its entry into the global economy has threatened many old values.

Nevertheless, you don't get a 10 much better lab experiment than this. In just 38 months, and with only one channel, a television-free culture that defined a fat person as robust has become a television culture that sees robust as, well, repulsive.

401

All that and these islanders didn't even get "Ally McBeal."

"Going thin" is no longer a social disease but the perceived requirement for getting a good job, nice clothes, and fancy cars. As Becker says carefully, "The acute and constant bombardment of certain images in the media are apparently quite influential in how teens experience their bodies."

Speaking of Fiji teenagers in a way that sounds all-too familiar, she adds, "We have a set of vulnerable teens consuming television. There's a huge disparity between what they see on television and what they look like themselves — that goes not only to clothing, hairstyles, and skin color, but size of bodies."

In short, the sum of Western culture, the big success story of our entertainment industry, is our ability to export insecurity: We can make

Calista Flockhart

any woman anywhere feel perfectly rotten about her shape. At this rate,

we owe the islanders at least one year of the ample lawyer Camryn Manheim in "The Practice" for free.

I'm not surprised by research 15 showing that eating disorders are a cultural byproduct. We've watched the female image shrink down to Calista Flockhart at the same time we've seen eating problems grow. But Hollywood hasn't been exactly eager to acknowledge the connection between image and illness.

Over the past few weeks since the Columbine High massacre, we've broken through some denial about violence as a teaching tool. It's pretty clear that boys are literally learning how to hate and harm others.

Maybe we ought to worry a little more about what girls learn: To hate and harm themselves.

Chapter 11 notes that causal arguments are often included as part of other arguments. Goodman's article reports on Anne Becker's research to support a larger argument.

········· LINK TO P. 165

RESPOND •

1. What is Goodman's argument? How does she build it around Becker's study while not limiting herself to that evidence alone? (Consider, especially, paragraphs 15–17.)

2. What cultural knowledge does Goodman assume her *Boston Globe* audience to have? How does she use allusions to American TV programs to build her argument? Note, for example, that she sometimes uses such allusions as conversational asides — "All that and these islanders didn't even get *Ally McBeal*," and "At this rate, we owe the islanders at least one year of the ample lawyer Camryn Manheim in *The Practice* for free" — to establish her ethos. In what other ways do allusions to TV programs contribute to Goodman's argument?

3. After reading both Goodman's op-ed column and Erica Goode's news article (p. 398), consider how the elements of argument are treated similarly or differently in op-ed and news articles. Look at how each

writer uses evidence, establishes ethos, and incorporates specific linguistic forms (such as questions in contrast to statements). Which selection do you find more argumentative? Persuasive? Agonistic? Invitational?

4. Many professors would find Goodman's conversational style inappropriate for most academic writing assignments. Choose several paragraphs of the text that contain information appropriate for an argumentative academic paper. Then **write a few well-developed paragraphs** on the topic. (Paragraphs 4–8 could be revised in this way, though you would put the information contained in these five paragraphs into only two or three longer paragraphs. Newspaper articles often feature shorter paragraphs, even paragraphs of a single sentence, that are generally inappropriate in academic writing.)

▼ This New York Times *news article reports on the 1999 annual conven-tion of the National Association to Advance Fat Acceptance (NAAFA), which met in Framingham, Massachusetts. As you read, note the arguments made by NAAFA members about why they should be accepted as they are.*

"People of Size" Gather to Promote Fat Acceptance
Group Celebrates Idea of Liberation

BY CAREY GOLDBERG

FRAMINGHAM, Mass., July 28 — The caramel lollipops at registration; the black thong bikini that Marilyn Wann, a proud 270 pounds, wore at the pool party; the very pool party itself, for people who are usually pool pariahs: All these were political statements of defiance here at the convention of the National Association to Advance Fat Acceptance, as political as the T-shirts that read, "Fat!So?"

Most of the year the association lobbies on behalf of fat people ("fat" is the preferred adjective, members said, a simple description they want to reclaim; "overweight" and especially "morbidly obese" are despised). With about 4,000 members, the association helps fat people cope in a society that hates their girth; it fights the diet industry, pointing out its overwhelming long-term failure rate, and it combats discrimination.

But once a year, it takes the added step of bringing together hundreds of members — nearly 500 this year — to create a place where "people of size" are just people, where everyone has a

story of an airplane-seat nightmare or gibes in a job interview, and where no one suggests a new diet.

"This particular one week a year when, in one particular hotel, everyone who's larger than average looks normal, is like a Brigadoon," Ms. Wann, a writer from San Francisco, said, referring to the Scottish village that comes to life for a day every 100 years. "It's odd to be in a place where you look like everyone else."

Odd, and for many, deeply affect-ing and energizing. In an orientation session for first-time convention-goers, several spoke about "coming out of the closet" as fat people, strange as that may seem when their size has always been visible to every-body. What they meant, they said, was the moment when they simply accepted their size and the likeli-hood that it would never change, and wanted others to do the same.

"Finally, after being tormented about being fat from the time I was a baby, I've decided I'm going to embrace it," said Barbara Lehmann, a social worker from Orono, Me., who estimated that she had gained and lost

thousands of pounds in her lifetime.

Looking around the circle of more than 20 members, mainly women, Ms. Lehmann commented, in a sort of wonderment, "This is the first time I've been in a room where I'm not the fattest person or close to it, and it's — it's — what am I trying to say?"

"Liberating?" suggested Frances White, the group leader.

The association has been pursuing such fat liberation — officially, it is known as the "size acceptance move-ment" — for 30 years now, with mixed success. Commenting on the current climate, Bettye Travis, the group's president, said there was good fat-acceptance news and bad: the popularity of Camryn Manheim, the television actress, is good; the portrayal of a gluttonous, disgusting character in the latest Austen Powers film is bad.

Others say it still rankles that Oprah Winfrey, with all her accom-plishments, has described losing weight as her greatest achievement.

More people are getting skeptical about diets, Ms. Travis said, but new diet drugs with dangerous side effects

Participants at the convention of the National Association to Advance Fat Acceptance. Notice their use of figurative language.

keep sweeping the country, and the medical establishment sometimes seems to be sending the message that "it's better to die than be fat."

The association's policy is to take the emphasis off dieting, which often does more harm than good, and put it on health, encouraging people to eat well, exercise and take care of them-

selves, and let their bodies settle into their natural weight — and then to work on getting comfortable as a person who takes up substantial space.

A strong current of pain ran through the convention — the accumulated wounds of rejection and ostracism, mean jokes, cruel remarks

that accrue to members of what Ms. Travis called "one of the last marginal groups that are still targeted, that it's still 'O.K.' to make fun of." There were stories about chairs that broke, about rude doctors, about ugly plus-sized clothes and the difficulties of buying a car with enough room or fitting into a hospital wheelchair, about people who assumed that fat meant ugly and lazy and dumb.

But there was also a strong current of humor and defiance, a celebration of snappy comebacks. Recently, in San Francisco, Ms. Travis said, a health club had a billboard advertisement showing an alien from space and saying, "When they come, they will eat the fat ones first." So some of the association's members did aerobics in front of the fitness club in protest.

The association is planning a sim- 15 ilar rally outside the Fanueil Hall Marketplace in Boston this Saturday, titled "Every Body-Good Body."

Last year the association staged a "million pound march" in Santa Monica, Calif. And in the San Francisco area, a fat women's swimming group calls itself "Making Waves."

The fat-acceptance cause has made some political progress. Although Michigan is the only state that includes a ban on size discrimination in its civil rights law, passed in the 1970s, Santa Monica has a similar city ordinance, and one is pending in San Francisco.

In Massachusetts, such a law has been proposed twice before but has never made it to the floor of the Legislature. Another effort is now under way, and convention organizers said today that the state's Governor, Paul Cellucci, had sent over a proclamation declaring that this would be "Size Acceptance Week" in Massachusetts.

In the past, said State Representative Byron Rushing, who has sponsored the size-discrimination bills, legislators have always sent them on for further study. "What they are studying," Mr. Rushing said, "is whether their constituents will elect them again if they vote for this."

Jody Abrams, an association 20 member who testified on behalf of Mr. Rushing's bill, said that legislators, like others who still believe in dieting, "haven't accepted that there are just going to be fat people in the world." And that, he added, is "a hard thing to come up against."

Association members say they pin many of their hopes on influencing the younger generation's attitudes toward fat people, and are setting up a special fat speakers' bureau to send members around to talk at schools.

Ultimately, said Ms. Wann, who has talked to students herself and has written a book called "Fat!So?" (Ten Speed Press, 1998), "the thing we have to do is, like drag queens, make it funky to be a rebel."

"I'm sorry, but Madonna has nothing on me as a rebel," Ms. Wann added. "Madonna in a thong, me in a thong—which one is more challenging to the status quo?"

Arguments are often difficult to categorize; one single article may contain a causal argument, a definition argument, an evaluation argument, and/or a proposal argument. Does Goldberg's article contain any features of a proposal argument? See Chapter 12 to read about the features of a proposal.

··· **LINK TO P. 192**

RESPOND •

1. The goal of the National Association to Advance Fat Acceptance (NAAFA) is to do exactly that: to convince the public to accept fat people as they are. What sorts of arguments (such as arguments of the heart or arguments based on character, facts and reason, or values) are put forth to support this position? How do members of the organization use humor as part of their arguments?

2. In some ways, Goldberg's argument is similar to the arguments by Erica Goode (p. 398) and Ellen Goodman (p. 401) about women's obsession with thinness being physically and psychologically unhealthy. However, the three authors make their points in very different ways. Compare this article with either the article by Goode or the one by Goodman in terms of the kinds of arguments put forth. (Obviously, answering question 1 gets you partway to an answer.)

3. How does the photograph accompanying this article influence your response to it? To the goals of NAAFA? Had the photograph not been included, do you imagine your response to the article would have been different? Why or why not?

4. **Write an essay** in response to the question posed by NAAFA member Marilyn Wann in the closing lines of the article: Who is the greater threat to the status quo in this society, Madonna in a thong bathing suit, or Wann, who weighs 270 pounds, in a thong bathing suit? How does each question the status quo? Who is the more rebellious? Why?

▶ *As the title of W. Charisse Goodman's 1995 book, The Invisible Woman: Confronting Weight Prejudice in America, implies, her thesis is that American society tolerates and even encourages prejudice against people, especially women, who are not thin. The chapter excerpted here, "One Picture Is Worth a Thousand Diets," focuses on the ways in which the media render invisible or treat with disdain women whom Goodman refers to as "large."*

One Picture Is Worth a Thousand Diets

W. CHARISSE GOODMAN

> Loyalty to petrified opinions never yet broke a chain or freed a
> human soul in this world—and never will.   –Mark Twain

In our consumption-addled culture, the mass media encourage us to absorb as many goods as possible far beyond the saturation point. We are urged to buy things we don't really need and luxuries we may not be able to afford. Not only is more better, but we are advised that it will make us sexier or more successful. But this rule has one notable exception: if a woman is perceived as having consumed too much food, she finds she has committed a social crime. By projecting the image of gluttony onto the large woman exclusively, our society can deny and rationalize its colossal overindulgence in the cult of conspicuous consumption. Greed, after all, is hardly restricted to a preoccupation with food. Movies, television, magazines, newspapers, and preachifying self-help books all reinforce and amplify the ignorant stereotypes about fat people that America holds so close and dear; taken together, they constitute a framework of "petrified opinions" which few dare to question.

A survey of merely eleven mainstream magazines, including *Vogue, Redbook, Time, McCall's,* even *Audubon* and *Modern Maturity,* turned up an astounding 645 pictures of thin women as opposed to 11 of heavy women. Scrutinizing the local newspapers over a period of several weeks left me with a body count of 221 thin women as opposed to nine large women; newspaper advertising inserts added another 288 pictures of individual thin women and approximately a dozen heavy women (most of whom were pictured in a single store flyer for large-size clothing). An examination of almost 160 commercials—after that point, it was either stop or incinerate the TV set—contributed 120 ads featuring thin women exclusively, 27 ads depicting heavy males, mostly in a normal or positive light, and all of 12 heavy women, half of whom, interestingly, were either African-American, older, or both. Of ads including fat women, one offered an evil old cartoon witch, another pictured two big women dressed as opera-singer Valkyrie types, and a third depicted *Alice in Wonderland*'s mean-tempered Red Queen. A . . . series of commercials for Snapple soft drinks featured a fairly heavy woman who read complimentary letters from consumers of the product; however, in most of the commercials this woman is visible only from the shoulders up, while the rest of her body is hidden by a very high counter. Ultimately, the burden of proof in this respect was no more than a counting exercise.

After drowning in an ocean of slender female figures everywhere I looked, it was easy to see how women are persuaded that thinness equals happiness and fulfillment. The women of the media are not only overwhelmingly small but also smiling, self-satisfied, exciting, dynamic, romantically involved, and generally having a splendid time. This is sheer marketing fantasy—and yet, as a society, we buy it, we eat it up, we swallow it whole and ask for more.

TELEVISION AND MOVIES

The most obvious pattern in television and movies, other than the predominant absence of large women, reflects the unsurprising fact that heavy men, although they suffer from the same general type of discrimination as heavy women, are not as severely censured for being large. Size in a man is often considered either a sign of physical power or a matter of no consequence. In a scene from the movie *Diner*, a large man eats plate after plate of sandwiches in a diner, apparently trying to set a personal record. The main characters, all male, are watching him in awe and cheering him on; no cracks are made about his size or his appetite. It is utterly impossible to imagine a big woman playing the same scene.

In even a cursory review of mass media presentations, one finds 5 many more large men than women. Take, for example, actors John Goodman, the late John Candy (whose death has been attributed not purely to his weight but also to a rapid and substantial weight loss), *Cheers'* George Wendt, Bob Hoskins, the late John Belushi (dead of an overdose of drugs, not food), the late comic Sam Kinison (car accident, not clogged arteries), French actor Gerard Depardieu, and British comic Robbie Coltrane, to name a few. All these men have played characters who, although heavy, are nonetheless portrayed as lovable and appealing enough to attract thin, conventionally attractive women.

John Candy

Can anyone imagine a female version of *Cheers'* Norm—a lazy, work-phobic, beer-guzzling woman who assiduously avoids home and husband—being hailed as funny, let alone "beloved," as one news article put it?

Of course, we're all well acquainted with that popular movie plot involving the sweet but physically unexceptional male who yearns after the beautiful, thin heroine and eventually, by means of his irresistible personality, wins his true love (*Minnie and Moskowitz* comes immediately to mind). The male-dominated film industry never misses an opportunity to remind us that men should always be loved for themselves. But what about women?

When Hollywood was casting for the 1991 film *Frankie and Johnnie,* a story about an ordinary-looking woman who falls in love with a plain-looking man, Kathy Bates, an Oscar-winning actress who portrayed Frankie on the stage and who just happens to be large, was passed over for the film role. The part went instead to Michelle Pfeiffer, a thin, conventionally glamorous blonde who obviously wanted to prove that she could play a character role. This is typical. If the heavy woman has any consistent role in commercial American films, it is as the peripheral, asexual mother or "buddy," and rarely, if ever, the central, romantic character. Message to all large women: You're not sexy. The only beautiful woman is a thin woman.

Bates herself pointed out in a 1991 interview that when she read for a part in the Sylvester Stallone movie *Paradise Alley,* the character breakdown showed that "after every single female character's name was the adjective 'beautiful,' even if the character was age 82." When Bates questioned the casting director about this, he replied, "Well if you want to make your own female version of *Marty* (a movie about a lonely, aging, unattractive man), be my guest" (Finke, 1991).

Of the approximately 70 movies I randomly surveyed—mostly mainstream commercial American films—only 17 had any large female characters at all in the script, most of whom represented the standard domineering mother figure, the comically unattractive woman, the whore figure, and Bates as her *Misery* psychopath character. Only six of these 17 films presented a big woman as a positive figure, and of these six, only three—*Daddy's Dyin'—Who's Got the Will?* and John Waters' *Hairspray* and *Crybaby*—featured fat women as romantic figures and central characters.

Television shows are not much better, although they occasionally 10 make an effort. Ricki Lake, who has since lost weight, was featured in the defunct series *China Beach,* Delta Burke once co-starred in *Designing Women* and had her own series; and Roseanne's show has long resided among the Top 10 in the Nielsen ratings. Although these women are encouraging examples of talent overcoming prejudice, they are too few and far between. At best, TV shows typically treat large female characters as special cases whose weight is always a matter of comment, rather than integrating women of all sizes and shapes into their programs as a matter of course.

On *L.A. Law,* heavy actress Conchata Ferrell played a new character who was dumped from the program after a relatively short tenure. Her role, that of a tough attorney, was variously described in reviews and on the show as "loud, brash and overbearing," "tubby," "aggressive," "bullying, overpowering," and "a real cash cow." At one point in the series, Ferrell's character marries a handsome, slender man amidst tittering speculation by the firm's slender female attorneys as to the groom's ulterior motive. Naturally, it turns out that he is a foreigner who has married the fat attorney solely to gain citizenship.

THE PERSONALS: "NO FAT WOMEN, PLEASE"

Although it's true the personals are not strictly part of the media establishment, they do constitute a public forum and mass-communication network, and they illustrate in a very raw fashion the reflection of media imagery in the desires of men.

The patterns of the personals reflect the usual stale stereotypes and sexism of weight prejudice. Out of 324 ads by men seeking women in which the men specified body size, 312 requested, or rather demanded, a thin body type, employing [no less than 17] synonyms for "thin." Men have a most creative vocabulary when it comes to describing a woman's body. Indeed, to judge by the phrasing of the ads, "slender" and "attractive" are one word, not two, in the same fashion as "fat" and "ugly."

It is most interesting that male admirers of big women are commonly portrayed as little boys looking for a mother figure; yet here, one finds men who appear to be looking for a very small, dependent, child-woman/daughter figure and status symbol. Could it be that they have

WM 46, 5'8" non-smoker looking for woman of my dreams: You are kind, helpful, caring, fun-loving, funny, polite, and smart. You like Sci-fi, comedy, travel, and cats. You're reasonably close to being height/weight proportionate.

NATIVE TEXAN NEW to town interested in SF between 24-34, slim or athletic, attractive, and intelligent. Must love to have fun and be positive about life. Non-smoker, light drinker.

A TALL, THIN woman. Yeah! That's what I want. 5'8" to 6'2", fun, pretty, seeking long-term relationship. I'm 6', muscular, grey and green, 40s, intelligent, V.I.P. businesses. Country life, boating, camping to limousine trips, dinners, tours.

TALL, FIT, HANDSOME, intelligent, emotionally stable, financially secure, laid back professional SWM, mid-40s, looking to fall in love with pretty, fit, SW/HF, 32-45, with varied interests. ☎1301

Surveys of newspaper classified ads or TV commercials can be rich sources of evidence for many kinds of arguments that deal with current cultural or social issues. See Chapter 18 for suggestions about other types of first-hand evidence.

···LINK TO P. 299

their own peculiar incest fantasies? Might one go even further and speculate that the preference for women with androgynous or boyish figures represents a closeted homosexuality in some men, or an unconscious fear of and hostility toward the more powerful femininity of the large woman?

In any case, the overall impression of the personals is that men still 15 care more about a woman's body and looks than her qualities as a human being. An S/B/M (single black male) summed it up perfectly when he wrote, in search of a woman who "weighs no more than 140. Be any race, be yourself, be beautiful." Or else?

NEWSPAPERS

The problem with mainstream newspaper journalism is twofold: first, its hearty participation in the national pastime of describing fat people in contemptuous terms; and second, that it purports to be an objective, unbiased observer and reporter of news and culture. But when entertainment journalists describe a large actress as "a blimp on the way to full zeppelin status" (Miller, 1992) or a bone-thin actress as "deliciously gorgeous," the reader can make a pretty good guess as to their personal views as well as their degree of impartiality.

One of the best—or worst—examples of journalistic weight prejudice was the local sports columnist reporting from the 1992 Barcelona Olympics on the Spanish beaches, and his disparaging remarks about local older women possessed of the sheer tasteless gall to walk on said beaches in "nothing but" their swimsuits. This same columnist also deplored women who dared to sunbathe undraped on a topless beach—not because they were naked, but because they lacked the flawless breasts and figures that appeal so to the male eye (Nevius, 1992).

Even in newspaper articles that have nothing to do with diet and weight, women are frequently described in terms of their approximate or specific weight and appearance. Phrases like "tall sexy . . . type," "the mountain of blond hair she balances on 102 pounds," "slender beauty," and "California girl beauty" appear in one article alone about female stand-up comics which includes, interestingly, a graphic description of a man helping himself to generous portions of a buffet while the women sit and drink only water (Kahn, 1991). One newspaper item about singer Ann Peebles refers to her as "the 99-pound vocalist) (Selvin, 1992); another article briefly profiling four blues musicians describes the one woman in the group as "5-foot-3 and 105 pounds" but makes no mention of any of the three men's physical attributes (Orr, 1992).

[M]ost newspaper items omit such detailed descriptions of men's sizes and body parts. One interview of director Robert Altman describes him in terms of his age and hair color, and compares him to a "bemused, slightly grumpy, extremely shrewd owl," but makes no mention of his weight, although the full-body shot accompanying the article reveals a clearly heavyset man (Guthmann, 1992).

As for print advertisements, they lack the dynamics of television 20 ads, and consequently they can come on quite strong in their promotion of thinness as the ultimate aphrodisiac. One diet product ad out of TV Guide depicts a thin woman in a leotard examining her hips. Superimposed upon the picture are the words "We'll help you turn on more than your metabolism." Next to the picture, the ad begins, "You're not only dieting for yourself. That's why it's so important to lose those extra pounds. . . ." Another item in a different issue of this magazine hawks an exercise machine, and while the words describing the health benefits are in rather small print, the impossibly slender and leggy female model in the ad is quite noticeable, as are the words, "Hurry! Get that NordicTrack figure you always wanted." Then there are the ubiquitous exercise club advertisements featuring women who are dressed, shaped, and posed more like centerfolds than athletes or average people.

The mass media do not really reflect an idealized reality, as its gurus would like us to think. From the movie studios and directors, to the ad executives and the TV producers and the novelists, rock stars, and music video producers, the media masters have constructed a universe of "petrified opinions" where the only valuable woman is a thin woman, while big women function primarily as shrewish, silly, asexual mommy figures or cheap jokes. Not only is this one-dimensional viewpoint warped and oppressive, it is crashingly dull, redundant, and predictable. Taken as a whole, this so-called creative product conspires to turn impressionable young women into insecure nervous wrecks trying to compete with image upon image of the same tiny-waisted, big-breasted dream girl.

If art really is a reflection of life, and the mass media in turn are a businesslike imitation of art, then when Americans struggle and strive to shape their lives in media's image, they are living life twice removed. The constricted vision of the world fabricated by Hollywood and Madison Avenue compresses the individual and her hopes, needs, and dreams into narrow channels, reducing life to a hopeless pursuit of false perfection in imitation of people who exist primarily for the illusions they can project.

"Be any race, be yourself, but be beautiful." Or else.

WORKS CITED

Finke, N. "Actress Is Weighed Down by Hollywood Attitudes." *San Francisco Chronicle,* February 17, 1991, Sunday Datebook: 33–34.

Guthmann, E. "Altman's 'Player' for the 90's." *San Francisco Chronicle,* April 23, 1992: E2.

Kahn, A. "The Women of the Night." *San Francisco Chronicle,* June 17, 1991: D3.

Miller, R. "Don't Expect Any Good, Clean Fun from 'Maid.'" *San Jose Mercury News,* January 13, 1992: 10B.

Nevius, C.W. "Life's a Beach—Just Barely." *San Francisco Chronicle,* July 28, 1992: E5.

Orr, J. "Twelve Bars and a Turnaround." *San Jose Mercury News,* July 19, 1992, West Magazine: 18.

Selvin, J. "Ann Peebles Redeems Her Rain Check." *San Francisco Chronicle,* April 16, 1992, Sunday Datebook: 51.

RESPOND •

1. Goodman contends that "[m]ovies, television, magazines, newspapers, and preachifying self-help books all reinforce and amplify the ignorant stereotypes about fat people that America holds so close and dear; taken together, they constitute a framework of 'petrified opinions' which few dare to question" (paragraph 1). What sorts of evidence does she use to support this claim? How is Goodman's evidence similar to the evidence used by Carey Goldberg in "'People of Size' Gather to Promote Fat Acceptance" (p. 404)?

2. Examine how Goodman uses quotations as evidence, especially the opening quote about "petrified opinions" from Mark Twain and the one from the personals section of a newspaper ("Be any race, be yourself, but be beautiful") in paragraphs 15 and 23. In what ways do quotations help structure the argument?

3. Personal ads are especially interesting as arguments because of their brevity. Examine some personal ads in a local newspaper, surveying systematically the images that emerge of the ideal male or female partner. What images emerge as the ideals for each group? To what extent are these ideals the ones that occur most frequently in television, movies, and magazines? Are you concerned about the gap between the ideal and the reality of everyday life? Why or why not?

4. Goodman challenges readers to scrutinize the world, looking to see how large women are or are not represented. Part of the persuasiveness of her argument for many readers, especially for readers who are not large women, likely comes from the volume of evidence she offers. Take the Goodman challenge: choose three familiar magazines or television shows, and survey them as systematically as possible. (For magazines, for example, you will want to distinguish between photographs in advertisements and those in articles.) **Write an essay** arguing for a particular position with regard to the representation of large women in the media.

Cutting Edge

JANICE TURNER

When Joseph hit the big four-oh, he certainly didn't feel old. But he felt he looked old.

"To me, I looked very tired," says the Metro businessman. "And I was getting a decent amount of sleep. I didn't look bad or excessively wrinkled up or that. But it wasn't the way I wanted to look."

After a year of shopping around, Joseph went under the knife. He had his brow lifted, the skin around his mouth and nose pulled back, his upper eyelids tucked and some laser skin resurfacing to ease the creases in his lower lids.

And he had it all done at once, for the relatively inexpensive price of $8,000.

A bit young for cosmetic surgery, you think? A little odd for a guy?   5

The answer is a firm no—to both. Today, men account for about a third of all facial cosmetic surgery done in the United States, up 6 percentage points since 1990. The bulk of clients are between the ages of 40 and 60.

Stressed out by corporate downsizing, many are looking for any edge to get or keep their jobs. They view cosmetic surgery as an investment in their careers.

Men are now grappling with the same kind of exacting beauty standards women have struggled with for decades, observes Shari Cartwright, a spokesperson for the Illinois-based American Society of Plastic Reconstructive Surgeons.

"Is it a bad thing? When it was just women it was fine."

"Perception is reality, in many cases," she adds. "When people look at you they   10
make an assumption, right or wrong."

The top five most popular procedures sought by men are hair transplants, nose work, eyelid work, and scar revision, according to the Washington, D.C.-based

American Academy of Facial Plastic and Reconstructive Surgery, the world's largest association of facial plastic surgeons. The fastest growing procedures for men are eyelid surgery, liposuction, and facelifts.

No comparable figures are available here, according to the Canadian Society of Plastic Surgeons, but anecdotal evidence suggests men here are flocking to cosmetic surgeons as well.

If you include all cosmetic work—face and body—men account for roughly 12 per cent of all procedures, notes the American Society of Plastic Reconstructive Surgeons. When it comes to body work, men favor liposuction (face and stomach), and chest reduction.

Men are having things "corrected" as they notice them, according to Dr. Peter Adamson, a Toronto facial plastic surgeon trained in head and neck surgery, an associate professor at the University of Toronto, and president-elect of the American Academy of Facial Plastic and Reconstructive Surgery. Sometimes that's in their 20s or 30s, often it's in their 40s and 50s.

"Women have tended to care more about their appearance than men have,"   15
Adamson says. "That's changing, and that's why more and more men are going further along that spectrum. They're not just dressing in a more fashion conscious way, they're also using more cosmetics and toiletries."

And they're taking their perceived physical flaws to surgeons.

Toronto cosmetic surgeon Dr. William Middleton says men now account for 30 per cent of his practice—double that of a year ago.

A decade ago, males represented less than 5 per cent of his business.

And the newcomers aren't necessarily actors, models, or even top executives. They're everyday guys with fairly everyday looks.

"It's obviously out of the closet," says Middleton, who also has a speciality in   20
head and neck surgery, but does figure surgery as well. "Men now know it's quite acceptable."

Intense competition in the workplace and on the dating scene appear to be the biggest reasons for the surge. Combine that with a youth-worshipping society and it's hardly surprising that more male boomers are feeling insecure.

As one client told Adamson: "I looked down the (boardroom) table and I looked like an old lion. I think they're looking to replace the old lion with a young lion."

The aging professional opted for eyelid surgery.

"Often men don't really want to look different," says Adamson. "They just want to look refreshed."

Joseph, who works in computer marketing and training, says he felt some busi-   25
ness pressure.

"I was getting older and the work force was getting younger," he relates. "My eyelids were saggy and when I would smile I had deep creases, from my nose to my chin."

Of the surgery he says: "It's not the most pleasant feeling afterward. When you're getting your body cut it's painful, there's no two ways about it. But the pain was manageable. It wasn't severe or excessive."

Cosmetic surgery, Joseph enthuses, "can do wondrous things. The growing acceptance, I think that's a good thing. If it makes you feel better then it's worth it."

Despite greater acceptance, Joseph and other surgery patients interviewed for this story still did not want to be identified. They all, however, said that they had shared their experiences with close friends and family.

The decision to have surgery, notes Joseph, "is a very personal thing."   30

He points out that it's considered fine for a man to spend money on a car, or finish his basement. So why shouldn't he be able to put some of his money into repairing his body's wear and tear?

"Getting work done helps you age how you want to age," he says. "It's not going to turn back that process, but you can make a difference. You can be more vital and rested.

Turner uses an analogy in arguing that "it's considered fine for a man to spend money on a car, or finish his basement" — and then asking why he shouldn't "be able to put some money into repairing his body's wear and tear." What kind of reasoning is Joseph trying to use here? See Chapters 7 and 14 for suggestions as to how you can use analogy in arguments you make.

·······················LINK TO PP. 85 AND 243

"I think it does increase your confidence, but not to any large degree. I'm still the same person. But when I walk by the mirror I like what I see."

For Bobby, the problem was dark circles under his eyes that had bothered him since he was a teen. It was a condition that seemed to run in his family.

At the ripe age of 27, he recently had the fat under his eyes removed, and the darkness has faded. It cost him $3,000.   35

"A woman can put on some makeup and hide that kind of thing, but I'd tried that and wasn't comfortable. I was still self-conscious," says Bobby, who, with short, wavy hair looks every bit a twentysomething. A couple of his friends are having hair transplants. No one his age has suggested he was nuts for doing what he did.

"The bottom line is people don't want to be old and they don't want to grow old," he says. "I think cosmetic surgery among men is going to become common-place. To me, it was very exciting."

He sees little difference between his surgery and the guy who goes out and spends thousands of dollars on new suits.

"Now I'm able to put my contact lenses in and go out and know that no one is going to say, 'Boy, you look tired.' I just feel better about myself."

Stephen, a man of average looks, has had $16,000 worth of work done over the past four years. First he had his nosed reshaped, then a hair transplant, then flab in his chest removed.   40

"Once you start, you can just continue," says Stephen, who boasts he's a 52-year-old in a 25-year-old's body.

He's delighted with the results, in part because younger women still find him attractive.

"It's the '90s and everything's changed. So has the philosophy on improving yourself.

"It's like going to the dentist for regular checkups. I could see myself at 75 going under the knife, no problem."

Adamson says although more men are having cosmetic surgery, "there's no 45 doubt that women will have a greater psychological imperative than the majority of men." He sees male interest as an extension of keeping fit and staying healthy.

"The major drive is that people want to have their outer appearance reflect their inner spirit, so that when they see themselves they say, 'Yes, that's me. My body reflects me.'"

"This kind of surgery can't in and of itself change their professional or social life, but it can help them indirectly," adds Adamson.

Looking good, projecting that current image is crucial today, says Roz Usheroff, a Toronto image and communications consultant who works with professionals and outplacement firms.

"If someone looks outdated, that's the way it's perceived they think," she says. "You have to look the part. Firms are looking at the employees as ambassadors. Sure, there needs to be substance, but it's not enough now. It's not just what you say and how you say it, but how you look as you say it."

More men are realizing their appearance is interfering with what they're trying to 50 convey.

"Whether that's good or not, it's realistic," she says. "A lot of companies are telling men they have to look good. It's not negotiable—if they want to rise within the ranks, or even stay where they are. That's still a shock to some of them."

Dr. Art Blouin, an Ottawa clinical psychologist who works with men and body image, says cosmetic surgery, in itself, isn't a bad thing. What can be troublesome is the intensity with which someone pursues physical perfection.

"From a psychological point of view it would probably be healthier for men to accept their bodies," he says.

But he isn't surprised that more men are dissatisfied with themselves.

"Look at the emphasis, culturally, on attractiveness," he points out.   55

"What we see in the media is a much greater emphasis on the male physique —and much less on character."

Blouin does find it disturbing that more men are now equating much of their self-worth, both personally and professionally, with their looks.

"The problem is that once you start this type of thing, you may never be satisfied," he says. "The more you look, the worse it gets.

"The harder you look, the more you find."

RESPOND •

1. List the generalizations Turner makes about men and cosmetic surgery; then attempt to turn them into a thesis statement that could be the basis for an academic essay on this subject. Shari Cartwright's statement comes close: "Men are now grappling with the same kind of exacting beauty standards women have struggled with for decades" (paragraph 8). Try yourself to produce a thesis statement that is more specific than Cartwright's general observation.

2. Turner uses several kinds of evidence in constructing her argument: statistics, facts, testimony (from experts and clients), and examples (real and hypothetical). Find instances of each of these types of evidence in the article and describe how each one contributes to the argument. How does Turner's use of such inartistic proofs contribute to her ethos?

3. **Rewrite this article** in the form of an academic essay. Remember that a major difference between journalistic writing and academic writing is paragraph length. To some extent, the difference is one of formatting: newspapers chop their texts into many paragraphs while academic writers consciously use longer paragraphs. To test this observation, group related paragraphs in Turner's piece into longer paragraphs of the sort common in academic writing. Are the longer paragraph groupings easy to determine? Why or why not? What makes your groupings "natural" in some sense? Do your paragraphs add up to something like an academic essay? Why or why not? What other revisions would an academic essay require?

▼ *In the two articles that follow, Angela Neustatter and Louisa Young debate whether or not men should avail themselves of cosmetic surgery. The two articles appeared together in the* Guardian, *a London newspaper, in 1997. As you read, examine the writers' arguments critically and consider how you'd respond to them.*

Men Are Becoming Concerned about the Way They Look and Are Seeking the Answer in Cosmetic Surgery. Should They? Shouldn't They? Two Women Give Their Views.

Why Shouldn't the Epidermally Challenged Get Help?

Men Should Have Better Things to Do

ANGELA NEUSTATTER

I have caught him in the mirror more than once, smoothing out a wrinkle here, contorting his lower jaw muscles, a copy of Eva Fraser's facial exercises taken furtively from the bookshelf. Then there was the day some Liv Tyleresque young thing, working with him on a film set in lights that would have made even Samuel Beckett look like a baby's bum, murmured that he looked not a day over 32. (He's not by a long stretch.) He paraded around like a demented peacock for days.

I am indulgent about all this, not being entirely free of human frailty myself. But if Olly° announced that he was planning a face-lift, how would I feel? Rather as I might if Sylvester Stallone turned out to be a woman—flabbergasted. It seems so far from anything I can imagine in my practical, child-of-the-sixties old man. But, who knows, he may be pondering on the Albert Camus thought: "After a certain age, every man is responsible for his own face" and wondering if the man in the street is muttering that he ought to do the decent thing and tighten up.

I've spent years pointing out the differences between men and women, but I think we are

LOUISA YOUNG

There are those who like to see the mighty fallen, to see their enemy humiliated. There are those who consider men the mighty, and the enemy. These people are delighted with the apparent growing trend of men having cosmetic surgery.

Me, I hate cosmetic surgery. I differentiate here between cosmetic and reconstructive: we all know that the world can be cruel to those it considers abnormal-looking, and for those who face that cruelty, it is a miracle when they can show themselves, "normalised," to this nasty world. But when it is only the person her or himself who thinks she/he looks abnormal, and only thinks it because she/he doesn't look like Pamela Anderson or Brad Pitt, perhaps the only treatment needed is between the ears.

And when it is a case of just wanting to look prettier—oh God, just mass-mail them Oxfam° leaflets, tell them how long a starving child could survive on the calorific value of their liposucted fat, and ask them if there really isn't anything better they can think of to do with the money.

Women have had the excuse of pressure to be pretty—yeah, yeah. Men apparently are now get-

remarkably similar when it comes to fears about ageing and how we are judged. Show me a middle-aged woman or man who hasn't looked at their face at some time and mourned, as Gypsy Rose Lee° did: "I have everything I had 20 years ago—except now it's all lower."

Then there would be the matter of where it left me. It's not that I'd fear him running off with a chick scarcely out o̶_____ _____ ____ but he'd be taking a decision ab____ ____ _____ _____ ___ probably exclude _____ _____ ___ ____ _____ cut, I can dissuade _____ _____ ____ ____ ____ him to water and g_____ ____ __ _____ __ __ ___ ing up the tummy _____ ___ __ _____ views on clothes. _____ __ _____ __ ___ ____ cosmetic surgery, ____ _ _____ __ ___ _____

ting the same pressure. So do we crow with delight that they are being reduced to our level? Or do we wonder at their sanity—haven't they noticed what succumbing to that pressure has done to women? Do we just quietly remind them that behind the whole thing is that age-old evil, money? Reaching some kind of saturation point in the profitability of pulchritude-paranoia among women, profit-makers have simply turned to the next market—men. And ____ ____ __ ___ falling for it.

_____ __ ____ rts. It takes time to get over it. It is   5 _____ ____ nless there is something that really _____ ____ why face it? Of course everybody ___ ____ ___ standard of what constitutes unbear-____ __ _____ ovable in their own appearance, but ___ ____ ___ s so much profit being made by the

Explore

Neustatter's reader_ _____ ___ _____ ___ _____ ably don't already k___ ___ ____ _____ _____ __ _____ "Olly" by name, bu_ ____ ___ ____ ___ ___ _____ __ have a good sense _ ____ ___ ____ ____ _____ _____ intimate domestic _____ ___ ____ __ _____ _____ tionship. Neustatt__ ___ ___ ___ ___ ____ _____ us right in to her d_____

Gypsy Rose Lee: stage name of Rose Louise Hovick (1914–1970), who danced in the Zeigfeld Follies and later became known as America's greatest strip-tease performer. The 1959 Broadway musical *Gypsy* is based on her life.

Oxfam: British-based privately funded organi-zation founded in 1942 to provide disaster relief and development assistance. This is an illustration from an Oxfam leaflet.

and seek guidance there. Would he ask me which bits to get bobbed and tautened? I doubt it and he might choose the wrong style.

Yet I couldn't and wouldn't condemn it or him because no way do I want to join the band of puritans who deify their wrinkles and castigate, for their failure to age naturally, anyone who so much as has a collagen implant, because puritanism is a far nastier vice than narcissism. I share the view that the Tony Curtis look, with skin so stretched is ugly and probably the desperate effort of someone who still wants to be a young man, but I've seen plenty of people use cosmetic surgery for a discreet lift rather as they might use car maintenance, to keep the equipment in good nick for as long as possible. And what is wrong with that? There is no divine justice in the different ways we age, so why shouldn't the epidermally challenged get a bit of help?

But of course the key question is: would I still fancy him? I don't think I'd go off him if he had a face-lift, but it would help if he emerged looking like Antonio Banderas.

very people who advise on whether or not the process is desirable or necessary, how can you know?

People often have cosmetic surgery because they think it will make them more attractive. Speaking as one who thinks men look better for looking the worse for . . . wear, I can't help thinking that men should have better things to do than this. So, of course, should women; our only excuse is the centuries of exaggerated value put on female beauty, and the fact that it has warped our minds. Men have no such excuse. They should know better.

RESPOND ●

1. Neustatter and Young take opposing views on the same issue. Make a brief list of the arguments each writer makes—both for her position and against the opposing position. Putting aside your own feelings on the issue, which writer do you think presents the stronger argument? Why?

2. Neustatter contends that "puritanism is a far nastier vice than narcissism" (paragraph 5). **Write an essay** in which you defend or refute this claim.

3. "Should They? Shouldn't They?" Now it's your turn to **write an essay** (of about seven hundred words) in which you argue why men should or should not see cosmetic surgery as an answer to at least some of their woes.

▼ In this 1998 article from the Toronto Sun, *Sandy Naiman treats some of the issues related to men and cosmetic surgery. As you read, consider the several goals she might have had in mind as she wrote the piece.*

Suck Out Your Gut

SANDY NAIMAN

There's something so endearing about the little bulge above a man's belt, which is why I regretfully report that today's newest cosmetic surgery trend is abdominal liposuction for men.

Sure, we love looking at Adonises, caressing the ripples of their muscular torsos with our eyes, even our fingers. But when it comes to feeling close to a man, there's nothing like a little cushion of flesh.

Our youth-beauty cult — so toxic for women — is now catching on with men, and not just in their guts. They're embracing all cosmetic surgeries, with liposuction tipping the scales.

This is the logical extension of the fitness and health craze in a culture where men are more comfortable demonstrating their concern for their looks, suggests Dr. Arnis Freiburg, a University of Toronto plastic surgery professor and director of its Academic Aesthetic Surgery Program.

"Fifteen years ago, men wouldn't have considered cosmetic surgery, but today they're motivated by a quest for youth — not unlike women, by beauty. In this, the double standard between the sexes is narrowing but may be moving in the wrong direction."

What exactly is liposuction? Dr. Frank Beninger of STHETX in Toronto explains it as a surgical fat-removal method working like a miniscule vacuum cleaner. "There are two variations — tumescent, the gold standard, and the newer, ultrasonic-assisted liposuction (ULA), still under investigation," he says. Both use a cannula or small hollow tube attached to a pump for vacuuming.

NO SUBSTITUTE FOR WEIGHT LOSS

In tumescent liposuction, fat cells are broken down in a solution of anaesthetic, saline and adrenaline, then vacuumed out. With ULA, fat cells are ruptured with ultrasonic energy before vacuuming.

Sounds great, huh? Why diet when you can just have your fat vacuumed away, nice and easy, right? Wrong.

Liposuction, by no means the perceived panacea for the obese as much media coverage portrays it, is an invasive surgical procedure. It has caused a number of deaths in the United States and if you think it's an alternative to diet, exercise and healthy eating, you're wrong, says Freiburg.

"It's not a good procedure if you are obese, and the majority of people who request it are obese," he stresses.

"Liposuction is no substitute for weight loss."

Yet, it's the most popular cosmetic surgery in North America and growing exponentially. Most liposuction patients are women between 30 and 50. Yet in 1997, Canadian and American members of the American Society of Plastic and Reconstructive Surgeons performed liposuction on 20,192 men, compared to 6,138 men in 1992.

"The ideal candidate for liposuction is in good shape, not overweight, and exercises," says Freiburg. "But this is not the majority of people who want liposuction. We don't do many in our clinic because we can't find the right ideal candidate."

Writing about pain or death almost always invokes strong emotional responses from readers. Is Naiman deliberately making emotional appeals in her article or are emotions simply an unavoidable part of her subject? See Chapter 4, "Arguments from the Heart," for more information about using emotional appeals effectively in your writing.

LINK TO P. 49·······························

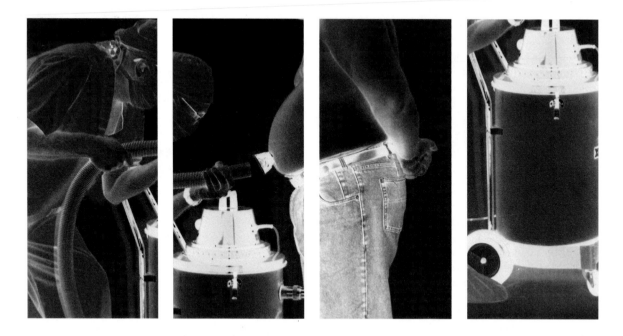

Kirk Brady, 37, was that "ideal candidate" when he walked into Beninger's office last November. In June 1996, he reviewed his life, quit smoking, drinking, joined a fitness club and re-invented himself, transforming his 6-foot-1, 162 pounds of flab into 154 pounds of muscular steel — with one exception. His gut wouldn't go away. Beninger agreed.

In January, Brady was wheeled into the clinic's operating room, given a local anaesthetic and for three hours, Beninger vacuumed 1.7 litres of marbled fat from the muscles of his entire abdominal area.

"There was no pain," recalls 15 Brady. "They froze the incision area. The scar is so minuscule, you can't see it now."

After an hour in recovery, he was taken home by a friend to rest for a week before returning to work, swollen and sporting an abdominal binder he would wear for six weeks.

Temporarily, he couldn't fit into his own clothes, but today, he says ebulliently, "I don't regret one penny (of the $4,700 plus GST) it cost. But I didn't realize what an invasive and serious procedure it is. Still, I heartily recommend it."

Dr. John E. Sherman, assistant clinical professor of surgery at the New York Hospital of Cornell Medical College in Manhattan, is an eminent liposuction specialist combining both ULA and tumescent liposuction to contour the body.

YOU END UP WITH LOOSE SKIN

"With today's economy, people are used to purchasing what they want," he observes.

Yet instant gratification doesn't 20 always pay when re-designing one's body, cautions Freiburg. "Gradual weight loss gives the skin a chance to shrink, but with liposuction, which takes a short time, a matter of hours, the skin has no time to shrink and you end up with loose skin."

Patients must also be in good psychological shape, stresses Sherman. "Medically stable, well-motivated, well-balanced. They must understand that 'sucking their gut' won't make them happy." He won't touch obese patients, but works with people 20 pounds overweight, trimming up to three inches off the waist, restoring self-image and improving confidence. "A patient can look and feel better."

"Still, liposuction is grossly overrated," Freiburg insists. "We treat it as an adjunct to other procedures or where there is no other surgery — with hips, knees, ankles or male breast reduction."

There is one critical caveat, Beninger adds emphatically. "Cosmetic surgery is just a name, with no licensing, no exams, no policing. It is not a recognized designation and it's often confused with plastic surgery. Virtually any physician can practise cosmetic surgery."

So, dear buyer, beware.

RESPOND •

1. You might argue that the purpose of Naiman's article is to inform or convince. What do you take her major purpose to be? What evidence would you cite for your claim?

2. Did you find this article informative, that is, did it provide you with information you did not already have? If so, what information was new for you? Does this information challenge your attitude toward liposuction? If so, how and why? If not, why do you think not?

3. Reread the selections by Naiman and Turner, noting how each writer uses testimony to support her argument. How many cases of testimony are used? Who "testifies"? About what? Why? How does each writer's use of testimony contribute (or fail to contribute) to her purpose? Then **write a short essay** in which you evaluate the credibility of the testimony used by each author.

▼ *In this excerpt from a 1998 issue of the* Washington Monthly, *Michelle Cottle uses humor to argue that popular men's magazines such as* Men's Health *encourage men to be obsessive about their appearance—in the way that women have long been expected to. The passage reprinted here is from the opening third of the article; later sections examine the sorts of advice offered by* Men's Health *on everything from exercise regimes to low-calorie snacks and the extent to which such advice is designed primarily to "move merchandise"—in fact, very expensive merchandise for a growing niche market.*

Turning Boys into Girls

How Men's Magazines Are Making Guys as Neurotic, Insecure, and Obsessive about Their Appearance as Women

BY MICHELLE COTTLE

I love *Men's Health* magazine. There. I'm out of the closet, and I'm not ashamed. Sure, I know what some of you are thinking: What self-respecting '90s woman could embrace a publication that runs such enlightened articles as "Turn Your Good Girl Bad" and "How to Wake Up Next to a One-Night Stand"? Or maybe you'll smile and wink knowingly: What red-blooded hetero chick *wouldn't* love all those glossy photo spreads of buff young beefcake in various states of undress, rippled abs and glutes flexed so tightly you could bounce a check on them? Either way you've got the wrong idea. My affection for *Men's Health* is driven by pure gender politics—by the realization that this magazine, and a handful of others like it, are leveling the playing field in a way that *Ms.* can only dream of. With page after page of bulging biceps and Gillette jaws, robust hairlines and silken skin, *Men's Health* is peddling a standard of male beauty as unforgiving and unrealistic as the female version sold by those dewy-eyed pre-teen waifs draped across the covers of *Glamour* and *Elle*. And with a variety of helpful features on "Foods That Fight Fat," "Banish Your Potbelly," and "Save Your Hair (Before it's Too Late)," *Men's Health* is well on its

way to making the male species as insane, insecure, and irrational about physical appearance as any *Cosmo* girl.

Don't you see, ladies? We've been going about this equality business all wrong. Instead of battling to get society fixated on something besides our breast size, we should have been fighting spandex with spandex. Bra burning was a nice gesture, but the greater justice is in convincing our male counterparts that the key to their happiness lies in a pair of made-for-him Super Shaper Briefs with the optional "fly front endowment pad" (as advertised in *Men's Journal*, $29.95 plus shipping and handling). Make the men as neurotic about the circumference of their waists and the whiteness of their smiles as the women, and at least the burden of vanity and self-loathing will be shared by all.

This is precisely what lads' mags like *Men's Health* are accomplishing. The rugged John-Wayne days when men scrubbed their faces with deodorant soap and viewed gray hair and wrinkles as a badge of honor are fading. Last year, international market analyst Euromonitor placed the U.S. men's toiletries market—hair color, skin moisturizer, tooth whiteners, etc.—at $3.5 billion. According to a survey

Men's Health

FEBRUARY 1998

Lose Your
GUT

**With Just
3 Exercises**

**FREE
POSTER
TOTAL BODY
WORKOUT**

TURN YOUR
GOOD GIRL BAD

2-Minute
Stress Test
(page 56)

FOODS THAT
FIGHT FAT

Save Your Hair
(Before it's Too Late)

BEST HEALTH
AND FITNESS TIPS
FOR 1998

$3.50 U.S. $3.95 CAN.

0 2

7 74820 08541 7

DISPLAY UNTIL FEBRUARY 9

conducted by DYG researchers for *Men's Health* in November 1996, approximately 20 percent of American men get manicures or pedicures, 18 percent use skin treatments such as masks or mud packs, and 10 percent enjoy professional facials. That same month, *Psychology Today* reported that a poll by Roper Starch Worldwide showed that "6 percent of men nationwide actually use such traditionally female products as bronzers and foundation to create the illusion of a youthful appearance."

What men are putting *on* their bodies, however, is nothing compared to what they're doing *to* their bodies: While in the 1980s only an estimated one in 10 plastic surgery patients were men, as of 1996, that ratio had shrunk to one in five. The American Academy of Cosmetic Surgery estimates that nationwide more than 690,000 men had cosmetic procedures performed in '96, the most recent year for which figures are available. And we're not just talking "hair restoration" here, though such procedures do command the lion's share of the male market. We're also seeing an increasing number of men shelling out mucho dinero for face peels, liposuction, collagen injections, eyelid lifts, chin tucks, and, of course, the real man's answer to breast implants: penile enlargements (now available to increase both length and diameter).

Granted, *Men's Health* and its journalistic cousins (*Men's Journal, Details, GQ,* etc.) cannot take all the credit for this breakthrough in gender parity. The fashion and glamour industries have perfected the art of creating consumer "needs," and with the women's market pretty much saturated, men have become the obvious target for the purveyors of everything from lip balm to lycra. Meanwhile, advances in medical science have made cosmetic surgery a quicker, cleaner option for busy executives (just as the tight fiscal leash of managed care is driving more and more doctors toward this cash-based specialty). Don't have several weeks to recover from a full-blown facelift? No prob-

5

lem. For a few hundred bucks you can get a microdermabrasion face peel on your lunch hour.

Then there are the underlying social factors. With women growing ever more financially independent, aspiring suitors are discovering that they must bring more to the table than a well-endowed wallet if they expect to win (and keep) the fair maiden. Nor should we overlook the increased market power of the gay population—in general a more image-conscious lot than straight guys. But perhaps most significant is the ongoing, ungraceful descent into middle age by legions of narcissistic baby boomers. Gone are the days when the elder statesmen of this demographic bulge could see themselves in the relatively youthful faces of those insipid yuppies on "Thirtysomething." Increasingly, boomers are finding they have more in common with the *parents* of today's TV, movie, and sports stars. Everywhere they turn some upstart Gen Xer is flaunting his youthful vitality, threatening boomer dominance on both the social and professional fronts. (Don't think even Hollywood didn't shudder when the Oscar for best original screenplay this year went to a couple of guys barely old enough to shave.) With whippersnappers looking to steal everything from their jobs to their women, postpubescent men have at long last discovered the terror of losing their springtime radiance.

Whatever combo of factors is feeding the frenzy of male vanity, magazines such as *Men's Health* provide the ideal meeting place for men's insecurities and marketers' greed. Like its more established female counterparts, *Men's Health* is an affordable, efficient delivery vehicle for the message that physical imperfection, age, and an underdeveloped fashion sense are potentially crippling disabilities. And as with women's mags, this cycle of insanity is self-perpetuating: The more men obsess about growing old or unattractive, the more marketers will exploit and expand that fear; the more marketers bombard men with messages about the need to be beautiful, the more they will obsess. Younger and younger men will be sucked into the vortex of self-doubt. Since 1990, *Men's Health* has seen its paid circulation rise from 250,000 to more than 1.5 million; the magazine estimates that half of its 5.3 million readers are under age 35 and 46 percent are married. And while most major magazines have suffered sluggish growth or even a decline in circulation in recent years, during the first half of 1997, *Men's Health* saw its paid circulation increase 14 percent over its '96 figures. (Likewise, its smaller, more outdoorsy relative, Wenner Media's *Men's Journal,* enjoyed an even bigger jump of 26.5 percent.) At this rate, one day soon, that farcical TV commercial featuring men hanging out in bars, whining about having inherited their mothers' thighs will be a reality. Now *that's* progress.   ∎

RESPOND •

1. What does Cottle mean when she claims that her "affection for *Men's Health* is driven by pure gender politics"? How well does she explain and support this claim? Do you find her argument persuasive? Why or why not?

2. Evaluate Cottle's use of humorous argument. Cite examples of humor from the text that you find especially effective or ineffective, and explain why you find them so. Would her argument be more or less effective if she had adopted a serious rather than a humorous tone? Why do you think Cottle uses humor in this piece? What goals does she hope to achieve by doing so?

3. Cottle's humorous argument is written for a specific audience: readers of the *Washington Monthly.* What other readers do you think she invokes? (See Chapter 3 on invoked readers.) Might some readers find her humor offensive? Who might they be, and on what grounds might they be less than amused? Why would Cottle risk alienating some of her readers with humor?

4. In paragraph 7, Cottle claims that "magazines such as *Men's Health* provide the ideal meeting place for men's insecurities and marketers' greed." How effectively does she support this claim? What consequences does she foresee for the situation she describes? Do you agree with her claim? Why or why not?

5. **Write a response** to Cottle. Imagine that you are an assistant editor of *Men's Health* and that your boss — who is steaming because he's just read Cottle's article — has given you the task of responding to her in a letter to the editor of the *Washington Monthly.* Your aim is to make the magazine look good while taking issue with Cottle's criticisms. The letter should be about five hundred words in length. Before you start writing it, you may want to examine a copy of *Men's Health* — the more you know about the magazine, the better your defense of it is likely to be.

Cottle knows she's walking into a minefield of stereotypes about her topic and establishes her credentials in the opening paragraph by referring to — and dismissing — each stereotype. Read about other ways to establish credibility in Chapter 3.

LINK TO P. 40 ·······

across the
Decades

▶ Several readings in this cluster contend that the high heel is now on the other foot: Men are being held to standards of "beauty" or physical appearance that formerly applied only to women. One way of testing such a claim is to examine the images of men used in advertising a product designed for them, such as underwear. Analyze the three advertisements that follow— an Esquire magazine ad from 1948, a Playboy ad from 1965, and a 1990 Calvin Klein billboard—in light of this claim. (For more on evaluating visual arguments, see Chapter 15.)

Figured rayon pajamas, A-D, about $10. • Rayon shorts, 30-44, about $1.75

Rayon satin
striped pajamas,
A-D, about $7
Rayon striped
shorts, 30-44,
about $1.75

Stop! Look! Such skillful tailoring...such slick designs

He's trying to engineer you into giving him Textron Menswear. He likes the special Textron tailoring—fuller seams, roomier armholes, longer trousers in the pajamas. He likes the "boxer" shorts with the famous "parachute" seat for extra comfort...the soft, non-restraining elastic at the waist. Finest Textron pajamas in rayon from about $7 to $10... shorts at about $1.75. At leading stores throughout the country. TEXTRON, INC., Textron Building, 401 Fifth Avenue, New York 16, N.Y.

TEXTRON

LINGERIE • BLOUSES • HOSTESS COATS • HOME FASHIONS • MENSWEAR

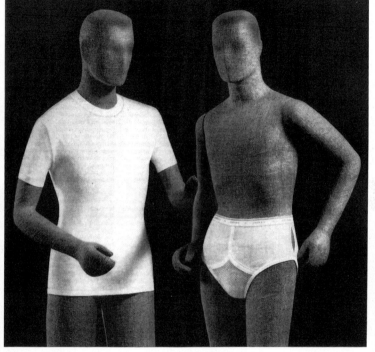

This tapered Brute shirt gives me a feeling of savoir faire —whatever that is.

Dummy! Savoir faire is what you have when you wear these Slim Guy briefs.

Look alive in new *Life* underwear by Jockey.

1. If we take these advertisements to be representative, how has the representation of the male body changed over the past five decades? Some commentators see the changes as evidence of a new "eroticiza-tion of the male body." What do they mean? Do you agree that such a process is occurring? Why or why not?

2. Collect ten other advertisements for female underwear or a product such as cologne from across the decades. You might choose a single magazine and take your advertisement from the same monthly issue in each year. What do changes in the advertisements tell you about the representation of the "ideal female"? How do the ads reflect larger shifts in societal attitudes toward what it means to be female?

3. **Write an essay** evaluating the evidence you gathered for question 2 and using your findings to argue for a specific point. Your essay should include examples of the ads, an explanation of how you chose them, and an evaluation of what you think they mean. You'll likely want to include copies of at least some of the ads in your paper and comment on them.

chapter twenty-four

What's Public?
What's Private?

What do supermarket discount cards, mail-order catalogs, and many Web sites have in common? For starters, they collect information about you and what you like every time you make a purchase, place an order, or visit a Web site. What becomes of that information? Does it go to some central repository where computers hum away, combining billions of discrete bits of information into profiles of you and everyone else? Who controls those computers? Does it matter? Should you care if someone else knows about your purchases? How about your medical records or financial transactions? Or your old love letters? And what of the details of one couple's sexual encounters described in newspapers and on the nightly news because the man happens to be the president of the United States and the woman is not his wife?

Each of these cases raises questions about what is public and what is private in American society today.

While Americans claim to cherish privacy, each of us defines it in a slightly different way, especially in specific situations. Legal experts don't always agree either. One famous definition from an influential 1890 article in the *Harvard Law Review* by Samuel D. Warren and Louis D. Brandeis claims that privacy is "the right to be let alone." A quite different perspective can be found in the work of Alan F. Westin, whose 1967 book *Privacy and Freedom* characterizes privacy as the right of individuals to determine when and how much information about them is made available to others. The readings in this chapter challenge you to consider how you define privacy, where you draw the line, and why.

The chapter opens with a group of arguments that raise questions about the nature of privacy in a range of situations—Internet marketing, pornographic images on office computers, strip searches of Americans returning home from abroad, and the bumper stickers on people's vehicles. Then comes a cluster of texts entitled "Who's Watching?" that focuses on the conflicting tendencies to want to be seen (and to see others) and to be left alone. Each challenges you to consider where you would draw the line between public and private.

▼ *The following two articles appeared during the summer of 1999 on the editorial page of the* Daily Texan, *the student newspaper of the University of Texas at Austin. Russ Cobb, a graduate student in Spanish, and Roahn Wynar, a graduate student in physics, argue about whether the sophisticated marketing devices made possible by high technology and the Internet are helpful or harmful to consumers. As you read, consider the tone of each piece, the relationship that each author is trying to establish with his audience, and the kinds of appeals each author uses.*

Point/Counterpoint:
They Know
What You're Buying

Point: Internet Target Marketing Threatens Consumer Privacy

Counterpoint: Paranoid Privacy Hawks Don't Realize How Good They've Got It

RUSS COBB

"78704—It's more than just a ZIP code, it's a way of life" a popular Austin bumper sticker proclaims. In the Information Age, numbers have become just as important markers of identity as the traditional demographics determined by income bracket, ethnicity and race. In the booming industry of Internet marketing, a seemingly unimportant postal code has become the means by which marketing specialists "target" and then "tailor" information to the unsuspecting consumer.

While super-hip Austinites may lay claim to a different "way of life" according to an arbitrary assignment by the post office, advertisers are realizing the true potential [of] a seemingly neutral code, investing millions of dollars into profiling consumers online. Ever bought a set of guitar strings from Mars, a TV antennae from Radio Shack, or a bike tube from Sears and wondered why you were

ROAHN WYNAR

The Internet is a target for college-of-liberal-arts-type demagogues who lately complain about invasive marketing practices. The claim is nebulous, but goes something like this: anytime you make a business transaction online, your demographic information is collected and exploited. Your privacy is invaded and there's nothing you can do about it.

For example, you sign up for an online newspaper, which is usually a free service. The newspaper collects a great deal of your personal information not only during sign-up, but also as you select articles and this information is used to route appropriate advertising your way, often while you browse. There is no doubt that this data can be stored and sold to direct mail and telephone marketing companies. In fact whenever you do business online you are broadcasting a piece of your personality.

Critics of this information gathering technique are making the absurd claim that some online com-

asked for your ZIP code? Whether you like it or not, you are slowly becoming part of [a] picture which is being painted by multinational marketing corporations to be sold to online advertisers.

ZIP codes have become all Internet users' de facto racial, ethnic and class identity indicators to a multimillion dollar advertising industry. By requesting your ZIP code in all online transactions, advertisers are allowed to construct a general profile of your interests. Likewise, the more your on-line activity is monitored by marketing experts, the more specific your profile becomes. You are then gently guided through the Internet Leviathan° by the people who know what's best for you—twenty-something techies with six figure salaries.

Internet technology works in mysterious ways . . .

To use an ostensibly "free" service like the *New* 5 *York Times Online*, for example, you must first register according to your gender, income bracket and ZIP code. This information is then given to a marketing firm which specializes in "tailoring" information for everyone on the Internet, making sure you know your virtual place in virtual reality.

While the *Times* may boast that it publishes "all the news that's fit to print," the advertisers who fund this free service will eventually be able to "tailor" it—in other words censor it—to give you only the news you want.

Want to be updated on the latest stock prices and sports scores without having to sift through all that garbage about refugees and welfare reform? It will be done, and best of all, free of charge. Even now, the cynical intellectual can be kindly guided from the *New York Times* Book Review straight to the

panies are evil because they're observant and have good memories.

A specific case is *Amazon.com*. When you browse for a book online a helpful message displays, "Other people who bought this book also bought. . . ." Don't even try to argue that this is not a handy resource. Of course they also know the names, credit card numbers and browsing habits of every one of their customers.

It's easy to picture some social studies major 5 somewhere, waxing nostalgic at their electric typewriter, wondering how they can make a name for themselves by inventing an unforeseen cultural consequence of Internet commerce.

Warnings about target marketing [have] become their—dare I say it?—zeitgeist. One can almost predict the title of the essay— *"Internet marketing and the contextualization of American self-identity: a critique of the new technocratic psychology—and its subtext of economic voyeurism."*

Target marketing is neither evil nor new. Marketing companies don't want to waste time advertising rosary beads to Mormons, as much as Mormons don't want to be bothered by such ads. What a wonderful day it will be when during the Superbowl I get to see commercials for photomultiplier tubes, diode lasers, computer games and violent action movies while our anti-progress Internet critics get to watch ads for kerosene lanterns, horse drawn buggies, bows and arrows and the latest play at the amphitheatre.

Then there are those who claim this is an invasion of privacy. Here's a good point to consider: nobody gives a damn about you. Nobody cares if you buy hockey equipment online or spend 15 hours a day at *hardcore.com*. Privacy freaks are mild conspiracy theorists who think someone is watching them. Get over it. It is not the responsibility of online businesses to place their customers into therapy for paranoia.

Leviathan: in Jewish mythology, a primordial sea monster, sometimes multiheaded.

Barnes & Noble home page to purchase the latest scathing indictment of capitalism.

Lest you assume that the people behind Internet profiling are involved in some sort of altruistic endeavor for the sake of your pursuit of knowledge, it is important to recognize that the same practice is used in tailoring pornography and violence. In fact, Web sites like the *Times* having nothing to do with your profile; there are larger corporations such as doubleclick.com which buy that information you unwittingly provided as a guest the first time you visited the site.

The executives at one billion dollar-plus Internet "solutions" companies like doubleclick.com would have us believe there is a benevolent, democratic force behind the "tailoring" of online news information services. After all, it is their multi-million dollar investments in the traditional news media that keeps news on the Internet free-of-charge.

So what's wrong with this picture?   10

The "tailoring" of news by means of sly demographic profiling, i.e. ZIP codes, amounts to free market censorship. Corporate consolidation by marketing companies such as doubleclick.com, which just bought out its largest competitor, will never restrict, per se, what you can and cannot see on the Internet. They will, however, lull you into conformity with what they have found to obviously be in your best interest.

The survival of a democratic society requires an open forum for ideas which runs contrary to conventional wisdom and across ZIP codes.

An opinion expressed this week in the *New York Times Magazine* was that quality of online news reporting will diminish as news sites focus on target marketing and abandon sections that don't produce many hits. Why report about Bosnia when the Yankees get a hundred times as many hits? There is no indication yet that this is happening, and the possibility that it will is empty speculation. There will always be a market for all sectors of news coverage and further specialization is good for consumers.

Will people ever stop inventing new reasons to   10
oppose technological advancement? It should be obvious by now that any notion of human progress is completely dependent on techno-nerds inventing better gizmos, and yet some people remain suspicious.

If I were in charge, Internet commerce would be run in such a way that every customer had their own special number. This number would connect to a database that has bucketloads of personal information ranging from clothing, food and travel tastes, to lifestyle habits, education, religion, legal histories, and credit ratings. You wouldn't be allowed to buy and sell on the Internet without this number. Soon all commerce will be done by computer and therefore everyone must have the number. No number, no food. Then, the fun part. After I implement the plan, I wait until the first 665 numbers have been issued, then I get mine!

Well, there's a reason to worry that is as logical as any I've heard.

Cobb invokes a powerful value for U.S. readers—the survival of a democratic society. See Chapter 5 for more information about making arguments based on values.

LINK TO P. 57

RESPOND ●

1. Summarize the position each writer takes on the question of Internet marketing and consumer privacy. To what extent do Cobb and Wynar directly address each other's arguments or evidence? What is each writer's attitude toward the other? Toward the audience? Cite evidence from the texts to support your answers.

2. Does either author engage in fallacious argumentation? How do you know? Cite examples. (You may want to review Chapter 19 on fallacies of argument.)

3. Which essay presents the better arguments based on fact and reason? Why? Which essay presents the better arguments based on values? Why? How and how effectively does each writer use humor?

4. **Write an essay** evaluating the relative effectiveness of Cobb's and Wynar's arguments. In the essay, you will need to state which writer's arguments you find superior and why. If your only reason for preferring one essay over the other is that the author's opinion matches yours, you will likely want to discuss the sorts of arguments necessary to persuade you that the other position is the more defensible one.

▶ *This essay by theologian and talk-show host Dennis Prager appeared in July 1999 in the* Weekly Standard, *a magazine that describes itself as "a weekly journal of conservative opinion." Prager criticizes the decision by the Harvard University Divinity School to ask for the resignation of its dean, Ronald Thiemann, after pornographic images of women were found on his office computer. Although the right to privacy and its meaning is a major focus of this essay, Prager simultaneously constructs another argument about what he terms "heterophobia," "the fear and loathing of male heterosexuals." As you read this essay, consider how the evidence Prager chooses relates to each of his arguments.*

Divinity and Pornography

BY DENNIS PRAGER

Last fall, after serving thirteen years as the dean of the Harvard University Divinity School, Ronald F. Thiemann resigned. The reason has just been made public.

Harvard president Neil L. Rudenstine asked for the resignation. According to Joe Wrinn, a university spokesman, the Harvard president was told that Dean Thiemann had pornographic images on his computer. The dean had apparently asked computer technicians to supply him with a bigger computer hard drive, and the technicians, transferring files, found the images.

All parties to the issue note that none of the images were of minors. There is not the slightest suggestion that the dean ever acted improperly toward a female, whether student or employee. Indeed there is not the slightest suggestion that he ever did anything improper at all. This Harvard University dean was told to give up his position because of what he looked at, not what he did.

We have entered an era that is beyond what George Orwell imagined in *Nineteen Eighty-Four*: a time wherein the fantasy life of citizens is monitored by authorities.

Those who defend Harvard's position argue as follows: 5

(1) Thiemann was the dean of the divinity school, from whom different behavior is expected than from the dean of any other school. Had he been the dean of, let us say, the business school, he would not have been asked to resign.

(2) Any man who consumes pornography is a misogynist or, at the very least, regards women as less than human (as sexual objects) and is unworthy of a position of moral or other authority.

(3) The computer with the pornographic images was owned by Harvard University and therefore should not have been used for private purposes.

There are a number of problems with the first argument. One is that it misrepresents the task of the contemporary school of divinity. Unlike seminaries, which seek to inculcate a religion in their students,

divinity schools teach their students *about* religion, just as schools of business teach about business and schools of education teach about education. Indeed, there are students and faculty at schools of divinity who believe in no religion or are even atheists.

It is true that Dean Thiemann is an ordained Lutheran minister, but that is only of concern to the Lutheran church. If it wishes to defrock a minister who has viewed pornography, that is its business and its prerogative. Religions are free to make any rules they want for their clergy. However, to the best of the public's knowledge, the Lutheran church has taken no steps toward punishing Pastor Thiemann, let alone removing him.

Harvard University clearly deems the private viewing of pornography more worthy of punishment than does the Lutheran church. I have long argued that contemporary liberalism serves for many of its adherents as a secular fundamentalist religion, and here is an example of that.

If Thiemann had been dean of another of its schools, would Harvard have ignored his pictures? Not likely. The Harvard feminists who protested against Dean Thiemann after they learned about the pornography—and who intimidate most universities' administrators—would have protested just as strongly against any other dean. The protesters' argument was not that Thiemann was the dean of a religious institution (which he was not), but that he engaged in a form of misogyny by consuming pornography. No politically correct college—which unfortunately means almost no college—has a president who will say the truth: that it is none of our business what legal pictures a man looks at in private, and that there is no correlation between viewing pornography and woman-hating. A university president who admitted that would be out of office before he could say "Catharine MacKinnon."°

This brings us to the second and most important argument—that men who use pornography demean women, or regard them as second-class beings, or simply harbor some conscious or unconscious hatred of them.

Those who make this argument either know very little about men's sexuality or are afraid of male heterosexuality (which is understandable—it can be frightening) and therefore demonize it. The plain fact of life is that normal and honorable heterosexual men enjoy looking at

Catharine MacKinnon: an American feminist and legal scholar (1946–) whose work has focused on pornography and sexual harassment. In the 1980s, MacKinnon came to public attention when she argued that pornography legitimizes the abuse and exploitation of women in society and thus constitutes a kind of sex discrimination. Thus, in her opinion, pornography is illegal.

partially clad and naked women. I feel a bit silly having to write in a publication read by college graduates what my unschooled grandmother knew. But the denial of unpleasant realities is one of the features of the highly educated at the end of the twentieth century.

Enjoying looking at pictures of naked women no more means a het- 15 erosexual man loathes women or wants them demeaned than looking at pictures of naked men means a homosexual man loathes men or wants them demeaned. In fact, it means absolutely nothing.

The Harvard affair is an example of heterophobia, the fear and loathing of male heterosexuality—a far more accepted condition among modern elites than homophobia. After all, if the dean had been a homosexual man who had pictures of naked men on his computer, the chances that Harvard would have asked him to resign his position are next to nothing. And if it had asked him to resign, charges of homophobia would have engulfed the university.

As it happens, the minister of Harvard University—the person who embodies whatever commitment Harvard has to religion—is a gay man. Presumably, Harvard has neither asked nor cares if the minister is chaste. Presumably, it is of no concern to Harvard University whether the minister it has chosen to embody its concept of the holy has sexual relations with another man, other men, or men and women. But Harvard cannot tolerate a dean who is married, who is the father of two children, who, to the best of Harvard's knowledge, is faithful to his wife, yet who, in private, looks at pictures of naked women! Such lunacy can only be explained by ideological fervor. And the ideology in question is heterophobia.

As for the third argument, that the computer was owned by Harvard —one wonders if those who offer this argument actually believe it or merely use it because they somehow know that having a dean resign because workmen found pictures of naked women on his computer is neither moral nor American. Harvard law professor Alan Dershowitz, who should be commended for his lonely defense of Dean Thiemann, has effectively refuted this argument. What if, Dershowitz asked, the dean had been a philatelist who had downloaded images of postage stamps—would anyone ask for his resignation because he kept these images on a Harvard-owned computer? Of course not. So, let's drop the pretense. At Harvard and in much of contemporary America, male

Why does Prager include the information that the Harvard University minister is gay? Is that fact relevant to his argument? Might it be a non sequitur? Check out Chapter 19 on logical fallacies, to help you answer that question.

·· LINK TO P. 323

heterosexuality is on notice not to rear its ugly head. (As for Prof. Dershowitz, I wonder when he will acknowledge that the greatest threats to liberty in America come from the left side of the political spectrum and from academia.)

Even if the three arguments had any merit, they would still pale in comparison to the deprivation of privacy in this case.

Why is abortion private and the viewing of pornography not?   20

Right to privacy—do these words ring a bell? The U.S. Supreme Court invoked this right in order to allow every woman the right to destroy a human fetus for any reason. I suspect that the president of Harvard and certainly all the feminists who protested Dean Thiemann's looking at pornography are pro-choice on abortion, on the grounds that society must protect a woman's right to privacy.

But do we not have a major contradiction here? On the one hand, these people declare the destroying of another being, a human fetus, an entirely private act that society has no right to judge, let alone restrict by legislation. On the other hand, they deny that what a man does in his most private world of sexual fantasy, by himself, to no one other than himself, is not private and that Harvard has every right to judge it and punish it.

How can we explain such a contradiction? Only by heterophobia—a hostility to heterosexual male sexuality.

And what is the reaction to this unprecedented violation of an entirely private area of a man's life? According to the *Los Angeles Times*, Thiemann's "colleagues at the school, known for its liberal philosophy, maintained a silence over the affair."

Why are Harvard's faculty members so quiet? Because at American 25 universities today there is no contest between feminist political correctness and a man's right to privacy. For a Harvard professor to come out in defense of Dean Thiemann's right to keep his fantasy life private would mean offending the feminist heterophobia that rules academia.

There is another fascinating contradiction here. I suspect that some of those who vociferously criticized Dean Thiemann were also among the most vocal defenders of President Clinton. They argued that society should allow the president of the United States to do whatever he wants sexually so long as it does not implicate his public duties. But how then can they criticize a college dean for his fantasy life? If looking at pictures of naked females alone in one's office fatally compromises a man's ability to be a university dean, why doesn't acting out sexual fantasies in the Oval Office with a real female compromise a man's ability to be president of the United States?

Too bad the dean resigned. I wouldn't have. I would have insisted on a public hearing. The only party in this matter deserving of humiliation is the party that did the humiliating—Harvard.

Fear and loathing of heterosexual male nature is a major problem in American life. That is why first-grade boys are kicked out of school for giving girls kisses on the cheek. The war on boys' natures also explains the desire to drug so many boys to calm them down. America is the first society ever to attempt to remake men's nature in the image of women's. Both men and women will suffer for it.

RESPOND •

1. Prager considers Thiemann's firing to be an example of "hetero-phobia." Do you agree with his assessment? Why or why not?

2. How would you describe Prager's treatment of opposing views? Is it fair or unfair? Does he provide sufficient information about them? To what degree? How does his discussion of opposing positions support his own? (Hint: Imagine his argument with the treatment of opposing views removed.)

3. In paragraph 15, Prager draws an analogy between heterosexual men looking at pictures of naked women and homosexual men looking at pictures of naked men in order to argue that men who look at pictures of naked women do not loathe or demean women in general. Do you think this analogy is a good one? Is it limited in any way? Why or why not?

4. Prager boldly claims in paragraph 11 that contemporary liberalism is for many a "secular fundamentalist religion." What does Prager mean by this provocative claim? (Hint: What do you think Prager's opinion of fundamentalism is? How do you know?) **Write an essay** in which you argue for or against his position and the effectiveness of his argumentation.

5. In paragraph 20 Prager asks, "Why is abortion private and the viewing of pornography not?" In the following two paragraphs, he sets up another extended metaphor, specifically an analogy that juxtaposes abortion and pornography on the one hand, and the nature of privacy and publicness (or perhaps public acceptability) on the other. **Write an essay** evaluating the appropriateness of this analogy. Be sure to pay special attention to Prager's word choice as he characterizes abortion.

Stripped of More than My Clothes

DARIA MONDESIRE

The most comforting part of a trip abroad used to be the part that brought me home.

There were only so many Yucatan pyramids to descend dizzily or Moorish castles to sigh over before not-to-be-denied nesting instincts kicked in and I missed the chaotic confusion of home. Souvenir mugs would get packed away, wet bathing suits tossed into carry-ons and unmailed postcards readied for repentant hand delivery.

Once aloft, I'd settle into a window seat, savor being above the clouds and think about the noisy welcome that awaited me.

Then came the day I found myself in a gray, windowless room in San Juan's airport politely being strip-searched by U.S. Customs agents.

There have, in my life, been two occasions when underwear was removed against my will. The first occurred at the hands of a rapist. The second time was at the hands of my government.

The agents told me they'd picked me out because I was dressed in bulky clothes: a backless sundress, a light cotton shirt and sandals. They told me that if they'd failed to stop me, their boss would have wanted to know why. They told me, after they'd made me remove my underwear and prove to their satisfaction the sanitary pad was there for its intended purpose, that I should consider working undercover as a drug agent.

Then they let me go.

Drugs have taken a numbing toll on this country. Lives have been lost, minds wasted. Heroin and cocaine should not be allowed to flow onto our shores unchallenged and unabated. Yet there's something chilling about a federal policy where law-abiding American citizens are forced to disrobe, detained without counsel, subjected to intrusive body cavity searches and at times held for as long as it takes laxatives to empty their stomachs.

Last year, 50,892 international airline passengers went through the rigors of some type of body search courtesy of the U.S. Customs Service — most of them "pat-downs" that fall short of the service's definition of a strip-search. One would surmise, given the professionalism of U.S. Customs officers, that drugs and maybe a mango or two would turn up on at least half the passengers subjected to such scrutiny.

Guess again. According to the Customs Service, 96% of them were found to be carrying nothing more than memories of a Caribbean honeymoon, gaudy sombreros destined to collect dust on a family room wall or mildewed laundry in need of a washer. Even three out of four of the 2,797 travelers subjected to partial or full strip searches, X-ray exams or cavity searches turned out not to be carrying drugs or contraband.

Those strip-searched were everyday people going about their everyday lives, until a federal agent labeled them with two loaded words: "potential courier." Had a municipal police department or a state police force attempted to do what U.S. Customs zealously did, constitutional safeguards against unreasonable search and seizure would bring the attempts to a screeching halt.

I can't say with absolute certainty why I, the one African-American on my flight, also was the one passenger on my flight singled out for that search several years ago. The official Customs line is that it focuses on high-risk flights from high-risk countries. Perhaps Grenada is famous for more than nutmeg and American intervention. Perhaps I should have taken care of those unpaid parking tickets. Perhaps I was a victim of a vast, right-wing conspiracy. It's all so wearying to think that, in addition to everything else being black in America entails, it may signal prima facie° grounds for agents of my government to strip me.

This much is clear: Minorities bear the brunt of the examinations. Of the total number of airline passengers who were searched in some manner in 1998 and on whom Customs kept race-identifying statistics, two-thirds were black, Latino or Asian.

---

prima facie: a Latin phrase that means "on first view" or "before additional examination."

MonDesire uses a rhetorical strategy when she defers the description of her proposal until the end of her article. You may wish to use a different strategy in your writing; see Chapter 12 for suggestions on ways of constructing a proposal argument.

·····················LINK TO P. 190

Customs officials, noting that three times as many whites as blacks were strip-searched, say they don't discriminate against blacks.

This official position, however, 15 does not include the opinion of Cathy Harris, a Customs inspector in Atlanta who has filed complaints alleging discrimination against black travelers. Nor is it supported by about four dozen black women who launched a class-action lawsuit in Chicago against the Customs Service alleging they were targeted for strip-searches because of their race. According to their attorney, Edward M. Fox, they include a 15-year-old searched while traveling with her white mother and aunt, who were not searched, a mentally retarded woman and a travel agent who has been repeatedly searched. Fox says he's now heard from more than 90 women from across the country.

The low number of body searches leading to drug seizures, the lawsuits and the complaints have convinced the Customs Service that things are not going swimmingly. A new commissioner Raymond W. Kelly, has a consultant examining the agency's policies. Customs officers are taking classes in cultural diversity. Some targeted passengers are being given the option of having machines scan their bodies.

Here's my proposal. Let's level the probing field and make it, indeed, a war against drugs.

Strip-search everyone who travels out of the country.

Strip-search Martha Stewart the second she steps off the Concorde. Strip-search Al Gore, members of Congress, all nine Supreme Court justices and every last one of the Daughters of the American Revolution. Strip-search Barbara Walters, Ivana Trump and ditto for The Donald. Strip search the Toujours Provence tourists, the Tuscany villa vacationers and the Hollywood-St. Barts brigade. Strip-search everyone who heretofore labored under the privileged assumption they could return to this country with some shred of dignity.

And then let the chips fall 20 where they may.

RESPOND•

1. MonDesire's proposal that all U.S. citizens returning home after a trip abroad be strip-searched is made for rhetorical effect; she knows (and so do we) that no such policy would ever be seriously considered. However, accept for a moment her proposal and analyze its logic. What are its strengths and weaknesses? What evidence can you provide for your position?

2. MonDesire incorporates statistics into her argument as part of the evidence for her claims. Sometimes she uses exact numbers (50,892; 2,797; 96 percent), and sometimes she uses prose figures (three out of four; two-thirds). Can you see any logic to her choices?

3. MonDesire offers one solution to what she sees as a major problem caused by U.S. Customs policy. Later in this chapter, you will find an essay by David Brin, "The Accountability Matrix" (p. 473). Brin would likely offer a very different proposal to problems like the one described by MonDesire. How would he propose responding to the overzealousness and inequities in the U.S. Customs' treatment of returning citizens? Which solution do you think would be the better one—MonDesire's or Brin's—and why?

4. How does the woodcut-style illustration accompanying this article contribute to its force? What visual symbols does Marcy E. Mullins, the artist, use to establish the power and authority of the Customs agents? The vulnerability of the woman, whom we take to be MonDesire?

5. Research the practices of U.S. Customs with regard to drug searches, the agency's rate of success, and the controversies surrounding these practices. **Write a letter** to U.S. Customs commissioners either proposing changes in the policy on searching returning citizens or urging the commissioners to maintain the current system. Provide solid evidence for your argument and establish yourself as knowledgeable about this subject.

▼ *This article appeared in 1997 in* Troika, *which describes itself as a "sophisticated, quirky, thought-provoking magazine covering arts, environment, ethics, travel, leisure, and business" for an "affluent, intellectual, society crowd." The author, Michael Perry, is a freelance writer and the author of* They Killed Big Boy *(1996),* Never Stand Behind a Sneezing Cow *(1996), and* Big Boy Out Loud *(1998). In this essay, Perry uses a comparison between two traffic incidents years apart to comment on the ways we adorn our vehicles to make claims (arguments, ultimately) about our place in the world—public statements about private commitments and even faith. As you read, consider the ways in which this article comments on privacy in a pluralistic (and exhibitionist) society like our own.*

Bumper-Sticker Bravado
Fear This

BY MICHAEL PERRY

My "fear" . . . is my substance, and probably the best part of me.
— FRANZ KAFKA

I don't get to town much, so being cut off in traffic should have been a novelty. A stream of bumper-to-bumper day jobbers droning homeward, doing sixty in a forty-five zone, light turning red 200 yards ahead, and this non-signaling knothead shoots in front of me like he's going for the pole at Daytona. Pinches himself between me and some four door, and then stomps the brakes like he's smashing a rat. And so I sat behind him, wondering if I had time to rip out his valve stems before the light changed. His baseball cap was on backward, of course, his stereo — as I am confident he would have put it — was "cranked," and he was driving one of those yappy little four-wheel drive pickups that have become the toy poodles of the truck world.

But while all of these things triggered my pique, it was the "No Fear" sticker in his rear window that sustains my rant. Irksomely ubiquitous on windshields, t-shirts, caps, billboards and bumper stickers, this bellicose bit of marketing has caused me to ponder what I know of fear. Very little, I suspect. Not because I am immune, or brave, or drive a hot little truck, but because of good fortune, and because what fear I have experienced — in the face of a Hungarian border guard, in the back of a fire engine, down a Belize City back street — has been, in the scope of things, fairly superficial. But in today's society, where rebellion amounts to a nipple ring, a Kool-Aid rinse, or an exquisite tattoo, superficial covers it.

Image — be it ephemeral as a cathode ray and thin as ink on a two-syllable bumper sticker — while so obviously nothing, is, in the age of identity purchased at retail, everything indeed. And every marketer

451

believes—that is not to say understands—the words of French playwright Jean Anouilh: "An ugly sight, a man who is afraid." Fear is ugly and ugly doesn't sell sunglasses. But what sort of vacuous buffoonery allows us to adopt such slogans? Consider the case of the lump of gristle with a pulse who cut me off in traffic. Cossetted in a society where rebellion has been co-opted by commerce, where individuality is glorified in fashion campaigns that put youth in worldwide lockstep with an efficiency despots only dream of (assuming, of course, that the people who own athletic shoe companies are not despots), raging youth finds itself sitting at a red light, steeped in the same hormonal invincibility that fuels ravaging armies, with nothing to do but wait to tromp the accelerator of a trendy little pickup. Who knows fear?

I once hitch-hiked a ride with a Belizian cane hauler. I couldn't speak Spanish; he couldn't speak English. It didn't matter: the bellowing engine precluded conversation. We simply grinned at each other as he hurled the truck through the twists in the road, the scorched sugar cane swaying high above our heads. The truck was of indeterminate vintage. The play in the steering was such that an entire half-spin of the wheel was required before the truck's vector was affected. The previous evening, on a blind corner, a pick-up had veered over the center line, crashing head-on with a tractor hauling cane. Two men had been killed. As we shot the same curve that morning, the wreckage still remained; grieving clusters of family stood along the roadside. We hit that curve full tilt, blowing a backwash of cane leaves over the upended tractor. I sneaked a peak at the speedometer. It was completely obscured by a circular decal of the Virgin Mary. We grinned at each other again.

Two men, both driving dangerously in trucks, both expressing themselves through adhesive symbology. And yet there is a difference; an instructive distinction.

Is the cane hauler wiser because he *knows* fear? Poverty, dangerous labor, the hungry faces of a brood at home—surely these cultivate acquaintance with fear. The Virgin Mary decal seems evidence of theistic fear. But these are presumptive conclusions, and, I think, just miss the point. That point being, if the cane hauler drives without fear it is because he has acknowledged fear, and then turned it over to the Blessed Virgin. The fellow in the four-wheel poodle, on the other hand, is fearless because he has never been forced through circumstance to acknowledge fear's existence. He has made the quintessentially American mistake of thinking his life is special, his bumper sticker is bold, his truck is shiny . . . because *he* is special. His fearlessness is an inane statement construed through an accident of birth. In contrast, the cane hauler may dispense with fear, but he knows better than to scoff at it.

Ernest Hemingway wrote about people living "essential, dangerous lives." Those three words say so much about what we are or aren't, and explain why, in a world filled with fear, we would choose to disguise the sheltered nature of our existence through mindless sloganizing. Perhaps the pickup driver could back up his bravado; swagger through a Rwandan refugee camp, exhort those pitiful laggards to get a set of decent basketball shoes, hoist a microbrew, and shake off this unattractive predilection to fear.

Perry employs various types of figurative language—simile, metaphor, and others. Check out Chapter 14 to see how many of the writing techniques described there you can find in Perry's article.

Virgen de Guadalupe

········LINK TO P. 239

Tell 'em this is Planet Reebok, and on Planet Reebok, we have no room for the fearful. Better yet, he could earn his "No Fear" decal by strapping on his favorite Nikes and sprinting down Sniper Alley beside a twelve-year-old Sarajevan on a water run.

Somehow, after that, I think he'd prefer to keep his rear window clear, the better to see what fearful thing might be creeping up on him.   ■

RESPOND •

1. Even while Perry denigrates the "No Fear" stickers, he includes himself in the question, "What sort of vacuous buffoonery allows us to adopt such slogans?" What might Perry's pronoun choice reveal about his attitude toward his audience? Toward people who have "No Fear" stickers on their vehicles? Toward himself?

2. In what ways is this article an article about the nature of public and private life in U.S. society? What is the real meaning of each of the vehicle decorations Perry describes? (What, specifically, does "No Fear" mean? Who is afraid or not afraid? Of what or whom? Why? Try providing a paraphrase of "No Fear.") How is each of the decorations described a declaration of faith? To what extent do you accept Perry's analysis of these decorations and declarations as arguments? Why?

3. Given what you know about the audience of *Troika*, do you think Perry's article uses style and tone appropriate for its readership? Why or why not? Try rewriting two or three paragraphs of the article, making them appropriate for an academic paper. Explain why you made the changes you did.

4. Spend several days observing the bumper stickers or other decorations on vehicles that you see where you live. Make notes on the messages on the bumper stickers you see, and the kind of vehicles on which they appear. Do any surprise you? **Write an essay** describing three or four of the vehicles and their decorations and analyzing the arguments the drivers might be trying to make about themselves.

This cluster of arguments considers the question **who's watching?** as it focuses on the conflicting tendencies many Americans have to see, to be seen, and to avoid being seen. Joshua Gamson, a scholar of popular culture at Yale University, considers these conflicting desires and the way in which they manifest themselves in our daily lives in his essay "Look at Me! Leave Me Alone!" Among the examples he cites are webcams and "reality" television, each represented in this cluster, appropriately enough, by first-person accounts. In "Why I Star in My Own *Truman Show*," Jennifer Ringley explains why she decided to set up JenniCam and what she's learned about people from doing so. In "My Taxicab Confession," Jennifer L. Felten recounts her experiences with the HBO "reality television" series of the same name. These two essays provide very different perspectives on what privacy might be and when it might be said to be violated. From a related perspective, Cathy Guisewite's *Cathy* cartoon "Here Comes the Bride" satirizes American wedding customs and our love of being watched even as it reaffirms poor Cathy's desire to be left alone. The cluster closes with a chapter from *The Transparent Society*, in which David Brin offers a provocative framework for analyzing issues of privacy. Brin's particular solution to questions of privacy is to put surveillance cameras everywhere, a suggestion we assume many readers will find startling.

Research on privacy in this country over the past twenty-five or so years shows that about a quarter of Americans are vigilant about their privacy, nearly a quarter seem to be indifferent to the issue, and the remaining 55 percent—whom Alan Westin labels "privacy pragmatists"—are interested in knowing how they might benefit from permitting information about themselves to be gathered. How would you characterize yourself? What do you think should be public, and what should remain private? Consider this question as you study the arguments in this cluster; perhaps they will challenge you to rethink your position. As you read, give some thought in particular to the ways in which the Internet and other trends in broadcasting continue to redefine the terms—and the stakes—of debates about privacy.

▼ *This article was originally published in 1998 in* **The American Prospect**, *a magazine of political news with a liberal viewpoint. In it, Joshua Gamson, a Yale sociologist who studies contemporary Western commercial culture and mass media, analyzes the interplay among three complex desires that Americans now simultaneously hold relating to privacy: the desires to watch others, to be watched, and to be free from being watched. We treasure our privacy, yet we want to cash in on the rewards of being watchable and being watched. Before you read, try to imagine a world without photography, without television, without video, and without webcams—the world during most of human history. How might your personality, appearance, or behavior be different in such a world?*

Look at Me! Leave Me Alone!

JOSHUA GAMSON

It's a beautiful fantasy, really, and a potent one right about now: you are sailing through stormy weather to the edge of this bright, false, pretty world, and ramming suddenly into what all of your life you had mistaken for the sky but turns out to be a wall, you climb out of your boat onto a staircase and up to a door, behind which things may be less pretty but certainly more real. Stepping through that door into a private darkness, you start a life that is unwatched, unproduced, unrecorded, unmarketed, unsold. This fantasy—the end of the popular dystopia° *The Truman Show*—is powerful exactly because of the world we seem to live in on this side of the backdrop sky, in which privacy is a scarce commodity, in which prying eyes are everywhere, and in which everything and everyone you see is for sale, operators standing by. In this world, it's tough to know just who and what is for real.

If you've seen the film, you know that Truman Burbank was the first baby to be legally adopted by a corporation, OmniCam. Directed by the God-artiste-mogul Christof ("the big guy," or, as he puts it, "the Creator [pause] of a television show"), Truman is the unknowing star of his own enormously popular television show; his entire life is recorded by 5,000 hidden cameras and is broadcast, with constant product placement, worldwide. The manicured and predictable little island town he lives in, Seahaven, is in fact the world's biggest studio, populated entirely by actors, including those playing his wife, his mother, his best friend. Everything in it, literally, is available by mail order. Truman is the only "real" thing on the set, kept there by a fear of water facilitated by the staged drowning of his father, TV shows proclaiming the joys of never leaving home, and travel agency posters featuring crashing jets. Gradually, through a series of glitches such as falling studio lights, the reappearance of his dead father, and a car radio playing control room instructions, Truman begins to suspect that things are not as they appear, a perspective aided by memories of an old girlfriend, now a leader of a "Free Truman" resistance movement, who before being dragged away by a thug posing as her father had shouted "Everybody's pretending! It's a set! It's a studio!"

And so Truman begins a ratings-grabbing escape, violently opposed and exploited by Christof and OmniCam, who put in his way forest fires, a nuclear plant leak from which he is chased and subdued by men in silver protective suits, betrayals by his wife and best friend, and a search by actors and hunting dogs lined up like a lynch mob, lit by a moon-turned-searchlight and a prematurely risen sun. Eventually he is found where he's not supposed to be, on the sea. Over the objections of network executives ("We can't let him die in front of a live audience!"), he is subjected to biblical punishments by Christof ("He was born in front of a live audience!"), who, using a weather program, sends storms and giant waves in an attempt to drown his boy rather than see the show

end. "There's no more truth out there than in the world I created," Christof warns Truman from his perch in the studio sky. Truman isn't buying it, and to the viewers' delight, still directed by Christof ("That's our hero shot," he says as Truman sails off defiantly), he plays the hero. "You're going to have to kill me," he screams, and he survives to hit the wall, and the staircase, and the doorway. Live free — camera-free, that is — or die.

WATCHING ME WATCHING YOU

The Truman Show is interesting not because of its originality; it borrows from and nicely updates quite a number of earlier stories of paranoid heroes starring unknowingly in films about themselves, of horrific Big Brother° surveillance and pacified publics and superpowerful media, from Samuel Beckett° and Aldous Huxley° and George Orwell° to

---

dystopia: an imagined place where life is dreadful; the opposite of "utopia."

Big Brother: fictional character from George Orwell's novel *Nineteen Eighty-Four* (1949) who, while appearing benevolent, actually personifies the evils of an authoritarian state.

Samuel Beckett: 1969 Nobel Prize winner (1906–1989) who wrote in English and French; Beckett is generally associated with the Theater of the Absurd, in which often paranoid characters find little or no meaning in life.

Aldous Huxley: British writer (1894–1963) best known for his 1932 novel *Brave New World,* which describes a future totalitarian society character-

ized by freedom from suffering and war, on the one hand, and by mass conformity and standardization, on the other.

George Orwell: pseudonym of Eric A. Blair (1903–1950), best known for *Animal Farm* (1946) and *Nineteen Eighty-Four* (1949), both of which illustrate his fear of mass movements and totalitarian states. They, along with Huxley's *Brave New World,* are considered the

best exemplars of English-language dystopic literature.

Philip K. Dick° and Robert A. Heinlein,° from *Blade Runner*° to *Network*° to *The Twilight Zone.*° It is, however, a timely satire, and one that has spurred waves of commentary about how it summarizes our current state of affairs in a big, entertaining metaphor, how we are all Truman Burbanks, trapped by the ever shrinking private life created by constant surveillance. "The movie's most frightening question comes down to this: Is the fictional specter of an all-knowing, all-seeing eye really so far removed from fact?" asked a typical *Chicago Tribune* report recently, going on to suggest it is not. Writing about information access more generally, novelist Richard Powers argued in the *New York Times* that "private life" might soon enough become a "term that had some shared meaning once but vaporized under the press of material progress." We have conceded the right to be recorded, Power claims, having "long forsaken any hope of preserving the private—that part of life that goes unregistered."

We are trapped, another version of the argument   5
goes, not so much by the constant registering of private life as by our insatiable appetite for the televised life. We may be victims of surveillance, but we are also its advocates, sad-sack Truman fans thrilled by the prying eyes of the cameras. The most provocative aspect of *The Truman Show,* Paul Brownfield wrote in the *Los Angeles Times,* for instance, "is not how thoroughly Big Brother can watch us but how the home viewers in the film blithely peer in at Truman's life, never stopping to consider their own complicity in the grand manipulation." If we are trapped, it is only because, as Christof asserts about Truman, we love our cell. "The captive of TV isn't Truman, it's the audience," Stanley Kauffmann suggested in the *New Republic.* "Us." And greedy media corporations are only too willing to shove cameras anywhere they can get them, feeding us the private until there's nothing left to eat.

What traps us, then, the constant watching by hidden others or our own constant watching? Which are we, the poor souls chased by camera crews or the chop-licking connoisseurs of other people's secrets? Which is the fantasy of freedom, the one in which we can see everything or the one in which we are safe from being seen? The weird thing, of course, is that both seem to be the case. Many of us are not, like Truman, running away from the cameras but running toward them, arms wide open, carrying our own spotlights—while complaining that we can't seem to get away from the lens. The fantasy of entering a camera-free realm coexists quite comfortably with the dream of a life in which all eyes are on you; the pronounced anxiety about eroded privacy (don't watch me! leave people alone!) lives happily with the avid worship of publicity (look at

---

Philip K. Dick: American novelist and science-fiction writer (1928–1982) whose characters repeatedly find that what they had assumed was real is, in fact, illusion.

Robert A. Heinlein: American engineer and science-fiction writer (1907–1988) best known for his 1961 novel *Stranger in a Strange Land,* which sought to question many of our culture's most basic assumptions about daily life.

Blade Runner: American cult sci-fi film (1982) whose protagonist seeks to rid the earth of android fugitives from another planet.

Network: American satiric film (1976) about "trash TV."

The Twilight Zone: American TV series (1959–1965) that depicted everyday situations that were never what they at first had seemed.

me! let me see!). What is new here is neither voyeurism nor exhibitionism — it is their strange relationship, in which watching and turning away, being on camera and hiding from it, are married impulses.

It's hard to know exactly where and when this all began but the two impulses are now relentlessly chasing each other's tails. The key to understanding the chase, where anxiety about diminution of privacy begets more craving for televised moments of privacy and vice versa, is that it is not the erosion of privacy alone that really seems to be bothersome, but the erosion of moments that can be *trusted*. It is not just crass voyeurism that drives growing popular interest in the nooks and crannies of everyday life, but a sense that those nooks and crannies look more and more like stage sets. The

growth of surveillance, industrialized voyeurism, and increased self-display add up to a situation in which "realness" seems harder to find; all the heightened recording of private and personal life, the invited kind and the uninvited, sets in motion a hunt for the authentic. Television, along with technological advances in surveillance technique and demographic-information capturing, has made the places where one is unwatched and unsurveyed, where one need make no adjustments for an audience, seem fewer and farther between (be careful what books you buy, your sales receipt might get subpoenaed; be careful what you do in the aisle of a drugstore, because hidden cameras are recording you). The look-at-me culture only makes the search for these moments even more untenable: the more people offer themselves for the

watching, the more like performers they become. And so the search for trustable moments, really private ones, intensifies.

Television, a prime purveyor of the look-at-me principle, has stepped in to satisfy the craving for the real, unobserved life that it has helped to undermine. Media conglomerates happily and effortlessly market the pursuit of realness, exploiting it for the old-fashioned goal of getting people to watch television. Television now commonly provides fare that promises a door at the edge of the studio — showing off private moments meant to reassure us that spontaneous behaviors, actions taken without regard to cameras and publicity, still exist. It can do this very easily by drawing on the heady dream of publicity that television culture has long since codified: the fantasy of being the star of your very own show (think of programs as disparate as *Oprah* or *America's Funniest Home Videos*), if only for a few minutes, with all its attendant rewards. Yet when all kinds of people take up these invitations to celebrity, as they have more and more, the sense of private life as a performance for the cameras, as somehow not quite real, gets even stronger. These rolling cameras to which we have by now grown so accustomed bring with them the giant suspicion that everyone might be partly acting, every candid moment part of the ongoing infomercial. And the TV solution to the worry that we are too watched to be real, our lives too public to be trusted, is more watching in the hope of glimpsing the real. We are invited to see the unobserved (a snoring

Truman, the unsuspecting criminals on *Cops*), the glitches in the observation system (the falling lights on Truman's stage set, goofy out-takes on *TV Censored Bloopers*), anything that takes us behind the door. But the TV offer comes with a funny sort of guarantee: the door gets farther away the faster you run toward it.

SOMEBODY'S WATCHING ME

It's an intriguing, reassuring, almost nostalgic kick to witness the innocence of the unwatched. Indeed, perhaps what makes the marketing of "private" reality an especially easy sell for television is the more and more common awareness that watchers could be pretty much anywhere. I myself, for instance, am careful not to do anything indelicate on elevators, at automatic teller machines, and in convenience stores these days, since it's hard to know if there's a camera in the corner watching me pick basil or poppy seeds out of my teeth. And I might also be well advised to compose my emails more carefully at work: along with many other such jarring examples in his [1998] book *The Transparent Society,* David Brin cites a 1997 survey of 906 employers, 35 percent of whom were found to be conducting one or more types of "close electronic surveillance" on their employees. I should probably also be more careful about what I do on the streets of New York City, where, as in Baltimore, my behavior in some areas is recorded by hidden cameras 24 hours a day. I'll be avoiding Roslyn Heights, New York, too, where, according to the *Boston Globe*, 35 hidden surveillance cameras feed live pictures onto the Internet of anyone moving on the streets.

It seems pretty clear that new technology has made hidden surveillance much more sophisticated, easier to do, and harder to detect. There's no question that everyone needs to be vigilant as ever about sleazy, ill-intentioned intrusions and restrictions on civil liberties, but it's also worth noting that, in order to be truly effective as social control tools—and these spying techniques have indeed proved to be remarkable crime reducers—people need to know the cameras are there. This kind of surveillance, unlike Truman's, operates on the knowledge that, at least potentially, someone is watching; the cameras must be both obscured and acknowledged. This is the effect of the Panopticon° famously noted by Michel Foucault:° people police themselves. Who's going to light up a joint in Washington Square Park when the cameras might be rolling? Who's going to have raunchy conversations online if their boss might be reading along? The awareness of being observed, not just the observing, is what Big Brother techniques promote.

Of course, the greatest recent increase in hidden watching is less Big Brother than big business. Driving records, Social Security numbers, credit ratings, marital status, purchasing habits, membership in organizations, taxes—pretty much anyone with a little skill and a computer can find those out with just your name and address. But who really wants to know? The increased recording of

---

Panopticon: a model prison, as envisioned by British philosopher Jeremy Benthan (1748–1832), where prisoners and all aspects of their behavior could be observed by unseen guards at all times.

Michel Foucault: French philosopher (1926–1984) whose writings on history, sexuality, madness, and power continue to have profound effects on thinking in a number of disciplines. Among his concerns are the ways in which members of societies contribute to their own domination.

information most of us thought was ours alone is not so much a matter of getting you to adjust your behavior as to generate information from which to sell you more things. America Online and others, for

"Anxiety about eroded privacy lives happily with the avid worship of publicity."

instance, compile names and addresses of their subscribers to sell to other companies; every magazine subscription begets unmerciful junk mail. An Internet site visit is tracked by a "cookie," a piece of software that makes note of what you look at, and the next thing you know you're getting messages from manufacturers of baldness cures or vacation resorts or people willing to take their clothes off for a small fee. A supermarket discount "club" card tracks what's in your shopping cart. It's not in fact paranoid to think that, at least when it comes to any activity that might remotely involve you in buying something, almost everything you do is on record. These surveillance activities, open or not, start to add up after a while, and you start to feel less certain that much information about yourself is yours to control, and more certain that in order to sell you things, companies of all kinds are keeping awfully close tabs.

While computerized recording of buying habits and convenience store cameras and nosy neighbors with video cameras are not bothersome in the same ways or to the same degree, together they do create the impression that not much is left unrecorded. It's this suspicion that is firmed up, popularized, and capitalized upon by the now ubiquitous phenomenon of "reality" television, in which people are filmed going about their everyday lives and those images converted into entertainment. Sometimes they know about the cameras ahead of time, sometimes they grant permission after the fact (or, more rarely, refuse to grant it) for some moment of their lives to be broadcast; some-

times the real life is loosely scripted, sometimes it's just edited for dramatic effect. A minor tradition precedes the 1990s explosion of reality TV — *Candid Camera* set people up to be the unknowing butts of televised jokes in the 1960s, the Loud family aired their laundry for PBS's *American Family* in the 1970s, David Letterman has had this cam and that cam roaming the streets and the studio since the 1980s, and daytime talk shows, for their part, have always made their money by the revelation of the everyday lives and emotions of their guests. But by now reality entertainment is a full-fledged genre, as cheap-to-produce programming meets up with an audience intrigued by dramas of "real life." MTV's *Real World* (and its spinoff *Road Rules*) brings together a combustible mix of good-looking young men and women and films them playing themselves as they might be if they had actually chosen to live together. Fox's *Cops* films police pursuing and arresting criminals, and the syndicated *Real TV* buys footage of car chases and dramatic rescue scenes. HBO's *Taxicab Confessions* places "lipstick cameras" in cabs and offers drivers, who are equipped with earphones through which they can hear producers' suggestions for questions to ask the fares. Local television news looks increasingly like some loony combination of *Cops* and *America's Funniest Home Videos*.

Watching these shows, it makes sense to wonder once again what there is left to live unobserved, whether there's a cam-less spot left. Truman may not have died on live television, but the airing of the Los Angeles freeway suicide earlier this year — and years before that, the O. J. car chase scene, which was riveting because he had a gun and was threatening suicide — has made it clear that it is indeed possible, if controversial, to watch someone die on live television. Or give birth on the Internet, as a woman named "Elizabeth" did this past summer before an audience estimated at two million. What seems especially striking in recent years is the enthusiasm with which so many people invite strangers to watch and listen to activities that are typically considered private, and the enthusiasm with which, despite the fear of lost privacy, strangers are willing to participate in the process. Apple software engineer John Kullmann has a webcam in his office that has fed his image so far to 76,000 strangers. "If I happen to be picking my nose, they catch me," he told a San Francisco reporter. Apple co-founder Steve Wozniak has four webcams in his office. "If I pick my nose," Wozniak told a Houston reporter, perhaps confirming the rumors of widespread computer industry nose-picking, "they see me." Jennifer Ringley allows you to witness her life on JenniCam for $15 a year, and Ana Voog's anacam.com allows you to watch the performance artist take baths, eat lunch, and paint herself blue in front of four webcams. According to one keeper of a list of webcam sites, between 20 and 30 people submit new sites every day.

And there's still the old-fashioned route. *The Jerry Springer Show* claims to get thousands of calls every week from people volunteering to fight with their two-timing/slut-dressing/thought-he-was-a-she wife/boyfriend/mother/cousin. According to the *Los Angeles Times,* about 14,000 people volunteered to be subjects for the most recent *Real World* and *Road Rules* casts. Clearly, not everybody is all that bothered by the idea of being watched. Picking noses, telling each other's secrets, eating a peanut butter sandwich, having a baby: there are more than enough people willing to invade their own "privacy." And more than enough people willing to watch, all the while complaining that "the media" are too intrusive, sticking their microphones in the midst of private grief and joy and intrigue.

The Currency of Publicity

Although people do routinely and vehemently object 15 to the erosion of privacy, it's puzzling that they also seem to be unbothered by quite a bit of it. For instance, while everyone pretty much agrees that the relentless, hidden information grabbing by companies is incredibly annoying, and that the companies should at least tell you when they're stealing your personal information for their own profiteering, to many people such activities seem relatively innocuous — after all, it's all about giving you what you want, and if someone wants to know what kind of cereal I like, or even what dirty pictures I like to look at, fine, go nuts.

But the story deepens a bit when one sees that privacy, while certainly also at stake, is not the key here. This is an extraordinarily ocular culture, and one that rewards the looked-at, so it ought not be surprising that lots of people are ready to be watched. Being looked at, being visible, being known about, is a currency. You can cash it in for money or office, and even if that's not what you're after, the logic of celebrity remains powerful: you aren't anybody until you've been on television. It's the pursuit of publicity, not privacy, that offers the big rewards in this culture. If the fantasy of sailing away from prying eyes is one potent vision, that may only be because the fantasy of being known is its jealous twin.

Indeed, it's the fact that publicity has such payoffs that sends the broadcasting of the "private" into high gear. Publicity culture makes a virtue of being watched, and reality television profits from the desire to witness something real behind self-interested publicity, to see how people look when they do not know they are being seen. The longing captured by *The Truman Show* is a craving for something "real." It's not so much the threats to privacy itself that are bothersome these days but what the private tends to make possible and has come to symbolize: a life you recognize as authentically your own because it is not there for the entertainment of others. The private moment has come to stand for realness, and the awareness of increased surveillance means that fewer and fewer moments qualify. "As private space shrinks," Ellen

Goodman has smartly pointed out, "the public's hunger for authenticity grows. As the hunger grows, the deeper we invade private life to find something real, and the shallower it gets." Reality television, moving its cameras into "private," promises exactly the unobserved moments that it makes impossible to deliver.

"Cue the sun," says *The Truman Show*'s Christof as he intensifies his search for Truman Burbank. Lately, entertainment media are smitten with this image of their own power, their role as gods manipulating the public and manufacturing reality—the reporter in *Mad City* who "controls" rather than reports a hostage story, the Hollywood producer in *Wag the Dog* who manufactures a made-for-TV war, the producers in *Bulworth* who make and break political careers. And although the manipulative power of media industries is plain and well documented, in many ways media are more like parasites than gods. They feed off social anxieties and broadcast them for profit. The disquieting sense that one is too often watched has more widespread creators than the media gods. Yet once they get in on the game, they set in motion a spiral that is hard to escape. Even if the creators are not as omnipotent as they appear in their own mirrors, that spiral itself is incredibly powerful, in part because the desire to feel one's own life remains, even if buried beneath a pile of *TV Guides,* very powerful. The simultaneous pursuit of publicity and distrust of it, once it enters the realm of television, builds a staircase back to the living room, where we can sit down to watch the watching in the blue-lit privacy of our own homes. As media critic Mark Crispin Miller once put it, "Big Brother is you, watching."

Perhaps in the end it is not really Truman Burbank and Christof who summarize the current state of affairs, but the *Teletubbies*. These four British imports, now trying to recreate their enormous U.K. popularity on America's PBS, are small, goofy alien creatures who bounce around the bright, colorful Teletubbyland ("the place where television is made") in fuzzy head-to-toe pajama-like outfits; their trippy show takes aim at the hither-to-untapped one- to two-year-old market. Po, Laa Laa, Dipsy, and Tinky Winky, who have antennas on their fluffy heads and television screens in their round tummies, live in a beautiful world in which life without television is literally unimaginable. Television lives inside of them. They are TV watchers who are also TV screens. During each show, what looks to be a windmill but turns out to be a TV transmitter begins to emit a signal, and one of the Tubbies' stomach screens starts to glow, until a video of a real-life child (riding a horse or a tricycle or some such thing) begins to play. When the video ends, the Teletubbies call for more. "Again, again," they cry, and we watch them as they turn to watch the mundane clip of life taking place again on one of their own small, glowing bellies. ∎

Teletubbies

Among the elements in Gamson's intricately woven article are definition arguments exploring the meanings of *privacy* and *reality.* See Chapter 9 for more on making definition arguments.

LINK TO P. 109

RESPOND.

1. Gamson uses many specific examples from daily life, including the media, as evidence for his claims that Americans' desires to watch, be watched, and avoid being watched are in conflict. Give examples from your own life that illustrate the conflicts among these desires.

2. What does Gamson mean by the claim, "It's the pursuit of publicity, not privacy, that offers the big rewards in this culture" (paragraph 16)? Do you agree with his claim? Why or why not?

3. Gamson concludes his article by suggesting that the Teletubbies "summarize the current state of affairs" (paragraph 19) with respect to privacy and the media. Do you think his suggestion is sincere, or is it simply a rhetorical device? What might be Gamson's purpose in ending with the image of the Teletubbies rather than a more "adult" reference?

4. Imagine that you are directing the sequel to *The Truman Show*. **Write** a description of the first experience Truman Burbank has after he walks through the door into the "real world."

5. Gamson contends in paragraph 7 that the erosion of privacy brings "the erosion of moments that can be *trusted*." He later notes, in paragraph 10, that increasingly, all Americans have an "awareness of being observed" in a range of ways across a variety of contexts. **Write an essay** exploring these claims, using personal experience—yours or that of friends or family—as one source of evidence.

▼ *Who knows how many Americans now broadcast part or all of their lives by webcam, but Jennifer Ringley was the first to put a webcam in her apartment. Her site has been operating since 1996 at <http://www .jennicam.com>, and she claims to receive between two and three million hits per day. This article by Ringley first appeared in* Cosmopolitan *in October 1998. You may already know about Ringley or others like her and have an opinion about what such people are doing. As you read, be aware of how your opinion is or isn't changing.*

Why I Star in My Own *Truman Show*

JENNIFER RINGLEY

For the past two and a half years, every minute of my life has been broadcast over the Internet to millions of people. But even though I have cameras in my bedroom and office at home, I'm not an exhibitionist. I enjoy my privacy. I just like to enjoy it with you — and the two million or so people who click into my life every day and night.

I had the idea to do my own *Truman Show* after seeing The Amazing FishCam Web site, where you can check in on a fish 24 hours a day. I thought, *What if you could watch a person living in a virtual fishbowl?* After all, you can turn to the Discovery channel and watch a lion in the wild — feeding, sleeping, and copulating. But the people you see on TV and in movies are actors. They're fictional — which is why their lives seem more exciting than yours does. Why not create a place where people

Mon, Nov 9, 1998 4:56 PM   http://www.jennicam.org ©JKR

could observe the behavior of another human being in her natural (actually, man-made) habitat?

Turns out, we really are fascinated by how other people live. JenniCam is the third most-visited site on the Internet. People tune in to me to watch me eat, work, sleep, even watch TV. And some, for sure, view with the hope — since it's happened before — that they'll see me during more intimate moments.

But I don't believe the site is really about me. It's about how normal people live and perform everyday functions. I feel it could focus on someone else and still be interesting. Maybe more so.

Like Truman, I never play for or hide from the cameras, which are tiny and unobtrusive. I don't even think about the cameras. If I have to scratch my butt, I do. (That's reality.)

465

Today, the Internet is the most efficient and widest-reaching vehicle by which to distribute information. I was surprised that people made a big deal about the online live birth. Why should anyone be shocked by a perfectly natural event broadcast on the Internet to educate people about childbirth?

My site also is for people to watch and learn. Through my ordinary existence, people can see that their lives are normal too — and maybe feel better about themselves. One guy E-mailed me on a Friday night, saying that he didn't feel like a loser for being home doing laundry because he saw I was also home, doing my laundry. And a 16-year-old girl recently

> **"I enjoy my privacy. I just like to enjoy it with the two million or so people who click into my life every day and night."**

thanked me because she saw that, though I too am not perfectly trim, I'm still comfortable with my body and sexuality. It's true undressing was awkward in the beginning, but I think it's a way of showing people that we all have essentially the same bodies.

The fact that Jenni-Cam gets more hits than the *Playboy* site shows that people are more intrigued by real individuals than they are by perfect air-brushed babes. People feel more comfortable watching humans who have flaws. It validates their normalcy. So if you're having a bad hair day, just tune in — I probably am too. ■

Chapter 8 explains how to do a Toulmin analysis of an argument, identifying such elements as enthymemes, warrants, or backing. Ringley's article could have as its enthymeme "My JenniCam site is good because broadcasting my life helps people feel regular." What would be the warrant for that enthymeme? Refer to Chapter 8 for help in answering the question.

············ LINK TO P. 95

RESPOND •

1. How credible do you find Ringley's assertion that she isn't an exhibitionist?

2. Ringley's argument is intensely personal, yet she uses more than simply an argument from the heart. What other lines of argumentation does she use? Provide specific examples from her text.

3. Ringley says nothing about money or profit in the article, but those who have visited the site know that members pay $15/year for access to more frequent updates. Would your attitude toward Ringley and JenniCam change if you thought she made no money from the site? Would the amount she made influence your opinion? Why? Is the question of profit connected to privacy for you at all? How so or how not?

4. Imagine that you are invited to a small party at Jennifer Ringley's house. If you go, your every move could be broadcast by webcam to thousands of unknown people. Would you attend? Why or why not? **Write an essay** explaining why you would or would not attend and what you would expect to find there if you were to attend it.

My Taxicab Confession

JENNIFER L. FELTEN

 In this essay, Jennifer Felten recounts her experience as someone who could have been on HBO's Taxicab Confessions. It first appeared in 1997 in the Weekly Standard, *a magazine that claims to be "America's premier political weekly," "conservative but independent." We found it on the Web using a search engine while following a lead from Joshua Gamson's essay, "Look at Me! Leave Me Alone!" (p. 456).*

We should have noticed something was up when a call to Yellow Cab from my friend Tracy's apartment brought a Checker cab to her doorstep. Since when are the Yellow and Checker guys even on speaking terms? But, then, headed out for a night on the town with the girls—Tracy, Kelly, Kerry, and me—who pays attention to details?

The front seat was broken, so we were told by the handsome, young, black cab driver; all four of us would have to squeeze into the back. We happily piled in, noisy, jostling, and giggling. As the cab pulled away, I noticed that the interior was awash in bright fluorescent lights radiating from above the front window.

"So what's with the crazy bright lights?" I asked.

"Oh, just my own security system, I don't want someone sneaking up on me in the dark," said the cabbie, who was quick to prompt a conversation. "Out for a big night on the town?" he prodded.

"Of course," we responded.   5

Before long the questions started getting more personal: "Are you all single?"

"Not this one," Tracy declared as she pointed to me.

"How long have you been married?" he asked.

"One year," I said.

"Happy?" he asked.   10

"Very," I said.

"She eloped," Kelly volunteered on my behalf.

"You eloped!" he exclaimed. "That's so cool."

It seems particularly appropriate that Felten would use her personal experience as the evidence in an argument about the privacy of personal experience. Check out what Chapter 18 has to say about using personal experience in your writing.

....LINK TO P. 304

"Tell him the story," Tracy chimed in.

"No no, it's such a long story," I protested.   15

"Who cares, I love good stories," said the cabbie.

It is a good story, I have to admit, and friends are always pumping me to retell it. And truth be told, I do love retelling it. I described how my husband's and my romantic adventure began when we crossed paths with each other at Dulles airport. You see, we had been engaged for a while, and then briefly disengaged. So over a late-day airport drink, Eric proposed that we forget about engagements and just elope instead. Europe seemed like a romantic spot and so we were off. We were too late for a transatlantic flight from Dulles so we cabbed to National, flew to JFK, cabbed to La Guardia, and just barely caught the last plane to London. Of course, we knew nothing of "posting banns," the English version of a two-week waiting period, which did complicate matters. So we ended up returning after a lovely, hectic weekend to the courthouse in Leesburg, Va.—about ten minutes away from our starting point at Dulles— where the only thing we had to do to get married was swear that we weren't brother and sister.

At every point in the story, the curious cabbie plied me with questions. "What did he say to you in the airport?" "How did you feel when that happened? . . ." Caught up in telling all, I didn't realize we were driving all over Washington in a very roundabout route to our destination. Tracy did question the cab driver's rather erratic navigational skills.

"It won't cost you any more," he reassured us.

Just as I had gotten through the grand finale, we arrived. Purses were opening   20 when our friendly cabbie turned around and calmly started reciting a prepared script: He was working with HBO on a "documentary" series called *Taxicab Confessions*. He was certain they would love to use my story. In fact, we could all be on TV if I would just sign this release. Collectively, we'd get $500, and the cab ride was free!

We all laughed nervously. Could this guy be a kook? Then Kelly pointed to the front window. "Hey, there's the hidden camera," cleverly concealed by a cheesy flower decal. It all clicked—the "security lights," the "broken front seat." This was for real, and I had been duped.

For a split second, as I looked at my starry-eyed friends, I thought that maybe this wasn't so bad. Maybe we would be discovered! But wait. Who said I ever wanted to be discovered telling all on HBO?

While I was struggling with the temptations of fleeting fame, out of nowhere (actually, out of a car that had been tailing us all the way) came Amber, HBO's producer. She popped up in the window and began to plead with me. "It is such a romantic story," she sighed dramatically. "Don't you want 5 million people to hear it?"

Yes, the story may be romantic, but on reflection I found that I really did not want to join the undignified ranks of the talk-show freaks haunting the sets of Sally, Oprah, Maury, and all the rest. They finally let me go when I promised to consider the offer overnight. Sure enough, Sunday afternoon Amber called. By then my husband was manning the phones, and her powers of persuasion got her nowhere.

So the alleged 5 million viewers will miss out on at least one honest story dis-   25
honestly obtained. These days we talk so much about the invasion of privacy visited on the rich and famous. But what about the rest of us?

━━━━━━━━━━━━━━━━━━━━━━━━━━━━━━━━━━━━

RESPOND ●

1. What was your reaction to Felten's account of her "taxicab confession"? Was her experience what you imagine being "discovered . . . on HBO" to be like? Why or why not? Were you surprised by the last paragraph of her essay? Why or why not? Why do you think Felten confessed in writing for the readers of *Weekly Standard* after refusing to be videotaped? Are there any contradictions in such a choice?

2. Was the privacy of Felten and her friends violated by HBO? Why or why not? Should the situation of Felten, who told her story, be considered different from those of her friends, who said little? Should they (collectively or each) have been given $500 even if Felten did not sign the release? Why or why not?

3. How does Felten use dialogue in developing her argument? Which parts of the argument are developed by dialogue? Which parts are developed by summarizing what was in fact said? Why do you think Felten sometimes uses dialogue and sometimes uses summary? If Felten had used only summary or only dialogue throughout, how would her argument have been different?

4. Should "the rich and famous" be treated differently from "the rest of us" when it comes to matters of privacy? Under what circumstances? On the basis of what criteria? **Write an invitational argument** in which you explore the situation of these two groups by considering the similarities and differences between the two groups with respect to matters of privacy. (As you'll recall from Chapter 1, invitational arguments are those that invite the reader to explore the complexity of an issue; although the writer may ultimately take or defend a position, the argument is characterized by respect for all parties involved.)

Cathy Guisewite's cartoon strip *Cathy* has been syndicated for more than twenty years and appears today in some 1,400 newspapers worldwide. This cartoon appeared in July 1999. The main character, Cathy, is the quintessential single, heterosexual "modern woman" who works hard to keep up with fashion and technology; much of her appeal lies in readers' ability to identify with her frailties, misgivings, and responses to the conflicting demands she feels in her life.

This cartoon could certainly be considered a visual argument, yet we never actually *see* Laura and Phillip's web page. Do you wish we could, or are we seeing everything we need to see? See Chapter 15 for more information about analyzing and constructing visual arguments.

LINK TO P. 251

1. Compare what Jennifer Ringley does on her JenniCam Web site with what Laura and Phillip do on their wedding Web page. (Ringley's Web site is discussed in her essay, "Why I Star in My Own *Truman Show*" (p. 465); the introductory note gives the webcam's URL.) What are the differences? What are the similarities? What different questions do these two uses of the Internet raise about issues of privacy? (Hint: whose privacy is being invaded in each case—that of the watcher or the watched? Why?)

2. In what ways are Web pages arguments? What sorts of arguments are they? **Write an essay** in response to these questions. If you have a personal Web page, consider how you decided what to put on it. Who do you expect goes to your page? Whom would you like to have viewing your page? Why? If you do not have your own Web page, write about the pages of others that you find on the Web. (You might want to review Chapter 16, "Arguments in Electronic Environments.")

The Accountability Matrix

DAVID BRIN

David Brin describes himself on his Web site as a "noted futurist." In this chapter from his 1998 book The Transparent Society, Brin advocates the use of technology to increase scrutiny of government and business officials as well as private citizens. Elsewhere in his book, he argues that placing surveillance cameras everywhere is the only path to true freedom. As you read, think about the relationship Brin seeks to establish with his audience and the kind of ethos he creates through his text.

> No man is so fond of freedom himself that he would not chuse to subject the will of some individuals of society to his own.
> —Oliver Goldsmith, *The Vicar of Wakefield*

In 1996 the famed muckraker and consumer advocate Ralph Nader was the presidential candidate of California's Green Party. At one point, after lecturing earnestly about the need to hold corporate officials accountable for every nefarious transaction and scheme, Nader was asked why he refused to publish his own financial records, as all other candidates had done. Without irony, Nader replied that his own bank and tax statements were private, and by refusing to comply he was making an important gesture for liberty. This despite the fact that he was running for the most powerful office in the land, and the one most urgently in need of relentless scrutiny.

Such unidirectionality of righteousness, so typical of our era, illustrates how people can be trusted to hold their foes accountable but are seldom as scrupulous in applying the same standards to themselves.

Information can flow in various ways that provoke people subjectively and powerfully, depending on their point of view. For instance, self-interest attracts us to any new development that increases our power to see others, especially our opponents, the better to observe their actions and stratagems. It is quite another matter when something comes along that makes *us* more naked and visible to our foes! Consider how this is illustrated in the following matrix.

1. TOOLS THAT HELP **ME** SEE WHAT **OTHERS** ARE UP TO	2. TOOLS THAT PREVENT **OTHERS** FROM SEEING WHAT *I* AM UP TO
3. TOOLS THAT HELP **OTHERS** SEE WHAT *I* AM UP TO	4. TOOLS THAT PREVENT **ME** FROM SEEING WHAT **OTHERS** ARE UP TO

Now, where it says "others," go ahead and insert some person or group, such as "government" or "aristocrats" or "corporations"—perhaps your worst foe, or whomever you perceive as a dangerous power center in the world. You are likely to call "good" any device, law, or technical advancement that enhances the effectiveness of categories 1 and 2. In contrast, whatever comes along that increases the effectiveness of 3 and 4 may raise your discomfort level, if not ire.

Illustrating this, EFF° cofounder John Gilmore has been outspoken about restricting government's ability to conceal (through tools like FOIA),° while also curbing its ability to see (by promoting encryption and denying the FBI court-ordered access to the coded communications of suspected criminals).

> The US government attracts a lot of people who like wielding power. We limit the power of our government for the health of our society. . . . We've seen what happens when states get those powers. We get governments that can't be voted out of office, that must be run out with guns; administrations that torture people, dictators who steal from their citizens. We get reigns of terror, inquisitions, star chambers, political prisoners, J. Edgar Hoovers.

Gilmore's statement sounds prudent. Government *does* attract the power hungry (though so do other walks of life). But historically, the ability of governments to oppress has always depended on maintaining a *one-way* flow of information. Kings, tyrants, and parties in power above all concealed things from the citizenry at large. In contrast, one would be hard pressed to show that restricting the amount of information flowing *to* government has more than a marginal impact on preventing the arrival of tyranny.

In fact, there is a vivid counterexample: *us*. Despite uncountable 5 flaws in our contemporary neo-Western world, there has never been a major urban society in which individuals of all social classes had more freedom than we do today. This is true despite the fact that our government knows far more about its citizens than any other in history. The one factor making this possible has been reciprocity of information flow.

Each time government acquired new powers of sight, citizens seized another tool for enforcing transparency and accountability *from* government. From open-meeting laws, to special prosecutors and

---

EEF (Electronic Frontier Foundation): nonprofit, non-partisan organization founded in 1990 that seeks to protect the rights of individuals, especially with regard to issues of censorship and freedom of expression in cyberspace.

FOIA (Freedom of Information Act): 1966 legislation that helped dismantle governmental secrecy; under FOIA, anyone can request copies of information held by any U.S. government agency.

conflict-of-interest prosecutions, to whistleblower protections, to financial disclosure codes and the vaunted FOIA, we have (so far) successfully used such tools to thwart the potential of tyranny that is inherent in any coercive bureaucratic system. Moreover, this was accomplished not by blinding our officials but by granting them the vision they claimed to need, and then insisting that they walk around (metaphorically) naked, observed, supervised, and forced to account for each marginal abuse of power.

Chastened by the Watergate experience, citizens seem to know almost instinctively that it is better to shine too much light than too little. Witness the so-called scandals that have transfixed U.S. news media in recent years. Would any past Speaker of the House have received so much attention for minor improprieties as Newt Gingrich° did for letting a Republican think tank pay for a minor lecture course? In former times, would anyone have bothered a First Lady for firing some members of the White House travel office?° And yet, I am not saying that lesser peccadilloes should be dismissed! Increased scrutiny and raising of standards may irk public officials who as a consequence find themselves living in a searchlight glare, with minor infractions receiving the attention of felonies, but that seems a small price to pay for the vigilance freedom requires.

And the trend continues. As terrorists, criminals, and bombers go more high-tech and lethal, each new heinous act will prompt government appeals for greater surveillance powers. Perhaps citizens will refuse these requests nine times in a row—until something truly grievous happens. Then, in the ensuing dread and panic, a frightened public will grant those new powers. No indignant posturing or bleating about sacred privacy rights will prevent it.

But we can make sure baby won't be thrown out with the bath water, *by doing the same thing we've done all along.* By demanding that officials be scrutinized every bit as much as they scrutinize us.

Two millennia ago Juvenal° posed the riddle, "Who shall watch the 10 watchman?"

There is just one answer. We all will.

Going back to the accountability matrix, one can take almost any contemporary privacy issue and see people choosing different boxes, depending on their point of view. As Ralph Nader vividly illustrated,

Newt Gingrich: former Speaker of the U.S. House of Representatives (1943–) responsible for the "Contract with America" campaign that helped sweep him and many Republicans into power in the mid-1990s. Later in the decade, he was the subject of dozens of violation-of-ethics charges and was formally reprimanded by the House, the first Speaker to suffer this fate. He resigned from office in 1999.

First Lady . . . firing some members of the White House travel office: this phrase alludes to a 1993 scandal that arose when then First Lady Hillary Clinton was accused of having played a role in the firing of seven aides in the White House travel office; five of the seven were later reinstated. A later investigation exonerated her of any criminal wrongdoing.

Juvenal: the most famous of Roman satiric poets (AD 55?–127?) who was banished to a remote province of the empire when he criticized the influence court favorites had on the emperor, Domitian.

Brin mentions Internet flaming and personal attacks as obstacles for genuine liberty and freedom of speech. See Chapter 16 for some key points to remember when you participate in arguments in electronic environments.

·······················LINK TO P. 282

CDA (Communications Decency Act): 1995 legislation, later ruled unconstitutional, that sought to control telecommunications facilities, and hence broadcast media and the Internet, with respect to material that might be considered obscene and practices that might be considered harassing.

any effort either to restrict or open up a data spigot is judged good or evil subjectively. When we enhance our own "privacy," this may be seen by others as a sneaky attempt to keep them in the dark, a conspiratorial veil that might conceal threats to their liberty.

Nowhere is this tendency more apparent than on the Internet, where the semi-official dogma is openness and liberty, but where unpopular opinions are often greeted with vicious attacks and masked retribution. *Wired* magazine columnist Jon Katz posed the problem in October 1996: "What exactly does freedom of speech mean here? Are we only to post opinions that young, angry males like, or things we all agree are politically correct?" Describing the behavior of many "netizens" whose subjective ethics fit the accountability matrix perfectly, Katz complained that: "Freedom of speech seems to mean we get to say whatever we want whenever we want. If people don't like it, tough. But hostility, personal attacks, and flaming, have, in some ways, already done more harm than the CDA° (Communications Decency Act) ever could."

Is this inevitable? Does human nature have to conflict with maturity and good sense?

Each of us would *personally* call boxes 1 and 2 good, and boxes 3 and 4 bad. But if our aim is to live in a society that is fair and free, the tools needed by our commons will be those favoring boxes 1 and 3, enhancing our ability to hold others accountable, and their ability to do the same to us.

The most dangerous trends, laws, and technologies are those promoting boxes 2 and 4, pitting citizens against one another in an arms race of masks, secrets, and indignation.

RESPOND●

1. What is Brin's attitude toward his audience? Would you, for example, characterize him as friendly or antagonistic? Does he establish himself as someone who identifies with his readers or as someone who sets himself apart? Give evidence for your assessment.

2. How does the 2 x 2 matrix that Brin incorporates into the chapter function as part of his argument? What functions does the matrix serve? For example, try to imagine examples of each of the four scenarios he describes. How would his argument have been different if he had not included this matrix?

3. Look back at paragraph 13, where Brin quotes *Wired* columnist Jon Katz as claiming that "freedom of speech seems to mean we get to say whatever we want whenever we want. If people don't like it, tough. But hostility, personal attacks, and flaming, have, in some ways, already done more harm than the CDA (Communications Decency Act) ever could." To what extent is Katz's criticism of "hostility, personal attacks, and flaming" similar to Michael Perry's criticism of "No Fear" in "Bumper-Sticker Bravado: Fear This" (p. 451)? How do both of these critiques concern the nature of privacy in this society? **Write an essay** in which you discuss privacy as freedom *from* certain kinds of expression.

chapter twenty-five

Time Off, Time Out

We Americans (or most of us anyway) like to think that our time off belongs to us: for a while, at least, we're free from work and bosses and a million other things. In fact, we generally see time off as an escape, a time out, a time when the problems of daily life fade into the background. But do they? The arguments in this chapter dare us to admit the obvious: like it or not, leisure activities cannot help but become arenas in which larger social issues play themselves out.

College athletics isn't just about having a good time, for the spectators or the players. In our society today, college athletics raises questions about gender equity: does supporting women's athletics mean denying male athletes a chance to play? From a different perspective, many college basketball players have to decide whether to gamble their collegiate eligibility against the possibility of being a first-round NBA draft pick. It is a choice that often comes down to dollars and common sense, though it also means leaving college without a degree. Other leisure-time activities are no less problematic. Movies full of carefully placed commercial products, so wittily satirized in *The Truman Show,* force us to question what the effects of such marketing might be. Public responses tend to be decidedly pro or con—product placement is great or horrible, Title IX is necessary or discriminatory. Are there alternatives to this sort of zero-sum thinking that assumes that if one side "wins," the other side has to "lose"?

The chapter comprises two clusters of readings. The first, "Grappling with the Implications of Title IX," examines what Title IX has and has not achieved with regard to gender equity in college sports since its passage in 1972. It considers the law's most contested repercussion, the reduction of athletic programs for men at some colleges, but goes further to examine some Title IX victories as well as areas where the progress seems much too limited. The readings in the second cluster, "Havin' a Good Time, or Just Chasin' the Benjamins?" scrutinize the way that cultural, media, and sporting events have increasingly become marketing opportunities. It may be time off, but it seems there's no time out from bigger social issues.

The arguments in this cluster ask you to consider critically the state of affairs brought about by a simple and seemingly clear federal policy enacted in 1972 known as Title IX. The policy states, "No person in the United States shall, on the basis of sex, be excluded from participation in, be denied benefits of, or be subjected to discrimination under any education program or activity receiving Federal assistance . . ." and then goes on to list a number of exceptions. Since that time, college athletes and sports fans have been **grappling with the implications of Title IX.** Nearly 30 years later, we're still arguing about the rules, their nature and extent, and even the goals of the games. In fact, the controversy has only continued to heat up since 1996, when changes to the law required that colleges and universities make public the participation rates of female and male students and the funding allotted to sports for each sex. Subsequent guidelines have given rise to even more debate.

The cluster begins with Ruth Conniff's defense of Title IX, "The Joy of Women's Sports," in which she bases her claims on the results of Title IX for women. Conniff's very positive view is followed by three perspectives on the increasingly common practice of reducing the number of men's sports teams in order to comply with Title IX guidelines. Welch Suggs, in "Colleges Consider Fairness of Cutting Men's Teams," Peter Monaghan, in "Dropping Men's Teams to Comply with Title IX," and Kate O'Beirne, in "Preferences for Women Hurting Athletic Programs for Males," weigh in with different perspectives on this practice. As the titles make clear, attitudes cannot be predicted by the author's sex. These arguments are likewise interesting because of the ways in which they support their claims, sometimes using the same statistics to different ends.

Leslie Heywood's essay, "Despite Positive Rhetoric about Women's Sports, Female Athletes Face a Culture of Sexual Harassment," argues that sexual harassment is still all too common an experience for female athletes in the United States. The texts about Title IX come from two popular magazines, the *Nation* and *National Review,* and from the *Chronicle of Higher Education,* a weekly newspaper reporting on items of interest to college and university administrators and professors. As should be clear, the *Chronicle*'s sports page is less about who's winning and losing than about issues of all kinds affecting college athletics. The cluster concludes with four cartoons commenting on the 1999 U.S. victory in the women's World Cup, an event that some commentators see as the fruit of Title IX. These cartoons remind us of the ways that current affairs become the stuff of arguments in the press and in the popular imagination.

As the introduction to this chapter promised, these arguments force us to recognize that leisure time activities often become arenas for much larger social struggles. Title IX and its enforcement raise numerous issues about the meaning and nature of fairness, the rights and responsibilities of government to engage in what some consider social engineering, and the remedying of past injustice.

Whatever we think about the implications of Title IX, one thing is clear: the final score isn't in.

▼ *This article appeared in a 1998 issue of the* Nation, *a weekly magazine of political analysis and commentary that takes a liberal point of view. Using specific assertions about women's participation in sports, Ruth Conniff, Washington editor for the* Progressive, *makes a general argument about the role of sports in U.S. society. Conniff's writing style is rich in descriptive detail. As you read, pay attention to how word choice enhances her argument.*

The Joy of Women's Sports

A Whole Generation of Girls Knows It's Not How a Body Looks, It's What It Can Do

RUTH CONNIFF

It has been my generation's great good fortune to grow up in the era of Title IX. Never before has a single law made it possible for so many previously disfranchised people to have so much fun. Since Title IX of the Education Amendments Act passed in 1972, requiring publicly funded schools to offer equal opportunities to male and female athletes, the number of American high school girls who play sports has jumped from one in twenty-seven to one in three. The effects are visible everywhere: an explosion of female Olympic stars, college and professional women's teams playing to packed stadiums, new magazines aimed at female athletes. But most of all, the effect of Title IX is evident in the freedom, strength and joy of a whole generation of young women.

In June I went to Buffalo, New York, to watch the NCAA track championships with Kamila Hoyer-

Weaver, a young woman I coached when she was a high school runner, and her mother, Joan.

"What must it be like to get this far—to be ready at this level?" Joan mused, as we stood near the starting line before the women's 1,500-meter race. College runners in ponytails and racing flats were doing their warmup strides and nervously shaking out their legs. Behind us, a high jumper made the best attempt of the meet so far, and the stands erupted in cheers.

"For women my age it's a foreign thing to understand this competition," she said. "We weren't even raised to be competitive."

Kamila, a freshman at the University of Wisconsin, has an entirely different point of view. She came to watch her teammates who have made it to this elite level—some of the best athletes in the country. She has been steeped in competition, as a high school 5 runner and basketball player, and now as part of a Division I college program.

I watched Kamila and her friends grow up during the six years I spent coaching runners at nearby Madison East High School—my alma mater. It was a joy to see those saucer-eyed kids on the starting line, pale and sometimes sick with nerves, propel themselves into accomplished, self-assured womanhood. This, it seems to me, is the whole project of adolescence—testing yourself, facing your fears, discovering what you can do. Sports provide the natural arena for it. Instead of turning inward, nurturing the crippling self-consciousness that often afflicts adolescent girls, these female athletes thrust themselves into the world. Along the way, they shed some of their peer group's cloying affectations and picked up an appealing jocky swagger. Kamila blossomed from a shy back-of-the-packer to a consistent varsity scorer in cross-country and track. At the end of her high school career, I traveled with her to the state meet where she ran a lifetime best in the 800, taking eighth place at 2:20.14. Now, she is reaching the next stage.

"She gets to run with the big girls," Kamila said admiringly of Kathy Butler, the NCAA cross-country champion from Wisconsin. The "big girls" are a group of Olympic hopefuls, including the famous Suzy Favor Hamilton, UW graduates who still train full time with their former college coach, Peter Tegen. "It's inspiring to see them on the track with us," Kamila says.

At Wisconsin, Kamila is in the center of women's track history. Coach Tegen, who founded the Wisconsin women's program twenty-five years ago, has nurtured a series of Olympians, beginning with Cindy Bremser, Wisconsin's first female All-American. In a speech at our girls' city banquet one year, Bremser told us how she began jogging for exercise in college and ended up at the Olympics, where she took fourth in the 1,500 meters in 1984.

"The talent that was developed while I was at Wisconsin has had an impact on the rest of my life," she said. "It's opened doors for me that I never would have dreamed of."

In the eighties, when I was running for East, Suzy 10 Favor was starting her career on one of our rival teams, Steven's Point Area High School. She and her teammates would warm up together, a pack of fierce-looking girls with French braids and black-and-red windsuits. At the start of each race their fans chanted "SPASH! SPASH! SPASH!" Their coach blew a horn you could hear for miles as his runners came charging over hills and through the woods. Favor, who was a rocket even then, went on to become the four-time NCAA champion in the 1,500 and the American record-holder in the 1,000 meters.

All this is ancient history to Kamila, who is well beyond the gee-whiz era of women's sports. She takes it for granted that there is a long line of female champions in whose footsteps she can follow. She says her heroes are Amy Wickus, a 1995 graduate of Wisconsin and the indoor collegiate record-holder in the 800 (2:01.65), Hazel Clark of Florida, this year's winner of the outdoor NCAA women's 800 (2:02.16) and Michael Jordan ("but I guess he's everybody's hero").

After the meet, back at the hotel, she talks with ABC track commentators Carol Lewis, the Olympic long jumper, and Dan O'Brien, Olympic gold medalist in the decathlon. It's nice to see how easily she moves among these female and male stars. For much of the weekend, she has been hanging out with Gabe Jennings, her classmate from high school, now a freshman at Stanford. Gabe took second in the men's 1,500 and made the national news. The day before his final race, he was sitting in the stands with Kamila and her mom, watching the men's and women's races, trading track stories.

One of the best things about the rise of women's sports is the friendship and camaraderie it engenders between boys and girls. In track and other individual sports, male and female athletes travel together, support each other and have fun as a team. Because the goal of each athlete is to improve his or her own best performance, and because men and women go through the same workouts and races, there is a feeling of equality.

"It's easier to build friendships with guys who do track," says Avrie Walters, Kamila's teammate, who made it to the 1,500 trials at the nationals. "There's a kind of respect," Stephanie Pesch, another Wisconsin runner, adds. "It's like they understand what you've achieved."

"I like it, even if you're just training at the track 15 and the guys yell for you," says Kamila.

At East High, the boys' and girls' cross-country runners were particularly close. They took turns hosting spaghetti dinners at their houses before meets. They ran along the course to cheer for each other during races. When both teams won the city meet, they did a victory dance together, beating on drums some of the boys had brought along, hopping around the finish chute, forming a crazy, mismatched can-can line and swinging each other by the arms in a spontaneous outburst of celebration.

These moments of coeducational enthusiasm are part of what's precious to me about my own experience in sports. Both in college and in a postcollegiate track club, I made lifelong friends with the men and women I ran with, shared the ups and downs of training and competition, and partied afterward. Hearing the encouraging words of my male track coaches, seeing my male teammates pound each other on the back and yell when my female teammates and I sprinted across the finish line to win, made an indelible impression on me. To the great benefit of us all, sports have changed how men look at women, and how women view themselves.

That's not to say there's no more conflict between the sexes when it comes to sports.

The *Washington Post* ran a story recently about the forty-six-year-old World Series for boys, which the Babe Ruth League is holding this August in Loudoun County, Virginia. In keeping with a musty tradition, tournament organizers have been advertising for local teenage girls to be "hostesses" to escort the players, entertain them and cheer for them during the tournament. Each girl, the *Post* reported, is supposed to wear a kind of modified baseball uniform with a skirt.

This idea went over like a ton of bricks with the 20 female high school athletes of Loudoun County.

"You can consider me a feminist . . . when they told me about that, I said 'Nope,'" Brooke Hoeltzel, a junior at Loudoun Valley High School, said. "A lot of my friends are athletes, and they have the same view I did."

Tournament organizers were quoted blaming the culture of Washington, with all its professional women, for the problems their hostess-recruitment effort encountered. "In Kentucky and Arkansas it does fine," said Erik Zimmerman, who heads the Loudoun organizing committee for the boys' World Series.

But girls like Hoeltzel say they don't have time to jump around in a little skirt. They have their own summer-league games to play. After getting a taste of playing, it seems, there's no going back.

"I'm an athlete," Hoeltzel told me. "I'm not a cheerleader, I know that. This would make me a cheerleader."

"What's the big difference?" I ask. 25

"With an athlete I think of an equal, a guy and a girl," she says. "And with a cheerleader it's sitting on the sidelines. I'm not one to sit there and watch."

Joy Miller, a Loudoun County mother of two daughters, ages 9 and 12, agrees. Her 9-year-old, who plays fast-pitch ball in a 10-and-under league, has been hitting and catching since she was 4. And both girls are now trying out for a summer travel team. They've been all fired up since they attended a clinic put on by Olympic softball player Dot Richardson.

"My daughters would rather be out swinging a bat than being a hostess for the boys," Miller told me.

When I get hold of Erik Zimmerman on the phone, he sounds weary from the media attention his event has been getting, first from the *Post,* then from the local television stations. "It's interesting, they've all been women interviewing me," he says dryly. He wants to set the record straight: For one thing, the hostess uniforms are not skirts. "We figured out a long time ago that skirts were not appropriate. After all, they're going to a ball game. So what they're wearing are skorts," he says.

Skorts?   30

"It's a pair of shorts that look like a skirt."

I try to picture the girl athletes' reaction to this.

Zimmerman seems nice enough. He tells me about his 15-year-old daughter, who played three sports last year. "I'm the last person to denigrate women's sports," he says. But when I ask him if the Babe Ruth League has considered adding a girls' program, he says no. "I don't think girls are interested in playing baseball."

In spite of the boom in women's sports, a backlash is brewing against Title IX. Opponents of the law say it forces schools to cut men's programs in order to give women money and facilities they don't want or need.

Earlier this year, John Stossel of ABC's *20/20* 35 offered one tale of the ravages of what he called "the equality police." At the Merritt Island High School in Florida, he reported, the boys' baseball team had a stadium with lights, bleachers, a concession stand and fancy scoreboard. The girls' softball team had a field just the other side of a locked fence, with patchy grass and no lavatories. Two softball players, Jennifer and Jessica Daniels, sued the school board for discrimination under Title IX.

"So the school board proposed a solution," Stossel intoned. "They would unplug the boys' scoreboard, shut down the concession stand and the press box and rope off the bleachers so no one could sit here. That would make things equal."

This scorched-earth response was not what the girls had in mind, of course. Stossel didn't bother to explain that their lawyer, Lisa Tietig of the ACLU, argued that it was unconstitutional to rope off the bleachers, since this would be discriminating against the boys. A judge agreed, and the boys got to keep their facilities.

I talked to Tietig after the *20/20* show aired. "I was so mad about that," she said. "It really distorted things. And of course everyone would hate the girls after seeing it."

The lawsuit, which has expanded to include all of the public schools in the county, is not scheduled for trial until the year 2000. But already for the girls in Merritt Island, the results of their legal action have been good. The school took down the locked fence between the boys' and girls' fields, so the girls and their fans can use the toilets. (Before the lawsuit, according to Tietig, the school had refused to consider unlocking the fence.) The school board paid for outdoor lights for the girls, and the community arranged to buy the girls a scoreboard and fix the grass. "The kids on the boys' and girls' teams have banded together," says Tietig. "And the parents of both teams helped each other out. They've been down on their hands and knees weeding the girls' field. It's a lot better."

In general, parents no longer accept the idea that 40 their sons deserve a better shot at sports than their daughters. That is the transformative effect of Title IX.

Still, according to Billie Jean King, who started the Women's Sports Foundation when she retired from tennis, after twenty-five years schools have come only about halfway to compliance with Title IX. Overall, boys still have almost twice as many opportunities to play in school athletic programs as girls do.

"The Office of Civil Rights has been incredibly in-effective in executing its responsibility" to enforce the law, King writes in a foundation report. "Moms and dads are being forced to go to court and suffer the expense and animosity generated by such judicial solutions. While they have won their cases, it is clear that the promises of Title IX will not be realized in my lifetime if each school not in compliance must be taken to court to force them to 'do the right thing.' "

Lately, opponents of Title IX have been trying to persuade people that you can be in favor of girls' sports and still be against Title IX. Leo Kocher, a wrestling coach who heads the National Coalition for Athletics Equity, argued this case on *20/20.* "We're just perpetrating an awful thing against the men," he said. "We're saying we're punishing you because you have more interest in sports than women."

It's true that Division I colleges across the country have been eliminating men's minor sports, from wrestling to gymnastics to baseball. And many coaches blame Title IX. But budget figures from the colleges don't support the argument that women's teams are the cause. The NCAA's latest gender-equity study shows that budget increases over the past five years for Division I-A men's sports was more than three times larger than the increase for women. More important, at the same time that Division I-A colleges have been cutting minor men's teams, spending on the big programs—mainly football—has increased dramatically.

Sixty-three percent of the $1.7 million increase in 45 funding for Division I-A men's sports over the past five years went to football. Just that extra money for football exceeded the total operating budget for *all* Division I-A women's sports combined.

"The real problem is that schools are refusing to hold the line on men's football and basketball budgets," says Donna Lopiano, executive director of the Women's Sports Foundation.

Football is the Pentagon of athletic department budgets. Big schools continue to pour the bulk of their money into it, leaving the other, small-budget sports to fight it out over the scraps.

Interestingly, the smaller Division II and III schools have actually added men's teams over the same period that Division I schools have been cutting them. As a result, men's participation in college sports is at an all-time high. When you count all men's teams in all divisions, men have seen a net increase of seventy-four teams since the advent of Title IX. "The poor schools are adding sports for men," Lopiano says. "The richest schools are dropping sports. Why? Because they're fueling the football monster."

Schools have a lot of control over how they allo-cate their sports budgets. And, contrary to popular belief, Title IX does not require that girls get the exact number of slots on a team as boys, nor the same amount of funding. Instead, it gives schools three options for meeting the requirements of the law. They can show (1) that female athletes are getting an opportunity to play sports proportional to their rep-resentation in the student population; or (2) that, even if female athletes are underrepresented, the school is making progress by gradually expanding the female sports program; or (3) that, even if female athletes are underrepresented, women and girls are getting as much opportunity to play as their interests demand.

It's a shame to see men's and women's minor 50 sports pitted against each other, because they have a lot in common. They are less about entertainment for sedentary fans than about participation. They are more inclusive than the big-time, quasi-professional programs. And they are subversive in a way, because they are driven by something other than the values of the market. You often hear the word "pure" bandied about to describe college women's teams. It's part of their charm that, as in minor men's programs, the athletes are playing for the love of it, not because they're raising revenue or planning on a multi-million-dollar professional career.

"Sports are the laboratory of the human spirit," says Anson Dorrance, the coach of one of the winningest teams in women's soccer, the University of North Carolina Tar Heels. He says he's learned to enjoy his sport more by coaching the women's game. In his book, *Training Soccer Champions,* he talks about how his coaching style has evolved. As a men's coach at UNC for thirteen years, Dorrance says, he used a lot of negative techniques, yelling at and bullying his athletes, waging a constant battle of egos with his players. "You basically have to drive men, but you can lead women," he writes. "And, in my opinion, the way you coach women is a more civilized mode of leadership."

Dorrance's female athletes responded badly to bullying, which forced him to become a more reasonable coach. On the flip side, he had to teach his players to overcome their training as girls to be sweet and passive. "They have this internal war going on between wanting to prove they are great soccer players and the social agenda of wanting to be accepted by the group," Dorrance writes of his younger players. "So when they go into direct confrontation with a veteran, it's almost like they feel they have to acquiesce."

To drill this out of his players, Dorrance throws them into what he calls a "competitive cauldron" at practice: "They sort of beat it into each other that it's okay to compete."

Clearly his athletes have got the message, winning national championship after national championship. Some have gone on to the world-champion US women's team, including April Heinrichs, the US team's assistant coach in 1996.

"I think women bring something incredibly positive to athletics," Dorrance told me. "They are won-

55

derfully coachable and so appreciative of anything you give them. If men could draw something from the women's model, their image would improve."

Out of the interaction of male and female athletes and coaches arises the prospect of a better approach to sports, and to life. That's good news not just for women but also for men. My colleague at East High, Ty Prosa, who switched from being a boy's coach to coaching the girls' track team, says this about his experience: "With boys, the old-fashioned idea is that coaches give orders, and the athletes are supposed to accept it. You're like a drill sergeant in the Marines. Girls have more questions. I was unprepared to deal with this questioning at first. It took me a lot of effort to overcome my feeling that it was a challenge to my authority. But now I really enjoy coaching girls. I'm more invested in their success, because they give me more feedback, and I've become a better coach."

Sports bring out the most fundamental parts of human nature. There's the potential for cruelty, cowardice and unethical behavior, as in any other social sphere. But sports can also put us in touch with the greatest parts of being human — our own courage, compassion and capacity for the sheer physical enjoyment of life.

The happiness and freedom sports bring us, as participants, is a radical notion in consumer culture.

Conniff makes extensive use of interviews, which she incorporates into her article as informal dialogue. See more about doing your own interviews in Chapter 18.

LINK TO P. 301 ·······························

There's all that pleasure to be had, from ourselves and each other, without buying anything. That potential slips away when, instead of participants, we become only spectators. We let professional athletes become stand-ins for ourselves. Games become a stand-in for war.

But sport is not war. It's just play. And the more we play, the better we are.   ∎

RESPOND ●

1. List the main points in Conniff's argument; then look at the various kinds of evidence she uses to support them — statistics, personal testimony, interviews with authorities, and so on. Which kind of evidence do you find most convincing — and why? Which kind does Conniff seem to favor or rely on most heavily? How might the article have appealed to a different audience if some other kinds of evidence had been emphasized?

2. Conniff uses a combination of rhetorical appeals in her article — argument from the heart as well as arguments based on values, on character, and on facts and reason. What kind of argument leaves the most lasting impression on you? Do you think it works similarly for other readers as well? Give reasons for your judgment.

3. Conniff claims that "[o]ne of the best things about the rise of women's sports is the friendship and camaraderie it engenders between boys and girls" (paragraph 13). Do you agree? Why or why not? Do you think everyone would see this camaraderie as a good thing? Who might not — and why?

4. Notice the way Conniff's word choice supports her argument. Look back at the text to find several instances of effective word choice, including figurative language, and state why you think they are effective. (For more information on figurative language, see Chapter 14.)

5. Reread the quotations from high school athlete Brooke Hoeltzel (paragraphs 21–26), who suggests that cheerleading is less serious and less valuable than conventional competitive sports. Using your personal knowledge or experience, **write an essay** that argues the value of cheerleading as an athletic activity. Is it a worthwhile endeavor for female students? For male students? Why or why not?

▼ *Welch Suggs is a sportswriter for the* Chronicle of Higher Education, *a weekly paper covering issues of concern to college and university faculty and administrators. This article, which appeared in February 1999, discusses a then-pending court case involving the wrestling program at California State University at Bakersfield. (A preliminary injunction was later issued, prohibiting the university from cutting the team or any individual wrestlers.)*

Colleges Consider Fairness of Cutting Men's Teams to Comply with Title IX

Advocacy Groups, Colleges, and Lawyers Differ on Who Should Pay to Achieve Gender Equity

BY WELCH SUGGS

College coaches cut unskilled and unfit players from their teams every day. Almost everyone — except perhaps for the cut players — would say that's fair.

But what happens when a university cuts an entire team of male players to make room for women? Is that fair?

The question arises as athletics departments try to create an equitable situation for female athletes while preserving revenue streams from football and men's basketball. Making the number of female athletes proportional to the number of enrolled female students is one way that universities can comply with Title IX of the Education Amendments of 1972, the law that bars discrimination at institutions that receive federal aid.

Last week, the Board of Trustees at Miami University in Ohio delayed for two months a decision on whether to drop men's golf, tennis, soccer, and wrestling, moves that it is considering for financial as well as gender-equity reasons. Also last week, a federal judge in Illinois dismissed a suit that had been brought by former male soccer players and wrestlers at Illinois State University after it dropped their teams to meet gender-equity goals. And later this year, wrestlers at California State University at Bakersfield will go to court to argue that the university's decision to drop their sport to meet proportionality goals violates their rights under Title IX.

Activists, athletics directors, and government officials all take different sides on the issue. A coalition of conservative groups contends that is unfair to both men and women to cut men's sports for gender-equity reasons. Men are more likely to be interested in playing sports than women, they say, and depriving men of opportunities just to meet proportionality guidelines is, on its face, discriminatory. Activists for women's sports say athletics administrators are making bad decisions on how to spend money.

Government officials who enforce Title IX say that the rights of women to participate in college sports outweigh the rights of individual men to participate in particular sports. And administrators say their hands are tied by financial constraints. Many of them say they can't afford to add women's sports.

"I think almost everybody in higher education believes the goal of Title IX is worthy," says James C. Garland, Miami's president. "The controversy is whether the end justifies the means, and that's the battleground where this is being fought."

GRAPPLING WITH THE FUTURE

At center stage in this debate is Stephen Neal, a senior wrestler at Bakersfield. The defending national collegiate champion in the

489

heavyweight division, Mr. Neal clearly prefers physical battles to legal ones.

"I'd rather talk about what I'm going to do out there," Mr. Neal says, gesturing to a wrestling mat during a meet at American University, "than what's going on with the suit."

Mr. Neal, who is unde- 10 feated this season and ranked No. 1 in the National Collegiate Athletic Association, has a great deal invested in the team's lawsuit. Besides being the lead plaintiff in the case, he hopes to coach wrestling after graduation. As more and more universities cut wrestling to meet proportionality standards, his chances of finding a college job dwindle.

He also has seen a number of friends and roommates lose direction after being cut from Bakersfield's team. In 1995, before it decided to abolish the team altogether, the university ordered the team to reduce its roster from 37 to 27, according to the wrestlers' suit.

"Sometimes in wrestling, it takes a couple of years for guys to develop," Mr. Neal says. "But they're the ones who come into their junior and senior years and get really good. And those are the guys who were cut."

At Bakersfield, the impetus to achieve proportionality is even greater than at most universities. The Cal State system is operating under a five-year-old consent agreement with the California chapter of the National Organization for Women. The agreement, reached after Cal-NOW (as it is known) filed a lawsuit, requires the 20 institutions in the system that have athletics programs to bring their pro-

> ## "Almost everybody in higher education believes the goal of Title IX is worthy. The controversy is whether the end justifies the means, and that's the battleground."

portion of female athletes within 10 percentage points of the proportion of undergraduate female students by the 1998-99 academic year. The requirement in the settlement is not quite as strict as Title IX, which requires universities to have proportionality within five percentage points, a condition known as "substantial proportionality." But unlike Title IX, the California consent agreement offers no other ways to achieve compliance.

"They've made some really tough decisions," says Linda C. Joplin, chairwoman of Cal-NOW's athletics equity committee. "I think it's unfortunate . . . but from what I've seen, there are too many administrators who continue to pay for things like hotels for football than to pay for women in minor sports. It's a matter of priorities."

Citing the lawsuit, Bakersfield 15 athletics officials declined to comment for this story.

Other lawsuits that have challenged gender-equity decisions by universities have not been very successful. This month, for example, a federal court in Illinois dismissed a 1995 lawsuit against Illinois State University that had been brought by former soccer players and wrestlers whose sports were dropped to bring the university into compliance with Title IX.

The court cited its own 1993 decision in *Kelley v. Board of Trustees of the University of Illinois,* a case in which male swimmers sued the university for dropping their sport. "Under Title IX, the university could cut men's programs without violating the statute because men's interests and abilities are presumptively met when substantial proportionality exists," the decision states.

That presumption goes straight to the question of fairness. Why should courts and administrators presume that men's interests in competing in college sports are being met simply by providing them with opportunities proportional to their enrollment at a university? Curt A. Levey, a lawyer for the Center for Individual Rights, a non-profit law group that is representing the Bakersfield wrestling team, says that athletics is the only area in education in which quotas are permitted.

Should a university's nursing school, he wonders, be forced to enroll men in numbers proportional

Stephen Neal (top) is the lead plaintiff in a suit seeking to block California State U at Bakersfield from eliminating its wrestling team.

to their overall enrollment at the university?

Sports programs are different, 20 responds Mary Frances O'Shea, who oversees Title IX compliance in athletics for the U.S. Department of Education's Office for Civil Rights.

"Athletic programs are the only programs wherein schools can establish [teams] set aside for men and women," Ms. O'Shea says. "You can't have Algebra I-A for boys and Algebra I-B for girls, but in athletics, because of the nature of the program, you can." As such, rules must be in place to insure that men and women are treated equitably in athletics programs, Ms. O'Shea says.

Donna A. Lopiano, executive director of the Women's Sports Foundation, says the "easiest solution is to double your resources and give the women the same opportunities as the men." But there's only one problem: "How many schools can double revenues?"

HARD CHOICES

None can. At Miami, trustees will decide April 16 whether to cut soccer, golf, tennis, and wrestling.

Miami's sports program is huge, with 22 varsity teams, but its revenue sources are limited. And even with 11 women's teams, the university is not close to meeting proportionality standards. Women make up 55 per cent of Miami's undergraduate student body but only 45 per cent of campus athletes. To meet "substantial proportionality" mandates, at least 50 per cent of athletes should be women. Based on the number of 1997-98 participants in the threatened sports, dropping them would make the number of men and women playing on Redhawks teams roughly equal.

"We do not have the budget, at 25 present, to fund 22 sports adequately," Mr. Maturi says. "Not only do we not have the budget for 22 sports, but we can't meet gender equity."

EQUITY BY OTHER MEANS

Officials from the Office for Civil Rights insist that institutions like Miami have options besides proportionality.

"The beauty of Title IX is that it recognizes the fact . . . that there might not be proportionally as many people in one group who are interested in athletics as in another group," says Ms. O'Shea.

Universities have two other ways to comply with the law. Institutions can demonstrate a continuing history of expanding opportunities for women to play sports. Alternatively, a university can demonstrate that it is fully and effectively meeting the identified needs, abilities, and interests of women on the campus.

Those options aren't available to Bakersfield, though, because of the Cal-NOW consent decree. And Mr. Garland, Miami's president, says the other goals aren't financially feasible for a university like his. "We've tried to comply with federal law by the continuing practice of adding women's teams," he says. "But any school can only do that for so long, because any time you add a sport, you add additional expenses."

Still more women at Miami have 30 proposed adding additional sports, which proves that their interests are not being met. But Miami can't afford to add additional sports. That leaves participation, Mr. Garland says.

In cases like Bakersfield's, Ms. O'Shea doesn't think men who sue will have much of a case. "Title IX does not grant individuals the opportunity to participate in a particular sport," she says. "It doesn't look to individuals as such; it looks to the overall program."

That doesn't sit well with Kimberly Schuld, the manager of special projects for the Independent Women's Forum. It smacks of a government-sponsored quota, she says.

Despite Ms. O'Shea's thoughts, Mr. Neal and the other Bakersfield wrestlers may have some cause for optimism. A federal court in California has issued a restraining order preventing the university from forcing the team to cut wrestlers, and it has denied the university's motions to dismiss the case.

Everyone seems to agree that it is wrong for universities to cut men's teams. The question remains, however, whether providing equitable opportunities for women is right enough to supersede that wrong.

Although Suggs is writing about the present, his article could be interpreted as an argument about the future. See more about such arguments in Chapter 1.

·· LINK TO P. 12

RESPOND •

1. Suggs interviews people who take different positions on the controversy, but does he take a position himself—implicitly or explicitly? Give evidence for your answer.

2. In several places Suggs asserts a broad generalization about public opinion among "almost everyone": "Almost everyone—except perhaps for the cut players—would say that's fair. . . . Everyone seems to agree that it is wrong for universities to cut men's teams. . . . 'I think almost everybody in higher education believes the goal of Title IX is worthy'" (paragraphs 1, 34, and 7). (This last sentence is a quotation Suggs uses.) What is implied about those who disagree with "everyone"? What effect would the use of the qualifiers "everybody" or "almost everybody" have on an audience of people who disagree with Suggs's generalizations?

3. Can you find fallacies in Suggs's reasoning at any point? For example, does he imply that because Stephen Neal may not be able to find a job coaching wrestling at the university level, Neal deserves sympathy and perhaps legal redress? Do you think Suggs would be equally sympathetic to Latin or anthropology majors who can't find jobs? Find two or three fallacies in the text; for each one, tell what type of fallacy it is and why you think so. (You may want to review Chapter 19, "Fallacies of Argument.")

4. In "Bad As They Wanna Be" (p. 519), Thad Williamson claims that "[a] sad rite of passage for most college athletes is the existential realization that they will never make it to the pros," and he quotes former Florida State football player Sheray Gaffney as saying, "What was astonishing was the number of scars that [the program] left on athletes. . . . It was painful to see athletes crying in distress because they see their dreams slowly fading away" (paragraph 15). Does Gaffney's statement affect how you respond to Suggs's description of the emotional distress of the Bakersfield wrestlers who get cut from the team? Why or why not? Should it? How do you predict Williamson and Gaffney would respond to Suggs?

5. Suggs compares the gender imbalance in athletics programs with that in nursing programs, asking whether schools should be forced to admit men to nursing programs "in numbers proportional to their overall enrollment at the university." Do you think this question is genuine or is it posed for rhetorical effect? Do you think nursing and athletics programs should strive for such gender balance? Why or why not? **Write an essay** explaining your position.

▼ *This article appeared in December 1998 in the* Chronicle of Higher Education, *a weekly paper covering issues of concern to college and university faculty and administrators. Although Peter Monaghan can safely assume that his audience is familiar with Title IX,* NCAA *regulations, Division I, and other terms related to college sports, he spends time defining some terms for his readers. As you read, pay attention to where Monaghan defines familiar terms and how the definitions support his argument.*

Dropping Men's Teams to Comply with Title IX

PETER MONAGHAN

In colleges' long, slow march toward gender equity in their athletics programs, nothing is more certain to generate heat than dropping men's teams to free up money for women's teams.

Yet that is the tactic that many institutions have employed—Providence College, the latest among them.

Providence quickly was met by protests when, in October, it said it would drop three men's programs as part of a four-year plan to comply with federal gender-equity law. The law in question, Title IX of the Education Amendments of 1972, forbids institutions that receive federal funds from discriminating on the basis of sex.

For many years, supporters of men's teams that have been dropped have claimed that such decisions demonstrate the ravages wrought by Title IX.

In one typical outburst, a sports 5 columnist in Providence, R.I., had this to say about the college's recent cuts: "How crazy is it that, in order to create athletic opportunities for women, Providence College has had to take athletic opportunities away from men?"

He added: "Eliminating sports was never the intent of Title IX. But it has been the result."

The facts don't necessarily back up that argument, says Janet M. Justus, director of education outreach at the National Collegiate Athletic Association. "Cuts get the attention, but study might show that most schools have not cut programs to meet Title IX. Most have added programs."

A 1997 report by the Women's Sports Foundation showed that from 1978 to 1996, 853 men's programs in Division I had been dropped, and 927 added. Women certainly did gain: In the same period, 1,658 women's programs were added.

National data show that the number of men's teams has not shrunk, but some campuses, like Providence, have made cuts—usually with great reluctance, and significant pain.

Title IX requires colleges with 10 sports teams to offer programs for men and women that are roughly proportional to their representation in the student body. If 50 per cent of a college's students are women, about 50 per cent of its athletes should be, too. And if 50 per cent of a college's athletes are women, they should get about half of the institution's athletics-scholarship budget as well, according to the U.S. Educational Department's guidelines for carrying out the law.

In fulfilling the obligations of Title IX, Providence has one edge over many other institutions: It has no football team. Colleges typically must sponsor more teams for women to offset the large number of players on a football squad.

Still, Providence's compliance with Title IX was complicated by its demographics. Its student body is 57 per cent female and 43 per cent male.

A survey last spring by *The Chronicle* showed that 52 per cent of Providence's athletes were men, and that male athletes got 54 per cent of the college's athletics-scholarship money (*The Chronicle,* April 3). Like many colleges in the survey, Providence's numbers indicated that it was in violation of Title IX.

Because government enforcement of Title IX compliance has been lackadaisical, colleges have typically made changes in their sports programs in response to lawsuits, or threats of lawsuits.

Providence officials say their changes were motivated by another factor: an impending peer review as part of the N.C.A.A.'s certification process.

Starting in 1993, the association began a process in which colleges in Division I, its top competitive level, undergo periodic reviews of their compliance with a variety of rules, such as those on recruiting, as well as their fiscal and academic soundness.

In the first round of certification reviews, institutions had to have a program in place to advance their progress toward gender equity. By 1999, they must prove that they actually have made progress.

Almost 300 of the 307 Division I institutions have been inspected over the last five years, and all but one have been certified. Twenty-nine were certified with conditions, such as that they improve their gender-equity plans. N.C.A.A. officials say they don't know how many colleges stumbled over that requirement, but some did.

As their review approached, Providence officials knew they had a gender-equity problem. How to fix it was less clear.

They knew they needed to change the proportions of male and female athletes. They also had to come up with enough money to add scholarships for women, either by starting new teams or by giving more grants for existing women's teams.

John M. Marinatto, the college's assistant vice-president for athletics, says Providence officials knew that adding to the number of women's teams — a costly proposition — was not a viable option.

"It became apparent to us that we could not add funding to athletics, and that reallocation was our only path," he says.

Providence did weigh other options, such as withdrawing from the Big East Conference — to try to find a stable but less expensive competitive level. It rejected that step, even though some of its teams have struggled to compete in the league.

The university's president, the Rev. Philip A. Smith, says, "The decision to drop any of our sports teams was very difficult but very necessary, given the college's limited financial resources and our desire to continue offering student-athletes the opportunity to participate at the highest level of varsity athletic competition without compromising academic priorities."

Once Providence decided that it had no option but to drop men's teams, that still left tough decisions about which ones to cut.

Mr. Marinatto says that the only programs not considered for cuts were men's and women's basketball — teams that a college must field to remain in Division I. Everything else was on the table, he says.

Providence assessed its existing sports based on their financial viability, the likelihood of their staying competitive, and their contribution to keeping total sports participation as high as possible, a factor in drawing students.

In October, officials announced that Providence would drop baseball, golf, and men's tennis at the end of this academic year, a decision that will affect 57 male athletes who have been sharing the equivalent of just under 11 athletics grants. Those scholarships will be redistributed to members of existing women's teams in field hockey, ice hockey, soccer, or softball. But the male athletes aren't being entirely cut off. They will be free to remain at Providence until after their fourth year of enrollment, at the same level of financial support.

The changes will leave the college with 19 sports, eight for men and 11 for women. But within four years, the most important goal will have been attained: Providence's gender breakdown in sports, and its spending on athletics scholarships for women and men, will be in proportion to the female-male ratio of its student body.

Facts like those have not assuaged supporters of the men's programs that will be dropped. Nor have they consoled the male athletes on those teams.

The day Providence administrators announced their plans, they called a meeting of the affected athletes. The officials describe the meeting as emotional. Players were tearful and angry.

A few days later, 200 students rallied on the campus to show support for the athletes. Much of the support came from female athletes; the women's volleyball team, for instance, wore baseball jerseys in warm-ups for a match soon after the decision was announced.

Officials met with the captains of all sports programs to explain their quandary. Mr. Marinatto says they told the captains what they later told members of support groups for the three men's sports, who had no warning that their teams were at risk and rushed to the campus for answers. Says Mr. Marinatto: "We told them we were happy to revisit it, but we don't think there's something out there. We believe we've covered every base."

Supporters and coaches are still trying to come up with creative alternatives to dropping the teams.

Says Charlie Hickey, a baseball 35 coach at Providence for eight years: "I don't believe that, from an alumni standpoint, there is an acceptance of

this decision. There is a tremendous outpouring of support. Most of it is anger. They were never contacted or asked if they could be of help or service."

He remains hopeful that his program will be spared, but not optimistic. "Not only would we have to generate revenues to support the baseball program, but we'd also have to raise additional money for women, to still be in compliance" with Title IX, he says. Supporters of the 77-year-old baseball program have been told that the $300,000 needed each year to

keep baseball alive would be only 43 per cent of the total they must raise.

He and other supporters are trying to convince the college that cutting the programs would hurt Providence financially. The college is having trouble attracting male students, and almost all of his players are paying part or full tuition fees.

Realistically, he says, he knows that most of his players will now leave the college. All 16 freshman and sophomore students on his roster as of last summer have said they'll transfer elsewhere.

Monaghan knows that many university administrators and policy makers are a large part of his audience. How did he choose his evidence with those readers in mind? Check out the section on considering audiences in Chapter 18.

························· LINK TO P. 308

RESPOND •

1. What is Monaghan's position on Title IX compliance? How sure are you? How do you know?

2. Even though newspaper and magazine authors rarely write their own titles, those titles become part of the argument because the title is the first thing readers see and the thing that often attracts readers to read the article. In light of Welch Suggs's admission in the previous article (p. 489)—that many schools are cutting smaller men's teams to help support football programs—how accurate or fair is the title of Monaghan's article?

3. Three of the articles in this section—those by Suggs, Monaghan, and O'Beirne—make similar arguments, but they use different rhetorical techniques. Evaluate each article as an argument from the heart and as an argument based on value. Which article does the most effective job of each argument type? Present evidence for your evaluation.

4. Read Ruth Conniff's article on "The Joy of Women's Sports" (p. 482). Consider how Conniff's and Monaghan's word choices create very different pictures of the effects of Title IX. Choose one passage in each article and change the language to create a more neutral impression, making as few changes as possible. Describe what you did and explain why.

5. **Write a letter** to the president of Providence College, supporting his decision or urging him to take a different course of action (be specific about your suggestion). Give reasons and evidence for your position.

▼ *This article appeared in 1997 in the* National Review, *a weekly magazine of political commentary that bills itself as "America's Conservative Magazine." As you read, think about Kate O'Beirne's use of humor and what it contributes to her argument.*

Preferences for Women Hurting Athletic Programs for Males

KATE O'BEIRNE

Opponents of race-based preferences are winning in the courts, but, thanks to the Clinton Administration, sex-based preferences have triumphed in the gym. In the name of "gender equity," colleges belonging to the NCAA have cut 20,900 male athletes from team rosters over the past five years. Male wrestling and gymnastics programs face extinction. Although eliminating men's teams does not improve athletic opportunities for women, a 25-year-old antidiscrimination initiative imposes strict quotas on collegiate playing fields.

Back when the Equal Rights Amendment was wending its way through the state legislatures, Congress approved Title IX of the Education Amendments of 1972, which prohibited sexual discrimination in federally assisted education programs. There's little evidence of discrimination in education today. The majority of students in college now are women, and women earn the majority of masters' degrees. But the feminists are not content.

The problem is that, while enjoying enormous educational success, women are not playing sports to the same extent as men: The number of female athletes has increased dramatically since the early Seventies, when young women were not encouraged to play competitive sports and only 300,000 high-school girls did. In my all-girl high school, neatly

pressed gym uniforms were the priority for our teacher, who presided over the class in stockings and heels. Apparently, ironing was thought to contribute to our physical fitness. One of my sisters abandoned competitive swimming when our mother pointed out that large shoulders would look terrible in evening clothes.

Today 2.4 million high-school girls enjoy the benefits of competitive sports. However, in both high school and college, the proportion of female students playing competitively has, after an initial surge, leveled off to less than 40 per cent. A sensible person might conclude that this reflects women's natural inclination to be less interested in sports. After all, men made up 60 per cent of the TV audience for the women's NCAA basketball finals. And female students are plenty engaged in other activities. Studies show that high-school girls are more involved than boys in nonsports extracurricular activities like choir, band, and debate and drama clubs.

Despite the evidence that women now freely 5
engage in sports in proportion to their interest, federal courts and the Clinton Administration are forcing colleges to eliminate men's teams in order to create an even ratio in male and female athletics.

The National Women's Law Center celebrated the 25th anniversary of Title IX by filing complaints with the Department of Education against 25 universities whose athletic teams don't have the same male–female ratios as the student body. (Who says girls can't do math?) The Department's own enforcement policies and a recent case involving Brown University will force colleges to adopt a strict proportionality between men's and women's teams or risk losing federal payments.

Although Brown was an early supporter of the women's athletic movement, it was sued when budget-cutting in 1991 led to the elimination of two women's teams and two men's teams, which affected 37 men and 23 women. The court recognized that Brown funded 32 teams, half for men, half for women. However, women accounted for 51 per cent of the enrollment and only 38 per cent of the varsity athletes. Brown argued that it provided athletic opportunities sufficient to meet the interest and abilities of its female students, but the courts ruled that under Title IX schools must structure teams so that the ratio of male to female athletes matches the ratio in the student body. Brown was told to fund any sport women might want to play, regardless of cost, or eliminate 213 slots for men. In April, the Supreme Court denied Brown's petition for review.

This interpretation of Title IX has led to the elimination of hundreds of men's programs — with no appreciable gains for women. As interpreted by the Clinton Administration and enforced by the courts, Title IX has been four times more effective in eliminating male athletes then in developing female athletes. The NCAA reports that there are now more women's teams than men's among its members, but male rosters remain larger, and so, as one university coach puts it, the "carnage" afflicting men's sports continues.

Over the past five years, NCAA Division III programs cut 9,000 male slots while adding a mere 178 female slots. In the last three years, 16 Division I schools have dropped their men's swim teams and more than 60 schools have eliminated men's track

programs. There were 133 men's gymnastics teams in 1975; there are only 32 today. In 1972, there were 777 college wrestling programs; there were only 315 by 1996 despite enormous interest at the high-school level. Florida has 253 high-school programs with 6,850 participants, but no college teams at any level.

Recent news accounts indicate that the number of men's high-school teams in Florida might also be facing a precipitous decline. State education officials have notified several schools that under state law and Title IX they risk being eliminated from all athletic competition if they don't recruit more female athletes. Officials at one Florida high school complain that they don't have sexual parity in athletics because 25 per cent of their female students are already or soon to be mothers. 10

Congressman Denny Hastert (R., Ill.), who spent 16 years as a high-school wrestling and football coach, has been leading congressional efforts to enforce the original anti-discrimination intent of Title IX. When higher-education programs are reauthorized next year, he wants Congress to clarify that colleges "shouldn't reduce opportunities for either gender to participate in order to satisfy proportionality." If Hastert's GOP colleagues prove too timid to eliminate reverse discrimination in collegiate athletics, they ought to be benched. ∎

O'Beirne uses many statistics in paragraph 9. Do they speak for themselves, or did O'Beirne set them up to make certain implications? Check out Chapter 7 for more information about using statistics in your writing.

LINK TO P. 77 ⋯⋯⋯⋯⋯⋯⋯⋯

RESPOND•

1. The use of sarcasm, a kind of humor, is always risky in argument. What does O'Beirne's use of sarcasm tell you about the relationship she wants to establish with her audience? Do you think her strategy of sarcasm is successful, or does it backfire? How would you expect your friends to respond to O'Beirne's article? Why? What sort of reader might not like it? (For more on humorous argument, see Chapter 13.)

2. How does O'Beirne use references to U.S. political parties to further her argument? Why, since Title IX was passed during the Nixon administration, does O'Beirne never mention Nixon by name? Although she never explicitly states her party affiliation, do you think O'Beirne is a Democrat, a Republican, or neither? Why?

3. What evidence does O'Beirne provide to support her assertion that "women now freely engage in sports in proportion to their interest" (paragraph 5)? How persuasive is this claim?

4. Consider how O'Beirne, Monaghan, and Suggs work to create ethos in their arguments. **Write an essay** summarizing the ethos each writer creates. Which of the three presents the strongest argument of character? Give evidence for your judgment.

▼ Leslie Heywood teaches English and cultural studies at the State University of New York at Binghamton. This article appeared in a January 1999 issue of the Chronicle of Higher Education, a weekly paper covering issues of concern to college and university administrators and faculty. In it she raises difficult questions about women's sports that have received little attention. The Chronicle published only one letter—a critical one—in response to Heywood's article. As you read, think about whether—and how—the issues she raises have been addressed at your school.

Despite the Positive Rhetoric about Women's Sports, Female Athletes Face a Culture of Sexual Harassment

BY LESLIE HEYWOOD

Last October, Nike and the Partnership for Women's Health at Columbia University announced Helping Girls Become Strong Women, an alliance formed in response to an on-line survey conducted by *Seventeen* and *Ladies' Home Journal*. That survey found that 50 per cent of the 1,100 girls polled reported feeling depressed at least once a week; 29 per cent felt somewhat or very uncomfortable with their bodies; and close to 50 per cent were unhappy with their appearances.

The alliance stresses sports as a major solution to those problems. It echoes a landmark study written under the auspices of the President's Council on Physical Fitness and Sports, which also emphasized the benefits of sports for girls and women. That report cited, for example, the way sports disprove gender stereotypes about female weakness and incompetency, and the ways in which

they foster better physical and mental health, self-esteem, and skills such as leadership and cooperation.

Certainly, sports can help with some of the problems faced by young girls and women. And female participation in sports has greatly increased in the years since the 1972 passage of Title IX of the Education Amendments, which barred schools and colleges receiving federal funds from discriminating against women. High-school girls' participation in sports grew from 300,000 in 1972 to 2.25 million in 1995, and today, one in three women in college participates in competitive sports.

But there is another, less-discussed side to the story. A discrepancy exists between the increasing equality and respect for female athletes on the one hand, and, on the other, behavior within the athletics culture that shows profound disrespect for female competitors.

For example, old assumptions that 5 women who excel at sports are really more like men (and must, therefore, be lesbians, because they're not conventionally feminine) are rearticulated in the kind of "lesbian baiting" of female coaches and athletes that happens on many campuses.

In her book *Coming on Strong* (Free Press, 1994) the women's-sports historian Susan K. Cahn discusses the recent rumor circulated among coaches that an anonymous list had been mailed to prospective high-school recruits identifying programs as lesbian or straight. "Oddly," Cahn writes, "concerns about lesbianism in sports may even have increased, in inverse relationship to the greater acceptance of women's sports in general." Such concern shows a profound disrespect, because it assumes that good athletes are not "real women," and that lesbianism is something to fear, which undermines the fundamental dignity and worth of all female athletes and fosters a homophobia that may discourage women from participating in sports.

Other denigrating coaching practices — although they are officially discouraged — include mandatory weigh-ins and criticizing athletes about their weight. Many coaches are inordinately preoccupied with what their female athletes eat, and subject them to public ridicule about their diets and bodies. One group of athletes, from an athletically successful university in the South, told me about a coach who dubbed one of his athletes "Janie Snax" because he thought she was overweight (she weighed 125 at 5 feet 8 inches tall), and had the male athletes make fun of her every time she tried to eat anything. I have heard similar tales on many campuses.

Such practices, though disturbing, may stem from assumptions about women's "natures" that are widely accepted. In a recent issue of the *Nation,* in "The Joy of Women's Sports," Ruth Conniff° applauds Anson Dorrance, who has coached the women's soccer team at the University of North Carolina at Chapel Hill to 15 national championships, for being responsive to women athletes by making changes in his coaching style. Conniff quotes Dorrance as saying, "You basically have to drive men, but you can lead women. . . . I think women bring something incredibly positive to athletics. They are wonderfully coachable and so appreciative of anything you give them."

Two weeks after the *Nation* article appeared, *The Chronicle* and other news media reported a sexual-harassment lawsuit filed by two of Dorrance's former players, Debbie Keller (now a player on the national women's soccer team) and Melissa Jennings. They charge that he "intentionally and systematically subjected his players to inappropriate conduct and unwelcome harassment and thereby created a hostile environment at U.N.C." The suit alleges that Dorrance made uninvited sexual advances, monitored players' whereabouts outside of practice, and sent them harassing e-mail messages.

The idea that women are "wonder- 10 fully coachable and so appreciative" has a sinister ring in light of these

---

The reading by Ruth Conniff is reprinted in this book on page 482.

Heywood claims that sexual exploitation of female athletes jeopardizes some of the benefits of sports for women. Would you agree that her article could be considered a qualitative evaluation argument? Check out Chapter 10.

LINK TO P. 135

charges (which Dorrance has denied), and highlights some questionable assumptions underlying the positive rhetoric about women in sports. Gender-based assumptions like Dorrance's, such as the idea that women are more "coachable" — that is, open and manipulable — and that they are "appreciative" of whatever attentions the coach chooses to give them, may lead to unethical behavior such as that cited in the charges against Dorrance.

Yet the issue of coaches' behavior toward female athletes — what is acceptable and what is not — has been swept aside, and reports of the lawsuit against Dorrance have had no effect on recruiting for the U.N.C. women's soccer team. One of the nation's top soccer recruits, in a recent article in *College Soccer Weekly,* said that the allegations weren't "an issue"; that the lawsuit, in her opinion, "doesn't exist."

That kind of dismissal is a common response when a female athlete comes forward with charges of sexual harassment. As is the case at U.N.C., teams often rally around the coach and ostracize the accuser, creating an environment in which most women are afraid to speak out. In the November 14 issue of *USA Today,* Dorrance noted that there was a "silver lining" to the lawsuit in that it "unified the team very quickly." High-profile cases such as this one, in

which the news media seem to stress support for the coach rather than for the athlete, communicate to other athletes that if they speak out, they will be brushed aside and disbelieved.

In fact, sexual harassment and abuse of female athletes are part of the reality of women's sports. The executive director of the Women's Sports Foundation, Donna Lopiano, has written on the foundation's site on the World-Wide Web: "Sexual harassment or even sexual assault is a significant problem in school and open

amateur sport settings across the country that often goes unreported."

Michelle Hite, an athlete who competed in track in the mid-'90s at a major Division I university, told me that "one of the reasons I gave up my athletics scholarship was because of the sexual harassment that I felt was as much a part of my athletics routine as practice was." Hite and her teammates cite coaches' preoccupations with their bodies and weight, inappro- 15 priate comments about their bodies and their sexuality (and policing of that sexuality, such as forbidding athletes to have romantic relationships),

direct sexual come-ons from members of the coaching staff, and romantic relationships between coaches and athletes — which were destructive and disruptive to the athletes involved and to the team as a whole.

It wasn't until recently, however, 15 that romantic relationships between coaches and athletes were seen as a problem. When Mariah Burton Nelson wrote *The Stronger Women Get, the More Men Love Football* (Harcourt Brace, 1994), she found that harassment was a part of everyday reality in sports culture. "Some of the 'best' male coaches in the country have seduced a succession of female athletes," she writes. "Like their counterparts in medicine, education, psychotherapy, and the priesthood, coaches are rarely caught or punished."

In a crucial first step, most athletics organizations have drawn a hard line against such behavior. In his 1994 article "Ethics in Coaching: It's Time to Do the Right Thing" in *Olympic Coach* magazine, William V. Nielsens, of the U.S. Olympic Committee, wrote: "One of the most pressing issues today that needs to be addressed concerning coaching ethics is sexual abuse and harassment." The Women's Sports Foundation and WomenSport International have developed extensive anti-harassment and training guidelines for coaches. In Canada, various sports organiza-

> **"Creating a climate that fosters open discussion about sexual harassment is crucial, so that athletes feel authorized and safe in speaking out."**

tions have joined to create the Harassment and Abuse in Sport Collective.

Athletics departments also claim to be sensitive to these issues, but it remains unclear how much action they have taken beyond paying lip service to the problem. Some more-progressive campuses have established preventive measures, such as educational training for coaches and athletes. The University of Arizona, for instance, has implemented an extensive education and support system, which includes seminars prepared for coaches by affirmative-action officers. The seminars specifically deal with the multi-faceted nature of sexual harassment, and include case studies and "real-life scenarios" to clarify what exactly constitutes harassment. Freshman orientation for athletes covers "social issues" like harassment, unethical coach/athlete relationships, and eating disorders. This is supplemented by orientation for parents that lets them know about potential problems that may develop in their daughters' athletics careers, and the resources that are available to these young women.

There are several problems, though, with such prevention and treatment strategies at even the most-progressive campuses. The first is that almost all such education programs are initiated by affirmative-action officers, rather than originating in the athletics departments themselves. The Women's Sports Foundation recommends that athletics departments have their own policies and programs,

because there is so much more personal contact and interaction in the world of athletics than in ordinary teacher-student relationships.

Furthermore, typical seminars given by affirmative-action offices involve outsiders coming in to lecture individuals who are caught up in an athletics culture that doesn't always take such education seriously. In fact, a conflict exists between athletics, which values winning at all costs, and

"sensitivity training," which many athletes see either as distracting or as not applying to them.

It is hard to convince coaches and 20 athletes that the problems of female athletes are real and significant: After all, what does the self-esteem of a few girls matter when we've got to go out and win the big game? The women themselves, who may feel that achieving success and respect is bound up with gaining the approval of coaches, view the people who come to talk about harassment as an intrusion or distraction from the larger goal of athletics success.

Many sports administrators also assume that the athlete herself will report any abuses to the proper authorities. But many women rightly believe that doing so would bring about reprisals, such as being ostracized by their teammates and coaches, and being given less playing time.

The problems are complicated, tied up as they are with assumptions inherent in the athletics culture itself. If we really want to create an environment that is supportive to all athletes, we need to change traditional cultural assumptions about which athletes and which sports are most valuable. As continual debates about Title IX reveal, despite the widespread acceptance of female athletes, in many universities male athletes are still seen as "the real thing," the more-valued players. Over all, universities trivialize issues such as harassment, because allegations are perceived as detracting from "business as usual" — that is, producing winning men's teams.

According to the Women's Sports Foundation, every sports organization, from university athletics departments to youth leagues, should have and implement its own code of ethics and conduct for coaches. Creating a climate that fosters open discussion about sexual harassment also is crucial, so that athletes feel authorized and safe in speaking out.

Often, athletes believe that they will be accused of consenting to sexual relations with coaches, or of making up incidents of harassment. Many athletes also feel ashamed to talk about sexual issues publicly. But harassment is an issue of power, not of sex, and college and university policies need to make that distinction clear.

Parents and athletes also should look for schools and colleges with education programs that inform coaches clearly about what kinds of behavior won't be tolerated, and that inform athletes of their rights and the recourse available to them if they should encounter harassment. If parents and athletes show a preference for institutions with such programs, others will follow suit. But the programs need to go beyond lip service and show real support for women who file complaints, by showing zero tolerance for harassment and not — as has historically been the case — immediately leaping to the coaches' defense.

Sports are great for women. Some of my best experiences have been, and continue to be, in competitive sports. But for sports to really improve self-esteem and provide character building, camaraderie, and learning, greater attention needs to be paid to coaching, the assumptions that coaches sometimes make about female athletes, and how much control coaches should have over female athletes' lives. If we want women to truly benefit from participation in sports, we need to find ways to prevent their exploitation.

25

RESPOND •

1. What solutions does Heywood recommend for eliminating the sexual abuse and harassment of female athletes by coaches? Do you think her proposal is viable? Why or why not?

2. The first two paragraphs of Heywood's article do not directly address the main topic. What is Heywood doing in these paragraphs? Why does she open the article in this way? How well does the strategy work?

3. Writing to an audience of educators and policy-making officials of sports organizations such as the NCAA, Heywood uses a combination of personal and statistical evidence to construct her argument. How might she have changed her article for an audience of parents? Of athletes? How might she alter her appeal in a speech to a coaches' conference?

4. In "The Joy of Women's Sports" (p. 482), Ruth Conniff portrays coach Anson Dorrance of the University of North Carolina in a favorable light. Heywood both quotes from Conniff's interview with Dorrance and discusses a sexual harassment suit filed against him (paragraphs 8–12). Does Heywood's article cause you to reevaluate Conniff's argument? Why or why not?

5. Heywood's article uses all four types of argument described in Chapters 4–7 of this book. Choose the type you think is most prominent in her article and **write an essay** analyzing the rhetorical techniques Heywood uses to construct that type of argument. Give examples from her text, and tell why you think her use of this type of argument is (or is not) effective.

Four Cartoons about the 1999 Women's World Cup

The first cartoon shown here was published in the *New Yorker*, a weekly magazine aimed at a sophisticated urban audience. The other three cartoons appeared on the editorial pages of daily U.S. newspapers. Notice that all four cartoons depict a male character and one or more female characters enacting some aspect of the gender-based debate discussed in this cluster of readings. Cartoons have the ability to represent succinctly events, abstract concepts, even arguments. As you study each cartoon, consider whether the characters represent ordinary people or symbolize something else—such as a particular group or attitude. Think about the argument each artist is making. Is it an argument from the heart or one based on values or character?

"I take it we got the account."

GARY MARKSTEIN
©Milwaukee Journal Sentinel
COPLEY NEWS SERVICE

THAT'S RIGHT-GET USED TO IT. WOMEN IN SPORTS MAGAZINES...AND I DON'T MEAN SWIMSUITS!...

Sports ILLUSTRATED
WNBA!
WOMEN'S WORLD CUP SOCCER

©1999 THE BIRMINGHAM NEWS
COPLEY NEWS SERVICE
STANTIS

STEREOTYPES

GOAL!

1. What does the placid demeanor of the man in Marisa Acocella's *New Yorker* cartoon indicate? Can you picture yourself as either character in this cartoon? Why or why not? How does knowing that Acocella is a woman help you interpret the cartoon? How might a male cartoonist have drawn this scene?

2. Both cartoons on p. 506 depict a version of Brandi Chastain's now-famous victory gesture. (Chastain was, of course, a member of the U.S. women's soccer team that won the Women's World Cup in 1999.) Considering the different audiences for the two cartoons, do you think the men in each cartoon are meant to depict an average male reader? Is either man symbolic of anything else? If so, what? Explain your judgment.

3. The second and third cartoons depict middle-aged couples, presumably married, and women who are making a pointed comment. In each cartoon, how are the characters portrayed? Favorably? Unfavorably? Do you think there is a more sympathetic character in either cartoon? Which character do you most strongly identify with— and why? Do you think the cartoonist intends for you to feel that way? Why or why not?

4. The characters in the last cartoon are drawn less realistically than are the characters in the other three cartoons. What was your first impression of this cartoon? Did you perceive the large character labeled "Stereotypes" as a male? Why or why not? How does your perception of that character's gender change upon closer analysis? What is the meaning of the difference in scale between the character representing stereotypes and the rest of the cartoon?

The arguments in this cluster ask you to examine and perhaps question the role of profit and the profit motive in two U.S. leisure-time activities, movies and television, on the one hand, and college athletics, on the other. Are these activities about **havin' a good time, or just chasin' the benjamins?** (This last expression is a great example of figurative language originating in hip-hop culture. Don't get its meaning? Stop and think whose picture appears on one-hundred-dollar bills.)

The first two readings consider the recent phenomenon of product placement, whereby companies donate goods or even pay to have the products they make worn by characters or strategically placed on the sets or in the backgrounds of movies and TV shows set in the present. (Nobody's gonna pay to put a soft drink can on the set of a Shakespeare play set in the Renaissance!) In a piece from the *Christian Science Monitor*, a paper known for its fairness, Shinan Govani argues that product placement is not necessarily a bad idea and might even have benefits. From a very different perspective, Julia Fein Azoulay, writing for *Children's Business*, offers a "how-to" set of instructions in her article, "Getting Product Placed in Film and TV." In addition to challenging you to watch TV shows and movies in a new way, these two texts should encourage you to think carefully about the issues raised by product placement. Why, after all, should product placement matter? Does the practice encourage us to buy the products we see stars we like using? Should it? If it does, what is that fact telling us? If it doesn't, should corporations engage in the practice anyway? For what reasons? And what about stars or characters we don't like?

Might corporations pay the makers of television programs and films to have villains wear their competitors' products?

The next four arguments in this cluster deal with the growing emphasis on profit in college sports, professional sports, and sporting events — even counterculture ones like the X Games. Thad Williamson, in "Bad as They Wanna Be," and William Hytche, in "The Cost of Hoop Dreams," focus on different aspects of what they see as problems associated with the professionalization of college basketball. In "Business Postures to Name New Team," Becky Yerak examines the growing practice of naming teams for the corporations that own them. Finally, in "X Games: 'Extreme' Athletes to Storm San Francisco with Counterculture Sports," Neva Chonin reports on controversies surrounding corporate sponsorship for an event that prides itself on *not* being part of this country's culture of business-as-usual. Are the concerns of these writers and those they quote trivial or misplaced? Must athletic and sporting events inevitably become even more commercialized than they currently are? Will someone always come up with some novel way to sell sports? When sports is sold, who profits and who loses?

These readings force us to ask hard questions. Has leisure time *ever* been only about leisure? Is it, by definition, about making bucks? Are we cynical to pose such questions, or is it just being honest about what has been going on all along?

▼ *Shinan Govani is a freelance writer. This article appeared in February 1999 on the editorial page of the* Christian Science Monitor, *a daily newspaper that offers an analytical view of current issues in public discourse. Many elements in Govani's article reveal his assumption that his position may be unpopular. As you read, make note of these elements and how Govani uses them to assist his argument.*

Product Placement in Movies—Is It Really So Bad?

BY SHINAN GOVANI

The recent cinematic release of "You've Got Mail" has cultural Chicken Littles all aflutter. Starring the familiar Tom Hanks-Meg Ryan duo, the Warner Bros. production has come under attack for casting America Online in a supporting role. Critics say the Internet carrier gets far too much screen time as the medium through which the two leads meet and fall in love. It is, according to industry insiders, the largest product placement deal in silver screen history—reportedly worth between $3 million and $6 million—and even the film's trailers come festooned with AOL's signature smiley-face logo.

Three thumbs up I say. Contrary to the squiggly wisdom that product placements in movies are a kind of Faustian bargain,° there really isn't much to lose sleep over. Corporate cameos have been around for decades—at least since Katharine Hepburn dumped Gordon's Dry Gin overboard in "The African Queen" or when Joan Crawford, in "The Caretakers," came head-to-head with

a Pepsi trade show display at a psychiatric-ward picnic.

While product placements have undoubtedly become more frequent

in recent years, it simply reflects the spiraling costs of making a movie today.

There are three overarching arguments demonstrating that product placements are not the bogeymen of Tinseltown.

First, these products give movies 5 an indelible imprint of realism. In real life, we eat, drink, wear, and drive brand-name products. It's part of our topography. What do we really want directors to do? Scratch out the logos? Last year's independent *cause célèbre,* "Boogie Nights," was all the more immersing because it dripped with references to Fresca, 7-Up, and Chevy Corvette as it wound its way through the 1970s disco-and-polyester era. Similarly, it was wholly believable when, following a visit to the Kennedy White House, Tom Hanks's Forrest Gump declared: "One of the best things about meeting the president was you could drink all the Dr. Pepper you wanted." Characters become more three-dimensional when shown with products.

Faustian bargain: the selling of one's soul to the devil, or the bargaining away of something of lasting value for some lesser, immediate benefit.

A second reason product placements are useful is that they often reinforce a film character's personality and history. Because products—like it or not—come encoded with a certain symbolism, they can provide a variety of nonverbal cues and near-universal reference points. When Matt Damon's character yaks about Dunkin' Donuts in "Good Will Hunting," he instantly earns his working-class credentials. When James Bond conspicuously consumes Rolex watches, Brioni suits, and BMW sedans, he immediately evokes the spirit of the gentleman spy who demanded only the very best.

A third reason product placements shine brightly is that they often give a movie an additional subtext, allowing moviegoers a chance to play spot-the-product. Actually, sometimes they provide a text, period. Oh, look, there's E.T. feasting on some Reese's

Pieces. And there, that's Richard Gere in "American Gigolo" strutting his stuff in Giorgio Armani. And—oh, Taco Bell's the only restaurant left standing in the grisly world of "Demolition Man."

Some may disparage this product treasure-hunt mentality, but it's something nearly all of us respond to. Even during the Clinton-Lewinsky saga—the year's most popular movie, according to Neal Gabler, author of "Life: The Movie"—we chuckled at mention of Monica's blue Gap dress or at Clinton taking a swig from a Diet Coke can during his grand jury testimony.

Critics, such as the Center for the Study of Commercialism, argue that movies have become "dangerously" saturated with products and that, in the name of full disclosure, they ought to list products in their credits. That's a counterproductive proposal,

considering that it would hand advertisers one more golden opportunity to see their names in lights. Perhaps a better suggestion would be a disclaimer at the beginning of every flick that reads: "This is just a movie."

Manufacturers obviously use product placement because they can in some cases boost sales, but there's nothing inherently venal about the practice. Some may argue that product placements upset artistic impression, but anyone who's going to a mainstream flick to find art in the first place may need to get their reality passport stamped. The bottom line is this: Anyone who goes out and buys a toothbrush just because he saw Sandra Bullock holding one just like it is a simpleton. So is anyone who signs up with AOL simply because he wants to find the gal of his dreams.

Products don't tarnish a movie: sometimes they enhance it.

10

Notice how clear the organization of Govani's article is. See the Guide to Writing an Evaluation in Chapter 10 for suggestions on how to structure an evaluation.

·································· LINK TO P. 149

RESPOND●

1. List the three reasons Govani gives in support of product placement in movies. Which one seems most persuasive to you? Why?

2. What does Govani mean by "squiggly wisdom" in paragraph 2? Is this expression familiar to you, or might Govani have created it? Although the tone of this article is generally informal, that phrase is particularly so. How does it contribute to Govani's argument? How effective a use of figurative language is it? See Chapter 14.

3. Product placements can include such diverse items as a brand of soda, a model of sports car, or an item of designer clothing. Choose a recent movie depicting present-day life that you have already seen and watch it again, paying particular attention to the presence of identifiable products. Do you now notice products that you hadn't noticed on your first viewing? Using your observations as part of your evidence, **write an essay** in which you take a stance on product placement—for, against, or neutral. Whatever your stance, be sure to acknowledge other possible stances.

Getting Product Placed in Film and TV

JULIA FEIN AZOULAY

Sixteen years ago, Reese's Pieces had a "walk-on" part in a "sweet little film" called "ET, The Extra-Terrestrial," and no one thought much about it. Not, that is, until the family-friendly movie turned into a blockbuster hit, and Reese's Pieces sales jumped a whopping 65 percent in the weeks following the film's release. Then, the product placement engines started spinning. It had become eminently clear that kids' movies were a powerful promotional vehicle for kid-oriented products. Today, product placement is a thriving business, and agencies specializing in placement are plentiful, readily-accessible, and relatively affordable—even for small-scale operations.

Marketing costs for feature films released by the major studios have skyrocketed in recent years, and can now range from $15 million to $50 million; production costs routinely reach $100 million. Any way to leverage overhead is welcomed by the entertainment industry. Donated products and props are one such very real way to save production costs. At the same time, a product's appearance in a major film can go a long way in establishing—or increasing—marketplace presence.

Here's how it works: after checking out a number of product placement agencies, you decide to retain Agency X. For an annual retainer fee ranging from $25,000 to $250,000, they agree to review hundreds of active scripts (those either in production or set to shoot in the near future), keeping a look-out for every scene that might call for your product. Once they find the right scripts and the right scenes, they get in touch with the wardrobe and prop departments associated with those productions and offer, or pitch for, your line. These are not necessarily cold calls, either: reputable agencies have developed ongoing working relationships with key personnel in the film and television industries; and often, they know ahead of time who and when to call. No money changes hands between the agency and the production team: placement agencies generally do not pay any fees to get a product into a shoot. Rather, the placement agency explains how and why your line is the right one for one or another character to be wearing, and what it is that you're willing to donate to the production. Thanks to the hard work of the right agency staff, your line does, indeed, ultimately make its way to the wardrobes of main characters in a number of

◀ *This article originally appeared in a 1998 issue of* Children's Business, *a trade magazine for advertisers and manufacturers of products for children. We found it on the Web. As is usually the case with trade magazine articles, this piece provides specific information with concrete application to help readers with business endeavors. Nonetheless, Julia Fein Azoulay's piece is more than a simple "how-to" article; she argues for a specific business strategy. As you read, think about what makes this article an argument. Remember there are opposing viewpoints for every argument; what might some opposing views to Azoulay's argument be?*

Is Azoulay's purpose here to inform? To explore? To convince? Something else? See Chapter 1 to decide.

LINK TO P. 5 ⋯⋯⋯⋯⋯⋯⋯⋯⋯⋯⋯⋯⋯⋯⋯⋯

movies and TV shows. A few of the scenes your line "stars" in make it to the screen, while others are cut out in the editing process. But one good scene in one hit film can do wonders for your brand recognition—at a fraction of the cost of a 30-second prime time spot.

Despite the phenomenal growth spurt in sales that Reese's Pieces enjoyed after the release of "ET.," however, product placement is not about a direct impact on sales. According to Dean Ayers, President of the all-volunteer Entertainment Resources and Marketing Association (ERMA), "It's rare that a placement all by itself will increase sales. The impact of product placement is more along the lines of brand awareness and brand imaging." If put to the "right kind of use," Ayers explains, film and television placement can firmly establish a powerful image.

The Gain-Gain Deal

Some might call product placement a gain-gain deal: you gain the exposure,   5
the production team gets free wardrobe and props. Wardrobe and prop masters have a tight budget to work with, and your "donated" line can take a real edge off the pressure. Also, if your line has a certain "panache" to it—or better yet, a quirky sort of pizzazz—it can tell the audience a lot more about the personality of the character wearing it onscreen. Lines "that have a brand character and profile help define the character onscreen," explains Devery Holmes, senior VP of marketing and promotion at Norm Marshall & Associates. "We review 600 feature film scripts per year and break them down as to product placement opportunities," continues Holmes, whose agency successfully placed Vans sneakers in "Brady Bunch, The Movie." "Is it part of the story line? Does it provide a positive brand image? How recognizable is the logo? Will it mean something to the public when they see it? Is it unique enough to register on the public when they see it at retail?"

Indeed, there's more to placement than just sliding a product into a shot. There are subtleties that a quality product placement agency will take into consideration, among them the nature of the film property, the type of character wearing your line, and the scene in which your line appears. The Catalyst Group, says president Gisela Dawson, works "on a hundred prime time shows, so we gear different products toward the right shows, the exact show we think the client should be in." For an annual retainer fee in the $50,000 range, the Catalyst Group (TCG) guarantees at least six placements over the course of a year.

"There's no problem meeting that minimum," Dawson assures, "because we read 400 scripts a year with an eye towards assisting studios with their needs." One such need has been successfully met by TCG client Duck Head, which has been placed on "Moesha," "Seventh Heaven," "Unhappily Ever After," "The Secret Life of Alex Mack," and other prime time hits. TCG pitches for the client's boys' line rather than girls' wear, explains account executive Caressa Douglas, because "the logo for girls isn't as clear. It's the client's goal to bring out brand awareness, and the boys' line does that better."

Efforts to involve a line of apparel in a movie don't always come from the clothing company or a placement agency. "'The Lost World' came in to our offices through a product request [issued by film personnel]," recalls Timberland's Kelly Leonard. "From that initial inquiry the whole opportunity grew into a sponsorship, not just product placement." Timberland dressed Jeff Goldblum's daughter's character in a men's Guide Shirt, which was then cut down by wardrobe to fit her. They also provided the production with classic boots and hiking boots. "We developed a whole point of sale merchandising program, which was at the time the largest promotional effort Timberland had ever been involved with." The company sponsored a contest that offered a 10-day excursion adventure, complete with a visit to "The Lost World" set, a reception with the film's stars, and dinosaur "tracking" in Canada and Montana. "It was a very successful contest," Leonard recalls. "We measured it in terms of sales and brand awareness—and it helped summer sales, whereas we'd been traditionally thought of as a winter line."

Starting Your Search

The best place to start your search for the right product placement match for your line? The Entertainment Resources and Marketing Association (ERMA). As the professional association for product placement agencies, ERMA has a member list of 85 agencies, studios and corporations. Head to their Web site at www.erma.org, which offers information on members, including product placement agency email addresses, telephone numbers and mailing addresses, complete profiles and client lists, a section on guidelines, and even tips on how to select an agency.

Whether you're a major player in the children's apparel and accessory business or a small-scale start-up, bear the following in mind when considering turning to a product placement agency:

You're not just looking for exposure, you're looking for positive exposure. Your   10
agent should be matching the brand image you're trying to build with the right
opportunity for placement. An audience will get a certain sense of your product
depending on which character's wearing it and in what context—and will bear
that image in mind when they see your line on the racks, in the street or down
the hall at school.

You'll enjoy the greatest bang for your buck if your clothing or shoe lines feature
a readily-identifiable, bold and visible logo or brand icon. Recognition is key in
product placement pay-off: even if your line is in every scene of the season's
biggest film, you probably won't realize any great increase in sales if your audience doesn't know it's your line—as opposed to the competition's. No matter
how many placements your agency secures for you, if you don't have a readily
identifiable brand or logo, the pay-off isn't there.

Consider enlarging your logo or strengthening its visible impact. Provide pieces
that display the logo proudly—and visibly. Make sure it's well-positioned for the
shot: it won't do you any good if it's on the back of a jacket, for example, while
the shot is a tight close-up of the character's face.

Even though your product might make it into a film shoot, that doesn't guarantee it will make it all the way to the screen. It might end up on the "cutting room
floor," which means that the scene or shot your product was in ultimately got
edited out for entirely unrelated reasons.

Make sure your prospective product placement agency takes these issues into
consideration when taking your product line to bat. For an annual retainer fee, a
good agency will scour hundreds of scripts over the course of a year to find the
best and potentially, most effective on-screen opportunities for your line. To
cover the bases, and to increase the likelihood that a shot featuring your line
makes it all the way to the public, a reliable agency will work to get you into a
variety of different films, not just one. And many agencies offer money-back
guarantees for the wholesale value of a product (or credit toward the future)
that they'll get you into a minimum number of films.

Steer clear of any agency that guarantees placement in a certain film: no one   15
can predict what shots and scenes are going to make it past the director's final
cutting decisions.

Remember that a film's "shelf life" continues well beyond its initial first-run theatrical release. Home video, network syndication, cable and even airplane screenings extend the reach of many films. When considering the cost versus the potential rewards of product placement exposure, bear the bigger picture in mind.

A good agency should have good industry relationships and a strong reputation. Ask prospective agencies for a list of references at studio prop and wardrobe departments. Also, ask to see a "reel" of what the agency's done. Make sure you feel comfortable with the nature of their past accomplishments.

Don't get involved in any "one-shot deals." A quality agency will generally have a target of a number of placements over the course of a retainer year.

Low-Budget Placement

Let's say you're a small start-up or a modest player in the kids' industry, and the fee for even a low-cost agency retainer is well beyond the bounds of your budget. Although agencies are a sure-fire way to get your product placed in film and TV, they're not the only way to go.

Studios keep their cards close to the vest about product placement, but a mem- 20
ber of the wardrobe department at Disney Studios said this on condition of anonymity: "Sometimes agencies make a lot of promises [to studios] they can't keep; or they just have the basics to offer wardrobe; or they don't come through on time; or they have a tendency to want a name actor to wear the line. It's not necessarily through agencies that we get our wardrobe placement. We have our own contacts, so we might not go through the standard route." Apparel manufacturers, he continued, can "call the production and talk to the costume designer, who would then come look at their stuff in a showroom. We've made direct contact with clothing companies ourselves. We leave the labels on, make sure it gets seen . . . and everybody's happy." Placement inquiries from small manufacturers or apparel industry start-ups, he concludes, "bring new product that we might not otherwise be aware of."

Or consider brokering your own deal with a low-budget "indie." Many independent films shot with skeleton crews and produced outside of the studio system nevertheless make it to screen and make it big. Student films shot at major film schools, such as UCLA or NYU, stand a good chance of reaching the public, and they all need wardrobe and props. Maybe your line would fit the bill. Depending upon the nature of your product, an appearance in an independent film may go even farther in establishing your image. If your target market is the kind of audience that would be inspired by an offbeat, perhaps bohemiam indie, then the cost of pursuing this route on your own may prove to be funds well-spent.

RESPOND ●

1. Is Azoulay's article more a case of argument or persuasion, as those terms are described in Chapter 1? Support your answer with evidence from the reading.

2. Does this article fit the description of a proposal argument discussed in Chapter 12? Why or why not? The article is not structured the way a traditional academic essay would be structured; for example, it does not end with a conclusion. How is it structured? Make a paragraph-by-paragraph outline of the article; then **write a paragraph** discussing why the article is structured as it is.

3. Might Shinan Govani, the author of the previous article, "Product Placement in Movies—Is It Really So Bad?", rethink his position if he were to read Azoulay's article? Why or why not?

4. Azoulay claims that product placement is a flawless strategy for man-ufacturers hoping to establish brand recognition for their products. Do you agree, or do you think unfavorable associations might result from product placement in certain cases? Could the image of a brand or product be harmed, for example, from its use by a villain in a movie? **Write a short essay** arguing whether and when a product placement could have undesirable results.

Bad As They Wanna Be

Loving the Game Is Harder As Colleges Sell Out Themselves, the Fans, the Athletes

THAD WILLIAMSON

Growing up in an American college town gives one a better than average chance of being infected with progressive politics, a certain intellectual curiosity and a love for intercollegiate athletics. Growing up in Chapel Hill, North Carolina, makes one susceptible to catching a strong dose of all three.

Such is the case with this writer, who grew up believing that Dean Smith, the legendary coach of the University of North Carolina Tar Heels basketball team (who retired recently after thirty-six years), embodied virtue and goodness as surely as Jesse Helms represented hate and ignorance. A passion for college basketball is *the* tie that binds in "The Triangle," where UNC, North Carolina State and Duke University all play. And if you live in this area, the team you root for inevitably becomes part of your identity. Duke is alternately denounced and adored as the South's answer to the Ivy League; UNC boasts of being the region's premier public university; North Carolina State, a school historically focused on agriculture and engineering, enjoys a large in-state following as the populist alternative to its liberal arts neighbors.

For decades young Tar Heels fans grew up aware of Dean Smith's unapologetic liberalism: a much-celebrated (albeit modest) role in integrating Chapel Hill in the late fifties and early sixties, opposition to the Vietnam War, support of a nuclear freeze and opposition to the death penalty. Smith's political bent and reputation for treating players like extended family made it possible to imagine that by rooting for UNC, you somehow showed support for doing the right thing.

No one held to that belief more than myself. From age 12 I watched Michael Jordan and others from a courtside perch as an operator of UNC's old manual scoreboard. Now, a decade after leaving Chapel Hill, I remain a devoted follower of Atlantic Coast Conference basketball. Writing a triweekly, inseason column for *InsideCarolina* (northcarolina .com), an independent magazine and Web site devoted to UNC sports,

◀ *Thad Williamson is an author of books and articles on theology, economic and social policy, and sports. This article was originally published in an August 1998 issue of the* Nation, *a magazine of social and political analysis that takes a liberal viewpoint. Williamson issues a call to action in this proposal argument. As you read, notice how he works to build his credibility and engender his readers' trust before he suggests that they take action on his proposal.*

Arguments based on character, such as Williamson's here, can be very effective. See more examples of effective arguments based on character in Chapter 6.

LINK TO P. 64

I fancy myself in the rare (but not entirely unknown) position of left-wing sportswriter. Like a Latin American soccer commentator, I strive to keep the game in perspective but still feel elation when the Tar Heels win and supreme dejection when they lose in the Final Four.

For the thoughtful fan of college sports, however, it's getting harder to check your critical intelligence at the door and simply enjoy the game. The appeal of college athletics has long rested on their "amateur" status, the notion that the kids play mostly for the love of the game, without the pressures and influences that suffuse professional sports. These days, however, it's increasingly clear that big-time college athletics—in particular, men's basketball and football—are as wrapped in commercial values as the pros, and the system is rapidly spinning out of control.

In college arenas the best seats are now routinely reserved not for students and die-hard fans but for big-money boosters and private donors to the universities. The arenas themselves are being turned into prime advertising venues: Georgia Tech's revamped Alexander Memorial Coliseum, for example, goes so far as to place the McDonald's trademark "M" on the floor. Meanwhile, the NCAA's lucrative television contracts—an eight-year, $1.7 billion deal with CBS for broadcast rights to the Men's Division I basketball tournament and similar deals in football—are changing the fabric of the game, as top competition is slotted for prime-time viewing hours and games are steadily lengthened by TV timeouts.

Even the school I cover, North Carolina, which to this day bans all corporate advertising inside arenas, has largely succumbed to the trend. In the eighties UNC used some $34 million in private funds to build a 21,500-seat basketball arena, in the process setting a precedent of entitlement for major boosters. Not only did they win rights to the best seats in the arena, they are also allowed to pass on those seats to their progeny. More recently, university officials convinced the state highway board to authorize $1.2 million for a special road to allow top-dollar Tar Heels donors a convenient exit from home games.

There's more. Last summer the university signed a five-year, $11 million contract to use Nike-provided gear in all practices (for all sports) and to wear the familiar swoosh. No faculty members or students were directly involved in the negotiations, and no serious questions were raised about Nike's notorious labor practices abroad.

Subsequently, concerned UNC students and faculty generated considerable public debate about the deal, but UNC plans to remain on the take.

Indeed, shoe companies like Adidas and Nike are now prime players in the college game. Most major Division I football and basketball coaches receive lucrative payments from the companies in exchange for outfitting their teams with the appropriate logo—and in some cases, such as the University of California, Berkeley, for encouraging their players to buy additional Nike gear. The sneaker sellers also operate most of the major summer camps for elite high school athletes, where schoolboy stars show their wares to college coaches (many of whom are themselves on Nike's or Reebok's payroll) in hopes of landing a top-flight scholarship. While the hottest prospects are showered with expenses-paid travel and free athletic gear, the companies develop relationships with future stars that might culminate in endorsement contracts. In his fine book *The Last Shot*, Darcy Frey likened the atmosphere at Nike's annual high school summer camp to a meatmarket, where the mostly black kids are herded around like cattle while the overwhelmingly white coaches and corporate sponsors look on.

Nowhere are the priorities of the new corporate order of college sports 10 clearer than in the treatment of athletes—though you'd never know it from the popular image of those athletes as coddled superstars. In *He Got Game*, Spike Lee depicts the campus as a pleasure dome for young men treated to unlimited cars, women and material perks for four blissfully hedonistic years.

The truth is often far less alluring. "It's not as glamorous as people think," cautions Sheray Gaffney, a former reserve fullback for the football powerhouse Florida State Seminoles. "If you're in the program, it's not glamorous at all."

One reason for this is the so-called grant-in-aid system that characterizes all athletic scholarships in the NCAA. Originally established in 1956, grant-in-aid was intended to level the playing field by providing a fixed set of benefits to college athletes. Schools were allowed to offer scholarships of one to four years and were bound to honor them even if the athlete quit the team altogether. In 1973, however, the NCAA abruptly shifted course and mandated that the grants be limited to a one-year, annually renewable grant. The purpose of this change was to enable schools—in actuality, coaches—to keep tabs on each player's performance from year to year, and to cut off the scholarships of those whom the coach considered dispensable.

"Colleges changed the rule so they could run off the athletes who weren't good enough," explains Walter Byers, who oversaw the growth of college athletics while serving as NCAA executive director from 1951 to 1987. Back in the fifties Byers coined the term "student-athlete," a romantic idea that the NCAA continues to use in its promotional literature. These days, he is one of the NCAA's leading critics. "Once the colleges gave coaches the power to control those grants," he says, "that was a perversion that permanently changed the way things were done. It used to be that at least athletes could get an education if they couldn't play for the team."

Indeed, under the new system athletes do as the coaches say or risk being kicked out. Coach Rick Majerus of Utah, whose team reached the NCAA basketball finals this year, recently "released" Jordie McTavish saying he just wasn't good enough. A year ago, Coach Bobby Cremins of Georgia Tech asked freshman point guard Kevin Morris to leave for the same reason. More often than direct dismissals, coaches pressure players to leave on their own. Indiana's Bobby Knight, seeking to clean house after a disappointing 1996–97 season, drove starting point guard Neil Reed out of town with one year of eligibility remaining. Reed left, but not before accusing Knight of physical and emotional abuse.

Given the pressures to stay in the good graces of coaches—players 15 know that missing even one session in the weight room risks incurring the coach's wrath—it's no wonder that graduation rates for Division I football and basketball players in the NCAA hover at roughly 50 percent, a figure that exaggerates the amount of learning that actually takes place. Instead of promoting a balance between sports and academics, the system forces athletes to pour every ounce of energy into the game, with little recognition that the vast majority of players are in a vocational dead end. A sad rite of passage for most college athletes is the existential realization that they will never make it to the pros. "What was astonishing was the number of scars that [the program] left on athletes that came to the surface behind closed doors," recalls Gaffney. "It was painful to see athletes crying in distress because they see their dreams slowly fading away. All of a sudden at age 20, 21, they are required to make a complete transition."

True, college sports still represent a way out for poor or working-class athletes. Some, with the help of coaches like Dean Smith, find jobs in coaching, pro leagues overseas or business. Others succeed in getting an education. But the inequities are glaring. While generating an enormous revenue stream for their universities through ticket sales, merchandising, advertising and TV deals, athletes are forbidden from sharing in any of the gains. "When these commercial activities came along," notes Byers, "the overseers and supervisors made sure that the benefits went to them, not the athletes." College coaches routinely earn six-figure salaries, sign endorsement deals with corporations and jump from school to school for more lucrative contracts. The athletes, meanwhile, are the focus of scandal and media outrage if they so much as accept money for an extra trip home. Under the grant-in-aid rule, athletes may not use their talent or name recognition to earn money while in school except under tightly defined conditions.

In Byers's view, the "gobs of money" now flowing to the universities make a return to the amateur ideal impossible. What is possible, he believes, is scrapping the current grant-in-aid system, which leads not only to the rampant exploitation of athletes but, he argues, violates antitrust laws because colleges essentially operate as a cartel, setting a national limit on what a whole class of students can earn. He would require athletes to apply for financial aid like any other student but would remove all restrictions on how they could earn money while in college.

Rick Telander, a *Sports Illustrated* writer and author of *The Hundred Yard Lie,* an exposé of college football, proposes a more radical solution: namely, severing big-time college football programs from the schools that lend them their name. In Telander's view, an NFL-subsidized "age-group professional league" could be established in which universities would own and operate teams, using university facilities and traditional school colors. Players need not be students but would earn a year of tuition for each year played, redeemable at any time, during or after their playing careers. College basketball would also benefit from the creation of an NBA-backed age-group league. Such leagues could offer gifted players with no interest in academics a credible alternative to college, and a second chance to earn an education should their professional dreams fade.

Of course, given the entrenched institutional support for the status quo, none of this can happen without a sustained demand from the public, including students, coaches not yet corrupted, and athletes themselves. In the meantime, students and faculty can make their voices heard by continuing—and expanding—their campaigns challenging the corporate sponsorship of university athletic departments. Over the past year campus activists at Duke and other universities have successfully pushed administrators to adopt rules requiring that all campus sweatshirts and athletic gear be produced in compliance with labor and human rights standards. These same activists should insist that corporate advertising be banned from all arenas; that universities cap athletic budgets for football and basketball and put an end to the "arms race" for bigger facilities and more amenities; and that the influence of big-money donors be limited so that students and fans can continue to attend athletic events at reasonable prices. Activists might also find unexpected common ground with coaches and fans concerned about how the integrity of the game has been subordinated to television, or how corporations are colonizing and poisoning the high school recruiting scene.

Speaking for myself, probably only death will cure my love affair 20 with North Carolina basketball, and no doubt there are millions of people who feel the same way about their own teams. But loving the game need not mean having a romantic view of how college sports are organized. College sports are far too visible an arena in American society to be simply thrown to the wolves. Ultimately, the only productive route forward is to insist that those who love the game also fight to change it.

RESPOND●

1. What evidence does Williamson provide to support his contention that "the [college athletics] system is rapidly spinning out of control"? What kind of appeals does he use? Arguments from the heart? Arguments of character? Other kinds? (See Chapters 4–7.)

2. Why does Williamson give us so much detailed information about North Carolina coach Dean Smith's political beliefs? Does that information contribute to the argument? How? Why? If not, why not?

3. Williamson's article ends with a strong call to action, yet there is no hint of such an appeal in the title or opening paragraphs of the article. Why do you think Williamson chose this rhetorical strategy?

4. Do you agree with Williamson's suggestion (in paragraph 16) that collegiate sports are "a way out" for poor and working-class students? Do you think that assertion is more (or less) true today than it was in the past? What evidence would you want to present to support or refute Williamson's claim?

5. Walter Byers, NCAA executive director from 1951 to 1987, has proposed removing all restrictions on how student-athletes can earn money while in college. Imagine that your school is considering adopting Byers's proposal. **Write a letter** to your college administrators supporting or rejecting Byers's plan. Provide detailed evidence for your position.

▼ William P. Hytche is president emeritus of University of Maryland
Eastern Shore. In this June 1999 opinion piece from the Christian Science
Monitor, *Hytche discusses several problems with college basketball and
argues that the newly formed Collegiate Professional Basketball League
(*CPBL*) can solve those problems. Although Hytche is a member of the* CPBL's
*board of directors, he chooses not to reveal this information about himself to
his readers. As you read, think about why he might not have mentioned his
official status with the* CBPL.

The Cost of Hoop Dreams
Let's Admit that the Bottom Line Is Money — Even in College

BY WILLIAM P. HYTCHE

There's a new and alarming trend in college basketball: young men forgoing college eligibility to enter the pros. Just five years ago only a handful took this option. Last year there were 28; this year 39.

Of the 28 underclassmen who entered last year's draft, 11 failed to be selected by any NBA team — ending not just their hoop dreams, but the opportunity to earn a college degree they might not otherwise pursue.

This is just one of the serious problems facing NCAA basketball, which has the lowest graduation rates of any collegiate sport and has suffered scandals involving gambling, criminal activity, and under-the-table booster money. But all of these problems stem from one thing — money. Or as hip-hop icon Sean "Puffy" Combs says: "It's all about the Benjamins, baby." (He's referring to the $100-bill image of Ben Franklin.)

The average NBA salary is almost $3 million a year, yet the new collective bargaining agreement that ended this year's lockout calls for a five-year rookie "salary cap." Put yourself in the players' shoes. If you knew it would take five years to be offered a contract worth more than $100 million, wouldn't you want to start as soon as possible?

Money confounds the college 5 game as well. Basketball is the NCAA's goose that lays the golden eggs — several hundred million of them. Yet under the current system,

the athletes who generate this tremendous wealth are permitted to earn only $2,000 to cover expenses. And if only 41 percent of these players actually obtain a college degree, the real benefit of an athletic scholarship is questionable.

The NCAA has recently proposed offering loans to athletes who stay in school, barring first-year men's basketball players from competition during their freshman year, and linking the number of athletic scholarships a school can offer in a particular sport to that program's graduation rate. The

Hytche is writing about basketball players, but the players are not his main audience here. Who is Hytche writing for in this article? How does he establish rapport with his readers? See Chapter 3 to learn techniques for connecting with your readers.

·············· **LINK TO P. 44**

NBA has discussed barring anyone under 20 from playing in the NBA.

But it's time for candid talk: Many of the athletes playing for this nation's best college basketball programs are not there for the education. And playing Division I basketball is equivalent to a full-time job. It's time to give these athletes more time to earn their degrees, or move some of their course load to the off-season. It's also time to share the tremendous wealth generated by the game of basketball.

This involves more than simply paying these talented young men to play. We should both reward and protect them as they pursue their hoop dreams by giving them a more realistic opportunity to eventually earn a college degree, and by giving them access for a longer period to tuition, room, and board.

The Collegiate Professional Basketball League (CPBL), scheduled to begin its first season in November 2000, is designed to do just that. Players 17 to 22 years of age—in Boston, Chicago, Cleveland, Detroit, New Jersey, New York, Philadelphia, and Washington—will not be paid multimillion dollar salaries. But they will be guaranteed access to up to eight years of tuition, room, and board at the school of their choice. The school doesn't even have to be a Division I school; it could be a smaller college or university, a community college, or even a prep or trade school.

Although the league has a manda- 10
tory minimum education requirement,

it will be fulfilled during the summer off-season.

As a result, by the time a player has spent four years in the CPBL, he will have earned the equivalent of an associate's degree, with access to four additional years of tuition, room, and board at the school of his choice. By offering eight years of academic scholarship money, players who "age out" of this league and who decide they will need a college degree, will still have the funds to pursue one.

As a former university president, I think it should be clear to everyone by now that we can't continue trying to force athletes to study against their will, or put them in circumstances that will lead to academic failure. But this doesn't mean we abandon the thought of educating these young men. Instead, why not offer college-age basketball players economic incentives to pursue a college degree?

While the NCAA uses punitive measures to force athletes to study, the CPBL will offer additional monetary compensation — outside tuition, room, and board — to those players who diligently pursue their college degrees.

What's more, CPBL players who earn their college degree in six years or less will receive an additional bonus of up to $10,000.

As the old saying goes: In order to 15 do good, you first must do well.

It's time that those of us who care about today's college basketball players do good, by enabling these gifted young men to do well.

"Division I basketball is a cash cow. Why not use more revenue on the players to keep them in college instead of jumping pro?"

RESPOND●

1. Hytche offers what we might call a "comparative advantage" argument, a kind of proposal claiming that a novel course of action will prove superior to the status quo. Which problems, specifically, does the CPBL seek to address, and how, in theory, will its results prove superior to those of the current system?

2. How does Hytche seek to establish his credibility with his audience? Provide examples and evidence. What does he gain by not mentioning in the article his status as a board member of CPBL? Would mentioning his status have strengthened or weakened his argument? Why?

3. There are no interviews in Hytche's article, but he does quote one person — Sean "Puffy" Combs. Based on what you know of the *Christian Science Monitor*, do you think its readers are familiar with Combs? Why do you think Hytche chose to quote Combs and not someone else?

4. Hytche relies heavily on an argument of values (see Chapter 5). Why do you think Hytche chose to emphasize that type of argument more than the other types? **Write an essay** discussing how Hytche develops his argument of values and evaluating its effectiveness.

▼ *This 1999 article reports on sponsorship issues surrounding the newly formed Collegiate Professional Basketball League (CPBL). The article originally appeared in the business pages of the Detroit News in 1999. Notice that this news article includes the results of an opinion poll at the end, which at first glance may seem unrelated to the text. Read the article through twice; on the second reading, think about how the survey functions as argument.*

Business Postures to Name New Team
Broadcast.com Near to Signing Deal for Detroit Hoops Squad

BY BECKY YERAK

DETROIT—A new men's professional basketball league for college-age players is negotiating to sell team naming rights for its Detroit team to Broadcast.com.

In what's expected to be a $1.8-million, three-year deal that should be completed and announced next week, Broadcast.com will join current Collegiate Professional Basketball League team sponsors Lycos and Acunet for the eight-city league.

In selling names, the league wants the teams to be called by the companies' names, not by their cities. "Sponsors are taking a significant risk," league founder Paul McMann said.

At a sports finance forum in New York this week, Chris Payne, chief operating officer for pro soccer team San Diego Flash, questioned whether fans will get attached to, say, Team Broadcast.com or Team Lycos, explaining that fans like rooting for the home team, so to speak.

Royal Oak sports fan Ross Howey 5 agrees. "They'd lose their geographic identity," the 80-year-old retiree said.

Broadcast.com is a Dallas-based public Internet provider of live and on-demand audio and video programs. "Anywhere in the world, you'll be able to tune in and watch a CPBL game via the Internet," McMann said.

While the league has talked of starting up in November, the price for team naming rights seems to be rising; the other deals were for $1.2 million and $1.6 million. In contrast,

NCAA sponsorships run from $2.5 million to $5 million a year.

The new league differs from the NCAA in a few respects: It will pay its players an annual stipend and put more of a focus on education by paying tuition and housing. Players also

Sponsor Influence

A Fox Sports/ROI poll earlier this year asked: "If a (company) sponsored an event or sport you follow, would you be more likely to consider trying that company's brand of product or service for the first time?"

	More likely to try
Soft drink	46.2%
Apparel	44.7%
Sneaker	40.4%
Car	35.6%
Computer	31.3%
Beer	24.4%
Long distance	20.5%
Credit card	16.7%

Note: Survey sample size is 3,637, ages 12 and older except for the beer category.

Source: The Sports Business Daily

What do we know about Ross Howey? Why might Yerak have included a comment from an "80-year-old retiree" at this point in an article written for the business pages? Chapter 7's discussion of testimonies, reports, and interviews can help you use these kinds of proofs strategically.

·············· LINK TO P. 80

get a bonus for graduating and taking extra classes.

It will recruit high school students who might lack the SAT scores to meet NCAA requirements. Fewer than half of Division 1 players graduate, and hardly any go on to the NBA.

Pax TV will broadcast Saturday 10 games. "We've got television in place. We're structuring deals with signifi-cant media outlets to ensure visibility for the league," said McMann, ex-pecting to have a national TV contract by year three. "Until then, we will buy the time."

RESPOND •

1. Yerak cites a Fox Sports/ROI poll that asked respondents if they would be likely to try for the first time a product that sponsored an event they followed. Do the poll figures seem plausible and accurate to you? Why or why not? For example, 46.2 percent of those contacted said they'd be likely to try a soft drink, but only 24.4 percent would try a new beer. Speculate on why there is so much difference between the two products.

2. Yerak and Hytche, the author of the previous article are both writing about the CPBL, but each focuses on different aspects of the league. How do the authors tailor their articles to appeal to their respective audiences? What do they do similarly? What do they do differently?

3. Do you think sports fans are ready to accept sports teams identified by corporations rather than hometowns? **Write an essay** arguing why they are or are not.

▼ *Neva Chonin is a staff writer for the* San Francisco Chronicle, *where "X Games" appeared in June 1999. Chonin reports on corporate sponsorship of "extreme" sports events in which "X athletes" compete in such nontraditional areas as bicycle stunt riding, skateboarding, and sky surfing. As you read, think about whether the writer reveals her views on such corporate sponsorship as she reports on it.*

X Games

"Extreme" Athletes to Storm S.F. with Counterculture Sports

BY NEVA CHONIN

Stunt biker Dave Mirra hopes he doesn't leave his heart in San Francisco. He's already left his spleen in Dallas, thanks to an accident in 1995.

Mirra, at 25 the world's premier stunt rider, is understated about what he expects from the 1999 X Games, which open tomorrow at San Francisco's Pier 30.

"A challenge. I've ridden in San Francisco before, and I'm hoping to break more records."

And, with a little luck, no bones.

Tomorrow through July 3, ESPN's 5 fifth annual extreme sports competition will bring more than 400 world-class alternative athletes to the Bay Area. The games were held in San Diego the past two years. The nine-day event should be an eye-opener for those who think the X Games cater to slackers.

This year's games will be televised on ESPN, ESPN2 and ABC. Corporate sponsors such as Sony and Adidas have been jockeying for position all year, and the U.S. Postal

Service is issuing more than 150 million commemorative stamps.

The stakes have never been higher for X athletes. They're competing for nearly $1 million in prize money in nine different categories and 24 disciplines—from aggressive in-line skating, bicycle stunt riding and

skateboarding to sky surfing, sport climbing and big-air snowboarding.

The graffiti are on the wall: Extreme sports are big and getting bigger.

"I liken what's happening now in extreme sports to what happened with rock 'n' roll in the early '60s," said ESPN Director of Programming Ron Semiao. "Traditional music critics said it wasn't real music and wouldn't last. But the kids dug it, and it's become an accepted part of our culture.

"With extreme sports, the initial 10 reaction was that these weren't real sports and these weren't real athletes. But the culture has gained acceptance over time. Parents understand now that their kids might be into skateboarding instead of baseball."

Executive Director Jack Wienert said people who are put off by extreme athletes' frequently extreme slacker appearance need to look closer. "Mainstream folks say that what these athletes do is extremely dangerous and that they're crazy. Well, it is extremely dangerous, but they're not crazy or they'd be crippled or dead. These are real athletes. They're serious about their sport."

Extreme sports culture was once easy to peg: a soundtrack of hardcore Southern California punk bands, colorful hair in bristling buzz cuts and clothes baggy enough to fit three people at once.

But as their ranks swell with enthusiasts from around the world, the clothes and music of X athletes have become as diverse as the sports they love. These days, not every skateboarder boasts multiple tattoos and listens to Pennywise or Blink 182;

they're just as likely to be low-key jazz enthusiasts or dreadlocked cosmic surfers with a Beastie Boys fixation.

X Games skateboarder Danny Gonzalez, 20, likes everything from punk to rap, preferably combined. He moved to San Francisco from Texas two years ago, he said, "because everyone in the entire world knows about San Francisco. You've got families in Japan sending their kids over here to skateboard. The scene at the Embarcadero started a new breed."

Whatever their stylistic prefer- 15 ences, extreme athletes cherish both their individuality and their sense of community. Skateboarders and stunt bikers consider each other friends, not competitors, insists San Francisco skater Drew Walker, 13.

"Real skateboarding is about bonding," he said. "It's more than just learning how to do tricks. It's the music, the people, it's all linked."

Kent Uyehara, 30, owner of FTC Skateboards in the Haight, said, "Mainstream recreation people are trying to make things more competitive, because they think that's what it's about. But the athletes don't care about that. They don't want to compete—their sponsors do."

With traditional sports stars' salaries going through the roof and stadium costs climbing even higher, these highly individualized, do-it-yourself athletes are increasingly being courted by the sports establishment. Skateboarders are featured in ads for everything from soft drinks to phone companies, and X Games prize money has increased by 166 percent since the first games in 1995. NBC

recently announced plans for its own extreme sports competition, the Gravity Games.

Uyehara concedes that such commercialization is inevitable. "At least if we're involved, we can give feedback and make sure it retains its essence."

To bolster the X Games' credi- 20 bility with kids on the street, ESPN has recruited an array of athlete commentators and reporters. Fans following the games on the Internet will have an opportunity to vote for the winner in the skateboarding vert trick event and to send in their own digital photos. A live chat crawl at the bottom of the screen will accompany some events, similar to the crawls used in MTV's video chats.

"We want to be real, and we're always learning," said Wienert. "We want our people to relate to this culture and these sports. We've given the athletes respect, and we've earned theirs."

Pros like Dave Mirra say they're grateful to finally be earning a living doing what they love.

"Some people think that riding for corporate sponsors is wrong," he said. "But I've lived this sport for a long time, and if I can get good endorsements, it helps me. We went a lot of years with no money involved. It's not like we're basketball players making millions of dollars. Money isn't a bad thing.

"I think it's giving a lot of people a lot of good opportunities. And it's nice to see a lot of people respecting what we do."

Fabiola da Silva, 20, a Brazil- 25 born, in-line skater from Santa Rosa,

is an X Games triple gold medalist who said she's not going to sweat over street credibility. "Some people don't like the idea of doing this stuff for TV, but I think it's fun. So I'm gonna relax and just do what I do."

Advertisers have always tried to link their products with the latest cool youth culture, Semiao said. He doesn't think extreme sports are in any danger of corruption, arguing that corporate sponsorship "doesn't take any of the soul out of the sports. The culture is becoming larger, but the rebelliousness and innovation are still there. And the benefit is that you're seeing more and more skate parks pop up, like ball fields, giving kids somewhere to practice besides the streets."

Unfortunately, San Francisco, the world skateboarding and stunt-biking mecca, doesn't have a skate park. And kids who try to skate on the sidewalk for lack of options can expect to have their boards confiscated.

That's why Jake Phelps, the 36-year-old editor of *Thrasher,* the locally based skateboard magazine, thinks the X Games "suck."

"Everyone talks about how dramatic they are. You want drama? Go skate in the streets where you can get run over by traffic. That's drama."

Chonin assumes that her readers are familiar with the groups Blink 182 and the Beastie Boys. Check out Chapter 7 to see more about how writers can use cultural assumptions to further their arguments.

LINK TO P. 83

"Regular kids can't skate the X Games. It's a Madison Avenue sham."

Even X Games fans see the irony. Rob Holmes, a 14-year-old San Francisco skateboarder, can't wait to watch his favorite athletes perform this coming week. But his excitement is tinged with frustration.

"We have a week to watch all these great pros skating, but we don't have a chance to have fun like they do," he said wistfully. "Wherever I 30 skate, people tell me to get lost. It's so stupid."

At least, he said, the events are free. And this year's games are the first during which on-site concerts will fill in the gaps between afternoon and evening competitions with an indie-rock lineup headlined by the rapper Coolio.

For some hard-core aficionados, though, the music and free admission are just part of a corporate package they'd rather not open.

"They can hype it until it's gone, 35 but the people who are really core will still be out there on the concrete when the corporate sponsors have forgotten about skateboarding," said Phelps, who won't be attending the games. "That's the bottom line: It's the concrete that teaches you how to skate."

RESPOND •

1. Is Chonin's own point of view discernible in this news article? Do you think Chonin is sympathetic towards extreme athletes? Why or why not? What evidence can you find in the article to support your conclusion?

2. Look back at where Chonin quotes Jake Phelps, editor of *Thrasher*, a skateboarding magazine (paragraphs 28–30 and 35). Why is Phelps critical of the X Games? Do you find his position surprising considering that he is involved in a business aspect of extreme sports? Why or why not?

3. How are the problems of extreme sports (and extreme athletes) different from or similar to those of other types of athletics (and athletes) in terms of funding and opportunities to compete? Present evidence to support your argument, including any evidence you find appropriate from any of the other readings in this section.

4. **Write an essay** supporting or rejecting corporate sponsorship of extreme sports events. Establish your authority on the subject by presenting the views and experiences of extreme athletes (yourself, perhaps, or others).

chapter twenty-six

Who Owns What?

You die tomorrow. Who owns your body? What about its parts—the kidneys or eyes or heart or skin or bone marrow? And what if you've left sperm in a sperm bank, eggs in an egg bank, or fertilized embryos stored for future implantation? How about the white blood cells in your spleen, which might become the source of a medical discovery that stands to make some scientific researchers and enterprising capitalists very wealthy? And who owns your bones when you're no longer alive? How long do those claims of ownership endure? Months? Years? Forever? Easy questions, you might think, and you just might be wrong.

And what about words? Can anyone be said to own them? Under what circumstances? If they're said in private and not recorded? If they're so well known that even schoolchildren can recite them? In this chapter, we examine what quickly becomes a complex problem, *who owns what*, by looking at two very different sets of issues —first, ownership of the body and its parts and, second, ownership of words, one form of "intellectual property." As the arguments here demonstrate, there is little agreement among the many contending parties who have an interest in ownership about much of anything—except, perhaps, the importance of whatever they're fighting over.

The arguments in this chapter challenge us to rethink assumptions we might hold about the nature of individual and communal ownership and to recognize the changing nature of each. They force us to consider the competing interests of the individual and the community, the individual and society, and the individual and social institutions like medicine, law, and even art. Especially because our society is simultaneously democratic, valuing "equality," and capitalist, valuing private ownership and financial profit, questions of ownership cannot help but become questions of how we, as Americans, define the nature of the self in our society.

This cluster of arguments offers a spectrum of attitudes about **who owns the body and its parts.** In the opening reading, "Lambs to the Gene Market," John Vidal and John Carvel examine the case of John Moore, whose cancerous spleen contained white-blood cells that became the basis of a medical breakthrough. The U.S. patent on the discovery is owned by a biotechnology company, which paid 1.7 million dollars for the rights of ownership; meanwhile, Moore got almost nothing. In the second text, "Weighing the Right to Own an Embryo," Mike McKee analyzes the ways in which American courts have dealt with questions regarding the ownership of embryos in cases of divorce or death.

The third and fourth readings raise the question of organs for transplant and ownership. Steven Walters and Marilynn Marchione's "Plan Would Alter Region for Organ Sharing" reports on disagreements among states in this country about sharing organs for transplants, while an unsigned article from the *Straits Times* of Singapore, "Organ Donor Drive by Muslim Group," gives details about legislation there that claims state ownership of kidneys for transplant when someone dies in an accident unless two relatives object. These texts remind us that societies—and groups within a society—may hold very different beliefs about the ownership of organs, even when the organs, if harvested, might be put to what many would consider "a good cause."

The final two pieces in the cluster consider property of a very different sort, ancestral remains, offering differing perspectives on Harvard University's decision to repatriate the remains of Native Americans, purchased early last century, by returning them to the Jemez Pueblo nation, which claims the sanctity of the body and, hence, bodily remains, for generations, for centuries, indeed, forever. The first of the texts, James Bandler's "A Long Journey Home," appeared in the *Boston Globe,* the major newspaper in the large city closest to Harvard, while the second, Miguel Navrot's "Ancestors Return Home," was published in the *Albuquerque Journal,* the major newspaper serving the area that includes the pueblo to which the remains were returned. These two texts report on the same basic story, but from different perspectives and for different communities. As a result, you'll see that they tell somewhat different stories about what happened, why, what it meant, and for whom.

In some of the cases examined in these readings, ownership of bodies or their parts, living or not, is seen as resting with a community and serving, in some way, to strengthen bonds among the living members of that community. Other cases, especially those relating to embryos and genes, pit individual against individual and individuals against social institutions like medicine and law, complicated by corporate quests for profit. All of them make clear that questions about who owns the body and its parts are anything but simple.

Lambs to the Gene Market

What Do Tracy the Sheep and John Moore Have in Common? Millions of Pounds Can Be Made from Cells Taken from Their Bodies. John Vidal and John Carvel Report on the Growing Debate about Who Owns Genetic Material and Whether Your Body Can Be Patented.

JOHN VIDAL AND JOHN CARVEL

John Moore says he has been "essence-raped." The genial Burl Ives° lookalike is effectively the world's first patented man. Yet he was grateful enough in 1976 when, as an oil worker, he came off the Alaskan pipeline to seek treatment for hairy-cell leukaemia. His doctor at the University of California found that Moore's spleen had enlarged from about half a pound to more than 14 pounds. It was removed and Moore recovered.

What he did not know then was that his doctor had been taking samples of the white blood cells from his cancerous organ. He had cultured them into an "immortal" cell line which, unusually, was capable of producing blood proteins of great value in treating immunosuppressive diseases.

Nor did Moore know that the university had applied for—and been granted—a United States patent on its "invention." He became suspicious only in 1983, when his doctor pressed him to sign over all rights to cell lines taken from his spleen. He refused. Only later did Moore learn that the "Mo line" had been sold to a bio-technology company for $1.7 million: about £ 1.1 million. He was stunned: "What the doctors had done," he told the *Guardian* this week, "was to claim that my humanity, my genetic essence, was their invention and their property. They viewed me as a mine from which to extract biological material. I was harvested."

Since then Moore's cell line has made a fortune for its owners and could, he says, generate more than $3 billion of business. Moore, meanwhile, makes a living through a small business marketing beers and soft drinks. He has received only a small settlement and token damages.

Moore sees himself as 20th-century Common Man. "How has life become a commodity?" he asks, rather innocently. "I believe that all genetic material extracted from human beings should belong to society as a whole, and not be patentable."

◀ *"Lambs to the Gene Market" originally appeared in a 1994 issue of the* Guardian, *a London daily newspaper. John Vidal serves as the paper's environment editor, and John Carvel is one of its education correspondents. Unlike U.S. newspapers, British daily papers often take overtly political viewpoints; the* Guardian *boasts a leftist perspective. In this article, Vidal and Carvel examine some of the complex conflicts between ethical and commercial considerations of genetic research. As you read, pay attention to how the writers employ the testimony of authorities—scientists, policy specialists, and others—to construct their argument and develop their ethos.*

5 *Burl Ives:* a large man with a full, white beard who was a popular folksinger in the 1950s.

But who does own your body? Should agri-business or a drug company be allowed to patent a body part or even an entire species? And who should have the rights to genetic material? Such questions, given immediate life by the experiences of John Moore, are only beginning to be faced. The nascent science of genetics is already raising new social, ethical, legal, political and financial problems that go far beyond individuals such as Moore. They are now to tax Europeans at the highest levels.

European Union: organization currently composed of 15 European countries; its ultimate goals include fostering balanced and sustainable social and economic progress among the member nations and ensuring a European presence on the international scene.

For more than a year the European Union° and MEPs° have been bitterly divided over the extent to which life should be patentable. The EU, heavily lobbied by more than 70 drug and seed companies, wants a directive that would allow the patenting of all human, animal and plant tissue throughout the community. It favours the American Supreme Court ruling that Moore's spleen ceased to be his property when it left his body.

But the European Parliament, by a qualified majority vote, has tabled an amendment. This would establish that genes and cell lines removed from the human body should not count as an "invention"; therefore they should not be patented. Firms could gain commercial protection for specific treatments, but not for the genetic material on which these are based. A conciliation period is about to start.

MEP: member of the European Parliament.

What *should* count as an invention? The method of framing a definitional argument in Chapter 9 could help you figure it out.

································· LINK TO P. 120

The pharmaceutical and seed companies argue strongly and uniformly that patents are the starter-motors of the genetic revolution. They are essential, they say, if agriculture, medicine and humankind are to enter a new age of advanced biological technology.

In the last year alone, they point out, genes have been identified that confer varying degrees of predisposition to breast, uterine, ovarian and colon cancer, to osteoporosis and Huntington's disease. They are optimistic that genetically modified, pest-resistant plants will soon be bred widely. None of this, they argue, would have been possible without patents.   10

"The industry depends on patents to protect its investments," says a Swiss patent attorney, who would not be named. "It makes no distinction between machines and life, but says that patents encourage new products. Without them there would be no investment and the new cures and discoveries would not come."

It is a powerful argument, much favoured by governments. But behind the industry's faith that medicine and agriculture can be transformed, and improved, there is increasing concern at the privatisation of life forms and at the speed and direction of developments.

When leading biomedical researchers launched the internationally-funded $2 billion Human Genome Project in the late eighties, the intention was to "decode" all DNA (the store of genetic information). Scientists estimated that this would take about 15 years, that it would be funded largely by governments, and that the information would be freely accessible.

But genetic research is moving at lightning speed. Each new bit of information is being patented and rushed into the marketplace. Within weeks of the discovery of the colon-cancer gene, 10 US companies had bought the rights to develop a screening test for it.

The research is also moving in some strange directions. "Tracy the Sheep,"   15 patented by an Edinburgh-based biotech company, produces Alpha 1, an anti-trypsin drug used in treating patients with emphysema, an inherited lung disease. "Herman the bull" has been given a human gene which may allow his daughters to produce in their milk an anti-bacterial drug called lactoferrin. Herman's owners hope it will make breast-milk substitutes more like human milk.

But the torrent of information and developments is coming not from government-funded or university laboratories, but largely from private companies. They are eager to recoup their investments and quick to see the commercial possibilities of the gene rush. Next week an OECD° report will predict that biotechnology is moving into its third, perhaps largest domain—the prevention and cleaning up of polluted environments, worth, it estimates, $75 billion a year within five years.

OECD: Organization for Economic Cooperation and Development; founded in 1961 to provide "governments a setting in which to discuss, develop and perfect economic and social policy" (<http://www.oecd.org/about/general/index.htm>). Its twenty-nine member nations are located principally in western Europe, North America, and Asia.

But the industry's immediate concerns are over free access to knowledge, the point at which genetic material should become patentable, and what information, if any, should remain in the public domain. Alarm bells rang this year when the director of the Centre for the Study of Human Polymorphisms, a French foundation which holds the DNA fragments of more than 5,000 diabetics, tried to sell the foundation's genetic database to an American biotech company with which it was associated.

The foundation's scientists were outraged and the government had to intervene. The deal was stopped, but no one established who owned the DNA—the families who gave their genes, the research foundation, the scientists, or even the state.

Further warning bells rang when Merck, a leading drug company, established exclusive rights to patent material taken from much of Costa Rica's forests. They also rang as the International Agricultural Research Corporations, built up in developing countries over decades on UN money, debate whether to patent seed bases containing samples donated freely by third-world farmers.

But they clanged loudest when Dr. Craig Venter, a scientist at the US National   20
Institute of Health, applied in 1991 for patents on more than 7,000 fragments of DNA which he and his team had identified with automatic gene-sequencing technology. Venter did not know the function of the fragments beyond that they came from the brain and were crucial for development, including memory and intelligence. Medical institutions and academics were furious, arguing that he was laying claim to vast stretches of life rather than products. Under pressure, the US Patent Office rejected the applications.

Institute for Genome Research (IGR): a not-for-profit research institute founded in 1992 by Dr. Craig Venter.

But Venter then upped the ante: after filing the applications, he left the NIH to set up the Institute for Genome Research.° There he began the mass-sequencing of human genetic material. He has now reportedly compiled the world's largest human genetic data bank, believed to contain 150,000 fragments of DNA sequences—between one-third and half of all the 100,000-odd human genes.

Wellcome Trust: a charitable foundation established by Sir Henry Wellcome in 1936, who also founded the pharmaceutical company Burroughs Wellcome (now Glaxo Wellcome, in which the Trust maintains a 4.7 percent interest).

"The data is worth a lot as it is," says Dr. Michael Morgan, programme director of the Wellcome Trust.° "But if these fragments could be placed on a 'gene map,' so researchers knew where they came on the chromosomes, they could be worth many billions."

In April this year, SmithKline Beecham (SB), a major drug company, invested £80 million for an exclusive stake in Venter's database. The company told scientists they could have access to it on one condition: that IGR/SB retained first rights on any patentable discovery.

"In other words," says David King, a former geneticist who edits *Gen-Ethics News,* "you have a corporation trying to monopolise control of a large part of the whole human genome—literally, the human heritage. Should this become private property?" Yes and no, argues Professor Peter Goodfellow, head of genetics at Cambridge University. "It's like having a library of books and randomly tearing pages out. You may know which books the pages came from but that doesn't tell you much about them."

He argues there should be no patenting of gene sequences without their func-   25
tion having been identified. "To patent the whole genome is not reasonable. You can make a case for a company or an academic who finds out the function of a gene which has economic potential. It could be disastrous. It is an economic and political act to try and stop other people working in the area." A few companies, he argues, are potentially colonising science.

Goodfellow echoes third-world activists who see genetically engineered, patented crops dominating poor countries in a new version of the Green Revolution of the sixties. "The privatisation of life," says Vandana Shiva, an Indian physicist and author, "is now broadening out and entering uncharted waters which society is not ready for or prepared to accommodate."

Last year, Agracetus, a subsidiary of W. G. Grace, a giant agro-chemical company, was given the patent on all future genetically engineered cotton. Grace itself has a patent on all products of the common neem tree.°

neem tree: a tropical evergreen related to mahogany and used for centuries for various medicinal purposes in India and elsewhere.

The implications were not lost on Indian farmers. In last year's run-up to the finalisation of the GATT Uruguay Round,° which extended western models of intellectual-property rights into third-world countries, more than 500,000 farmers demonstrated against Grace and other seed companies. They believed the companies were being given the legal right to usurp traditional skills and knowledge. As Jerry Quisenberry, of the US Department of Agriculture, puts it: "These patents are like Ford getting the patent on the automobile."

GATT Uruguay Round: General Agreement on Tariffs and Trade; meetings held in 1995 in Uruguay during which the World Trade Organization (WTO) was founded.

For many, the gene rush and the patenting of life is offensive. The Hagahai people of Papua New Guinea first made contact with the West in 1984. Five years later, health workers collected blood samples from 24 members of the tribe. These were sent to the gene bank of the US National Institute of Health. Seven people were found to have HTLV-1 in their genetic make-up, a virus it was thought would help fight leukaemia. So last year the Hagahai DNA chain was patented by the US Department of Commerce.

Similar "gene-prospecting" episodes have led to the Solomon Islands' govern-   30
ment demanding that patents taken out by the US government on some of its
citizens' cell lines be retracted. One on a Guatemalan woman was withdrawn
only after pressure.

Meanwhile, the Human Genome Diversity Project (HGDP), a $20 million
(£ 13 million) multi-government funded programme, has been working to establish a gene bank of endangered peoples. It has so far identified 722 indigenous
groups. Researchers are now collecting genetic data from tribes including the
Penans of Malaysia, Australian aborigines, peoples of the Sahara, Latin
American Indians, and the Saamis of northern Norway and Sweden.

The programme is furiously opposed by indigenous groups, many of whom
have not even been told they were on the HGDP's hitlist. "After being subject to
ethnocide for 500 years, which is why we are endangered, the alternative now
is for our DNA to be collected," says Victoria Tauli-Corpuz, who has represented
indigenous peoples at the UN. "Why don't they address the causes of our being
endangered instead of spending millions to store us? How soon before they
apply for intellectual property rights and sell us?"

Yet the first signs of patenting peace may be emerging. In July, Merck
announced it would set up a database of genetic information to which everyone,
including competitors, would have access. The initiative was welcomed, but
widely interpreted by other companies and academics as an attempt by Merck
to claw itself back from a weak commercial position. A consortium from within
academia and industry is now trying to establish a free-access "gene map"—
vital for making sense of gene fragments.

But this is small comfort for the broader public, which has been only marginally
involved in the debate, and may still not see the full implications of the revolution. "Much of this genetic information will be perilous," warns Jessica Mathews,
a senior fellow at the US Council on Foreign Relations. "It will tell us whether
we are likely to die young of an untreatable disease. . . . It will reveal predispo-
sitions to various forms of mental illness, and what the future holds for a
prospective spouse, and the characteristics of an unborn child."

The information will undoubtedly save lives; it will also open up many other pos-   35
sibilities, such as in-vitro fertilisation, to ensure that parents do not pass along
dangerous genes. Yet, as Mathews puts it: "The options may only be available

to those who can afford to pay for them." Others proffer a more chilling scenario. After some years of screen-testing, as some geneticists see it, the gene pools of the rich and the poor would begin to diverge. At the top there would be improved genomes; and at the bottom, a "genetic underclass."

Still, the revolution is well under way, and we ignore it at our peril. "New genetic technologies will increasingly dominate existing health care and agriculture, adding to existing costs," says David King of *Gen-Ethics News*. "Private companies, rather than publicly funded science, are now setting the new healthcare and agricultural agenda. The ethical debate is still failing to take the basic commercial facts of life into account."

John Moore, who is US Patent number 4,438,032, would understand that.

RESPOND ●

1. As noted, the *Guardian* takes an overtly liberal political position. Would this article need to be written differently for a U.S. newspaper? If so, how? Do Vidal and Carvel reveal their positions on genetic research? Give examples to support your answers.

2. Vidal and Carvel begin the article with an extended example, the case of an Alaskan pipeline worker, John Moore. Why do you think the authors chose to begin and end the article with this example? What kind of argument is it? How does it compare or contrast with the arguments in the remainder of the essay?

3. Vidal and Carvel present a great deal of complex information about genetic research, yet you may still want to know more about the topic before you formulate your own position on proprietorship of genetic information and material. What else, if anything, would you have wanted Vidal and Carvel to tell you? Why? Consider the credentials of the experts cited in the article. What other authorities, if any, would you like to have heard from in the article?

4. John Moore, whose DNA was patented without his knowledge, believes that "all genetic material extracted from human beings should belong to society as a whole" (paragraph 5). Do you find his suggestion worthwhile and viable? Why or why not? What has happened since this article appeared in 1994 to make Moore's suggestion more or less appealing? Research recent developments in the field of human genetics, and **write an essay** arguing for or against Moore's suggestion. Provide evidence to back up your position.

▼ This article made the front page of the Recorder, a daily legal newspaper published in San Francisco that reports on news and topics of interest to attorneys and others involved in legal practice, in June 1998. The topic here—human reproduction—formerly one of the most personal and private of all acts, is increasingly the subject of arguments involving medicine, law, and technology. As these arguments make clear, the interests of researchers, doctors, judges, legislators, potential parents, donors, surrogates, and, ultimately, the offspring themselves often stand in direct conflict. As you read, remember that Mike McKee is writing to an audience of attorneys.

Weighing the Right to Own an Embryo

MIKE MCKEE

Before he killed himself in a Las Vegas hotel in 1991, William Kane deposited 15 vials of sperm at a Los Angeles cryobank so that his girlfriend could eventually use them to have his baby.

"If she does," he wrote nine days before his Oct. 30 death, "this letter is for my posthumous offspring . . . with the thought that I have loved you in my dreams, even though I never got to see you born. . . . I wanted to leave you something more than a dead enigma that was your father."

As it turned out, what the 48-year-old Kane left behind was worse than an enigma. It was a legal morass, as his two adult children contested his girlfriend Deborah Hecht's right to his sperm.

This was the first and only case in California to deal with the cutting-edge social, legal and ethical issues raised when one party objects to another using frozen genetic material to achieve pregnancy. Advances in technology will only propel arguments over frozen sperm, frozen embryos and increasingly complex surrogacy arrangements into the next century. So far, there are few, or conflicting, laws offering guidance nationwide, and courts have turned to competing contract law and public policy holdings to guide their decisions.

"There definitely needs to be legislation in this area," says Yueh-ru Chu, a former attorney at the New York Civil Liberties Union and an expert on the subject. "It's basically a void at the moment and state courts are dealing with these issues as they come up."

Attention was focused on this subject on May 7 when New York's highest court held that a woman could not use her frozen embryos to impregnate herself without her ex-husband's consent.

Maureen Kass had unsuccessfully argued that the privacy rights established by *Roe v. Wade*, 410 U.S. 113, empowered her to determine the fate of her embryos. But the New York court rejected that argument and held that Kass must abide by a contract she had signed that required both her and her ex-husband's consent before the embryos could be used.

"Advance agreements as to disposition would have little purpose if they were enforceable only in the event the parties continued to agree," the court said.

A similar case is moving forward in New Jersey. But Tennessee's high court is the only other in the nation to have already tackled the touchy topic of frozen-embryo usage without invoking *Roe*. Tennessee reached the same conclusions as New York—siding with the unwilling father-to-be—but for slightly different legal reasons.

While both rulings can be used as persuasive authority by other states' courts, neither carries precedential weight outside their own state borders. And most state legislatures haven't exactly rushed to fill the vacuum.

5

10

"No one wants to live with the legacy of having guessed wrong on these topics," says Leslie Shear, an Encino solo practitioner who specializes in family law issues. "Science and society are changing at a rate faster than courts and legislatures can anticipate and respond."

To Birth or Not to Birth

In the California probate case, the Los Angeles-based Second District Court of Appeal—in its third foray into the area—sided with the hopeful mother, Hecht, by declaring that her deceased lover's intent was the crucial factor in determining the fate of his sperm.

"Seldom has this court reviewed a probate case where the decedent evidenced his or her intent so clearly," Justice Earl Johnson Jr. wrote on Nov. 13, 1996. "Neither this court nor decedent's adult children possess reason or right to prevent Hecht from implementing decedent's preeminent interest in realizing his 'fundamental right' to procreate with the woman of his choice."

Any precedential value that *Hecht v. Superior Court,* 50 Cal.App.4th 1289, could have offered, though, was lost when the California Supreme Court unexpectedly depublished ° it two months later. If, as expected, another dispute over frozen sperm or embryos eventually lands in court, California lawyers will basically have to start from scratch.

Experts say that the lack of judi- 15 cial or legislative guidance isn't entirely surprising.

"You aren't exactly playing God, but it's not something far from it,"

says Chu, now an associate at New York's Kornstein, Veisz & Wexler. "And I think that's why courts don't want to get in there and start grappling with it."

But Fourth District Justice David Sills—whose San Diego court has been saddled with all of California's precedent-setting cases on surrogacy—says judges and legislators can't hide their heads in the sand much longer.

"Both the judicial system and the legislative process are going to have to learn to deal with scientific advances that are coming much quicker than in the last century," he says. "Not only in regard to reproduction law, but also with end-of-life decisions, how to deal with scientific evidence and with different genetic questions."

Sills, who has tweaked legislators' noses more than once about their lack of guidance on scientific issues, did so again in a March 10 case involving a child birthed by a surrogate mother using a donor egg and sperm—neither from the intended parents. (The couple filed for divorce a few days before the child was born and the prospective father attempted to back out of the contract.)

"Courts can continue to make 20 decisions on an ad hoc basis without necessarily imposing some grand scheme," he wrote in *In re Marriage of Buzzanca,* 61 Cal.App.4th 1410. "Or the Legislature can act to impose a broader order, which, even though it might not be perfect on a case-by-case basis, would bring some predictability to those who seek to make use of artificial reproductive technologies."

New York legislators attempted to do exactly that late last year in anticipation of their high court's frozen-embryo ruling in *Kass v. Kass,* 98 N.Y. Int. 0049.

Introduced on Nov. 24, New York Senate Bill 5815 would require advanced written directives from couples about how to dispose of their frozen eggs or embryos in the event of divorce, death or other unforeseen factors.

Maureen and Steven Kass had signed consent forms in May 1993 giving them sole responsibility for determining what to do with the five frozen embryos stored by their fertilization clinic. But about three weeks later, they instituted divorce proceedings and began clashing over the embryos: Maureen wanted to use them to become pregnant, and Steven opposed that.

That's when Maureen argued that the U.S. Supreme Court's 1973 *Roe* ruling, which gave a woman "exclusive control over the fate of her nonviable fetus," should also apply to the fate of a woman's embryo. The New York Court of Appeals—the state's highest bench—disagreed, stating flatly that the disposition of the embryos "does not implicate a

---

depublication: courts designate some, but not all of their decisions for publication in legal case reports, which can then be cited as precedents for future decisions. Depublication occurs when the court changes its mind about the status of a case and withdraws it from inclusion in legal case reports.

woman's right of privacy or bodily integrity in the area of reproductive choice."

The ruling required Maureen Kass 25 to abide by the original contract that demanded both parties' consent for use of the embryos.

That dovetailed with the thinking of the New York Civil Liberties Union, which had argued in an *amicus curiae* brief° that in situations where no clear agreement exists, the court "should adopt a strong presumption in favor of the party wishing to avoid parenthood.

"To allow implantation over the objection of the unwilling party is to impose affirmative, irrevocable and lifelong emotional attachments and moral responsibilities as well as substantial financial obligations on an unconsenting individual," then-NYCLU lawyer Chu wrote. "While the loss of a possibly unique opportunity to become a parent is without doubt a significant one, such a loss will not carry with it the many and significant obligations of parenthood."

The Tennessee Supreme Court had said something similar in its 1992 ruling in *Davis v. Davis,* 842 S.W.2d

---

amicus curiae brief: "amicus curiae" is a Latin phrase meaning "friend of the court." An *amicus curiae* brief is presented by some individual or group not involved in the specific legal case to provide the court with relevant legal information about the potential impact of the court's decision.

588. While holding that there were two rights of equal significance in the case—"the right to procreate and the right to avoid procreation"—the court said that in most cases "the party wishing to avoid procreation should prevail."

The court indirectly touched on *Roe v. Wade,* which was raised by neither party, by saying: "None of the concerns about a woman's bodily integrity that have previously precluded men from controlling abortion decisions is applicable here."

And although there was no con- 30 tract at issue in *Davis,* the court foreshadowed New York's *Kass* by holding that if there had been, it likely would have been valid.

CONTRACT V. INTENT

The contract rationale of *Davis* and *Kass* pleases Joseph Gitlin, co-chairman of the American Bar Association's genetics and reproductive technologies committee. His group hopes by January to debut a model law, called the Assisted Reproductive Technologies Act, that could be adopted by states to require written agreements between couples about the disposition of genetic material.

"You tell the fertilization clinics that they can't do this work unless they have a contract between the parties saying what the intentions of the people are," says Gitlin, a partner in Woodstock, Illinois' Gitlin & Gitlin. "Why should you have to try to divine what the intent was" later in court?

But Encino solo Shear, who filed an *amicus* brief for the Association of Certified Family Law Specialists in

California's *Buzzanca* surrogacy case, says she worries about reproduction rights being regulated by contract.

"When you have private contract law, it's protecting only the rights of the adults and not the prospective child," she says. "Society can't tolerate this core area of law to be governed by contract."

Intent is a better barometer, Shear 35 says.

That issue played out in *Buzzanca,* when John Buzzanca tried to deny fatherhood to Jaycee, a child birthed for the Buzzancas by a surrogate who had agreed to be implanted with an egg and sperm provided by neither Buzzanca or his wife.

The contract signed by the Buzzancas was "evidence that this procreation was deliberate," says Shear. "It was a means by which he symbolically took responsibility for the child."

Sills was even more blunt in his ruling.

"Let us get right to the point: Jaycee never would have been born," he wrote, "had not Luanne and John both agreed to have a fertilized egg implanted in a surrogate."

Intent also played a role in both 40 the New York and Tennessee frozen-embryo cases. The couples in both states intended to be parents while married, but those intentions divided upon divorce. That forced the courts to determine intent—New York doing so based on a written contract and Tennessee on statements by the ex-husband that he had sought parenthood while married, but not afterward.

Even *Hecht,* the California probate case, turned on intent. "The intent of the sperm donor — and no one else's — controls the disposition and use of the sperm," the court held.

But as Justice Sills points out in *Buzzanca,* case-by-case handling of such issues isn't ideal. "These cases will not go away," he notes, and likely will just get more complex as artificial reproduction technology progresses. Legislation would help.

"We'd best come to grips with the problem because I don't think we've dealt very rapidly with these questions," Sills says. "The challenge for the courts . . . in the next century is how they deal with science and technology."

Use the criteria given in Chapter 18 to determine whether you think McKee chose appropriate evidence and used it effectively.

LINK TO P. 308 ·······································

····· **RESPOND** ●

1. McKee sets up several dualities in his article — "To Birth or Not to Birth" (paragraphs 12–30), "Contract v. Intent" (31–43), and judicial versus legislative authority (4). Why do you think McKee frames his article as a set of *either-or* propositions? Consider his audience here. Would such a structure be effective for an audience of researchers in reproduction technology? For an audience of legislators? Of prospective parents? Why or why not? How would you present the issues differently to each of these audiences — and why?

2. Are all of the *either-or* oppositions identified in the preceding question really a matter of only two options? Do any other options exist, even some that productively combine the two poles McKee sets up? Choose one of the dualities he sets up, and outline all the possible variations of it you can think of.

3. What do you think should happen with frozen embryos of couples who have divorced? Research *Kass v. Kass* or a similar case, and **write an essay** proposing a particular course of action. In constructing your essay, use artistic argument based on facts and reason as your primary mode of argumentation (see Chapter 7).

▼ *Steven Walters and Marilynn Marchione wrote this article in July 1999,
when it appeared on the front page of the* Milwaukee Journal Sentinel,
*a daily newspaper. The article reports on a speech given by Wisconsin
Governor Tommy Thompson at a ceremony he hosts annually for transplant
recipients. Thompson used that ceremonial occasion to speak about his
opposition to pending federal rules for the allocation of donated organs. As
you read, think about why Thompson chose this audience to hear "his first
public comments" on the proposed federal rules. Also think about the kind of
argument Walters and Marchione are making in the article.*

Plan Would Alter Region for Organ Sharing
Thompson, UW Hope to Keep Donated Livers Out of Illinois and Still Meet Rules

**STEVEN WALTERS
AND MARILYNN MARCHIONE**

MAPLE BLUFF — Gov. Tommy G. Thompson on Monday endorsed creating an organ-sharing region with Minnesota and North and South Dakota as a way to keep Wisconsin organs out of Illinois and still meet new federal rules for sharing organs.

The new region, proposed by the head of the University of Wisconsin-Madison's transplant program, would replace the five-state region that includes Illinois.

Speaking at his annual ceremony for transplant recipients, Thompson denounced the pending federal rules, saying they would penalize the state that's doing the best job of persuading grieving relatives to give organs that allow others to live.

In his first public comments since several recent setbacks for the state on organ transplant policy, Thompson railed against "dictatorial" federal rules that would send more organs to sicker patients out of state.

"Voice your concern to those in Washington," Thompson told about 450 people invited to the governor's mansion for the tearful ceremony. "We have a system in Wisconsin that works. Don't take from the state that is doing the best job."

At the ceremony, Hans Sollinger, the surgeon who heads UW-Madison's transplant program, proposed a way to avoid having the rules harm Wisconsin by creating the new organ-sharing region that excludes Illinois.

"We want to be good neighbors and to play a fair game," but Chicago-area transplant programs won't agree to a payback system for organs sent to them from Wisconsin or other states in the region, Sollinger said.

Sollinger agreed with Thompson, saying we have "a very special problem" in this state where successful organ transplant programs are threatened. "We can't allow that to happen to Wisconsin," he said.

Thompson said the federal rules would result in more organs perishing because they'd have to travel greater distances. The rules also could lead fewer Wisconsinites to donate organs if they knew organs were destined for another part of the country, he said.

One reason Wisconsin's transplant program is the best nationally is "the personal connection that's felt saving the life of someone down the street," Thompson said.

Instead of "reversing the hard work we have done" and forcing Wisconsin to export organs, other states should model this one's procurement efforts, he said. "Take what is right and pass it on."

Wisconsin's problems with organ transplant policy began in March 1998, when U.S. Health and Human Services Secretary Donna Shalala ordered that the system be overhauled to give the sickest patients priority for organs regardless of where they live. All organs would be affected by the policy, but livers have been most hotly contested because that's where the shortage is most acute.

The United Network for Organ Sharing, or UNOS, the agency that has a federal contract to run the organ allocation system, fought Shalala's order, and about a dozen states, including Wisconsin, adopted laws requiring organs to remain in the state in which they were donated.

Congress delayed Shalala's order from taking effect until this October and ordered the Institute of Medicine, a group of physicians who advise the government, to study the issue.

Meanwhile, in June, UNOS 15 adopted new guidelines requiring regional sharing of livers for the sickest, or Status 1 patients. Now, organs are offered locally to all transplant candidates, regardless of medical status, and then regionally. The new UNOS guidelines mean that Wisconsin residents would have to compete for livers with busy programs in Chicago, which nearly always have Status 1 patients.

The existing five-state region has 24 million people, and dropping Illinois would cut that number in half — an ideal size, Sollinger said. He said he would seek an agreement within the new four-state region so that any transplant program receiving a liver from outside its organ procurement agency would send back a liver at a later date.

It would mean "a very healthy back-and-forth sharing" by Midwestern neighbors, Sollinger said. "The give-and-take would be about equal." With 12 million residents, Illinois is large enough to be a region by itself, he said.

Wisconsin needs UNOS's approval to create a new region or redraw regional boundaries.

Mark Adams, a professor of surgery at the Medical College of Wisconsin who heads Froedtert Memorial Lutheran Hospital's liver transplant program, said Sollinger's plan "makes a lot of sense" because the four states involved have "a long history of working cooperatively together."

"We trust each other," Adams said, 20 "but we don't trust Chicago."

Officials at the Mayo Clinic, whose liver transplant program serves North and South Dakota as well as Minnesota, declined comment on the proposal.

A transplant recipient and several people who authorized donation of a relative's organs also spoke at the ceremony.

Gladys Penne of Greenfield recalled the day in 1991 when physicians told her and her husband that their daughter, Donna, 22, would never recover from brain injuries suffered when she was abducted, robbed and thrown from a speeding car in Waukesha County.

She said family members have "an overwhelming sense of joy" knowing that Donna's heart, kidney, liver, eyes, skin and bones "continue to sustain life for others."

Michael Medland, 57, of Madison 25 received the liver of a 14-year-old New Holstein boy killed in an ATV accident almost six years ago. He said he, his wife, four sons, mother, brothers and sisters understand "that most wonderful gift of life" — organ transplantation.

"I'm very happy to be alive," Medland said. "There are thousands of us."

What function does Donna Penne's story serve here? See Chapter 4, "Arguments from the Heart," to find the answer.

LINK TO P. 52 ···

RESPOND •

1. Is this front-page newspaper article an example of unbiased reporting, or does it take a particular position on the issue it discusses? How do you know? Provide evidence for your conclusion.

2. Do you find Walters and Marchione's article cohesive? Why or why not? The requirements of a journalistic article and an academic essay are very different. What would you have to do to convert this newspaper article into an academic argument? Explain the changes you would make in structure, organization, and style.

3. Walters and Marchione quote a brief comment made by the head of a Milwaukee hospital's liver transplant program: "We trust each other [Wisconsin, Minnesota, North and South Dakota], but we don't trust Chicago" (paragraph 20). How might that comment, given with very little other explanation, be an effective argument based on values for the audience of the *Journal Sentinel* in particular? (Hint: Why might Wisconsinites not trust Chicagoans?)

4. Do you think state boundaries should be an important consideration in the allocation of donated organs in the United States? If not, what would you recommend as a fair method? Research the issues involved in the current controversy in this country and, perhaps, the policies of other countries on organ recipients. **Write an essay** defining your position on this issue. Rely primarily on argument based on facts and reason (see Chapter 7), and provide examples and other types of evidence to support your position.

▼ *"Organ Donor Drive by Muslim Group," an unsigned article, appeared in a July 1999 issue of the* Straits Times, *a daily English-language newspaper published in Singapore, the smallest nation in Southeast Asia. Singapore has the lowest birth and population growth rates in that region, as well as a high literacy rate, a high life expectancy, and a low infant mortality rate. The population is quite diverse; ethnically, Singaporeans are prin- cipally Chinese, Malay, and Indian. About two-thirds of the population observe the traditional Chinese religions of Confucianism, Buddhism, and Taoism; about 17 percent—virtually all of the Malays and Indians—practice Islam; and about 10 percent, almost all of whom are Chinese, practice Christianity. Singapore is a parliamentary democracy; voting is compulsory, as is military service for males over eighteen years of age. The Human Organ Transplant Act of 1987, discussed in this article, authorizes hospitals to remove the kidneys of patients who die as a result of an accident (of unspecified type) unless the patient had previously filed official forms to opt out. No other organ or cause of death is addressed by the law. At the end of this Web text, you'll find text for a graphic that likely accompanied the original article. The information summarizes the legislation and provides readers with quick information about its consequences and origins.*

Organ Donor Drive by Muslim Group

STRAITS TIMES (SINGAPORE)

A group proposing legislation to make it easier for Muslims here to become kid- ney donors will launch [a] six-month effort to garner support and feedback.

New organ donation legislation is being proposed to get more Muslims to be kidney donors.

It will be similar to the Human Organ Transplant Act, which provides for Singaporeans between the ages of 21 and 60 to become kidney donors auto- matically upon death, unless they opt out.

However, Muslims are exempted from the Act and must instead choose to become donors. They also need the consent of two male next-of-kin if they want to pledge their kidneys.

The proposed legislation will assume that every Muslim is a potential kidney   5 donor but with one important caveat: a pledger's kidneys cannot be removed if two male next-of-kin object.

An intensive six-month campaign begins next month to get the Muslim community's feedback and support on the legislation.

The group behind the proposal is the Muslim Kidney Action Committee, which was set up to increase the number of potential kidney donors among the 400,000 Muslims in Singapore.

At a press briefing yesterday, the committee said that if Muslims here are in favour of its suggestion, it will draft a detailed proposal.

This will be submitted to the Islamic Religious Council of Singapore (MUIS) and Minister-in-charge of Muslim Affairs Abdullah Tarmugi for further action.

Committee chairman Ameerali Abdeali said it would ask Malay/Muslim organisations here for feedback, and use road shows, seminars and mailers to reach out to the community.   10

Kidney donation has long been a sensitive issue for the Muslim community here because Muslims believe they must be buried with their organs intact.

Under the Medical (Therapy, Education and Research) Act that governs only Muslims, they have to pledge their kidneys or opt in if they want to become donors. By doing so, they can, if their kidneys fail, get subsidised dialysis treatment and priority for kidney transplants.

The number of Muslim kidney patients is on the rise. There is now an average of 80 new cases a year, compared with 50 five years ago, said Mr. Ameerali.

Only 11,400 Muslims out of a possible 250,000 have pledged their kidneys. But this small number does not necessarily mean the community does not support kidney donation.

"It is just that the process of pledging kidneys is laborious," said Mr. Ameerali.   15

A Muslim spokesman said it would review the community's feedback fully before making a statement.

KIDNEY DONATION: a new legislation?

UNDER the existing legislation, Muslims must choose to become donors.

PROPOSED LEGISLATION: Will assume that all Muslims are potential kidney donors, unless the person has opted out of the scheme, or if his kidney donation is vetoed by two male next-of-kin upon his death.

RESPOND •

1. What is your response to this article on kidney donations in Singapore? Why might many American readers be shocked to learn that the Singaporean government assumes the right to remove a person's kidneys? Does this article lead you to question some of your basic presumptions about "ownership" of your body? Why or why not?

2. The Muslim Kidney Action Committee aims to persuade more Muslims to become kidney donors. What types of arguments do you think it might employ? How might its appeals differ from a similar campaign to Muslims in the United States? (You may need to do some research on Islam in order to answer this question.)

3. What kind of debate do you think would ensue if a bill similar to Singapore's Human Organ Transplant Act (HOTA) were introduced in the United States? On what grounds would the issue be argued? Are there any U.S. groups (by region, religion, social class, and so on) that might advocate or oppose such a bill? What might their arguments be? **Write an essay** in which you state your position on the issues raised by Singapore's HOTA and justify it.

▼ *This story appeared on May 19, 1999, on the first page of the metro/regional news section of the* Boston Globe. *James Bandler reports on the return of two thousand skeletal remains of the Pecos Pueblo people to New Mexico by Harvard's Peabody Museum of Archeology and Ethrology, some eighty-four years after they were unearthed in 1916. As you read, think about who might make up the readership of the Boston newspaper and what interest that audience might have in the event reported here.*

A Long Journey Home
Decades after Dig, Remains Returning to N.M. Tribe

JAMES BANDLER

Alfred V. Kidder offered 50 cents to the man who found the first skeleton.

It was 1916, and Kidder, a pipe-smoking archeologist fresh out of Harvard's graduate school, stood atop a rocky knoll overlooking New Mexico's Pecos Valley. On this tongue of land, Kidder's team had begun unearthing the ruins of an American Indian pueblo.

The Pecos dig, later hailed by scholars as the coming of age of American archeology, would propel Kidder into prominence in his field. It would create one of the most important collections of human remains in the United States, leading to ground-breaking research in the study of osteoporosis.

But it would also cause wrenching pain to the descendants of the Pecos Indians whose remains were exhumed. Today, with the return of the remains to New Mexico imminent, they regard the excavation as a desecration, and they wonder how anyone could have so thoughtlessly violated holy ground.

But on that early summer day as his team picked through the red soil, Kidder had his mind on more temporal matters. He was thinking about bones. "I was very anxious, of course, to find skeletons, because they would lead to pottery," Kidder wrote in his memoirs. "We began to find skeletons pretty soon."

On the second day of digging, a single skeleton was uncovered. Kidder reduced the reward to 25 cents. The more they dug, the more skeletons they discovered, and the finder's fee was lowered to a dime.

"I finally said if they found any more skeletons, I would fine them," Kidder recalled years later. "That rubbish heap was literally full of skeletons."

That "rubbish heap," actually a resting place where the Pecos buried their dead alongside ordinary objects, and the hundreds of rooms next to it ultimately yielded more than 2,000 human remains. The Kidder excavation also took thousands of artifacts, including ceramic vessels, shell pendants, and effigies. The bones and artifacts date from the 12th century to the 1830s.

While most of the bones were taken to Harvard's Peabody Museum of Archeology and Ethnology, the artifacts have been kept at Phillips Academy of Andover's Robert Peabody Museum of Archeology, which sponsored Kidder's excavation.

Yesterday, 84 years after Kidder began his work in Pecos, the remains and remaining artifacts finally started their journey home after a ceremony at the Harvard museum. On Saturday there will be a private reburial ceremony in Pecos, N.M., marking the largest repatriation of American Indian remains.

"It's a phenomenal event," said William Whatley, tribal preservation officer for the Pueblo of Jemez, a tribe that traces its lineage to the Pecos Pueblo. "It's a closing of the circle."

Is Whatley being literal or metaphorical about the closing of the circle? It could be argued both ways; check out Chapter 14 to help you decide.

⋯⋯⋯LINK TO P. 242

The reburial ends years of negotiations between tribal officials and the two museums—a process that began four years after the passage of the federal Native American Graves Protection and Repatriation Act in 1990. The law requires museums to inventory their collections of items that might have sacred or special tribal significance and to return them to those tribes that can make strong claims.

Jemez tribal representatives paid their first visit to Harvard's Peabody Museum in 1996. They were led to a sprawling, two-storied storage room filled with thousands of boxes of human remains. The Pecos remains occupied nearly the entire second level of the room—and the sight of them caused the tribal leaders to weep. The tribal leaders then consulted the spirits of the ancestors, Whatley said. The answer, he said, was unequivocal: "We want to go home."

Anthropologists and medical researchers have regarded the Pecos collection as a scientific treasure. The bones, by and large, are in remarkably good condition, and the collection, which is demographically representative of a single population, is large enough to be statistically significant. The bones have been studied by dozens of researchers, from eugenicists in the 1930s who equated cranial size with intelligence, to scientists who have engaged in more legitimate inquiries—everything from head injuries to tooth decay.

One of the most significant pieces 15 of research was performed by Johns Hopkins University anthropologist Christopher Ruff. His studies demonstrated that exercise could strengthen aging bones by enlarging them to compensate for the shrinkage associated with osteoporosis.

Ruff called the repatriation of the bones a "significant loss to science," but he said he also understands the fiercely emotional sentiments of the Jemez people.

The Jemez, who say their ancestors migrated from Pecos Pueblo in 1838, said they are glad some good came from the bones' presence at Harvard. But they said no amount of scientific research would compensate for Kidder's desecration. "It's our belief that no one has the right to disturb the graves of another man's ancestors," Whatley said.

Yet Whatley said the tribe bore no animosity toward Kidder, Harvard, or Andover. He said Harvard's Peabody Museum curators had handled the remains with the care of parents. Representatives from both the Harvard and Andover museums, he said, would be invited to Pecos for the May 22 ceremony. "Even though it's a private family funeral, those representatives will be standing side by side with us," Whatley said. "They're considered family."

As for Kidder, he died of heart failure in 1963 after an illustrious career and was buried in Mount Auburn Cemetery. But his story didn't end there.

Before she died, Kidder's wife, 20 Madeleine, requested that upon her death, her husband's remains be exhumed from his grave in Cambridge, cremated, and reburied in New Mexico, next to hers. Today, a simple, flat stone by a stream bed marks the grave, a half mile or so from the site of Kidder's famous dig.

"It was a place he deeply loved," said Kidder's only surviving son, James. "He was repatriated, too."

RESPOND●

1. Bandler describes the first visit made by Jemez tribal representatives to the Harvard museum to begin negotiating for the repatriation of their Pecos ancestors' remains, writing that "the sight of [the remains] caused the tribal leaders to weep" (paragraph 13). Do you think this statement is an argument of emotion? Why or why not? Are there any arguments of emotion in this article? What are they?

2. "A Long Journey Home" appeared in the regional news section of a Boston newspaper, near where Harvard University is located. Compare it with Miguel Navrot's "Ancestors Return Home" (p. 559), which appeared in the *Albuquerque Journal* a few days after Bandler's article was published in the *Globe*. Which events or features of the story does each author and newspaper choose to emphasize? Why might the authors and newspaper editors have made these choices? What is the central argument of each piece?

3. Why do you think Bandler ends his article with an anecdote about archaeologist Alfred Kidder? Is the anecdote relevant? What does it contribute to the article as a whole?

4. What basic assumptions permitted early twentieth-century researchers, scholars, and speculators in archaeology to think it was acceptable to "own" human remains? What factors do you think may have led more recent researchers, scholars, and the general public to rethink these assumptions? Would you visit a museum to see an exhibit of Egyptian mummies or of the remains of people from various social groups, including your own? Why or why not?

5. Read the article on organ sharing by Steven Walters and Marilynn Marchione (p. 550). How is the Jemez view on ownership of human remains similar to the view of Governor Thompson of Wisconsin? How is it different? On the surface there may not appear to be any common characteristics between the two views, yet both make similar claims of group propriety. **Write an essay** in which you compare and evaluate these two views of body ownership.

▼ This story about the repatriation of ancestral remains to the Jemez Pueblo appeared on May 23, 1999, on the front page of the Albuquerque Journal, a daily newspaper with the largest circulation in New Mexico. Another article of similar length covering this event appeared on the front page on May 17, the day that the remains left Massachusetts. As you read, look for ways in which Miguel Navrot is writing to a local audience.

Ancestors Return Home

Jemez Pueblo Turned Out in Force as Bones of Almost 2,000 Native Americans Were Reburied Saturday

MIGUEL NAVROT

PECOS NATIONAL HISTORICAL PARK—Escorted by hundreds of tribal officials, elders and members, the ancestral remains of nearly 2,000 Native Americans returned home Saturday. Their return, touted as the largest act of Native American repatriation in the nation's history, capped years of work among tribal leaders, museum administrators and government officials.

The remains and hundreds of artifacts had been exhumed from Pecos Pueblo roughly 75 years ago by archaeologist Alfred V. Kidder, and some date back to the 12th century.

"This repatriation is a very, very important political victory, not only for the Pueblo of Jemez, but for all Native Americans across the United States," said 2nd Lt. Gov. Ruben Sando of Jemez after Saturday's private burial ceremony.

Saturday's reburial of ancestors of the Pecos, Comanche, Kiowa, Apache, Navajo and other Native

A TIME OF JOY: Dolores Toya, from Jemez Pueblo, celebrates the return of American Indian remains to Pecos National Historical Park on Saturday.

Americans brought a dramatic end to the Jemez quest to reinter the remains. Many of the Jemez people trace their ancestry to the last of the Pecos survivors who abandoned the site in 1838.

The remains and artifacts arrived at the park under escort of law enforcement and more than 600 tribal officials, elders, members and invited guests, who walked just over a mile to the park entrance under Saturday's early morning sun. Boxed in cardboard, the remains and artifacts had been trucked from Massachusetts last week in a tractor-trailer.

The procession into the park stretched about the length of a football field as walkers brimmed over the sides of two-lane N.M. 63. A delegation of tribal officials and elders, clad in brightly colored traditional clothing, walked at the head.

Bearing the Pecos Pueblo Governor's Cane given to the pueblo while Spain claimed possession of present-day New Mexico, Sando led the walk, eyes fixed straight ahead throughout. Tribal member Ada Romero walked near the procession front, sprinkling corn meal along the path from a small woven basket she carried.

Saturday's procession also marked the final leg of a four-day march by hundreds of Jemez members from their pueblo to the national park. Tribal officials calculated the distance of the trek at 100 miles over sand, rocks, sun-baked asphalt, sections of the Santa Fe River and stretches of road under construction.

The journey left walkers with blistered and bruised feet, although many, like Jemez resident Julian Vigil, said they weren't concerned with pain Saturday.

"It's a sacrifice," Vigil said. "It's a sacrifice for our people, and a sacrifice for our ancestors."

Elvera Gachupin, a cousin to tribal Gov. Raymond Gachupin, spoke of the walkers' arrival at Pecos. I'm proud of our accomplishment," she said. "I'm very happy about what we've done. I'm sore, I guess, but I'm happy."

Upon their approach to the park gate, procession participants followed the truck into a closed-off section for private burial rites for the remains and artifacts.

Following the ceremonies, participants gathered for acknowledgments of the work that went into the event. An emotional Sando, whose voice halted occasionally during his speech, said Saturday's reburial symbolized a new beginning for the Jemez people.

"Our ancestors and other tribes who were born here, played here, sang and danced along this beautiful Pecos River valley and mountain, who were taken away for so many years, are now home," Sando said. "I guarantee to all of you that they are joyously happy, as we all are."

Reclaiming the remains was a long, quiet process for the tribe. In September 1991, then-Gov. Jose Toledo, other officials and tribal archaeologist William Whatley began formal meetings with the park service about returning the skeletal remains dug up in the 1910s and 1920s at the long-deserted pueblo. Their meetings began shortly after then-President George Bush signed the Native American Graves Protection and Repatriation Act of 1990 into law.

Tribal leaders pursued their goal with tribal and federal officials and museum representatives for nearly eight years, telling few outsiders of their efforts.

Last month, those efforts finally paid off.

"We have completed that journey," Gov. Gachupin said Saturday. "This may be a political victory for our people, and maybe for all Native American people throughout the country."

The remains had been kept for study at the Peabody Museum of Archaeology and Ethnology.

Michele Morgan, an associate of osteology at Peabody, said that unlike some other acts of repatriation the museum is working on, no disputes arose as to the rightful owners of the "Pecos Collection."

"The Jemez case presents no real gray areas for us," Morgan said in a recent interview. The museum, mandated by federal law to return sections of its collection to the rightful Native American owners, also is compelled to ensure remains and artifacts go to the proper people.

"That's what can take more time than (we) or the tribes would sometimes like," Morgan added.

The eight years of work by the Jemez people, though, have yielded more than just the return of their ancestral remains, Sando said.

"It proves on a very large scale that Native Americans do have rights to the artifacts, objects and human remains that have been taken from their ancestral lands."

RESPOND●

1. The readership of the *Albuquerque Journal* would certainly include many Native American and other readers supportive of the goal of the Pueblo of Jemez, but there would also likely be a significant number of readers who are not sympathetic to Native American claims. Although this article appeared on the front page of a daily newspaper, it may not necessarily assume a neutral stance on the event. Does Navrot take a position in this article? How do you know? Give evidence from the text to support your answer.

2. Compare Navrot's article with the preceding article on the same event published in the *Boston Globe*. Note that both articles quote Jemez official William Whatley; the Boston article identifies Whatley as "tribal preservation officer," while the Albuquerque article identifies him as "tribal archaeologist." (Whatley holds both offices, and both titles are accurate.) Why might each paper have chosen the single title that it did to identify Whatley? What are the denotative differences in meaning between the two titles? The connotative differences?

3. Anthropologist Christopher Ruff, who had used the Pecos remains for medical research, is quoted in the previous article as saying that "the repatriation of the bones [is] a 'significant loss to science'" (paragraph 16). Do you think the needs of science would ever prevail over Native Americans' right to own their ancestors' remains? (You'll likely find that this is not a simple "yes" or "no" situation.) Under what conditions, if any, would science have a legitimate claim to human remains? Within a certain time period after death? Whose remains? Would some types of research have more legitimate claims than others? **Write an essay** in which you propose research guidelines that would address these questions and argue for the adoption of your guidelines. What types of argument will you rely on to make your case? What authorities will you want to quote?

Use the criteria for assessing sources in Chapter 21 to determine if Navrot's article would be a good source for a paper on the repatriation of Native American remains. Would it be a good source for a paper on Jemez history? On the Peabody Museum?

LINK TO P. 334

The second cluster of arguments in this chapter deals with issues of intellectual property and, more specifically, **who owns words.** You've likely never given it much thought, but about 20 percent—one-fifth—of the price you paid for this textbook went to cover the cost of intellectual property—not just royalties paid to the book's authors but also permission fees paid to the authors, photographers, and artists to reprint the arguments you're analyzing. In fact, some texts and illustrations were not used in this book because the cost of using them—the price to be paid for reproducing the intellectual property—was simply too expensive.

The cluster begins with an excerpt from Charles C. Mann's essay "Who Will Own Your Next Good Idea?" The essay originally appeared in the *Atlantic Monthly* and serves as a quick overview of the sorts of issues associated with intellectual property. Next comes a cartoon representing a very real conflict in the realm of intellectual property—the rights of musical artists and those of technosavvy consumers who download music from the Internet.

The remainder of the cluster offers a case study in intellectual property by focusing on reactions to a court case involving the estate of Dr. Martin Luther King Jr. and the Columbia Broadcasting Service (CBS). While CBS contends that Dr. King's "I Have a Dream" speech (reprinted in this book in Chapter 28) is in the public domain—that is, that anyone can reproduce the words without seeking permission or paying royalties—the King family contends that it is not and that CBS must pay the estate for its use of excerpts from the speech. Do King's words belong to the estate, or do they belong to us all—not merely in some abstract sense but in the very real sense that we can use them, even as the basis for seeking profit? We begin with Bill Rankin's "King's Speech: Who Owns Soul-Stirring Words?" from the *Atlanta Journal and Constitution*, which serves the city that, in many ways, claims Dr. King as its own. Rankin's discussion of the issue elicited a letter to the editor from Margaret Curtis, who argues that the King family does not own King's words. Ellen Goodman, the nationally syndicated columnist who regularly writes for the *Boston Globe* and whose column also appears in the *Journal and Constitution*, weighs in on the issue with "Who Owns Dr. King's Words?" Like Rankin's article, Goodman's column elicited a response, and Thomas Burnett disagrees with Goodman's position in his letter, which is titled "Promoting an Extreme Case of Sharing."

As all the readings in this cluster demonstrate, new technologies and new means of mechanically reproducing words, sounds, and images have brought a burgeoning interest in intellectual property: it's not just about plagiarism anymore.

▶ *Charles C. Mann wrote the article from which this excerpt was taken for the September 1998 issue of* The Atlantic Monthly, *a magazine that offers in-depth coverage of current events, arts, politics, and technology. Mann explores issues surrounding copyrights, a U.S. institution established in the Constitution and now being complicated by recent technological developments. Every one of us has a large stake in how these issues of copyright are resolved—either as authors/ artists, or as readers and consumers, or often as both. As you read, think about what interest(s) Mann may be representing in this article.*

Who Will Own Your Next Good Idea?

CHARLES C. MANN

> Some corporations want to lock up copyright even tighter. Some naive intellectuals want to abandon copyright altogether. Where is a "do-nothing" Congress now that we need one?

About twelve years ago I walked past a magazine kiosk in Europe and noticed the words *"temple des rats"* on the cover of a French magazine. Rat temple! I was amazed. A few months before, a friend of mine had traveled to northwestern India to write about the world's only shrine to humankind's least favorite rodent. The temple was in a village in the Marusthali Desert. That two Western journalists should have visited within a few months of each other stunned me. Naturally, I bought the magazine.

The article began with a Gallic tirade against the genus *Rattus. Le spectre du rat, le cauchemar d'humanité! Quel horreur!*—that sort of thing. Then came the meat: an interview, in Q&A form, with a "noted American journalist" who had just gone to the rat temple. The journalist, who was named, was my friend. No such interview had occurred: the article was a straight translation, with fake interruptions by the "interviewer" such as *"Vraiment?"* and *"Mon Dieu!"*

I was outraged. To my way of thinking, these French people had ripped off my friend. I telephoned him immediately; he had the same reaction. Expletives crackled wildly across the Atlantic. Reprinting his copyrighted article without permission or payment was the same, we decided, as kicking down his door and stealing his CD player.

We were wrong. Although the magazine had done my friend wrong, what was stolen was not at all like a CD player. CD players are physical property. Magazine articles are *intellectual* property, a different matter entirely. When thieves steal CD players, the owners no longer have them, and are obviously worse off.

But when my friend's writing was appropriated, he still had the   5 original manuscript. What, then, was stolen? Because the article had been translated, not one sentence in the French version appeared in the original. How could it be considered a copy? Anomalies like this are why intellectual property has its own set of laws.[1]

Intellectual property is knowledge or expression that is owned by someone. It has three customary domains: copyright, patent, and trademark (a fourth form, trade secrets, is sometimes included). Copyrighted songs, patented drugs, and trademarked soft drinks have long been familiar denizens of the American landscape, but the growth of digital technology has pushed intellectual property into new territory. Nowadays one might best define intellectual property as anything that can be sold in the form of zeroes and ones. It is the primary product of the Information Age. All three forms of intellectual property are growing in importance, but copyright holds pride of place. In legal terms, copyright governs the right to make copies of a given work. It awards limited monopolies to creators on their creations: for a given number of years no one but Walt Disney can sell Mickey Mouse cartoons without permission. Such monopolies, always valuable, are increasingly lucrative. For the past twenty years the copyright industry has grown almost three times as fast as the economy as a whole,

according to the International Intellectual Property Alliance, a trade group representing film studios, book publishers, and the like. Last year, the alliance says, copyrighted material contributed more than $400 billion to the national economy and was the country's single most important export.[2]

These figures may actually understate the value of copyright. Today it is widely believed that personal computers, cable television, the Internet, and the telephone system are converging into a giant hose that will spray huge amounts of data—intellectual property—into American living rooms. As this occurs, according to the conventional scenario, the economic winners will be those who own the zeroes and ones, not those who make the equipment that copies, transmits, and displays them. Because copyright is the mechanism for establishing ownership, it is increasingly seen as the key to wealth in the Information Age.

At the same time, the transformation of intellectual property into electronic form creates new problems. If the cost of manufacturing and distributing a product falls, economic forces will drive down its price, too. The Net embodies this principle to an extreme degree. Manufacturing and distribution costs collapse almost to nothing online:

What kind of figurative language is Mann using with his image of a giant hose? See Chapter 14 to help you find the answer.

···LINK TO P. 242

zeroes and ones can be shot around the world with a few clicks of a mouse. Hence producers of digital texts, music, and films will have trouble charging anything at all for copies of their works—competitors can always offer substitutes for less, pushing the price toward the vanishing point.

In addition, creators must deal with piracy, which is vastly easier and more effective in the digital environment. People have long been able to photocopy texts, tape-record music, and videotape television shows. Such leakage, as copyright lawyers call it, has existed since the first day a reader lent a (copyrighted) book to a friend. With the rise of digital media, the leakage threatens to turn into a gush. To make and distribute a dozen copies of a videotaped film requires at least two videocassette recorders, a dozen tapes, padded envelopes and postage, and considerable patience. And because the copies are tapes of tapes, the quality suffers. But if the film has been digitized into a computer file, it can be E-mailed to millions of people in minutes; because strings of zeroes and ones can be reproduced with absolute fidelity, the copies are perfect. And online pirates have no development costs—they don't even have to pay for paper or blank cassettes—so they don't really have a bottom line. In other words, even as digital technology drives the potential value of copyright to ever greater heights, that same technology threatens to make it next to worthless.

This paradox has engendered two reactions. One is to advocate 10 eliminating copyright altogether. Led by a small but surprisingly influential cadre of libertarian futurists, anti-copyrightists believe that the increased ease of copying effectively obviates the © symbol and all it entails. "Information wants to be free"—a phrase apparently coined by the writer Stewart Brand—is the apothegm° of choice here. In this view, copyright restricts what people can do with the intellectual property coming through the wires. Futilely but dangerously, it tries to fence the electronic frontier. It unjustly creates monopolies in the basic commodity of the Information Age. It is a relic of the past and should be expunged.

apothegm: a short, pithy saying.

The other, opposing reaction is to strengthen the hand of copyright owners. Realizing the growing economic import of copyright, Congress is rapidly trying to overhaul the nation's intellectual-property regime. The changes would give copyright owners more control for longer times; some would make it a crime to work around copyright-protection schemes. A different tack is being taken by state governments, which may bypass copyright altogether by amending the laws governing sales contracts. If they succeed, copyright owners will be able to ask individual customers to agree to contracts regulating the zeroes and ones flowing into their homes. *Before we send this vintage episode of Seinfeld to your computer, please read the following conditions and terms, paying careful attention to the clauses that forbid taping or replaying the program even once. After you click "OK," the transmission will start.*

Because I make much of my living from copyright, I find the to-and-fro fascinating, and have a vested interest in the results. But issues bigger than the financial status of writers are involved. Copyright is the regulatory authority for the marketplace of ideas. It lays out the economic ground rules to create the hubbub of debate that the Founders believed necessary for democracy—one reason that they included copyright in the Constitution (Article I, Section 8, instructs Congress to "secur[e] for limited Times to Authors and Inventors the exclusive Right to their Respective Writings and Discoveries"). Copyright law allows Michael Jackson to make a fortune from the Beatles catalogue, and Bill Gates to add to his untold wealth by licensing electronic reproductions of the photographs of Ansel Adams. But its real purpose is to foster ever more ideas and ever more innovation from ever more diverse sources. When, in 1790, George Washington asked Congress to enact copyright legislation, he argued that it would increase the national stock of knowledge. And knowledge, he said, is "the surest basis of public happiness."

Today the marketplace of ideas is being shaken up by the competing demands of technology, finance, and law. Large sums of money are at stake. Change seems inevitable. One way or another, we will lay a new institutional foundation for literary culture in the United States. How we do it will play a big role, according to the logic of the Founders, in determining our future well-being. It would be comforting to believe that decisions will be made thoughtfully and well. But little evidence suggests this is true. Indeed, we may be heading into a muddle that it will take us a long time to escape.

Notes

1. A translation is not a copy? Could anyone believe this? In 1853 Harriet Beecher Stowe sued to stop an unauthorized German translation of *Uncle*

Tom's Cabin—and lost. Copyright, ruled Judge Robert Grier, applies only to the "precise words." Calling a translation "a copy of the original," he opined, is "ridiculous." Only in 1870 did Congress include translations in the Copyright Act.

2. "Most people do not realize the extent to which copyright pervades their lives," says L. Ray Patterson, a professor at the University of Georgia School of Law and the author of a standard history of copyright. "They get their education from copyrighted books, they get their news from copyrighted papers and TV programs, they get their jobs from copyrighted want ads, they get their entertainment from copyrighted music and motion pictures—every aspect of life is affected by the law of copyright."

RESPOND •

1. Mann suggests two thumbnail definitions of *intellectual property* in paragraph 6—the traditional "knowledge or expression that is owned by someone," and the more current "anything that can be sold in the form of zeroes and ones." What kind of definition does each one represent—a formal definition, an operational definition, or a definition by example? What are the fundamental differences between Mann's two definitions? Are they mutually exclusive? Do you think one definition is more accurate than the other? Why or why not?

2. Although Mann has a strong personal stake in the outcome of the copyright debate (as he notes in paragraph 12), he doesn't take a clear position in this article. Why might he have chosen not to do so?

3. Mann's article deals mainly with the written word as intellectual property. Read "Lambs to the Gene Market" by John Vidal and John Carvel (p. 539). Does that article on the patenting of genetic material lead you to rethink your notions of intellectual property? Why or why not?

4. How the copyright debate is ultimately resolved will depend in part on a determination of what constitutes intellectual property. Using the guidelines in Chapter 9 for developing arguments of definition, **write an essay** in which you draw the boundaries of intellectual property as you see them. (Hint: your responses to question 1 will help you get started.)

"Wow, thanks. I'm a big fan. I've downloaded all your stuff."

RESPOND.

1. What makes this cartoon humorous? What argument(s) is it making?

2. Have you ever considered downloading music as an intellectual property issue? What are the intellectual property issues in downloading a song—from the perspective of the downloader? The owner of the Web site providing the songs? The recording company? The recording artist? Research the pro's and con's of downloading intellectual property using an Internet search engine, and **write an essay** in which you argue for or against the practice of downloading. (If you have not read the excerpt from Charles C. Mann's "Who Will Own Your Next Good Idea?" [p. 564], you'll find that it offers a quick introduction to many intellectual property issues.)

The next four arguments all appeared in 1999, between May 12 and May 20, in the Atlanta Journal and Constitution, the largest-circulation daily newspaper in the city where the Martin Luther King Jr. Center for Nonviolent Social Change is located. All four texts deal with a then-pending federal appeals court case to determine who owns the rights to King's famous 1963 "I Have a Dream" speech (p. 666). The first article, by Bill Rankin, appeared as a front-page news story. Margaret Curtis's letter to the editor responded to Rankin's article. The third piece, "Who Owns Dr. King's Words?" was written by nationally syndicated columnist Ellen Goodman. Thomas Burnett's letter to the editor responds to Goodman's column. As you read, try to determine what the central issues of the controversy are and to consider the extent to which the four authors bring other issues into the debate. In July 2000, CBS and the King family reached an agreement so that both parties can use the speech. CBS agreed to make a contribution of an undisclosed amount to the King Center and to provide the estate with footage for its own use. The settlement does not, however, resolve the issue of who ultimately owns King's words.

BILL RANKIN

When the Rev. Martin Luther King Jr. spoke to a divided nation from the steps of the Lincoln Memorial more than 35 years ago, he wanted his oratory to reach as many people as possible.

His "I Have a Dream" speech, climaxing the March on Washington, not only ignited a crowd of more than 200,000 people on the Washington Mall, it was broadcast live to millions of television viewers. But today the family of the slain civil rights leader is waging a court battle to control the rights to King's legacy, including the famous Aug. 28, 1963, speech.

Before the 11th U.S. Circuit Court of Appeals in Atlanta on Tuesday, a lawyer for the family asked a three-judge panel to rule that the rights to the speech belong to King's estate and should not be used by others who want to profit from it. The lawsuit by the King estate against CBS News was dismissed by a district court, which said King forfeited his rights to the speech because it was widely disseminated. It could be several months before the appeals panel decides, but it is not a debate that is likely to fade.

This is more than an argument of free speech vs. copyright law. It is a battle over who will profit from one of the most widely quoted pieces of this century's oratory, said David Garrow, a King historian and Emory University professor.

The First Amendment and copyright claims set forth in the suit

by CBS and the King estate, respectively, are "the kind of case in which an historian can laugh at the arguments made by both sides," he said.

CBS is accused in the pleadings of also profiting from the speech by licensing the use of its archival film at rates of up to $2,500 per minute.

Garrow added, "If the Kings are able to successfully beat up on CBS, which may deserve it a little, the end result of a King victory could be to further restrict and constrict public access to King's work."

That is not the intention of the Kings or the Martin Luther King Jr. Center for Nonviolent Social Change, said Dexter Scott King, the center president.

"We're simply following my father's conduct and trying to respect his wishes and intent," he said outside the courthouse. "My father's actions and his conduct were to protect the speech. He filed for many copyrights for his works. This is a very important case."

King's widow, Coretta Scott King, 10 sat with her son on the front row of the courtroom during Tuesday's hour-long arguments.

Over the past few years, the King family has moved aggressively to protect King's legacy. It has brought a lawsuit to prevent companies from using King's image on refrigerator magnets. It lost a lawsuit in 1993 seeking to remove thousands of

King's personal papers from his alma mater, Boston University, and bring them back to Atlanta.

Henry Hampton, who produced "Eyes on the Prize," the public television series on the civil rights movement, was sued and later settled with the King estate. When USA Today reprinted the "I Have a Dream" speech in 1993 to mark the 30th anniversary of the March on Washington, it, too, was sued and also settled with the family.

By holding the copyrights, the family can prevent the misuse of King's works, said Ray Patterson, a copyright law professor at the University of Georgia. If the court rules the "I Have a Dream" speech is in the public domain, anyone could use the speech for any purpose, he said.

Nine minutes — or 62 percent — of the speech were broadcast in "The 20th Century with Mike Wallace," a documentary that CBS produced in 1994 with the cable network Arts & Entertainment. The documentary, in which the civil rights movement was featured in one segment, was broadcast and sold as a boxed set by A&E.

The King family filed suit against 15 CBS in November 1996, saying the network infringed upon the family's copyright. But in a ruling last summer, U.S. District Judge William O'Kelley dismissed the lawsuit.

"As one of the most public and most widely disseminated speeches in history, it could be the poster child for general publications," O'Kelley wrote.

Many of the key passages in "I Have a Dream" — about 600 words that are among the most quoted — were not in the advance text given to reporters. The trademark "I have a dream" phrase and the thoughts that follow from it were not in that text, nor were the passages introduced with "let freedom ring." It is the use of these specific words, among others, that has prompted the King family to sue organizations that reprint or replay them without their permission.

Joseph Beck, a King family lawyer, told the federal appeals court Tuesday that King registered the speech with the U.S. Copyright Office a month after giving the speech and also successfully sued a company in 1964 that sought to sell tapes of the speech in its entirety.

"His conduct shows an attitude to protect his work," Beck said. Simply itself was published in its entirety," Anderson said. "It would have only been a matter of courtesy . . . to make sure it's all right with him, would it not?"

Beck said he believes that King did not authorize the publication in the newsletter. As for the advance text, the most well-known passages of the speech were not in it because they

Newspaper articles like this one often incorporate quotations. See Chapter 21 for a guide to the proper form and procedure for using quotations in your work.

LINK TO P. 338 ···

CBS, which taped and broadcast the "I Have a Dream" speech, licenses segments or "clips" of the speech. . . . The network charges $2,500 a minute for the clips to private entities and $1,000 a minute to churches, schools and other non-profits.

---

giving the speech to such a large audience also did not cause the copyright to be forfeited, Beck said, adding, "When someone makes a speech in public, one doesn't have to stand up and say, 'All rights reserved.'"

During the hearing, Judges Lanier Anderson III and Paul Roney expressed concern that King had allowed an advance copy of his speech to be handed out to the news media and that the Southern Christian Leadership Council, of which King was president, later reprinted the entire speech in its newsletter, without listing any copyright protection.

"It's hard for me to believe that 20 Dr. King didn't know what was in that newsletter . . . when the speech were in King's extemporaneous remarks, Beck added, noting that CBS broadcast 90 percent of the ad-libbed portion in the A&E program.

The newsletter shows King did not move to protect his copyright of the speech, Floyd Abrams, a lawyer for CBS, told the court.

After the hearing, Beck responded sharply to questions as to whether the King family is seeking to profit from King's legacy.

The King family routinely provides the speech free for use by schools, but CBS charges as much as $2,500 a minute for its broadcast rights to the speech, he said. "Let's talk about who's being greedy here," he said.

Kings Don't Own Words

On first hearing the Rev. Martin Luther King's "I Have a Dream" speech, my startled reaction was, "God is speaking through that man!" I have no problem with the King family's desire to prosper ("King's speech: Who owns soul-stirring words?" Page One, May 12). Blacks have too long been denied a fair reward for their labor, but trying to copyright King's speech is like trying to copyright the Bible, from which much of his speech is borrowed. Even the phrase "let freedom ring" did not originate with him. How can the speech be divided into which part was his invention and which was not? More important, any attempt to copyright and profit from that speech trivializes and dishonors something many believe is sacred.

–Margaret Curtis

Curtis is a homemaker living in Vinings.

Who Owns Dr. King's Words?

ELLEN GOODMAN

At first it sounds like a question for a panel of philosophers: Who owns a dream? What happens when a vision that's formed in the words of one person is released like a balloon into the air to be shared with everyone? Whose property is it then?

The dream in this case was described by Martin Luther King Jr. Standing before a crowd of 200,000 at the Lincoln Memorial on that August day in 1963, he found the language to match the moment. "I Have a Dream," he told the country in a speech that became a part of our collective eloquence, as much a part of our heritage as the Gettysburg Address.

Dr. King had a gift. Now people are wrangling over the value of that gift.

Coretta Scott King, widow of Martin Luther King Jr.

Today the question of dreamers and owners, words and property, history and money, has been set before a panel of three judges in Atlanta. The King family is asking an appeals court to rule that CBS must pay them to use the dream speech in a documentary sold on videotape. They

> ## "He had a gift. Now people are wrangling over the value of it."

claim that they—not the public— own Dr. King's words.

For years, the King family has 5 been protective or litigious—choose one or the other. They sued and settled with Henry Hampton, who produced the "Eyes on the Prize" documentary. They sued and settled with USA Today. They regard themselves as keepers of the legacy . . . and the accounting books.

In 1963, no one would have believed there was money to be made from civil rights history. In his lifetime Dr. King was interested in justice, not profit. His family at times lived on the salary of a $6,000-a-year minister. He contributed everything, even his Nobel Prize money, to the Southern Christian Leadership Conference.

When Dr. King was assassinated, the sum total of his estate was a $50,000 insurance policy bought for him by Harry Belafonte. That, plus his words.

These words are what the family lawyers call "intellectual property." It's property that will soon be worth an estimated $50 million from multimedia deals, licensing, and real estate.

I do not mean to suggest that the family is in the protection racket solely for the money. Schools are granted the use of the "Dream Speech" freely. At the same time, one of the many lawsuits was against a company that wanted to use Dr. King's image on refrigerator magnets.

It's not surprising that the family 10 would resist the trivialization of a man's magnetism into a refrigerator magnet. It's far too easy in our culture to slip from being a martyr on a pedestal to a pop icon on a T-shirt.

While we are talking about King and commercialism, it is fair to ask the difference between the family profit—much of which goes to the Center for Nonviolent Social Change in Atlanta—and CBS's profit.

But nevertheless there is still the little matter of public history and private property.

In the appeals court, the case will not be decided on the grounds of greed but of copyright law and free speech. On the one hand Dr. King gave the press advance copies of the speech; on the other hand, the most eloquent passages were extemporaneous. On the one hand he copyrighted the speech after it was given; on the other hand he characterized it as "a living petition to the public and the Congress."

Those of us who work with words for a living understand the desire to control our ephemeral "product." We are sensitive to the notion of intellectual property and do not take kindly to bootlegged editions of CDs or books or software that show up on black markets.

But Martin Luther King Jr. was 15 not a rock star. Or a software designer. He was a preacher, a leader, a prophet, a martyr. He was, in every sense of the word, a public figure.

One day, 36 years ago, he gave voice to our collective idealism and words to our best collective yearnings: "I have a dream that my four little children will one day live in a nation where they will not be judged by the color of their skin but by the content of their character."

This is not a private dream. It doesn't belong to his family estate. It belongs to all of us.

Why does Goodman use *our* and *us* at the end? See Chapter 3 for details on ways of using language to build common ground.

LINK TO P. 42

Promoting an Extreme Case of Sharing

If syndicated columnist Ellen Goodman is not a Democrat, she would make a good one ("Who Owns Dr. King's Words?"). She wants to take something owned by a private party (the King family) and convert it to public use—without paying for it, of course. If Goodman owned the rights to something worth $50 million, would she give it to the public?

–Thomas R. Burnett

Burnett, of Chamblee, is an environmental engineer.

RESPOND ●

1. The front-page news story by Rankin reports on a court case and gives some background information. Everything in the article is factual, and Rankin does not overtly display any particular point of view. Do you think the article is completely neutral? What evidence do you have for your conclusion? As a staff writer for the *Atlanta Journal and Constitution*, Rankin wrote this article expressly for an Atlanta audience. What features of Rankin's article reveal his awareness of a local audience?

2. In her letter to the editor, Curtis comments on selected elements of the case while ignoring others. Do you think she addresses the central issues of the controversy? Why or why not? What do you see as the central issues of the case? How does Curtis employ an argument of values in her letter? Do you think her argument is effective? Why or why not?

3. In his short letter, Burnett uses humor—sarcasm, in fact—to make his point. How does the humor contribute to his argument? Is it persuasive for you? Why or why not? How would not using humor have affected the effectiveness of Burnett's argument?

4. Goodman and Burnett both frame the controversy in terms of money and profit. Do you think this representation of the issue is an accurate one? Why or why not?

5. The *Atlanta Journal and Constitution* gives the occupation of its letter writers. Why might the paper want to include that information? Does occupational information about Curtis and Burnett influence your evaluation of the letters? Should it? Why or why not?

6. The three overtly opinion pieces—by Curtis, Goodman, and Burnett—approach the controversy as a conflict between the King estate and the public interest, with little consideration of CBS, the other party in the lawsuit. Goodman briefly mentions CBS once in her column in paragraph 11 while neither Curtis nor Burnett makes any reference to CBS at all. Why did these writers not discuss CBS? How, if at all, is the public interest involved in this case? Should "public interest" be used to resolve the controversy? Why or why not?

7. Professor David Garrow is cited in Rankin's article asserting, "This is more than an argument of free speech vs. copyright law. It is a battle over who will profit from one of the most widely quoted pieces of this century's oratory" (paragraph 4). Do you agree? Why or why not? Should the status of Dr. King, his role in American history, or the national significance of this speech be a factor in how the judge interprets the law? Why or why not? **Write an essay** in which you explore the role that the literary, social, or historical importance of a work might or should play in arguments about ownership of intellectual property like "I Have a Dream."

8. Who should own Dr. King's words and why? All of his words or some of them? **Write an essay** responding to these questions. As you plan your essay, give special consideration to the kinds of arguments you use and to your reasons for using them.

chapter twenty-seven

Language(s) and Identities

Language isn't just a tool for communicating. It also works as a symbol we use to create identities for ourselves as individuals and as members of myriad social groups. The ways we use language, whether spoken, signed, or written, tell others who we are or want to be— and who we don't want to be mistaken for. Take a moment to list ten groups you belong to. Odds are that all these groups are in some way defined by the language they use.

The arguments in this chapter examine the topic of languages and identities from many perspectives. The specific questions raised here ask you to consider the roles that language in general and specific varieties of language in particular play in how you tell the world who you are and who you want to be seen (and heard) as being. The chapter begins with several arguments that consider the connection between language and identity. Is there a link between patriotism and how you speak English? Should bilingualism be encouraged in the United States? Are laws mandating signs in English good or bad—and for whom? Can a person come to be proud of speaking many different "Englishes"—or other language varieties? Do women and men use language differently? Does it matter? What role has language played in creating "America"?

The second half of the chapter examines public opinion about Ebonics, the label for what linguists term African American Vernacular English, the variety of American English spoken some of the time by many African Americans. The most recent round of public debate about Ebonics began in December 1997, when the Oakland school board declared that it would begin using Ebonics as the language of instruction. Responses were immediate and polarized, revealing a range of strong opinions inside and outside the African American community.

"Don't believe everything you think." Or so states one of our favorite bumper sticker arguments. The arguments in this chapter should challenge you to recognize—and reexamine—some of your assumptions about language and identity, yours and everyone else's.

PLEDGE FOR CHILDREN

CHICAGO WOMEN'S CLUB

I love the United States of America. I love my country's flag.
I love my country's language. I promise:

1. That I will not dishonor my country's speech by leaving off the last syllables of words.

2. That I will say a good American "yes" and "no" in place of an Indian grunt "um-hum" and "nup-um" or a foreign "ya" or "yeh" and "nope."

3. That I will do my best to improve American speech by avoiding loud, rough tones, by enunciating clearly, and speaking pleasantly, clearly, and sincerely.

4. That I will learn to articulate correctly as many words as possible during the year.

◀ *This pledge was distributed by the Chicago Women's Club American Speech Committee to the school-children of the city in 1918.*

Not all arguments based on values are as overt as this one. See examples of more subtle arguments in Chapter 5.

LINK TO P. 57

RESPOND ●

1. What sorts of arguments are being made by this pledge? In other words, how is Americanness defined in general? With respect to language use in particular? According to the pledge, how does the "ideal American," or the American who loves his or her country, speak?

2. According to the criteria of the pledge, do you qualify as an "ideal American"? Does that trouble you in any way? Why or why not? How do you think you'd respond if you'd been given such a pledge as, say, an eighth grader? Why?

3. Consider the table on p. 580, which presents statistics about immigrants in Chicago in 1900, 1910, 1920, and 1990. At the time the pledge was issued, many of the immigrants living in Chicago had come from

Germany, Austria, Poland, and Russia and, to a far lesser extent, Ireland, Sweden, and Italy. Upon arrival, they were generally poor and uneducated. How do these figures, along with the 1918 pledge, construct an argument? What, specifically, is the argument?

Immigrants in Chicago

Year	Population	Foreign Born	Foreign-born Stock*
1900	1,698,575	35%	77%
1910	2,185,283	36%	78%
1920	2,701,705	30%	72%
1990	2,783,726	17%	Not Available

*Foreign-born stock = Immigrants to Chicago from other countries and their US-born children.

4. **Write an essay** analyzing the goals of the pledge in the historical context of the census data presented. Is the pledge, for example, a case of forensic, epideictic, or deliberative rhetoric? Why?

▼ *Ariel Dorfman teaches literature and Latin American studies at Duke University. His most recent book,* Heading South, Looking North: A Bilingual Journey *(1998), which appeared in both English and Spanish, expands on issues raised in this piece. The essay reprinted here originally appeared in the* New York Times *in June 1998.*

If Only We All Spoke Two Languages

BY ARIEL DORFMAN

DURHAM, N.C.—Ever since I came to settle in the United States 18 years ago, I have hoped that this nation might someday become truly multilingual, with everyone here speaking at least two languages.

I am aware, of course, that my dream is not shared by most Americans: if the outcome of California's referendum on bilingual education earlier this month is any indication, the nation will continue to stubbornly prefer a monolingual country. California voters rejected the bilingual approach—teaching subjects like math and science in the student's native language and gradually introducing English. Instead, they approved what is known as the immersion method, which would give youngsters a year of intensive English, then put them in regular classrooms.

The referendum was ostensibly about education, but the deeper and perhaps subconscious choice was about the future of America. Will this country speak two languages or merely one?

The bilingual method, in spite of what its detractors claim, does not imprison a child in his or her original language. Rather, it keeps it alive in order to build bridges to English. The immersion method, on the other hand, wants youngsters to cut their ties to the syllables of their past culture.

Both methods can work. I should know. I have endured them both. But my experience was unquestionably better with bilingual education.

I first suffered the immersion method in 1945 when I was 2½ years old. My family had recently moved to New York from my native Argentina, and when I caught pneumonia, I was interned in the isolation ward of a Manhattan hospital. I emerged three weeks later, in shock from having the doctors and nurses speak to me only in English, and didn't utter another word in Spanish for 10 years.

That experience turned me into a savagely monolingual child, a xenophobic all-American kid, desperate to differentiate himself from Ricky Ricardo° and Chiquita Banana.° But

Ricky Ricardo: the husband of Lucy in *I Love Lucy,* a TV series in the 1950s. In real life, Lucille Ball (1911–1989), who played Lucy, and Desi Arnez (1917–1986), who played Ricky, were married from 1940 to 1960. Arnez had immigrated to the United States at age 16 from Cuba.

Chiquita Banana: a brand of banana; the reference here is to commercials from the 1950s that included a dancing banana and/or a woman, both wearing large-brimmed hats full of fruit. See and hear them at <http://www.chiquita.com/discover/media/origjingle.wav>.

when my family moved to Chile in 1954, I could not continue to deny my heritage. I learned Spanish again in a British school in Santiago that used the gradualist method. Thus I became a bilingual adolescent.

Later, during the ideologically charged 1960's, I foolishly willed myself to become monolingual again, branding English as the language of an imperial power out to subjugate Latin America. I swore never to speak or write in English again. The 1973 military coup in Chile against the democratically elected Government of Salvador Allende Gossens sent me into exile—and back into the arms of English, making me into this hybrid creature who now uses both languages and writes a memoir in English and a play in Spanish as if it were the most ordinary thing to do.

I have developed a linguistic ambidexterity that I will be the first to admit is not at all typical. Even so, it is within reach of others if they start early enough, this thrilling experience of being dual, of taking from one linguistic river and then dipping into the other, until the confluence of the two vocabularies connects distant com-

munities. This is an experience I wish all Americans could share.

Or maybe I would be satisfied if 10 voters in this country could understand that by introducing children from other lands to the wonders of English while leaving all the variety

---

Bilingualism as a bridge to other cultures.

---

and marvels of their native languages intact, the American experience and idiom are fertilized and fortified.

If people could realize that immigrant children are better off, and less scarred, by holding on to their first languages as they learn a second one, then perhaps Americans could accept a more drastic change. What if every English-speaking toddler were to start learning a foreign language at an early age, maybe in kindergarten? What if these children were to learn Spanish, for instance, the language already spoken by millions of

American citizens, but also by so many neighbors to the South?

Most Americans would respond by asking why it is necessary at all to learn another language, given that the rest of the planet is rapidly turning English into the lingua franca of our time. Isn't it easier, most Americans would say, to have others speak to us in our words and with our grammar? Let them make the mistakes and miss the nuances and subtleties while we occupy the more powerful and secure linguistic ground in any exchange.

But that is a shortsighted strategy. If America doesn't change, it will find itself, let's say in a few hundred years, to be a monolingual nation in a world that has become gloriously multilingual. It will discover that acquiring a second language not only gives people an economic and political edge, but is also the best way to understand someone else's culture, the most stimulating way to open your life and transform yourself into a more complete member of the species.

No tengan miedo. Don't be afraid.

Your children won't be losing 15 Shakespeare. They'll just be gaining Cervantes.

Dorfman is obviously making a proposal argument, but how good is it as a proposal? Use the criteria under "Developing Proposals" in Chapter 12 to decide.

·· LINK TO P. 193

RESPOND •

1. What event motivated Dorfman to write this essay? What seems to be his ultimate argument: that the United States should be multilingual (or encourage multilingualism), that it should be bilingual (or encourage bilingualism), or that it should become bilingual in English and Spanish (or encourage such bilingualism)? What evidence can you provide for your position?

2. What experiences led to Dorfman's bilingualism? How are his experiences similar to or different from those of the typical immigrant to the United States? Why is this question in particular important when thinking about generalizing Dorfman's experiences to other situations?

3. Supporters of the California referendum on bilingual education would likely argue that immigrants are free to speak, use, and pass on to their children any languages other than English that they might speak but that they should not expect publicly funded schools to teach their children these languages. Does Dorfman anticipate or respond in any way to this criticism? If he does not, why not? Can an argument that does not address the concerns of those taking an opposing view still be effective? Give reasons for your answer.

4. Those who write about bilingual education distinguish among three types of programs: *transitional programs,* which seek to help children make the transition from the home language to the school language as quickly as possible; *maintenance programs,* which seek to produce bilinguals able to speak and write both the language of the school and that of the home community; and *enrichment programs,* which enable students who already speak the language of the school to learn a second language that they (or their parents) believe will be of use to them. (Legally mandated bilingual programs in the United States are transitional programs.) **Write an essay** evaluating the advantages and disadvantages of each of the three kinds of programs for the individual, the community, and the society. (Note that you are not being asked to support bilingual education for this or any other country; rather, you're being asked to evaluate objectively the different kinds of bilingual programs.)

▶ Chang-rae Lee is author of
Native Speaker (1995), a
powerful novel about lan-
guage as a locus of identity,
especially for immigrants and
their children, in which the
protagonist, a Korean
American, tries to make sense
of who he is—and isn't. In
"Mute in an English-Only
World," which was published
on the op-ed page of the
New York Times in 1996, Lee
writes of his mother's experience as a nonnative speaker of
English, using her situation to
offer an unexpected perspective on a Palisades Park law
requiring that commercial
signs be written at least half
in English.

Mute in an English-Only World

CHANG-RAE LEE

When I read of the troubles in Palisades Park, N.J., over the proliferation of Korean-language signs along its main commercial strip, I unexpectedly sympathized with the frustrations, resentments and fears of
the longtime residents. They clearly felt alienated and even unwelcome in a vital part of their community. The town, like seven others in
New Jersey, has passed laws requiring that half of any commercial sign
in a foreign language be in English.

Now I certainly would never tolerate any exclusionary ideas about
who could rightfully settle and belong in the town. But having been
raised in a Korean immigrant family, I saw every day the exacting price
and power of language, especially with my mother, who was an outsider in an English-only world.

In the first years we lived in America, my mother could speak only
the most basic English, and she often encountered great difficulty
whenever she went out.

We lived in New Rochelle, N.Y., in the early 70's, and most of the
local businesses were run by the descendants of immigrants who,
generations ago, had come to the suburbs from New York City. Proudly
dotting Main Street and North Avenue were Italian pastry and cheese
shops, Jewish tailors and cleaners and Polish and German butchers
and bakers. If my mother's marketing couldn't wait until the weekend,
when my father had free time, she would often hold off until I came
home from school to buy the groceries.

Though I was only 6 or 7 years old, she insisted that I go out shop- 5
ping with her and my younger sister. I mostly loathed the task, partly
because it meant I couldn't spend the afternoon playing catch with my
friends but also because I knew our errands would inevitably lead to
an awkward scene, and that I would have to speak up to help my
mother.

I was just learning the language myself, but I was a quick study, as
children are with new tongues. I had spent kindergarten in almost
complete silence, hearing only the high nasality of my teacher and

Do you think Lee's article is an
example of an argument from the
heart? Check out Chapter 4 to
find out exactly what such arguments are—and aren't.

······································LINK TO P. 49

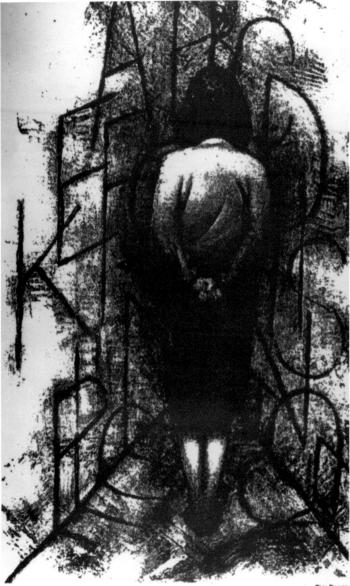

Tim Bower

comprehending little but the cranky wails and cries of my classmates. But soon, seemingly mere months later, I had already become a terrible ham and mimic, and I would crack up my father with impressions of teachers, his friends and even himself. My mother scolded me for aping his speech, and the one time I attempted to make light of hers I rated a roundhouse smack on my bottom.

For her, the English language was not very funny. It usually meant trouble and a good dose of shame, and sometimes real hurt. Although she had a good reading knowledge of the language from university classes in South Korea, she had never practiced actual conversation. So in America, she used English flashcards and phrase books and watched television with us kids. And she faithfully carried a pocket workbook illustrated with stick-figure people and compound sentences to be filled in.

But none of it seemed to do her much good. Staying mostly at home to care for us, she didn't have many chances to try out sundry words and phrases. When she did, say, at the window of the post office, her readied speech would stall, freeze, sometimes altogether collapse.

One day was unusually harrowing. We ventured downtown in the new Ford Country Squire my father had bought her, an enormous station wagon that seemed as long—and deft—as an ocean liner. We were shopping for a special meal for guests visiting that weekend, and my mother had heard that a particular butcher carried fresh oxtails— which she needed for a traditional soup.

We'd never been inside the shop, but my mother would pause 10 before its window, which was always lined with whole hams, crown roasts and ropes of plump handmade sausages. She greatly esteemed the bounty with her eyes, and my sister and I did also, but despite our desirous cries she'd turn us away and instead buy the packaged links at the Finast supermarket, where she felt comfortable looking them over and could easily spot the price. And, of course, not have to talk.

But that day she was resolved. The butcher store was crowded, and as we stepped inside the door jingled a welcome. No one seemed to notice. We waited for some time, and people who entered after us were now being served. Finally, an old woman nudged my mother and waved a little ticket, which we hadn't taken. We patiently waited again, until one of the beefy men behind the glass display hollered our number.

My mother pulled us forward and began searching the cases, but the oxtails were nowhere to be found. The man, his big arms crossed, sharply said, "Come on, lady, whaddya want?" This unnerved her, and she somehow blurted the Korean word for oxtail, soggori.

The butcher looked as if my mother had put something sour in his mouth, and he glanced back at the lighted board and called the next number.

Before I knew it, she had rushed us outside and back in the wagon, which she had double-parked because of the crowd. She was furious, almost vibrating with fear and grief, and I could see she was about to cry.

She wanted to go back inside, but now the driver of the car we were 15 blocking wanted to pull out. She was shooing us away. My mother, who had just earned her driver's license, started furiously working the pedals. But in her haste she must have flooded the engine, for it wouldn't turn over. The driver started honking and then another car began honking as well, and soon it seemed the entire street was shrieking at us.

In the following years, my mother grew steadily more comfortable with English. In Korean, she could be fiery, stern, deeply funny and ironic; in English, just slightly less so. If she was never quite fluent, she gained enough confidence to make herself clearly known to anyone, and particularly to me.

Five years ago, she died of cancer, and some months after we buried her I found myself in the driveway of my father's house, washing her sedan. I liked taking care of her things; it made me feel close to her. While I was cleaning out the glove compartment, I found her pocket English workbook, the one with the silly illustrations. I hadn't seen it in nearly 20 years. The yellowed pages were brittle and dog-eared. She had fashioned a plain-paper wrapping for it, and I wondered whether she meant to protect the book or hide it.

I don't doubt that she would have appreciated doing the family shopping on the new Broad Avenue of Palisades Park. But I like to think, too, that she would have understood those who now complain about the Korean-only signs.

I wonder what these same people would have done if they had seen my mother studying her English workbook—or lost in a store. Would they have nodded gently at her? Would they have lent a kind word?

RESPOND.

1. Throughout the piece, Lee offers numerous insights into the strategies those who do not speak English well use to negotiate American society. List some of these strategies along with their consequences for people like Lee's mother and their loved ones.

2. One of the interesting things about this essay from a rhetorical perspective is the way in which Lee bucks reader expectations. Many readers would assume that the son of an immigrant, writing about his mother's struggles with English, would oppose a law mandating the use of English in signs. How and why does Lee challenge reader expectations? How does this use of his mother's experiences contribute to his ethos and authority?

3. Read Ariel Dorfman's essay, "If Only We All Spoke Two Languages" (p. 581), which also discusses bilingualism in American society. Then, **write a dialogue** representing the conversation Lee and Dorfman might have about bilingualism in the United States. Lee became bilingual because he grew up in an immigrant household while Dorfman learned English under different circumstances. What, if anything, might the authors share in terms of experience or stance? How and why might they differ? The conversation you construct should take the form of an argument—perhaps exploratory, perhaps antagonistic.

4. Lee's essay describes a series of events relating to language that were embarrassing for his mother (and, one imagines, sometimes for the author himself). **Write an essay** about an experience in your life when you were embarrassed by someone's use or misuse of a particular language. Reflecting on the experience, discuss what you learned from the experience about yourself and about language and identity.

Mother Tongue

AMY TAN

I am not a scholar of English or literature. I cannot give you much more than personal opinions on the English language and its variations in this country or others.

I am a writer. And by that definition, I am someone who has always loved language. I am fascinated by language in daily life. I spend a great deal of my time thinking about the power of language—the way it can evoke an emotion, a visual image, a complex idea, or a simple truth. Language is the tool of my trade. And I use them all—all the Englishes I grew up with.

Recently, I was made keenly aware of the different Englishes I do use. I was giving a talk to a large group of people, the same talk I had already given to half a dozen other groups. The nature of the talk was about my writing, my life, and my book, *The Joy Luck Club.* The talk was going along well enough, until I remembered one major difference that made the whole talk sound wrong. My mother was in the room. And it was perhaps the first time she had heard me give a lengthy speech—using the kind of English I have never used with her. I was saying things like, "The intersection of memory upon imagination" and "There is an aspect of my fiction that relates to thus-and-thus"—a speech filled with carefully wrought grammatical phrases, burdened, it suddenly seemed to me, with nominalized forms, past perfect tenses, conditional phrases—all the forms of standard English that I had learned in school and through books, the forms of English I did not use at home with my mother.

Just last week, I was walking down the street with my mother, and I again found myself conscious of the English I was using, the English I do use with her. We were talking about the price of new and used furniture and I heard myself saying this: "Not waste money that way." My husband was with us as well, and he didn't notice any switch in my English. And then I realized why. It's because over the twenty years we've been together I've often used that same kind of English with him, and sometimes he even uses it with me. It has become our language of intimacy, a different sort of English that relates to family talk, the language I grew up with.

◀ *Amy Tan, best known for her novels* The Joy Luck Club *(1989) and* The Kitchen God's Wife *(1991), writes most often about relationships between Chinese American daughters and their mothers and about each group's struggles with generational and cultural differences. Her work is often praised for its sensitive and realistic rendering of dialogue. During her adolescence, Tan lost her father and her brother to brain tumors. As she recounts, she went on to study English at San Jose State University rather than becoming a neurosurgeon, as her mother had hoped. Tan began as a technical writer but started writing fiction after reading a novel by Louise Erdrich, a Native American writer. This text is a talk Tan gave as part of a panel entitled "Englishes: Whose English Is It Anyway?" at a language symposium in San Francisco in 1989. As you read, try to imagine hearing Tan deliver this speech.*

Tan's open, informal style may make you feel as if you are part of a conversation among friends, but her speech is carefully prepared in ways that casual conversation rarely is. See Chapter 17 to learn some of the techniques that Tan uses so effectively.

·· LINK TO P. 285

So you'll have some idea of what this family talk I heard sounds like, I'll quote 5 what my mother said during a recent conversation which I videotaped and then transcribed. During this conversation, my mother was talking about a political gangster in Shanghai who had the same last name as her family's, Du, and how the gangster in his early years wanted to be adopted by her family which was rich by comparison. Later, the gangster became more powerful, far richer than my mother's family, and one day showed up at my mother's wedding to pay his respects. Here's what she said in part:

"Du Yusong having business like fruit stand. Like off the street kind. He is Du like Du Zong—but not Tsung-ming Island people. The local people call putong, the river east side, he belong to that side local people. That man want to ask Du Zong father take him in like become own family. Du Zong father wasn't look down on him, but didn't take seriously, until that man big like become mafia. Now important person, very hard to inviting him. Chinese way, came only to show respect, don't stay for dinner. Respect for making big celebration, he shows up. Mean gives lots of respect. Chinese custom. Chinese social life that way. If too important won't have to stay too long. He come to my wedding. I didn't see, I heard it. I gone to boy's side, they have YMCA dinner. Chinese age I was 19."

You should know that my mother's expressive command of English belies how much she actually understands. She reads the Forbes report, listens to Wall Street Week, converses daily with her stockbroker, reads all of Shirley MacLaine's books with ease—all kinds of things I can't begin to understand. Yet some of my friends tell me they understand fifty percent of what my mother says. Some say they understand eighty to ninety percent. Some say they understand none of it, as if she were speaking pure Chinese. But to me, my mother's English is perfectly clear, perfectly natural. It's my mother tongue. Her language, as I hear it, is vivid, direct, full of observation and imagery. That was the language that helped shape the way I saw things, expressed things, made sense of the world.

Lately, I've been giving more thought to the kind of English my mother speaks. Like others, I have described it to people as "broken" or "fractured" English. But I wince when I say that. It has always bothered me that I can think of no way to describe it other than "broken," as if it were damaged and needed to be fixed, as if it lacked a certain wholeness and soundness. I've heard other terms used, "limited English," for example. But they seem just as bad, as if everything is limited, including people's perception of the limited English speaker.

I know this for a fact, because when I was growing up, my mother's "limited" English limited my perception of her. I was ashamed of her English. I believed that her English reflected the quality of what she had to say. That is, because she expressed them imperfectly her thoughts were imperfect. And I had plenty of empirical evidence to support me: the fact that people in department stores, at banks, and at restaurants did not take her seriously, did not give her good service, pretended not to understand her, or even acted as if they did not hear her.

My mother has long realized the limitations of her English as well. When I was 10 fifteen, she used to have me call people on the phone to pretend I was she. In this guise, I was forced to ask for information or even to complain and yell at people who had been rude to her. One time it was a call to her stockbroker in New York. She had cashed out her small portfolio and it just so happened we were going to go to New York the next week, our very first trip outside California. I had to get on the phone and say in an adolescent voice that was not very convincing. "This is Mrs. Tan."

And my mother was standing in the back whispering loudly, "Why he don't send me check, already two weeks late. So mad he lie to me, losing me money."

And then I said in perfect English, "Yes, I'm getting rather concerned. You had agreed to send the check two weeks ago, but it hasn't arrived."

Then she began to talk more loudly, "What he want, I come to New York tell him front of his boss, you cheating me?" And I was trying to calm her down, make her be quiet, while telling the stockbroker, "I can't tolerate any more excuses. If I don't receive the check immediately, I am going to have to speak to your manager when I'm in New York next week." And sure enough, the following week there we were in front of this astonished stockbroker, and I was sitting there red-faced and quiet, and my mother, the real Mrs. Tan, was shouting at his boss in her impeccable broken English.

We used a similar routine just five days ago, for a situation that was far less humorous. My mother had gone to the hospital for an appointment, to find out about a benign brain tumor a CAT scan had revealed a month ago. She said she had spoken very good English, her best English, no mistakes. Still, she said, the hospital did not apologize when they said they had lost the CAT scan and she had come for nothing. She said they did not seem to have any sympathy when she told them she was anxious to know the exact diagnosis since her husband and son had both died of brain tumors. She said they would not give her any more information until the next time and she would have to make another appointment for that. So she said she would not leave until the doctor called her daughter. She wouldn't budge. And when the doctor finally called her daughter, me, who spoke in perfect English—lo and behold—we had assurances the CAT scan would be found, promises that a conference call on Monday would be held, and apologies for any suffering my mother had gone through for a most regrettable mistake.

I think my mother's English almost had an effect on limiting my possibilities in life 15 as well. Sociologists and linguists probably will tell you that a person's developing language skills are more influenced by peers. But I do think that the language spoken in the family, especially in immigrant families which are more insular, plays a large role in shaping the language of the child. And I believe that it affected my results on achievement tests, IQ tests, and the SAT. While my English skills were never judged as poor, compared to math, English could not be considered my strong suit. In grade school, I did moderately well, getting perhaps *B*s, sometimes *B*+s in English, and scoring perhaps in the sixtieth or seventieth percentile on achievement tests. But those scores were not good enough to override the opinion that my true abilities lay in math and science, because in those areas I achieved *A*s and scored in the ninetieth percentile or higher.

This was understandable. Math is precise; there is only one correct answer. Whereas, for me at least, the answers on English tests were always a judgment call, a matter of opinion and personal experience. Those tests were constructed around items like fill-in-the blank sentence completion, such as "Even though Tom was _____, Mary thought he was _____." And the correct answer always seemed to be the most bland combinations of thoughts, for example, "Even though Tom was shy, Mary thought he was charming," with the grammatical structure "even though" limiting the correct answer to some sort of semantic opposites, so you wouldn't get answers like "Even though Tom was foolish, Mary thought he was ridiculous." Well, according to my mother, there were very few limitations as to what Tom could have been, and what Mary might have thought of him. So I never did well on tests like that.

The same was true with word analogies, pairs of words, in which you were supposed to find some sort of logical, semantic relationship—for example, "sunset" is to "nightfall" as _____ is to _____. And here, you would be presented with a list of four possible pairs, one of which showed the same kind of relationship: "red" is to "stoplight," "bus" is to "arrival," "chills" is to "fever," "yawn" is to "boring." Well, I could never think that way. I knew what the tests were asking, but I could not block out of my mind the images already created by the first pair, "sunset is to nightfall"—and I would see a burst of colors against a darkening sky, the moon rising, the lowering of a curtain of stars. And all the other pairs of words—red, bus, stoplight, boring—just threw up a mass of confusing images, making it impossible for me to sort out something as logical as saying: "A sunset precedes nightfall" is the same as "a chill precedes a fever." The only way I would have gotten that answer right would have been to imagine an associative situation, for example, my being disobedient and staying out past sunset, catching a chill at night, which turns into feverish pneumonia as punishment, which indeed did happen to me.

I have been thinking about all this lately, about my mother's English, about achievement tests. Because lately I've been asked, as a writer, why there are not more Asian-Americans represented in American literature. Why are there few Asian-Americans enrolled in creative writing programs? Why do so many Chinese students go into engineering? Well, these are broad sociological questions I can't begin to answer. But I have noticed in surveys — in fact, just last week — that Asian students, as a whole, always do significantly better on math achievement tests than in English. And this makes me think that there are other Asian-American students whose English spoken in the home might also be described as "broken" or "limited." And perhaps they also have teachers who are steering them away from writing and into math and science, which is what happened to me.

Fortunately, I happen to be rebellious in nature, and enjoy the challenge of disproving assumptions made about me. I became an English major my first year in college after being enrolled as pre-med. I started writing non-fiction as a freelancer the week after I was told by my former boss that writing was my worst skill and I should hone my talents toward account management.

But it wasn't until 1985 that I finally began to write fiction. And at first I wrote   20 using what I thought to be wittily crafted sentences, sentences that would finally prove I had mastery over the English language. Here's an example from the first draft of a story that later made its way into *The Joy Luck Club,* but without this line: "That was my mental quandary in its nascent state." A terrible line, which I can barely pronounce.

Fortunately, for reasons I won't get into today, I later decided I should envision a reader for the stories I would write. And the reader I decided upon was my mother, because these were stories about mothers. So with this reader in mind — and in fact, she did read my early drafts — I began to write stories using all the Englishes I grew up with: the English I spoke to my mother, which for lack of a better term, might be described as "simple"; the English she used with me, which for lack of a better term might be described as "broken"; my translation of her Chinese, which could certainly be described as "watered down"; and what

I imagined to be her translation of her Chinese if she could speak in perfect English, her internal language, and for that I sought to preserve the essence, but not either an English or a Chinese structure. I wanted to capture what language ability tests can never reveal: her intent, her passion, her imagery, the rhythms of her speech and the nature of her thoughts.

Apart from what any critic had to say about my writing, I knew I had succeeded where it counted when my mother finished reading my book, and gave me her verdict: "So easy to read."

RESPOND●

1. How have Tan's attitudes toward her mother's English changed over the years? Why? Have you had similar experiences with your parents or other older relatives?

2. Why, ultimately, is Tan suspicious of language ability tests? What are her complaints? What sorts of evidence does she offer? Do you agree or disagree with her argument? Why?

3. Tan's text was written to be read aloud by the author herself. In what ways might this fact be important? (You may wish to consult Chapter 17 on the features of spoken arguments.) What would it be like, for example, to have heard Tan deliver this text? How would such an experience have been different from reading it on the page? Had Tan written the piece to be read silently by strangers—as her novels are, for example—how might she have altered it? Why?

4. What does Tan mean when she claims that she uses "all the Englishes [she] grew up with"? What are these Englishes? What are her problems in giving them labels? Do you agree with Tan's implied argument that we should use all our Englishes and use them proudly? Why or why not? Are there any limits to this position? If so, what are they? **Write an essay** evaluating Tan's position. (In preparing for this assignment, you might think about the Englishes that you know and use. Do they all have recognizable names or convenient labels? Do you associate them with certain people or places or activities? What does each represent to you? About you? Do you have ambivalent feelings about any of them? Why?)

Teachers' Classroom Strategies Should Recognize That Men and Women Use Language Differently

DEBORAH TANNEN

▼ *Deborah Tannen, a socio-linguist who teaches at Georgetown University, is the author of several popular books, including the best-selling* You Just Don't Understand: Women and Men in Conversation *(1990),* Talking from 9 to 5: Women and Men in the Workplace: Language, Sex, and Power *(1994), and* The Argument Culture: Stopping America's War of Words *(1998); and numerous scholarly works. In this essay, which appeared in 1991 in the* Chronicle of Higher Education, *a weekly newspaper that deals with issues of interest to college and university administrators and faculty, she applies some of her research findings to classrooms, including her own. Notice how Tannen characterizes the differences between female and male conversational styles and how she sees evidence of these styles in the college classroom.*

When I researched and wrote my latest book, *You Just Don't Understand: Women and Men in Conversation,* the furthest thing from my mind was reevaluating my teaching strategies. But that has been one of the direct benefits of having written the book.

The primary focus of my linguistic research always has been the language of everyday conversation. One facet of this is conversational style: how different regional, ethnic, and class backgrounds, as well as age and gender, result in different ways of using language to communicate. *You Just Don't Understand* is about the conversational styles of women and men. As I gained more insight into typically male and female ways of using language, I began to suspect some of the causes of the troubling facts that women who go to single-sex schools do better in later life, and that when young women sit next to young men in classrooms, the males talk more. This is not to say that all men talk in class, nor that no women do. It is simply that a greater percentage of discussion time is taken by men's voices.

The research of sociologists and anthropologists such as Janet Lever, Marjorie Harness Goodwin, and Donna Eder has shown that girls and boys learn to use language differently in their sex-separate peer groups. Typically, a girl has a best friend with whom she sits and talks, frequently telling secrets. It's the telling of secrets, the fact and the way that they talk to each other, that makes them best friends. For boys, activities are central: Their best friends are the ones they do things with. Boys also tend to play in larger groups that are hierarchical. High-status boys give orders and push low-status boys around. So boys are expected to use language to seize center stage: by exhibiting their skill, displaying their knowledge, and challenging and resisting challenges.

These patterns have stunning implications for classroom interaction. Most faculty members assume that participating in class discussion is a necessary part of successful performance. Yet speaking in a classroom is more congenial to boys' language experience than to girls', since it entails putting oneself forward in front of a large group of people, many of whom are strangers and at least one of whom is sure to judge speakers' knowledge and intelligence by their verbal display.

Another aspect of many classrooms that makes them more hos-   5 pitable to most men than to most women is the use of debate-like formats as a learning tool. Our educational system, as Walter Ong argues persuasively in his book *Fighting for Life* (Cornell University Press, 1981), is fundamentally male in that the pursuit of knowledge is believed to be achieved by ritual opposition: public display followed by argument and challenge. Father Ong demonstrates that ritual opposition—what he calls "adversativeness" or "agonism"—is fundamental to the way most males approach almost any activity. (Consider, for example, the little boy who shows he likes a little girl by pulling her braids and shoving her.) But ritual opposition is antithetical to the way most females learn and like to interact. It is not that females don't fight, but that they don't fight for fun. They don't *ritualize* opposition.

Anthropologists working in widely disparate parts of the world have found contrasting verbal rituals for women and men. Women in completely unrelated cultures (for example, Greece and Bali) engage in ritual laments: spontaneously produced rhyming couplets that express their pain, for example, over the loss of loved ones. Men do not take part in laments. They have their own, very different verbal ritual: a contest, a war of words in which they vie with each other to devise clever insults.

When discussing these phenomena with a colleague, I commented that I see these two styles in American conversation: Many women bond by talking about troubles, and many men bond by exchanging playful insults and put-downs, and other sorts of verbal sparring. He exclaimed: "I never thought of this, but that's the way I teach: I have students read an article, and then I invite them to tear it apart. After we've torn it to shreds, we talk about how to build a better model."

This contrasts sharply with the way I teach: I open the discussion of readings by asking, "What did you find useful in this? What can we use in our own theory building and our own methods?" I note what I see as weaknesses in the author's approach, but I also point out that

the writer's discipline and purposes might be different from ours. Finally, I offer personal anecdotes illustrating the phenomena under discussion and praise students' anecdotes as well as their critical acumen.

These different teaching styles must make our classrooms wildly different places and hospitable to different students. Male students are more likely to be comfortable attacking the readings and might find the inclusion of personal anecdotes irrelevant and "soft." Women are more likely to resist discussion they perceive as hostile, and, indeed, it is women in my classes who are most likely to offer personal anecdotes.

A colleague who read my book commented that he had always taken 10 for granted that the best way to deal with students' comments is to challenge them; this, he felt it was self-evident, sharpens their minds and helps them develop debating skills. But he had noticed that women were relatively silent in his classes, so he decided to try beginning discussion with relatively open-ended questions and letting comments go unchallenged. He found, to his amazement and satisfaction, that more women began to speak up.

Though some of the women in his class clearly liked this better, perhaps some of the men liked it less. One young man in my class wrote in a questionnaire about a history professor who gave students questions to think about and called on people to answer them: "He would then play devil's advocate . . . i.e., he debated us. . . . That class *really* sharpened me intellectually. . . . We as students do need to know how to defend ourselves." This young man valued the experience of being attacked and challenged publicly. Many, if not most, women would shrink from such "challenge," experiencing it as public humiliation.

A professor at Hamilton College told me of a young man who was upset because he felt his class presentation had been a failure. The professor was puzzled because he had observed that class members had listened attentively and agreed with the student's observations. It turned out that it was this very agreement that the student interpreted as failure: Since no one had engaged his ideas by arguing with him, he felt they had found them unworthy of attention.

So one reason men speak in class more than women is that many of them find the "public" classroom setting more conducive to speaking, whereas most women are more comfortable speaking in private to a small group of people they know well. A second reason is that men are more likely to be comfortable with the debate-like form that discussion may take. Yet another reason is the different attitudes toward speaking in class that typify women and men.

Students who speak frequently in class, many of whom are men, assume that it is their job to think of contributions and try to get the floor to express them. But many women monitor their participation not only to get the floor but to avoid getting it. Women students in my class tell me that if they have spoken up once or twice, they hold back for the rest of the class because they don't want to dominate. If they have spoken a lot one week, they will remain silent the next. These different ethics of participation are, of course, unstated, so those who speak freely assume that those who remain silent have nothing to say, and those who are reining themselves in assume that the big talkers are selfish and hoggish.

When I looked around my classes, I could see these differing ethics 15 and habits at work. For example, my graduate class in analyzing conversation had 20 students, 11 women and 9 men. Of the men, four were foreign students: two Japanese, one Chinese, and one Syrian. With the exception of the three Asian men, all the men spoke in class at least occasionally. The biggest talker in the class was a woman, but there were also five women who never spoke at all, only one of whom was Japanese. I decided to try something different.

I broke the class into small groups to discuss the issues raised in the readings and to analyze their own conversational transcripts. I devised three ways of dividing the students into groups: one by the degree program they were in, one by gender, and one by conversational style, as closely as I could guess it. This meant that when the class was grouped according to conversational style, I put Asian students together, fast talkers together, and quiet students together. The class split into groups six times during the semester, so they met in each grouping twice. I told students to regard the groups as examples of interactional data and to note the different ways they participated in the different groups. Toward the end of the term, I gave them a questionnaire asking about their class and group participation.

I could see plainly from my observation of the groups at work that women who never opened their mouths in class were talking away in the small groups. In fact, the Japanese woman commented that she found it particularly hard to contribute to the all-woman group she was in because "I was overwhelmed by how talkative the female students were in the female-only group." This is particularly revealing because it highlights that the same person who can be "oppressed" into silence in one context can become the talkative "oppressor" in another. No one's conversational style is absolute; everyone's style changes in response to the context and others' styles.

Some of the students (seven) said they preferred the same-gender groups; others preferred the same-style groups. In answer to the question "Would you have liked to speak in class more than you did?" six of the seven who said Yes were women; the one man was Japanese. Most startlingly, this response did not come only from quiet women; it came from women who had indicated they had spoken in class never, rarely, sometimes, and often. Of the 11 students who said the amount they had spoken was fine, 7 were men. Of the four women who checked "fine," two added qualifications indicating it wasn't completely fine: One wrote in "maybe more," and one wrote, "I have an urge to participate but often feel I should have something more interesting/relevant/wonderful/intelligent to say!!"

I counted my experiment a success. Everyone in the class found the small groups interesting, and no one indicated he or she would have preferred that the class not break into groups. Perhaps most instructive, however, was the fact that the experience of breaking into groups, and of talking about participation in class, raised everyone's awareness about classroom participation. After we had talked about it, some of the quietest women in the class made a few voluntary contributions, though sometimes I had to insure their participation by interrupting the students who were exuberantly speaking out.

Americans are often proud that they discount the significance of 20 cultural differences: "We are all individuals," many people boast. Ignoring such issues as gender and ethnicity becomes a source of pride: "I treat everyone the same." But treating people the same is not equal treatment if they are not the same.

The classroom is a different environment for those who feel comfortable putting themselves forward in a group than it is for those who find the prospect of doing so chastening, or even terrifying. When a professor asks, "Are there any questions?," students who can formulate statements the fastest have the greatest opportunity to respond. Those who need significant time to do so have not really been given a chance at all, since by the time they are ready to speak, someone else has the floor.

In a class where some students speak out without raising hands, those who feel they must raise their hands and wait to be recognized do not have equal opportunity to speak. Telling them to feel free to jump in will not make them feel free; one's sense of timing, of one's rights and obligations in a classroom, are automatic, learned over years of interaction. They may be changed over time, with motivation and effort, but they cannot be changed on the spot. And everyone assumes his or her own way is best. When I asked my students how the class could be changed to make it easier for them to speak more, the most talkative woman said she would prefer it if no one had to raise hands, and a foreign student said he wished people would raise their hands and wait to be recognized.

My experience in this class has convinced me that small-group interaction should be part of any class that is not a small seminar. I

Tannen is using personal experience as evidence, but she's also presenting evidence from surveys and questionnaires she systematically conducted with her own students. Read more in Chapter 18 about what counts as evidence.

·· LINK TO P. 297

also am convinced that having the students become observers of their own interaction is a crucial part of their education. Talking about ways of talking in class makes students aware that their ways of talking affect other students, that the motivations they impute to others may not truly reflect others' motives, and that the behaviors they assume to be self-evidently right are not universal norms.

The goal of complete equal opportunity in class may not be attainable, but realizing that one monolithic classroom-participation structure is not equal opportunity is itself a powerful motivation to find more-diverse methods to serve diverse students—and every classroom is diverse.

RESPOND •

1. To what extent do you agree with Tannen's characterization of female and male conversational styles? With her discussion of the consequences of these different styles on classroom interaction? Why?

2. Do you prefer classes in which the "male" or "female" style of interaction, as described by Tannen, is rewarded? Why? How do you respond when you are in a classroom where the kind of interactional style you do not prefer is rewarded? If you are male and prefer the "female" style of interaction or if you are female and prefer the "male" style of interaction, should you be worried? Why or why not?

3. Tannen claims that "[o]ur educational system . . . is fundamentally male in that the pursuit of knowledge is believed to be achieved by . . . argument and challenge" (paragraph 5). Similar claims have been made about the style of argumentation required of college students and that required of professors in their research. To what extent do you agree? Why or why not?

4. Describe Tannen's own style of argumentation. Is it antagonistic or adversarial? Does it seek common ground? Is it absolutist ("There is only one right answer, and I have it")? Why or why not?

5. In paragraph 23, Tannen argues that "small-group interaction should be part of any class that is not a small seminar." Do you agree or disagree? To what extent? Why? Using personal experience, and what you have learned from this article, **write an essay** in which you respond to Tannen's argument about including small-group interaction in all classes. Be careful to discuss not only its benefits but also any drawbacks you might see.

▼ *In this column from the June 1999 issue of* Sports Illustrated, *Steve Rushin describes and critiques one aspect of what we might term "the American character." Crucially, the patterns of behavior he criticizes are linguistic in nature, involving ways we use language to create our identities. As you read, pay special attention to the sorts of examples Rushin uses to support his claim that the United States has become "Wise Guy Nation."*

Hip Unchecked

In Sports and on TV, Sarcasm and Cynicism Are Drowning Out Sincerity and Compassion

STEVE RUSHIN

LAST WEEK, at an amusement park in middle America, I saw a seven-year-old boy in a basketball-themed T-shirt that read KNOW YOUR ROLE — SHUT YOUR MOUTH. Within minutes came another kid, maybe 12, in a trash-talking T-shirt that said YOU SHOULD BE IN A MUSEUM — YOU'RE GETTIN' WAXED. Moments later, yet another child walked world-wearily by in a T-shirt that commanded SPEAK TO MY AGENT. He was, at most, five years old.

All day these pip-squeaks passed, like the little boy in a T-shirt manufactured by the No Fear, Inc. apparel company, one that declared IF YOU CAN'T WIN, DON'T PLAY. (He was holding his father's hand.) Retreating to my hotel, I switched on ESPN2 in time to see a commercial in which a man dressed as a giant Slim Jim was yelling, "Eat me!" Flipping to *The Late Late Show* on CBS, I watched former ESPN anchor Craig Kilborn read a phony news item about drug agents seizing several tons of

cocaine before it reached its intended destination of — smirk, leer, arched eyebrow — "Darryl Strawberry's left nostril." So ended an unremarkable day in the life of America, where every citizen is a snarky, cynical, hipper-than-thou, irony-dripping icon of comedy and cool.

I don't know when, exactly, everyone became a smart-ass, only that it has happened. "Everybody I know is sarcastic all the time, in everything they say," a guy named Scott Dikkers recently told *The New Yorker.* Dikkers is editor-in-chief of — what else? — a satirical newspaper called *The Onion,* and he and I seem to know all the same people. In sports the smart-aleck attitude is inescapable, be it on *SportsCenter,* in ads for EA Sports, or wherever two sportswriters gather — invariably to make fun of everyone, including each other.

It is exhausting, all this clever contempt for everything. I have seen major league baseball trainers wearing T-shirts bearing the slogan I WILL GIVE TREATMENT, NOT SYMPATHY. On such seemingly minor everyday messages—call them incidental incivilities—a popular culture has been built.

So remind me: Why is it wrong to give sympathy to someone who might need it? What is uncool about occasional earnestness, sincerity or genuine human emotion? Does every TV commercial have to be a winking, we-know-that-you-know-that-this-is-a-cheesy-commercial commercial? With the spoofed-up news on *The Daily Show with Jon Stewart,* and "Headlines" on *The Tonight Show,* and the mock newscast on *The Late Late Show,* and the mock newscast on *Dennis Miller Live,* and the mock newscast on *Saturday Night Live,* television now broadcasts more news parodies than actual news programs. We have become Wise Guy Nation. On our one-dollar bill George Washington ought to smirk like Mona Lisa. On the five, Lincoln's fingers could form a *W,* the international symbol for *whatever.*

In an interview broadcast during halftime of the Knicks-Pacers playoff game on NBC last Friday night, Indiana guard Mark Jackson spoke movingly about the recent death of his father. It was telling that Jackson felt it necessary to point out, "There's no shame in crying and saying 'I love him to death.'"

You wouldn't think so. But people now feel shame for their virtues (e.g., loving one's parents) and no shame for their sins (e.g., loving one's White House intern). Losers—socially or athletically—deserve ridicule. As I left the amusement park last week, I saw an adult in a T-shirt that bore the image of a high school wrestler and the following slogan across the chest: WIN WITH HUMILITY, LOSE WITH DIGNITY.

The earnest and simple sentiment gave me hope, so I nodded solemnly as the man passed. Only then did I see the back of his shirt. It read BUT DON'T LOSE! ■

RESPOND •

1. How well does the article's subtitle—"In Sports and on TV, Sarcasm and Cynicism Are Drowning Out Sincerity and Compassion"—summarize Rushin's argument? Why do you think that Rushin does not include an explicit thesis in his essay? How might doing so have altered the tone of the piece?

2. How would you describe the tone of Rushin's essay? To what extent does his tone enact the very attitudes and behaviors he is criticizing? Do you think the tone contributes to or detracts from his argument? Why or why not?

3. Nearly all of Rushin's examples involve males. Is the pattern of behavior Rushin describes and criticizes "a guy thing" or "an American thing"? Why? (Imagine, for example, how Deborah Tannen (p. 595) might respond to this piece.)

4. Rushin claims in paragraph 7 that "people now feel shame for their virtues . . . and no shame for their sins. . . ." **Write an essay** supporting or rejecting this claim.

Rushin's article is about values, but is his appeal based on values? Emotion? A combination? Check out Chapters 4 and 5 to help you decide.

LINK TO PP. 49 AND 57 ·

The most acerbic public debate about language and identity in the United States in recent years began on December 18, 1996, when the school board in Oakland, California, passed a resolution concerning the language variety many of its African American children spoke at home and brought into the classroom. The resolution referred to the home language variety of these students as Ebonics, a label first used in 1975. Importantly, the resolution treated Ebonics not as a variety of English but as a separate language related to the West and Niger-Congo languages, the African languages spoken by the ancestors of American slaves. An accompanying statement compared the situation of speakers of Ebonics to that of students from homes where a language other than English is used, arguing that speakers of Ebonics should be eligible for Title VII programs, federally mandated programs in bilingual education and English as a second language.

The response was immediate and intense. Newspapers and news programs across the nation carried reports about the resolution. For several weeks, it was a favored topic on editorial pages and talk shows, and many of the critics were African American. The Linguistic Society of America even passed a resolution about the issue at its annual meeting early in 1997. (See <http://www.lsadc.org/web2/ebonicsfr.htm>.)

Here, we offer a range of opinions about **the Ebonics debates,** which are of course ultimately about issues of language and identity. As you will note, little agreement exists among the general public about what exactly Ebonics is and what it represents. (As Chapters 1 and 9 remind us, when there is no agreement on the definition of a basic term in an argument, the likelihood of reaching shared conclusions is minimal.) Similarly, there is little agreement among commentators about the exact nature of Standard English, although they write as if its nature were clear. Many Americans believe that because of their background or education, whatever comes out of their mouth (or pen) is Standard English. Assuming that their English is standard permits them to assume that those who speak English differently do *not* speak Standard English. Hence, part of the power of Standard English (or the standard variety of any language) is its symbolic value. Because of its prestige as the "correct" or "best" variety, its users see themselves and are often seen by others as educated, intelligent, industrious, hardworking, and a host of other positive values. In contrast, speakers of other varieties are seen as embodying the opposite of these values. Nonstandard varieties are seen as "bad language," and their speakers are perceived in negative ways.

Whatever a person thinks about the Ebonics debates, the issues that remain concern how best to educate children who arrive at school speaking something other than Standard English, whether a nonstandard variety of English or a language other than English. The debates also raise complex questions about how we, as individuals and as a society, deal with linguistic difference. Because of the close links between language and identity in this society, the challenges remain even as the most recent series of debates about what we term Ebonics recedes into the past.

Both Ebonics and the decision itself were popular topics for editorial cartoons during public debates about the Oakland school board's decision. Here are two, the first by Chris Britt and the second by Jim Borgman. A bit of background information is useful in understanding both. After the 1896 Supreme Court decision Plessy v. Ferguson, "separate but equal" accommodations and treatment for African Americans and Whites were legally inscribed, giving rise, especially in the South, to Black and White train cars, segregated housing mandated by law, "Whites Only" lunch counters, and what were termed "Colored" and "White" rest rooms and water fountains. The Court's 1954 decision Brown v. Board of Education, which desegregated American schools, overturned the doctrine of "separate but equal." A major goal of the Civil Rights movement in the 1960s was obtaining equality in accommodations and treatment for African Americans.

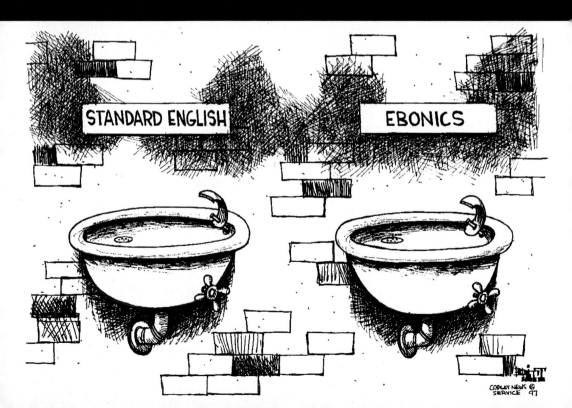

RESPOND.

1. Summarize the point of Chris Britt's cartoon. (Hints: Why are Standard English and Ebonics juxtaposed as the labels for water fountains? What are the links between the cartoon's title, American history, and the debate about Ebonics?)

2. What argument is Jim Borgman making about Ebonics? Show evidence. Consider, for example, why Borgman has written "Jus'" instead of "Just" as the first word in the speech bubble. How does this spelling represent speakers of Ebonics? Is this a fair representation? Do you, for example, always pronounce all of the letters in the word *just*, or do you sometimes say *jus*, especially in rapid, informal speech?

3. Britt's and Borgman's cartoons make related arguments. Which is the more effective? Why?

4. **Write an essay** explaining either Britt's or Borgman's cartoon to an English speaker who is not from the United States (that is, someone who knows English but does not know enough about American history and culture to understand the cartoon). Agree or disagree with the stance the cartoonist takes, justifying your position. (Be sure to state explicitly its creator's argument.)

▼ *James Hill is a staff writer for the* Chicago Tribune, *where this article first appeared. It was reprinted, along with several others, in a* San Francisco Examiner *series that ran during January 1997 about the controversies that arose in light of the Oakland school board's resolution about Ebonics. As you read, consider both Hill's own use of language and the evidence he uses to support his arguments.*

Say What? Watch Your Language

BY JAMES HILL

I must admit, the recent decision by the school board in Oakland left me in quite the quandary at first.

I didn't know whether I should be excited as an American of African descent that the language I had heard and used growing up on the streets in Detroit was being held up as legitimate. Or if I should be mad as hell at the fact that a language I was always told was "improper," was being viewed as "unique" and "important."

Now, I'm just insulted.

I think back to Mrs. Tribble's 3rd-grade class at a racially diverse private school in Detroit. I remember how whenever someone would "axe" a question—that's

Hill embeds a definition argument into his article as evidence for his principal argument. See more about definition arguments and how to use them effectively in Chapter 9.

LINK TO P. 109

Ebonics for "ask"—Mrs. Tribble would cringe and say "ouch." And yes, Mrs. Tribble was African-American, and a very down sister, I might add.

To this day, I cringe when I hear 5 people say "axe" or use an elongated -ed ending, such as, "He was light skin-ded." It's not because I am now some uppity middle-class brother who has forgotten his roots, but because I have been taught differently.

And it's not that I don't still occasionally use Ebonics. I can't tell you how many times I have "axed" the question "Where he at?" But that doesn't make me bilingual. Ebonics is a dialect, not a language.

Webster's defines dialect as "popularly, any form of speech considered as deviating from a real or imaginary standard speech. The form or variety of a spoken language peculiar to a region, community, social group, occupational group, etc. (in this sense, dialects are regarded as being, to some degree, mutually intelligible while languages are not mutually intelligible)."

Even if I said, "I be going to the store," I'm sure someone of, say, the Caucasian persuasion would know what I mean or at least could figure it out relatively easily. It's clumsy, but it's "mutually intelligible."

The term black English (and we really need to talk about this lower-case b) itself is contradictory to the argument. The name would lead you to believe it is a variation or even an innovation of the English language. Therefore, it could not be a different language.

The Tribune reported Dec. 20 that 10 the American Speech, Language and Hearing Association has classified black English as a legitimate social dialect with unique lexicon, grammar, phonology, syntax and semantics.

Yeah, well the same could be said for the concocted metaphors and drawl of many Southerners. (Being of a family originally from the South, I can say that. Am I now trilingual?)

Or what about that long-O sound many people from Minnesooota are sooo fond of using? They aren't considered bilingual. Nor are they considered to be using a lazy tongue. It is a dialect or accent, not a separate language.

The fact that the Oakland school system is thinking of applying for federal bilingual funding for Ebonics shoots down the whole issue of "understanding" that Willie Hamilton, an Oakland high school principal, tried to get across. It turns their argument into a gimmick and not even a cleverly crafted one.

Oakland school officials looking to institute the Ebonics program said the "motivation for the program was the dismal achievement scores posted by African-American students, 71 percent of whom are enrolled in special education classes."

However, I would be willing to bet 15 money that you won't find Ebonics in the ACT, SAT, Iowa or other standardized achievement tests. So Ebonics won't help on that front.

It seems Oakland's alleged noble effort is a scheme to get more money from the government to come up with new ways to move African-American students out of the mainstream. I suspect they already are getting money from the state by classifying so many of them as "special

> ## "It's not that I don't still occasionally use Ebonics. I can't tell you how many times I have 'axed' the question 'Where he at?' But that doesn't make me bilingual."

education," and I'll lay another wager that many are "low-income" students entitling the school system to more state funds.

Now they are seeking to make even more money off the backs of African-American students by trying to quantify their speech as exploring a new language. Maybe they will even teach Ebonics in the special education classes, eh?

The fact that 71 percent of the African-American students, who make up 53 percent of the district's population, are in special education speaks to the fact that teachers and administrators there seem to have already given up on trying to understand and educate them. Now they appear to be using African-American students, even mocking them, to save their collective assets.

The fact that linguists have traced Ebonics to African languages spoken by slaves is no real argument.

The Africans who 20 were brought here didn't speak English and weren't taught it. It was a tactic used to keep the slaves from being able to learn, communicate effectively and move forward socially. While they picked up words from their masters, they were never taught how to use them, thereby damning them to the lower rungs of society.

In short, they spoke Ebonics because they didn't know any better. I would like to think that we, as African-Americans, know better now. And I also would like to think that the Oakland school board should know better.

RESPOND ●

1. Which parts of the original resolution from the Oakland school board most disturb Hill? Why? How does he structure his argument against the board's contention that Ebonics is a separate language? What sorts of evidence does he offer?

2. According to Hill, how does Ebonics fit into the history of African Americans? What role should it play and not play today?

3. Does Hill consider himself a speaker/writer of Standard English? Of Ebonics? How does he establish his credibility as either or both? (Hint: Does he claim this status with respect to either variety? Does he employ either or both varieties? Equally? Why or why not?)

4. Analyze Hill's essay using Toulmin's categories. Note Hill's claim, reason(s), and backing. (See Chapter 8 for information on Toulmin arguments.)

5. In paragraph 4, Hill recounts his experiences with Mrs. Tribble, his third-grade teacher, who taught him to avoid certain forms associated with Ebonics and to use "proper English" instead. On the basis of what Hill was taught, he judges others' use of language. Can you recall an episode in which you were made aware of differences in language use — for example, a time when you were overtly corrected by a teacher or parent; a time when you figured out that people of different backgrounds use language differently; or a time when you realized that many people make judgments about others on the basis of their language use? **Write an essay about the incident**, reflecting on and evaluating this practice of judging people, their character, or their worth on the basis of their language.

▼ In this piece, Ted Rall, a freelance cartoonist and columnist based in New York, draws a parallel between Ebonics and office jargon. As you read, try to determine Rall's attitude toward the Oakland school board's decision to declare Ebonics a separate language and to apply for bilingual education funds to help pay for programs to teach Standard English to African American students. This feature is reprinted from the January 1997 San Francisco Examiner's series on Ebonics.

Office Jargon: Language or Dialect?

TED RALL

Taking a cue from the Oakland school board, Fortune 500 companies should request federal funds to teach workers Standard English.

"We need more than just the usual corporate welfare for this project," says a statement that could have come from Microsoft chairman Bill Gates. "How will our employees compete in the global village if they can't speak the same proper English used in Japan and Taiwan?"

Business leaders express concerns about the prevalence of such office slang as "touching base" and "the distribution channel"—terms that refer to, respectively, talking and the market.

While many office workers describe their dialect as lingo they use only among their upper-middle-class peers and in their office parks—while reverting back to normal English in public—some linguists consider it to be a language separate from Standard English.

There are key characteristics. 5

FREQUENT USE OF SPORTS METAPHORS

White-collar types pepper their speech with obscure references to various spectator sports, particularly football and baseball.

Example: "Let's touch base on this next week; if sales drops the ball, we can always huddle on that later."

(As an interim step toward re-establishing the preeminence of standard English, some experts suggest introducing references to other sports, like soccer and cricket, that are better known overseas.)

OBSCURE ACRONYMS

Speakers use acronyms that even someone familiar with a particular business wouldn't know.

Example: "The RFPs for the IRBs 10 still haven't come back from the OSPs. I'll call the CBOE."

CREATION OF NEW VERBS

Converting nouns into transitive verbs usually occurs by silencing the last syllable and using the suf- fix "-ize." Speakers of Corporate-American-English Vernacular use nouns as verbs that can only be understood through context.

Example: "We've got to strategize our response."

OVERZEALOUS USE OF EUPHEMISMS

Particularly in discussions of mass firings, workers invent new words such as "rightsizing."

Examples: "Henry got destaffed. Betty was externalized."

Some academics theorize that cor- 15 porate, or "straight," English first developed as a defensive strategy. By discussing such potentially distasteful topics as toxic waste dumping and effective use of child labor in terms that were understandable only within a specific field, executives hoped to

What values does Rall assume you share with him? How do you know? Chapter 3 discusses how writers establish credibility by highlighting shared values.

LINK TO P. 41 ·············

avoid uncomfortable questions about the true nature of their jobs.

Over time, the thinking goes, the jargon became increasingly specific, resulting in terminology comprehensible only within a certain division of a particular company.

Eventually, wannabes in the word-processing pool adapted the dialect in an effort to communicate more effectively with their superiors, completing the vernacular structure of the white-collar ghetto.

Nonetheless, many Anglophones outside the corporate world agree that office argot is a separate language — and, in fact, indicative of a different subculture.

"I find them incomprehensible," said one Harlem pastor. "Nobody knows what the hell they're talking about, much less what they're thinking. It's not just the idioms either — it's the walk, the clothes, the whole attitude. It's distasteful."

RESPOND●

1. How does Rall define and illustrate office jargon? (By the way, his list of "key characteristics" parodies many linguistic accounts of Ebonics, which cite the most notable differences between Ebonics and other varieties of English.)

2. Reread the final paragraph of Rall's article. Why might he have chosen to end his article with a fictitious quotation from a Harlem pastor?

3. How effective is Rall's humor? Might it be misunderstood? (Here you may wish to discuss with some classmates what you take Rall's opinion about Ebonics to be.)

4. The Ebonics debate gave rise to a number of comedy routines, email chain messages, and newspaper parodies of linguistic descriptions of Ebonics — Hebronics, Fratonics, Gayonics, Redneckonics, and so on. How would you respond to the charge that such parodies are inherently racist? How might someone who claims that such parodies are, by definition, racist support that claim? **Write an essay** arguing that such Ebonics parodies are or are not racist using Rall's article as evidence.

Defining Who We Are in Society

DAVID D. TROUTT

◀ *David D. Troutt is a professor at the Rutgers School of Law at Newark and also author of a recent collection of short stories,* The Monkey Suit *(1998), based on famous legal cases involving African Americans. In this essay, he seeks to analyze why the actions of the Oakland school board caused such an uproar in Black and non-Black communities. This article originally appeared in January 1997 in the* Los Angeles Times.

When passing a controversial resolution to help black schoolchildren learn standard English through Ebonics, the speech patterns many use at home, the Oakland School District reminded the nation of what language means to us. It is our very beginning. Once we as toddlers are given the gift of the communicating self, we can forever discover, learn and expand in a world of common symbols.

Perhaps nothing defines us more than our linguistic skills; nothing determines as much about where we can and cannot go. How we talk may be the first—and last—clue about our intelligence and whether we're trusted or feared, heard or ignored, admitted or excluded.

But we treat our fluency like property. Depending where we are, our ability to speak in certain ways entitles us to access, membership and social riches, such as employment or popularity. As a culture, the greatest benefits go to those who write and speak in standard English, ways identified by most of us as "white," specifically middle-class white.

But participating in the benefits of communication doesn't require being white. It only requires that people around us—wherever we are—understand what we're saying. Ebonics merely validates the distinctive talk among people on a margin far from the majority's view of competence and invites them in. It recognizes that a voice developed amid inequality does not bespeak inferiority.

The problem with Ebonics is not that it will teach children what they already know, which, as critics point out, would be silly. The problem is that its public acceptance might throw into question claims of ownership to intelligence and belonging. After all, Ebonics is not as much the language of blackness as it is the only dialect of persistently poor, racially segregated people—the so-called black underclass. It is the dumbness against which all smartness is measured. But if we reached consensus that Ebonics is a real linguistic system born of difference whose use in schools may facilitate inclusion for children of the excluded, we must deal frankly with the exclusion itself.

5

Ebonics therefore becomes a troubling measure of separation. For many whites, it measures the contradictions of colorblind convictions. For many blacks, Ebonics measures the complications of assimilation and the resiliency of shame.

The ridicule and disparagement on talk radio confirm why an Ebonics program makes sense. Many whites have used the issue as an opportunity to vent racist jokes ordinarily kept underground or in sports bars. Others invoke it in order to restrict black cultural influences, such as banning rap music or canceling TV shows in which black characters use slang.

Meanwhile, more serious mainstream criticism sees the colorblind vision of the republic at stake. Suddenly interested in the achievement of poor black schoolchildren, pundits, federal officials and policymakers unanimously condemn Ebonics for lowering standards. Inadvertently echoing English-only advocacy, they argue that Oakland's resolution would replace children's individuality with militant group identification and promote black "separatism." The standard English language, they say, belongs to all of us.

Such hypocrisy is hard to beat. Of course, language, like intelligence, is no group's personal property. But despite the well-meaning ring of colorblind ideals, you cannot demand sameness of language while perpetuating segregated education. Privately, any master of the language will admit, the best thing you can do for your kids is get them into schools with the tiniest percentage of (poor) blacks. Thus, it is no coincidence that the public school districts experimenting with Ebonics have long been abandoned by white parents. In fact, many public schools are funded by property taxes, making direct the connection between residential and education segregation. This separatism is quite normal. It is how social advantages are reproduced. But you can't enjoy them at a distance and demand conformity, too.

Since the Supreme Court declared separate-but-equal school facili-   10 ties unconstitutional in Brown vs. Board of Education,° most urban school districts have become more, not less, segregated. Moreover, as wealth and resources develop the suburbs, the residential segregation that accompanies separate schooling has produced a degree of racial isolation among inner-city blacks that approaches complete homogeneity.

Brown v. Board of Education: landmark 1954 U.S. Supreme Court decision that declared segregated schooling unconstitutional and put an end to the doctrine of "separate but equal."

To be sure, the Oakland resolution's description of Ebonics as a "primary" language was unfortunate. Such a language would not be English, and non-English cannot be criticized for being "bad English." It is enough that Ebonics has a distinct lexicon and grammatical rules that are spoken exclusively by some blacks. It then qualifies as a reliable measurement of the gulf between many poor blacks and the middle-class world where standard English is spoken.

Recognition of this fact by sociolinguists and its application in school settings are at least three decades old. In addition to Los Angeles and Oakland, schools in Michigan, Texas and New York use what scholars call Black English Vernacular (BEV) as a teaching tool. The principle is hardly new: Begin teaching from where students are and bridge the familiar with the untried.

Another principle at work, however, is assimilation. If Ebonics measures distance, it also measures a closeness more successful blacks have to mainstream culture. Formally educated blacks who use both standard English and Ebonics depending on social context, or "code switching," remain close to two worlds that seem at odds with each other. For white co-workers, they may introduce black English idioms into common parlance. Among less-assimilated family and friends, they may be ostracized for "talking white." As a result, they often both bemoan and boast of their bidialectalism. It is a mark of cross-cultural identification, involving a complicated mix of pride, achievement and lingering shame.

Jesse Jackson illustrated this when he immediately denounced the Oakland resolution as an "unacceptable surrender," then, soon after, changed his mind. His first reaction honored a long, revolutionary tradition of black educators teaching standard English to children at a time when white institutions and hate groups forcibly and deliberately denied us the written and spoken language. Much of the NAACP's legacy—including the Brown decision—was built on such demands for access. It is not surprising, then, that its current director, Kweisi Mfume, denounced Ebonics by resurrecting the memory of Frederick Douglass,° the freed slave who taught himself to read five languages.

Jackson inherits that tradition of civil-rights leadership. He under- 15 stands how the social benefits of assimilation come primarily through language acquisition. Surely, he also recognizes a deep-seated shame many blacks feel at the persistent inability of less-advantaged blacks

Notice how Troutt makes value-based arguments by invoking the authority of respected Black writers. Arguments based on values often work in combination with arguments based on character; see Chapters 5 and 6 for more on both kinds of argument.

LINK TO PP. 57 AND 64·····

Frederick Douglass: African American orator, autobiographer, and journalist (1818–1895), much involved in the abolitionist movement and considered by many to have been the most significant Black American writer and speaker of the nineteenth century.

Zora Neale Hurston: African American writer (1891–1960) who wrote novels and short stories as well as book-length folklore and anthropological studies of African American, Haitian, and Jamaican culture.

Amiri Baraka: African American writer, political activist, and theatrical director (1934–) especially known for his influence on Black American writers of the last third of the twentieth century who, following his example, proudly drew on their own cultural heritage.

to cross over and speak both tongues. The public and institutional denigration of black speech patterns for so long contributes to an undeniable sense of stigma against which blacks from a variety of class backgrounds still struggle.

But in his second reaction, Jackson must have resolved that Ebonics does not dignify some shameful difference. If done right, it should validate, then transcend difference. This reaction also enjoys a long tradition in black culture, as illustrated by the diverse work of writers such as Zora Neale Hurston° and Amiri Baraka.° Many wrote powerfully in standard English, only to return at times to black dialect and write just as beautifully there.

Although Ebonics may prove valuable in teaching underperforming black children standard English, implementing Ebonics programs probably shouldn't be confused with bilingualism. This would create potential competition for scarce funds between blacks and students for whom English is not a primary language. Hopefully, we will find a better way than pitting outsiders against outsiders. There are important differences in the experience of a Guatemalan or Vietnamese third-grader, who returns from school to immigrant parents. The stigma may not result from associating her language with ignorance, but the unkindness is just as real.

Instead, the Ebonics debate should heighten our appreciation of differences among us, as well as the special difficulties faced by students on the margins, who, along with their families, are trying, against long odds, to belong.

RESPOND●

1. Troutt begins with the assertion that "[p]erhaps nothing defines us more than our linguistic skills" (paragraph 2). Throughout the rest of the essay, what evidence does he offer for such a strong assertion?

2. According to Troutt, how did the responses of Blacks and Whites to the Ebonics controversy differ? What were the origins and consequences of these differences? Again, what sorts of evidence does Troutt offer to support his position? How, specifically, does he use the example of Jesse Jackson to demonstrate the ambivalence of most African Americans toward Ebonics?

3. Troutt argues that American society is not exactly honest about Standard English. "As a culture, the greatest benefits go to those who write and speak in standard English," but, according to Troutt, these "ways [of using language are] identified by most of us as 'white,' specifically middle-class white" (paragraph 3). At the same time, "[t]he Standard English language, they say, belongs to all of us" (paragraph 8). Does Standard English belong to everyone? To what extent is it linked implicitly or explicitly to issues of class and ethnicity (and perhaps other axes of social difference such as gender or region)? **Write an essay** in which you explore the ownership of Standard English.

torials, letters to the editor, and cartoons, Ebonics became the subject of public service advertisements during 1997 and 1998. The ad reprinted here ran in several major American newspapers, sponsored by various groups.

I HAS A DREAM.

Does this bother you? It should. We've spent over 400 years fighting for the right to have a voice. Is this how we'll use it? More importantly, is this how we'll teach our children to use it? If we expect more of them, we must not throw our hands in the air and agree with those who say our children cannot be taught. By now, you've probably heard about Ebonics (aka, black English). And if you think it's become a controversy because white America doesn't want us messing with their precious language, don't. White America couldn't care less what we do to segregate ourselves.

The fact is language is power. And we can't take that power away from our children with Ebonics. Would Dr. Martin Luther King, Malcom X and all the others who paid the price of obtaining our voice with the currency of their lives embrace this? If you haven't used your voice lately, consider this an invitation.

SPEAK OUT AGAINST EBONICS

1. Who is the ad's intended audience, that is, those the writer consciously intends to address? Who are its invoked readers, those who can be seen represented in the text? (See Chapter 3 for information about intended and invoked audiences.) What evidence can you offer? (Clue: Who are the "you," the "we," and the "their" of the text?)

2. Who is the African American man standing with his back to us? What is the allusion in the caption "I has a dream"? Why is the allusion especially powerful and apt?

3. **Write an essay** in which you outline the ways in which David Troutt ("Defining Who We Are in Society," p. 613) or John Rickford (Suite for Ebony *and* Phonics," p. 620) might see this ad as being overly simplistic in its representation of Ebonics and the controversies surrounding it.

▼ *John Rickford teaches linguistics and directs the Center for African American Studies at Stanford University. A native speaker of Guyanese Creole, Rickford has devoted much research to documenting the links among various Caribbean creoles and their links to the language used by African Americans. In this essay, which originally appeared in* Discover *in 1997, he explains how linguists look at Ebonics and why.*

Suite for Ebony *and* Phonics

BY JOHN RICKFORD

To James Baldwin, writing in 1979, it was "this passion, this skill . . . this incredible music." Toni Morrison, two years later, was impressed by its "five present tenses" and felt that "the worst of all possible things that could happen would be to lose that language." What these novelists were talking about was Ebonics, the informal speech of many African Americans, which rocketed to public attention a year ago this month after the Oakland School Board approved a resolution recognizing it as the primary language of African American students.

The reaction of most people across the country — in the media, at holiday gatherings, and on electronic bulletin boards — was overwhelmingly negative. In the flash flood of e-mail on America Online, Ebonics was described as "lazy English," "bastardized English," "poor grammar," and "fractured slang." Oakland's decision to recognize Ebonics and use it to facilitate mastery of Standard English also elicited superlatives of negativity: "ridiculous, ludicrous," "VERY, VERY STUPID," "a terrible mistake."

However, linguists — who study the sounds, words, and grammars of languages and dialects — though less rhapsodic about Ebonics than the novelists, were much more positive than the general public. Last January, at the annual meeting of the Linguistic Society of America, my colleagues and I unanimously approved a resolution describing Ebonics as "systematic and rule-governed like all natural speech varieties." Moreover, we agreed that the Oakland resolution was "linguistically and pedagogically sound."

Why do we linguists see the issue so differently from most other people? A founding principle of our science is that we describe *how* people talk; we don't judge how language should or should not be used. A second principle is that all languages, if they have enough speakers, have dialects — regional or social varieties that develop when people are separated by geographic or social barriers. And a third principle, vital for understanding linguists' reactions to the Ebonics controversy, is that all languages and dialects are systematic and rule-governed. Every human language and dialect that we have studied to date — and we have studied thousands — obeys distinct rules of grammar and pronunciation.

What this means, first of all, is that Ebonics is not 5 slang. Slang refers just to a small set of new and usually short-lived words in the vocabulary of a dialect or language. Although Ebonics certainly has slang words — such as *chillin* ("relaxing") or *homey* ("close friend"), to pick two that have found wide dissemination by the media — its linguistic identity is described by distinctive patterns of pronunciation and grammar.

But is Ebonics a different language from English or a different dialect of English? Linguists tend to sidestep such questions, noting that the answers can depend on historical and political considerations. For instance, spoken Cantonese and Mandarin are mutually unintelligible, but they are usually regarded as "dialects" of Chinese because their speakers use the same writing system and see themselves as part of a common Chinese tradition. By contrast, although Norwegian and Swedish are so similar that their speakers can generally understand each other, they are usually regarded as different languages because their speakers are citizens of different countries. As for Ebonics, most linguists agree that Ebonics is more of a dialect of English than a separate language, because it shares many words and other features with other informal varieties of American English. And its speakers can easily communicate with speakers of other American English dialects.

Yet Ebonics is one of the most distinctive varieties of American English, differing from Standard English — the educated standard — in several ways. Consider, for instance, its verb tenses and aspects. ("Tense" refers to *when* an event occurs, "aspect" to *how* it occurs, whether habitual or ongoing.) When Toni Morrison referred to the "five present tenses" of Ebonics, she probably had usages like these — each one different from Standard English — in mind:

1. He runnin. ("He is running.")
2. He be runnin. ("He is usually running.")
3. He be steady runnin. ("He is usually running in an intensive, sustained manner.")
4. He bin runnin. ("He has been running.")
5. He BIN runnin. ("He has been running for a long time and still is.")

In Standard English, the distinction between habitual or nonhabitual events can be expressed only with adverbs like "usually." Of course, there are also simple present tense forms, such as "he runs," for habitual events, but they do not carry the meaning of an ongoing action, because they lack the "-ing" suffix. Note too that "bin" in example 4 is unstressed, while "BIN" in example 5 is stressed. The former can usually be understood by non-Ebonics speakers as equivalent to "has been" with the "has" deleted, but the stressed BIN form can be badly misunderstood. Years ago, I presented the Ebonics sentence "She BIN married" to 25 whites and 25 African Americans from various parts of the United States and asked them if they understood the speaker to be still married or not. While 23 of the African Americans said yes, only 8 of the whites gave the correct answer. (In real life a misunderstanding like this could be disastrous!)

Word pronunciation is another distinctive aspect of dialects, and the regularity of these differences can be very subtle. Most of the "rules" we follow when speaking Standard English are obeyed unconsciously. Take for instance English plurals. Although grammar books tell us that we add "s" to a word to form a regular English plural, as in "cats" and "dogs," that's true only for writing. In speech, what we actually add in the case of "cat" is an *s* sound; in the case of "dog" we add *z*. The difference is that *s* is voiceless, with the vocal cords spread apart, while *z* is voiced, with the vocal cords held closely together and noisily vibrating.

Now, how do you know whether to add *s* or *z* to ₁₀ form a plural when you're speaking? Easy. If the word ends in a voiceless consonant, like "t," add voiceless *s*. If the word ends in a voiced consonant, like "g," add voiced *z*. Since all vowels are voiced, if the word ends in a vowel, like "tree," add *z*. Because we spell both plural endings with "s," we're not aware that English speakers make this systematic difference every day, and I'll bet your English teacher never told you about voiced and voiceless plurals. But you follow the "rules" for using them anyway, and anyone who doesn't — for instance, someone who says "bookz" — strikes an English speaker as sounding funny.

One reason people might regard Ebonics as "lazy English" is its tendency to omit consonants at the ends of words—especially if they come after another consonant, as in "tes(t)" and "han(d)." But if one were just being lazy or cussed or both, why not also leave out the final consonant in a word like "pant"? This is not permitted in Ebonics; the "rules" of the dialect do not allow the deletion of the second consonant at the end of a word unless both consonants are either voiceless, as with "st," or voiced, as with "nd." In the case of "pant," the final "t" is voiceless, but the preceding "n" is voiced, so the consonants are both spoken. In short, the manner in which Ebonics differs from Standard English is highly ordered; it is no more lazy English than Italian is lazy Latin. Only by carefully analyzing each dialect can we appreciate the complex rules that native speakers follow effortlessly and unconsciously in their daily lives.

Who speaks Ebonics? If we made a list of all the ways in which the pronunciation and grammar of Ebonics differ from Standard English, we probably couldn't find anyone who always uses all of them. While its features are found most commonly among African Americans (*Ebonics* is itself derived from "ebony" and "phonics," meaning "black sounds"), not all African Americans speak it. The features of Ebonics, especially the distinctive tenses, are more common among working-class than among middle-class speakers, among adolescents than among the middle-aged, and informal contexts (a conversation on the street) rather than formal ones (a sermon at church) or writing.

The genesis of Ebonics lies in the distinctive cultural background and relative isolation of African Americans, which originated in the slaveholding South. But contemporary social networks, too, influence who uses Ebonics. For example, lawyers and doctors and their families are more likely to have more contact with Standard English speakers—in schools, work, and neighborhoods—than do blue-collar workers and the unemployed. Language can also be used to reinforce a sense of community. Working-class speakers, and adolescents in particular, often embrace Ebonics features as markers of African American identity, while middle-class speakers (in public at least) tend to eschew them.

Some Ebonics features are shared with other vernacular varieties of English, especially Southern white dialects, many of which have been influenced by the heavy concentration of African Americans in the South. And a lot of African American slang has "crossed over" to white and other ethnic groups. Expressions like "givin five" ("slapping palms in agreement or congratulation") and "Whassup?" are so widespread in American culture that many people don't realize they originated in the African American community. Older, nonslang words have also originated in imported African words. *Tote,* for example, comes from the Kikongo word for "carry," *tota,* and *hip* comes from the Wolof word *hipi,* to "be aware." However, some of the distinctive verb forms in Ebonics—he run, he be runnin, he BIN runnin—are rarer or nonexistent in white vernaculars.

How did Ebonics arise? The Oakland School 15 Board's proposal alluded to the Niger-Congo roots of Ebonics, but the extent of that contribution is not at all clear. What we do know is that the ancestors of most African Americans came to this country as slaves. They first arrived in Jamestown in 1619, and a steady stream continued to arrive until at least 1808, when the slave trade ended, at least officially. Like the forebears of many other Americans, these waves of African "immigrants" spoke languages other than English. Their languages were from the Niger-Congo language family, especially the West Atlantic, Mande, and Kwa subgroups spoken from Senegal and Gambia to the Cameroons, and the Bantu subgroup spoken farther south. Arriving in an American milieu in which English was dominant, the slaves learned

English. But how quickly and completely they did so and with how much influence from their African languages are matters of dispute among linguists.

The Afrocentric view is that most of the distinctive features of Ebonics represent imports from Africa. As West African slaves acquired English, they restructured it according to the patterns of Niger-Congo languages. In this view, Ebonics simplifies consonant clusters at the ends of words and doesn't use linking verbs like "is" and "are" — as in, for example, "he happy" — because these features are generally absent from Niger-Congo languages. Verbal forms like habitual "be" and BIN, referring to a remote past, it is argued, crop up in Ebonics because these kinds of tenses occur in Niger-Congo languages.

Most Afrocentrists, however, don't cite a particular West African language source. Languages in the Niger-Congo family vary enormously, and some historically significant Niger-Congo languages don't show these forms. For instance, while Yoruba, a major language for many West Africans sold into slavery, does indeed lack a linking verb like "is" for some adjectival constructions, it has another linking verb for other adjectives. And it has *six* other linking verbs for nonadjectival constructions, where English would use "is" or "are." Moreover, features like dropping final consonants can be found in some vernaculars in England that had little or no West African influence. Although many linguists acknowledge continuing African influences in some Ebonics and American English words, they want more proof of its influence on Ebonics pronunciation and grammar.

A second view, the Eurocentric — or dialectologist — view, is that African slaves learned English from white settlers, and that they did so relatively quickly and successfully, retaining little trace of their African linguistic heritage. Vernacular, or non-Standard features of Ebonics, including omitting final consonants and habitual "be," are seen as imports from dialects spoken by colonial English, Irish, or Scotch-Irish settlers, many of whom were indentured servants. Or they may be features that emerged in the twentieth century, after African Americans became more isolated in urban ghettos. (Use of habitual "be," for example, is more common in urban than in rural areas.) However, as with Afrocentric arguments, we still don't have enough historical details to settle the question. Crucial Ebonics features, such as the absence of linking "is," appear to be rare or nonexistent in these early settler dialects, so they're unlikely to have been the source. Furthermore, although the scenario posited by this view is possible, it seems unlikely. Yes, African American slaves and whites sometimes worked alongside each other in households and fields. And yes, the number of African slaves was so low, especially in the early colonial period, that distinctive African American dialects may not have formed. But the assumption that slaves rapidly and successfully acquired the dialects of the whites around them requires a rosier view of their relationship than the historical record and contemporary evidence suggest.

> **Media uproar over Ebonics missed the point. What's really important is not what kind of language Ebonics isn't, but what kind it is.**

A third view, the creolist view, is that many African slaves, in acquiring English, developed a pidgin language — a simplified fusion of English and African languages — from which Ebonics evolved. Native to none of its speakers, a pidgin is a mixed language, incorporating elements of its users' native languages but with less complex grammar and fewer words than either parent language. A pidgin language emerges to facilitate communication between speakers who do not share a language; it becomes a creole language when it takes root and becomes the primary tongue among its users. This often occurs among the children of pidgin speakers — the vocabulary of the language expands, and the simple grammar is fleshed out. But the creole still remains simpler in some aspects than the original languages. Most creoles, for instance, don't use suffixes to mark tense ("he walk*ed*"), plurals ("boy*s*"), or possession ("John'*s* house").

Creole languages are particularly common on the islands of the Caribbean and the Pacific, where large plantations brought together huge groups of slaves or indentured laborers. The native languages of these workers were radically different from the native tongues of the small groups of European colonizers and settlers, and under such conditions, with minimal access to European speakers, new, restructured varieties like Haitian Creole French and Jamaican Creole English arose. These languages do show African influence, as the Afrocentric theory would predict, but their speakers may have simplified existing patterns in African languages by eliminating more complex alternatives, like the seven linking verbs of Yoruba I mentioned earlier.

Within the United States African Americans speak one well-established English creole, Gullah. It is spoken on the Sea Islands off the coast of South Carolina and Georgia, where African Americans at one time constituted 80 to 90 percent of the local population in places. When I researched one of the South Carolina Sea Islands some years ago, I recorded the following creole sentences. They sound much like Caribbean Creole English today:

1. E. M. run an gone to Suzie house. ("E. M. went running to Suzie's house.")
2. But I does go to see people when they sick. ("But I usually go to see people when they are sick.")
3. De mill bin to Bluffton dem time. ("The mill was in Bluffton in those days.")

Note the creole traits: the first sentence lacks the past tense and the possessive form; the second sentence lacks the linking verb "are" and includes the habitual "does"; the last sentence uses unstressed "bin" for past tense and "dem time" to refer to a plural without using an *s*.

What about creole origins for Ebonics? Creole speech might have been introduced to the American colonies through the large numbers of slaves imported from the colonies of Jamaica and Barbados, where creoles were common. In these regions the percentage of Africans ran from 65 to 90 percent. And some slaves who came directly from Africa may have brought with them pidgins or creoles that developed around West African trading forts. It's also possible that some creole varieties — apart from well-known cases like Gullah — might have developed on American soil.

This would have been less likely in the northern colonies, where blacks were a very small percentage of the population. But blacks were much more concentrated in the South, making up 61 percent of the population in South Carolina and 40 percent overall in the South. Observations by travelers and commentators in the eighteenth and nineteenth centuries record creole-like features in African American speech. Even today, certain features of Ebonics, like the absence of the linking verbs "is" and "are," are widespread in Gullah and Caribbean English creoles but rare or nonexistent in British dialects.

My own view is that the creolist hypothesis incorporates the strengths of the other hypotheses and avoids their weaknesses. But we linguists may never be able to settle that particular issue one way or another. What we can settle on is the unique identity of Ebonics as an English dialect.

So what does all this scholarship have to do with the Oakland School Board's proposal? Some readers might be fuming that it's one thing to identify Ebonics as a dialect and quite another to promote its usage. Don't linguists realize that nonstandard dialects are stigmatized in the larger society, and that Ebonics speakers who cannot shift to Standard English are less likely to do well in school and on the job front? Well, yes. The resolution we put forward last January in fact stated that "there are benefits in acquiring Standard English." But there is experimental evidence both from the United States and Europe that mastering the standard language might be easier if the differences in the student vernacular and Standard English were made explicit rather than entirely ignored.

To give only one example: At Aurora University, outside Chicago, inner-city African American students were taught by an approach that contrasted Standard English and Ebonics features through explicit instruction and drills. After eleven weeks, this group showed a 59 percent reduction in their use of Ebonics features in their Standard English writing.

But a control group taught by conventional methods showed an 8.5 percent increase in such features.

This is the technique the Oakland School Board was promoting in its resolution last December. The approach is not new; it is part of the 16-year-old Standard English Proficiency Program, which is being used in some 300 California schools. Since the media uproar over its original proposal, the Oakland School Board has clarified its intent: the point is not to teach Ebonics as a distinct language but to use it as a tool to increase mastery of Standard English among Ebonics speakers. The support of linguists for this approach may strike nonlinguists as unorthodox, but that is where our principles — and the evidence — lead us.

■

Rickford constructs his argument on a very emotionally loaded subject using evidence based on fact and reason — historical fact, statistics, and studies. Find out about other kinds of fact- and reason-based evidence in Chapter 7.

LINK TO P. 73

RESPOND●

1. In light of Rickford's argument, what does the following sentence from p. 624 mean: "Media uproar over Ebonics missed the point. What's really important is not what kind of language Ebonic isn't, but what kind it is"?

2. What are the three theories of the origins of Ebonics that Rickford discusses? How effectively does he summarize each theory? (In other words, how clear an idea do you have of what each theory argues?) What does he say are the strengths and weaknesses of each? How persuasive is he in arguing for the creolist view, given the evidence he offers? Do you think Rickford assumes you will agree with him? Why or why not?

3. As Rickford notes, linguists contend that they study language scientifically. Assuming they do, how much knowledge about language or linguistics do you find in the other pieces about Ebonics in this cluster? What, in your opinion, accounts for the fact that the knowledge claimed by linguists, as scientists, is generally absent from public debates about language?

4. What does Rickford's final sentence mean? How does it support his own position and that of other linguists? How does it indirectly criticize the negative responses to the Ebonics resolution summarized in paragraph 2 of the essay? **Write an essay** evaluating the evidence Rickford provides for taking a linguistically informed stance on Ebonics.

1. How does Trudeau satirize Mike's attitudes toward African Americans and the varieties of English they use? What variety of English, for example, does Thor use throughout all but the last frame of the cartoon? Why does he switch to Ebonics in the final frame? How does it simultaneously strengthen Thor's authority to speak and the power of his criticism of Mike's condescending attitude?

2. Considering the writers you have read on Ebonics, which of them would find this cartoon most humorous and persuasive? Which do you think would not find it amusing? Why?

3. Part of the humor (and power) of this cartoon comes from Thor's switching between Standard English and Ebonics. **Write an essay** about a situation you have observed in real life, on TV, or in a movie, when someone strategically switched between language varieties or languages to convey an extra message. Be sure to describe the situation clearly (providing translations, if necessary), explaining why switching was an effective rhetorical tool, and demonstrating how the switch linked language and identity in some way.

chapter twenty-eight

Beliefs and Stances

What does it mean to take a stance on an issue, especially a controversial one, in a society as diverse and pluralistic as the United States? Does the American commitment to freedom of religion include the right to talk about or practice one's religion publicly? Or does freedom *of* religion mean freedom *from* religious discourse of any kind in public settings? What about freedom of expression or of speech? Should those who hold strong political beliefs be allowed to express them? Is the right to speak—that is, to express an opinion—the same as the right to be heard? Can speech ever be free, or are there costs that society must bear for "free speech"? If so, what are those costs, and how does society pay them? Can Americans learn to talk with one another in spite of their differences?

The arguments in this chapter call upon you to consider these issues. Regardless of your own ideological commitments, these readings will force you to examine those commitments and the ways in which you argue for them. Is your argumentative strategy to silence those with opposing views, figuratively or literally? Do you seek to "defeat" those with whom you disagree? Do you instead agree to disagree? Or do you seek common ground in order to find "win-win" solutions to what would otherwise remain disagreements? How can you—as an individual and as a member of society—determine what might be appropriate responses in particular situations?

The chapter begins with a cluster of readings about religious beliefs in the public arena, followed by a cluster of arguments about free speech and whether certain views can be freely expressed on college campuses.

One thing distinguishing the United States from perhaps all other countries is its constitutional separation of church and state. There is no "state religion," and Americans aren't required to pay dues or taxes to any religious institution. And most Americans—even (or especially) those who are religious—are generally happy with that state of affairs because they don't want others dictating what they should believe or practice. At the same time, we cannot deny that "In God We Trust" appears on all American currency, a practice begun in 1861 with the two-cent piece and extended to all coins in 1908 and all currency in 1955, nor that if businesses close, they generally do so on Sundays and holidays associated with the Christian tradition. Further, a higher percentage of Americans claim to attend religious services regularly than do the citizens of any other "first world" country.

These facts remind us that there is little common ground among Americans on the proper role of **religious beliefs in the public arena.** Should the government be neutral with matters of faith and religion? Should it vigorously protect the rights of those who are religious? Of those who are not? Of the majority? Of the minority? Is it possible to protect simultaneously the rights of those who are and are not religious? Of the majority and the minority? These questions will likely endure unresolved as long as this country does.

The arguments in this cluster all focus in some way on matters of religious belief and their expression in the public arena. Sometimes the audience for that expression is limited to members of the writer's community of faith; often, however, it is much larger, encompassing the entire society. The issues raised, however, certainly extend beyond the particular texts. Does the freedom to espouse one's religious beliefs entail a commitment to the right of others to espouse the beliefs of other religions—or even no religion at all? Can believers from many religious traditions "join hands across the divide of faith" to work together, or must such cherished beliefs separate believers, making it impossible for them to cooperate, even as they seek to "do good"? Should cartoonists of a particular faith be surprised if some newspapers refuse to print their cartoons when they explicitly espouse that faith? How do the children of immigrants who practice a minority religion make sense of who they are in a culture quite different from the one their parents left? How do gays and lesbians engage with religious traditions that encourage a decidedly negative view of homosexuality and homosexuals? How does a White fundamentalist Christian seek to persuade other White fundamentalists that they, on religious grounds, should apologize to African Americans for slavery?

As the response to each round of Supreme Court rulings reminds us—whether the cases concern abortion, prayer at graduation ceremonies, or the right of the Boy Scouts to reject gay men as scout leaders—religious beliefs have always been present in our country's public debate, and it's likely they'll stay there. For that reason alone, it's in everyone's best interest to spend some time evaluating how such beliefs manifest themselves in our public discourse and how they work as parts of arguments.

Wiley Miller's syndicated cartoon Non Sequitur *appears daily in newspapers across the United States. (As you may know, a non sequitur is a common logical fallacy; for details, check out Chapter 19.) In this May 1999 cartoon, which we've entitled "Complete Tolerance," Miller takes on a controversial topic, the balancing of faith and tolerance. On his Web site, <http://www.wileytoons.com/bio.html>, Miller describes the work of cartoonists as "conveying a thought, giving a perception. We are making a comment, not necessarily a big comment on a big issue—but an observation. Cartoonists are essentially columnists; we perform exactly the same function . . . in a different format." As you study the cartoon, think about how the argument it makes could be expressed in prose form.*

Miller's characters are dressed to suggest ancient Romans—does that mean he is intending his argument to refer to ancient times? Check out Chapter 15 for suggestions on how to analyze visual arguments.

LINK TO P. 251

1. What is Miller's argument? In what ways does it represent a paradox? People from many other societies where the issues of freedom of religion and freedom of expression are not endlessly debated might see this cartoon as especially "American" in nature. Why, might you think?

2. To what extent do you think America lives up to its promise of freedom of speech? Of freedom of religion? What events or other factors have affected your views on these matters?

3. As the United States has become more diverse culturally, Americans have in turn become more diverse with regard to religion. The fastest-growing religious denominations and faiths in the United States are no longer Christian. How do you anticipate that the changing demographics of society will influence the country, which often refers to its Judeo-Christian heritage? Will the response likely be one of tolerance, intolerance, or a complex mixture of both? In what ways? By whom? **Write an essay** in which you address these questions. You may want to begin by doing library or Internet research on the demographics of various U.S. religious groups, using such keywords as *religion, census, demographics,* and *U.S.*

Join Hands across the Divide of Faith: Different Religions Must Begin to Cooperate to Overcome Society's Major Problems

CARDINAL FRANCIS ARINZE

◀ *Cardinal Francis Arinze, born in Nigeria in 1932, serves as president of the Pontifical Council for Interreligious Dialogue. Frequently mentioned as a possible successor to Pope John Paul II, he delivered the commencement address at Wake Forest University in May 1999, when he received an honorary doctorate from that institution. This excerpt from that address appeared in early June of that year in the Charlotte Observer. As you read, pay special attention to how Cardinal Arinze uses elements of definition to develop his argument about what he terms "interreligious collaboration."*

Cardinal Francis Arinze

There is not only one organized religion in the world. There are many. There are Christians and Muslims. There are Jews. But there are also Hindus, Buddhists, followers of traditional religions, Sikhs, Zoroastrians, and so on. Religious plurality is a fact.

Collaboration between the followers of the various religions is necessary both for theological and sociological reasons. Theologically, we consider that all human beings were created by the same God, they have the same human nature and, according to the Christian faith, they have all been redeemed by the same Savior, Jesus Christ.

Sociological reasons for interreligious collaboration come from considerations of joint promotion of the good of humanity and also of mutual enrichment. If citizens of the same country, for example, adhere to differing religions, it is better for them and their country that they accept and respect one another and that they join hands to seek solutions to major problems of their society.

Many problems and challenges do not respect religious frontiers. There is no Catholic hurricane or Baptist drought. There is no Jewish inflation or Muslim unemployment. There is no Buddhist drug addiction or Hindu AIDS.

Interreligious collaboration therefore calls on the followers of the various religions to join hands—for example, to defend the family and its positive values, to

5

Arinze's article is a good example of a Rogerian argument. See more about Rogerian arguments in Chapter 1.

LINK TO P. 6 ···

promote a society where the individual is appreciated, respected and cared for in case of need, to defend life in all its stages from conception right up to natural death, to tackle problems of unemployment, drug addiction and AIDS, and to defend religious freedom for citizens, not only in some countries but everywhere.

Religions are expected to contribute to a more just economic, social and political order. If the free play of market forces means that a few big companies stifle or snuff out the smaller industries, if an over-liberal economic and social system makes very acute the gap between rich and poor, so that a few over-rich people banquet every day as if in an oasis of opulence and enjoyment while others languish in a desert of misery, if the pitiless political system evolves into full-blown dictatorship that ridicules individual freedom, then the religions are definitely called upon to come all out and help to produce a solution.

The moral virtue of solidarity teaches us to share with others. Solidarity is interdependence accepted, loved and lived. And respect for the dignity of the human person means that democracy is no empty word, but that every citizen has the right, and the duty, of participation in public affairs, in ways to be worked out in each country and cultural area.

When, therefore, we talk of interreligious collaboration, we are referring to everyday needs and not to an elitist entertainment. When we say interreligious dialogue, we do not mean necessarily an international conference in which learned theologians and professors read their paper's 40 pages with 20-page bibliography. We need such professors, but most people are not of that level. They just want to interact at the level of daily life.

This plea for interreligious collaboration is not support for the foundation of more religions. We already have far too many. Nevertheless, much as it might be beautiful if there were only one religion, we should not deny any human being the exercise of the right to religious freedom, within due limits.

To argue in favor of interreligious collaboration, on the other hand, does not aim 10 at depriving any religion of its identity. It is not an effort to persuade the various religions to cast their various beliefs, rites and moral codes into a melting pot for the brewing of a syncretistic product. We are not trying to make an omelet of the religions. Such a religion would be the religion of nobody. Meant to fit anybody, it could not offer anyone a dynamic and satisfactory philosophy of life, a clear enough road map. It would not stand anyone in good stead in a moment of great moral crisis.

Interreligious cooperation presumes that the participating believers belong each to a religion with clear self-identity. Such a genuine religion should be one that has clear beliefs, ritual and code of conduct. It should equip the believer with a unified view of life. It should present a vital synthesis of the details that make up a person's daily life.

We must not ignore the objection raised by some people who fear that in the seeking of harmony, religions may be part of the problem rather than part of the solution. Some even argue that along the corridors of history, religions have caused tension, violence and war. For them, discussion on interreligious collaboration is so much pious but unrealistic talk.

Let us begin by admitting that prejudices generated or occasioned by religions, and handed on from generation to generation, are not easy to discard. And de facto in history, and even at present, some people have alleged or tried to hijack religious considerations to justify or motivate tension, violence or even war.

But it must be asserted that every religion worthy of the name teaches the golden rule: Do unto others as you would have them do to you. Genuine religion is about love of God and consequent love of neighbor. "Anyone who says, 'I love God,' and hates his brother, is a liar," St. John tells us, "since a man who does not love the brother that he can see cannot love God, whom he has never seen."

The promotion of hatred, violence and war is the opposite of what true religion is 15 all about. When a careful analysis is made of a particular case of tension, violence or war, it will be found that often considerations that are racial, political and economic have contributed to the disaster. There may also be the burden of history, unhealed memories of past injustices, real or merely perceived. Religion has sometimes been abused and exploited and blamed in order to hide these motivations and explain outbursts of violence, economically oppressive measures, massacres, so-called ethnic cleansings or other acts of injustice which fallen human nature is all too prone to perpetrate.

A true believer, on the other hand, is known by love of neighbor, readiness to admit guilt where there has been any, openness to reconciliation and positive promotion of solidarity between peoples, cultures and religions. Give us such people in large numbers, and our societies will be able to look to the future, to the forthcoming millennium, with a sense of renewed hope that greater harmony is not impossible.

<u>**RESPOND**</u> •

1. What does Arinze mean by "interreligious collaboration"? What are its characteristics? What sort of definition (Chapter 4) does he offer? How does Arinze anticipate and respond to potential criticisms of his arguments in favor of such collaboration?

2. Arinze's speech contains elements of Rogerian argument (Chapter 1), particularly in the way it attempts to find and build on common ground. Cite examples from the text where Arinze tries to create common ground with his listeners. Why might Rogerian argument be especially appropriate for a college graduation ceremony?

3. We can assume that Arinze's argument was written to be delivered orally. What elements of spoken arguments (Chapter 17) does Arinze use to help listeners follow the structure of his argument? How does he use figurative language (Chapter 14) to help structure his argument and make it memorable for his listeners?

4. What might Arinze mean by the claim that "we should not deny any human being the exercise of the right to religious freedom, within due limits" (paragraph 9)? What might such limits be? How might differences in opinion about "due limits" be resolved? **Write an essay** in which you define the "due limits" (if any) that you believe should be placed on the exercise of the right to religious freedom. (An interesting example to consider here involves the Wiccans, neo-Pagans who found themselves at the center of a controversy in 1999, when the U.S. military first permitted them to practice their faith on military bases. You should be able to find information about this controversy using the Internet.)

▼ Nationally syndicated columnist Leonard Pitts writes about politics, culture, and everyday life. He has won several journalism awards for his outstanding columns and written a book, **Black Men and the Journey to Fatherhood** (1999). In this column, which appeared in major U.S. newspapers in late April 1999, Pitts examines a controversy about religious themes in public discourse generally and in newspaper comics specifically by focusing on the work of Johnny Hart, some of whose cartoons are reprinted following this selection (p. 641). As you read, notice the way Pitts's writing style works as a rhetorical tool.

A Little Matter of Faith

LEONARD PITTS

Ordinarily, Johnny Hart is not a guy I'd be rushing to defend.

Politically speaking, he's a little to the right of Attila the Hun. Adheres to an unswervingly literal interpretation of the Bible. Believes God may have been behind the assassination of Israeli Prime Minister Yitzhak Rabin as punishment for negotiating holy land away. Thinks Muslims, Jews and gays are on the afterlife express to hell. Not exactly on the same page, Johnny Hart and I. Till now.

It seems that in the last few years, Hart — creator of a popular comic strip called "B.C." that runs in many newspapers — has been at the center of a minor media controversy. Angry readers have complained. And some of the more than 1,200 newspapers that carry his work have either dropped it entirely or reserved the right to excise strips they don't like. Count among them such powerhouses as the *Chicago Sun-Times,* the *Los Angeles Times* and the *Washington Post.*

You might be wondering what Hart did to raise such a stink. According to a profile that recently ran in the *Post,* the answer is simple: He mentioned Jesus. Meaning that from time to time, particularly around the religious holidays, Hart uses the comic strip as a forum for Christian doctrine: birth, death, resurrection, salvation.

That, apparently, is more than 5 some folks can stand.

It's a funny thing about the funny pages. People don't like it when you mess with 'em. That's why so many strips seem to unfold in some dimension beyond time, an eternal '50s where nothing changes and safe, in-offensive gags recycle without end.

In such an environment, it doesn't take much to stir controversy. Garry Trudeau's "Doonesbury" does it with pointed sociopolitical satire. Lynn Johnston's "For Better or for Worse" does it with a recurring character who's gay. And Johnny Hart does it by talking Jesus. Which seems to illustrate the looming difficulty we have with discussing issues of faith.

It's a private matter, we say, but there's a certain hypocrisy in that argument, given that we discuss private matters in public forums all the time. What's it say to you that some of us find it easier to discuss penile implants than the fact that some people believe a man named Jesus was killed and then lived again? Or that others believe their ancestors were led from slavery to freedom by a man named Moses? Or that still others believe an angel imparted divine wisdom to a man named Mohammed?

I'm not here to argue the verities of faith. The point I'm trying to make has nothing to do with what people believe. Rather, it deals with the fact that people believe. Believe over-whelmingly, according to the polls. In a higher power, a force, a man or woman upstairs, a God.

639

Media—from the funny pages to 10 the 6 o'clock news—often seem ill at ease with that. Outside the easy hooks—Islamic terrorists, Christian zealots—they tend to pass the subject in silence, for reasons I'm not sure I understand. But I certainly understand the result: Media miss a large portion of the lives they purport to reflect.

I appreciate the misgivings of newspaper editors regarding Hart. They have a right—an obligation— to police their pages for inappropriate content. And there have been times his work teetered uncomfortably close to sheer proselytizing. Other times when it was, arguably, ugly toward those who don't believe as he does.

I'm convinced, however, that the larger part of media—and public— disaffection with Hart's work has less to do with how he says what he says than that he says it at all. That he transgresses the unspoken rule by which issues of faith are not to be openly discussed.

But the American creed of free speech has always demanded that we consider more views, not fewer. Has always held that the ability to countenance diverse opinions is a source of strength, not a sign of weakness. Guided by that principle, we've survived some pretty extreme characters.

I have to believe we can survive Jesus, too.

Causal arguments often focus on the claim that something *will* happen; here Pitts is arguing that a particular result *won't* occur. See more about how to formulate a causal argument in Chapter 11.

··· LINK TO P. 161

RESPOND ●

1. Why does Pitts, a religious believer who generally does not agree with Johnny Hart's religious beliefs, defend the cartoonist's right to use religion explicitly as a theme in his cartoons? What sorts of arguments does Pitts make? What sorts of evidence does he offer for his claims? How effective are they? What does Pitts mean in his final sentence when he writes, "I have to believe we can survive Jesus, too"?

2. Pitts's column is written in a very casual style: the reader can easily imagine him *saying* more or less exactly what he has written. He achieves this conversational tone by using sentence fragments and syntax that sound much like that of everyday speech. Rewrite paragraphs 6–9 in a style appropriate for an academic essay, recasting fragments into complete sentences, altering at least some of the informal syntax, and perhaps making other changes as well.

3. Among Pitts's arguments is the claim (paragraph 10) that with a few key exceptions, the media ignore religion and religious believers because they are "ill at ease" with religious belief. (Note that Pitts makes two separate but related claims here—he claims that the media ignore matters of faith and he offers his analysis of their reason for doing so.) Do you agree? Why or why not? **Write a column** of about five hundred words for a newspaper you regularly read addressing the paper's coverage of matters relating to faith or beliefs and support or critique its current practice with respect to these topics.

B.C. is an award-winning comic strip
drawn by Johnny Hart since 1958. The B.C.
cartoons reprinted here address directly
matters of faith from a decidedly Christian
perspective. The title of the strip is, of course,
part of Hart's argument. As you study these
cartoons, consider how readers from a range
of faiths and with a range of attitudes about
the role of religious belief in public life might
respond to them and their appearance in newspapers across the United States.

How does Hart use symbols in
the arguments B.C. makes? See
more about visual arguments in
Chapter 15.

LINK TO P. 251

1. What is Hart's argument in each cartoon? Who is the intended audience? The invoked audience? The "real" or actual audience? (See Chapter 3.) How do you know? (Consider, for example, how members of each of the following groups might respond to the cartoons: evangelical Christians; Christians who find evangelism offensive or at least unwarranted; members of other faiths; atheists and others who believe there should be no mention of religious beliefs in public forums; those who believe that certain religious groups should have the right to mention their beliefs, even if others may find the beliefs offensive; and those who believe that "free speech" means all people can say anything they like.)

2. What are the meaning and history of the symbol that appears in the last panel of the fourth cartoon (which is a visual argument based on a Greek acronym)? This symbol often appears affixed to the rear end of automobiles, and it has given rise to at least two other "arguments," both of which are also often stuck to cars: a fish with small feet that has the name DARWIN written inside, and a fish with the word GEFILTE written inside. Explain each of the three arguments, discussing the sort of people who are likely to display each one on their cars. How effective are the two arguments that allude to the original one? How effectively do they use humor? To what ends? What is the purpose of making such arguments (that is, why do people affix such symbols to their automobiles in the first place)?

3. In "A Little Matter of Faith" (p. 639), Leonard Pitts points out that some newspapers no longer carry Hart's *B.C.* cartoons or "reserve . . . the right to excise strips they don't like" (paragraph 3). This decision was made in response to readers' complaints about the cartoons' overtly Christian content. **Write an essay** in which you respond to the question of whether such a decision constitutes censorship, good business, or something else. The most well-reasoned responses will not be those that merely reply "yes" or "no" but those that address both the limits placed on the expression of religious faith in forums like the comics of a commercial newspaper and the heterogeneous nature of U.S. society with respect to matters of faith and their public discussion.

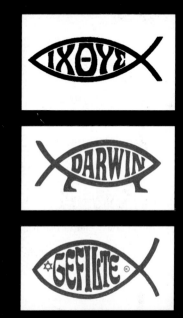

A Hindu Renaissance

DEBORAH KOVACH CALDWELL

COPPELL, Texas — A few years ago,
Manmadhan and Radha Nair enclosed the patio off their trim suburban ranch house and turned it into a
Hindu oasis.

The white-tiled room is a tranquil
place for lighting candles, draping
deities — Vishnu, Shiva, Ganapathi
and others — with garlands and offering rose water and grapes.

They wouldn't have considered
such a room 20 years ago.

"Honestly, we were kind of
embarrassed," said Manmadhan Nair,
45, who likes to be called Mike. "We
were a little worried whether we
could expose this kind of thing to
other people."

Then their born-and-reared-in- 5
America teenage kids came along.

For more than a generation, most
of the nation's approximately 1.5 million Hindus — the vast majority of
them Indian immigrants — have paid

little attention to their ancient faith.
Busy building careers and families,
they've tried to blend into America.
But now the first generation of
American-born Indians is coming of
age. They are forcing their baby-
boomer parents to reckon with a long-
neglected faith.

Prayer rooms like the Nairs' are
appearing in subdivisions everywhere. Nationwide, a wave of Hindu
temple construction is going on;
perhaps 1,000 communities are in
various stages of planning or construction, according to observers.
About 200 temples have already been
built.

Devotees are starting the Hindu
version of Bible studies and Sunday
schools, unheard of in India.

There is a Web site — http://www
.hindunet.org/ — aimed at the young.
And there is a glossy monthly called
Hinduism Today that bills itself as a
leader in the Hindu "renaissance." On
campuses, Hindu awareness groups
are popping up. There is even a small

organization called the American
Hindu Anti-Defamation Council.

What is going on?   10

"Religion is becoming very
important for the second generation
because that is the way immigrants
maintain ethnic identity," said Prema
Kurien, a sociology professor at the
University of Southern California
who studies Indian immigration.
"They first tried to be just American,
and they weren't accepted as just
American. This is a reaction to that."

But older Hindus are also in the
midst of an intense struggle over how
to make the religion attractive to their
youth. Young Hindus want to know
why they should practice the faith,
but their parents often don't know
the answer. Most baby-boomer
Hindus learned only the rituals, not
the theology, when they were growing up in India.

The Gen-Xers want more. And
they, too, are struggling. Those
who've learned the faith from their
parents want to keep it. But every day

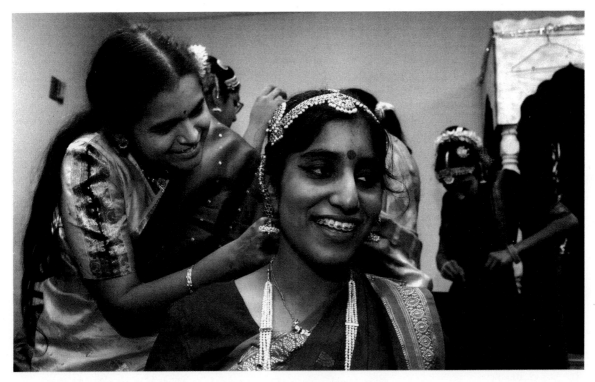

Three generations of Hindu women prepare for a ceremony in a Dallas/Fort Worth temple.

they battle against two opposing forces: American culture and their parents' Indian ways.

Some Hindus believe that if they can rejuvenate their faith, it can become an important new American force, like Islam. Everyone agrees, however, that the path will be difficult.

CULTURE VS. FAITH

Manish Nair, 16, plopped in a 15 chair in his living room on a Saturday afternoon. He wore shorts and a T-shirt but said when he goes to the temple, he wears a "juba" — loose-fitting pants and a shirt.

"Religiously, I'm settled," he said. "I'd like to follow Hinduism. But culturally, it's hard. What we do in the home is completely different from what I do out there."

He eats meat outside his house — a practice that goes against Hindu teaching. On the other hand, he doesn't expect to date; it is simply not done in India. And he intends to marry an Indian woman.

His father sat next to him, smiling his approval.

"Mike" Nair came to the United States from India in 1980. After graduating from the University of North

Texas in 1989, he went to work for J.C. Penney as a systems analyst.

He and his wife, Radha, who is 42 20 and owns a home health care business, also have a daughter, Asha, 13.

In the early years, the Nairs found it difficult to keep up the daily prayers; they were busy coping with jobs, a young family and the overwhelming American culture. So for a while, they let the rituals slide.

Then the children got older.

"They have pushed us a lot," Nair said. "We picked up all our knowledge of Hinduism from our parents, and we felt if we were not giving it to our children, a great culture would be lost. It's our moral duty to show them."

Asha has become heavily involved in Hindu classical dance and practices in the prayer room. Before school and work each day, the Nairs bathe; then they pray in their special room. At the end of the day they repeat the process.

"It's a very sacred place in this home," Nair said.   25

Still, the disconnect between the two cultures is sometimes wearying.

"I bring my friends home and they ask, 'Why do you worship elephants?' " Manish said, referring to the god Ganapathi, with his elephant face.

Manish hopes Hinduism lasts into the next generation in America—but he isn't sure it will.

"It's hard to keep up the traditions and values," he said. "You're being pulled between two societies."

RITUALS VS. BELIEFS

That is the anxiety for Hindus.   30
Even though some Hindu families like the Nairs are working to create a vibrant faith in America, many Hindu leaders worry that their numbers are small.

"What good things we have, I don't know if we'll preserve them," says Dr. Asmukh Shah, 73, a cardiovascular surgeon who came to the United States 40 years ago.

Nearly 20 years ago, Shah organized a local group that got together to read the Bhagavad Gita, a Hindu scripture. Today, Shah leads weekly religion classes at the Dallas/Fort Worth Hindu Temple in Irving. But out of an estimated local Hindu popu-lation of 20,000, only 150 people come, he said. On festival days, perhaps 2,000 people show up.

Perhaps that is because understanding Hinduism is so difficult. It is a complex 5,000-year-old village tradition with various beliefs across India. Most Indians learn the faith from their families during rituals passed down through generations. As a result, most Hindus don't understand their faith as a system of ideas.

That leads to another of Hinduism's unique challenges: It isn't demanding or rule-bound. One of the few ideas around which Hindus rally is that "You can have what you want." Hindus are taught to lead moderate, generous lives, but they are not given a list of do's and don'ts. That is one reason Hinduism has historically been tolerant of other religions.

But in the West, this causes a   35
problem because Christianity, Judaism and Islam are all faiths with more rigid boundaries—and thus a lack of understanding of a looser set of beliefs.

Hindu observers worry the faith won't adapt to American culture.

Most Hindu priests are trained only in leading rituals—which don't interest the vast majority of American Hindus, observers say. Most Hindu leaders have no training in teaching, counseling or programming, according to Arumugaswami, managing editor of Hinduism Today. He and others believe an American-style menu of services like classes and activities will draw Hindus.

"We need to adapt our religion to another country," he said. "That's what other religions did. But we're not even in a good position to convert our own people."

Hinduism Today recently published an article about the organizing efforts of American Muslims, and added an editor's note suggesting Hindus could learn from those efforts. In many ways Islam, which claims about 6 million American adherents, was in Hinduism's situation a decade ago.

But the road ahead will be harder   40
for Hindus, experts say.

"The Hindu community is not anywhere near as well-organized as Muslims," says Diana Eck, director of the Pluralism Project at Harvard University and an expert on Hinduism. "The Islamic community has a very large national infrastructure, and also they've prioritized Islamic education over and above building religious institutions like mosques. And there is also a core teaching to Islam that makes it a bit easier for young Muslims to get hold of.

"I don't know that you'll ever see American Hindus with the same kind of assertiveness," she said.

TWO WORLDS

When Mallika Rao was small, she dreamed of painting herself white and having white children.

"I wanted to fit in," said Mallika, 15, a sophomore at Ursuline Academy in Dallas.

That feeling has disappeared. But   45
Mallika and her brother, Siddartha, a 17-year-old junior at St. Mark's School in Dallas, still struggle.

They talk to their parents about Hinduism occasionally, but they get frustrated because their parents don't understand what it's like to be a questioning American teenager.

Mallika eats meat, although her brother does not. They both plan to date, and they both go to parties — and feel a little guilty about it.

Sometimes they make fun of their elders' Indian accents, and that makes them feel guilty, too. They're embarrassed when their mother wears saris to school functions but they're not sure why.

Still, they sense an emergence of Hindu pride.

"All of a sudden there is this big 50 rush of people liking Indian stuff," said Mallika.

One of her friends sports a bindi, the brown dot many Indian women wear to represent the third eye of Shiva, the protective goddess. She notices popular musicians also wearing bindis.

Mallika's mother, Dallas neurologist Dr. Kalpana Rao, said she ran into a white American middle-schooler at an Indian restaurant recently. The boy pointed to a bronze statue and said, "That's Shiva, right?" He was correct.

For Rao, 47, the emergence of pop Hinduism isn't surprising. The world is getting smaller, after all, she said.

Rao believes that while American Hindus are struggling to keep the faith, so are Indians.

Rao remembered her grandmother's rigid Hindu practices: She forced everyone to bathe before they entered the kitchen, where she wore a special sari. But her parents didn't practice such rituals, and she doesn't either.

"India is changing and so are we," 55 she said. "If there is going to be a Hindu renaissance, it's going to be more in a practical sense."

But how?

In small pockets around America, change is happening.

According to Kurien of the University of Southern California, temples are beginning to hold rituals and special celebrations on Sundays, when most people aren't working. Many American temples, including the one in Irving, practice a kind of "ecumenical Hinduism." They display deities popular in various parts of India to satisfy their diverse congregations. The Irving temple has three priests, each from a different Indian region.

And some communities, including the Irving temple, have started offering American-style celebrations,

such as Graduation Day or Mother's Day — all unheard of in India.

But more needs to happen, said 60 Gurumurthy Kalyanaram, 42, a Dallas marketing consultant.

"How are these temples going to survive?" he said, gesturing as he ate lunch at India Palace restaurant in North Dallas. "We are not telling the next generation what we're about."

Kalyanaram wants to see more programs at the temple and more discussion groups to help Hindus understand their tradition.

"I'm hopeful about the younger generation," he said. "The great joy of being born in this country and not being constrained is that you rediscover Hindu thought in a meaningful way. But the anxiety is this: Between that generation and the older generation there is a gap of about 20 years — the baby boomers who immigrated here. That generation is anchored neither in the joy of Hindu thought nor in the rituals."

And that leaves the difficult question.

"Who," he asked, "is going to 65 bridge this gap?"

Not all causal arguments are intended to convince or persuade. We can interpret Caldwell's article as an argument to explore. See more about the many purposes of arguments in Chapter 1.

⋯⋯⋯⋯⋯⋯⋯⋯⋯ LINK TO P. 3

RESPOND ●

1. According to the Hindus interviewed by Caldwell, what sorts of tensions do U.S. immigrants who practice a minority religion face? How do these tensions manifest themselves in different ways for different generations of immigrants? How do the faiths of immigrants become adapted to American culture? What, ultimately, is Caldwell's argument?

2. As in most feature articles, much of Caldwell's support for her argument comes from testimony. What sorts of testimony does she use, and how effectively do these testimonies work to support her argument?

3. Investigate the issues discussed in this article by interviewing two or three people whose families immigrated to this country within the past few decades, or people who were born in the United States but have lived in another country or culture where the predominant religion was not their own. Ask them to describe the accommodations they had to make and the conflicts they experienced—perhaps internal conflicts or conflicts with family members or people in the home community—with respect to matters of religious faith and practice. **Write an essay** in which you report on and analyze the situations of the people you have interviewed.

An Open Letter to My Christian Friends

ED MADDEN

Ed Madden teaches in the English Department at the University of South Carolina. A scholar and poet, he is also a committed Christian. This letter, written in 1997, originally circulated as email; the version reprinted here was forwarded to one of the authors from a friend rather than coming directly from Madden. Readers from the Christian tradition will be well aware of the importance of the epistolary tradition in their faith. Most of the books of the New Testament began as letters written to distant churches or believers, prompted by particular historical events. The event that prompted Madden's letter was the controversy following Ellen DeGeneres's coming out on the Ellen show.

An open letter to my Christian friends, and to my Harding University brothers and sisters, after reading many email messages and forwardings about "Ellen":

I, like many young Christian men and women, grew up in a loving and warm Christian home, attended an active and devoted rural church, went to a spiritually enriching Christian college, and spent a great deal of my life devoted to the work of Christ. As a high school student I won the state Bible bowl competitions several years in a row and played an active leadership role in my church. As a college student I went on mission trips to Europe, and actively pursued study of the Bible. As a graduate student I took time to attend (and graduate from) a Christian seminary, and I worked with the educational programs of my church.

Like many young men and women, though, I also grew up knowing that I was different, realizing later that that difference was and is homosexual orientation. And I spent a great part of my life learning how to lie, how to deceive, and how to hate myself. Sexual issues were rarely discussed in my church and family, except in cases of condemnation, and homosexuality was even more rarely discussed, except as something absolutely abhorrent, unspeakable, and disgusting. When you're a little kid, and when you are beginning to sense that the difference you feel from your culture is something so hated, you learn your lessons well. Often you spend your time working for God's favor and praying for change. Sometimes you spend your time cultivating the favor of your parents, knowing that there is something about you that they might (and often do) reject. Sometimes you cultivate asexuality, and avoid love or devotion altogether. Sometimes you date women to keep up appearances. Always you learn to be silent. Always you learn to lie, when necessary. Always you learn how to hate yourself.

After I left Harding University, a good Christian school that was essential to my spiritual development, I decided to be honest, both with myself and others. I have known I was gay at least since I was eight years old, if not before. I spent most of my life learning to hide my feelings, or worse, learning to fake feelings I didn't have. I tried to become engaged, in an act of desperation. I felt almost suicidal when my girlfriend (wisely) broke up with me—she seemed my last hope, my last bargaining chip with God.

I spent a great deal of time in reading and prayer, trying to understand. I do not 5 fit the usual right-wing or pathological explanations of homosexuality. I was never abused as a child. I did not have a smothering mother, nor did I have an especially distant father. Nor did I *choose* to be gay. My orientation is a preconscious condition, not a willful choice or a perverse preference. I realized that being gay is not a choice; being honest is. I prayed and prayed for God to change me. He did: he changed my mind.

I left the Church of Christ for the Methodist Church, a church at least willing to discuss the issue and have compassion and understanding for gay and lesbian Christians. I may have been wrong about the Church of Christ, and your particular church may be different, but my only sense of things there was that it was a church that refused to deal with the issue, a group that felt a compulsion to silence those who wished to address it, and a community that demonized those who, by no choice of their own, found themselves to be lesbian or gay. You were rejected, that is, unless you were dying of AIDS, and then you were welcomed back into the church as a prodigal son. Dying as a precondition for acceptance.

It was also a church in which homosexuality was treated simply as a behavior, not as a condition, much less an identity. The experience of most gays and lesbians is that being gay is not something we do. It's who we are, regardless of what we do. The failure of our community to recognize that distinction (it's not what you do, it's who you are) only complicates our attempts to deal with the issue as gay or lesbian Christians. Furthermore, homosexuality is more often than not treated as the worst sin, an unforgivable sin, something unspeakable. It is demonized, pathologized, and silenced. And those of us who grow up knowing we are gay or lesbian, but also knowing we are Christian, find ourselves in an impossible situation. We are both part of the community, and we are its object of hatred.

For example, when I once worked with preteen boys on a biblical drama, a "parable project" in which we acted out parables from the gospels, those little boys made it clear to me that early on we learn in Christian families that homosexuals are people to be hated. We were modernizing the parables for them to act out (the kids wrote the scripts, planned the costumes, worked on props, and talked about the important Christian lessons being taught). We were working on the parable of the good Samaritan.° My female co-teacher and I talked about the Jewish contempt for the Samaritans, and suggested that they come up with

good Samaritan: one of Jesus' parables (Luke 10:25–37) told in answer to the question, "Who is my neighbor?" The parable recounts how both a priest and a religious man walked past a man who had been robbed and left to die by the side of the road, offering no assistance, while a Samaritan, a member of the group most despised by Jesus's listeners, stopped to offer assistance. When Jesus asked the questioner which of these men had acted as a neighbor, the petitioner responded, "The one who showed mercy." Jesus then told him to go and do likewise.

a modern equivalent. Since the church was a progressive urban church, the boys did not choose the obvious parallels of racism or even religious hatred. Without any prompting, they suggested two groups that people (including their parents, they said) hate or despise: homeless people and gay men. Although they chose to act out the parable using a homeless man as a good Samaritan, which was probably the wisest choice given the context, I learned the lesson that they had also learned all too well: it is okay for Christians to despise and hate homosexuals. Wisdom from the mouths of children.

(Read Bette Greene's adolescent novel _The Drowning of Stephan Jones_, based on a true story, about teenage boys killing a gay man, and justifying that murder with the hatred they learned in their Christian communities.)

When I decided to be honest with my family, I further learned how Christian and 10 family values are acted out when you happen to be gay. What are those family values? That honesty has a cost. That family love is conditional. That brother may reject brother. That the use of scripture is selectively enforced. (Although Jesus has a lot to say about greed, homosexuality is the condition that requires that you reject your own loved ones.) That dishonesty is a virtue. (I was told that I should spend my life lying, that I should "lie to [my] grave.") That homosexual is the worst possible thing one can be. (If only, as one family member said, I could be addicted to drugs or had murdered someone, they could deal with that.)

My students tell me horror stories. One kid's father asked him to leave his house when he found out that his son was gay. While this student was hurriedly packing up some things and preparing to leave, he decided to run to the hall-way and grab a family photo. All the photos with him in them were gone, and his father was in the backyard destroying them. The last words he ever heard from his brother, a respected Southern Baptist minister, were: "I hope you get AIDS and die like all the other faggots." Another kid I know had his father write to him: "Tell me if you're ever coming home, so that I can leave town." Another man I know opened his mail in January to find that his father had returned to him all the Christmas gifts he had sent to him, all of them unopened.

The ultimate value most gay kids learn in the church is dishonesty. We learn that being dishonest, lying, is a good Christian practice. How many closeted gay men have I known who have stayed in the church, only on the condition of their own dishonesty? If they are honest, they will be rejected, stigmatized, effectively driven away. If they remain closeted, they can stay in the church. They may secretly "fall" with a frequency that would appall most of their companions, they may indulge in bad sexual behavior. Or they may remain celibate and silent and perpetuate the stigma and the lie that we are not part of the Christian community. Or they may even marry to keep up appearances. They are good citizens of the church, good brethren, and good liars. Those of us who try to live with honesty and integrity, who wish to be honest about who we are, are often rejected by our families, despised and rejected by our communities, and sometimes silenced by our churches.

I realize some gay men and lesbians may try to change, or deny and repress the deep fact of their orientation. I respect them for their decisions. But what if they were allowed to be honest?

It is no wonder that 1/3 of teenage suicides can be tied to issues of sexual identity. Many of us know we are gay, and we imagine ourselves therefore fully deserving of hatred and rejection, even though we may have never had sex or fallen in love. We hear of the "lifestyle" we lead that deserves condemnation, even though we may never wear leather, dress in drag, or pursue anonymous or promiscuous sex. And, as the outrage about "Ellen" demonstrates, our friends and companions make it clear that discussion about or even awareness of homosexuality is something to be silenced. It is a chilling monologue, not a conversation that results: "Hate yourself!" "Shut up!" Or, more often than not, "Leave."

Regardless of what you think about homosexuality, please remember that you 15 know homosexuals and lesbians, whether you are aware of them or not. Remember that most of us experience our sexual orientation as an essential part of who we are, an identity, not an isolated act or a behavioral choice. Remember that some of us found ourselves rejected by our families and our churches, and many of us have not experienced compassion or understanding from the Christian communities in which we grew up. Remember that most of us were, in fact, forced to find other communities in order to be honest people.

Remember that there are lots of frightened gay teenagers, who are studiously learning how to hate themselves and how to lie, who have all their self-hatred and fear affirmed every time they hear messages of demonization rather than messages of compassion. Remember that lots of other teenage kids have grown up in a Christian community that taught them that it is perfectly acceptable to despise and hate gays and lesbians, even if they're in your own family, and it is perfectly within the bounds of Christian love to reject your own brother or sister if they happen to be gay or lesbian.

We are your invisible sons and daughters, your invisible brothers and sisters. Please at least think about that.

In Christian love,

Ed

RESPOND ●

1. What sort of ethos does Madden establish for himself as author? How does he do so? What do you believe Madden is asking of his audience? In other words, what does he hope the outcome of his letter will be? Why? What is the tone of his letter? Is it effective, given the writer's purpose and argument? Why or why not?

2. In paragraph 7, Madden writes, "We [gay and lesbian Christians] are both part of the community, and we are its object of hatred," a point to which he returns in the letter's closing paragraphs. Why does he characterize the situation of lesbian and gay Christians in this way? Can you think of other groups about whom a similar claim could be made?

3. Think of Madden's letter as an apology, in the original sense of the term — that is, a genre that aims to explain or justify a strongly held idea or position about a matter of importance. Madden's letter addresses a particular situation about which he feels a need to take a stand and to do so honestly, though he is aware that doing so will likely cost him a great deal. Part of the power of his letter comes from the nature of the situation and how it is viewed by our society at this time. **Write a letter** in which you explain to someone — a friend, your parents, a teacher, for example — why you have been moved to take a stance on some issue with which they disagree.

▶ *The author of this excerpt explains why she, a lesbian rabbi, has chosen to use the pseudonym La Escondida ("the hidden one") in writing this essay, which originally appeared in* Twice Blessed: On Being Lesbian, Gay, and Jewish *(1989), one of the earliest collections of writings by lesbians and gay men of faith.*

crypto-: hidden, secret.

Journey toward Wholeness: Reflections of a Lesbian Rabbi

LA ESCONDIDA

Recently, I heard a report on National Public Radio about "the secret Jews of New Mexico," remnants of the *Marranos,* the crypto-Jews° of late medieval Spain who hid their Jewish identities in order to escape persecution at the hands of the Spanish Inquisition. These New Mexican Jews, outwardly Catholics, call themselves "los escondidos" (the hidden ones). They still live in secret, quietly teaching their children ancient Jewish rituals, quietly observing as much of Jewish practice as they know after centuries of separation from mainstream Judaism. Even now, in 1988, they hide, fearful that revealing their true identities will bring them harm, fearful that someone, somewhere, will persecute them for being who they really are.

As I listened to the report, my emotions were stirred. As a student of Jewish history, I was fascinated by the tenacity of these people and their success in surviving through centuries of clandestine life, without validation and support from the larger Jewish world. As a Jew who lives much of her own life in secret, fearful of revealing all of who I am, fearful of the harm that may come to me if I do, I felt the pain and sadness of my co-religionists in New Mexico.

Because it is risky for me to reveal my true identity at this point in my career, I write this essay under a pseudonym. Like the Jews of New Mexico, I too am an "escondida," a hidden one. I am a Jew. I am a woman. I am a rabbi. I am a lesbian.

Being a Jew has always been the axis around which my life has rotated. I grew up in a deeply committed Jewish home, with ardently Zionist parents who were dedicated to the birth and growth of a Jewish homeland in which the highest ideals of social justice would be realized. My home was filled with love for the Hebrew language, a fascination with Jewish history and culture, and a deeply ingrained commitment to the survival of the Jewish people. Though not "religious" in the traditional sense, my parents were profoundly Jewish in a cultural, historical, and emotional sense. I can imagine no other way of being in the world than being a Jew who is actively and passionately connected to my people.

As an adult I spent several years in Israel, where I saw my Jewishness in cultural, historical, and national terms. I took great pride in my people's growth, in the country we were building, in Israel's artistic flowering, in the intellectual achievements of this small nation. I thought that being a Jew and an Israeli were synonymous — and that my life was whole.

After completing my B.A. in Israel, I returned to the United States to pursue graduate studies in Jewish history. Back in America, I soon came to realize that my life as a Jew was incomplete — it had always focused on the historical and cultural evolution of my people, but I knew little about the spiritual and religious aspects of Judaism. I felt the need to connect with God, with my own soul, and with my people's faith and belief system. I realized that there was a whole world within Judaism that I hadn't yet explored and that I needed in my life. While my intellect was being nourished, my soul, too, needed to find its home within Judaism.

Simultaneous with this realization came another powerful discovery about myself: I am a lesbian. I had fallen in love with a woman. After fighting society's frightening and confusing stereotypes, I acknowledged that I had felt most comfortable and most whole throughout my life in close relationships with other girls and women. My deepest emotional attachments had always been with women, my most profound feelings of love, affection, intimate connection, and physical attraction had always been for women. With this acknowledgment, I was able to shake off the oppressive stereotypes and begin a long-term relationship with the woman whom I loved deeply.

For several years I lived a bifurcated existence. My academic and professional life as a scholar of Jewish history was entirely separate from my personal life, and my spiritual quest was done alone. Typical to the intellectual that I am, I read books about Jewish spirituality and faith, but I was not actively engaged in seeking my *own* life within the spiritual context of Judaism. Wholeness for me as a Jew was still an elusive goal.

I know now that part of the reason I didn't venture forth into a living community of Jews was that I feared being rejected as a lesbian.

Soon, to my great relief, I discovered there was a lesbian and gay outreach synagogue where I lived. I remember how I felt as my partner and I walked through the synagogue doors for the first time. The conflicts within me began to abate, as I sensed the possibility of integrating the different aspects of my being. In this modest building, I began to feel that I could be a Jew and a lesbian. I could pray as a Jew, learn as a Jew, rejoice in my loving relationship with a woman, and have others celebrate with me.

This synagogue, Beth Ameinu ("House of Our People"; the syna- 10 gogue's name is fictitious), indeed offered to me possibilities of an enriching new connection with my people. I became actively involved in the congregation, serving on the synagogue's board, as head of its ritual committee and as a frequent leader of Shabbat° services. Soon, I found that this piece of Judaism that had been missing for me, its spiritual and religious dimension, was coming alive. I no longer needed to sit alone and read books—I could pray and sing with a community as a *whole* human being: Jewish and lesbian.

Over time, I began to feel that my professional life, though intellectually challenging, was also incomplete. As Judaism's horizons expanded for me, I felt that teaching it from a purely intellectual perspective was not enough. As a professor of Jewish history, I did not experience wholeness. In this capacity, my task was to teach Judaism in a consciously clinical and objective manner. I often felt like a disembodied mind, imparting knowledge about Judaism without also sharing its *ruach,* its spirit. It became increasingly difficult for me to offer my students a dispassionate Judaism. It simply meant too much to me to do that.

A new awareness pushed me forward on my journey. I came to realize that I wanted my professional life to reflect my deepest personal commitments: I knew that I wanted to be a rabbi. After several years of thinking seriously about the direction my life should take, and considering the life changes my decision might require, I applied to a rabbinical seminary. In my application I explained my motivations for becoming a rabbi:

> What I really want to do is help people reach the more profound spiritual dimension connected with their Judaism. I want to be able to work with other Jews to create meaningful rituals, to find their way toward their own religious/spiritual evolution. . . . I want to teach

Shabbat: Hebrew name for the Jewish Sabbath, from sundown Friday until sundown Saturday.

within a Jewish context (not exclusively in a secular university) where I am not constrained by the obligation to be objective and coldly intellectual.

I want to help provide that food for the soul as well as the mind. I find that as a woman, as a feminist, there are worlds to be found within Judaism, worlds to explore, principles to be studied and challenged, a history of Jewish women to be reclaimed and a life of ritual for women to be developed. I want to be a part of that process. . . .

Now, in the final stages of my rabbinical studies, and after working for two years as a rabbi of a small congregation, these are still ideals that energize me.

Along with my idealism about becoming a rabbi have come some terribly disturbing realizations about how I must live my life as a congregational rabbi. Sadly, even as I pursue wholeness in my professional life, I have found that some of the personal integration I felt at Beth Ameinu has left me. Again I live a bifurcated life. Though I have a wonderful support system of good friends with whom I can be fully myself, the fact that I cannot be wholly honest about who I am to my congregants is painful to me. Nevertheless, despite the pain that I feel, I know that it would be professionally foolish to reveal to them who I am in my totality. If I were to come out to my congregants, in all probability I would lose my job as their rabbi. I do not believe that these warm and lovely people are ready to know that their rabbi is a lesbian.

Two years ago, I gave an impassioned sermon about AIDS to my congregation on the High Holy Days.° In the context of the emotional self-evaluation that Jews engage in at this time of year, I spoke about empathy and compassion, acceptance and marginalization—and I suggested that our congregation become involved, even in a small way, in the struggle against AIDS. I suggested that we collect food for people with AIDS who are no longer able to shop for themselves and who may be financially impoverished by the astronomical costs of medical care. My suggestion was received well by my congregants and we engaged in a fairly successful food collection. Every few weeks, I delivered the collected cans of food to the local AIDS project.

A few months after the High Holy Days, in reporting the gratitude 15 that the AIDS project had expressed to our congregation, I suggested that we might wish to let the project know that if there were Jewish people with AIDS who wished to worship in a community, the doors of

High Holy Days: the festivals of Rosh Hashana, the Jewish New Year; and Yom Kippur, the "Day of Atonement"; and the days in between.

our synagogue would be open to them. I was immediately confronted by a storm of reaction from my congregants, who are usually fairly receptive to my suggestions. I was told not to extend such an invitation to people with AIDS, that my congregation did not wish to be known as "the gay synagogue," and that they did not wish to be "ostracized" or "marginalized" within the larger Jewish community. I felt the pain of this incident deep within me: "If they only knew that their rabbi was a lesbian," I thought. I remained silent and accepted my congregants' instructions. I felt hurt and deeply ashamed at my inability to reveal myself to them, and to force them to confront their own prejudices. I also understood that I needed to protect myself professionally.

In the High Holy Day sermon I mentioned earlier, I spoke about a young Jewish woman with AIDS who lives in the same city where my congregation is located. Having learned about her from an article in a national magazine, I wondered out loud "if she is in a synagogue praying with a community." I wondered whether she had a community of Jews, "who will nurture her and give her the loving, the caring, the respect, and the support she needs."

I had thought seriously about *not* delivering my sermon on AIDS for fear of appearing too "outspoken," for fear of appearing too involved in an issue that was still mistakenly thought of by many as "a gay men's issue." I wondered whether I should steer clear of anything even remotely connected to gay concerns because someone might make a connection between gay issues and me. But after worrying about it for a while, I concluded that there are limits to how much one should worry about such things. I decided that as a member of an often invisible minority, I could not make myself even more invisible by remaining silent about an issue of great concern to me and to our society in general. There were limits even to my own "hiddenness." I made a conscious decision, *which stems from my identity as a lesbian,* that however controversial my sermon might be, I could not remain silent.

I will always be grateful that I gave that sermon. After services were over, a thin woman stood apart from the crowd and waited to speak with me. After almost everyone else had left, she approached me and asked to speak with me alone. Once we had gone into another room, the woman told me that *she* was the person about whom I had just spoken. Of course, I did not know that she would be in my synagogue that Yom Kippur° day. But the fact is that *she* had heard me. Taking my

Yom Kippur: the "Day of Atonement," the holiest day of the Jewish year, during which Jews fast and say prayers of penitence.

hands in hers, she said to me: "I haven't been in a synagogue in years. When I got AIDS, I was sure that God had abandoned me. But now that my life may be over soon, I felt the need to come back to my Jewish roots. I have never heard a rabbi speak the way you did today. Thank you. I want you to know that it means a great deal to me. I think you've helped me come home." We embraced and we cried together — and I offered what help I could; a listening ear, compassion, a connection with her Jewishness by a connection to me as her rabbi.

This young woman does not attend services regularly. She is now too ill to do so, but I have visited her, and we have talked. I believe that my being available to her as a rabbi is helping. In all likelihood, I will officiate at her funeral, and I hope that I can provide some solace to her family. There is deep sadness here at the loss of a fine human being. But I feel that my decisions *based on the entirety of who I am* and my work as a rabbi have been redeemed by my encounter with this woman.

There are other positive and valuable aspects to my identity as a 20 lesbian and my work as a rabbi. I believe that I am more sensitive to "the stranger who walks in our land," those Jews who sit at the edges of our communities, somewhat marginalized, somewhat outside of the mainstream. I believe that I may be more attuned to them because I, too, often feel like an outsider, unable to reveal my full self to my community. I believe that because many people judge me and my lesbian identity harshly, I may be more sensitive to judgmentalism in general. I have learned that there are many, many ways of living one's life as a decent human being — and that my responsibility is not to judge but to establish human connection.

My experience as a rabbi in a mainstream (rather than exclusively gay or lesbian) congregation has brought me great satisfaction, but it has also brought me doubts. When I dream of my work as a rabbi, I envision working with *Jews* — not exclusively young Jews, not exclusively old Jews, not exclusively gay and lesbian Jews, not exclusively heterosexual Jews. I simply want to work with *Jews*.

I often fear that I will not be given a chance (by a mainstream community that so often rejects gay people) to simply work with Jews if I come out. I fear that I will become marginal, ostracized from the general community of Jews and confined to working only with lesbian and gay Jews. While my experience at Beth Ameinu was precious to me, and I would not have traded my life in that congregation for anything, I dream of a time when there will be no need for a separate gay and lesbian congregation. As I seek wholeness for myself, an integration of all aspects of myself, I pray for such wholeness for my people as well.

I began this essay by writing about the hidden Jews of New Mexico, "los escondidos." It is my deepest hope that there will come a time when they and I will come out into the light of day and feel unthreatened, able to reveal the *totality* of our identities, able to be safe and valued in a world they know will fully accept us. May this day come speedily and in our time.

RESPOND ●

1. How does the author use the comparison of her situation with that of the Marranos to frame her essay? How does her choice of a pseudonym strengthen her association with that marginalized group? How effective are these choices, given her purposes for writing? What of the essay's title? How does it contribute to the author's argument?

2. According to La Escondida, what are the links between her sexuality and her faith? How does her identity as a lesbian influence her Jewish faith, her work as a rabbi, and Judaism? How might her faith have an impact on the lesbian and gay community?

3. What conflicts does La Escondida continue to experience with respect to her faith? Her sexual identity? The two together? Might her experiences be different if she were a gay man? Do you think that all of her conflicts would disappear if she were heterosexual? How? Why or why not?

4. How does La Escondida portray contemporary American Judaism? The Judaism she envisions as ideal? **Write an essay** in which you outline La Escondida's views on Judaism—as it exists and as it might be—as well as the values on which she bases her argument; then give your response to that argument. For example, do you find it appealing or surprising? Why or why not? You will need to acknowledge the understanding of and experience with Judaism that you bring to La Escondida's text in your essay.

▼ Gordon Marino is associate professor of philosophy at Saint Olaf College in Northfield, Minnesota. His specializations are the history of philosophy, the philosophy of religion, and the work of Danish philosopher Søren Kierkegaard (1813–1855), considered by many to be the founder of existentialism. The article reprinted here appeared in October 1998 in Christianity Today, a magazine that characterizes itself as "the definitive news voice for evangelical Christians around the world."

Me? Apologize for Slavery?

I May Not Have Owned Slaves, but I've Benefited from Their Having Been Used

GORDON MARINO

Gestures of collective repentance have become popular in recent years. In 1994, the pope offered an apology for past sins committed against non-Catholics. In the summer of 1995, the Southern Baptists, who number over 15 million, voted to express a resolution of repentance that read in part, "We lament and repudiate historic acts of evil such as slavery from which we continue to reap a bitter harvest." Last year [1997], President Clinton apologized to the African Americans who were the unwitting subjects in the infamous Tuskegee study of syphilis,° and he seriously considered the possibility of apologizing for slavery in general.

Reactions to Clinton's proposed mea culpa° varied. Ward Connerly, an African-American entrepreneur, regent of the University of California, and architect of the California antiaffirmative action referendum, Proposition 209, pronounced this verdict on the idea: "Apologizing for slavery is probably one of the dumbest things anyone could do." Conversely, civil-rights leader Julian Bond maintained that an apology for slavery would be a good and important symbolic gesture.

Tuskegee study of syphilis: American medical research project that has become synonymous with unethical scientific investigation. From 1932 to 1972, the U.S. Public Health Service sponsored the project, which examined the effects of untreated syphilis on a group of men, all of whom were poor African American sharecroppers. The research subjects were not informed about their health status, nor were they educated about the disease. After initial treatment proved useless, the decision was made to withhold any treatment and follow the subjects until their death in order to study the long-term effects of the disease, a decision that held even after penicillin was discovered to be an effective treatment for the disease, and after legislation mandating the disease's treatment was enacted. The study ended only in 1972, after it was the subject of articles in a Washington, D.C., newspaper.

mea culpa: expression of guilt or apology (Latin, "my fault," an expression used in the Roman Catholic Church's prayer of confession in the Latin liturgy).

Last summer, in between Little League baseball games in a largely white Minnesota town, I did some informal polling of my own. Though none of the people I talked to took the President's proposed apology to be an urgent matter, about half expressed mild support for the idea. Others scoffed at repenting for what they took to be ancient history. The wife of a professor commented, "Why should I apologize for something done to blacks more than a hundred years ago?" A fair question, which might be restated: "Why should I apologize for a crime that I had nothing to do with?" Or more to the point, "By what authority can I apologize for someone else's actions?" It would, after all, be hubristic° for me to think that I could repent for a mugging that I did not participate in.

As a professor of philosophy, I have encountered many white students over the years who accurately or out of paranoia believe that they are constantly being asked to feel guilty and repent for racist institutions and actions in which they themselves had no hand. When it comes to race and repentance, these students are of the Aristotelian opinion that we should only be praised or blamed for our own voluntary actions. Oddly enough, many of them feel no qualms about taking pride in the accomplishments of the various communities with which they identify—their college, church, country, or for that matter, their local major league baseball team.

This minor inconsistency aside, many of those 5 who sneer or snarl at the suggestion of apologizing for deeds from the deep past need to consider the possibility that we may bear a moral connection to actions that we did not ourselves commit. In this regard, it would be useful to distinguish between actions that one neither commits nor profits from and actions not committed but profited from.

Suppose, for example, that unbeknownst to me, a friend of mine robs a bank and makes off with $7 million. Clearly, I am neither responsible for the robbery nor am I in a position to apologize for it. However, if after telling me about the theft, my friend offers me a

million dollars of the stolen loot, and I accept it, then I am no longer innocent of the robbery, despite the fact that I had nothing at all to do with the heist. It could be argued that white people have profited from our racist past, and thus, relative to slavery, we are more like receivers of stolen goods than innocent bystanders who just happen to bear a physical likeness to slave owners.

Paradoxically enough, Americans do not shy away from admitting that we profit from access to cheap foreign labor, and yet whites find it hard to believe that we have benefited in any way from hundreds of years of free labor. Obviously, this lack of awareness would be exculpatory if, in fact, slavery and discrimination did not serve the interests of whites. However, if ignorance of being privileged is an ignorance we ourselves are responsible for producing, then we become morally reproachable receivers of stolen goods. And to be psychologically realistic, whites have a strong investment in blinkering their assessment of the broad effects of racism.

Let's return to my earlier example: assume that when I accepted the gift of a million dollars, I had no reason to think that the money had been stolen. Years later I came to understand that the funds upon which I had built a comfortable and respectable life had been pilfered from the accounts of your great-grandparents. Would the fact that many years had gone by cover the sin to such a degree that I would not bear any responsibility to the

---

hubristic: exceedingly prideful, especially the sort of pride that precedes the fall of a hero in ancient Greek tragedy.

Marino uses an extended analogy of a bank robbery to support his argument. See more about analogies in Chapter 14.

LINK TO P. 243

descendants of my great-grandparents' victims who, thanks to my ancestors, now led a distinctively unprivileged existence?

Individuals who benefit from a crime are mistaken in thinking that they have nothing to do with the crime. If responsibility does not extend from the robber baron to his children, then the material benefits of his wrongdoing can be passed along with impunity to future generations.

Once again, it is essential to distinguish between 10 cases in which one generation is entirely innocent of a transgression committed by an earlier generation and those in which the sins of the father continue to bear fruits of advantage for his descendants. Although I am not sure that a presidential apology would have the healing effects that some anticipate, I do know that white Americans have profited from slavery and discrimination. In a competitive society, whites have always had a leg up on African Americans, whether it be in hunting for a job, loan, house, or a position in a corporate firm.

Consider the Texaco scandal in 1996, when unsuspecting white corporate executives were caught on tape espousing racist sentiments. Or consider a story that a friend recently shared with me. My friend, who is about 35, recently returned to his hometown in a Detroit suburb for a class reunion at his richly integrated public high school. After the reunion, four of his old school chums convinced him to go out and play a few rounds of golf. All were corporate executives and registered Democrats. And yet, when the issue of race came up, all of them swore they would never "take the risk" of hiring an African American to fill a leadership role in their respective companies. In other words, any white applicants who sought employment in one of their firms would have a decisive advantage over all African American applicants.

> **Apologies are becoming all too easy to make today. But abuse is no argument against use.**

I was not involved in the civil-rights struggle of the sixties. While I have huffed and puffed and shaken my head about racial injustice, I have made no significant sacrifices for the cause of racial justice. I have no special authority to preach on the matter, and yet I have lived long enough in this country to recognize by whose sweat and on whose backs this country has been built and why. Because of slavery and discrimination, African Americans have provided an endless supply of cheap labor. They still work the fields, wash white babies and white octogenarians, shake drinks in country clubs, and mop floors in the classrooms in which white folks debate about race. It was not by chance that a black woman closed my dead father's eyes. It was no accident that a black woman was there when my child first opened his blue eyes.

As a result of institutionalized racism, African Americans have been cornered into doing more than their fair share of protecting, building, and preserving this land. For that reason, I suggest that even white Americans who have cursed racism have unwillingly and perhaps unwittingly benefited from it. Thus, whites are in no position to slough off the call for an apology by insisting that they have no connection to slavery.

The Hebrew scriptures ring with intimations that blessings and blandishments can be passed on from generation to generation. The children of Abraham are blessed because of Abraham's faith. On the other side, there was clearly a time when the Israelites believed that the sins of the fathers would be punishable unto the fourth generation.

The revolutionary prophet Ezekiel inveighs against 15 the notion of cross-generational responsibility. Attempting to focus his people's attention on their individual actions, Ezekiel proclaims that if a man "has a son who sees all the sins that his father has done, considers, and does not do likewise, . . . he shall not die for his father's iniquity" (Ezek. 18:14, 17, NRSV). When we refuse to acknowledge the harm that our community has inflicted upon others, when we the unoppressed refuse to acknowledge that, at least for a time, oppression benefits those who are not forced to walk on the other side of the street, then we fail to turn away from the sin of oppression.

By turning a blind eye, the sins of the father become the sins of the more passive son. By refusing to acknowledge who has been doing what for the last four hundred years, we fail to turn away from the grievous sins of our forefathers.

There is some sense today that apologies are becoming all too easy to make. Perhaps so. But as the philosopher Stephen Toulmin° has pointed out, abuse is no argument against use. If Americans ought to feel sorry that people in our community ever permitted slavery, then we ought to be willing to say that we are sorry for slavery. Clearly, it is a sorry character who does not regret our slaveholding past. ■

RESPOND ●

1. Marino clearly believes that White Americans should apologize to African Americans for slavery. Where and how does he use appeals to logic, emotion, values, or character? How well does he anticipate and respond to readers' potential rebuttals?

2. Assuming that most readers of *Christianity Today* are comfortable with the label "evangelical Christian," how does Marino tailor his arguments to his intended audience? What sorts of readers are invoked in the text?

3. Evaluate the likely effectiveness of his argument with a much more diverse audience—the readers of this textbook. Are you persuaded by Marino's argument? If you identify yourself as an evangelical Christian and are not persuaded by Marino's argument, how might he have argued to convince you of his position (or would such a task be impossible because of beliefs you hold)? If you do not identify yourself as an evangelical Christian and are not persuaded by Marino's argument, how might he have argued to convince you (or would such a task be impossible)?

4. Marino's argument raises complex questions about collective responsibility for the past actions of groups and even entire societies. As he notes, Americans, like people of probably all countries, are quick to claim the successes and accomplishments of groups with which they identify and quick to shun association with any of their failures or shortcomings. To what groups, if any, might Americans owe an apology? Why? If there are situations in which an apology is warranted, why is an apology sufficient? If you cannot think of any circumstances under which Americans or others might owe a group an apology, what does collective responsibility mean to you? **Write an essay** in which you explore the nature and limits of collective responsibility.

Stephen Toulmin: British philosopher (1922–) concerned especially with the nature of practical, everyday reason; Chapter 8 discusses his model of argument.

▶ *Martin Luther King Jr. (1929–1968), winner of the 1964 Nobel Prize for peace, played a significant role in helping shape twentieth-century American history. From the mid-1950s until his assassination, he worked tire-lessly for the cause of civil rights for African Americans, arguing always that nonvio-lence is the strongest strategy a group struggling for fairness and justice can use.*

The speech here was deliv-ered on August 28, 1963, at the Lincoln Memorial during the March on Washington, when a quarter of a million Americans, the majority of them African Americans, came together in the name of justice. Many Americans old enough to remember hearing the speech in 1963 are still moved to tears today when hearing recordings of it; phrases from the speech like "the content of their charac-ter" have become part of the way that Americans talk and argue, especially about matters of difference and equality. In short, King's speech reminds us of the power of words and of argu-ment to transform a moment in time into a significant part of a country's history.

I Have a Dream

MARTIN LUTHER KING JR.

Five score years ago, a great American, in whose symbolic shadow we stand, signed the Emancipation Proclamation. This momentous decree came as a great beacon light of hope to millions of Negro slaves who had been seared in the flames of withering injustice. It came as a joyous daybreak to end the long night of captivity.

But one hundred years later, we must face the tragic fact that the Negro is still not free. One hundred years later, the life of the Negro is still sadly crippled by the manacles of segregation and the chains of discrimination. One hundred years later, the Negro lives on a lonely island of poverty in the midst of a vast ocean of material prosperity. One hundred years later, the Negro is still languish-ing in the corners of American society and finds himself an exile in his own land. So we have come here today to dramatize an appalling condition.

In a sense we have come to our nation's capital to cash a check. When the archi-tects of our republic wrote the magnificent words of the Constitution and the Declaration of Independence, they were signing a promissory note to which every American was to fall heir. This note was a promise that all men would be guaranteed the inalienable rights of life, liberty, and the pursuit of happiness.

It is obvious today that America has defaulted on this promissory note insofar as her citizens of color are concerned. Instead of honoring this sacred obligation, America has given the Negro people a bad check which has come back marked "insuffi-cient funds." But we refuse to believe that the bank of justice is bankrupt. We refuse to believe that there are insufficient funds in the great vaults of opportunity of this nation. So we have come to cash this check — a check that will give us upon demand the riches of freedom and the security of justice. We have also come to this hallowed spot to remind America of the fierce urgency of *now*. This is no time to engage in the luxury of cooling off

Martin Luther King Jr.

or to take the tranquilizing drug of gradualism. *Now* is the time to rise from the dark and desolate valley of segregation to the sunlit path of racial justice. *Now* is the time to open the doors of opportunity to all of God's children. *Now* is the time to lift our nation from the quicksands of racial injustice to the solid rock of brotherhood.

It would be fatal for the nation to overlook the urgency of the moment and to   5 underestimate the determination of the Negro. This sweltering summer of the Negro's legitimate discontent will not pass until there is an invigorating autumn of freedom and equality. Nineteen sixty-three is not an end, but a beginning. Those who hope that the Negro needed to blow off steam and will now be content will have a rude awakening if the nation returns to business as usual. There will be neither rest nor tranquility in America until the Negro is granted his citizenship rights. The whirlwinds of revolt will continue to shake the foundations of our nation until the bright day of justice emerges.

But there is something that I must say to my people who stand on the warm threshold which leads into the palace of justice. In the process of gaining our rightful place we must not be guilty of wrongful deeds. Let us not seek to satisfy our thirst for freedom by drinking from the cup of bitterness and hatred.

We must forever conduct our struggle on the high plane of dignity and discipline. We must not allow our creative protest to degenerate into physical violence. Again and again we must rise to the majestic heights of meeting physical force with soul force. The marvelous new militancy which has engulfed the Negro community must not lead us to distrust of all white people, for many of our white brothers, as evidenced by their presence here today, have come to realize that their destiny is tied up with our destiny and their freedom is inextricably bound to our freedom. We cannot walk alone.

And as we walk, we must make the pledge that we shall march ahead. We cannot turn back. There are those who are asking the devotees of civil rights, "When will you be satisfied?" We can never be satisfied as long as our bodies, heavy with the fatigue of travel, cannot gain lodging in the motels of the highways and the hotels of the cities. We cannot be satisfied as long as the Negro's basic mobility is from a smaller ghetto to a larger one. We can never be satisfied as long as a Negro in Mississippi cannot vote and a Negro in New York believes he has nothing for which to vote. No, no, we are not satisfied, and we will not be satisfied until justice rolls down like waters and righteousness like a mighty stream.

King shifts frequently and seamlessly between long, complex sentences and short, simple sentences. Remember that hearing an argument is different from reading one; listeners need frequent breaks from complexity. For more suggestions on how to construct a spoken argument, see Chapter 17.

LINK TO P. 285

I am not unmindful that some of you have come here out of great trials and tribulations. Some of you have come fresh from narrow cells. Some of you have come from areas where your quest for freedom left you battered by the storms of persecution and staggered by the winds of police brutality. You have been the veterans of creative suffering. Continue to work with the faith that unearned suffering is redemptive.

Go back to Mississippi, go back to Alabama, go back to Georgia, go back to 10 Louisiana, go back to the slums and ghettos of our northern cities, knowing that somehow this situation can and will be changed. Let us not wallow in the valley of despair.

I say to you today, my friends, that in spite of the difficulties and frustrations of the moment, I still have a dream. It is a dream deeply rooted in the American dream.

I have a dream that one day this nation will rise up and live out the true meaning of its creed: "We hold these truths to be self-evident: that all men are created equal."

I have a dream that one day on the red hills of Georgia the sons of former slaves and the sons of former slaveowners will be able to sit down together at a table of brotherhood.

I have a dream that one day even the state of Mississippi, a desert state, sweltering with the heat of injustice and oppression, will be transformed into an oasis of freedom and justice.

I have a dream that my four children will one day live in a nation where they will 15 not be judged by the color of their skin but by the content of their character.

I have a dream today.

I have a dream that one day the state of Alabama, whose governor's lips are presently dripping with the words of interposition and nullification, will be transformed into a situation where little black boys and black girls will be able to join hands with little white boys and white girls and walk together as sisters and brothers.

I have a dream today.

I have a dream that one day every valley shall be exalted, every hill and mountain shall be made low, the rough places will be made plain, and the crooked places will be made straight, and the glory of the Lord shall be revealed, and all flesh shall see it together.

This is our hope. This is the faith with which I return to the South. With this faith 20 we will be able to hew out of the mountain of despair a stone of hope. With this faith we will be able to transform the jangling discords of our nation into a beautiful symphony of brotherhood. With this faith we will be able to work together, to pray together, to struggle together, to go to jail together, to stand up for freedom together, knowing that we will be free one day.

This will be the day when all of God's children will be able to sing with a new meaning, "My country, 'tis of thee, sweet land of liberty, of thee I sing. Land where my fathers died, land of the pilgrim's pride, from every mountainside, let freedom ring."

And if America is to be a great nation this must become true. So let freedom ring from the prodigious hilltops of New Hampshire. Let freedom ring from the mighty mountains of New York. Let freedom ring from the heightening Alleghenies of Pennsylvania!

Let freedom ring from the snowcapped Rockies of Colorado!

Let freedom ring from the curvaceous peaks of California!

But not only that; let freedom ring from Stone Mountain of Georgia!   25

Let freedom ring from Lookout Mountain of Tennessee!

Let freedom ring from every hill and every molehill of Mississippi. From every mountainside, let freedom ring.

When we let freedom ring, when we let it ring from every village and every hamlet, from every state and every city, we will be able to speed up that day when all of God's children, black men and white men, Jews and Gentiles, Protestants and Catholics, will be able to join hands and sing in the words of the old Negro spiritual, "Free at last! free at last! thank God Almighty, we are free at last!"

RESPOND.

1. Is King's argument primarily forensic, epideictic, or deliberative (Chapter 1)? Give evidence to support your choice.

2. Investigate the 1963 March on Washington, including press coverage of King's speech. How was it received at the time? Why do you think scholars of public discourse now consider it the most significant American speech of the past century?

3. "I Have a Dream" is remembered for many reasons. As an argument, it certainly embodies appeals based on values and on character, emotional appeals, and logical appeals. Analyze each of these sorts of appeals (discussed in Chapters 4–7). First, consider the ethos King creates for himself as author and speaker. Then examine how King makes appeals to the emotions of his audiences—those present and those who heard the speech on radio or television at the time and even to those who would read or hear the speech in the future. Finally, consider the sorts of logical appeals King uses. Choose one type of appeal, and **write an essay** in which you describe and illustrate King's successful use of it in his speech.

4. The power of King's speech comes in part from his use of figurative language and the artfulness of his delivery. Both of these strengths draw on King's experience as a minister in the African American Baptist church. Analyze the speech for the types of figurative language (Chapter 14) King uses—metaphor, simile, analogy, parallelism, repetition, allusion—and for the elements of spoken argument discussed in Chapter 17. If you are able to listen to a sound clip of the speech, pay attention to how King uses breathing, phrasing, and volume strategically. **Write an essay** describing how King uses figurative language to move his audience. In order to do a thorough analysis, limit your discussion to two or three consecutive paragraphs of King's speech.

The arguments in this cluster challenge you to examine complex questions regarding freedom of speech—specifically the speech of those whose opinions are unpopular and, to some, offensive. The readings here include a number of articles and letters about one specific event and two other essays that help put that event in a broader context. We have deliberately limited the discussion to arguments about the question of **free speech on campus: can conservative views be heard?**

The event in question is a speech given by Ward Connerly in March 1999 at the Law School of the University of Texas at Austin (UT). Connerly, a former regent of the University of California, is chair of the California Civil Rights Initiative, a group that seeks to dismantle affirmative action programs in education and business. In 1996, Connerly spearheaded the successful campaign for Proposition 209, which ended affirmative action in California public schools and universities. An African American, Connerly contends that affirmative action constitutes preferential treatment and that whether on the basis of race, ethnicity, sex, or other categories, such treatment constitutes unlawful discrimination and should not be allowed.

The topic of affirmative action was already a source of great debate at UT because of the 1996 "Hopwood decision," in which Cheryl Hopwood and three other White law school applicants filed suit against the UT Law School, charging reverse discrimination because their applications for the class of 1995 had been rejected. In 1996, a federal circuit court ruled UT admissions policies unconstitutional and issued an injunction barring UT from using race or ethnicity as a consideration in law school admissions. UT students quickly formed organizations opposing or supporting the court's decision. Into this highly charged atmosphere came Connerly, invited by several politically conservative campus groups. He was repeatedly heckled during his address, while students outside the auditorium staged a loud demonstration. Connerly did not finish his prepared remarks, and even a question-and-answer period deteriorated into a shouting match and was terminated.

Most of the texts here come from the *Daily Texan*, the student newspaper. Many of the texts refer to AROC (Anti-Racist Organizing Committee), a student group formed to protest the Hopwood decision, whose members support continued use of affirmative action.

In addition to the texts from the *Daily Texan*, we include a nationally syndicated column, "How Leftists 'Debate,'" by Jeff Jacoby and "News from the Ladies' Room," an essay about affirmative action from a collection by law students at U.C. Berkeley, where the consequences of Proposition 209 were soon visible.

We present these arguments *not* as a debate about affirmative action or other issues Connerly addresses. Rather, our purpose is to examine questions of freedom of speech on college campuses: Can we create an atmosphere on college and university campuses that accommodates a truly free exchange of ideas? How? Can such an exchange be civil in nature? Is the silencing of a voice ever appropriate? If so, whose voice? Why? When? Or must we accept the notion that democracy is sometimes messy?

These two pieces appeared on the editorial page of the Daily Texan, *the student newspaper of the University of Texas at Austin (UT) prior to Ward Connerly's visit there. The first text, a guest column by Carl Villarreal, chair of the UT student organization Anti-Racist Organizing Committee (AROC), is a call to action during Connerly's upcoming visit. The second reading, an unsigned* Daily Texan *editorial, calls for moderation on the part of UT students who oppose Connerly's ideas. Although it does not directly refer to Villarreal's column, the editorial appears to be a response to it.*

Anticipating Ward Connerly's Visit

An Enemy of Civil Rights

CARL VILLARREAL

Ward Connerly, the man who is driving the anti-affirmative action movement in this country, is scheduled to speak on campus Monday night. At other universities, fed-up students have forced him off stage. He should be strongly opposed at this university as well.

Connerly has described the actions and discourse of his opponents as "scare tactics." But there is good reason to be scared of Connerly's agenda. His actions are contributing to increasing racial and ethnic inequality in this country. After Connerly made his mark on California, black student admissions at the University of California at Berkeley dropped 80 percent.

Now he is looking to resegregate other locations. In Texas, he has considered the city of Houston, but he now seems to be focusing on statewide initiatives in places like Florida. But his anti-affirmative action stance is so conservative, even Florida Republican Gov. Jeb Bush has refused to support Connerly's crusade because he feels it's too divisive. The Republican party of Florida has also denied Connerly's campaign any financial support.

Martin Luther King III has said of Connerly's actions, "Any initiative to dismantle the safeguards

Free Speech for Both Sides

DAILY TEXAN EDITORS

Members of the U. Texas Anti-Racist Organizing Committee plan to protest Ward Connerly's speech at the UT Law School auditorium at 8 p.m. Monday. We strongly support their right to free speech and their right to peaceably assemble. But AROC and other student protesters should be careful not to diminish the liberties of others or stifle the free exchange of ideas.

Connerly is a controversial figure. As a University of California System regent, he championed the passage of Proposition 209, which outlawed affirmative action across the state. His visits to other college campuses have usually been marked with student protest. Last October at the University of Wisconsin at Madison, audience members interrupted Connerly's speech and nearly forced him to leave the stage after speaking for 15 minutes, according to the *Badger Herald,* UW's student newspaper.

Concerned that another episode like this could occur, the student organizers of Connerly's visit will allow questions from audience members to be submitted on index cards and read by a moderator. This could be an effective means of promoting productive and thoughtful debate — the same means, in

of equal opportunity under the guise of 'civil rights' is an affront to the very memory of Dr. Martin Luther King Jr." In an interview with the *Sacramento Bee,* King continued, "I resent and I am prepared to resist Ward Connerly's latest divisive tactics."

Despite the fact that Connerly's message seems   5 clearly opposed to the Civil Rights Movement, some people are fond of pointing out that the man is black. But as far as politics goes, that is irrelevant. Before black suffrage, there were African Americans who publicly argued against their own right to vote. Like Connerly, these men were often held up by white bigots as spokespersons and models for others to follow. Today the problem is that not enough African Americans are represented in positions like Connerly's, yet they are over-represented in prisons and low-class, inner-city neighborhoods.

If a powerful man like Connerly isn't doing anything about these issues, then he is part of the problem. If his actions are making this situation worse, which they are, then he is aligned with the enemy. When we see Connerly, we should identify him first as a wealthy enemy of equality and opportunity for all Americans, and second as an African American. His message of maintaining the unequal status quo should not be tolerated.

Why is he doing this? Fellow UC regent William Bagley has explained, "He's become a celebrity and he enjoys that. He walks into a white Rotary Club and he gets a standing ovation." A man who lives in a half-million dollar home on a half-acre lot in a neighborhood where he is the only black home-owner is bound to seek out the respect of the community and social class to which he belongs.

And Connerly has gained their respect. Former right-wing California Gov. Pete Wilson chose Connerly to head the Proposition 209 campaign to

fact, used during AROC-sponsored Town Hall meetings with UT administrators during recent months.

But last week, AROC members circulated fliers stating: "Open it up or shout him down." This is precisely the kind of tactics they should avoid.

Disrupting Connerly's speech with chants or   5 heckles would only hurt student protesters' credibility and needlessly give their opponents argumentative ammunition. In Madison, conservatives denounced the protesters as bullies who showed contempt for anyone else's ability to practice free speech. Heckling a guest speaker diverts attention from the issue at hand and does not make sense strategically for students who defend affirmative action.

There are more constructive ways to protest Connerly's visit. Last week, MEChA [Movimiento Estudiantil Chicano/ade Aztlan]° held a West Mall

---

MEChA [Movimiento Estudiantil Chicano/a de Aztlan] (Chicano/a Student Movement of Aztlan): political organization composed of Mexican American university students begun in 1969 in Santa Barbara, California; Aztlan refers to the mythical homeland of the Aztecs, claimed by some to have been what is now the southwestern U.S. (The Web address for UT's chapter of MEChA is <http://www.utexas.edu/ftp/student/mecha/>.)

The phrase "scare tactics," which Villarreal mentions in paragraph 2, is a familiar one, but do you really know exactly what they are and why they work? Check out the explanation of scare tactics in Chapter 19.

·················· LINK TO P. 314

end affirmative action in California. But Wilson was merely returning a favor. According to Common Cause, a political watchdog group, Connerly had supported Wilson's various election campaigns with financial help totaling $108,000.

In addition to Wilson, Connerly has also allied himself with the Center for Individual Rights, which has taken on the judicial front in the war on equal opportunity. The Center is the legal group that represented Cheryl Hopwood in her lawsuit against the University, which eventually was used as an excuse for ending all affirmative action programs here. The Center has defended such people as Michael Levin, a New York professor who has argued that blacks are less intelligent and less law-abiding than other races. According to *The Independent of London,* the Center for Individual Rights has received financial support from the Pioneer Fund, a group that supports "research asserting the genetic superiority of whites." Connerly hasn't had a problem working with Michael S. Greve, the co-founder and executive director of the Center.

This is clearly a battle of people versus money. 10 Right now money is winning, but that is only more reason for more people to get involved. Connerly is set to speak at 8 p.m. in the law school auditorium. Concerned students should arrive at 7:30 p.m. to send a clear message that his anti-equality rhetoric will not be tolerated at the University of Texas, and his money shouldn't be wasted here.

teach-in on Texas Independence Day. Instead of disrupting a campus rally to mark the occasion, they opted to educate students about how Hispanics were adversely affected following Texas' independence from Mexico. Through education, MEChA promoted its views effectively.

AROC would do well to follow this example. Holding their own forum or teach-in immediately before Connerly's speech gives everyone a chance to hear both sides of the affirmative action issue. But trying to "shout him down" has a chilling effect on free speech.

Last semester, AROC members held a sit-in at the Tower, partly to gain an open, honest dialogue with policy-makers. It worked. Now that another student group has arranged another dialogue on the same issue, it remains to be seen whether this debate will be met with the same respect.

Like it or not, Connerly is a guest speaker on our campus. At an institution devoted to the free exchange of ideas, we all have a responsibility to remain civil.

RESPOND •

1. To what extent does Villarreal's column match Chapter 19's description of an *ad hominem* argument? Cite evidence from the text to support your conclusions.

2. The standards for academic papers require authors to document the sources for information used; American newspapers are not held to such stringent standards although newspaper writers often make clear the sources of their information. Villarreal makes several assertions of fact without citing the sources of his information. Reread his column carefully, marking the passages that would require source documentation in an academic paper. Choose one assertion of fact, and do the research necessary to determine whether or not he has related the fact accurately.

3. Villarreal's column and the *Daily Texan* editorial appeared together on the same page in the same issue of the newspaper. Like editorials in many newspapers, this one is titled but unsigned—indicating, indirectly perhaps, the official stance of the newspaper's editors and perhaps the entire staff. How does the absence of the author's name affect the ethos of the argument? Would the editorial have been more or less persuasive had the author been listed? Why? Would Villarreal's column have been more or less persuasive if it had appeared unsigned? Why?

4. The *Daily Texan* editorial argues that all people's ideas are worthy of being heard, whereas Villarreal argues that Ward Connerly's ideas are so odious as to warrant UT students' sending him "a clear message that his [ideas] . . . will not be tolerated." **Write an essay** in which you argue why UT students should or should not have permitted Connerly's ideas to be heard based on the information you have from these two articles and your own beliefs.

Connerly Booed at Talk

States Should Look Past Race, Says Speaker Amid Protest

LAURA OFFENBACHER

Amidst shouts of protest, Ward Connerly, chairman of the American Civil Rights Institute and a key figure in the abolition of affirmative action in California, spoke Monday at the UT School of Law.

The forum, featuring discussion about affirmative action and race relations in the United States, was limited to about 230 people due to the size of the room. Nearly 50 people gathered to protest Connerly outside the entrance of the auditorium.

Michael Sharlot, dean of the UT School of Law, introduced Connerly, but noted that Connerly's opinion of affirmative action differs from that of law school administrators.

"The views of the law school with respect to affirmative action and the views of Mr. Connerly are totally opposed," Sharlot said, adding that the University has been fighting to establish the constitutionality of affirmative action for the past five years.

Connerly's speech, punctuated by 5 interjections from audience members, focused on his goal for a colorblind society.

Lori McMullen, left, and Jeannine King argue after Ward Connerly's speech. Connerly, a former regent of the University of California-Berkeley, spoke Monday night against affirmative action. Many in the audience ignored Connerly or booed him.

"Civil rights are not just for black people—civil rights are for everybody," he said. "We have to get beyond our obsession with race."

Connerly said he is opposed to racial preferences, but admitted that racism is a problem in the United States that must be addressed.

Notice how Offenbacher qualifies the number of protestors with the word *nearly,* which makes her statement more truthful. Find a list of other useful qualifiers in Chapter 8.

⋯⋯⋯⋯⋯⋯⋯⋯⋯⋯⋯LINK TO P. 102

677

Ward Connerly shows signs of frustration during his speech at the UT School of Law. Connerly, who is against affirmative action, was heckled throughout his talk by affirmative action supporters.

dents at a community college where he once spoke.

"The level of discourse was far superior than that here," he said.

Despite the interruptions, Ken Emanuelson, president of the Texas Federalist Society for Law and Public Policy, said he was satisfied with the event.

"I think Ward was able to get his message across," said Emanuelson, a third-year law student. "That's the bottom line — if people can't express their viewpoints, we can't move forward in this."

But Marlen Whitley, a first-year UT Law student and former Student Government president, said Connerly was unable to provide students any solutions to the problem of racism in the U.S.

any chocolate chips, and all-white-bread sandwiches that consisted of mayonnaise spread between two pieces of bread with no crust.

They also kept dark-colored food on a separate table to indicate racial segregation in the absence of affirmative action, said Tanya Clay, a third-year law student and one of the organizers of the cookie giveaway.

"Ward Connerly has half-baked ideas, so we thought, what better way to support this than with a 'half-baked sale,'" Clay said.

J. Reed, an RTF °/English junior and member of the Anti-Racist Organizing Committee, said Connerly treated some audience members in a demeaning manner.

"I think that Ward Connerly 20 attempts to cast our questions as shallow, and I think that's an inaccurate conception of our opinion," Reed said. "Ward Connerly oversimplifies the issues and that was made clear tonight."

Reed said the forum was an opportunity for people to exercise their right of free speech, adding that students used their collective voice to send a message.

"In that sense, what we have seen today is democracy at work," he said.

But Marc Levin, a UT alumnus and executive director of Campaign for a Colorblind America — a non-campus supporter of the event, countered that members of AROC are not

---

"Civil rights are not just for black people — civil rights are for everybody. We have to get beyond our obsession with race."

– Ward Connerly,
former regent of the University of California-Berkeley

"It is an issue that, if we do not solve it in our time, then the next generation will have to resolve that issue," Connerly said.

Some students frequently shouted at the speaker while others held up *The Daily Texan* as a sign of protest.

Connerly responded to repeated 10 interruptions by audience members at one point by comparing them to stu-

"For him to speak of a colorblind 15 society and to not outline any steps just show he's blind to the problem that exists in the first place," Whitley said.

Several law students held a "half-baked sale" to protest Connerly's position on ending affirmative action. They were giving away "chocolate-chip cookies," which didn't include

---

RTF: radio/television/film.

representative of the views of the UT student body.

"I don't think they're taken seriously by most students," Levin said. "It's in their tactics and the way they go about pursuing their agenda that puts them so radically far out."

Levin said the forum was open to 25 community members as well as students so that a wide range of people could participate.

"We wanted this to be a chance for everybody whether they agreed with us or not to have a dialogue with Mr. Connerly," Levin said.

He said the forum was a good opportunity for students to learn another view on affirmative action, adding that people should welcome all opinions.

"It's beneficial for leaders on all sides of the political and ideological spectrum to visit the University," Levin said. "It's ludicrous to suggest that he shouldn't be able to speak at the University, and it shows a tremendous intolerance of ideas," Levin said.

Despite the amount of noise, UT police said there were no serious problems and nobody was arrested.

The Texas Federalist Society for 30 Law and Politics, Texas Review for Law and Politics, Young Conservatives of Texas and Students for a Colorblind Society also sponsored the event.

RESPOND●

1. Do you think Offenbacher presents a complete account of the Ward Connerly event? What information might be missing? What else would you want to know about the event? Offenbacher was likely not able to interview Connerly himself, but what other constituencies' comments might have been valuable in this article? Why?

2. In paragraphs 19–22, Offenbacher summarizes and quotes an AROC member: "Reed said the forum was an opportunity for people to exercise their right of free speech, [and to use] their collective voice to send a message" (21). How would you describe that "message"? Reed also calls the event "democracy at work" (22). Based on what you know of the event, do you agree with Reed? Why or why not?

3. As you are no doubt aware, even "objective" news articles often take a position, however subtle. What position do you think Offenbacher takes in this article? Is she objective, or does she appear to favor one side over others? **Write a short essay** in which you evaluate Offenbacher's objectivity, presenting evidence for your argument.

▼ *These two pieces, which appeared on the editorial page of the* Daily Texan *on March 10, 1999, present different interpretations of what happened during Ward Connerly's visit to UT. The first text, an unsigned* Texan *editorial, criticizes Connerly's performance. The second article, by student reporter Brian Winter, criticizes* AROC *and its actions. Both pieces presume readers' familiarity with the event discussed. As you read, think about whether the interpretation you've formed of the event from the other readings in this cluster is similar to either of the views offered in these articles.*

From the *Daily Texan:* What Happened?

Waste of Time

DAILY TEXAN EDITORS

U. Texas students are certainly among the best activists in the nation, but the quality of our discourse is now questionable.

Organizers of Ward Connerly's speech Monday touted the event as a dialogue on affirmative action and the future of race relations in America. At the University, where fallout from the Hopwood ruling is still fodder for discussion in classrooms and on the West Mall,° one would expect thoughtful debate from both sides. Not a chance.

Hecklers in the audience, planning to shout Connerly off of the stage, fired the first volleys in what quickly deteriorated into more than an hour of snide comments between Connerly and activists in the audience.

"Whoever is controlling the event: I will not continue speaking until that person is removed," Connerly said, requesting that organizers either silence or arrest one of the hecklers.

Nothing Gained without Respect

BRIAN WINTER

Remember the belligerent heckler from junior high who sat in the back of the class and blurted out stupid comments about the English teacher's dress? Well, chances are that he was sitting in the back of the UT Law School Auditorium at Ward Connerly's speech on Monday, and unfortunately, the years haven't made him any more clever.

The tactics of the Anti-Racist Organizing Committee, which lists the sit-in at the Tower° last fall among its more impressive accomplishments, went several steps too far on Monday night when some of its members repeatedly interrupted Connerly's speech with childlike, ignorant attempts at insult. AROC's actions during the speech accomplished nothing except the further alienation of students — many of whom, ironically, agree completely with the organization's political agenda.

Many of the verbal attacks screamed out during Connerly's 15-minute monologue were personal in

---

West Mall: area of the UT campus designated as a "free speech area" that can be reserved by student organizations for holding rallies about particular issues.

the Tower: the tallest building on the UT campus and the location of the university's administrative offices.

"Then why do you claim that this is an open forum for discussion?" one student yelled in reply. Though organizers had originally planned for Connerly to answer questions submitted on index cards just before the event, Connerly quickly struck a deal with protesters: let me speak, and I'll answer your questions for 30 minutes when I'm finished. But Connerly never finished his speech, and he answered few of the questions.

The guest speaker made half-hearted attempts to discuss the value of K-12 education and a color-blind government in the future of the nation's race relations. For the most part, however, Connerly was content to answer hecklers' rhetoric with sarcastic commentary of his own.

When one student yelled that Connerly was "standing behind the white man," he quickly quipped: "Your mental capacity is being reflected by that kind of stupid comment."

At least two students in the audience of 200 repeatedly begged for Connerly to ignore the insults and continue his speech.

But he didn't, and even students who remained respectful received no reward for their patience.

Cicely Reid, a first-year law student who is African American, asked Connerly to specify his proposals to improve race relations. "I am one of eight in my class. How do I become one of 28, one of 30?" she asked.

nature, almost all were irrelevant, and some were quite obviously racist. When Connerly spoke of his segregation-era childhood, one AROC member screamed "With a white mother!" After Connerly requested that the police remove the vocal protesters, another member thundered, "You gonna stand behind the white man again?" For a group that decries racism so vehemently, some members of AROC sure did use it unabashedly when it suited their needs.

AROC member J. Reed defended his organization's tactics. "In the face of someone like Ward Connerly, we feel that it is appropriate to be disruptive." According to Reed, Connerly's corporate backing affords him the luxury of a monologue behind a podium (in theory, at least), while AROC is forced to resort to other tactics to attract media attention.

"One of the ways that has been historically successful and necessary is protest and visibility," Reed added.

Indeed, there is a time and place for active protest. But AROC should have simply kept the protest outside the auditorium doors. Any kind of picket, informational session, or opposing speaker would have still captured the attention of local media. More importantly, AROC would not have seemed so completely intolerant of another side's views.

Opportunity lost: the continued disruptions forced Connerly to cut his speech short, eliminating much of the empirical data that he had originally planned to present. Was AROC so afraid of what Ward Connerly had to say that they couldn't let him speak without interruption?

AROC has done some good things for this campus. Last fall's sit-in produced healthy debate at Town Hall meetings with UT administrators. Also, their protests Monday did yield a modification of

---

What is the effect of the phrase "half-hearted" as used in this editorial? Check out the section in Chapter 14 on the dangers of unduly slanted language.

················· LINK TO P. 248

Connerly replied by polling the audience on the language of the Bakke ruling.° It was an opportunity for him to outline his vision for colorblind social reform, and he didn't take it.

When Marlen Whitley, former SG president, asked Connerly what he has done to promote colorblind justice, Connerly replied that his original speech included the evidence of the anecdotes Whitley requested, "but a funny thing happened on the way to the mic," Connerly said. However, he did not offer or try to return to his prepared presentation.

The result: students who managed to get into the packed auditorium were forced to listen to bickering and political grandstanding. Yelling matches on the West Mall have generated more substantial ideas.

True, student organizers had expected a controversial evening, but this wasn't even substantive controversy.

Connerly led the fight for Proposition 209 in 15 California and has since become a national spokesman against affirmative action. But for a man who has tackled one of the hottest and certainly one of the most emotional issues of this decade, his performance Monday was deplorable.

Connerly chastised UT students Monday.

"You know, I gave a speech at a community college in Massachusetts one day, and the level of discourse was far greater than here. I expected more from the University of Texas," he said.

Sadly, we also expected far more from him as well.

the poorly contrived debate format, allowing students to speak directly to Connerly in a question and answer session.

But even that accomplishment ended up betraying evidence of the arrogance and elitism openly displayed by some AROC members. When Connerly accepted questions from non-AROC audience members, some members of the group had the unbelievable gall to repeatedly exclaim, "We were the ones who were supposed to ask questions!"

AROC member Carl Villarreal expressed the 10 group's apparent general sentiment after Connerly's speech: "Breaking into the debate was more important for us than a few bad remarks in the paper about not respecting discourse." Well. The other 200 people in that auditorium were there to hear Connerly speak. Maybe they didn't agree with his views, but they at least wanted to know what the man had to say. Thanks to the protesters, they were mostly deprived of that opportunity. Way to go, AROC. Still think "any press is good press"?

Bakke ruling: controversial 1978 Supreme Court decision regarding "reverse discrimination" in educational programs. In it, a divided court agreed on a judgment but issued no majority opinion. Nevertheless, the case is often cited as evidence that while quotas are illegal, considerations of an applicant's ethnicity are acceptable.

RESPOND•

1. The *Daily Texan* editorial never mentions AROC by name or its organized interruption of Connerly's speech. What might be the unsigned author's attitude toward the AROC demonstration? How can you tell? Cite evidence from the text to support your answer.

2. Winter makes concessions to AROC about the good work it has accomplished at the University of Texas. How does this Rogerian strategy contribute to the ethos Winter wants to establish? To the persuasiveness of his argument?

3. The editorial presents a very different interpretation of Ward Connerly's UT visit than you have seen in the other readings in this cluster, including Winter's column. How, if at all, does the editorial change your views on the event? Why or why not? Which interpretation—the editorial's or Winter's—is more plausible or persuasive to you? (Are their different interpretations mutually exclusive? Why or why not?) **Write a short essay** in which you lay out and justify your interpretation of the events surrounding Connerly's visit to UT as reported in this cluster.

▼ The five letters to the editor here represent a small sampling of those published by the Daily Texan in the days following Ward Connerly's visit to UT. We have chosen these particular letters because of the information they offer—what actually happened—and the kinds of arguments they make. Three of the letters, "Poor Discourse," "Hey AROC You Can't Hide," and "AROC Responds," were written by students; one, "Disclaimer," was written by the dean of the Law School; and one, "No Insight," came from a UT law alum. As you read these arguments, consider the role letters to the editor play in public discourse: in addition to whatever other ends they might serve, they are part of the public process of arguing about what in fact happened and what the meanings of events might be.

Daily Texan Readers Respond

Poor Discourse

I was present at Ward Connerly's speech on Monday night. I must say that AROC's presence in the audience and outside detracted greatly from the event. The chanting and thumping from protesters outside was so great I could not hear much of the time and my seat vibrated when the thumping became particularly violent. Interruptions were frequent as AROC members laughed, booed, or made numerous statements of disbelief in response to Connerly's statements. Ad hominem attack was answered by ad hominem attack on both sides, to the detraction of Connerly, who, in response to, "[You're] hiding behind the white man," stated, "You know, your mental capacity is being reflected by that kind of stupid statement."

What exactly is an "ad hominem attack"? Check out Chapter 19.

LINK TO P. 319

Unfortunately, it was hard to pin Connerly down on his position of what to do if not affirmative action, as he either couldn't hear, dodged the question, or was interrupted in the process of giving an answer. He did mention once, right after AROC interrupted the speech for five minutes to complain about the methodology for questioning, that he wanted every student to have the same education level out of high school. It would level the quality of students entering university and is a reasonable goal and a fine idea which should be pursued here in Texas. Imagine, if allowed to enunciate his whole speech, maybe we would have been given another good idea.

– Michael Lebold
Economics/government sophomore

Hey AROC You Can't Hide

I tried to attend the speech by Ward Connerly on Monday but was stopped just outside the entrance because the auditorium was full. Some AROC members in the hall were trying to organize people to stay and protest, so I figured I should stay and find out what their position was. What I found out was that they had no interest in a rational discussion of affirmative action. They just wanted to be loud and get Connerly to leave. I have a few tips for AROC protesters to help them out:

1. Make up some intelligent slogans (they started out OK, with a reasonable "Educate, don't Segregate!", but progressed to the infantile "Hell no, we won't go!").

2. Don't put up hypocritical signs like "Protect Free Speech—Shut Connerly Up!"

3. Acknowledge reporters from conservative papers such as the *Austin Review* instead of chanting in their faces when they ask for a comment. A little tolerance will only promote your views.

4. When someone is making fun of your mob-like behavior by shouting "Stomping! We need more stomping!", don't respond by stomping loudly.

5. Don't brand me a racist for writing this letter—I agree with affirmative action but not with all of your methods.

–Donny Lucas
Mechanical engineering freshman

AROC Responds

Ward Connerly's speech wasn't cut short by protesters. Members of the audience protested that they would not be allowed to directly address Connerly after his speech, being forced to write questions on cards before the speech and have them read by a moderator. Whenever Connerly mentioned the "free exchange of ideas" or the "open dialogue," angry audience members objected. So Connerly said he would allow 30 minutes of Q & A after his speech if the audience was respectful and quiet. At that point, the heckling and protests from the audience ceased.

Monday's speech made it clear that the reason Connerly is protested everywhere is because his idea of "free speech" and "open dialogue" is restrictive and misleading. He believes in a dialogue where he can control any dissenting opinion and always have the last word. When Connerly is willing to open himself up to real and productive dialogue he finds that his opponents do not boo and jeer him because they fear what he has to say; it's because they realize

the manipulative hypocrisy behind his rhetoric of "free speech."

–David Hill
Philosophy/African-American studies senior
Anti-Racist Organizing Committee

Disclaimer

I wish to correct one statement in your first-page article Tuesday on the attempt by Ward Connerly to speak at the Law School. I did not introduce Mr. Connerly. Indeed, as is indicated by the enclosed text of my remarks, the administration had nothing to do with inviting Mr. Connerly or sponsoring his appearance. I did attempt to appeal to the audience to respect the right of free speech expression embodied in the First Amendment to our Constitution; normally the favorite Amendment of journalists.

I would add that the behavior of the minority law students who were present was inspirational. Despite their understandably strong negative feelings about the speaker's message, they tried to engage him in a lawerly manner and did not participate in the efforts to suppress his talk. Unfortunately, there were others who arrogated to themselves the power to determine what speech is to be permitted at the University. Their efforts, outside the auditorium, to drown out his remarks were reminiscent of totalitarian mobs throughout the ages and the world.

–M. Michael Sharlot
Dean, UT School of Law

No Insight

I would like to compliment my former dean, M. Michael Sharlot, on his keen observation in Wednesday's Firing Line that the minority students who attended Ward Connerly's lecture on March 8 had "understandably strong negative feelings about the speaker's message." However, sadly, I cannot so compliment my former dean. His comments evidence ignorance, not insight.

Mr. Sharlot has no means to know what kind of feelings every minority student (a ridiculous phrase in itself) among over 200 lecture attendees held about Mr. Connerly's message. It is sad that Mr. Sharlot cannot see past his prejudice to realize that not all minority individuals think alike.

What is so hard about accepting that some minority students at the lecture may have held neutral or positive feelings about Mr. Connerly's message? Nothing—if you believe that a person's mind is not a prisoner to his ancestry.

So, why did Mr. Connerly's presence at the University upset some people so much? Maybe, by presenting a non-stereotypical viewpoint, Mr. Connerly reminded them that they have chosen prison over freedom.

–Adam Dick
UT Law, class of '97

RESPOND.

1. The first four of these letters were written by people who were present at Ward Connerly's lecture. How does each of these letters contribute to your understanding of what, in fact, happened the night of the lecture? How does each of these letters, along with the fifth, complicate your understanding of the meanings of what happened that night for the participants? For the reading public?

2. Lebold criticizes both Connerly and AROC for making ad hominem attacks (opening paragraph). What is Lebold's attitude toward AROC's demonstrations? How do you know? Some readers might argue that Lebold's final sentence is facetious and that his letter is, in fact, a critique of Connerly's position. Offer reasons to accept or reject such an interpretation of Lebold's letter.

3. Lucas addresses two different audiences in his letter. Who are they? Where and how does he make an appeal based on character? How effective is his use of humor? Although Hill's letter does not refer to Lucas's letter by title or its author by name, it is a response to it and other letters and articles critical of AROC. Much like Lucas, Hill has written a letter addressed to the readership of the daily student paper, but he appears to be writing primarily to a subgroup of readers that, in contrast to Lucas's letter, goes unnamed. What group is Hill addressing, and what beliefs do they hold? How do you know?

4. How does Sharlot's status as dean of the UT law school contribute to his ethos? Would his comparison of the demonstrators to "totalitarian mobs" have been as effective if it had been written by a student? Why or why not? In his response to Sharlot's letter, how does Dick establish ethos? His letter begins with the expression of an unrealized — and unrealizable — compliment to Sharlot. How effectively does this device, including the syntactic repetition, work to support Dick's argument?

5. Like most letters to the editor, these letters all make agonistic or combative arguments rather than invitational ones in any way. What features of this genre do you think contribute to the preponderance of agonistic argument?

6. **Write an essay** in which you respond to the question of whether it is ever appropriate to silence a speaker in a public forum like the one described in this cluster of readings. If it is appropriate to do so, under what conditions and for what reasons? If it is not, why not?

▼ *This nationally syndicated column by Jeff Jacoby appeared in May 1999 in major newspapers throughout the country. In it, Jacoby links the Ward Connerly event at the University of Texas with an incident that occurred at Duke University in Durham, North Carolina. See whether you think Jacoby is accurate in his analysis that the two incidents are examples of the same phenomenon.*

How Leftists "Debate"

JEFF JACOBY

Another blast of leftist intolerance for Ward Connerly: The remarkable man who led the fight to abolish racial preferences in California was invited to speak about civil rights at the University of Texas Law School a few weeks back. Connerly is normally an eloquent speaker, but he had no hope of winning hearts and minds in Austin on March 8. A gang of bullies, the self-styled Anti-Racist Organizing Committee, turned out to prevent him from being heard. They resorted to the usual thuggish tactics, yelling insults, pounding the walls, stomping their feet, waving placards. One poster demanded: "Protect Free Speech — Shut Connerly Up!"

For days before Connerly's appearance, AROC had distributed flyers egging students to "shout him down." On the day he arrived, a columnist in the school paper urged students to show that Connerly's "rhetoric will not be tolerated," noting that "at other universities, fed-up students have forced him off stage." Time and again, this is how liberals debate: Not by joining the conversation, but by stifling it.

Michael Sharlot, the law school dean, introduced the program with a stern warning that mob censorship would not be tolerated. The police, he said, would eject anyone who tried to silence Connerly. But that was just for show. The disruption began as soon as Sharlot finished, and he did nothing to stop the hecklers. The mob got its way. Connerly's message was drowned out.

At least he's used to it. Connerly has been getting this treatment ever since the Proposition 209 campaign three years ago. He has been labeled an Uncle Tom, a Ku Klux Klansman, a traitor to his race. It's vile, but it no longer shocks him. By contrast, Jay Strader and Berin Szoka, two freshmen at Duke University, have just had the shock of their lives.

Duke has been debating whether to establish a major in Hindi, a language widely spoken (though far from universal) in India. The call for a Hindi major has more to do with multicultural cheerleading than with actual student demand; Duke already offers four sections of Hindi instruction and 72 percent of the available seats go begging.

Proponents argue for a Hindi major not on academic grounds, but as a vehicle for "diversity" and for "welcoming" Indian students. A letter to the *Chronicle,* Duke's campus daily, declared that "by not implementing a Hindi major, this university is . . . perpetuating racism and white supremacy." A *Chronicle* editorial endorsed the major as a way to foster an "accommodating climate for Hindu culture" and "provide Hindi professors with job security."

After watching the action for a while, Strader and Szoka weighed in with letters of their own.

Strader contrasted Hindi with statistics, another field in which Duke does not offer a major. "Consider the relative usefulness of each subject: The former is a language spoken in a Third World country overwrought by disease and poverty, while the

687

latter is a science of proven, inestimable value in all branches of industry and science." A bit strident, to be sure (and he meant overrun, not "overwrought"), but clearly relevant and well within the bounds of campus discourse.

Strader's letter triggered a flurry of rebuttals, most of which sprinkled him with insults — "ignorant," "blatantly racist," "disgusting" — while praising India's rich and important culture.

Szoka's letter, a week later, came 10 to Strader's defense, and took on the multiculturalists full-tilt.

"The values of the West — the power of reason, the sanctity of individual rights, and the unfettered pursuit of happiness — are superior to the values of a primitive, impoverished country like India," he wrote. "Were it not for the British, whatever 'ancient traditions and rich culture' existed before their arrival would be enjoyed only by the very top of India's feudal caste system." There was more in that vein, highly provocative stuff, a biting retort in the tradition of anti-egalitarian polemicists from H. L. Mencken° to William A. Henry III.°

Of course Szoka expected a response; he and Strader are excited by intellectual combat and unafraid of jabbing sacred cows. What they didn't expect was hate mail, physical confrontations, and death threats.

"If we ever see you out of your room. . . . We will beat you within one inch of your life and step on you like the little shit that you are," one e-mail to Szoka warned. Another advised, "Be particularly careful when showing your face around campus for a while. It might not be a bad idea to bring some sort of a mask or protection." Vandals broke into Strader's room and wrote on his computer: "We're going to kick your ass — Mother India." Szoka says three students came to his room and threatened to beat him; Strader was likewise menaced.

The freshmen found themselves likened to Nazis, cursed with four-letter words, and repeatedly denounced as racists. They've turned the threats over to the police — "After Littleton," Szoka says, "you have to take them seriously" — but what jolted them most was the realization that their opponents have no interest in arguing. They had imagined that at a university anything was open to debate, even — or especially — the axioms of political correctness.

Now they are disabused. "It seems 15 like people don't care about ideas here," Strader says. "All they care about is protecting their racial or ethnic turf. That wasn't what I expected when I came to college."

H. L. Mencken: American journalist and satirist (1880–1956) known for social commentary that mocked the values of many Americans, especially those of the comfortable middle class. During the 1920s, he was among the most influential American writers.

William A. Henry III: Award-winning American journalist (1950–1994) whose posthumous book, *In Defense of Elitism,* argued against affirmative action, contending that "a fair society is one in which some people fail."

RESPOND•

1. Jay Strader and Berin Szoka, the Duke University freshmen discussed by Jacoby, are coeditors of a conservative student newspaper at Duke. Do you think this fact is relevant to Jacoby's description of the events at Duke? Why or why not? Why might Jacoby not have mentioned their other roles on campus?

2. Do you find Jacoby's comparison of Strader and Szoka with H. L. Mencken and William A. Henry III reasonable? Why or why not?

3. Jacoby claims that the Ward Connerly event at the University of Texas and the experiences of Strader and Szoka at Duke University are both examples of "how liberals debate" (paragraph 2). Do you agree with his assessment? Why or why not?

4. In what ways does Jacoby's argument make an appeal based on values? How does he go about creating that appeal? **Write an essay** in which you analyze how Jacoby's use of metaphor, description, comparison, and other rhetorical tools contributes to his argument's appeal based on values.

▶ *The following essay by Megan Elizabeth Murray is from* The Diversity Hoax *(1999), a collection of essays written by students at Boalt Hall, the law school at U. C. Berkeley, during the troubled year following the passage of Proposition 209 forbidding affirmative action in admissions. Of particular interest in this piece is Murray's reminder that public debates can take place in the most private of places—bathroom stalls.*

News from the Ladies' Room

MEGAN ELIZABETH MURRAY

This piece was written from my heart. It is not prize-winning writing. It is not first-rate storytelling. It is how I feel, poured out onto paper with little editing. It is the true experience of a second-year Boalt Hall student.

Diversity. What a joke. Webster's dictionary defines diversity as, "quality, state, fact, or instance of being different or dissimilar; varied." Boalt diverse? Not even close. On the biggest issue facing the university today, affirmative action, only one voice is heard. That is the voice of the tyrannical few.

Boalt is the most homogenous place I have been. Everywhere I look I see signs and stickers about the racist regime of Proposition 209. In every class I hear how each and every regulatory scheme is racist— even organ transplant distribution schemes (how dare they prefer donees with the same blood type?). Half the student body wears T-shirts that say "Educate, Don't Segregate." I do not believe a word of it. Yet, I virtually never speak up. Why is that? I am one of the most outspoken people around. I have never shied away from making outrageous remarks. I am the one who will shout out that the emperor is wearing no clothes. But for some reason, I stay silent at Boalt. I stay silent because the atmosphere is so hostile. I stay silent because the arguments are irrational.

The latest sign posted talks about declining minority admissions to the school. It says, and I really do quote, "No more of this shit." This is what is hanging in my face when I go to check my mailbox at school. The only thing I ever see in the weekly bulletin from the Dean's office to the students is that it is against school rules for anyone to remove such signs. There is never a word about the profanity or the attacking nature of the signs. So I get to walk around my own school with messages cursing about the racism of school policies. Of course, these same signs make no mention of the decline in applications for minorities. It is awfully hard to get admitted if you do not apply. However, I know that if I put up a sign mentioning that, it would be torn down in a heartbeat, and no one would do a thing about it.

There are other signs. There are ones referring to 209 as "racist legislation" and implying that all of us who voted for it are racist. Slap an ugly label like that on us, combine it with an irrational refusal to listen to opposing arguments, and none of us are going to speak.

The stickers have to be the best, though. In every bathroom stall, on almost every locker, and in all kinds of odd places, like the middle of walls, there are stickers again calling Proposition 209 racist, and rallying to support affirmative action. Stickers are not removed nearly as easily as posters. Believe me. I have tried. I have never been one to criticize others for speaking. All year I have fought the urge to tear these signs and posters and stickers off the walls. My feeling has been that it is everyone's prerogative to speak how they please. After many months it finally got to me, though, and I tried to take a sticker off the stall door in a bathroom. Forget it. They will have to be sanded off, literally. 5

I gave up for a while after that. I decided it was my conscience telling me it was the wrong thing to do. It was not my place. So I dropped it. A few weeks later, though, I got really steamed. In a stall, someone had partially torn off a sticker. It left a white sheet of backing paper behind. Someone had written on that sheet, "Affirmative action is racism." The next person had scribbled over it. What right did that person have, I thought, to cross it out? My whole philosophy of leaving everything behind had been premised on the belief that we all have a right to speak, but here the very people whose rights I was trying to respect were not respecting the rights of others. So, I stooped as low as I ever have. I wrote on the leftover sticker. I could not believe I did it, because I am one of those goody two-shoes who would never vandalize or deface property. I suppose I justified it by thinking that I only wrote on the sticker, not the wall. I still felt guilty, though. I did. I do not anymore.

What I wrote was, "You can't ignore the truth by scratching it out. Affirmative action is racism." I checked back a few weeks later. Someone had written, and again, I apologize for the profanity, "You fucking idiot! Prop. 209 allows the racist regime to continue." I stopped feeling guilty right then and there. Why have I been so careful in respecting the rights of people whose arguments consist of name-calling and profanity? I suddenly felt obligated to respond. Maybe that is what they wanted. I do not know. All I know is that suddenly, writing on the leftover sticker on a bathroom wall was not vandalism. It was almost a right I had to respond to being torn down.

So, I wrote back. First, I circled "fucking idiot" and wrote, "Brilliant," next to it. Then I went to the end of the last woman's message and wrote, "NO. Giving one race preference over another is RACISM." I used up the sticker on that message. I have not heard back. Maybe she feels the same way I do about vandalizing the wall. Maybe she can only bring herself to write on the sticker, too. Maybe I should bring in a new sticker. I would feel terrible about sticking it on in the first place though. They don't come off.

My bathroom experience sums up my frustration with the lack of true diversity at Boalt. How can we call the school diverse when a segment of the population speaks out only in bathroom stalls? This school touts itself as one of the best in the country. How can that be when students are not truly free to speak and share ideas? How can meaningful intellectual discourse take place when every word is chosen so carefully so as not to offend? It cannot. How can a school claim to be one of the best when no meaningful discourse takes place? It cannot. Those of us who believe in Proposition 209, who believe that racial preference is racist, and who are proud card-carrying Republicans lurk about in the shadows. We are not holding rallies, wearing T-shirts, or posting profanity-filled signs. Yet we are here. You would not know it from listening in classes or reading posters around school, but we are here. True diversity can only come about if we come out of the stalls and show our faces.

RESPOND •

1. What is Murray's thesis? How does she go about supporting it? Specifically, what sorts of arguments among students at Boalt Hall does she cite to support her claim about the intolerance of diversity at Berkeley Law School? How do you respond to this argument? Does it surprise or shock you, for example? Does it make you laugh or shake your head in disbelief? Why or why not?

2. What sort of ethos does Murray attempt to create for herself in this essay? How does that ethos contribute to or detract from her thesis?

3. Murray describes an interesting kind of debate — one that is public but anonymous, taking place in college rest rooms via graffiti written on the stalls. What are the features or characteristics of effective graffiti arguments in men's or women's rest rooms? How does the physical situation influence the criteria for effective argument? Why, according to Murray, do some arguments take place only via bathroom graffiti? Is this fact good or bad? Why?

4. **Write an essay** in which you compare and contrast the values espoused by Murray in this reading and by Gordon Marino in "Me? Apologize for Slavery?" (p. 661). (Note that you can only make assumptions about Marino's views on affirmative action in college admissions policy and Murray's stance on White America's need to apologize for slavery, but you can come to some conclusions about how the two authors espouse very similar — and very different — values in these readings.)

chapter twenty-nine

Technology Redefining the Meaning of Life

The book of Ecclesiastes claims there is nothing new under the sun. Certainly, the book's writer understood an important truth about human existence: we are all born, and we all die. But a moment's reflection reminds us that although science and technology may not have changed the human condition during the past century, they surely altered the terms of many debates about conception and birth as well as death and dying. Late in 1999, a billboard on a busy Austin thoroughfare boldly inquired, "Who's the father? Call 1-800-DNA-TYPE," against a background of what at first glance appeared to be the outlines of party balloons but were, on closer inspection, sperm. In January 2000, a CNN news item reported that French secondary school nurses had begun distributing "morning after" pills to female students on demand in an effort to reduce unwanted pregnancies. Meanwhile, a growing number of Americans question whether we should want medicine to keep us alive as long as possible. What does "quality of life" mean when a longer life span raises the likelihood of Alzheimer's disease? And what is "death with dignity" in the current era? The arguments in this chapter challenge you to examine your own convictions about issues ranging from reproductive technologies to physician-assisted suicide now that technology, fueled by science, continues to make everyday events of situations that were a few decades ago unimaginable and redefines the terms of ongoing debates about birth and death.

These arguments are likely the most challenging in the book. Certainly, they raise some of life's most difficult questions. But these texts are ultimately challenging because they confront us with our own mortality and that of those we love. You may well have a visceral response to many of these readings as you imagine your-self or someone you care about in the situations de-scribed or recall similar experiences that you've already known. Such responses, so real and so personal, remind us of why life matters and why its meanings are so contested.

When does human life in fact begin? When fertile eggs or fertile sperm are produced? When a fertile sperm successfully penetrates a fertile egg? When a fertilized zygote implants itself in the uterine walls? At some specifiable point during a pregnancy? At the moment of birth? And how has the answer to this question changed across time as technology has permitted women and men to intervene in the processes of **conception and birth?** Some evolutionary biologists claim that even heterosexual attraction between those able to reproduce represents intervention in these processes and is therefore a kind of technology. Folk wisdom about how a woman or man can act to increase—or decrease—the likelihood of the woman's getting pregnant or having a child of a particular sex represents technology of another sort. Fueled by experimental science, more recent technological advances confront us with the possibility of intervening in the process of conception in far more direct and calculated ways than were formerly possible.

The arguments in this cluster challenge you to examine how such technological advances affect the terms of public debate about conception and birth. What are generally called "morning after pills" prevent pregnancy from occurring by making it impossible for the fertilized egg to implant itself in the uterine wall, as you'll see when you examine the Web site for a product named "Plan B": <www.go2planb.com>. Links to this page carefully distinguish this product from another recent medicine that acts to expel a fertilized egg from a woman's body when it is no larger than a grape, thereby redefining abortion as a medical, rather than surgical, procedure. Next, you will analyze the arguments made by ads in magazines and college newspapers that now routinely offer large sums of money for egg donors of a certain profile (generally, tall, attractive, intelligent, and talented in any number of ways) and two accounts of the ethical debates to which such ads gave rise. Do such ads represent a new instance of eugenics, or are they the logical coupling of reproductive technology and market economics? The designer babies of comedy routines and the technophobe's jeremiad, with features and abilities chosen from a checklist by parents, are not yet a reality, but as the transcript of a National Public Radio feature explains, reproductive technology now enables parents-to-be to determine the sex of their child-to-be. (In fact, the range of genres represented in this cluster reminds us that information about these reproductive technologies is all around us, transmitted via traditional media like print ads and radio as well as the Internet—another way that technology permits intervention in the process of conception.)

The arguments in this cluster encourage you to examine carefully how possibilities for influencing the likelihood or outcome of conception, all resulting from technology and science, continue to shape how we as individuals and as a culture define and debate the meaning of conception and birth. As we should, we debate the availability of contraception and the ethics of abortion, but the arguments here remind us that the terms of these ongoing arguments—and a host of others—are by no means settled.

▼ This argument is a commercial Web site for Plan B, a new contraceptive marketed by the Women's Capital Corporation (WCC). As you examine the site (and perhaps some of its related links), spend some time thinking about how Web sites—especially commercial Web sites—are ultimately arguments and what kinds of arguments they make. Consider as well how the technology of the Internet makes possible access to information about conception and birth that was far less readily available just a few short years ago. Go to <http://www.go2planb.com> to access WCC's Plan B Web site.

[Links]   Consumer's Guide to Plan B   Info for Health Care Providers

If Plan A Fails, Go To Plan B..

This website is intended to give women, men, and health care providers more information about a new emergency contraceptive option - Plan B™ (levonorgestrel).

Plan B is emergency contraception. It can prevent pregnancy if taken within 72 hours after unprotected sex (if a contraceptive fails or if no contraception is used). Plan B contains levonorgestrel, which is a synthetic hormone (progestin) commonly used in birth control pills. Plan B does not protect against sexually transmitted diseases and should not be used in place of regular contraception.

What's New   Informacion en Español   Who is WCC?

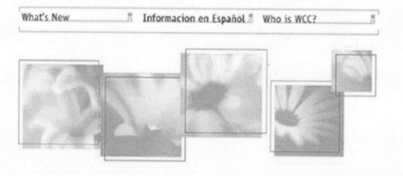

1. The Plan B home page states that its intention is to give information to "women, men, and health care providers." Based on your experience with advertising and your knowledge of visual arguments, who might the site producers intend as their primary audience? Why? Give evidence to support your answer.

2. If you are familiar with the kind of "look" that many popular Web sites have, you may find that the Plan B site has an unusual appearance with its pale, single-color graphics and small, somewhat difficult-to-read type. Does the site's visual design appeal to you? Why or why not? What might be the purpose of such a design? (Consider, for example, the range of people who might be seeking information on such a product and the many places where the computer terminals they use might be located.)

3. What kind of argument is contained in the product name, Plan B, and the site address, go2planb? Is it effective? Why or why not?

4. While a Web site and an essay can each present a unified, cohesive argument, a Web site has a great deal more flexibility with regard to its presentation of information than a traditional essay or article. What is the main argument of <go2planb.com>? What is the most important evidence presented by the site in support of its argument? If the same argument was to be made in essay format, how might it be structured? **Write an outline of an essay** version of the Plan B site's argument, using the basic information given at the site.

How effectively does this Web site use techniques of making an argument in an electronic environment? Evaluate this site according to the criteria for a good visual argument set out in Chapter 15.

LINK TO P. 258

Two Advertisements Soliciting Egg Donors

Here are two ads of a sort that became the subject of controversy in 1999: ads soliciting egg donors from particular categories of women. The controversy began when such an ad appeared in student newspapers at Stanford, MIT, CIT, Harvard, and Yale late in February, 1999. Similar ads

RESPOND.

1. What sorts of appeals are made by each of the ads? How are the ads
   similar in content and appeal? How do they differ? Why?

2. Which do you think is more effective? Which is less effective? Why?

3. Do you find either of the ads offensive? Why? Why might some readers find them controversial? What would you expect to be the grounds
   for the controversy? **Write a letter** to the editor of one of the publications in which the ads appeared, expressing your dismay at the editor's decision to run the ad or supporting its publication, despite any
   controversy it might have given rise to.

▼ Gina Kolata writes regularly on science and medicine for the New York Times. She is the winner of numerous writing awards and author of several books, including The Baby Doctors: Probing the Limits of Fetal Medicine (1990); Sex in America: A Definitive Survey (with Edward Laumann, John Gagnon, and Robert Michaels) (1995); and Clone: The Road to Dolly and the Path Ahead (1999). In 1971, she dropped out of the doctoral program in microbiology at MIT to pursue a writing career. In this news article, Kolata offers the New York Times's initial discussion of the ad first run at Stanford, Yale, MIT, CIT, and Harvard in February 1999, presenting factual information about the ad and reporting responses from an attorney, the director of an assisted-reproduction program at a major hospital, and a medical ethicist.

$50,000 Offered to Tall, Smart Egg Donor

GINA KOLATA

The advertisements started appearing last week in newspapers at the nation's top schools — Ivy League colleges, Stanford University, the Massachusetts Institute of Technology, the California Institute of Technology.

"Egg Donor Needed," the advertisements said, adding, "Large Financial Incentive." The advertisements called for a 5-foot-10, athletic woman who had scored at least 1400 on her Scholastic Achievement Test and who had no major family medical problems. In return for providing eggs, she would receive $50,000.

Already, more than 200 women have responded to what is believed to be the largest amount of money offered for a woman's eggs. Darlene Pinkerton, who with her lawyer-husband, Thomas Pinkerton, placed the advertisement on behalf of an infertile couple, said that most respondents were from Ivy League institutions and that she was starting to get calls from women in countries as far away as Finland and New Zealand. Women from state colleges and universities are calling, Ms. Pinkerton said, as are women who are too short or whose S.A.T. scores are too low.

When she ran the same advertisement in October, without mentioning the price the couple would pay, Ms. Pinkerton said, she got only six responses.

Until now, ethicists argued 5 whether $5,000 was too much to pay for an egg donor. They debated whether it was coercive for couples to ask for S.A.T. scores or height or favorite books when they sought egg donors. But, some ethicists say, a $50,000 price, in a donor market that just a year ago was reeling from offers of $7,500 for donors, makes them wonder whether the business is getting out of control.

The couple offering $50,000 wants to remain anonymous, Ms. Pinkerton said. But, she said, they decided to offer $50,000 "because they can."

The couple also realized that it might be hard to find a donor who met their criteria. They are "highly educated," Ms. Pinkerton said, and want a child who can be highly educated as well. They are tall, so they want a child who is tall.

"We have heard that only one percent of the college population is over 5-feet-10 inches with over 1400 S.A.T. scores," Ms. Pinkerton said.

Lori Andrews, a professor at Chicago-Kent College of Law, is taken aback by the heights that payments are reaching. "I think we are moving to children as consumer products," Ms. Andrews said.

"When prices for donors reach 10 $50,000, it gets to be a meaningful, life-altering sum," she said.

Dr. Mark Sauer, who directs the assisted-reproduction program at Columbia University's College of Physicians and Surgeons in New York, said he found women, even Ivy League women, who were willing to donate their eggs for $5,000. And so, Dr. Sauer asks, why would a couple want to pay $50,000?

"I can understand the motive for the donor—it's like winning the lottery," Dr. Sauer said.

After all, he said, it takes just three to four weeks to produce eggs. The donor takes fertility drugs to stimulate her ovaries to produce more than a dozen eggs, has regular ultrasound exams so a doctor can follow the eggs' development, and then is anesthetized while a doctor aspirates the eggs from her ovaries through a needle.

But, Dr. Sauer asked, what are the egg recipients thinking when they offer to pay so much for a donor with such specific traits?

"What genetics textbook did they 15 read," he asks, "that would tell them that they could order up a tall, smart, athletic child by paying $50,000 for a donor?

But other experts say they fail to see what is so wrong with looking for specific traits in a donor and paying $50,000 for them. Dr. Norman Fost, who directs the program in medical ethics at the University of Wisconsin in Madison, said it was not so crazy to ask for height and S.A.T. scores.

Dr. Fost said he worried more about parents who tried to engineer their children after they were born, pushing them to get perfect grades and to take endless S.A.T. tutoring courses.

"I don't think that genetic engineering is any more pernicious," he said.

As for the $50,000 payment to the egg donor, why not? "It's like offering someone a million dollars to play professional football," Dr. Fost said. "You are perfectly free to walk away from it. People make these choices all their lives."

In the end, he said, "whether chil- 20 dren are valued and how they are treated has very little to do with how they are conceived."

RESPOND•

1. Do you agree with Dr. Norman Fost's statement that parents' efforts at "engineering" children after they're born are worse than engineering their conception (paragraphs 17–18)? Why or why not?

2. How do you respond to Fost's claim that "[y]ou are perfectly free to walk away from [the $50,000]" (paragraph 19)? Is his claim true or relevant in all cases? Why or why not?

3. How does Kolata describe the procedure used for egg extraction? Do you think her article gives an accurate summary of this procedure? (You might consult another characterization of the process, one presented in far less neutral terms, that appears in Rebecca Mead's "Eggs for Sale," *The New Yorker*, August 9, 1999, pp. 55–56.) How does Kolata's discussion of the procedure serve her rhetorical purpose?

4. How should the going rate for donated eggs be established? Should there be a "free market" with no regulation or intervention by government bodies or professional organizations? Why or why not? If there were to be a fixed rate of compensation for donors, what criteria should be used to establish that rate? **Write an essay** exploring these issues.

Kolata's evidence comes mainly from interviews with "experts." This strategy works especially well for arguments based on character; check out Chapter 6 for more suggestions on using arguments based on character.

LINK TO P. 65

▼ *David Lefer is a staff writer for the* New York Daily News, *a newspaper that targets a different audience from the* New York Times. *In this article on the controversy following in the wake of the first smart-egg ad, Lefer focuses on the responses of several potential egg donors, the director of the center for reproductive medicine and fertility at a majority university, an NCAA spokesperson, a sociologist who specializes in biotechnology, and an Ivy League admissions officer.*

An Ad for Smart Eggs Spawns Ethics Uproar

DAVID LEFER

An advertisement seeking egg donors among the nation's tallest and smartest college women has resulted in a flaring controversy on some of the nation's top campuses. Athletic officials even have suggested that women accepting money for eggs might violate intercollegiate eligibility rules.

The so-called smart-egg ad, placed in school newspapers from Harvard and Yale to Stanford and the California Institute of Technology, offered the unprecedented sum of $50,000 for the ova of healthy, athletic women who stand taller than 5-foot-10 and have SAT scores greater than 1400. The anonymous couple who paid for the ad is said to be tall, well-educated and wealthy enough to pay for such a super egg.

So far, say the couple's Los Angeles-based lawyers, between 200 and 300 hopefuls have volunteered to donate eggs. Still, reaction to the ads on campuses has provoked heated debate among students, doctors and ethicists about the morality of donating eggs for big bucks.

EGG DONOR NEEDED

LARGE FINANCIAL INCENTIVE

Intelligent, Athletic Egg Donor Needed

For Loving Family

You must be at least 5'10"

Have a 1400+ SAT score

Possess no major family medical issues

$50,000

Free Medical Screening

All Expenses Paid

Columbia University student Brie Cokos. An advertisement offering $50,000 for the eggs of tall, brainy women like Cokos for a couple seeking to have a baby has caused controversy on the nation's top college campuses.

704

"People are really split on the issue," said Megan Bramlette, a 6-foot-1 freshman on Columbia University's women's basketball team who scored high on her SATs. "Some people are totally morally opposed to it. Others say, 'For $50,000, I'd do just about anything.'"

"I think it's a coercive amount of money," said Dr. Zev Rosenwaks, director of the Center for Reproductive Medicine and Fertility at Cornell University. "This is something that should not be done." 5

"College students don't have a concept of that amount of money," said a 6-foot senior on Harvard's women's basketball team with SAT scores higher than 1400.

Brie Cokos, a 5-foot-11 sophomore biology major at Columbia University who scored 1410 on her SATs, said she doesn't think she could go through with donating her eggs. But she admits the money is enticing.

"For that amount of money, why would you not at least find out what all this is about?" she said. "For one thing, my loans would be out of the way."

Despite the extraordinary sum involved, there might be another hitch in getting student athletes to participate. Although the National Collegiate Athletic Association has no policy on egg donations, an NCAA spokesman confirmed that any student who receives money based directly or indirectly on athletic ability would be ineligible for play.

"If you say you can't play basket- 10 ball anymore, that's going to take a lot of people out of the running," said Columbia's Bramlette.

Religious beliefs also would keep some students from donating eggs.

"I'm a Catholic, and I would probably have to see what the Church would say about it," said a 6-foot-1 Harvard senior with SATs of more than 1400. Money aside, doctors and ethicists are quick to point out that exceptional genes don't necessarily produce exceptional offspring.

"[The offer] reflects an extraordinarily naive view of genetics that you can pay for a certain kind of heredity and think that it will come out exactly as you planned," said Dorothy Nelkin, a professor of sociology at New York University who specializes in the ethics of biotechnology and genetics.

But at least one Ivy League admissions officer already foresees the possibility that the smart-egg controversy might be around for some time.

"If there are two applicants for 15 admission and one space, would the person who came from a Harvard egg get the spot?" asked Marlyn McGrath-Lewis, admissions director for Harvard and Radcliffe colleges.

"The only good news is it will be another 18 years before we really have to deal with this."

Lefer's article raises many questions, many of which are causal in nature, including one about the consequences for college athletes who accept payment for their ova. See more about causal arguments in Chapter 11.

LINK TO P. 161

RESPOND●

1. The technology permitting human egg donation raises a number of ethical issues, yet many of the negative responses touched off by the smart-eggs ads focused on the high payment involved. Which, if any, of the ethical questions would a legally set fixed rate resolve? Would you support such a move? Why or why not?

2. Why do you think Lefer includes comments from McGrath-Lewis about the "Harvard egg" applicant (paragraph 15) and the issue of legacy admission, that is, preference in the admissions process because one's parents or other relatives attended a school? Assuming that legacy admission will continue to exist, should admissions

committees include in the pool of legacy applicants those who can demonstrate that the egg donor or sperm donor who helped give them life is an alum? Should, for example, admissions committees be privy to such information? Should they be able to ask for it? Should they refuse to consider it? Why or why not?

3. Do you think tall, athletic, and intelligent couples are more entitled to solicit eggs from a tall, athletic, and intelligent donor than prospective parents who may be short, clumsy, and less than brilliant? Why or why not?

4. Read Gina Kolata's article on smart-egg ads (p. 702), noting the similarities and differences with Lefer's piece. **Write an essay** in which you compare and contrast the two articles, focusing particularly on the sources each writer consulted, her or his ultimate purposes, and her or his likely audience.

5. **Write a proposal** in which you define and propose how best to regulate the business of "eggs for sale." A likely part of the justification for your proposal will be your own beliefs about this practice.

New Technology Allows Couples to Choose Gender of Child

BOB EDWARDS, *ANCHOR*
CHRISTOPHER JOYCE, *REPORTER*

◀ *Radio news stories and features often constitute complex, multilayered arguments worthy of careful analysis, partly because of the many voices that listeners can literally hear (even though what these voices say is carefully edited by radio reporters and producers). This feature aired on National Public Radio's Morning Edition on June 2, 1999. As you read the transcript, consider the many competing arguments being made here about new advances in reproductive technology.*

BOB EDWARDS, host: This is NPR's *Morning Edition*. I'm Bob Edwards.

Technology has taken a lot of the guesswork out of human reproduction. Couples who can't conceive the old-fashioned way can create embryos in a test tube, and those embryos can be excluded if they carry inherited disease. But choosing the gender of your child with any certainty was beyond reach, until last year when a clinic in Virginia introduced a gender-selection technique called MicroSort. The technique has now produced more than 90 pregnancies. Between 70 percent and 90 percent of the children born have been of the chosen sex. NPR's Christopher Joyce talked to one of the first couples to try this procedure.

MRS. CATHERINE REED: My name is Catherine Reed. Our baby is due on June 10th.

CHRISTOPHER JOYCE reporting: Catherine Reed is a 38-year-old housewife. She used to write war plans for the Navy. She now makes her home in a tree-shaded neighborhood of a southern city with her husband, William, and their two-year-old son, Hunter.

MRS. REED: There you go, sleepyhead.

MR. WILLIAM REED: Hunter, are you a happy boy?

MRS. REED: Get him some milk, please.

MR. REED: Say hi.

MRS. REED: Can you say, thank you?

HUNTER REED: Thank you.

MR. REED: *(Chuckling)*

MRS. REED: *(Chuckling)* Good for you, sweetheart.

MR. REED: Very good.

5

10

Although this piece from *Morning Edition* isn't a speech delivered by a single individual, it is still a form of spoken argument and employs many of the techniques of spoken argument described in Chapter 17, such as considerations of diction and syntax. Learn more of the techniques for spoken arguments in Chapter 17.

LINK TO P. 285

MRS. REED: You're very good.

JOYCE: William Reed had been married before he met Catherine. He had five 15 sons, who now live elsewhere. Enough boys for a basketball team, he jokes. Then Catherine had her first child. It was another boy.

MRS. REED: When we had our beautiful boy, Hunter, the first time we were just overjoyed to have him. And yet I began to think after that, if we're going to have just one more, a gift I can really give my husband and particularly to make this still an even more enjoyable experience is to give to him something he's never had, which is to have a little girl.

JOYCE: Catherine Reed got on the Internet and discovered something called MicroSort offered by Genetics and IVF Institute in Fairfax, Virginia. The technique was invented in 1989 to breed livestock. A device called a flow cytometer distinguishes between sperm carrying X chromosomes—those are the ones that make girls—and Y-bearing sperm. Those make the boys. The machine can distinguish the two because the X chromosome is 2.8 percent heavier than the Y. When a dye is added to the sperm, the X chromosome absorbs more and shines brighter under a special light. X sperm can then be separated from the Y's. Last year the institute started signing up volunteers. The Reeds were among the first. Instead of buying furniture for their new home, they decided to invest their savings on trying to have a girl.

MR. REED: I want a daughter. And I'm going to protect her and love her and spoil her and then turn her over to Mom. So I'm going to have my little princess.

MRS. REED: I don't know why, I always sort of summed it up in that I always imagined brushing a ponytail. And on all the things that, sort of, that encompasses for me, it's just another experience in life so very singular. And I thought how beautiful to have the balance of one child of each and the different unique properties that each one brings.

JOYCE: There were certain things Catherine Reed had to be sure of first: that 20 there would be no genetic manipulation of the sperm, and that the selection process didn't somehow select less hardy sperm than natural conception. GIVF assured her that neither was the case.

The Reeds were seeking what GIVF calls family balancing. Other women signed on because they carried certain genetic flaws on the X chromosome. These can cause any of some 350 so-called X-linked diseases; for example, hemophilia or Duchenne's muscular dystrophy. Women can carry these diseases, but usually only boys get them. So couples can try the MicroSort procedure to increase the chance of having a girl. Given these benefits, Bill and Catherine Reed decided the risk of a relatively untried procedure was worth it. And they are now about to have a baby girl.

MR. REED: We are—I think we were—glad to be part of that process because there are a lot of people out there, for a number of reasons, that want to balance their families or prevent sex-linked transmission of diseases and things like that. There's good reasons. And the people that we've shared this with, which is all of our friends and co-workers, they have all shown a keen interest in a procedure like this being available.

MRS. REED: The one reason we're speaking with you today is we wanted to let people know that it was possible. And you don't have to go on having child after child hoping that the next one will be the sex that you don't yet have in your family.

JOYCE: The Genetics and IVF Institute experiment with humans followed more than 400 births among five species of animals using this technique. GIVF's Edward Fugger, who modified the technology for human use, says about 90 women have become pregnant and over 30 have given birth using sperm sorting. And he says all the children are normal and healthy. Fugger says GIVF does not accept everyone, though, who wants a child of a particular gender.

MR. EDWARD FUGGER (Genetics and IVF Institute): We're not offering this technol- 25 ogy to first-child conceptions. If they have at least one child of one gender, then they can select for the opposite gender. Example, if they had five boys and one girl and they wanted another girl, then they would be able to select for a girl. In other words, by definition, there would be no gender bias issues and no gender ratio issues.

JOYCE: Once sorted, sperm is introduced into the woman's uterus using a catheter, a standard technique in artificial insemination. Each attempt costs $2,500. Three attempts is the average for a pregnancy. The majority of couples applying for the procedure are seeking to balance a family. Fugger says just over half the applicants want a girl.

Choosing a girl offers better odds. GIVF figures show 90 percent of those who choose a girl get one. The success rate is just below 70 percent for boys. That's because the boy, or *Y*-bearing, sperm are harder to separate out.

History is replete with notions of how to pick the gender of your child, from the timing of intercourse to an assortment of sperm-sorting devices. GIVF says its technology is the most successful, but with success has come some criticism.

Ms. Carrie Gordon (Focus on the Family): God is the creator of life, and for us to control our ability to procreate, to have children, is one thing, but to control the kind of children that we create is another.

Joyce: Carrie Gordon is with the religious group Focus on the Family. She 30 advises Christian families about new reproductive technologies. She says this technique is a hard call. It would be difficult telling people they can't choose gender to avoid having a disabled child, but she says the technology is too easy to abuse.

Ms. Gordon: Tomorrow it may be athletic ability or intelligence or beauty, and it's just going to be too tempting for the general public to be allowed to genetically manipulate babies to their custom or to their specific specification.

Joyce: There are more secular concerns as well. Thomas Murray heads the Hastings Center, a bioethics think tank in New York. Speaking as an ethicist and a father, he says he views children as a kind of surprise. The more control people have over what kind of children they have, he says, the more children become commodities.

Mr. Thomas Murray (Hastings Center): To value them according to their characteristics, that really begins to look like we're treating them the way we would with a—choosing our child the way we choose a new car, you know. You choose the style. Do you want two doors or four doors, or do you want a station wagon? Do you like—what color do you like? What accessories do you want with the car? That concerns me deeply.

Joyce: Yet others who work in bioethics and reproductive medicine downplay the effect of MicroSort. They say its potential for harm is less than proposed techniques to genetically manipulate embryos created in the laboratory. And Catherine Reed argues that there are worse ways to select the gender of a child.

Mrs. Reed: I think you'd have to agree that deliberate sex balancing done at the 35 conception, of course, is so much better than practices in some countries where they're using sonograms to determine that it may not be, for example, a male, and they may abort the child. So I think this is still preferable.

Joyce: Yet there are still unknowns, and the procedure remains experimental, says GIVF, until they have enough births to prove that gender selection is no more harmful than natural selection. Christopher Joyce, NPR News, Washington.

Edwards: It's 11 minutes before the hour.

RESPOND●

1. Because of time constraints and the need to appeal directly to audiences, radio features are carefully edited in certain ways to remove extraneous or irrelevant material. In other words, listeners can assume that everything they hear has been included for a reason. What is the purpose of including the lengthy interchange between the Reeds and their toddler son (paragraphs 5–13)? How does the dialogue contribute to the argument? What sorts of appeals does it make? Is it effective? Why or why not?

2. What impression do you have of each of the people interviewed for this feature? Are you inclined to agree with their assessments of the MicroSort technology? Why or why not? Is this inclination based on the arguments those interviewed make, the assumptions you previously held, or both?

3. What might Thomas Murray (paragraph 33) say about the smart-eggs controversy discussed in the three previous readings ("Two Advertisements Soliciting Egg Donors," p. 700; Gina Kolata's "$50,000 Offered to Tall, Smart Egg Donor," p. 702; and David Lefer's "An Ad for Smart Eggs Spawns Ethics Uproar," p. 704)? About egg or sperm donation in general? Why?

4. Characterize the response of Carrie Gordon, who is associated with Focus on the Family, advising Christian families about reproductive technologies, to this technology (paragraphs 29–31). What particular challenges does this reproductive technology present for those who believe, with Gordon, that "God is the creator of life"? How might Gordon respond to those, more conservative than she, who would claim on religious grounds that a woman should not use technology like MicroSort even if it means giving birth to a disabled child?

5. Quite clearly, GIVF screens its potential customers. What are its criteria? Do they seem appropriate, fair, and necessary? Why or why not? **Write an essay** proposing appropriate criteria for access to GIVF's services or arguing that any couple or any woman should be able to use the company's services. (You may want to discuss who should pay the cost of these procedures—the couples or individual involved, their health plans, the government for those without health insurance, or some combination of these. Tackling this latter topic will require you to do some research on the financing of reproductive technologies—many health plans, for example, provide partial coverage at best for the use of such technology.)

No less than conception and birth, **death and dying** are being reshaped by technological advances. Over the past century, the life expectancy of Americans has risen to just over seventy-six years; some researchers estimate that twenty-five years of this longer life expectancy are due to advances in public health, resulting from scientific research and the technology that followed in its wake. Yet, except in the world of science fiction, technology cannot make death and dying disappear. What has changed is the nature of our understanding of these life processes and the debates we have about them.

The arguments in this cluster challenge you to examine the stance you take in these debates as well as the values informing the assumptions you hold about death and dying. The cluster opens with the introductory chapter from a 1997 book called *The Good Death: The New American Search to Reshape the End of Life,* by Marilyn Webb; this reading serves as a road map of sorts to the landscape of death and dying in contemporary America. As Webb argues, many Americans now question the biomedical model of death and dying in which one dies in a hospital, kept alive as long as possible by all the medical care and technology one can afford. The remaining arguments examine two major alternatives to the biomedical model of death and dying at this time, hospice care and physician-assisted death. (This latter alternative covers a continuum of possibilities, from a physician administering medication to end a patient's life to prescribing such medication to withholding treatment that might keep a patient alive. With rare exceptions, advocates of such practices assume that the patient has, at some point, specifically requested one of these forms of treatment.) Faye Girsh's title, "Should Physician-Assisted Suicide Be

Legalized? Yes!" makes her stance quite clear, as does Joe Loconte's title "Hospice, Not Hemlock." (Loconte's allusion to hemlock recalls not only the poisonous drink with which Socrates ended his life but more importantly the Hemlock Society, which advocates death with the help of a physician.) These contrasting views of physician-assisted suicide and hospice care are followed by two especially personal responses to death and dying, each involving the loss of loved ones who chose hospice care. In "The Long Goodbye," Alicia Shepard offers a diary account of losing her mother, who died at home, and Cyrus Cassells writes of the loss of four friends in residential hospices in his poem "Evening Lasting as Long as Life." The cluster ends with a legal argument, the complete text of the Oregon Death with Dignity Act, which permits Oregonians with a terminal illness to request medication to end their lives. The last section of the measure provides a model of the letter one must submit in order to request and receive the necessary medication while remaining within the confines of the law, a sobering testament to the power of the written word and written argument.

All of these texts, even (and perhaps especially) the Oregon statute, remind us that debates about death and dying are not just questions of law; rather, they spill over into the domains of philosophy and ethics, clinical medicine, public policy, economics, and spirituality, forcing us to acknowledge the ultimate mystery of life and the complexity of dying and death.

► *Marilyn Webb is author of* **The Good Death: The New American Search to Reshape the End of Life** *(1997), in which this reading serves as introduction. As you read, reflect on the sorts of arguments that book introductions make as well as Webb's perspective on how technology and medicine can and cannot change death and dying for Americans.*

The Good Death

MARILYN WEBB

During the six years it has taken to research and write this book, people have asked me whether it wasn't depressing, even morbid, to report about death in America. They are surprised when I say that not only has this been the most inspiring work of my life, but the most magnificent times were spent with people who were dying.

I came to this book haltingly, no doubt out of personal need, but in the end I realized I have been preparing to do this book all my life. I was a child of the fifties, when death was not spoken of, most particularly not to children. So when death came, it came as a shock.

I was sixteen when my sister died, and she was thirteen and a half. Her name was Netta, after my mother's sister, Nettie, who'd also died at thirteen and a half, when my own mother was sixteen.

Nettie was run over by a hit-and-run taxicab driver one afternoon on her way to buy bread for dinner. She lingered in a Brooklyn hospital in a coma for nearly a month before she died, but the family had known it was just a matter of time.

It was different with my sister. Netta died in 1959 at North Shore 5 Hospital on Long Island, after she'd been sick for three years. We thought all along that modern medicine would cure her.

Netta contracted nephrosis, a kidney infection, as a complication of a strep throat when she was ten. Those were the days just before kidney dialysis or transplants. What she had was fatal, but I never knew, not for any part of those three long years it took her to die. I later learned that her doctor had told my father, but he'd tried to "protect" my mother by not telling her. The doctors went along with the lie. My mother still says she never knew. She functioned on dreams, fantasies of medical miracles, and denial.

I lived in dreams of my own. I remember nights of dreams pockmarked by noise outside my bedroom door. My room was at the end of a long hall; my sister's was closer to my parents' room, the bathroom between her room and theirs. Many nights they were all up, dashing back and forth from their bedrooms to the bathroom. Sometimes I'd

What kind of evidence does Webb present in her article? She describes her interviews with many other people and her intensive studies in various places, yet it is all framed in terms of her own personal experience. Does Webb make effective use of personal experience in her argument, according to the criteria in Chapter 12?

··· LINK TO P. 198

wake up and get ready for school with just a neighbor in the house, telling me that my parents had to take Netta to the hospital once again.

The last time I saw Netta alive was a Friday afternoon, the day before I went off to a boarding school weekend dance. By then, I'd already gotten used to what I saw. Her body had swelled, she'd grown weak, she'd long been vomiting blood, her skin had yellowed. She never complained, but—also by then—she'd become nearly tyrannical toward me. Maybe I should have known the end was near when she gave me her vanilla ice cream.

When I returned on Sunday evening, my house was filled with people, many of them strangers. My mother was in the living room, crying. Crowds enveloped her. That wall of people soon symbolized for me the muzzle our family put on talk of death.

Years later, I discovered that Netta had had a final heart attack 10 while my mother rushed to change the sheets on her hospital bed. She'd soiled herself—as frequently happens in death—but my mother didn't know, or couldn't admit, that Netta was in the process of dying.

When I came home, someone at the front door merely told me that Netta had died, and also that my mother needed me to be strong. It was better if I would try not to ask too much. Our family shut down. I imagined that Netta had died in great pain, and the not-knowing made me scared. I didn't know what death was; I wasn't prepared, nor was I helped afterward to understand or to grieve. I adopted a pose of black humor, with a literary twist. I called Netta's story "Death by Vanilla Ice Cream."

In 1963, while I was away at college, my father died. He went to dinner and never made it home. The police found him slumped over the steering wheel, his car parked around the corner on the side of the road. My mother later identified him in a drawer at the morgue. They said he'd had a heart attack. I thought he'd died of a broken heart.

We never talked about this death either, but this time there was something more: My dad and I had been in the midst of a feud about someone I was dating. No surprise, we broke up, but my relationship with my father remained unresolved. Now I was filled with guilt, unfinished business, and anger. I called this story "Death by Bad Boyfriend."

Over the next few years, all four of my grandparents died. By then, my family—or what was left of it—began using black humor, too. On a scale of deaths, my paternal grandfather's was the best: He died at home at the age of ninety-five, sitting in his dark leather chair, feet up, reading the *Wall Street Journal*. It was still open to the page with the stock market quotes when they found him. On that day, Grandpa's stocks had gone way up.

I've since learned that the way death occurs in families has tremen- 15 dous weight and can leave a legacy that is lasting. Those deaths that are good pull families together and leave a legacy of peace. Those that are bad leave a legacy of grief, anger, and pain that can continue across many generations. Our family used silence, which compounded the pain. And I've since learned that our way was no different from that of most families in America.

When my sister became ill, antibiotics were still so new that her doctor didn't even know the correct one to prescribe for her infection, and later, as her kidneys failed, there were no dialysis machines or transplants. My father died swiftly because that was what heart conditions meant at the time. But America was on the cusp of enormous change.

Today, thanks to modern antibiotics, heart bypasses, cancer treatments, organ transplants, life-support equipment, dialysis, and intravenous fluids, medicine has changed the way this nation dies, giving us a life expectancy at birth of an extra twenty-seven years since the turn of the century. But, as I discovered in researching this book, it has also made the dying process harder.

In defeating many previously lethal diseases, new ailments have taken their place that instead keep people in long-term decline and even less sure than my family was about when an illness is likely to lead to death. Medical success may have even allowed death to become *more* hidden, lulling Americans into losing knowledge not just of the physical process of dying, but of the psychological and spiritual dimensions of death.

This was brought home to me by a later family death. My stepfather, Macy, was a funny, street-smart attorney, but during the mid-1980s, this ruddy and raucous man began dying inch by terrible inch of Alzheimer's disease.

[A]s his dementia grew worse, his doctors continued to treat his physi- 20 cal ailments aggressively—heart attacks, diverticulitis, infections, pneumonia—as if there were something they might do by treating his body that would end up curing his mind. All of this in the face of our explicitly stated family wishes against such treatment. In a way, it was lucky his mind was gone, though, since Macy's death was so slow and so debased that had he known what was going on he would have been humiliated beyond all enduring.

About the time my stepfather had already lost track of our names and faces, he was hospitalized for pneumonia. One day I found him sitting alone in a regular chair. He wasn't braying, or hanging off his walker or wheelchair, or cursing, as he usually did. In fact, he looked almost normal. He turned to me when I walked into the room, and with full recognition, he said, "Your father was here to see me this morning."

By then, my father had been dead for twenty-five years. My step-father had never met him, nor did he know a lot about our relation-ship, yet when I asked what my father had to say, he answered, "He told me to tell you that he loves you very much, even though you don't think so." He also said some personal things my father would likely have said, things my stepfather could never have known. Then he went back to his braying.

Over the next few months, this incident ended up unraveling and ultimately healing my unresolved anger with my father. It also made me realize that far more is going on as we prepare to die than medi-cine might have us think.

Journalists cope with their personal lives by writing stories about other people. After Macy died in 1989, I wrote an article for *New York* maga-zine about how Americans are coping with the vastly altered land-scape of modern medicine and with illnesses like Alzheimer's, cancer, and AIDS.

I learned that such cataclysmic changes are occurring in how we 25 die that these issues may well be among the most crucial challenges we face as we enter the twenty-first century.

In fact, a confluence of crucial events occurred in June 1990:

- Dr. Jack Kevorkian, a retired Michigan pathologist, helped Janet Adkins, an Alzheimer's patient from Oregon, die in the back of his rusty Volkswagen van, using a makeshift suicide machine.

- Dr. Timothy Quill, a former hospice physician from Rochester, New York, helped Patricia Diane Trumbull, a leukemia patient of his, die by giving her a prescription for "barbiturates for sleep," knowing that she would take them when she felt it was time. But to protect him and her family from prosecution, she would have to take them and die alone.

- The U.S. Supreme Court decided in the case of Nancy Beth Cruzan—a thirty-three-year-old woman who lay comatose in a Missouri hospital, subsisting on a feeding tube and in a persistent vegetative state—that patients legally could refuse feeding tubes, just as they could any other medical treatment, even if that refusal meant death. The Cruzan decision spurred Congress to pass the Patient Self-Determination Act, requiring hospitals and nursing homes to let patients know they had the right to sign an advance directive about the kind of treatment they preferred at the end of life.

- The family of eighty-five-year-old Helga Wanglie appealed to a Minnesota court to prevent doctors from disconnecting Mrs. Wanglie's respirator and feeding tube against her family's wishes. Her doctors called her condition hopeless, but the Wanglies argued that Helga, a religious woman who'd suffered irreparable brain damage after a heart attack, would not have wanted life supports removed.

Changes in medicine and the law have now penetrated into the most intimate areas of life, confounding all our prior ways of handling illness and death. As this book was being finished, the Supreme Court ruled on the issue of legalizing assisted suicide. The nation as a whole was struggling with what improvements might need to be made in health-care finance and in the care of the dying. More significant, it was also struggling with the question: When it comes to each of our own deaths, who decides? and how?

I realized at the start of my reporting that individual deaths—like those in my family—are played out against a vast scope of medical, legal, social, cultural, political, and financial issues. I began to search this larger background, trying to examine death not just as the private ordeal it always is, but as part of an enormous and shifting social fabric.

In undertaking this book, I wanted to take death out of the shadows of secrecy. I wanted to talk to those who are dying about what their dying is like, to learn more about what happens to our fading bodies and minds. I wanted to look at how the seriously ill and dying are treated, and what we might do to bring about an eventual *good* death for ourselves and for those whom we love.

That search set me on a lengthy investigative path. For six years I 30 immersed myself as a reporter in America's medical and health-care system, probing the medical environments and styles in which most people die.

At the very beginning of my work, I practically moved onto the inpatient unit of Cabrini Hospice in Manhattan for a month. There I spent days and nights with patients and staff members and was lucky enough to learn at the start about the psychological dimensions of dying. My guide was Sister Loretta Palamara, one of the most gifted people in the care of the dying that I have ever met, who died of a cerebral hemorrhage just as I was finishing this book.

At Cabrini Hospice I also met two extraordinary patients. Audrey Hill, who died of ovarian cancer, helped me understand the spiritual dimensions of dying, and that those moments like the one I had with my stepfather are available to many, if we know how to listen. Peter Ciccone, who died of AIDS, was the first to show me that pain management in America is not always what it could be.

They were the first of some fifteen patients and their families who allowed me into their lives, who let me follow them, talk with them—in person, on the phone, at their deathbeds—week after week, month after month, telling me in detail what they were feeling and thinking, nearly until the moment they died. I am particularly honored that except in those few places noted in the text, everyone I interviewed or wrote about allowed me to use his or her real name. They helped me to know the dying process itself, and in sharing that process with me, they allowed me to reshape the private puzzle of my life. It was an immense gift, and for that I will always remain grateful.

Needing to understand more, I began attending intensive medical training seminars at major teaching hospitals and their nursing home affiliates. I also went to conferences held by professional organizations—for example, the American Society of Clinical Oncology, the National Hospice Organization, and the Academy of Hospice Physicians—and to workshops and training intensives on more highly focused medical issues held by a variety of medical groups.

I crisscrossed the nation, going to small communities like Pass 35 Christian, Mississippi, or Sebastian, Florida, places where there are modest hospitals and quieter ways of death, and visiting or interviewing those at large teaching hospitals and medical centers in New York, Detroit, San Francisco, New Haven, Washington, Boston, Los Angeles, San Antonio, Chicago, Minneapolis, Montreal, Philadelphia, and Houston.

I went on cardiology rounds at Mount Sinai Medical Center and to pain management sessions at Memorial Sloan-Kettering Cancer Center and Beth Israel Hospital, all in New York City. I visited palliative care centers and hospices like the Royal Victoria Hospital in Montreal, the Hospice of Michigan and its inpatient affiliates at the Detroit hospitals, and the Coming Home Hospice in San Francisco's Castro district.

To learn what doctors are taught about dying I studied textbooks—often under the guidance of medical school faculty members—used in the best medical schools today. I focused particularly on texts on internal medicine, pain management, and palliative care. And I pored over the history of medicine in the reading rooms and rare book rooms of the New York Academy of Medicine's vast library. I also interviewed nearly three hundred physicians, nurses, and health-care workers about their work, their training, their relationships with patients, and about their general understanding and views of modern medical care.

Among those interviewed were people who now play a significant part in our modern saga of dying—familiar names like Dr. Elisabeth Kübler-Ross, Dr. Joanne Lynn, Dr. Jack Kevorkian, and Dr. Timothy Quill, as well as countless other people actively involved on the front lines in shaping, and changing, our American culture of dying: doctors, nurses, psychologists, social workers, hospice volunteers, hospital administrators, ethicists, lawyers, spiritual advisers, and philosophers on death.

While I talked extensively with Jewish, Catholic, and other Christian clerics and theologians, I also explored how influences from the East, particularly Tibetan Buddhism, are changing the terrain of dying in America. And I reported on the new kind of spirituality emerging from hospice care and from popular accounts of near-death experiences.

I was also interested in differing political points of view and what 40 impact they have on our care of the dying. To that end, I interviewed people with diverse opinions—from pro-choice liberals involved with the Hemlock Society, Choice in Dying, and AIDS organizations to pro-life conservatives involved with the National Committee for the Right to Life, or disability activists with a group called Not Dead Yet.

I tried to understand the new ethical and legal issues involved in dying, spending a month as a journalist-in-residence at the Hastings Center in Briarcliff Manor, New York, and interviewing noted end-of-life attorneys and ethicists. I listened to the families who were key to the growing body of ethics and case law that we are learning to live by—the Quinlans, the Cruzans—and I talked with their lawyers, their doctors, their priests.

When I began reporting, I could not understand why someone might want to die in the back of Dr. Jack Kevorkian's rusty van. Now I do. But I also learned that if we are to have good deaths, the culture of dying needs to change.

These needed changes involve the way we make our own personal decisions, and they involve altering the sociomedical context in which we die. We need to change the way ill patients are treated, the way health-care financing is handled, the way we care for those who are at the edges of life. I also learned that there is hope, since many of the changes that I found were needed in medicine, end-of-life care, and the law may now be on the way.

Surely, none of us wants to die, but there are decisions to be made that can make our dying easier. Each person, of course, will make his or her own choices and they will not be the same for everyone. I have learned in writing this book which choices can help make death less painful.

All decisions require open conversations rather than secrecy about death. Against the backdrop of confusion and sorrow that is always there when someone we love dies, I have also learned something more: It is possible to have a good death in America, but as a nation that has grown used to medical miracles, we now have to develop the will to learn how to bring closure to life when a cure is no longer likely.

RESPOND ●

1. What goals does Webb appear to have in writing the introduction to *The Good Death*? What sort of ethos does she create? How does she do so? How would you characterize Webb's perspective on death and dying in America? Are you interested in reading her book? Why or why not?

2. What does Webb mean when she argues that medical advances have both increased life expectancy for Americans and "made the dying process harder" (paragraph 17)? Do you agree? Why or why not? What sorts of evidence do you find yourself offering to support your position? What do you think Webb means by the final sentence of the introduction?

3. Investigate laws in your state about matters relating to an individual's rights with regard to death and dying. Are advance directives to physicians outlining the kinds of treatment desired at the end of life permitted? What form do they take? What laws (if any) govern such matters as physician-assisted suicide or a family's right to discontinue life support?

4. **Write a letter** to Webb in which you describe your personal experiences with matters of death and dying, outlining what you think you have learned about Americans' attitudes toward death from your experiences. Have you found, for example, that we in America do not talk about death and do not want to talk about it? If so, is this practice good or bad? Why? Have you had an experience similar to Webb's experience with her stepfather, who claimed to have been visited by Webb's father? If so, how did you make sense of the experience? If you have considerable familiarity with life and death in another country or culture, you may wish to use this knowledge as the basis of your essay. If your experience with death and dying has been very limited, you might explain how you anticipate dealing with these matters when they arise.

In this essay, Faye Girsh, executive director of the Hemlock Society, a nonprofit organization seeking to help legalize "voluntary physician aid in dying for terminally ill consenting adults," argues that physician-assisted suicide should be legalized in the United States. According to the society's Web page, <http://www.hemlock.org>, "Hemlock believes that people who wish to retain their dignity and choice at the end of life should have the option of a peaceful, gentle, certain and swift death in the company of their loved ones. The means to accomplish this is with legally prescribed medication as part of the continuum of care between a patient and a doctor." We found Girsh's article on the Web, but it was originally published in 1999 in Insight on the News, a weekly news magazine covering politics and cultural issues for a national audience. As you read, pay special attention to how Girsh deals—or fails to deal—with potential counterarguments.

Should Physician-Assisted Suicide Be Legalized? Yes!

FAYE GIRSH

Q: Should physician-assisted suicide be legalized by the states?
Yes: Don't make doctors criminals for helping people escape painful terminal illnesses.

Many people agree that there are horrifying situations at the end of life which cry out for the help of a doctor to end the suffering by providing a peaceful, wished-for death. But, opponents argue, that does not mean that the practice should be legalized. They contend that these are the exceptional cases from which bad law would result.

I disagree. It is precisely these kinds of hard deaths that people fear and that happen to 7 to 10 percent of those who are dying that convince them to support the right to choose a hastened death with medical assistance. The reason that polls in this country—and in Canada, Australia, Great Britain and other parts of Europe—show 60 to 80 percent support for legalization of assisted suicide is that people want to know they will have a way out if their suffering becomes too great. They dread losing control not only of their bodies but of what will happen to them in the medical system. As a multiple-sclerosis patient wrote to the Hemlock Society: "I feel like I am just rotting away. . . . If there is something that gives life meaning and purpose it is this: a peaceful end to a good life before the last part of it becomes even more hellish."

Socrates drinking hemlock and thus ending his life. Accused by Athenian authories of "impropriety," most likely because they disagreed with his political affiliations and ideas about education, Socrates was sentenced to die. During and after his trial, he refused to take actions that might have resulted in a lighter sentence because he viewed such actions as compromising; similarly, he did not escape from jail although he easily might have. Instead, he drank hemlock (to the despair of friends), thus forcing the Athenians to face the unjust consequences of their decision.

723

Even with the best of hospice care people want to know that there can be some way to shorten a tortured dying process. A man whose wife was dying from cancer wrote, "For us, hospice care was our choice. We, however, still had 'our way,' also our choice, as 'our alternative.' We were prepared. And the 'choice' should be that of the patient and family."

It is not pain that causes people to ask for a hastened death but the indignities and suffering accompanying some terminal disorders such as cancer, stroke and AIDS. A survey in the Netherlands found that the primary reason to choose help in dying was to avoid "senseless suffering."

Hospice can make people more comfortable, can bring spiritual solace and can   5
work with the family, but—as long as hospice is sworn neither to prolong nor hasten death—it will not be the whole answer for everyone. People should not have to make a choice between seeking hospice care and choosing to hasten the dying process. The best hospice care should be available to everyone, as should the option of a quick, gentle, certain death with loved ones around when the suffering has become unbearable. Both should be part of the continuum of care at the end of life.

We have the right to commit suicide and the right to refuse unwanted medical treatment, including food and water. But what we don't have—unless we live in Oregon—is the right to get help from a doctor to achieve a peaceful death. As the trial judge in the Florida case of Kirscher vs. McIver, an AIDS patient who wanted his doctor's help in dying, said in his decision: "Physicians are permitted to assist their terminal patients by disconnecting life support or by prescribing medication to ease their starvation. Yet medications to produce a quick death, free of pain and protracted agony, are prohibited. This is a difference without distinction."

The Oregon example has shown us that, although a large number of people want to know the choice is there, only a small number will take advantage of it. During the first eight months of the Oregon "Death with Dignity" law, only 10 people took the opportunity to obtain the medications and eight used them to end their lives. In the Netherlands it consistently has been less than 5 percent of the total number of people who die every year who choose to get help in doing so from their doctor.

In Switzerland, where physician-assisted death also is legal, about 120 people die annually with the help of medical assistance. There is no deluge of people wanting to put themselves out of their misery nor of greedy doctors and hospitals encouraging that alternative. People want to live as long as possible. There are repeated testimonials to the fact that people can live longer and with less anguish once they know that help will be available if they want to end it. Even Jack Kevorkian, who says he helped 130 people die since 1990, has averaged only 14 deaths a year.

To the credit of the right-to-die movement, end-of-life care has improved because of the push for assisted dying. In Oregon, end-of-life care is the best in the country: Oregon is No. 1 in morphine use, twice as many people there use hospice as the national average and more people die at home than in the hospital. In Maine there will be an initiative on the ballot in 2000 to legalize physician aid in dying, and in Arizona a physician-assisted-dying bill has been introduced. In both states the Robert Wood Johnson Foundation has awarded sizable grants to expand hospice care and to improve end-of-life care.

It is gratifying that the specter of assisted dying has spurred such concern for   10
care at the end of life. Clearly, if we take the pressure off, the issue will disappear back into the closet. No matter how good the care gets, there still will be a need to have an assisted death as one choice. The better the care gets, the less that need will exist.

The pope and his minions in the Catholic Church, as well as the religious right, announce that assisted dying is part of the "culture of death." Murder, lawlessness, suicide, the cheapening of life with killing in the media, the accessibility of guns, war—those create a culture of death, not providing help to a dying person who repeatedly requests an end to his or her suffering by a day or a week. Not all religious people believe that. The Rev. Bishop Spong of the Episcopal Diocese of Newark, N.J., said: "My personal creed asserts that every person is sacred. I see the holiness of life enhanced, not diminished, by letting people have a say in how they choose to die. Many of us want the moral and legal right to choose to die with our faculties intact, surrounded by those we love before we are reduced to breathing cadavers with no human dignity attached to our final days. Life must not be identified with the extension of biological existence. Assisted suicide is a life-affirming moral choice."

The Catholic belief that suicide is a sin which will cause a person to burn in hell is at the root of the well-financed, virulent opposition to physician aid in dying. This has resulted in expenditures of more than $10 million in losing efforts to

A word like *minions* carries a strong connotation. Sometimes the choice of such a powerful word is an effective rhetorical strategy, but other times less potent words are more effective. Check out the section on the dangers of unduly slanted language in Chapter 14 for suggestions on word choice.

LINK TO P. 248

defeat the two Oregon initiatives and a successful campaign to defeat the recent Michigan measure. And $6 million was spent in Michigan, most of which came from Catholic donors, to show four TV ads six weeks before voters saw the issue on the 1998 ballot. The ads never attacked the concept of physician aid in dying, but hammered on the well-crafted Proposal B. Surely that money could have been spent to protect life in better ways than to frustrate people who have come to terms with their deaths and want to move on. The arguments that life is sacred and that it is a gift from God rarely are heard now from the opposition. Most Americans do not want to be governed by religious beliefs they don't share, so the argument has shifted to "protection of the vulnerable and the slippery slope." Note, however, that the proposed death-with-dignity laws carefully are written to protect the vulnerable. The request for physician-assisted death must be voluntary, must be from a competent adult and must be documented and repeated during a waiting period. Two doctors must examine the patient and, if there is any question of depression or incompetence or coercion, a mental-health professional can be consulted. After that it must be up to the requester to mix and swallow the lethal medication. No one forces anyone to do anything!

The same arguments were raised in 1976 when the first "living-will" law was passed in California. It again was raised in 1990 when the Supreme Court ruled that every American has the right to refuse medical treatment, including food and hydration, and to designate a proxy to make those decisions if they cannot. This has not been a downhill slope in the last 22 years but an expansion of rights and choices. It has not led to abuse but rather to more freedom. Those who raise the specter of the Nazis must remember that we are in greater danger of having our freedoms limited by religious dogma than of having them expanded so that more choices are available. When the state dictates how the most intimate and personal choices will be made, based on how some religious groups think it should be, then we as individuals and as a country are in serious trouble.

One observer said about the Oregon Death with Dignity law: "This is a permissive law. It allows something. It requires nothing. It forbids nothing and taxes no one. It enhances freedom. It lets people do a little more of what they want without hurting anyone else. It removes a slight bit of the weight of government regulation and threat of punishment that hangs over all of us all the time if we step out of line."

Making physician aid in dying legal as a matter of public policy will accomplish   15
several objectives. Right now we have a model of prohibition. There is an
underground cadre of doctors — of whom Kevorkian is the tip of the iceberg —
who are helping people die. The number varies, according to survey, from 6 to
16 percent to 20 to 53 percent. The 53 percent is for doctors in San Francisco
who work with people with AIDS where networks for assisted dying have
existed for many years. This practice is not regulated or reported; the criteria
and methods used are unknown. There is some information that the majority of
these deaths are done by lethal injection. Millions of viewers witnessed on *60
Minutes* the videotape of Kevorkian using this method to assist in the death of
Thomas Youk. If the practice is regulated, there will be more uniformity, doctors
will be able to and will have to obtain a second opinion and will have the option
of having a mental-health professional consult on the case. Most importantly for
patients, they will be able to talk about all their options openly with their health-
care providers and their loved ones.

Another consequence is that desperately ill people will not have to resort to
dying in a Michigan motel with Kevorkian's assistance, with a plastic bag on
their heads, with a gun in their mouth or, worse, botching the job and winding
up in worse shape and traumatizing their families. They won't have to die the
way someone else wants them to die, rather than the way they choose. As
Ronald Dworkin said in *Life's Dominion*: "Making someone die in a way others
approve, but he believes a horrifying contradiction of his life, is a devastating,
odious form of tyranny."

RESPOND•

1. Briefly summarize Girsh's arguments for legalizing physician-assisted
   suicide as well as her counterarguments against those who oppose
   such legalization. Although she does not explicitly mention changing
   technology as an impetus for physician-assisted suicide, how is the
   existence of such technology invoked in the text?

2. What sorts of appeals does Girsh use in constructing her argument?
   List the specific appeals that she uses, providing examples from the
   text. How effective are they? On the basis of these appeals, what sorts
   of readers might you deduce Girsh expects to read her article?

3. How effectively does Girsh deal with the opposition to legalizing physician-assisted suicide? (Note that this opposition might take several forms — those who oppose it in principle, those who argue that physician-assisted suicide is unnecessary if adequate hospice care is provided, etc.) How fairly does she characterize and deal with opposing views and concerns in general? What is the likelihood that Girsh's arguments will persuade readers who do not already agree with her position? Why? What is the likelihood that Girsh will persuade religious readers, particularly those who are Catholic (given her comments in paragraphs 11–12)?

4. Girsh formulates her argument as the "correct" answer to a purely legal question about physician-assisted suicide. In a recent collection of papers, *Physician-Assisted Suicide: Expanding the Debate* (1998), the editors, Margaret P. Battin, Rosamond Rhodes, and Anita Silvers, argue that the issue is much larger than a legal question, encompassing what they label the philosophical landscape; the clinical or medical landscape; the social, political, economic, and public policy landscape; and the religious landscape. **Write an essay** in which you define what you see as the most appropriate terms in which to formulate questions about issues of death and dying, evaluating the potential consequences of the various questions you devise.

▼ *Joe Loconte is author of* Seducing the Samaritan: How Government Contracts Are Reshaping Social Services *(1997) and deputy editor of* The Journal of American Citizenship, *the source from which this reading was excerpted. The original article appeared in March–April 1998. As this reading's title implies, it makes a strong argument for the use of hospice treatment for the terminally ill and against physician-assisted suicide.*

Hospice, Not Hemlock

JOE LOCONTE

In the deepening debate over assisted suicide, almost everyone agrees on a few troubling facts: Most people with terminal illnesses die in the sterile settings of hospitals or nursing homes, often in prolonged, uncontrolled pain; physicians typically fail to manage their patients' symptoms, adding mightily to their suffering; the wishes of patients are ignored as they are subjected to intrusive, often futile, medical interventions; and aggressive end-of-life care often bankrupts families that are already in crisis.

TOO MANY PEOPLE IN AMERICA
ARE DYING A BAD DEATH

The solution, some tell us, is physician-assisted suicide. Oregon has legalized the practice for the terminally ill. Michigan's Jack Kevorkian continues to help willing patients end their own lives. The prestigious *New England Journal of Medicine* has come out in favor of doctor-assisted death. Says Faye Girsh, the director of the Hemlock Society: "The only way to achieve a quick and painless and certain death is through medications that only a physician has access to."

This, we are told, is death with dignity. What we do not often hear is that there is another way to die — under the care of a specialized discipline of medicine that manages the pain of deadly diseases, keeps patients comfortable yet awake and alert, and surrounds the dying with emotional and spiritual support. Every year, roughly 450,000 people die in this way. They die in hospice.

"The vast majority of terminally ill patients can have clarity of mind and freedom from pain," says Martha Twaddle, a leading hospice physician and medical director at the hospice division of the Palliative Care Center of the North Shore, in Evanston, Illinois. "Hospice care helps liberate patients from the afflictions of their symptoms so that they can truly live until they die."

The hospice concept rejects decisions to hasten 5 death, but also extreme medical efforts to prolong life for the terminally ill. Rather, it aggressively treats the symptoms of disease — pain, fatigue, disorientation, depression — to ease the emotional suffering of those near death. It applies "palliative medicine," a team-based philosophy of caregiving that unites the medical know-how of doctors and nurses with the practical and emotional support of social workers, volunteer aides, and spiritual counselors. Because the goal of hospice is comfort, not cure, patients are usually treated at home, where most say they would prefer to die.

"Most people nowadays see two options: A mechanized, depersonalized, and painful death in a hospital or a swift death that rejects medical institutions and technology," says Nicholas Christakis, an assistant professor of medicine and sociology at the University of Chicago. "It is a false choice. Hospice offers a way out of this dilemma."

Hospice or Hemlock?

If so, there remains a gauntlet of cultural roadblocks. Hospice is rarely mentioned in medical school curricula. Says Dale Smith, a former head of the American Academy of Hospice and Palliative Medicine, "Talk to any physician and he'll tell you he never got any training in ways to deal with patients at the end of life."

The result: Most terminally ill patients either never hear about the hospice option or enter a program on the brink of death. Though a recent Gallup Poll shows that nine out of 10 Americans would choose to die at home once they are diagnosed with a terminal disease, most spend their final days in hospitals or nursing homes.

And, too often, that's not a very good place to die. A four-year research project funded by the Robert Wood Johnson Foundation looked at more than 9,000 seriously ill patients in five major teaching hospitals. Considered one of the most important studies on medical care for the dying, it found that doctors routinely subject patients to futile treatment, ignore their specific instructions for care, and allow them to die in needless pain.

"We are failing in our responsibility to provide humane care for people who are dying," says Ira Byock, a leading hospice physician and the author of *Dying Well*. George Annas, the director of the Law, Medicine and Ethics Program at Boston University, puts it even more starkly: "If dying patients want to retain some control over their dying process, they must get out of the hospital."

Since the mid-1970s, hospice programs have grown from a mere handful to more than 2,500, available in nearly every community. At least 4,000 nurses are now nationally certified in hospice techniques. In Michigan — Kevorkian's home state — a statewide hospice program cares for 1,100 people a day, regardless of their ability to pay. The Robert Wood Johnson Foundation, a leading health-care philanthropy, has launched a $12-million initiative to improve care for the dying. And the American Medical Association, which did not even recognize hospice as a medical discipline until 1995, has made the training of physicians in end-of-life care one of its top priorities.

There is a conflict raging in America today over society's obligations to care for its most vulnerable. Says Charles von Gunten, a hospice specialist at Northwestern Memorial Hospital, in Chicago, "It is fundamentally an argument about the soul of medicine." One observer calls it a choice between hospice or hemlock — between a compassion that "suffers with" the dying, or one that eliminates suffering by eliminating the sufferer.

A New Vision of Medicine

The modern hospice movement was founded by English physician Cicely Saunders, who, as a nurse in a London clinic, was aghast at the disregard for the emotional and spiritual suffering of patients near death. In 1967, she opened St. Christopher's Hospice, an in-patient facility drawing on spiritual and practical support from local congregations.

"She wanted to introduce a distinctly Christian 10 vision to mainstream medicine," says Nigel Cameron, an expert in bioethics at Trinity International University, in Deerfield, Illinois. The staples of the hospice philosophy quickly emerged: at-home care; an interdisciplinary team of physicians, nurses, pharmacists, ministers, and social workers; and a heavy sprinkling of volunteers.

Saunders' vision got a boost from *On Death and* 15 *Dying*, Elisabeth Kübler-Ross's book based on more than 500 interviews with dying patients. The study, in which the author pleaded for greater attention to the psychosocial aspects of dying, became an international bestseller. By 1974, the National Cancer Institute had begun funding hospices; the first, in Branford, Connecticut, was regarded as a national model of home care for the terminally ill.

Early hospice programs were independent and community-run, managed by local physicians or registered nurses. Most operated on a shoestring, relying on contributions, patient payments, and private insurance. Many were relatively spartan, consisting of little more than a nurse and a social worker making home visits.

Religious communities were early and natural supporters. "The questions people ask at the end of life are religious questions," says Rabbi Maurice Lamm, the president of the National Institute for Jewish Hospice, "and they must be answered by somebody who knows the person's faith." Synagogues, which usually support visitation committees for the sick, formed commissions to establish a Jewish presence in hospitals offering hospice care. The Catholic Church took a leadership role: Through its hospitals, health-care systems, and parishes, it began providing hospice beds, nurses, and priests.

A hospice patient at home during the final months of her life

By the mid-1980s, the movement started to take off. As hospital costs escalated, Medicare joined a growing number of insurance companies that offered reimbursement for hospice's home-care approach. In 1985, President Ronald Reagan signed legislation making the Medicare hospice benefit a permanent part of the Medicare program.

Today nearly 80 percent of hospices qualify. Medicare picks up most of the bill for services, from pain medications to special beds. The majority of managed-care plans offer at least partial coverage, and most private insurance plans include a hospice benefit. Since becoming a part of Medicare, hospice has seen a four-fold increase in patients receiving its services.

REDEFINING AUTONOMY

The starting place for any hospice team is the patient: 20 What kind of care does he or she really want? "It's not about our goals for a patient," says Dorothy Pitner, the president of the Palliative Care Center of the North Shore, which cares for about 200 people a day in Chicago's northern suburbs. "They tell us how they define quality of life, and then together we decide the course of action."

This is how hospice respects patient autonomy: not by hastening death, but by working closely with patients and families to weigh the costs and benefits of care. "Patients have the right to refuse unwanted, futile medical care," says Walter Hunter, the chairman of the National Hospice Ethics Committee. "But the right to refuse care does not mean the right to demand active assistance in dying."

Though physicians and medical directors may make only a few visits to a patient's home over the course of an illness, they supervise all caregiving decisions by the hospice teams. No one fills a prescription, inserts a tube, or gives medication without their OK. The central task of getting a person's pain under control falls to doctors, working closely with pharmacists.

Registered nurses serve as case managers. Usually they are the first to enter the home of the dying, make an assessment, and describe symptoms to physicians. They visit the home weekly and are on call 24 hours a day for emergencies. Nurses, along with nurse's aides, not only act as the go-between for families and physicians; they also bear much of the burden for making sure patients are comfortable, from administering drugs to drawing blood to suggesting medications or therapies.

Volunteers are also important to that work. For several hours a week they help out at home, cooking or doing household chores, keeping an eye on bedridden patients, or just listening as family members struggle with grief. Last year, about 100,000 volunteers joined 30,000 paid staff in hospices nationwide. They are, as one veteran caregiver puts it, the "sponges" in the mix, soaking up some of the anguish that accompanies death and dying.

THE DEATH WISH

Hospice care usually begins where traditional medi- 25 cine ends: when it becomes clear that a person's illness will not succumb to even the most heroic of medical therapies. "This is the toughest problem for doctors and families, the issue of letting go," says Alan Smookler, the Palliative Care Center's assistant medical director. "There's a lot of technology out there—feeding tubes, antibiotics, oxygen, ventilators, dialysis—and the hardest problem is saying that these interventions are no longer beneficial."

Hospice [of the Florida Suncoast] president Mary Labyak says many people come in eager to hasten their own deaths, but almost always have a change of heart. Of the 50,000 patients who have died under the group's care, she says, perhaps six have committed suicide. "The public perception is that people are [choosing suicide] every day. But these are people in their own homes, they have the means, they have lots of medication, and they don't choose death."

Hardly anything creates a more frightening sense of chaos than unrelieved pain and suffering. "We know that severe pain greatly reduces people's ability to function," says Patricia Berry, the director of the Wisconsin Cancer Pain Initiative. "If we don't control symptoms, then people can't have quality of life, they can't choose what they want to do or what to think about."

Hospice has understood this connection between pain and overall well-being from the start. After conventional treatments fail, says Martha Twaddle, "you'll often hear doctors say 'there's nothing left to do.' There's a lot left to do. There is a lot of aggressive care that can be given to you to treat your symptoms."

Hardly anyone doubts that more energetic caregiving for the dying is in order. A 1990 report from the National Cancer Institute warned that "undertreatment of pain and other symptoms of cancer is a serious and neglected public health problem." The New York State Task Force on Life and the Law, in arguing against legalizing assisted suicide, cited the "pervasive failure of our health-care system to treat pain and diagnose and treat depression."

The best studies show that most doctors still 30 undertreat pain and that most people with chronic and terminal illnesses experience needless suffering. A survey was taken a few years ago of 1,177 U.S. physicians who had cared for more than 70,000 patients with cancer during the previous six months. Eighty-five percent said the majority of cancer patients with pain were undermedicated; nearly half of those surveyed rated their own pain management techniques as fair or very poor.

A Debt to Hospice

The pain-control approach of hospice depends on an aggressive use of opioid drugs — narcotics such as morphine, fentanyl, codeine, or methadone. Despite the effectiveness of these drugs in clinical settings, euthanasia supporters often ignore or contest the results. Timothy Quill, a leading advocate of doctor-assisted suicide, writes that "there is no empirical evidence that all physical suffering associated with incurable illness can be effectively relieved."

Ira Byock, the president of the American Academy of Hospice and Palliative Medicine, says that's medical bunk. A 20-year hospice physician, Byock has cared for thousands of patients with terminal disease. "The best hospice and palliative-care programs have demonstrated that pain and physical suffering can always be alleviated," he says. "Not necessarily eliminated, but it can always be lessened and made more tolerable." Physicians and other authorities outside the hospice movement agree that most pain can be controlled. Authors of the New York Task Force report assert that "modern pain relief techniques can alleviate pain in all but extremely rare cases."

Living until They Die

Even the goal of easing people's suffering, as central as it is to hospice care, is not an end in itself. The aim of comfort is part of a larger objective: to help the terminally ill live as fully as possible until they die. This is where hospice departs most pointedly both from traditional medicine and the advocates of assisted suicide.

Hospice, by shining a light on the emotional and spiritual aspects of suffering, is challenging the

---

Loconte's article makes an evaluation argument by examining the question, "What is a good death?" Chapter 10 explains other ways of using evaluation arguments.

LINK TO P. 135 ·······················

medical community to re-examine its priorities. The period at the end of life, simultaneously ignored and micro-managed by conventional approaches, can be filled with significance. To neglect it is to diminish ourselves. "Spiritual inattentiveness in the face of dying and death can lead to the sad spectacle of medical technology run amok," says Laurence O'Connell, the president of the Park Ridge Center, a medical ethics think tank in Chicago.

Those who have spent years tending to the dying 35 say there is a mystery at life's end, one that seems to defy the rules of medicine. Walter Hunter, a medical director at the Hospice of Michigan, recalls a patient with end-stage kidney disease who entered hospice and quickly asked to be taken off the hemodialysis (a kidney machine) needed to keep her alive. Conventional medical wisdom put her life expectancy at two to three weeks without the technology, but the woman said she was eager to die.

Eight months later she was still alive. She asked Hunter, then her primary doctor, why she was still breathing. "I don't know," the doctor replied. "According to the textbooks, you should be dead."

Hospice staff had been busy in those months, keeping the patient comfortable, providing emotional and spiritual support. They later learned that just two days before the woman died, she had reconciled with one of her estranged children.

Sharon McCarthy has been a social worker at the Palliative Care Center of the North Shore for 18 years. She has cared for thousands of dying patients, getting a ringside seat to the grief of countless families. For the vast majority, she says, hospice provides the window of opportunity to get their lives in order. One of the most common desires: forgiveness, both extended and received. "There's a lot of nonphysical pain that goes on when these things aren't done." Says Mary Sheehan, director of clinical services and a 12-year veteran in hospice: "Ninety-nine percent of the time they have unfinished business."

SAVING THE SOUL OF MEDICINE

Hospice or hemlock: Though both end in death, each pursues its vision of a "good death" along radically different paths. At its deepest level, the hospice philosophy strikes a blow at the notion of the isolated individual. It insists that no one dies in a vacuum. Where one exists, hospice physicians, nurses, and social workers rush in to help fill it.

For many hospice staff and supporters, such work 40 is motivated and informed by a deeply moral and religious outlook. "I do not work within a specific religious context," writes Byock in *Dying Well,* "but I find more than a little truth in the spiritual philosophies of Christianity, Buddhism, and Judaism." Karen Bell, the hospice director of the Catholic-run Providence Health System in Portland, Oregon, says her organization is propelled by religious values. "The foundational principle is that life has a meaning and value until the very end, regardless of a person's physical condition or mental state."

Faith communities have always been involved in caring for the desperately ill, founding hospitals, clinics, medical schools, and so on. Though not usually connected to religious institutions, nearly all hospice programs make spiritual counseling available; rabbis, chaplains, and ecumenical ministers make frequent home visits and regularly attend hospice team meetings.

For many religious physicians, tackling the issue of personal autonomy is a crucial step in end-of-life care. "This is the Christian answer to whose life it is: 'It is not your own; you were bought at a price,'" says Yale University Medical School's Dr. Diane Comp, quoting the apostle Paul. "But if we are not in control of our lives, then we need companionship. We need the companionship of God and the companionship of those who reflect the image of God in this broken world."

Leon Kass, a physician and philosopher at the University of Chicago, says the religiously inspired moral vigor of hospice sets itself squarely against the movement for assisted death. "Hospice borrows its energy from a certain Judeo-Christian view of our obligations to suffering humanity," he says. "It is the idea that company and care, rather than attempts at cure, are abiding human obligations. These obligations are put to the severest test when the recipient of care is at his lowest and most unattractive."

We seem, as a culture, to be under such a test, and the outcome is not at all certain. Some call it a war for the soul of medicine. If so, hospice personnel could be to medical care what American GIs were to the Allied effort in Europe—the source of both its tactical and moral strength and, eventually, the foot soldiers for victory and reconstruction.   ■

RESPOND ●

1. What seem to be Loconte's purposes in writing this essay? Does he seem more concerned with arguing against physician-assisted suicide or arguing for hospice care? What evidence can you cite for your claim? Are the two mutually exclusive? Why or why not?

2. How do you imagine Faye Girsh ("Should Physician-Assisted Suicide Be Legalized? Yes!" p. 723) would respond to Loconte's essay? Which of his claims in particular would she find most problematic? Why? Loconte paints an especially positive and trouble-free view of hospice care. Might there be problems (or potential problems) he is ignoring or overlooking? How do you respond to Loconte's essay? Does he persuade you of his position? Why or why not?

3. *The Journal of American Citizenship* is published by the Heritage Foundation, a conservative think tank. Does Loconte's essay strike you as "conservative" in any way? Why or why not? Can you imagine people who might label themselves "liberals" sharing many (or all) of Loconte's views? Why or why not?

4. In paragraph 6, Loconte quotes Professor Nicholas Christakis as saying, "Most people nowadays see two options: A mechanized, depersonalized, and painful death in a hospital or a swift death that rejects medical institutions and technology. . . . Hospice offers a way out of this dilemma." Here, Christakis sets up the biomedical model of death and dying and physician-assisted suicide as bad alternatives and hospice care as a good alternative. Must it be so? Can you imagine a society in which all three might have a role to play? Why or why not? **Write an essay** in which you discuss the proper role of one or more of these in American society.

▼ "The Long Goodbye," which is excerpted here, originally appeared in July 1999 in the Washingtonian, a monthly magazine published in Washington, D.C. It chronicles in diary form Alicia Shepard's experiences dealing with her mother's dying and death. As Shepard notes, after aggressive medical treatment for cancer, her mother chose to die at home with the assistance of home hospice care. As you read, reflect on how diaries and personal narratives can function as arguments and on the rhetorical situations in which they might be most effective.

The Long Goodbye

ALICIA SHEPARD

Three years ago, my mother, Florence Shepard, gave me a gift. She moved from Montclair, New Jersey, into the Jefferson, a senior complex that provides meals and medical services, five minutes from my house in Arlington.

At 80, "Luzzie," as most everyone called her, was healthy, independent, and a companion for my then nine-year-old son, Cutter. My dad had died when I was 12, so my mother was my world. As I got older, she became my best friend.

Mom was crazy about the theater. She had several administrative jobs over the years, but above all she was an actress. In the 1940s, she was a television pioneer, cohosting a morning talk show called *Hi, Ladies* for WGN in Chicago. While raising a family in New Jersey, she acted in community theater, and at 68 she quit her desk job and shot for stardom in New York City. At an age when most grandmothers are gardening, my mother landed an appearance on *One Life to Live*. At 80, she joined us for a tubing trip down the Rappahannock River.

My mom was cool—even my friends thought so. I loved her, but more than that, I liked her. When she was diagnosed with lung cancer, I was lucky to be able to give something back.

JANUARY 10, 1998

Today we got the diagnosis we'd been expecting. Mom had been having trouble breathing and sounded horrible.

"I'm scared," she said.

"Me too, Mom."

The chest x-ray indicated fluid in her lungs; there was also a spot on her right lung. They would do a CT scan.

I thought: Mom's going to beat this. The spot will turn out to be an infection. Despite the fact that she smoked Chesterfields for more than 60 years, doctors have always marveled at her heart and lung capacity.

Dr. Mueller came in, closed the curtain, and sat down. He said, "We got the results of your CT scan, and I don't like what I see. Looks like lung cancer, but we can't be sure without a biopsy."

My stomach tightened. I couldn't even move over to Mom. She was sitting in her hospital gown trying to be stoic, tears rolling down her cheeks.

My mother is going to die. The spot on her lung will define the rest of our relationship.

She's already making jokes: "Glad I didn't get that two-year subscription to *Time*." "Good thing I never got those expensive hearing aids."

When we go up to her hospital room, she motions for me. I lie down next to her and she holds me and we cry. I think of all the times when I was a little girl and she held me the same way.

JANUARY 12

Feeling angry at Mom for having smoked. Sorry for myself as I realize the burden will fall on me because I'm the child living closest to her. Guilty for feeling those things.

My husband, Robert, advised me to keep thinking about how I will feel two years from now. The only thing that will matter to me is how I treated my

---

After Florence Shepard was diagnosed with lung cancer, her daughter chronicled the emotional journey, her mother's courageous fight, and the lifesaving help they received from hospice care.

---

mother, not that I couldn't go to an exercise class or had to postpone a trip.

Mom and I talk around things. Endless phone calls from people wanting information. I have no answers. I know it's cancer. The language in the hospital is changing; there is no "if" anymore. Today Mom had the needle biopsy; tomorrow, the results. She asked my brother to come; he can't.

I tell her she doesn't have to do any treatment. Treatment can be rough. Maybe you get an extra month, but you've spent two miserable months to gain that one.

Will I feel that way when the end is in sight?

JANUARY 15

Mom is overwhelmed. Phone ringing nonstop. The odd thing is the sick person is put in the position of comforting people who love her, and then feeling bad about upsetting them. My sister, Judy, wants to dash here from Florida. We discourage her; she'll be needed later on. My brother's having a hard time knowing what to do.

My husband's been a help. Sending my mother flowers, leaving work to be there when the doctors told Mom the news, climbing onto the bed to hold her as I took notes from the oncologist.

JANUARY 16

E-mail to family members:

"Mom looks fantastic. That throws you. It is Stage 3, inoperable lung cancer, nonsmall-cell, which means it doesn't grow quickly but it also doesn't respond well to treatment. There is no cure."

My dad died 33 years ago today.

JANUARY 23

Took Mom and x-rays to the Lombardi Cancer Center at Georgetown University. Georgetown is more aggressive and experimental. Mom isn't keen on aggressive therapy. But as Robert tells her: "Luzzie, we're just getting information. What if it turned out that spreading peanut butter on your back would relieve pain? Wouldn't you want to know that?"

JANUARY 31

Mom agreed to try the more toxic Georgetown chemo cocktail. These drugs can extend and improve the quality of her life, the doctor says.

Mom was reluctant to do the chemotherapy largely because she didn't want to lose her hair.

"Mom, you hardly have any hair."

"I do too. I have a lot of hair."

"No, you don't. If you had a lot of hair, you wouldn't wear a hairpiece."

The doctor interrupted: "Time out! This discussion is not about how much hair your mother has."

Later, Mom asked me to go to a wig place. Her hairdresser has offered to come on her day off. Mom, a bottle blonde, wants a red wig.

"Might as well try something different," she says.

FEBRUARY 7

Mom had her first chemo session yesterday. I was braced for the worst when I picked her up after five hours. She was up and complaining to the nurse about my being late. She was starving.

Since Mom lives in a retirement community, she 35 didn't want to go home and answer questions. So we got takeout and watched *Some Like It Hot* at my house. Mom was giddy, like she had dodged a bullet. She'd expected to feel much worse. She's taking these megapills at $46 a pop to ward off nausea, and they seem to be working.

MARCH 3

My sister, Judy, says Mom isn't doing cancer right! Mom hasn't lost her appetite, nor has she lost a pound. But she did lose her hair a few days before the second treatment. That sent her spirits into the dumps.

My nephew Courtney has signed Mom up for a Wig-of-the-Month Club he invented. When "Chartreuse Ruse" arrived, Mom wore it to dinner.

My son, Cutter, and I went over last night to get her dinner. Cutter, 11, asked her before entering her apartment, "Luzzie, are you bald?" It was a sight he'd prefer not to see.

MARCH 11

Mom is feeling better. She'd been feeling pretty terrible. I took her to a health-food store and bought her a ginseng concoction to restore energy. I'll try anything. Mom told me yesterday in tears, "I don't care what the results are from the CT scan. I don't want to do anything else. I want to die."

I offered that if she were dead, she'd also bring a 40 lot of pain. We need to take this one step at a time.

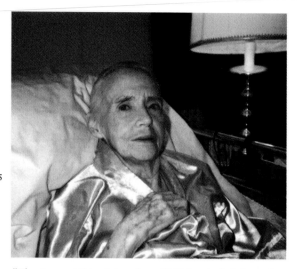

"The strangest thing is how beautiful Mom looks," the author wrote during her mother's illness. In 1935, Florence Shepard had movie-star looks at age 19. A few months before her death, although she no longer wore a wig to hide her hair loss, she always made sure her face was made up.

MARCH 25

Finally, news. The tumor on her right lung was two centimeters by two centimeters in January. It's now six by eight. The chemo didn't work.

MARCH 27

The doctor wants to start radiation. He said someone would call us from Georgetown to let us know when we start. But they didn't, and I got mad at how inconsiderate they were about my time because I have a friend from California visiting. Robert said, "I'd give anything to have a mother to take to radiation." Ouch. His mother died three years ago from lung cancer.

APRIL 3

Mom started radiation. She'll have 35 sessions, five times a week. The doctor said, "I have to tell you that it's not good news that the tumor grew as much as it did while she was undergoing chemotherapy."

Midway through radiation, she'll begin to feel tired. "I couldn't possibly feel more tired than I already do," Mom snapped. There was a spark of Mom there.

When the doctor left, she confided, "I don't ever want to be described as a good patient. My M.O.° is to be as difficult as possible. Then, when you have a good moment, you spread a little ray of sunshine."

While Mom was off getting tattoos etched on the places where radiation should aim, the nurse told me about the American Cancer Society's volunteer-driver service. I started crying. "I'm sorry," I kept saying, "I don't know where this is coming from." The nurse knew.

APRIL 23

Every day, no matter how exhausted and defeated she feels, Mom goes to radiation. It may be touted as painless, but it causes fatigue. One patient talks about taking an hour to get dressed. What amazes me about Mom is that she still puts on makeup and squeezes into her girdle every day.

For some reason — age, fatigue, remnants of chemo, radiation — she's really unsteady. She's fallen a few times. Lucky for her, she's got strong bones. Now she uses a cane.

APRIL 27

Just back from radiation. The strangest thing is how beautiful Mom looks. She admitted she felt better today.

It's my birthday. Will she be here for my next one?

MAY 3

Today was rough for Mom. I sometimes think: How much more can I take? How selfish. How much more can Mom take?

I feel desperate to find some way to make Mom's life better. Last weekend, I raced to a medical-supply store after a soccer game because a friend suggested a four-pronged cane. Also bought Mom a Caller ID box

to help her screen calls. I feel frantic: Try this, buy that.

The four-pronged cane lasted a week. Mom needs a walker. Found another medical-supply store, where I bought a purple walker. Purple is snazzy and right up Mom's alley. On my way home, I called from my car phone. Her friend Lee answered. Mom had fallen, and a nurse was checking for broken bones. This was the third fall that day.

Mom was pretty shaken when I got there. She hadn't been wearing her wig when she fell, and Lee sweetly got it for her. I still haven't seen her without it.

MAY 5

Today is the last day of radiation. I worry that it provided structure to Mom's life. Now what will happen to her?

MAY 9

My sister Judy and her daughter, Lydia, 15, arrive from Florida. My brother, Jay, and his son Sam, nine, drove in from Connecticut. Judy has arranged to bring in Hospice of Northern Virginia.

Mom was scared. Confused. Why were Jay and Judy here at the same time? Why was hospice involved?

It's time for hospice. They can provide equipment, a nurse to visit once a week, a social worker for Mom and us, an aide to bathe her, a volunteer for respite care, and a triage nurse who's always on duty.

Hard to absorb so much information. Especially for Mom. I ask her, "You've said your bags are packed and you're ready to go — why are you resisting this?" (Mom was under the impression that hospice means death is imminent. A common misconception. Hospice means our mother can stay in her apartment

---

M.O.: modus operandi (Lat. "way of operating").

with our help and have a comfortable and, hopefully, painless death.) Mom says she isn't resisting; she just hates to talk about this in front of her kids. We leave her and her questions for the hospice worker.

MAY 19

At Mom's tonight. Cutter needed help with his science homework. Mom needed me to test her medical alarm system and cut her pills in half. Felt caught. Got testy. Later, when it was past Cutter's bedtime and we were still struggling with homework, he said: "Mom, calm down. You are losing it."

I quieted down.

"Are you okay?" he asked.

I told him. "I guess I am losing it."

"Yes," he said. "Dad and I had a little talk about how you're doing." Then he burst into tears. "I love Luzzie so much. Thank you for taking such good care of her."

MAY 25

We are dealing in moments, as I call them. Mom sleeps a lot. She's not eating much. Getting food into her is a daily pitting of wills.

Don't know where I'd be without hospice. It's like having a wiser, more experienced friend by your side to help make the many tough and sometimes menial decisions.

Mom isn't Mom as most of us know her — up and around and in the thick of things. But the hospice nurse recently upped her to a morphine-based drug, and that seems to have made a dramatic difference.

JUNE 1

I asked Mom if she was ready to check out. She says as long as she's feeling the way she is now, she'd like to stick around.

Hospice tells us there are only weeks left. But I'm there day in and day out, and she seems stronger.

I've talked to her about dying, told her that I know she'll always have her arms around me. I asked her to make a special visit every year on my birthday.

Last night Judy and Lydia arrived for another visit. She genuinely appreciates the love and support that flood in daily. Her two best friends have each flown down to say goodbye.

JUNE 3

I asked Lydia how she thought Mom was doing. She said, "I'm not a doctor. I think we should just enjoy the good days and help her through the bad." I was stunned. She's 15.

JUNE 5

Thursday, Jay had duty with Mom. She threw up. He called me in a panic: "Get over here right now, please!" Mom reported that Jay had been sobbing in the living room. He just can't handle that his mother is dying. Who can?

I made arrangements today for George Washington University to take Mom's body when she dies. I heard myself saying, "So when my mother dies, you'll come pick up the body, right?" Like I was arranging for someone to come get our old refrigerator.

JUNE 7

Mom is getting weaker. She's losing her balance more. Should I continue to browbeat her into eating? She gets mad at me for always sticking food in her face. Hospice has said to feed her only when she's hungry. That would be never. I have a different philosophy: Keep her eating so she'll live. She's in no pain; she's lucid.

JUNE 8

Think I've hit the wall. Last night, Mom woke at 2:30 AM, then 4, then 6:30 and 8:30 to go to the bathroom.

I hear the walker. I pop up and hover. She gets annoyed to see me standing there, saying: "Need help?" I find myself feeling angry. She says, "Are you mad at me?"

No, I'm mad at the situation. I feel claustrophobic. I've been spending every night here. When the hospice aide comes, I bolt. I don't like how I feel. I know I'll be miserable when Mom is gone.

JUNE 10

Each day seems like a blur. Today my brother said to me, "Lisa, you've got to get help. You cannot do this alone."

I burst into tears. I'm living at Mom's. I wash my clothes in her washing machine and wear them the next day. Every time I go home for the hour and 45 minutes the hospice aide is with her, I have more important tasks than getting clothes. My stuff is strewn around Mom's apartment. My briefcase is jammed between a chair and a table. My sister's makeup bag is stuffed in a closet.

Is this what dying is? Camping out?

JUNE 11

Cutter's teacher called. He's behaving inappropriately at school. The kid's grandmother is dying, and his mom has abandoned him — what does she expect?

Rough day after being up all night. Mom slept until 4 PM. We had a heart-to-heart talk tonight. She told me it was important for us to be honest and open with each other. She was Mom — comforting but explaining that I was overreacting to things. As I went down to get her dinner, I wept in the elevator. Here she is comforting me.

I hired an aunt-niece team today who are home health aides. One will sleep at Mom's from 11 to 7 so I can get a good night's sleep.

JUNE 14

The morning at my house doesn't go well. It's raining. Cutter's required school T-shirt is wet. The dog needs to be walked. Everyone is irritable.

As I drive Cutter to school, he says, "Don't you think Luzzie would like you to get a nurse so you can take care of us, too?" And then a little later: "When am I going to get my mom back?"

JUNE 17

I've taken over paying her bills. Should I buy the *Post* for her up until August 16? I encouraged her to rest while I dashed to get Cutter a wheel for his inline skate.

By the time I returned, Mom was ready to go. Borrowed a wheelchair, got outside, and the sky darkened and it began to drizzle. We rolled around the courtyard, then over to a nearby art gallery. I love my mom: she's such a trouper.

JUNE 18

Cutter graduated from fifth grade today. A friend sat with Mom while I was gone.

It's lonely sitting in her apartment while she sleeps. I feel like I'm a centurion guarding her from death.

So much sleep and not eating is making Mom weaker again. I feel less trusting of letting her go to the bathroom alone. I must confess that I don't like taking my mother to the bathroom.

JUNE 22

This morning on the radio, *The Diane Rehm Show* had a panel on caregivers. I sat in the driveway listening to the guests talk about isolation, being forced to do a job for which you have no training, and abandoning every problem of your own to focus on the sick person. It was so familiar. The women — of course they were women — talked about finding yourself doing unimaginable things to your loved one. Judy and I cringe when we have to pull down our mother's underwear.

JULY 6

Mom is like her old self. She's eating a lot, and I can leave her. She goes out to play bridge. The doctor thinks it's because the toxicity of radiation and chemo has left her body. It's like getting a stay from the governor just before an execution. Although Mom may live a little longer, we'll have to go through the rituals of preparing to die all over again.

JULY 26

Tonight Mom came over for a "chick" barbecue at my house. Never thought she'd come to my house again.

AUGUST 2

We keep a notebook at Mom's so the caregivers can 95 write notes to each other. Judy wrote: "She's lying in that crooked way with her feet falling out, almost touching the floor. She's conscious if you talk to her, but otherwise she babbles to herself."

SEPTEMBER 1

Judy leaves to get Lydia back in school, but we decide she'll come spend the fall taking care of Mom. Hired nursing care.

SEPTEMBER 4

Mom is slipping away. It's hard even to have a conversation with her. She says her left ribs hurt. I don't feel as compelled to force-feed her now.

SEPTEMBER 18

Took the red-eye and got back at 10 AM [from a conference where Shepard had been for a few days]. Mom isn't having a good day. Judy will call the minute Mom's awake. At 4 PM Judy wakes me: Come right away. I scrap plans to meet Cutter after school. Haven't seen him for a week. I leave him a note.

The nurse and the social worker are there saying Mom may die this evening.

Whoa. Whoa.

They say the change in one hour has been 100 dramatic.

I call Robert and ask him to come home and get Cutter. I'm crying. Mom is pretty out of it. I don't know if she knows I'm there.

Cutter comes. "Mom, Cutter's here," I say, and she makes a face at him. We all laugh. She makes another one. Cutter makes one back. We're desperate to see this as a positive sign.

Later, Cutter is holding her hand by her bedside. He's stroking her hair, crying, telling her how much he loves her. She reaches out to comfort her grandson. "My baby," she says. "My baby."

At 4:30 AM Judy calls: Mom is lucid—come right 105 over. But I'm so tired. Never will I take a red-eye again. I decline, feeling guilty. Five minutes later, Judy calls. Mom has gone back to sleep. No need to come.

SEPTEMBER 19

Jay and his family arrive from Connecticut to say goodbye. I spend part of the afternoon at Mom's with Judy. Mom hasn't really talked.

William, Cutter's best friend, arrives. He leans over to say hello. Both boys are so natural with her, so unafraid. As William pulls back, Mom tugs his arm. "Come here," she says, indicating she wants William to kiss her as he usually does. It makes my heart jump when he kisses her.

SEPTEMBER 20

Jay and his wife take their two older boys to say goodbye to Mom. They know they'll never see her again. Mom looks awful. She doesn't bother with the wig.

E-mail sent Sunday night:

"For all who are praying for my mom and sending 110 good thoughts, I wanted to tell you that she's at the end of the road. Should be this week. She's not eating.

She's semi-comatose now. But I think she can hear us. She looks up every once in a while, but there's no doubt that it's time for her to move on to her next journey."

SEPTEMBER 21

Mom died last night.

Hours earlier, I'd felt this urgency to get to Mom's apartment as soon as my brother left. Robert was with Mom so Judy could join us for dinner and put Cutter to bed.

When I arrived, Mom was lying in bed, mouth agape, oxygen tank humming.

I told Robert how I had no regrets. That I'd loved her as much as she'd loved me and had been the best daughter I could. Not out of a sense of duty but because I wanted to give back what she gave me. Robert talked about how she had handled her illness with grace, dignity, and style — just as she had lived her life.

After Robert left, I told Mom all the things we'd said. An aide came at 10 PM to care for her. I left the room. Mom started making a gurgling noise, as though her lungs were filling with fluid. I kept waiting for it to stop. It didn't. We called hospice. The aide left at 11, and I climbed into bed with Mom.

I held her and told her how much I loved her, that it was time to let go. This wasn't how she wanted to live. I told her I knew she'd always be in my heart, and I always in hers. I was crying, and Mom wasn't responding. She was breathing so hard I could see her heart beating against her chest.

Hearing is the last to go. So I said, "Mom, if you can hear me, please wink." She did, ever so slightly. I said, "Wink again, so I'll know it wasn't a reflex." She did. It was my mother saying goodbye.

Judy came about 11:20, the hospice nurse ten minutes later. She tried to take Mom's blood pressure, but there wasn't any. She instructed us to give Mom liquid morphine every two hours and told us we should begin our vigil. *Our vigil?* Would Mom die that evening, with just me and Judy alone in her little apartment? The nurse started to leave.

"Please don't go. I'm scared," I said. The nurse's supervisor let her stay. The three of us sat in Mom's room. Judy held Mom's left hand and I her right, and we talked to her, telling her we loved her and that it was okay to go.

Mom's breathing lapsed into apnea, where she'd breathe, stop, then breathe again.

I held Mom's clammy hand, a hand attached to a body ravaged by cancer, a body I barely knew. She stopped breathing. At 12:15 AM she was gone, and the three of us said the Lord's Prayer.

In one sense, it was exhilarating. We were there, her two daughters, holding her hand the moment she died. I'd been there when she got the diagnosis, holding her hand, and I was there at the end, holding the same hand. The hand always there for me whenever I needed it.

SEPTEMBER 27

The memorial service was incredible. Yesterday was one of the most intense days of my life. The priest was wonderful, didn't pretend to know Mom and say sappy things. And the grandchildren were phenomenal. Five of them — the youngest ten years old — climbed the steps to the pulpit and spoke about their grandmother with poise and a sense of humor that made my heart burst. I could barely breathe as my own son, 11, told stories of my mother with a timing that caused the church to erupt in laughter. I know Mom — ever the showgirl — was there, beaming.

For years I've thought about speaking at my mother's memorial service. I knew I had to do it. But I worried that I couldn't. When the time came, it was easy. When I faltered, I asked Mom, out loud, to help me.

Luzzie's memorial-service program celebrated her love of the theater and her trademark black hair bow. "I know Mom— ever the showgirl—was there, beaming," the author wrote.

OCTOBER 8

Judy left. Over the last days, we cleaned out Mom's 125 apartment.

Judy's leaving made it seem real. She's my main connection to Mom. I feel numb.

OCTOBER 14

Attended a hospice lecture for people like me. I felt I had it pretty good in that room of 30 people. Mom lived a long life, and we got to help her die. We had the gift of time.

My calm about Mom makes me nervous. Why am I not more despondent?

OCTOBER 16

It's 11 o'clock. I can hear my son upstairs crying. He's had a hard time falling asleep, and I've already gone up for the second time. There are times, like now, when I can't comfort him. I know his tears will provoke mine, that his pain will reach into that safe place where I've stored my own. Robert's away, so I let him cry.

OCTOBER 23

The hospice social worker said the other night, "You 130 cannot go through watching or helping a person you love die and not be different at the other end."

I want to shake anyone who isn't kind to their parents: Love them while you can.

As time passes, I feel lonelier. Can Mom really be dead? Couldn't I just pick up the phone and call her?

By 5:15 PM yesterday, I felt like I needed to pull the car over, get out, and start running. When I came home, there were ten letters from hospice about people who had donated money for Mom. I held them close to my face and thought: I can't possibly live without my mother.

OCTOBER 30

Received hospice's "Signs of Grief" brochure in the 125 mail.

"Feeling Worse: Most people find that it takes 135 almost six weeks before the full effects of grief hit. It can be a terrible surprise to find that you feel worse after two months than you felt after two weeks.

"Outbursts: Sudden tearfulness even though you were fine the moment before; sudden anger, for example, over an insensitive statement or a piece of mail addressed to the person who has died."

It's reassuring. I'm right on track.

EPILOGUE

APRIL 27, 1999

My birthday. All day I was nervous: Will Mom find a way to come to me, as I asked her to when she was dying? What if she doesn't?

As I drove home alone on Nebraska Avenue, a six-inch branch with white flowers suddenly dropped onto my windshield. There was no wind, no rustling branches. My stomach jumped. I know it was her. ■

In the context of this chapter, Shepard's article argues for the value of hospice care by informing readers about her experiences surrounding her mother's death. See Chapter 1 to read about other purposes arguments may have.

LINK TO P. 5

RESPOND ●

1. Shepard quotes a hospice social worker as having commented, "You cannot go through watching or helping a person you love die and not be different at the other end" (paragraph 130), echoing sentiments expressed by Webb and other writers in this cluster. How was Shepard changed by her mother's dying and death? By the fact that her mother, declining aggressive medical treatment, chose to die at home? Do you see this text as an argument for—or against—hospice care or some other way of dying? Why?

2. Much of the power of this reading comes from its genre—the diary entry—and its use of detail. Which details do you find most effective? Why? How might this text have been different if it had been written in another genre—for example, an essay, a letter (to whom?), an argumentative pamphlet or tract? Why? Would such a change be a change for the better or the worse? Why?

3. How do you imagine other authors in this cluster might respond to Shepard's article? Why? **Write a dialogue** between Shepard and at least one other author in this cluster in which they address issues of death and dying, including how advances in medical technology are changing the nature of the decisions to be made about these issues.

▼ An award-winning poet, Cyrus Cassells teaches at Southwest Texas State University in San Marcos, Texas. This poem comes from Soul Make a Path through Shouting (1994). Like Shepard, he writes from personal experience with hospice care, in his case, four friends who died in residential hospices, rather than at home or in hospitals. As you read, pay particular attention to the way that Cassells uses figurative language to strengthen his argument.

Evening Lasting as Long as Life

CYRUS CASSELLS

in memory of four friends

The force, the aureole
Of all you were,
Flooding the hospice,
On this evening lasting as long as life,
Streaming round the husk, the hollowed   5
Dovecote of your skin—
I am not disease only;
Hold me as you would hold
The body of Christ—
Everywhere echoes: 10
Words spoken in chatterhappy mischief,
Words spoken in dream-bitten anger and grief
That we will never grow old together:
Brushstrokes, hammerstrokes,
The uppermost passion to be—   15

It was a privilege
To wipe away your sweat and ordure,
To talk as never before,
To hush the ravings

The world ranged against you in fear,   20
The great aphrodisiac of the earth—
And always you were teaching me
The time-at-hand:
This moment, *this* pain,
This marvel, then the next—   25

Now you join the many
Men, women, and children,
"A generation of grass,"
Gone from us
In the plague time,   30
And the world of countinghouse glitter,
The knockabout, warring world,
Will never know rest
Or rightness,
Till the suffering of millions is quilted   35
Into a usable splendor—

On this evening lasting as long as life,
Let me dream your wick-thin arms
As estuaries—brisk, emboldened,
Outspanning the distance between   40
The life we imagined
And the life we had to learn:
The pageant-sure thrust of rivers
To the sea,
The urge and clement drift   45
Into the calmest lap,
The clear, the cradling light
Of death.

We expect poetry to use figurative language of the types described in Chapter 14. Is the title (and theme) of Cassells's poem, "Evening Lasting as Long as Life," an example of hyperbole (overstatement)? Understatement? Or is it simply literal? See the descriptions of these two tropes in Chapter 14 to help you figure out your answer.

LINK TO P. 244 ···

RESPOND ●

1. What argument is Cassells making about death and its meaning for both the dying and the living? How does his use of figurative language contribute to this argument?

2. Cassells's poem represents his response to the loss of four friends to AIDS. What evidence can you find in the poem that its subject is, at some level, AIDS and its consequences? Are the sentiments expressed in the poem limited to people who lose or have lost loved ones to AIDS? Why or why not?

3. Both Alicia Shepard ("The Long Goodbye," p. 736) and Cassells write about their experiences caring for dying loved ones receiving hospice care. On the basis of these two readings, think about how hospice care creates an environment for dealing with issues of death and dying different from the one found in hospitals. What possibilities does hospice care create? What responsibilities or burdens does it entail? **Write an essay** in which you discuss these differences and evaluate them for yourself.

The Oregon Death with Dignity Act

Ballot Measure No. 16

Oregon Revised Statutes, 1996 Supplement §127.800–127.897

SECTION 1: GENERAL PROVISIONS

1.01 Definitions

The following words and phrases, whenever used in this Act, shall have the following meanings:

(1) "Adult" means an individual who is 18 years of age or older.

(2) "Attending physician" means the physician who has primary responsibility for the care of the patient and treatment of the patient's disease.

(3) "Consulting physician" means the physician who is qualified by specialty or experience to make a professional diagnosis and prognosis regarding the patient's disease.

(4) "Counseling" means a consultation between a state licensed psychiatrist or psychologist and a patient for the purpose of determining whether the patient is suffering from a psychiatric or psychological disorder, or depression causing impaired judgment.

(5) "Health care provider" means a person licensed, certified, or otherwise authorized or permitted by the law of this State to administer health care in the ordinary course of business or practice of a profession, and includes a health care facility.

(6) "Incapable" means that in the opinion of a court or in the opinion of the patient's attending physician or consulting physician, a patient lacks the ability to make and communicate health care decisions to health care providers, including communication through persons familiar with the patient's manner of communicating if those persons are available. Capable means not incapable.

(7) "Informed decision" means a decision by a qualified patient, to request and obtain a prescription to end his or her life in a humane and dignified manner, that is based on an appreciation of the relevant facts and after being fully informed by the attending physician of:

◀ This reading is the text of a ballot measure Oregonians voted into law first in November 1994 and again in 1997 by refusing to repeal it. The Oregon Death with Dignity Act makes physician-assisted suicide legal in that state under certain conditions, even though the law never actually uses that particular phrase. The measure has six sections, each of which defines as explicitly and unambiguously as possible the specific terms and limits of the law. If you have little experience reading legal texts, you may find this one hard-going at first; you may find it helpful to think about the text in terms of stasis theory (Chapter 1), with its concern for fact, definition, quality, and a proposed course of action. As you read, consider why each condition is included and why it is presented as it is. Pay special attention to Section 6, which offers a model request form of the sort that must be filed by those requesting medications to end their life within the confines of the law. (As this book goes to press in late summer 2000, Congress is considering legislation that may override this law.)

Would you agree that the name of this law could be interpreted as a definition argument? What exactly is a definition argument? See Chapter 9 for an explanation and examples.

·······························LINK TO P. 109

(a) his or her medical diagnosis;

(b) his or her prognosis;

(c) the potential risks associated with taking the medication to be prescribed;

(d) the probable result of taking the medication to be prescribed;

(e) the feasible alternatives, including, but not limited to, comfort care, hospice care and pain control.

(8) "Medically confirmed" means the medical opinion of the attending physician has been confirmed by a consulting physician who has examined the patient and the patient's relevant medical records.

(9) "Patient" means a person who is under the care of a physician.

(10) "Physician" means a doctor of medicine or osteopathy licensed to practice medicine by the Board of Medical Examiners for the State of Oregon.

(11) "Qualified patient" means a capable adult who is a resident of Oregon and has satisfied the requirements of this Act in order to obtain a prescription for medication to end his or her life in a humane and dignified manner.

(12) "Terminal disease" means an incurable and irreversible disease that has been medically confirmed and will, within reasonable medical judgment, produce death within six (6) months.

SECTION 2: WRITTEN REQUEST FOR MEDICATION TO END ONE'S LIFE IN A HUMANE AND DIGNIFIED MANNER

2.01 Who may initiate a written request for medication

An adult who is capable, is a resident of Oregon, and has been determined by the attending physician and consulting physician to be suffering from a terminal disease, and who has voluntarily expressed his or her wish to die, may make a written request for medication for the purpose of ending his or her life in a humane and dignified manner in accordance with this Act.

2.02 Form of the written request

(1) A valid request for medication under this Act shall be in substantially the form described in Section 6 of this Act, signed and dated by the patient and witnessed by at least two individuals who, in the presence of the patient, attest that to the best of their knowledge and

belief the patient is capable, acting voluntarily, and is not being coerced to sign the request.

    (2) One of the witnesses shall be a person who is not:

        (a) A relative of the patient by blood, marriage or adoption;

        (b) A person who at the time the request is signed would be entitled to any portion of the estate of the qualified patient upon death under any will or by operation of law; or

        (c) An owner, operator or employee of a health care facility where the qualified patient is receiving medical treatment or is a resident.

    (3) The patient's attending physician at the time the request is signed shall not be a witness.

    (4) If the patient is a patient in a long term care facility at the time the written request is made, one of the witnesses shall be an individual designated by the facility and having the qualifications specified by the Department of Human Resources by rule.

SECTION 3: SAFEGUARDS

3.01 Attending physician responsibilities

The attending physician shall:

    (1) Make the initial determination of whether a patient has a terminal disease, is capable, and has made the request voluntarily;

    (2) Inform the patient of:

        (a) his or her medical diagnosis;

        (b) his or her prognosis;

        (c) the potential risks associated with taking the medication to be prescribed;

        (d) the probable result of taking the medication to be prescribed;

        (e) the feasible alternatives, including, but not limited to, comfort care, hospice care and pain control.

    (3) Refer the patient to a consulting physician for medical confirmation of the diagnosis, and for determination that the patient is capable and acting voluntarily;

    (4) Refer the patient for counseling if appropriate pursuant to Section 3.03;

    (5) Request that the patient notify next of kin;

    (6) Inform the patient that he or she has an opportunity to rescind

the request at any time and in any manner, and offer the patient an opportunity to rescind at the end of the 15 day waiting period pursuant to Section 3.06;

(7) Verify, immediately prior to writing the prescription for medication under this Act, that the patient is making an informed decision;

(8) Fulfill the medical record documentation requirements of Section 3.09;

(9) Ensure that all appropriate steps are carried out in accordance with this Act prior to writing a prescription for medication to enable a qualified patient to end his or her life in a humane and dignified manner.

3.02 Consulting Physician Confirmation

Before a patient is qualified under this Act, a consulting physician shall examine the patient and his or her relevant medical records and confirm, in writing, the attending physician's diagnosis that the patient is suffering from a terminal disease, and verify that the patient is capable, is acting voluntarily and has made an informed decision.

3.03 Counseling Referral

If in the opinion of the attending physician or the consulting physician a patient may be suffering from a psychiatric or psychological disorder, or depression causing impaired judgment, either physician shall refer the patient for counseling. No medication to end a patient's life in a humane and dignified manner shall be prescribed until the person performing the counseling determines that the person is not suffering from a psychiatric or psychological disorder, or depression causing impaired judgment.

3.04 Informed decision

No person shall receive a prescription for medication to end his or her life in a humane and dignified manner unless he or she has made an informed decision as defined in Section 1.01(7). Immediately prior to writing a prescription for medication under this Act, the attending physician shall verify that the patient is making an informed decision.

3.05 Family notification

The attending physician shall ask the patient to notify next of kin of his or her request for medication pursuant to this Act. A patient who declines or is unable to notify next of kin shall not have his or her request denied for that reason.

3.06 Written and oral requests

In order to receive a prescription for medication to end his or her life in a humane and dignified manner, a qualified patient shall have made an oral request and a written request, and reiterate the oral request to his or her attending physician no less than fifteen (15) days after making the initial oral request. At the time the qualified patient makes his or her second oral request, the attending physician shall offer the patient an opportunity to rescind the request.

3.07 Right to rescind request

A patient may rescind his or her request at any time and in any manner without regard to his or her mental state. No prescription for medication under this Act may be written without the attending physician offering the qualified patient an opportunity to rescind the request.

3.08 Waiting periods

No less than fifteen (15) days shall elapse between the patient's initial and oral request and the writing of a prescription under this Act. No less than 48 hours shall elapse between the patient's written request and the writing of a prescription under this Act.

3.09 Medical record documentation requirements

The following shall be documented or filed in the patient's medical record:

(1) All oral requests by a patient for medication to end his or her life in a humane and dignified manner;

(2) All written requests by a patient for medication to end his or her life in a humane and dignified manner;

(3) The attending physician's diagnosis and prognosis, determination that the patient is capable, acting voluntarily and has made an informed decision;

(4) The consulting physician's diagnosis and prognosis, and verification that the patient is capable, acting voluntarily and has made an informed decision;

(5) A report of the outcome and determinations made during counseling, if performed;

(6) The attending physician's offer to the patient to rescind his or her request at the time of the patient's second oral request pursuant to Section 3.06; and

(7) A note by the attending physician indicating that all requirements under this Act have been met and indicating the steps taken to carry out the request, including a notation of the medication prescribed.

3.10 Residency requirements

Only requests made by Oregon residents, under this Act, shall be granted.

3.11 Reporting requirements

(1) The Health Division shall annually review a sample of records maintained pursuant to this Act.

(2) The Health Division shall make rules to facilitate the collection of information regarding compliance with this Act. The information collected shall not be a public record and may not be made available for inspection by the public.

(3) The Health Division shall generate and make available to the public an annual statistical report of information collected under Section 3.11(2) of this Act.

3.12 Effect on construction of wills, contracts and statutes

(1) No provision in a contract, will or other agreement, whether written or oral, to the extent the provision would affect whether a person may make or rescind a request for medication to end his or her life in a humane and dignified manner, shall be valid.

(2) No obligation owing under any currently existing contract shall be conditioned or affected by the making or rescinding of a request, by a person, for medication to end his or her life in a humane and dignified manner.

3.13 Insurance or annuity policies

The sale, procurement, or issuance of any life, health, or accident insurance or annuity policy or the rate charged for any policy shall not be conditioned upon or affected by the making or rescinding of a request, by a person, for medication to end his or her life in a humane and dignified manner. Neither shall a qualified patient's act of ingesting medication to end his or her life in a humane and dignified manner have an effect upon a life, health, or accident insurance or annuity policy.

3.14 Construction of act

Nothing in this Act shall be construed to authorize a physician or any other person to end a patient's life by lethal injection, mercy killing or active euthanasia. Actions taken in accordance with this Act shall not, for any purpose, constitute suicide, assisted suicide, mercy killing or homicide, under the law.

SECTION 4: IMMUNITIES AND LIABILITIES

4.01 Immunities

Except as provided in Section 4.02:

(1) No person shall be subject to civil or criminal liability or professional disciplinary action for participating in good faith compliance with this Act. This includes being present when a qualified patient takes the prescribed medication to end his or her life in a humane and dignified manner.

(2) No professional organization or association, or health care provider, may subject a person to censure, discipline, suspension, loss of license, loss of privileges, loss of membership or other penalty for participating or refusing to participate in good faith compliance with this Act.

(3) No request by a patient for or provision by an attending physician of medication in good faith compliance with the provisions of this Act shall constitute neglect for any purpose of law or provide the sole basis for the appointment of a guardian or conservator.

(4) No health care provider shall be under any duty, whether by contract, by statute or by any other legal requirement to participate in the provision to a qualified patient of medication to end his or her life in a humane and dignified manner. If a health care provider is unable or unwilling to carry out a patient's request under this Act, and the patient transfers his or her care to a new health care provider, the prior health care provider shall transfer, upon request, a copy of the patient's relevant medical records to the new health care provider.

4.02 Liabilities

(1) A person who without authorization of the patient willfully alters or forges a request for medication or conceals or destroys a

rescission of that request with the intent or effect of causing the patient's death shall be guilty of a Class A felony.

(2) A person who coerces or exerts undue influence on a patient to request medication for the purpose of ending the patient's life, or to destroy a rescission of such a request, shall be guilty of a Class A felony.

(3) Nothing in this Act limits further liability for civil damages resulting from other negligent conduct or intentional misconduct by any persons.

(4) The penalties in this Act do not preclude criminal penalties applicable under other law for conduct which is inconsistent with the provisions of this Act.

SECTION 5: SEVERABILITY

5.01 *Severability*

Any section of this Act being held invalid as to any person or circumstance shall not affect the application of any other section of this Act which can be given full effect without the invalid section or application.

SECTION 6: FORM OF THE REQUEST

6.01 *Form of the request*

A request for a medication as authorized by this Act shall be in substantially the following form:

REQUEST FOR MEDICATION
TO END MY LIFE IN A HUMANE AND DIGNIFIED MANNER

I, _____, am an adult of sound mind.

I am suffering from _____, which my attending physician has determined is a terminal disease and which has been medically formed by a consulting physician.

I have been fully informed of my diagnosis, prognosis, the nature of medication to be prescribed and potential associated risks, the expected result, and the feasible alternatives, including comfort care, hospice care and pain control.

I request that my attending physician prescribe medication that will end my life in a humane and dignified manner.

INITIAL ONE:

_____ I have informed my family of my decision and taken their opinions into consideration.

_____ I have decided not to inform my family of my decision.

_____ I have no family to inform of my decision.

I understand that I have the right to rescind this request at any time.

I understand the full import of this request and I expect to die when I take the medication to be prescribed.

I make this request voluntarily and without reservation, and I accept full moral responsibility for my actions.

Signed: _____

Dated: _____

DECLARATION OF WITNESSES

We declare that the person signing this request:

(a) Is personally known to us or has provided proof of identity;

(b) Signed this request in our presence;

(c) Appears to be of sound mind and not under duress, fraud or undue influence;

(d) Is not a patient for whom either of us is attending physician.

_____Witness 1/Date

_____Witness 2/Date

NOTE: One witness shall not be a relative (by blood, marriage or adoption) of the person signing this request, shall not be entitled to any portion of the person's estate upon death and shall not own, operate or be employed at a health care facility where the person is a patient or resident. If the patient is an inpatient at a health care facility, one of the witnesses shall be an individual designated by the facility.

RESPOND.

1. Are all parts of the Oregon Death with Dignity Act clear to you as reader? Do they all seem necessary? Why or why not? Why must laws be written in as exacting a form as this one is? How does the specificity of the definitions influence the sorts of arguments that can be made against the law? (Hint: Remember stasis theory!)

2. Examine the model request letter, "Form of the Request," presented in Section 6. What sort of argument does this document represent? Why is it presented in the form that it is? Why are all of the parts it includes necessary, given the way in which the law is written? Are any conditions that should have been included overlooked? Why or why not? Comment on the sort of language used in the document; how, for example, might the document be different if terms like "physician-assisted suicide" or "euthanasia" were used?

3. Can you foresee or imagine cases in which the law, as written, could not be carried out? Which particular parts of the law seem most likely to be violated? Why?

4. **Write an essay** in which you argue for or against the Oregon Death with Dignity Act. Note that your purpose is not to argue for or against physician-assisted suicide in some general way or at an abstract level; rather, you are arguing for or against this particular measure as it is written. (Feel free to suggest revisions to the law in order to improve it if doing so strengthens the argument you wish to make.)

GLOSSARY

accidental condition in a definition, an element that helps to explain what is being defined but is not essential to it. An accidental condition in defining a bird might be "ability to fly" because most, but not all, birds can fly. (See also *essential condition* and *sufficient condition*.)

ad hominem **argument** a fallacy of argument in which a writer's claim is answered by irrelevant attacks on his or her character.

analogy an extended comparison between something unfamiliar and something more familiar for the purpose of illuminating or dramatizing the unfamiliar. An analogy might, for example, compare nuclear fission (relatively unfamiliar) to an opening break in pool or billiards (more familiar).

anaphora a figure of speech involving repetition, particularly of the same word at the beginning of several clauses.

antithesis the use of parallel structures to call attention to contrasts or opposites, as in *Some like it hot; some like it cold.*

antonomasia use of a title, epithet, or description in place of a name, as in *Your Honor* for *Judge.*

argument (1) a spoken, written, or visual text that expresses a point of view; (2) the use of evidence and reason to discover some version of the truth, as distinct from *persuasion,* the attempt to change someone else's point of view.

artistic appeal support for an argument that a writer creates based on principles of reason and shared knowledge rather than on facts and evidence. (See also *inartistic appeal.*)

assumption a belief regarded as true, upon which other claims are based.

assumption, cultural a belief regarded as true or commonsensical within a particular culture, such as the belief in individual freedom in American culture.

audience the person or persons to whom an argument is directed.

authority the quality conveyed by a writer who is knowledgeable about his or her subject and confident in that knowledge.

background the information a writer provides to create the context for an argument.

backing in Toulmin argument, the evidence provided to support a *warrant.*

bandwagon appeal a fallacy of argument in which a course of action is recommended on the grounds that everyone else is following it.

begging the question a fallacy of argument in which a claim is based on the very grounds that are in doubt or dispute: *Rita can't be the bicycle thief; she's never stolen anything.*

ceremonial argument an argument that deals with current values and addresses questions of praise and blame. Also called *epideictic,* ceremonial arguments include eulogies and graduation speeches.

character, appeal based on a strategy in which a writer presents an authoritative or credible self-image in order to dispose an audience well toward a claim.

claim a statement that asserts a belief or truth. In arguments, most claims require supporting evidence. The claim is a key component in Toulmin argument.

connecting (1) identifying with a writer or reader; or (2) crafting an argument to emphasize where writers and audiences share interests, concerns, or experiences.

connotation the suggestions or associations that surround most words and extend beyond their literal meaning, creating associational effects. *Slender* and *skinny* have similar meanings, for example, but carry different connotations, the former more positive than the latter.

context the entire situation in which a piece of writing takes place, including the writer's purpose(s) for writing; the intended audience; the time and place of writing; the institutional, social, personal, and other influences on the piece of writing; the material conditions of writing (whether it is, for instance, online or on paper, in handwriting or print); and the writer's attitude toward the subject and the audience.

conviction the belief that a claim or course of action is true or reasonable. In a proposal argument, a writer must move an audience beyond conviction to action.

credibility an impression of integrity, honesty, and trustworthiness conveyed by a writer in an argument.

criterion in evaluative arguments, the standard by which something is measured to determine its quality or value.

definition, argument of an argument in which the claim specifies that something does or does not meet the conditions or features set forth in a definition: *Affirmative action is discrimination.*

deliberative argument an argument that deals with action to be taken in the future, focusing on matters of policy. Deliberative arguments include parliamentary debates and campaign platforms.

dogmatism a fallacy of argument in which a claim is supported on the grounds that it is the only conclusion acceptable within a given community.

either-or **choice** a fallacy of argument in which a complicated issue is represented as offering only two possible courses of action, one of which is made to seem vastly preferable to the other. *Either-or* choices generally misrepresent complicated arguments by oversimplifying them.

emotional appeal a strategy in which a writer tries to generate specific emotions (such as fear, envy, anger, or pity) in an audience to dispose it to accept a claim.

enthymeme in Toulmin argument, a statement that links a claim to a supporting reason: *The bank will fail* (claim) *because it has lost the support of its largest investors* (reason). In classical rhetoric, an enthymeme is a *syllogism* with one term understood but not stated: *Socrates is mortal because he is a human being.* (The understood term is: *All human beings are mortal.*)

epideictic argument see *ceremonial argument*.

equivocation a fallacy of argument in which a lie is given the appearance of truth, or in which the truth is misrepresented in deceptive language.

essential condition in a definition, an element that must be part of the definition but, by itself, isn't enough to define the term. An essential condition in defining a bird might be "winged": all birds have wings, yet wings alone do not define a bird since some insects and mammals also have wings. (See also *accidental condition* and *sufficient condition*.)

ethical appeal see *character, appeal based on*, and *ethos*.

ethnographic observation a form of field research involving close and extended observation of a group, event, or phenomenon; careful and detailed note-taking during the observation; analysis of the notes; and interpretation of that analysis.

ethos the self-image a writer creates to define a relationship with readers. In arguments, most writers try to establish an ethos that suggests honesty and credibility.

evaluation, argument of an argument in which the claim specifies that something does or does not meet established criteria: *The Nikon F5 is the most sophisticated 35mm camera currently available.*

evidence material offered to support an argument. See *artistic appeal* and *inartistic appeal*.

example, definition by a definition that operates by identifying individual examples of what is being defined: *Sports car — Corvette, Viper, Miata, Boxster.*

experimental evidence evidence gathered through experimentation; often evidence that can be quantified (for example, a survey of students before and after an election might yield statistical evidence about changes in their attitudes toward the candidates). Experimental evidence is frequently crucial to scientific arguments.

fact, argument of an argument in which the claim is a statement that can be proved or disproved with specific evidence or testimony: *The winter of 1998 in the United States was probably the warmest on record.*

fallacy of argument a flaw in the structure of an argument that renders its conclusion invalid or suspect. See *ad hominem argument, bandwagon appeal, begging the question, dogmatism, either-or choice, equivocation, false authority, faulty analogy, faulty causality, hasty generalization, moral equivalence, non sequitur, scare tactic, sentimental appeal*, and *slippery slope*.

false authority a fallacy of argument in which a claim is based on the expertise of someone who lacks appropriate credentials.

faulty analogy a fallacy of argument in which a comparison between two objects or concepts is inaccurate or inconsequential.

faulty causality a fallacy of argument in which an unwarranted assumption is made that because one event follows another, the first event causes the second. Faulty causality forms the basis of many superstitions.

forensic argument an argument that deals with actions that have occurred in the past. Sometimes called judicial arguments, forensic arguments include legal cases involving judgments of guilt or innocence.

formal definition a definition that identifies something first by the general class to which it belongs *(genus)* and then by the characteristics that distinguish it from other members of that class (species): *Baseball is a game* (genus) *played on a diamond by opposing teams of nine players who score runs by circling bases after striking a ball with a bat* (species).

genus in a definition, the general class to which an object or concept belongs: *baseball is a* sport; *green is a* color.

grounds in Toulmin argument, the evidence provided to support a claim or reason, or *enthymeme*.

hasty generalization a fallacy of argument in which an inference is drawn from insufficient data.

hyperbole use of overstatement for special effect.

hypothesis an assumption about what the findings of one's research or the conclusion to one's argument may be. A hypothesis must always be tested against evidence, counterarguments, and so on.

immediate reason the cause that leads directly to an effect, such as an automobile accident that results in an injury to the driver. (See also *necessary reason* and *sufficient reason*.)

inartistic appeal support for an argument using facts, statistics, eyewitness testimony, or other evidence the writer finds. (See also *artistic appeal*.)

intended readers the actual, real-life people whom a writer consciously wants to address in a piece of writing.

invention the process of finding and creating arguments to support a claim.

inverted word order moving grammatical elements of a sentence out of their usual order (subject-verb-object/complement) for special effect, as in *Tired I was; sleepy I was not.*

invitational argument a term used by Sonja Foss to describe arguments that are aimed not at vanquishing an opponent but at inviting others to collaborate in exploring mutually satisfying ways to solve problems.

invoked readers the readers directly addressed or implied in a text, which may include some that the writer did not consciously intend to reach. An argument that refers to *those who have experienced a major trauma,* for example, invokes all readers who have undergone this experience.

irony use of language that suggests a meaning in contrast to the literal meaning of the words.

line of argument a strategy or approach used in an argument. Argumentative strategies include appeals to the heart (emotional appeals), to values, to character (ethical appeals), and to facts and reason (logical appeals).

logical appeal a strategy in which a writer uses facts, evidence, and reason to make audience members accept a claim.

metaphor a figure of speech that makes a comparison, as in *The ship was a beacon of hope.*

moral equivalence a fallacy of argument in which no distinction is made between serious issues, problems, or failings and much less important ones.

necessary reason a cause that must be present for an effect to occur; for example, infection with a particular virus is a necessary reason for the development of AIDS. (See also *immediate reason* and *sufficient reason*.)

non sequitur a fallacy of argument in which claims, reasons, or warrants fail to connect logically; one point does not follow from another. *If you're really my friend, you'll lend me five hundred dollars.*

operational definition a definition that identifies an object by what it does or by the conditions that create it: *A line is the shortest distance between two points.*

parallelism use of similar grammatical structures or forms to create pleasing rhythms and other effects, as in *in the classroom, on the playground, and at the mall.*

parody a form of humor in which a writer transforms something familiar into a different form to make a comic point.

pathetic appeal see *emotional appeal.*

persuasion the act of seeking to change someone else's point of view.

precedents actions or decisions in the past that have established a pattern or model for subsequent actions. Precedents are particularly important in legal cases.

prejudices irrational beliefs, usually based on inadequate or outdated information.

premise a statement or position regarded as true and upon which other claims are based.

propaganda an argument that seeks to advance a point of view without regard to reason, fairness, or truth.

proposal argument an argument in which a claim is made in favor of or opposing a specific course of action: *Sport utility vehicles should have to meet the same fuel economy standards as passenger cars.*

qualifiers words or phrases that limit the scope of a claim: *usually; in a few cases; under these circumstances.*

qualitative argument an argument of evaluation that relies on nonnumerical criteria supported by reason, tradition, precedent, or logic.

quantitative argument an argument of evaluation that relies on criteria that can be measured, counted, or demonstrated objectively.

reason in writing, a statement that expands a claim by offering evidence to support it. The reason may be a statement of fact or another claim. In Toulmin argument, a *reason* is attached to a *claim* by a *warrant*, a statement that establishes the logical connection between claim and supporting reason.

rebuttal an answer that challenges or refutes a specific claim or charge. Rebuttals may also be offered by writers who anticipate objections to the claims or evidence they offer.

rebuttal, conditions of in Toulmin argument, potential objections to an argument. Writers need to anticipate such conditions in shaping their arguments.

reversed structures a figure of speech, referred to more formally as "chaismus," that involves the inversion of clauses, as in *What is good in your writing is not original; what is original is not good.*

rhetoric the art of persuasion. Western rhetoric originated in ancient Greece as a discipline to prepare citizens for arguing cases in court.

rhetorical questions questions posed to raise an issue or create an effect rather than to get a response: *You may well wonder, "What's in a name?"*

ridicule humor, usually mean-spirited, directed at a particular target.

Rogerian argument an approach to argumentation that is based on the principle, articulated by psychotherapist Carl Rogers, that audiences respond best when they do not feel threatened. Rogerian argument stresses trust and urges those who disagree to find common ground.

satire a form of humor in which a writer uses wit to expose—and possibly correct—human failings.

scare tactic a fallacy of argument in which an issue is presented in terms of exaggerated threats or dangers.

scheme a figure of speech that involves a special arrangement of words, such as inversion.

sentimental appeal a fallacy of argument in which an appeal is based on excessive emotion.

simile a comparison that uses *like* or *as*: *My love is like a red, red rose* or *I wandered lonely as a cloud*.

slippery slope a fallacy of argument in which it is suggested that a relatively inconsequential action or choice today will have serious adverse consequences in the future.

species in a definition, the particular features that distinguish one member of a *genus* from another: *Baseball is a sport* (genus) *played on a diamond by teams of nine players* (species).

stasis theory in classical rhetoric, a method for coming up with appropriate arguments by determining the nature of a given situation: *a question of fact; of definition; of quality;* or *of policy*.

sufficient condition in a definition, an element or set of elements adequate to define a term. A sufficient condition in defining God, for example, might be "supreme being" or "first cause." No other conditions are necessary, though many might be made. (See also *accidental condition* and *essential condition*.)

sufficient reason a cause that alone is enough to produce a particular effect; for example, a particular level of smoke in the air will set off a smoke alarm. (See also *immediate reason* and *necessary reason*.)

syllogism in formal logic, a structure of deductive logic in which correctly formed major and minor premises lead to a necessary conclusion:

Major premise	All human beings are mortal.
Minor premise	Socrates is a human being.
Conclusion	Socrates is mortal.

thesis a sentence that succinctly states a writer's main point.

Toulmin argument a method of informal logic first described by Stephen Toulmin in *The Uses of Argument* (1958). Toulmin argument describes the key components of an argument as the *claim, reason, warrant, backing,* and *grounds*.

trope a figure of speech that involves a change in the usual meaning or signification of words, such as *metaphor, simile,* and *analogy*.

understatement a figure of speech, more formally called "litotes," that makes a weaker statement than a situation seems to call for. It can lead to very powerful as well as to humorous effects.

values, appeal to a strategy in which a writer invokes shared principles and traditions of a society as a reason for accepting a claim.

warrant in Toulmin argument, the statement (expressed or implied) that establishes the logical connection between a claim and its supporting reason.

Claim	Don't eat that mushroom;
Reason	it's poisonous.
Warrant	What is poisonous should not be eaten.

ACKNOWLEDGMENTS

Chapter-Opening Art

Dilbert and Ruby slippers: Photofest; Breast Cancer Ribbon: Joel Gordon; Red Rose: Superstock; James Bond: Photofest.

Texts

Sherman Alexie. "The Exaggeration of Despair" reprinted from *The Summer of Black Widows.* Copyright © 1996 by Sherman Alexie, by permission of Hanging Loose Press.

John Anderson. "Shot on Ethnic Grounds and Side Streets" from *Newsday,* July 4, 1999. Copyright © 1999 by Newsday, Inc. Reprinted with permission.

Cardinal Francis Arinze. "Join Hands Across the Divide of Faith" from *The Charlotte Observer,* May 24, 1999. Reprinted by permission of the Charlotte Observer. Copyright owned by The Charlotte Observer.

Julia Fein Azoulay. "Getting Product Placed in Film and TV" from *Children's Business,* October 1, 1998. Copyright © 1998 by Julia Fein Azoulay.

James Bandler. "A Long Journey Home" from *The Boston Globe,* May 19, 1999. Republished by permission of Boston Globe; permission conveyed through Copyright Clearance Center Inc.

Dennis Baron. "Don't Make English Official: Ban It Instead" from *The Washington Post,* September 8, 1996. Copyright © 1996 by Dennis Baron. Reprinted by permission of the author.

Dave Barry. "A Look at Sports Nuts—And We Do Mean Nuts." From *Dave Barry Talks Back* by Dave Barry. Copyright © 1991 by Dave Barry. First printed in *Tropic Magazine.* Reprinted by permission of the author. Excerpts from *Dave Barry's Couples Guide to Guys* by Dave Barry. Copyright © 1995 by Dave Barry. Reprinted by permission of Crown Books, a division of Random House, Inc.

David Brin. "The Accountability Matrix" from *The Transparent Society: Freedom vs. Privacy in a City of Glass Houses* by David Brin. Copyright © 1998 by G. David Brin. Reprinted by permission of Perseus Books Publishers, a member of Perseus Books, L.L.C.

Thomas R. Burnett. "Promoting an Extreme Case of Sharing" from *The Atlanta Journal and Constitution,* May 20, 1999. Copyright © 1999 by Atlanta Journal and Constitution. Republished with permission from the Atlanta Journal and Constitution; permission conveyed through Copyright Clearance.

Deborah Kovach Caldwell. "A Hindu Renaissance" from *The Dallas Morning News,* February 20, 1999. Copyright © 1999 by the Dallas Morning News. Reprinted with permission of the Dallas Morning News.

Cyrus Cassells. "Evening Lasting as Long as Life" from *Soul Make a Path Through Shouting.* Copyright © 1994 by Cyrus Cassells. Reprinted by permission of Copper Canyon Press, P.O. Box 271, Port Townsend, WA 98368.

Neva Chonin. "X-Games: Extreme Athletes to Storm S.F. with Counterculture Sports" from *San Francisco Chronicle,* June 24, 1999. Copyright © 1999 by San Francisco Chronicle. Reprinted by permission.

Russ Cobb. "Internet Target Marketing Threatens Consumer Privacy" in *The Daily Texan,* July 15, 1999, Point/Counterpoint. Copyright © 1999 by the Daily Texan, University of Texas-Austin. Reprinted with permission from the Texas Student Publications.

Ruth Conniff. "The Joy of Women's Sports." Reprinted with permission from the August 10, 1998 issue of *The Nation.* Copyright © 1998 by The Nation.

Leslie Heywood. "Despite the Positive Rhetoric About Women's Sports, Female Athletes Face a Culture of Sexual Harassment" from *The Chronicle of Higher Education*, January 8, 1999. Copyright © 1999 by Leslie Heywood. Reprinted by permission of the author.

James Hill. "Say What? Watch Your Language" from *The Chicago Tribune*, December 29, 1996. Copyright © 1996 by Chicago Tribune Company. All rights reserved, used with permission.

David Hill. "AROC Responds," from *The Daily Texan*, March 11, 1999. Copyright © 1999 by the Daily Texan, University of Texas-Austin. Reprinted with permission from the Texas Student Publications.

Robert Hughes. Excerpt from article in *The New York Review of Books*, February 16, 1995. Copyright © 1995 by NYREV, Inc. As used in "Who Cares If Johnny Can't Read?" by Larissa MacFarquhar. Reprinted with permission from The New York Review of Books.

William P. Hytche. "The Cost of Hoop Dreams" from *The Christian Science Monitor*, June 24, 1999. Copyright © 1999 by William P. Hytche.

Jeff Jacoby. "Political Discourse on the College Campus: How 'Leftists' Debate" from *The Boston Globe*, May 3, 1999. Copyright © by The Boston Globe. Republished by permission of the Boston Globe; permission conveyed through Copyright Clearance Center, Inc.

Martin Luther King Jr. "I Have a Dream." Reprinted by arrangement with The Heirs to the Estate of Martin Luther King, Jr., c/o Writers House, Inc. as agent for the proprietor. Copyright © 1963 by Martin Luther King, Jr., copyright renewed 1991 by Coretta Scott King.

Gina Kolata. "$50,000 Offered to Tall, Smart Egg Donor" from *The New York Times*, March 3, 1999. Copyright © 1999 by The New York Times Company. Reprinted with the permission of the New York Times.

Michael Lebold. "Poor Discourse" from *The Daily Texan*, March 10, 1999. Copyright © 1999 by the Daily Texan, University of Texas-Austin. Reprinted with permission from the Texas Student Publications.

Chang-rae Lee. "Mute in an English-Only World" from *The New York Times*, April 18, 1996. Copyright © 1996 by the New York Times Company. Reprinted with permission.

David Lefer. "An Ad for Smart Eggs Spawns Ethics Uproar" from *The Daily News*, March 7, 1997. Copyright © New York Daily News, L.P. Reprinted with permission.

John Leo. "Fu Manchu on Naboo" from *U.S. News & World Report*, July 12, 1999. Copyright © 1999, U.S. News & World Report. Visit us at our Web site at <www.usnews.com> for additional information. Reprinted with permission.

John Levesque. "Sitcom Dads Rarely Know Best, Study of TV Laments" from *Seattle Post Intelligencer*, June 10, 1999, C1, C8. Reprinted with permission of Seattle Post-Intelligencer. Copyright © 1999 by Seattle Post-Intelligencer.

Joe Loconte. "Hospice, Not Hemlock: The Medical and Moral Rebuke to Doctor-Assisted Suicide" from *Policy Review: The Journal of American Citizenship*, March/April 1998, published by the Heritage Foundation. Copyright © 1998 by the Heritage Foundation. Reprinted with permission of the Heritage Foundation.

Donny Lucas. "Hey AROC, You Can't Hide . . ." From *The Daily Texan*, March 10, 1999. Copyright © 1999 by the Daily Texan, University of Texas-Austin. Reprinted by permission of Texas Student Publications.

Larissa MacFarquhar. "Who Cares If Johnny Can't Read?" First published in *Slate* Magazine, April 23, 1997. Reprinted by permission of the author.

Ted Rall. "Office Jargon: Language or Dialect?" Copyright © Ted Rall. Reprinted by permission of Universal Press Syndicate.

Bill Rankin. "King's Speech: Who Owns Soul-Stirring Words?" from *Atlanta Journal and Constitution*, May 12, 1999. Copyright © 1999 by the Atlanta Journal and Constitution. Republished with permission of the Atlanta Journal and Constitution; permission conveyed through Copyright Clearance.

John R. Rickford. "Suite for Ebony and Phonics" from *Discover* magazine, December 1997. Copyright © 1997 by John Rickford. Reprinted with permission of Discover magazine.

Jennifer Ringley. "Why I Star in My Own Truman Show: JenniCam's Jennifer Ringley on Why She Broadcasts Her Life Online" from *Cosmopolitan*, October 1998. Copyright © 1998 by Jennifer Ringley.

Slate letters to the editor: Ann W. Schmidt, "Lying Illiterates" and Harvey Scodel, "Illiteracy Test" in response to "Who Cares If Johnny Can't Read?" by Larissa MacFarquhar. First published in *Slate*, www.slate.com. Copyright © 1997 by SlateTM. Reprinted by permission.

Steve Rushin. "Hip Unchecked: In Sports and on TV, Sarcasm and Cynicism Are Drowning Out Sincerity and Compassion." Reprinted courtesy of *Sports Illustrated*, June 31, 1999. Copyright © 1999, Time, Inc. All rights reserved.

M. Michael Sharlot. "Connerly More than Interrupted," from *The Daily Texan*, March 10, 1999. Copyright © 1999 by the Daily Texan, University of Texas Publications. Reprinted with permission of the Texas Student Publications.

Alicia Shepard. "The Long Goodbye." Originally from *The Washingtonian*, July 1999. Copyright © 1999 by Alicia Shepard. Reprinted by permission of the author.

James Sterngold. "Able to Laugh at Their People, Not Just Cry for Them" from *The New York Times*, June 21, 1998. Copyright © 1998 by the New York Times Company. Reprinted by permission of the New York Times.

Straits Times. "Organ Donor Drive by Muslim Group" from *The Straits Times*, July 1999. Copyright © 1999 by Singapore Press Holdings. Reprinted by permission of Singapore Press Holdings.

Welch Suggs. "Colleges Consider Fairness of Cutting Men's Teams to Comply with Title IX" from *The Chronicle of Higher Education*, February 19, 1999, A53. Copyright © 1999, The Chronicle of Higher Education. Reprinted with permission.

Amy Tan. "Mother Tongue." Copyright © 1990 by Amy Tan. First appeared in *The Threepenny Review*. Reprinted by permission of the author and the Sandra Dijkstra Literary Agency.

Deborah Tannen. "Teachers' Classroom Strategies Should Recognize That Men and Women Use Language Differently," from *The Chronicle of Higher Education*, June 19, 1991. Copyright © 1991 by Deborah Tannen. Reprinted by permission.

Lester Thurow. "Why Women Are Paid Less Than Men." From *The New York Times*, March 9, 1981. Copyright © 2000 by the New York Times Company. Reprinted by permission.

David D. Troutt. "Defining Who We Are in Society" from *The Los Angeles Times*, January 12, 1977. Copyright © 1997 by David D. Troutt. Reprinted by permission of the author.

Janice Turner. "Cutting Edge: Men Are Having Cosmetic Surgery in Growing Numbers to Compete with Younger Guys in the Workplace and Social Scene" from *The Toronto Star*, June 1, 1996. Copyright © 1996 The Toronto Star. Reprinted with permission of The Toronto Star Syndicate.

John Vidal and John Carvel. "Lambs to the Gene Market" from *The Guardian*, November 12, 1994. Copyright © 1994 by the Guardian News Service, Ltd. Reprinted by permission.

Illustrations

Chapter 26. 559: Eddie Moore/*Albuquerque Journal,* © 1999; 564, 566: Illustrations by Theo Rudnak; 571: UPI/CORBIS-Bettmann; 574: Joe Marquette, AP/Wide World Photos.

Chapter 27. 581 (l): Photofest; 581 (r): Ed Bailey, AP/Wide World Photos; 585: Illustration by Tim Bower; 597: Illustration by Christophe Vorlet; 602: Illustration by Dan Picasso; 616: Photo by Carl Van Vechten, reprinted with permission of his estate; photo courtesy of the James Weldon Johnson Memorial Collection; Beinecke Library, Yale University; 621: Illustration by Christian Clayton, © 1997, reprinted with permission of *Discover* Magazine.

Chapter 28. 635: Gregorz Galazka/CORBIS; 643 (middle and bottom): EVOLVE FISH.com /Fish/Emblems (Colorado City); 645: R.E. Grothe/*Dallas Morning News;* 650: Engraving by Gustave Doré, courtesy New York Public Library—Picture Collection; 652: CORBIS-Bettman; 666: UPI/CORBIS-Bettmann; 677: Courtesy, *The Daily Texan,* University of Texas at Austin; 678: CORBIS-Bettmann.

Chapter 29. 704: Susan Watts/*N.Y. Daily News;* 723: Courtesy, New York Public Library—Picture Collection; 731: Joel Gordon; 738, 744: Courtesy, Alicia Shepard.

Cartoons and Advertisements

Marisa Acocella. "I Take It We Got the Account." © The New Yorker Collection 1999 by Marisa Acocella from cartoonbank.com. All rights reserved.

Jim Borgman. "A New Ghetto." Reprinted with special permission of King Features Syndicate.

Chris Britt. "Funny How You Had No Interest Until They Started Disrobing on Live TV." Copyright © 1999. Reprinted by permission of Copley News Service.

Chris Britt. "Standard English." Copyright © 1999. Reprinted by permission of Copley News Service.

Pat Byrnes. "This Diaper Makes My Butt Look Big." Copyright © The New Yorker Collection 2000 by Pat Byrnes from cartoonbank.com. All rights reserved.

Egan/St. James Advertising. "I Has a Dream" advertisement. Reprinted by permission of Egan/St. James Advertising.

Cathy Guisewite. "Here Comes the Bride." CATHY © 1999 Cathy Guisewite. Reprinted with permission of Universal Press Syndicate. All rights reserved.

Johnny Hart. *B.C.* cartoons. By permission of Johnny Hart and Creators Syndicate, Inc.

Jockey underwear advertisement. Used by permission of Jockey International.

Gary Markstein. "That's Right—Get Used to It. Women in Sports Magazines." Copyright © Copley News Service.

Wiley Miller. "Non Sequitur." © 1999, The Washington Post Writers Group. Reprinted with permission.

Scott Stantis. "Goal." Copyright © 1999. Reprinted by permission of Copley News Service.

G. B. Trudeau. "Sho 'Nuff," *Doonesbury.* Copyright © G. B. Trudeau. Reprinted with permission of Universal Press Syndicate. All rights reserved.

Jack Ziegler. "Wow, Thanks. I'm a Big Fan. I've Downloaded All Your Stuff." Copyright © The New Yorker Collection 2000 by Jack Ziegler from cartoonbank.com. All rights reserved.

INDEX